T0344195

Virtual Work and Human Interaction Research

Shawn D. Long
University of North Carolina – Charlotte, USA

Information Science
REFERENCE

Managing Director:	Lindsay Johnston
Senior Editorial Director:	Heather A. Probst
Book Production Manager:	Sean Woznicki
Development Manager:	Joel Gamon
Development Editor:	Hannah Abelbeck
Acquisitions Editor:	Erika Gallagher
Typesetter:	Adrienne Freeland
Cover Design:	Nick Newcomer, Lisandro Gonzalez

Published in the United States of America by
Information Science Reference (an imprint of IGI Global)
701 E. Chocolate Avenue
Hershey PA 17033
Tel: 717-533-8845
Fax: 717-533-8661
E-mail: cust@igi-global.com
Web site: http://www.igi-global.com

Library of Congress Cataloging-in-Publication Data

Virtual work and human interaction research / Shawn Long, editor.
     p. cm.
 Includes bibliographical references and index.
 Summary: "This book uses humanistic and social scientific inquiry to explore how humans communicate, behave, and navigate in their new virtual work spaces, providing scholars and practitioners an opportunity to study virtual work from quantitative and qualitative research approaches"--Provided by publisher.
 ISBN 978-1-4666-0963-1 (hardcover) -- ISBN 978-1-4666-0964-8 (ebook) -- ISBN 978-1-4666-0965-5 (print & perpetual access) 1. Telecommuting. 2. Virtual work. 3. Social interaction--Research. I. Long, Shawn.
 HD2336.3.V5697 2012
 331.25'68--dc23
                              2012003702

British Cataloguing in Publication Data
A Cataloguing in Publication record for this book is available from the British Library.

All work contributed to this book is new, previously-unpublished material. The views expressed in this book are those of the authors, but not necessarily of the publisher.

Editorial Advisory Board

Table of Contents

Preface...xiii

Acknowledgment...xviii

Section 1
Virtual Work and Human Interaction Research

Chapter 1
The Way We Work: Past, Present, and Future.. 1
  Wendy Wang, Trident University International, USA

Chapter 2
Shadowing Virtual Work Practices: Describing Subjects and Objects as Action Nets....................... 10
  Craig Lee Engstrom, Elmhurst College, USA

Chapter 3
Teleworkers' Boundary Management: Temporal, Spatial, and Expectation-Setting Strategies 31
  Kathryn L. Fonner, University of Wisconsin – Milwaukee, USA
  Lara C. Stache, University of Wisconsin – Milwaukee, USA

Chapter 4
Thinking Outside the Office: The Impact of Virtual Work on Creative Workers' Attitudes................. 59
  Beth A. Rubin, University of North Carolina – Charlotte, USA
  April J. Spivack, University of North Carolina – Charlotte, USA

Chapter 5
Virtual Vines: Using Participatory Methods to Connect Virtual Work with Community-Based
Practice.. 78
  Marianne LeGreco, University of North Carolina at Greensboro, USA
  Dawn Leonard, Urban Harvest Greensboro, USA
  Michelle Ferrier, Elon University, USA & LocallyGrownNews.com, USA

Chapter 6
Reply Timing and Emotional Strategy in Mobile Text Communications of Japanese Young People:
Replies to Messages Conveying Four Different Emotions..99
    Yuuki Kato, Sagami Women's University, Japan
    Shogo Kato, Tokyo Woman's Christian University, Japan
    Kunihiro Chida, Toei Animation Institute, Japan

Chapter 7
Australian Users' Interactions with E-Services in a Virtual Environment... 115
    Kamaljeet Sandhu, University of New England, Australia

Chapter 8
High-Touch Interactivity around Digital Learning Contents and Virtual Experiences: An Initial
Exploration Built on Real-World Cases.. 127
    Shalin Hai-Jew, Kansas State University, USA

Section 2
Virtual Work Research Methods and Approaches

Chapter 9
The Role of Experiments in the Study of Virtual Groups.. 149
    Lisa Slattery Walker, University of North Carolina – Charlotte, USA
    Anita L. Blanchard, University of North Carolina – Charlotte, USA
    Heather Burnett, Bank of America, USA

Chapter 10
Grounded Theory Approaches to Research on Virtual Work: A Brief Primer.................................... 160
    Danna M. Gibson, Columbus State University, USA
    Lynne M. Webb, University of Arkansas, USA

Chapter 11
Exploring Organizational Cultures through Virtual Survey Research... 176
    Eletra S. Gilchrist, The University of Alabama – Huntsville, USA
    Pavica Sheldon, The University of Alabama – Huntsville, USA

Chapter 12
Conducting Effective Interviews about Virtual Work: Gathering and Analyzing Data Using a
Grounded Theory Approach... 192
    Kerk F. Kee, Chapman University, USA
    Marceline Thompson-Hayes, Arkansas State University, USA

Chapter 13
Virtual Matters: Exploring the Communicative Accomplishment of Virtual Work and Virtual
Ethnography.. 213
    Natalie Nelson-Marsh, Boise State University, USA

Chapter 14
Mapping a Typology for Identifying the Culturally-Related Challenges of Global Virtual Teams:
A Research Perspective 230
    Norhayati Zakaria, University of Wollongong in Dubai, UAE
    Andrea Amelinckx, University of Lethbridge, Canada
    David Wilemon, Syracuse University, USA

Chapter 15
Considering Phenomenology in Virtual Work Research 248
    Shawn D. Long, University of North Carolina – Charlotte, USA
    Cerise L. Glenn, University of North Carolina – Greensboro, USA

Chapter 16
Case Study Findings from Human Interaction with Web E-Services: Qualitative Data Analysis 257
    Kamaljeet Sandhu, University of New England, Australia

Chapter 17
Applying Dramaturgy to Virtual Work Research 277
    Shawn D. Long, University of North Carolina – Charlotte, USA
    Frances Walton, University of North Carolina – Charlotte, USA
    Sayde J. Brais, University of North Carolina – Charlotte, USA

Compilation of References 286

About the Contributors 316

Index 323

Detailed Table of Contents

Preface..xiii

Acknowledgment...xviii

Section 1
Virtual Work and Human Interaction Research

Chapter 1

The Way We Work: Past, Present, and Future.. 1
    Wendy Wang, Trident University International, USA

Information technology provides unprecedented opportunities to work virtually. Despite a handful of perceived drawbacks, telecommuting offers society, organizations, and individuals numerous benefits. However, the embrace of telecommuting has been lukewarm at best. One possible explanation is that the traditional idea of a commuter workforce is so strongly ingrained that it will take more time before people begin to regard the office as superfluous. This chapter examines what the idea of "work" looked like in the past, looks like in the present, and what it may look like in the future. By examining the factors that contributed to how we worked both before and after the industrial revolution, and questioning whether these factors are still valid today, this chapter prompts us to reevaluate our assumption about the way we work, and prepare for the changes that are presently taking place. Lastly, this chapter will explore the practical and research implications of virtual work.

Chapter 2

Shadowing Virtual Work Practices: Describing Subjects and Objects as Action Nets......................... 10
    Craig Lee Engstrom, Elmhurst College, USA

Without modification, traditional ethnological approaches cannot fully attend to the translocation of practices into and out of virtual spaces. The ethnographer can observe the dislocation of a particular work practice from a specific place when he or she observes a research subject "log on," but accounting for the translocation of others' practices into the shared virtual space, which is necessary to conduct hermeneutical (or constitutive) research in virtual environments, remains an elusive methodological practice. In this chapter, interpretive shadowing, as it has recently been described (e.g., Czarniawska, 2007), is offered as one way to address some of the limitations of virtual ethnography. By describing (virtual) action nets vis-à-vis the "hybrid character of actions," researchers are able to follow subjects and objects as they move through various spaces/places and describe how these actants constitute fields of practices. Drawing upon examples from two years of shadowing research within the field of private investigations, this chapter describes how shadowers can observe both immediate and virtual practices. Specifically, descriptions of how to account for institutional practices that transcend space, place, and time are provided. Though interpretive research is theoretically sound, examples of specific methodological techniques are provided to address some of the technical limitations of the method when using it to study virtual practices.

Chapter 3

Teleworkers' Boundary Management: Temporal, Spatial, and Expectation-Setting Strategies 31

Kathryn L. Fonner, University of Wisconsin – Milwaukee, USA
Lara C. Stache, University of Wisconsin – Milwaukee, USA

Building on boundary theory, this chapter analyzes the open-ended responses of home-based teleworkers (N = 146) to identify the temporal and spatial strategies used by teleworkers to manage the boundary between work and home domains, and the expectation-setting strategies teleworkers use to uphold this boundary with family and work contacts. Teleworkers used temporal routines and physical space to segment work from home domains, but also maintained a degree of permeability between work and home domains in order to preserve the flexible benefits of their work arrangement. Teleworkers employed direct and indirect strategies with their families and colleagues to manage the work-home boundary. Relationships between boundary management choices, demographic variables, work-life conflict, and life-work conflict are also examined.

Chapter 4

Thinking Outside the Office: The Impact of Virtual Work on Creative Workers' Attitudes 59

Beth A. Rubin, University of North Carolina – Charlotte, USA
April J. Spivack, University of North Carolina – Charlotte, USA

This chapter draws on labor process theory and builds on a previous paper by Spivack and Rubin (2011) that explored workplace factors that might diminish the autonomy of creative knowledge workers. Using data from the National Study of the Changing Workforce, this chapter tests hypotheses linking creative workers' ability to work virtually, control their task and temporal autonomy to their well-being, job satisfaction, and commitment. The authors find that creative workers that have spatial autonomy have more positive work attitudes and better mental health. Further, they show that along with task and temporal autonomy, the conditions of the new workplace make spatial autonomy an important consideration. These findings contribute both to literature about the changing workplace and to practitioners concerned with maximizing the well-being of creative knowledge workers.

Chapter 5

Virtual Vines: Using Participatory Methods to Connect Virtual Work with Community-Based
Practice.. 78

Marianne LeGreco, University of North Carolina at Greensboro, USA
Dawn Leonard, Urban Harvest Greensboro, USA
Michelle Ferrier, Elon University, USA & LocallyGrownNews.com, USA

This chapter focuses on the somewhat unexpected relationship between participatory research methods, virtual work, and community-based practices. More specifically, the authors' contribution outlines different conceptual foundations and methodological approaches related to participatory and community-based research. Embedded within this review, they address two key connections between participatory methods and virtual work. First, participatory and community-based methodologies provide a useful set of concepts and practices that can be applied in virtual contexts. Second, virtual work can facilitate participatory initiatives and achieve community-based goals. The chapter also offers two short case studies that illustrate how community-based groups often rely on virtual work to move their local initiatives forward.

Chapter 6

Reply Timing and Emotional Strategy in Mobile Text Communications of Japanese Young People: Replies to Messages Conveying Four Different Emotions...99

Yuuki Kato, Sagami Women's University, Japan

Shogo Kato, Tokyo Woman's Christian University, Japan

Kunihiro Chida, Toei Animation Institute, Japan

In this chapter, the authors present two studies that examine the timing of replies to mobile text messages, especially the behavior of intentionally waiting before replying. As the first step in Study 1, 42 Japanese university subjects were asked by questionnaire survey whether they would wait before replying to mobile text messages they received, and if so, in which situations they would they wait. A large percentage of respondents suggested that they would sometimes wait before replying to a mobile text message. The freeform responses also indicated the involvement of an emotional aspect in most cases where subjects did not immediately reply to a mobile text message, even when they were capable of doing so. For Study 2, 224 Japanese university students were asked to rate on a 6-point scale whether they would wait before replying to mobile text messages from senders conveying each of four emotions: happiness, sadness, anger, and guilt. They were also asked to give a freeform answer as to why they would respond in such a way. The results showed that for each of the four emotional settings, subjects adjust the timing of message replies in order to manipulate the emotions of others or their own emotions, according to the situation. Individual differences were also observed in subjects' thoughts about adjusting reply timing and manipulating emotions.

Chapter 7

Australian Users' Interactions with E-Services in a Virtual Environment..115

Kamaljeet Sandhu, University of New England, Australia

Research into human interaction with computers requires a clear understanding about "user learning experience" on websites that shape user perceptions about virtual work. This chapter investigates issues that impact users' learning based on experience in using the e-services system. This research aims to address some of the important characteristics of user learning experience and how it can positively/ negatively impact user attitudes towards e-service tasks in virtual work. The adoption, use, and then continued use of an e-services system in terms of e-services system characteristics based on service-user interaction will be studied.

Chapter 8

High-Touch Interactivity around Digital Learning Contents and Virtual Experiences: An Initial Exploration Built on Real-World Cases...127

Shalin Hai-Jew, Kansas State University, USA

In high-demand learning, such as in higher education, high-touch interactivity between the subject matter experts and learners is critical as is the mutual creative frictions between the learners themselves. Technological affordances have enabled digital learning contents and immersive spaces to promote high-touch interactivity, intensive long-term conversations, interactions, co-designs, collaborations, and innovations between people. A majority of the digital contents and immersive experiences have been designed for particular purposes; some others are more free-form. In addition, these digital contents may be human-mediated or automated. This chapter examines real-world cases in the uses of digital contents and mediated virtual experiential contents for high-touch interactions.

Section 2
Virtual Work Research Methods and Approaches

Chapter 9

The Role of Experiments in the Study of Virtual Groups 149

Lisa Slattery Walker, University of North Carolina – Charlotte, USA

Anita L. Blanchard, University of North Carolina – Charlotte, USA

Heather Burnett, Bank of America, USA

In this chapter, the authors discuss the use of experimental methods in the study of virtual groups. For some time, experimentalists have hoped, as noted in Bainbridge (2007), that virtual worlds would provide a locale for research. The authors discuss practical techniques for doing so, and provide a detailed example of one such experiment as a platform for discussing opportunities and potential pitfalls for conducting research on virtual work groups. For convenience, they divide the steps in creating and conducting an experiment into several stages: design of the experiment, pre-testing, and statistical power of the data it produces. Each stage in any experiment presents challenges and requires decisions on the part of the experimenters; experiments conducted with virtual groups are certainly no exception.

Chapter 10

Grounded Theory Approaches to Research on Virtual Work: A Brief Primer 160

Danna M. Gibson, Columbus State University, USA

Lynne M. Webb, University of Arkansas, USA

This chapter explains how researchers can effectively employ grounded theory to study virtual work. The chapter defines grounded theory, reports the history of its development, describes its data collection and analysis, as well as offers guidelines for writing research reports of grounded theory analyses of human interactions surrounding virtual work.

Chapter 11

Exploring Organizational Cultures through Virtual Survey Research 176

Eletra S. Gilchrist, The University of Alabama – Huntsville, USA

Pavica Sheldon, The University of Alabama – Huntsville, USA

The survey is regarded as the most commonly used methodological tool in gathering information. There are many types of surveys, but this chapter discusses how to conduct and analyze quantitative and qualitative survey research in virtual environments via online or computer-administered surveys. Corporations are increasingly relying on virtual surveys to acquire knowledge about their employees' morale, satisfaction, and productivity. Hence, this chapter is intended as a tutorial guide for exploring organizational cultures through virtual survey research. This chapter explains in detail how to design survey questionnaires, sample subjects, analyze data both quantitatively and qualitatively, and finally how to interpret survey results. Strengths and limitations associated with using virtual surveys are highlighted. The chapter also considers future directions for understanding employees' needs through virtual survey research.

Chapter 12

Conducting Effective Interviews about Virtual Work: Gathering and Analyzing Data Using a
Grounded Theory Approach... 192

Kerk F. Kee, Chapman University, USA

Marceline Thompson-Hayes, Arkansas State University, USA

This chapter explicates interviewing as a viable research method for studying virtual work. The chapter begins with a review of the existing interdisciplinary scholarship on qualitative interviewing along with three modes of interviewing, interviewing techniques, formats, and rigor. Next, the chapter reviews exemplary research reports on virtual work to illustrate best practices in interviewing and data analysis. Finally, suggestions for collecting, analyzing, and interpreting interview data about virtual work are discussed.

Chapter 13

Virtual Matters: Exploring the Communicative Accomplishment of Virtual Work and Virtual
Ethnography 213

Natalie Nelson-Marsh, Boise State University, USA

Recent research highlights the complexity of virtual work and calls on researchers to examine virtual work as more than simply doing a job, but as negotiating a state of being virtual (Leonardi, Jackson, & Marsh, 2004; Long, 2010). A similar call has been made by virtual ethnographers to move away from cataloguing the differences between virtual ethnographic practices and co-located ethnographic practices and instead reflexively reconsider how and why to conduct a virtual ethnography (Hine, 2005). This chapter responds to both calls by exploring how virtual workers communicatively construct distance not as geographical absence, but as presence (Leonardi, et al., 2004; Broadfoot, Munshi, & Nelson-Marsh, 2010). Based on this knowledge, the chapter then develops a heuristic methodological framework that embraces reflexivity as a starting point and privileges communication as the mode through which virtual work is constituted and through which academics arrive at a deeper understanding of both virtual work and virtual ethnography.

Chapter 14

Mapping a Typology for Identifying the Culturally-Related Challenges of Global Virtual Teams:
A Research Perspective.. 230

Norhayati Zakaria, University of Wollongong in Dubai, UAE

Andrea Amelinckx, University of Lethbridge, Canada

David Wilemon, Syracuse University, USA

This chapter presents and synthesizes the culturally oriented challenges of managing distributed projects by Global Virtual Teams (GVTs) and examines the distinctive issues intrinsic to GVT work structures from a research perspective. In the first section, the authors define the concept of the global virtual team and explore the differences between global virtual teams and traditional co-located team structures. In the second section, they draw upon the cross-cultural theories (Hall, 1976; Hofstede, 1984) as a framework to explore the unique aspects of managing GVTs and then further develop a cultural typology illustrating the challenges of GVTs. Next, the authors discuss the research approaches to examine the cultural impacts on the success of GVTs, as well as highlight the practical implication in the light of the wide-ranging training programs needed by multinational corporations. In the final section, they assert that in order to be effective, GVTs need to develop new patterns of communication, team structure, knowledge exchange, and project management capabilities, and thus, the authors conclude with the future research directions.

Chapter 15
Considering Phenomenology in Virtual Work Research 248

    Shawn D. Long, University of North Carolina – Charlotte, USA
    Cerise L. Glenn, University of North Carolina – Greensboro, USA

Phenomenology provides a framework for understanding the dynamic, complex processes of everyday lived experiences. We suggest that the virtual work environment is fertile ground to utilize a phenomenological approach. Centralizing the lived experiences of organizational members frames the utility of this method throughout this chapter. A historical discussion of the roots of phenomenology, its application to the virtual work environment, a potential research study, and recommended uses and limitations of this approach are offered in this chapter.

Chapter 16
Case Study Findings from Human Interaction with Web E-Services: Qualitative Data Analysis......257

    Kamaljeet Sandhu, University of New England, Australia

Case study findings may provide a deeper insight into human interaction with web e-services. The qualitative data that was captured in this study suggests that human interaction with web e-services may make the user task difficult, and that the user expectation about the system not meeting user requirements may downgrade the system's use. Introducing an e-services system without integrating the user-friendly characteristics may have the effect of introducing complexity. Initial staff impressions of the system were formed on the basis of their expectations. When task outcomes did not meet their expectations, staff tried and then avoided its use.

Chapter 17
Applying Dramaturgy to Virtual Work Research...277

    Shawn D. Long, University of North Carolina – Charlotte, USA
    Frances Walton, University of North Carolina – Charlotte, USA
    Sayde J. Brais, University of North Carolina – Charlotte, USA

Dramaturgy as a research approach is a creative and useful tool to fully understand the complex dynamics of individuals interacting in a virtual work environment. Following Goffman's seminal dramaturgical research techniques, this chapter applies the principles and tenants of dramaturgy to virtual work. The authors examine the historical and theoretical underpinnings of dramaturgy and offer a potential research design integrating this methodological approach. The chapter extends the dramaturgical approach to offer challenges and opportunities of using this research approach in an electronic work domain.

Compilation of References 286

About the Contributors 316

Index..323

Preface

We are in the midst of an organizational technological revolution. This is a revolution, not a transition, primarily because we are in a time of redefining and reconstituting the workplace and rethinking about *what* and *how* it means to *do* work. This historic period in time is marked as one in which forward-thinking organizations and the subsequent scholarship reconsiders the *what, when, where, why,* and *how* questions of how work is accomplished, and more importantly, the inextricable influence and impact of technology in the workplace.

There is a seismic paradigmatic shift afoot for organizations and those who study them. This is not the dawn of the information age, but the accelerated push toward a new work paradigm; something I term the virtual work paradigm. New rules, language, artifacts, culture, beliefs, ideologies, jargon, assumptions, epistemologies, theories and methods of investigating organizations and those who work within them are quickly, and quietly, emerging. Some of the traditional applications to the virtual work environment are complementary; while others are severely incongruent to this new shape and form. New thoughts and methods of studying virtual work must emerge at a rapid pace to keep up with the quickly changing workplace.

This is indeed an exciting time for organizational scholars, especially those who conduct interdisciplinary and trans-disciplinary organizational research. We are witnessing first-hand the third nameable era in organizational history. Briefly the eras are: the agrarian era; the industrial age; and currently, the information age. The information age is so radically different from the former two eras in that there is less reliance on an actual physical organization, and even less reliance on organizational members actually being together in the same space at the same time to accomplish work tasks. The information age era centers on connectivity—electronic connectivity facilitated by innovative communication technologies—rather than physicality. Connectivity, rather than physicality, allows for remote work, dislocated organizational presence, geographically dispersed members and boundary-less spatial and temporal structures. This is clearly a shift in thinking, working and understanding work, which are evident signs of a radical shift to a virtual work paradigm.

In my earlier book, *Communication, Relationships and Practices in Virtual Work* (2010), I offered the first social scientific definition of virtual work. At the time I thought:

Virtual work should be considered as both an organizational noun and verb. There are inherently objective and subjective components associated with virtual work. Virtual work is a value-laden, politically rich, nuanced form of organizational functioning that has significant ecological considerations and implications. Virtual work is complicated by the constant energy given to tasks, social concerns, informal and formal communication, labor (emotional, psychological, and physical), impression management, face-saving techniques, virtual dramaturgy, managing up and down, motivating employees, rewarding and punishing virtual work behaviors, decision-making, socializing, organizational change, diversity issues, leading a virtual work team/group, etc. In essence, virtual work is work! In light of the electronic terrain, this virtual work is structurally complex due to the lack of nonverbal cues that are heavily relied upon and taken for granted in traditional face-to-face work arrangements.

Virtual work is much more than dislocated space. Virtual work is much more than just "doing" something. Virtual work is a state of being in a dislocated space operating under a new and emerging (and always changing) social contract between the organization and its members. Virtual work is political, social, economic, cultural, financial, legal, and ecologically paradoxical. Virtual work can be viewed as tacit and overt, confusing and stable, local and global, rational and irrational, dynamic and static and fraught with similar tensions that enable and inhibit this emerging work arrangement.

At the time of my earlier writing, I considered the concept of virtual work as complex and multidimensional with serious ecological considerations. I still do, and even more so today.

The title of this book, *Virtual Work and Human Interaction Research*, is inspired by the socio-humanistic interactions between humans, organizations, and technology. This intersection is becoming more normative and the overall spirit of this book is to serve as a methodological and research companion to the current and past scholarship emerging in virtual work. I believe that researchers and practitioners should work in concert to develop valid and rigorous methodological approaches and techniques to fully understand, describe and predict the virtual work environment and its organizational members. This book is a critical contribution to this effort.

This book brings together international and interdisciplinary scholars with diverse theoretical and methodological orientations, from a variety of legacy disciplines. This is an interdisciplinary and international project. My hope is that this book and the diverse contributions in this volume signal the importance of focusing on the broad opportunities the virtual work paradigm offers to researchers and practitioners worldwide and that spirited disciplinary and international conversations will continue around this topic.

This is an authoritative scholarly book that serves a specific purpose of advancing the conversation about virtual work research. Although this book may easily serve as an advanced undergraduate or graduate textbook, that was not my primary intention. My initial intention was motivated around shaping and contributing original scholarship to the area of virtual work research by bringing together international and interdisciplinary scholars focused in the emerging organizational domain of virtual work. I certainly welcome and encourage textbook adoption for training of the next generation of virtual work scholars and practitioners. I think this is a good resource for these populations.

The seventeen chapters that follow address a number of virtual work and human interaction research concerns including, but not limited to, the history of virtual work, research human interactivity around digital learning content, conducting virtual work experiments, virtual work environment's impact on creativity, case studies in virtual work, and virtual work boundary management, along with other salient topics. The chapters reflect a broad mix of conceptual, empirical, methodological, and historical points of view related to virtual work.

ORGANIZATION OF THE BOOK

This book is organized into two sections, consisting of 17 chapters. The two sections are: "Virtual Work Human Interaction Research" and "Virtual Work Research Approaches and Methods." The seventeen chapters embedded in the sections offer contemporary studies of virtual work, as well as the opportunities, dilemmas, complexities, methods, and approaches of studying virtual work.

Section 1: Virtual Work and Human Interaction Research

The chapters in this section offer quantitative and qualitative empirical studies of virtual work. The eight chapters in this section highlight current research in the virtual work environment.

Chapter 1, "The Way We Work: Past, Present, and Future": Wang, in her chapter, provides a historical road map of the evolution of work in America and the impact of technology on this change. She calls attention to our embedded and innate assumptions about working in contemporary society and the impact these assumptions have on virtual work.

Chapter 2, "Shadowing Virtual Work Practices: Describing Subjects and Objects as Action Nets": Engstrom advances the methodological technique of interpretative shadowing. He provides an explanation of the hybrid character of actions and then situates this approach by describing how shadowers can observe both immediate and virtual practices.

Chapter 3, "Teleworkers' Boundary Management: Temporal, Spatial, and Expectation-Setting Strategies": Fonner and Stache analyzed open-ended responses of virtual workers to identify the temporal and spatial strategies the virtual workers use to negotiate and manage work and home boundaries.

Chapter 4, "Thinking outside the Office: The Impact of Virtual Work on Creative Workers' Attitudes": Rubin and Spivack explore workplace factors that impact and ultimately reduce creativity in virtual work. Using secondary data, this chapter tests a number of hypotheses linking creative processes and autonomy with the virtual work environment.

Chapter 5, "Virtual Vines: Using Participatory Methods to Connect Virtual Work with Community-Based Practice": LeGreco, Leonard, and Ferrier explore the surprising relationship between participatory research methods, community-focused practices, and virtual work. They offer a number of different conceptual and methodological approaches to participatory and community-based research.

Chapter 6, "Reply Timing and Emotional Strategy in Mobile Text Communications of Japanese Young People: Replies to Messages Conveying Four Different Emotions": Kato, Kato, and Chida offer two studies examining the timing of replies to mobile text messages, particularly the behavior of waiting before replying. Emotion manipulation, individual differences and the time adjustment of replies were all uncovered in their results.

Chapter 7, "Australian Users' Interactions with E-Services in a Virtual Environment": In this chapter, Sandhu investigates the impact of the e-services system on users' learning in a virtual work environment. Specifically, he addresses important characteristics of the e-learning user experience and the implications of this experience on the user's attitudes and future use and adoption.

Chapter 8, "High-Touch Interactivity around Digital Learning Contents and Virtual Experiences: An Initial Exploration Built on Real-World Cases": In this chapter, Hai-Jew examines contemporary cases in the utilization of digital contents and the virtual experiences for high-touch interactions. The chapter situates high-touch interactions within the context of higher education and highlights the inherent creative conflicts between the learners of this technology.

Section 2: Virtual Work Research Methods and Approaches

This section offers a variety of research methods and approaches applied to virtual work. The nine chapters in this section cover a broad spectrum of qualitative and quantitative approaches in virtual work.

Chapter 9, "The Role of Experiments in a Study of Virtual Groups": Walker, Blanchard, and Burnett discuss the application of experimental methods in the study of virtual work groups. Opportunities, limitations and a research design example are provided in this chapter.

Chapter 10, "Grounded Theory Approaches to Research on Virtual Work: A Brief Primer": Gibson and Webb provide broad coverage of the utility of employing grounded theory to the study of virtual work. A history of this approach, data collection techniques and analysis, and effective report writing of grounded theory situated in the virtual work environment is provided in this chapter.

Chapter 11, "Exploring Organizational Cultures through Virtual Survey Research": Gilchrist and Sheldon discuss the advantages and disadvantages of using quantitative and qualitative survey research in virtual work. Survey research design, sample considerations, and analyses are explained in this chapter.

Chapter 12, "Conducting Effective Interviews about Virtual Work: Gathering and Analyzing Data Using a Grounded Theory Approach": In this chapter, Kee and Thompson-Hayes offers interviewing as a viable research method in the study of virtual work. Various forms of interview techniques in the virtual work research are discussed in this chapter.

Chapter 13, "Virtual Matters: Exploring the Communicative Accomplishment of Virtual Work and Virtual Ethnography": Nelson-Marsh develops a heuristic methodology embracing reflexivity as an initial start in employing ethnographic methods to the study of virtual work. Communication is privileged in this chapter, while underscoring the importance of closely considering virtual ethnographic research as a viable research approach.

Chapter 14, "Mapping a Typology for Identifying the Culturally-Related Challenges of Global Virtual Teams: A Research Perspective": Zakaria, Amelinckx, and Wilemon detail the challenges of managing distributed projects by Global Virtual Teams (GVTs). Additionally, the authors highlight the research issues and challenges of studying global virtual teams.

Chapter 15, "Considering Phenomenology in Virtual Work Research": Long and Glenn apply and modify traditional phenomenological research to the study of virtual work. The authors offer a mini-research design to illustrate the critical need of integrating phenomenology in virtual work research.

Chapter 16, "Case Study Findings from Human Interaction with Web E-Services: Qualitative Data Analysis": Sandu offers the case study approach as a salient method in virtual work research. This chapter focuses on the qualitative data captured from human interactions with web e-services in a virtual work platform. Challenges and opportunities of using this method are addressed in this chapter.

Chapter 17, "Applying Dramaturgy in Virtual Work Research": Long, Walton, and Brais explore the methodological opportunities and consequences of utilizing dramaturgy as a methodological approach in virtual work research. A brief history of dramaturgy as well as a mini-research design is offered in this chapter.

Shawn D. Long
University of North Carolina – Charlotte, USA

REFERENCE

Long, S. D. (Ed.). (2010). *Communication, relationships and practices in virtual work.* Hershey, PA: IGI Global. doi:10.4018/978-1-61520-979-8

Acknowledgment

There are several people that I would like to thank and acknowledge who were involved in this book project. Several people made this book come to life. To begin, I would like to thank all of the dedicated authors and contributors to this book. The contributors are forward-thinking, insightful, and committed thought leaders in the area of virtual work research. I enjoyed working with each of the authors throughout the book process, and I deeply appreciate their commitment to expand the boundaries of virtual work.

Many thanks to my exceptional editorial board: Dr. Brenda J. Allen, University of Denver; Dr. Tyler Harrison, Purdue University; Dr. Stacey Connaughton, Purdue University; Dr. Anita Blanchard, The University of North Carolina at Charlotte; and Dr. Gaelle Picherit-Duthler, Zehid University, UAE. Their expert guidance and advice were invaluable as I was shaping this book project.

I would like to thank the numerous reviewers who blind reviewed each of the chapters and offered insightful and instructive feedback to the contributors and me. Special thanks to my research team—Sadie Brais, Frances Walton, Jamon Flowers, and Ryan Arakaki.

The support of the College of Liberal Arts and Sciences, Department of Communication Studies, and the Organizational Science Program at the University of North Carolina at Charlotte has been invaluable in completing this project. The vibrant intellectual and interdisciplinary culture at UNC Charlotte makes working on projects like this one a real pleasure.

Thanks to the great team at IGI Global. Special thanks to Hannah Abelbeck, Editorial Assistant, for her expert guidance and support on this book.

Finally, and most importantly, I wish to thank my terrific family and friends, near and far, for their ongoing and tireless support of me in all of my endeavors, especially providing a constructive ear and sounding board on this project.

Shawn D. Long
University of North Carolina – Charlotte, USA

Section 1
Virtual Work and Human Interaction Research

Chapter 1
The Way We Work:
Past, Present, and Future

Wendy Wang
Trident University International, USA

ABSTRACT

Information technology provides unprecedented opportunities to work virtually. Despite a handful of perceived drawbacks, telecommuting offers society, organizations, and individuals numerous benefits. However, the embrace of telecommuting has been lukewarm at best. One possible explanation is that the traditional idea of a commuter workforce is so strongly ingrained that it will take more time before people begin to regard the office as superfluous. This chapter examines what the idea of "work" looked like in the past, looks like in the present, and what it may look like in the future. By examining the factors that contributed to how we worked both before and after the industrial revolution, and questioning whether these factors are still valid today, this chapter prompts us to reevaluate our assumption about the way we work, and prepare for the changes that are presently taking place. Lastly, this chapter will explore the practical and research implications of virtual work.

INTRODUCTION

It is impossible to overestimate the impact of information technology on every aspect of our lives. What was unthinkable in the past has become a routine convenience: we can play tennis with an avatar in front of a TV set, customize a dream car online, shop at online stores that stay open 24/7, and catch up on what our friends were up to last night on Facebook. In so many areas, we have responded enthusiastically to the opportunities and possibilities that information technology has offered us. However, in terms of where we work, we are reluctant to take full advantage of the flexibility it brings.

DOI: 10.4018/978-1-4666-0963-1.ch001

Information technology has made telecommuting possible: instead of being physically present at workplace, employees are able to work from home, a café, the library, or any place with internet connection. Nonetheless, in spite of the convenience and flexibility, many of us still consider the *Man in the Gray Flannel Suit* (Wilson & Franzen, 2002) the archetype of the working man; going to work implies proper dress and a daily commute.

Telecommuting provides numerous benefits, however, such as saved time from eliminated commutes, fewer cars on the roads, cleaner air, less dependence on gasoline, lower operational costs for businesses, widening talent pools, greater appeal to prospective employees, and an easier time balancing work and family responsibilities. Despite the benefits, telecommuting has not yet received widespread acceptance. We seem to welcome the idea of telecommuting, yet we are either not ready or not willing to commit to it in practice. In 2008, 52 million people could have done their jobs virtually, and yet just over 2 percent of non-self-employed workers were telecommuters, and the number of full-time telecommuters is significantly smaller than the number of occasional telecommuters (Center for Democracy and Technology & Earnest and Young, 2008). Companies such as IBM had offer telecommuting opportunities, and yet only a few employees showed interest; it appears most still prefer to be road warriors (Telework Research Network, 2011).

There are many possible explanations for telecommuting's lack of popularity. One of them is our natural resistance to change and our reluctance to experiment with the unfamiliar. We have been commuting to workplaces for so long, it may seem like that is how we have always worked and always will work. Both employees and employers are accustomed to this arrangement: employees understand what is expected of them in order to function effectively in the workplace, and employers have well-established guidelines for employee management. It is hard for both parties to think

differently. Given these attitudes, telecommuting can cause uneasy feelings for both employees and employers. Employees fear the loss of benefits that "face time" at an office can bring, including being up to date with the latest news in the organization, maintaining visibility that could lead to a promotion, or satisfying the need for social contact by interacting with colleagues. Employers, on the other hand, are concerned about issues such as telecommuters' organizational commitment, evaluation, and management of virtual workers, remote IT security, and other similar concerns.

The purpose of this chapter is to motivate us to evaluate assumptions behind the resistance to telecommuting. First, we will take a look at the historical record to see how we used to work, and then we will examine how and why work is done today. In the end, we will consider how we may work in the future. We will also discuss the challenges that wider embrace of telecommunication may bring, and how we might better prepare ourselves.

Telecommuting is commonly defined as employees doing their job from home or another location besides the employer's site, using information and telecommunication technologies. However, there remains some ambiguity regarding the actual amount of time spent working remotely; does telecommuting one hour per week, five hours per week, or ten hours per month really constitute true telecommuting? Since telecommuting 100 percent of the time does the most to save on office costs, alleviate congestion problems on highways, and reduce air pollution, in this chapter, we define the concept as employees telecommuting full time during regular work hours.

AGRICULTURAL PERIOD

Work from Home

Looking back through history, it becomes clear that going to the office every day is a very new phenomenon. Most people were either farmers or individual craftsmen; there were no offices to go to. People worked either in or close to their residence, whether making handicraft products, attending to their stores, following a master craftsman as apprentices, or plowing fields. There was little specialization at the time, since people did almost everything on their own, working on materials directly either manually or with the assistance of simple tools (Dudley, 1998). Since raw materials and working tools were usual individual possessions that were available at or close to home, where people lived also tended to be where they worked. This arrangement remained the primary mode of work from Roman times until the eighteenth century. The process of making goods was time consuming and tedious. The products of work (e.g., produce from the fields and handicrafts from family operated shops) were small in quantity (Dudley, 1998). With the limited means of transportation available, traveling any distance was more challenging as well, which meant products were mostly consumed and traded locally.

Craftsmanship is for the Uncultured

With the simple tools available at the time, productivity was low: the hard work of the entire family could generate only about 20 percent more produce beyond what was needed for the year, and even children had to work (Brown, 2009). Although there were many technological breakthroughs, their adoption and application was often very slow due to unfavorable attitudes towards skills that were seen to be solely "practical." These skills were not considered knowledge worth recording by the educated few who could actually read and write, and thus there were few books and schools teaching skills with practical value. Instead, people interested in these skills served as apprentice to a master for a couple of years and would learn by doing. These practices and attitudes contributed to the slow advance,

spread, and adoption of scientific knowledge for practical purpose, preventing technological breakthroughs to be converted into productivity increases (Drucker, 1993).

INDUSTRIAL REVOLUTION

Starting in the eighteenth century, people began to exhibit a more favorable attitude toward knowledge that had practical applications, and this in turn led to an increase in the adoption of many technological inventions. Textile manufacturing benefited tremendously during this time. Several important inventions helped to create the earliest mechanized textile factories, such as the flying shuttle and the spinning jenny that greatly expedited the process of turning cotton to cloth, and James Watt's steam engine that provided more powerful and reliable energy than that of the traditional water engine. These advances in technology revolutionized the textile industry, which in turn became the locomotive force that drove the industrial revolution.

Beginning of the Workplace

It was during the industrial revolution that the now-familiar division between "workplace" and "home" began to become widespread. Some of the earliest workers in the modern sense were farmers who chose to work in mechanized textile factories or were driven there because of changes in the nature of farming. In the eighteenth century, more sophisticated farming tools and technologies, like iron ploughs, seed drills, and irrigation systems, enabled farmers to produce much more than they needed, and this freed some of them work in factories.

Other farmers turned to work in factories because they were driven from their land by the enclosure movement. The enclosure movement started as far back as the twelfth century, but peaked in the mid-eighteenth century. During this period, many farmers lost their land to big land-owners. Without their former means of providing a livelihood, these farmers turned to the factories for work. For the first time in history, people were disconnected from the resources they needed for work; they lived in one place, while the raw materials and tools required to work them were located in dedicated factories. This work arrangement remains the dominant mode of work today.

In the early stages of the industrial revolution, due to lack of public transportation, workers often lived either in places close to the factories or on the grounds of the factories themselves. With the development of public transit in the late nineteenth century, and particularly with the jump in private ownership of cars in the 1950s, factories moved further away from urban areas, and the distance of workers' daily commutes got longer (Wells, 2003).

The separation of residence and workplace was the result of the nature of work in an industrial society. Work became highly specialized in order to improve productivity; instead of one person doing everything, each person was assigned to work on one or a few repetitive tasks in front of machines. Products were usually huge and mass-manufactured by machines at the factories; manufacturing and transportation of these products required the cooperation of many workers. It was thus crucial for people to work in proximity to each other at one location.

Workplace Management

In the agricultural period, work was done in small volume, farmers and craftsman owned the means of work, and since they worked independently from each other, they could decide when and how to work. Employers took a more laissez-faire attitude toward their hired hands. With the emergence of workplaces with large numbers of people working together, there were new questions that needed to be answered: how to streamline the work processes, coordinate individual workers' efforts, motivate employees while maximizing employers'

benefits, etc. These issues demanded a new style of management. Devising that management style has been a journey of trial and error, from the ad hoc management style in early factories to today's modern management science, and the quest for the optimum management practice continues.

The management style in early factories of the industrial revolution was very abrasive. Workers were under close supervision and had to endure very long hours in poor working environments (Dudley, 1998). Their conditions were condemned by many critics at the time. Later on, Frederick Taylor's more amiable management gained popularity. Taylor believed workers and managers could have a cooperative relationship. He proposed performance-based criteria to reward and manage workers. Eventually, Taylor's method was widely adopted, until it was shaken by the next workplace development: the advent of minimum hourly wages in the 1930s (Drucker, 1993). The influence of hourly wages has been far-reaching: even for salaried employees, managers tend to use the amount of time spent in the office to evaluate employee contribution and organizational commitment. Employees realized this as well, and often demonstrate loyalty by spending more hours in a workplace.

There are numerous books meant to help coach employers in better management of their employees, and to help employees excel in the workplace, but all of them are written with the assumption that employees work on site. In the post-industrial society, this assumption is being challenged.

POST-INDUSTRIAL SOCIETY

Work Goes to Workers

Working in an employer-provided workspace has been the expectation in mass manufacturing since the industrial revolution. In post-industrial society, however, this work mode is becoming dated. The number of workers in manufacturing has dropped significantly. In Taylor's time, nine out of ten people worked in manufacturing; in 2008, only one out of ten did so. With the diminishing manufacturing workforce comes an increase in the number of knowledge workers. Knowledge workers are those who are specialized in processing concepts and ideas. Similar to workers in the pre-industrial time, knowledge workers own the tools they use (most often a computer) and the materials they work with, namely, their knowledge and ideas. They have a lot of autonomy at work, and they require minimum supervision. With the assistance of telecommunication tools and information technology, there is no need for knowledge workers to maintain physical proximity to each other. One of the unique facets of knowledge workers is the product of their work. These products are very often abstract in nature: an algorithm, a new marketing plan, a new formula, a book, a research proposal, a cost and benefits analysis report, a new airplane design, etc. Transportation of these products is easily accomplished over the internet, obviating the need for transportation systems (Coyle, 1999). Hence, in post-industrial society, commuting to the employer's provided workplace is no longer an imperative; people can work and transfer their products anywhere with an internet connection. As the astronomical successes of companies such as Google, Apple, and Facebook have demonstrated, knowledge workers and their products have replaced the traditional resources such as land, equipment, and factories as the crucial ingredients in creating value.

Ready for Telecommuting?

Telecommuting suits the characteristics of work in post-industrial society. The technology is already here. Computers are getting cheaper and more powerful; technologies such as Voice over IP (Skype), virtual private networks, and video conferencing systems are mature and inexpensive. More people have access to the internet every day.

By 2012, there will be more than six billion mobile cellular subscriptions worldwide, more than two and a half billion people online, and nearly one out of three people in the world will surf the internet regularly (Touré, 2011). However, there remains a sizable gap between telecommuting policies and the number of people who actually take the telecommuting option. In 2008, it was estimated that over 50 million people, about 40 percent of the working population, telecommuted at least part time, 17.2 million people did it occasionally (World at Work, 2009), and only 2.5 million employees considered their home primary place of working (Lister, Harnish, & Nille, 2009). What could have contributed to the lack of enthusiasm for telecommuting? It appears that we, like farmers reluctant to adapt to working in factories, are reluctant to adapt to this new form of work.

Working in an employer-provided workspace definitely has its advantages for employees: face-to-face meeting is still the most effective mode of human interaction, and the quickest way to establish relationships with fellow employees; at best, technology can attempt to replicate this experience. The workplace can also be a place that showcases employee's efforts to climb the corporate ladder, such as the corner office or accolades on the wall. Furthermore, the predictable nine-to-five routine provides structure for many people, especially those who have no family. Hence, employees stand to lose these things in a move towards telecommuting. Another issue raised by working from home is that it makes people feel lonely and isolated. A survey about both the federal government and private sector confirmed that many employees worried about the feeling of isolation and loss of human interaction if they were to telecommute (CDW, 2008).

Since the industrial revolution, employers have established systematic ways to manage, monitor, and evaluate employees in the workplace. The traditional organizational structure has management perform functions such as selecting qualified individuals, monitoring employee performance, and conducting training. To better accommodate the telecommuting work mode, employers need to change their management style and create corresponding procedures and policies. For telecommuting to truly flourish, employers need to create a telecommuting-friendly environment and adopt a management style that is conducive to this new work mode. For example, they could consider flattening an organization's structure to give the highly educated employees a maximum of autonomy in their work, evaluating employees' performance by result rather than the numbers of hours they stay in the office, and experimenting with traditional policies for vacations and personal leaves. The main concern of employers however, is how to ensure IT security in telecommuting environment. According to the CDW teleworking report (CDW, 2008), IT security was listed as the number one concern of IT professionals regarding telecommuting. This concern is especially prevalent among governmental agencies.

As more knowledge workers become freelancers, consultants, and telecommuters, some spend more time on the road, while others occasionally need a place to escape the distractions of home. Yet alternative workplaces that are telecommuting-friendly are not easy to find. Telecommuters often must settle for noisy cafes or libraries that are not always conducive to work. Fortunately, this situation has been improving. In recent years, "coworking," a new way of working, has been quietly coming onto the scene. Coworking provides a comfortable alternative workspace to those enrolled in the service. Members enjoy all the amenities of a typical office, without the hassle of dealing with administrative staff. Members may have 24-hour access and are even able to bring along their pets (Reed, 2007). Similar to gyms that allow people to exercise together 24/7, coworking enables people that are not affiliated with the same organization to share a workspace and interact with each other at any time.

The first coworking organization, Citizen Space, started in San Francisco in 2007. Four hundred similar spaces have now spread to six continents. However, places like citizen space are still few in number, and their viability remains questionable.

WORK IN THE FUTURE

We live in a world that is constantly changing. It is hard to predict what the tomorrow will bring. Gaining a better understanding of our current experiences may help us glimpse into the future. The industrial revolution changed the old tradition of working from home, and the information and telecommunication technology available today may enable more people to go back home again. People of tomorrow will likely enjoy even more flexibility and become nomadic in their work lives.

Work: Nomadic Style

Tomorrow's workers are nomadic workers. They are able to work at any place at any time. This mobility will be enjoyed not only by knowledge workers, but also people whose work now still requires a daily commute, such as those in manufacturing. Mass manufacturing in factories will be replaced with customized manufacturing; using technologies such as 3-D printing, people will be able to make products at their home offices or garages. 3-D technology allows users to first tinker with the design at their computers using 3-D software, and then once the design is complete, "print" the design using a special device that would build the product gradually with material such as plastic or metal. With 3-D printing, workers can make small objects such as a wheel, a bottle, or even a violin in their home office. With a big enough printer, it would even be possible to print an airplane (Economist, 2011a).

Compared to traditional manufacturing, technologies such as 3-D printing put more weight on creativity, knowledge, and the ability to apply that knowledge to work, all of which makes the role of manufacturing secondary (Economist, 2011b). People will spend more time experimenting with ideas and product design where value is added the most. How and where we work would be changed fundamentally, as workers will be free to work from any locations. Thus, even manufacturing could go nomadic.

Challenges of Nomadic Work

Work in the future would be more flexible. Telecommuting will make geographical distance irrelevant in terms of hunting for talent or jobs. Employers would be able to recruit the best talent worldwide, while employees could seek opportunities globally. Such flexibility brings associated risks: work in the future would be less secure, and competition for jobs will not be confined to one geographical area. The assumption of long-term organizational commitment to employees and employees' lifelong loyalty to their employers would be dealt a significant blow. It would be rare for people to stay in one job in one career with one organization; people would change jobs or even careers frequently during their lifetime.

To prepare for tomorrow's work, individuals, society, and governments still have a long way to go. It will be crucial for individuals to acquire the skills and habits of being lifelong learners, updating knowledge every five to seven years to stay current. The current payment, tax, health care, and benefit systems were designed with the assumption of comparatively stable jobs. To adapt to a more risky and highly changeable environment, governments and organizations will need to work together to create a more flexible environment to accommodate the coming changes (Wells, 2003; Coyle, 1999; Shapiro, 2008).

PRACTICAL AND RESEARCH IMPLICATIONS

This chapter has examined factors that have contributed to changes in the way we work from the agriculture period, through the industrial revolution, and into post-industrial society. Reviewing historical changes helps us to better understand what we are experiencing today, and enables us to prepare for increasingly mobile work in the telecommuting age.

From the enclosure movement in the twelfth century to the industrial revolution in the eighteenth, it took hundreds of years to gain momentum for the separation of workplace and home, and another two centuries to make the daily commute the dominant arrangement we are familiar with today. Remembering the past helps us to better understand our behaviors. Similar to people's suspicion of the idea of working in factories at the beginning of the industrial revolution, it is natural to have concerns over working from home full time. As it took time for employers to change the ad hoc management style prevalent in early factories to the modern management of an office, organizations will also need time to formulate and fine tune policies and procedures that will help to ease them into the telecommuting age.

The move to the telecommuting era will not take very long. In spite of the initial slow adoption of telecommuting, the process is definitely speeding up. On December 9, 2010, President Obama signed the Telework Enhancement Act. The passage of this law will allow eligible federal workers to telecommute. It also made it mandatory for federal agencies to formulate telework policies within six month. However, for telecommuting to truly flourish, management still needs to wrestle with many issues.

Privacy and security is a major concern for telecommuting. In late 2007, the Earnest and Young and Center for Democracy and Technology (CDT) surveyed a diverse group of 73 organizations from ten industries in the US, Canada, and

Europe, and found that allowing employees to telecommute poses security and privacy risks that are not being addressed adequately by business or government. Many organizations did not have formal telecommuting security policies implemented in practice, and have not trained their employees working from home to protect their data. There was a sizable gap between organizations' recognition of the risk factors and their efforts to address them (Center for Democracy and Technology & Earnest and Young, 2008).

Another concern that must be addressed is the loss of personal interaction. Organizations need to design policies to ensure that telecommuters will get the same treatment as employees who go to offices. To accomplish this, performance evaluations need to be more result-driven. Furthermore, in the traditional work environment, it is easy to draft policies to cover personal leave, holidays, and work-related injuries. People can ask for leave to pick up children or go to the dentist's office, and they can receive compensation for work-related injuries. In the telecommuting environment, however, the line is more difficult to draw.

Studies on telecommunications and virtual organizations are rather limited. There are many unanswered questions that need to be addressed. What will be the impact of the federal government's embrace of telecommuting? What are the long-term effects of full time telecommuting on employees' careers? How do full time telecommuters compare with part time ones in terms of productivity? How can organizations manage employee loyalty and job satisfaction in an environment where employees have less identification with their employers? What habits should employees cultivate to thrive in an increasingly unpredictable and uncertain environment, and how can society accommodate an increasingly mobile work force?

According to the International Telecommunication Union (ITU), in 2010, 83.7 percent of South Koreans and 80 percent of Japanese citizens have internet access, higher than the percentage of internet users in the US, currently at 79 percent (International Telecommunication Union, 2010). It would be interesting to study adoption of telecommuting by these Asian cultures. The literature to date has focused almost exclusively on organizations in Western society.

In a world where work is becoming increasingly unstable, gaining an understanding of virtual work is crucial. This is a call to action for researchers to thoroughly examine the social, economic, psychological, and managerial implications of telecommuting.

REFERENCES

Brown, L. (2009). *European agriculture: Farming in Europe from 1500 to 1815*. Retrieved from http://www.suite101.com/content/european-agriculture-a114546.

CDW. (2008). *Telework report: Feds stuck in second gear: Private sector puts the pedal to the metal.* Retrieved from http://webobjects.cdw.com/webobjects/media/pdf/2008-CDW-Telework-Report.pdf.

Center for Democracy and Technology & Earnest and Young. (2008). *Risk at home: Privacy and security risks in telecommuting.* Retrieved from http://www.cdt.org/privacy/20080729_riskathome.pdf.

Coyle, D. (1999). *The weightless world: Strategies for managing the digital economy*. Cambridge, MA: The MIT Press.

Drucker, F. P. (1993). *Post capitalist society*. New York, NY: HarperCollins.

Dudley, W. (Ed.). (1998). *The industrial revolution opposing viewpoints*. San Diego, CA: Greenhaven Press, Inc.

Economist. (2011a, February 10). *Print me a Stradivarius: How a new manufacturing technology will change the world.* Retrieved from http://www.economist.com.

Economist. (2011b, February 10). *Three-dimensional printing from digital designs will transform manufacturing and allow more people to start making thing.* Retrieved from http://www.economist.com.

International Telecommunication Union. (2010). *Internet user.* Retrieved from http://www.itu.int.

Lister, K., Harnish, T., & Nille, J. M. (2009). *Undress for success -- The naked truth about making money at home.* New York, NY: John Wiley & Sons.

Reed, B. (2007). Co-working: The ultimate in teleworking flexibility: Co-working sites make space, build community for telecommuters. *Network World.* Retrieved from http://www.networkworld.com/news/2007/102307-coworking.html.

Shapiro, R. J. (2008). *Futurecast: How superpowers, populations, and globalization will change the way you live and work.* New York, NY: St. Martin's Press.

Telework Research Network. (2011). *How many people telecommute.* Retrieved from http://www.teleworkresearchnetwork.com/research/people-telecommute.

Touré, H. I. (2011). *ITU telecom world 2011 forum closing speech.* Retrieved from http://www.itu.int/en/osg/speeches/Pages/2011-10-27.aspx.

Wells, W. (2003). *American capitalism, 1945-2000: Continuity and change from mass production to the information society.* Chicago, IL: Ivan R. Dee.

Wilson, S., & Franzen, J. (2002). *The man in the gray flannel suit.* New York, NY: Da Capo Press.

World at Work. (2009). *Telework trendlines, 2009.* Retrieved from http://www.worldatwork.org/waw/adimLink?id=31115.

Chapter 2
Shadowing Virtual Work Practices:
Describing Subjects and Objects as Action Nets

Craig Lee Engstrom
Elmhurst College, USA

ABSTRACT

Without modification, traditional ethnological approaches cannot fully attend to the translocation of practices into and out of virtual spaces. The ethnographer can observe the dislocation of a particular work practice from a specific place when he or she observes a research subject "log on," but accounting for the translocation of others' practices into the shared virtual space, which is necessary to conduct hermeneutical (or constitutive) research in virtual environments, remains an elusive methodological practice. In this chapter, interpretive shadowing, as it has recently been described (e.g., Czarniawska, 2007), is offered as one way to address some of the limitations of virtual ethnography. By describing (virtual) action nets vis-à-vis the "hybrid character of actions," researchers are able to follow subjects and objects as they move through various spaces/places and describe how these actants constitute fields of practices. Drawing upon examples from two years of shadowing research within the field of private investigations, this chapter describes how shadowers can observe both immediate and virtual practices. Specifically, descriptions of how to account for institutional practices that transcend space, place, and time are provided. Though interpretive research is theoretically sound, examples of specific methodological techniques are provided to address some of the technical limitations of the method when using it to study virtual practices.

INTRODUCTION

Qualitative inquiry has come of age in human studies research. It is especially fashionable in the fields of communication, sociology, and organization studies (Denzin & Lincoln, 2005; Lindlof & Taylor, 2011; Prasad & Prasad, 2002). In *The Sage Handbook of Online Research Methods*, Christine Hine (2008) notes, "Ethnography has become embedded in academic culture as an appropriate way to explore how people make sense of the possibilities that the Internet offers them" (p. 260). I therefore assume that readers are already

DOI: 10.4018/978-1-4666-0963-1.ch002

familiar with the intricacies of conducting qualitative research and writing descriptive, ethnographic accounts. For readers who desire a more thorough introduction to ethnography, there is a healthy amount of scholarship and guides on the subject of conducting and writing qualitative research in and of organizational and virtual environments (see, among other references, Atkinson, Coffey, Delamont, Lofland, & Loftland, 2007; Fielding, Lee, & Blank, 2008; Hammersley & Atkins, 1983; Harper, 2000; Hine, 1994; Kozinets, 2009; Markham & Baym, 2008; Neyland, 2007; Prasad, 2005; Ybema, Yanow, Wels, & Kamsteeg, 2009). Instead of describing how to write ethnographies of virtual work, my goal in this chapter is to describe how to account for virtual work practices that are constitutive of action nets.

Interpretive shadowing, the method described in this chapter, is an amalgam of traditional ethnography, in which "the ethnographer participates, overtly or covertly, in people's daily lives for an extended period of time, watching what happens, listening to what is said, asking questions" (Hammersley & Atkinson, 1983, p. 2), and "virtual ethnography" which, according to Hine (2008), "transfers the ethnographic tradition of the researcher as an embodied research instrument to the social spaces of the Internet" (p. 257). Other than the fact that shadowing involves following a single person or object for a period of time, rather than studying the practices of a culture, the methods used to collect information and write up interpretations are largely consistent with other forms of qualitative research. The *a priori* assumptions, the types of observations collected, and the analysis of data, however, distinguish *interpretive shadowing of action nets* from other forms of qualitative inquiry.

My contribution to qualitative scholarship on virtual work, and the central purpose of this chapter, is to further legitimize *interpretive shadowing of action nets*, as described by Barbara Czarniawska (2004, 2007, 2008), as an approach to studying work practices that occur, often simultaneously,

in virtual and non-virtual contexts. Drawing upon fieldwork observations of private investigators collected over a two year period (2008-2010) as examples, I demonstrate how neither traditional nor virtual ethnological research can account for, by itself, the *a priori* conditions that make possible professional work and business transactions. In this sense, I argue that interpretive shadowing of action nets—which is characterized more by a particular attitude toward epistemology and ontology than a distinctive methodology—brings together features of traditional and virtual qualitative research in such a way that it overcomes one of the central problems in observational qualitative studies of work in organizational and professional contexts—accounting for the unobserved practices that make up virtual work.

In order to achieve the objective of this chapter, I first explain the limitations of virtual and traditional ethnographies in conducting interpretive research on professionals' (virtual) work. Second, I provide an account from the field and, by way of analogy, demonstrate why it is important to account for the often "unobserved but noticed" relationships among actants[1] engaged in virtual work. Third, I describe interpretive shadowing and by drawing upon the initial field account, along with other examples, demonstrate how interpretive shadowing of action nets overcomes these methodological shortcomings. In the conclusion, I discuss some of the challenges of this methodology.

A NEED TO BE CREATIVE: LIMITS OF VIRTUAL AND TRADITIONAL ETHNOGRAPHIES OF PROFESSIONALS' WORK

Virtual ethnography, also frequently referred to as "cyberethnography," "network ethnography," or "netnography" (Kozinets, 2009; Wilson, 2002), is a confusing term that has been defined in conflicting and unclear terms (Driscoll & Gregg,

2010). On the one hand, it can refer to the study of online communities as cultures. Researchers, in this scenario, often join a pre-existing or emerging community via a private terminal and engage in participant-observation research: observing passively or engaging in activities, conversations, and interviews that happen online. The subject and objects of study are bound by the "space" as defined by the cultural participants or researcher (see Wilson, 2002). This form of research, as with early urban and some organizational ethnography, has been criticized for being fast, easy, and convenient. Challenging this argument, virtual ethnographic researchers have thoroughly defended it as a legitimate method (see Hine, 2008). What is more, it is not "easy research" as there are significant ethical and methodological challenges to doing ethnographic work virtually in virtual environments—i.e., when and how to gain "informed consent," how to define membership, how to determine boundaries, how long to spend "in the field," and so on.

On the other hand, the term can describe ethnography that looks at the social meaningfulness of online activity, regardless if the research is conducted virtually. In this sense, virtual ethnographers do not assume that what makes the internet culturally or socially meaningful must be observed online, and accept that ethnographic research of internet communities is only partial. This definition assumes that studies can account for how people "use the internet" by observing their activities in an over-the-shoulder manner (see Hine, 2004). As Hine (2008) notes:

Ethnographers in online settings have...found that the model of the online community fails to do justice to the full spectrum of Internet social interactions. More recently virtual ethnography has continued to emphasize the social reality of the Internet, but has begun to explore the complex connects between online and offline social spaces. A key challenge for the future is to develop forms of ethnography that takes seriously the social

reality of online settings, whilst also exploring their embedding within everyday life. [This is a primary goal of action net researchers.] How far 'virtual ethnography' should continue to be a marked category of ethnography is debatable (pp. 257-258).

Since the introduction of smart phones, Hine's argument against a sole focus on the internet has become clearer. However, the term "virtual ethnography" is still mostly treated as synonymous with descriptions of internet community or internet-mediated practices. It is, therefore, a loaded term for descriptions of "everyday work" (hence the proposed term: shadowing) of professional and organizational stakeholders, which includes both face-to-face and virtual praxis. Qualitative research of professions and organizations should attend to both online and offline practices that continue to be mediated by networked connections, regardless if the connection is immediate. Also, other technology that mediates virtual relationships, such as telephones, text messages, voice mail, email, and even postal service, should not be left unaccounted for in descriptions of social life.

In traditional organizational ethnographic research, researchers observe the situated practices of organizational stakeholders as they interact with one another. Ethnographers document interpersonal dynamics, environmental features, and objects when observed in situ *and* determined to be relevant (Goodall, 2000; van Maanen, 2006). Ethnographers, especially in studies of the entrepreneur (Hjorth & Steyart, 2004), have become interested in capturing the quotidian experiences of people entrepreneuring and organizing (Ybema, et al., 2009). This research may hardly seem exciting; however, for organizational ethnographers much of the intriguing mystery of everyday, professional life is hidden in the ordinary exchanges among ordinary people and ordinary objects on an ordinary sort of day. To capture these prosaic practices, researchers are increasingly oriented toward following a person (Czarniawska, 2007;

McDonald, 2005), or a specific organizational practice, an object, or "fact" (Cooren, 2004; Frandsen, 2009; Harper, 1998). As Ybema et al. note, "[Shadowing] can take place at any level of the organizational hierarchy—studying up or studying down—or across departmental and organizational boundaries; it can be done within a clearly demarcated organization 'space' or in more fragmented, diffuse, and even 'virtual organizations'" (p. 5). Following non-human objects often requires being able to trace movements of non-concrete entities, such as data, facts, and information, which often move rapidly through virtual networks.

Without modifications to data analysis by researchers, ethnographic research, though still very important to understanding organizational culture and work processes, is somewhat impractical in many of today's professional and business environments, which are marked by the hybridization and translocation of work practices through virtual networks (Czarniawska, 2008). Due to its democratization, technology now mediates, often with political implications, most work practices (Long, 2010). Workers and institutional stakeholders labor together and communicate in virtual spaces (e.g., conference calls, online bulletin boards, wikis, and second-life forums), and documents and information are shared asynchronously. The ethnographer can observe the dislocation of a particular work practice from a specific *place* when he or she observes a research subject "log on," but accounting for others' practices that make up an ethnographic interaction is difficult. It is necessary to account for practices that are imported into the shared virtual *space*, if we hope to better understand professional work. The methodological techniques necessary to conduct thorough hermeneutical research in virtual environments remain, however, under explained. Traditionally, the researcher's gaze is on the immediate practices of particular subjects, but this leaves unnoticed the ways in which people, objects, and ideas rapidly move and connect through organizations' virtual

systems. What is more, organizations have become loosely coupled and professional practices diffused; thus, work, information, and artifacts are *always already elsewhere* (Strannegård & Friberg, 2002). Methodologically speaking, researchers must adapt to these changing conditions. The following example, taken from field notes, and the corresponding analogy, reveal why.

FROM THE FIELD: A SITUATED ACCOUNT OF A PRIVATE INVESTIGATOR'S PROSAIC WORK

Shadowee 5 (S5)[2], an agency owner located near Dallas, Texas, and I begin our third day together as we had each day prior. We drive from his home office in Lewisville to Plano, a suburb of Dallas. He's collecting evidence on a plaintiff in a lawsuit for his client, a large insurance company. We set up surveillance just down the street and begin our lackluster wait for the surveillance target to do something. As with the days prior, he accesses the internet using a laptop and cellular connection. He's already listened to his voice mails during the drive, so, according to him, "[his] first task is to contact an attorney to see if his [the attorney's] client [a woman seeking custody] wants us to 'set up' surveillance on a 'deadbeat father.'" He notes that it is critical to his business that he is "able to remain connected while in the field," and further comments that "it is amazing private investigators ever worked without this technology." He further explains that he sometimes uses his iPhone to send and receive email, "but the laptop is faster because it's easier to type on." [About five hours later the attorney confirms, by telephone, the surveillance. We "sit on the target" (i.e., do the surveillance) later that day, from 4:30 p.m. to midnight.]

After he sends the email, he, as on days prior, logs into Google Analytics (google.com/analytics) to "check how many visitors [his] website has received." He mentions that traffic is down a bit from the previous day, and complains that most of his traffic comes from Google Adwords, i.e., paid advertising, rather than basic search results. His goal, as he states, "is to increase his placement, through search engine optimization, in results for the search: 'Dallas private investigator.'" [Later that day he receives a call from a new client, who found the website through Google Adwords.] He then reads news reports. Today, unlike days prior, he finds an interesting article on a private investigator who helped uncover some illegal activities at an assisted-living facility in San Antonio. He copies the article's URL and posts it in his blog (hosted by Blogger.com) under the tag "positive industry news." He informs me that this work is important because it "works against the negative image of the profession." He then posts a link to the blog on Facebook, Twitter, and LinkedIn. He explains, "Because the blog is hosted on my website, people who follow the link will tell Google, Yahoo, and Bing that my website is relevant, which will improve my ranking."

Intermittently, S5 records the investigation target's house and other details of the scene. This, he notes, is proof of his presence when billing clients. During our 7.5 hour stay at the location, we do not observe much activity. People come and go from the house under surveillance, but we never visually see the target. Between the brief episodes of recording data, S5 engages in some of the following practices:

- Fields three phone calls from potential clients (averaging 20 minutes in length each), eight phone calls from currently clients (averaging eight minutes each), five phone calls from his wife and children (averaging six and a half minutes each), and one sales calls from a phone book company seeking renewal of a contract (approximately 18 minutes).
- Makes 12 phone calls, primarily to his other field investigator to "check in" and to receive status reports on a "cheating spouse" case.

- Checks a website that gives him updates on "trackers" (GPS tracking devices) on targets' vehicles. (This is legal in Texas, so long as the client's name is on the title of the vehicle. These devices are mainly used for small business investigations on employees driving company vehicles and for infidelity investigations.) His field investigators are required to have trackers on their vehicles while doing work for the company, so he also checks in on the field investigator to make sure the investigator is "staying put."
- Sends and receives 23 text messages on various topics and with various individuals.
- Emails a contract to a potential client for a "domestic surveillance" (i.e., cheating spouse) for the following day. (The client returns the contract and inputs her credit card information into a web-based form on the company's website.) S5 confirms the transaction by processing the credit card payment through the bank's website.
- In preparation for the forthcoming surveillance for the attorney, S5 looks up the target's address and, by using Google Map's "walk around feature," does "pre-surveillance" on the location. As Figure 1 demonstrates, he is able to determine potential entry and exit points from the neighborhood, determine an optimal location to park his vehicle, and figure out, in advance, what some of the potential visual obstructions could be.

When the client, i.e. the insurance company, decides to terminate the surveillance for the day, we take a short break by eating a late lunch with S5's wife. We then drive to the next surveillance location, where we remain until after midnight. From the activities above, it may seem that the investigator is generally distracted. However, these activities are always, as I observed during other surveillances with this shadowee and others, put on hold whenever there is any activity at a target location.

This Google map (http://maps.google.com) (Figure 1) allows private investigators to do pre-surveillance work virtually. Though there are obvious limitations (the video is not live), Google Maps allows investigators to know a location without having to physically commute to it. From this image alone, researchers can account for numerous action net connections, such as a photographer for Google (usually a volunteer), website programmers, and private investigators using it as a tool.

The activities above are part of the everyday multitasking routines of a small private investiga-

tions company in which the agency owner doubles as a private investigator and business person. They show how doing the business and doing the professional work of private investigating simultaneously require virtual work. But in order to capture the complexities of this work, qualitative researchers must notice more than what is immediately visible. Researchers need to be able to account for the constitutive elements, including subjects and objects, that make the various intersecting interactions of the above practices possible. But what does this entail? It entails accounting for what is not immediately observed. While this may seem counter-intuitive to the notion of "participant-observation," searching for and describing

Figure 1. Private investigator using Google maps for pre-surveillance activity

©2011 Google, © 2011 Teremetrics, ©2011 Europa Technologies

what is not observed but present is a common ethnological practice, as the following analogy demonstrates.

A COMPARATIVE ANALOGY: FOLLOWING A VENDOR AT A FARMERS' MARKET

Imagine a scenario in which a farmers' market is being studied by an organizational ethnographer. Having already spent several months in the field, the ethnographer spends time with specific informants when the market assembles. On an early fall day, the ethnographer observes one informant, a friendly fruit vendor, prepare her stall. The market has just opened, and the weather is poor, so business is slow. The fruit vendor indicates that she wants coffee. The ethnographer follows her to another vendor's stall, where she buys a cup of fresh, locally roasted coffee. Before departing for the coffee vendor's stand, the fruit vendor asks a nearby vegetable vendor to watch her stall. She instructs him: "Do as before and sell to customers within 20% of the advertised price." After the fruit vendor expresses her gratitude—"Can I bring you back something?"—she vacates her stand for some time.

While purchasing her coffee and for about 15 minutes thereafter, the fruit vendor "gossips" with the coffee vendor about local politics and various customers. They also discuss issues related to the market, including increases in insurance premiums and a proposed increase in stall fees. The coffee vendor then asks about the fruit vendor's inventory. The fruit vendor discusses which fruits, jams, and fresh-baked products are worth purchasing, and she presses the coffee vendor to buy cranberries, which are in season. The coffee vendor indicates that she will send her husband over to pick up some cranberries, and other fruits, before the market closes.

When the fruit vendor returns, the vegetable vendor indicates that he sold several kilograms of apples and assorted berries within five percent of the price point. He gives the fruit vendor her money who, in turn, offers the vegetable vendor a bag of apples. The fruit vendor resumes doing what the ethnographer has observed market vendors do for several months—organizes her produce so the best ones stand out, converses with customers, negotiates, and sells.

In this hypothetical situation, the fruit vendor does many things typical for farmers' market vendors. That is to say, they take breaks and, during these breaks, catch up with friends and market their products to each other. Thus, these practices would eventually be described in the ethnography. But that which is not observed, at least not immediately, also needs to be noticed. For starters, the ethnographer observes a conversation that is a persuasive attempt by both the fruit and coffee vendors to shape each other's attitude towards pending political actions (e.g., an increase in stall fees). At a later date, should the ethnographer learn that vendors had formed a coalition against market organizers, this rhetorical effort would be a critical observation. Second, the ethnographer knows that while the fruit vendor is buying coffee (and simultaneously engaging in self-interested promotion), another vendor is selling her produce. Though the ethnographer does not directly observe this practice, there is evidence that it happened. When the fruit vendor returns to her stall she is informed of the outcome and handed money. Just because the ethnographer does not observe these "sells" directly does not mean they are not important to vending.

This example demonstrates that working in a farmers' market requires relationships among various stakeholders that are "unobserved but noticed" by the ethnographer. Conversations are mobilizing future political actions and moderating relationship among vendors, who take turns selling for each other. Pre-established relationships, in short, make the various practices that the ethnographer observed possible. Of course, the ethnographer would need time to see which conversations, relationships, and practices matter, but we are unlikely to question how conclusions regarding what occurred in the ethnographer's absence were derived. But similar observations within virtual environments are likely to be met with more suspicion, largely because in place of human actors there are computer algorithms monitoring in the absence of humans. Many of the constitutive features of virtual work, therefore, are likely to be left unobserved by researchers who do not pay attention to the (virtual) *connections* among human and non-human actants involved in the processes of organizing.

AN ATTITUDE ADJUSTMENT: OBSERVING (NON-)VIRTUAL WORK CONNECTIONS

The hypothetical example provides a good starting point for describing how to collect qualitative data of virtual work. Just because a practice is not immediately observed does not make it irrelevant. An ethnographer, due to nothing more than timing in the field, may not observe research subjects create and manage their websites or Google AdWords (the advertisement displayed in search results). However, whenever an ethnographer observes a phone call motivated by Google AdWords or knows that a customer completes a transaction on a website (data obtainable by looking at website analytics) while the website's owner is doing other things, whether this is online or not, there is significantly rich data motivating the actions, which need to be noted. By comparison, this is like a vendor selling on behalf of another vendor, who happens to be temporarily away from his or her stall. (Instead of a person, it is a "robot" or HTML code. So, while a private investigator is doing research online, while observing a client, while a potential client is reading the website and planning a phone call, while a GPS tracking devise is keeping tabs on an employee, the ethnographer is limited to observing only one or two of these

activities, even though the others are important to the overall professional field. The "market" for the investigator encompasses all of these other practices, and the ethnographer should account for them. Other unobserved information is important, especially if the ethnography is concerned with virtual work. Unlike the farmers' market, however, the qualitative researcher cannot learn of the practices by chance; she or he must go looking for them and accept that there are non-humans, such as search engines, websites, credit card terminals, and so on "working" too. Leaving all of these other practices unaccounted for reduces the potential that the ethnographer will meet an important requirement of quality qualitative research—thick descriptions (Hammersly & Atkinson, 1983). Two central issues are where and how to find evidence of these practices, and how to make sense of these observations and data.

To study virtual work qualitatively, various methods are modifiable. As noted, *interpretive shadowing* can be used to resolve some of the pitfalls of ethnography described above. Below, I specifically describe an emergent approach to shadowing called action net research (Czarniawska, 2004) that seeks to simultaneously account for virtual and non-virtual practices of both human and non-human actants as they move across space, place, and time. By shadowing the "hybrid character of actions" (Meunier & Vasquez, 2008), instead of just observed practices, and by thinking of practices as forming *action nets* (thoroughly explained below) rather than a demarcated ethnographic space, researchers interested in professional practices of virtual work will be able to write thicker descriptions of virtual work.

While *interpretive shadowing of action nets* cannot resolve all of the methodological challenges faced by ethnographers studying virtual work practices, and undoubtedly creates others, my hope is to inspire readers to use this emergent approach, which has become increasingly popular in Scandinavian organization studies (e.g., Del Bosco & Misani, 2011; Korneliussen & Panozzo,

2005; Lindberg & Czarniawska, 2006). In order to fully understand shadowing of action nets, it is important to describe shadowing and action nets. So that explanation of the methods remains clear, I continue to use examples from the field of private investigations to describe the pragmatics of taking this attitude toward this method of research.

ON SHADOWING: OLD AND NEW APPROACHES

While a variety of ethnological approaches can be used to understand practices mediated by and embedded in virtual work practices (e.g., interviewing could be used to understand how subjects make sense of their virtual work practices), shadowing action nets (Czarniawska, 2007) is an emerging method that provides researchers with new fieldwork possibilities. Shadowing, most frequently defined as "a research technique which involves a researcher closely following a member of an organization over an extended period of time" (McDonald, 2005, p. 456) first appeared as "structured observation" (Mintzberg, 1970). There are a variety of studies that appear from the 1970s onward; however, this method has only recently become more fashionable (see Czarniawska, 2007; McDonald, 2005; Meunier & Vasquez, 2008).

Shadowing provides researchers with many advantages. Among other things, shadowers may obtain access to events, meetings, and spaces not easily accessed by other researchers. This is an outcome of having gained rapport and trust with the shadowee over an extended period of time. Shadowing also presents researchers with various challenges, such as interpreting and reporting data that emerge from intimate access to others' personal and professional lives.

Most descriptions of the method and studies using shadowing still tend to use more traditional participant-observation techniques and produce traditional ethnographies (Czarniawska, 2007).

The disadvantage of the more traditional approach is that the researcher focuses on human action and still "lurks at a distance," in the sense that she or he does not move beyond the immediately observable practices of a particular individual. In recent years, several scholars have advocated for researchers to abandon the more structured approaches, and to use the actor-network-theory maxim of "follow the actors themselves" (Latour, 2005, p. 12) and to "accept that [they] may be surprised by [their] fieldwork" (Meunier & Vasquez, 2008, p. 180; see also Czarniawska, 2007; Frandsen, 2009). Such an unstructured approach allows the researcher to be a creative *bricoleur* in the field and to follow all actants, even non-human objects (e.g., texts that *act* by mobilizing human action; see Cooren, 2004). When researchers approach fieldwork through this epistemic frame, they "follow the hybrid character of actions" (Meunier & Vasquez, p. 167), which repositions the researcher's gaze from specific human subjects to specific hybrid actions—e.g., from a private investigator observing to the data derived from observing and the connections required to make observing possible.

This approach requires an epistemological shift in attitude, as noted in the analogous examples above. The researcher must be willing to look for information that clues him or her into ongoing practices that make possible the interactions that are observed. In the example above, the researcher at the farmers' market looks for references to action (e.g., "here is the money, which proves I engaged in negotiation on your behalf"); in regard to the private investigations example, data show a "tracker *followed* the target of an investigation from location 'x' to location 'z.'" Note how the tracker is given agency, it *followed* someone and *produced* data (a map of driving behavior), which are followed by the researcher from the tracking device, assumedly to a satellite, to an account on a website, to a private investigative report, which is handed to a client, which in turn shows up as courtroom testimony. By following data instead of a human, the researcher can observe how these data move virtually (e.g., by email) and reveal how professionals works with these data virtually (e.g., by calculating information and writing a report with others in a cloud-based document, such as Google Docs)[3].

Observing hybrid actions requires researchers to refocus their attention toward the connections of virtual actions, discourses, and objects and to describe how actors translate hybrid characters into symbolically meaningful entities. While the researcher may still follow a specific human actor, she or he can also follow actions in, into, and out of virtual networks. By de-centering the human actor (as the focus of research), shadowers not only gain a better sense of the particularities of virtual work among different professions, but they are also able to better describe the virtualness of this work. Rather than look solely for human actions that mobilize artifacts, shadowers look for artifacts that mobilize actions. Artifacts are treated as both outcomes and inputs of professional actions. Thus, researchers are able to "go into" and "explore" the virtual environment without the concerns of space, place, and time, which are significant limitations of more traditional participant-observation methods. Researchers, therefore, can more easily follow data as they move (asynchronously) between and among virtual and (non-)virtual environments.

Latour (1994) was one of the first researchers to introduce the notion of following non-human actants. Czarniawska (2007), more recently, introduced the field practice of shadowing objects to ethnographers; and, Meunier and Vasquez (2008) provide an operational procedure for actually doing this type of research. Drawing upon Actor-Network-Theory's (ANT) maxim to "follow the actors [i.e., actants]" (Latour, 2005), Meunier and Vasquez propose that researchers do the following: 1) document the flows of actions as they are mobilized in interactions, 2) apply an equivalent analytical strategy to both human and non-human actants, and 3) describe the material and discursive dimensions of communication as action. This outlines an approach that is consistent with other ethnological research in general and shadowing research in particular; however, how to document flows of actions and objects, how to apply an equivalent analysis to each, and how to describe findings remains under explained. From a methodological point of view, shadowers taking this newer approach to shadowing must seek to document the flows of material and discursive textual artifacts (i.e., objects and accounts) as they are mobilized and stabilized in a series of interactions. I propose that one way to conduct such research is through the concept of action net.

ON SHADOWING ACTION NETS

Action net, as described by Czarniawska (2008), is a term that "has no analytical ambitions" (p. 18). Instead, it connotes an approach to studies of organizing that minimize *a priori* assumptions about organizations. Typically, at the outset of research, researchers begin a study with the assumed existence of organizational objects, such as properties, places, people, and events. While these entities do exist, the action net researcher does not assume that they are stable or that they are inputs into organizational processes. Instead, an action net approach presupposes that these are contextual and fluid *outcomes* of organizing. When observing private investigators' practices, therefore, the researcher would not assume that "clients," "targets," and "investigative reports" exist without particular connections among particular actants. It is more important to focus on the intersections, the relationships, and the conditions that make possible such interactions. How an investigator and "tracking device data" interact, in other words, is of greater interest than what these entities are or do by themselves.

Czarniawska (2004, 2008) describes action net research as an amalgam of three larger sociological projects. The first is organization studies turn toward a "sociology of verbs," in which researchers describe *organizing* processes

(Weick, 1979). The second is neo-institutional theory's focus on institutionalized practices within *interorganizational fields*, as well as its attempt to account for actual and virtual connections among actors within these fields (DiMaggio & Powell, 1991; Selznik, 1948). The third is sociology of translation's tenet that social connections create actants' (i.e., human actors' and objects') identities (Latour, 1999a, 1999b; Law, 1999). The first two are well known fields. A lesser known and significant contribution to shadowing research of virtual practices is "sociology of translation." Thus, this requires special attention.

SOCIOLOGY OF TRANSLATION

Practices of translation are the vehicle of organizing (Czarniawska & Sevón, 2005). Successful organizing processes "require a knotting together of different types of action by 'translating' them into one another" (Lindberg & Czarniawska, 2006, p. 292). The sociology of translation is most commonly associated with Bruno Latour (1986) and Michel Callon (1986), and is a primary activity in actor-network-theory. Specifically, the concept "translation" is borrowed from Michel Serres, and as Czarniawska and Sevón note:

For Serres, translation is a generalized operation, not merely linguistic, and it takes many different forms. It may involve displacing something, or the act of substitution; it always involves transformation. Consequently, that which is involved in translation—be it knowledge, people or things—has an identity. Each translation changes the translator and what is translated (p. 8).

Translation thus "involves creating convergences and homologies by relating things that were previously different" (Callon, 1986, p. 211). It is an expression of the agency of actors who interact with various artifacts spread through time and space, and who make these artifacts meaningful by transforming, modifying, deflecting, betraying, adding, or appropriating them (Latour, 1986).

Translation does not apply solely to linguistic translations—from the language of private investigators into the language of clients, for example. Translating applies to any organizational artifact (e.g., object, image, and action), which "means that words can be translated into objects or into actions. But translation can also work the other way around; actions and objects can be translated into words" (Lindberg & Czarniawska, 2006, p. 295; see also Czarniawska, 2000). By focusing on acts of translation, we are able to identify how disparate practices, such as a debtor avoiding the payment of debts, private investigators' professional training and marketing activities, and credit bureaus' data entry, connect with one another to form a particular type of investigative activity, which is translated into a single word, i.e., "skip tracing," which describes this complex process of relationships. Skip tracing is a colloquial term used to describe the process of locating someone's whereabouts, often, though not always, for creditors. In other words, to trace the path that someone who "skipped town" took. This definition, however, is somewhat irrelevant. For the shadower, the (virtual) relationships and objects that must exist before the stabilization of this activity into a recognizable practice (and term) is what counts, and therefore should be accounted for in ethnographies. Skip tracing, as a practice, requires pre-established connections among creditors, lenders, credit bureaus, data bases of information, legislation, regulations, forms, and so on. While these connections existed before the internet, they have certainly changed how actants work together.

An action net forms through the stabilization of connections (i.e., translation nodes). The primary difference between the more familiar actor-network and action net, according to Czarniawska (2008), is time: "the difference between action net and networks lies not in space but in time. Network assumes that actors exist to forge connections, building a network. Action net reverts this assumption, suggesting that connections between and among actions, when stabilized, are used to construct identities of actors" (p. 19). For example, the familiar practices of "reading," "advising," "field working" and "writing" are practices that can be accomplished by many, but they intersect and are translated in particularly meaningful ways to forge "an academic identity" (see Czarniawska, 2008, pp. 19-20, 30).

UNDERSTAND ACTION NETS THROUGH SHADOWING HYBRID CHARACTERS

As described above, the theoretical rationale for conducting action net research is sound. The issue for researchers interested in virtual work remains methodological. Czarniawska and her colleagues provide evidence of empirical uses of action net (e.g., Frandsen, 2009; Gherardi & Nicolini, 2000; Korneliussen & Panozzo, 2005); however, to do this research, scholars must accept that texts (and other objects) have agency (Cooren, 2004), that actions are hybrid (Meunier & Vasquez, 2008) and always already elsewhere (Strannegård & Friberg, 2002).

Researchers can focus on the *agency* of organizational texts, without falling into anthropomorphism (Cooren, 2004) by capturing in writing the qualitative and "…active contribution of texts (especially documents) to organizational processes; that is, on the ways that texts, such as reports, contracts, memos, signs, or work orders, *perform something*" (p. 374; italics in original). Rather than giving primary attention to what organizational stakeholders do with texts, researchers reverse (and therefore expand their attention) the order and study what texts do to stakeholders. Methodologically, the researcher is looking for action verbs in statements made by shadowees and informants:

- "The camera *caught* him in the act."
- "Google Maps *gives me* an opportunity to do pre-surveillance activities for free."
- "The credit card form on my website *makes* [it assists] my work easier."
- "GPS units *track* people's movements."

By focusing on textual performance, researchers are able to avoid the overreliance on face-to-face interactions and, instead, explore the *translocation* of institutional practices. For example, if we know that Google Maps "*gives* an opportunity," then the focus of research can be on how the map and research subjects interact with one another, and for what purpose.

If focus is solely on performative texts, we risk leaving unaccounted the descriptions of *how* textual artifacts and other objects originate. Thus, researchers should simultaneously seek to account for the "hybrid character of actions," i.e., the "association between subjects and objects, humans and nonhumans" across space, place, and time (Meunier & Vasquez, 2008, p. 183). When approached through the lens of action net, researchers document textual agency and hybrid characters in order to account for interactional connections, as these are possible sites of artifact-activity and activity-artifact production. For example, in Figure 2, which is a visual representation of a virtual action net that I have modified (see Czarniawska, 2008, p. 19), an actor (e.g., private investigator) is engaged in familiar practices: social networking, researching, internet browsing, etc.

The center of Figure 2 builds upon Czarniawska's (2008) model. It seeks to represent the institutional work practices that take place in both non-virtual and virtual environments. The "ribbons" are not stable, but move around until they find intersections of activity that are produced by and are productions of identities, texts, and other actants. The four-sided-and-arrowed boxes marked (1) and (2) seek to capture non-virtual interactions. These interactions are also constitutive of and constituted by data and other actants

Figure 2. Private investigating and shadow research as (virtual) action nets

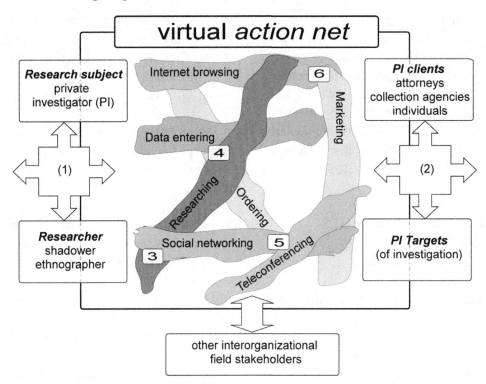

that are imported into or exported out of virtual environments. Because these interactions are also describable vis-à-vis action net research, we can visualize the "streaming ribbons" in the white spaces of each of these boxes.

Each ribbon represents a collection of complex practices that are themselves translated representations of complex activities (e.g., the word "researching" represents a complex activity). Unpacking the complexities is the qualitative researcher's task. When practices overlap (see point 3, for example), these connections make possible another translation. Through the process of translating, actants create other meaningful artifacts (e.g., Facebook wall posts). Overlapping practices reveal the hybrid character of actions, and the types of practices that are observable or accountable in each particular case is what constitutes a field of practices. For example, the private investigator can "pre-text" an investigative target by pretending to be a friend, gain access to

a target's social network, and begin collecting data on the target. However, preexisting artifacts (e.g., a Facebook page) *facilitate* the interaction (i.e., the Facebook page has "textual agency"). At this particular intersection of "social networking" and "researching," a private investigator interested in a particular person or social group maintaining a Facebook page could "follow" the Facebook page and observe status updates ("wall" comments). The researcher could then see how other followers interact with the particular update. In particular, the researcher will pay attention to comments made by the "friends" of the Facebook profile. Thus, the ribbons in Figure 2 represent not only a single actor's practices, but also the intersection of several actors' practices.

In another example (Figure 2, point 4), the researcher could take notice of the connected practices that generate a background report on a target. Though they are not immediately observed, they can be developed by reasonable analysis or by asking the shadowee what kinds of "background practices" go into the production of these reports. Among many other things, these would include: 1) a banker putting financial information into a web-based program; 2) a credit bureau tracking information on people and maintaining a database of this information; 3) a private investigator ordering a report from a third-party vendor (i.e., filling out a website form); and 4) a web program (algorithm) communicating with a database to generate a report. By accounting for as many of these intricacies as we can, the everyday, mundane practices that are normally taken for granted (e.g., filling out a website form) become more meaningful and provide more detail for thicker ethnographic descriptions. The web-based form, as a virtual object, the practice of filling out the form (virtual work), and the aggregation of data by codes tell a more compelling story of what it means to accomplish private investigative work.

PRAGMATICS OF VIRTUAL SHADOWING

As Figure 2 and the above discussion demonstrate, social practices are often translated into texts or "objective data" that can flow through virtual space. Points 1 and 2 in Figure 2 represent the fact that transactions occur in non-virtual social interactions as well, such as an individual who borrows money and fails to pay it back. As I have argued, a shadower ought not to focus solely on the observable practices, but should seek out additional practices (or data of practices) that point to necessary mobilizing actions that make others' (non-)virtual work possible. In the following brief example, I describe some data collection activities that were useful as I conducted my fieldwork. Since each field of practices is likely to be different, researchers will need to be *bricoleurs* and decide what data could be relevant for capturing the various intersecting virtual work practices that constitute their field of research interest. As

always, researchers have to show how these connections are relevant in their writing. Nevertheless, the example I provide is likely to be similar in many fields.

MARKETING PRACTICES

For agency owners, investigating and entrepreneuring are entwined practices. Many private investigators maintain a website and engage in virtual marketing by, for example, maintaining blogs and purchasing content-directed advertisements through Google Adwords. In the latter case, companies bid for advertising placement in internet search results. When the right key words are typed into a search engine and the company's bid is high enough, an advertisement is placed in the search results and the individual searching can click on it. This will send him or her to the investigator's webpage. Notice the translocation and time difference of events. In this example, the investigator is "bidding [in advance] on advertisement space" and "marketing," perhaps while following a cheating spouse. In a sense, the investigator is always already doing virtual work, and although these actions are not observable to the ethnographer, they are very relevant to a private investigator's success as a business owner.

Consistent with the virtual action net research method proposed, focus is not solely on the phone call or the AdWord either, but on the ongoing translation of action. Therefore, it is important to find sources of data that reveal and make sense of relevant, though unobserved actions. The private investigator's virtual marketing through Google Adwords enabled the "Adword" to perform its function—marketing. The action of many consumers today is to use the internet to find companies. Thus, as Figure 3 demonstrates, Google analytics on a company's website is something that ought to be obtained by qualitative researchers. From these data, many things can be traced. For example, these data reveal the "Top Traffic Sources" based on source and keywords (Figure 3, point 1). These reveal the search practices of potential clients. Particularly, we observe that the Google Adwords ("google [cpc]," Figure 3, point 2) sent the greatest amount of traffic to this particular investigator's website during the period March 17 to April 16, 2011. The data also reveal that the top key word search was "private investigator dallas" (Figure 3, point 3). These data reveal that there are many connections being formed at the intersection of a potential client's "internet browsing" and the private investigator's "marketing" practices (Figure 2, point 6). It reveals a pattern of word combinations and "key word density" that inform consultants and researchers about consumer practices within the field of private investigations. In short, field notes, when doing participant observation research of virtual work, account for practices that intersect in virtual spaces. Other artifacts to obtain access to as way to identify action net connections include the following: telephone records, documents stored in filing cabinets, certain data stored on hard drive, social networking statistics (e.g., who follows a particular twitter feed), and so on.

Obtaining analytic information from websites is one way to account for connections among virtual work practices. Among other practices, this figure reveals the practices of virtual marketing and web browsing. It reveals how people arrive to a website and how long they stay. In other screens of this program, a free service of

Figure 3. Google analytics: interactions with company website via internet search

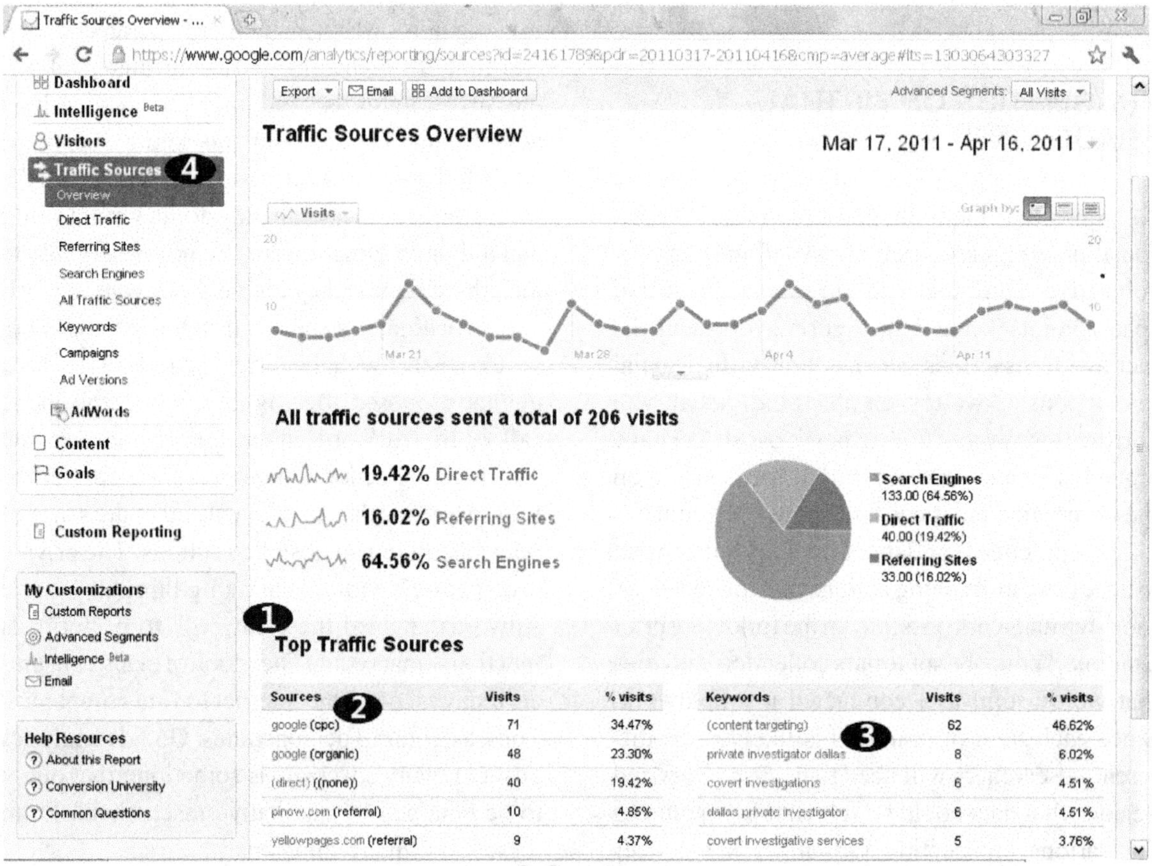

© Google

Google, it shows what specific links people click on. Qualitative interviews could reveal how shadowees make sense of these data.

By focusing only on what the private investigator does, rather than also on the data that reveal action ("connections" within action nets), significant amounts of important field data are lost. All of the investigators I shadowed and interviewed (30 in total) understood the importance of internet advertising for "exciting" the Google algorithms. Thus, shadowers (and ethnographers) observing the practices of human subjects need to gain access to data of virtual practices that make a particular organization fields possible. However, the importance of spending time with human subjects should not be minimized. Without data of both online and offline practices, the importance of "Google searching"—and the particular ways in which subjects in a particular field make sense of and use search engines—would mean little in ethnographies of organizational practices.

CONCLUSION: IMPLICATIONS AND CHALLENGES OF SHADOWING

In this chapter, I have argued that shadowing aimed toward describing action nets can facilitate qualitative research for scholars interested in better understanding interorganizational field practices, many of which occur virtually. Qualitative methods of traditional ethnography apply to this type of research, but the assumptions that we bring to the field need to be changed in order to do effective qualitative research of and on virtual work. The product of this approach to research is likely to be richer ethnographies; however, I should note that such research could also be used to write a taxonomy or theoretical analysis (Czarniawska, 2008). As shadowing matures as an important qualitative research methodology, it is necessary for researchers to engage in ongoing dialogue about how to improve fieldwork, analysis, and writing. As an approach to studying

work that moves between non-virtual and virtual environments, I have articulated some theoretical underpinnings and provided examples of doing shadowing fieldwork of virtual work.

Despite the exciting possibilities that this method offers, there are some challenges to such fieldwork that need to be addressed—access, time, and cost. *Access.* One of the primary benefits and distinguishing features of shadow research, as compared to general ethnological observation, is that it focuses on one specific individual (often someone in a position of authority or power) or object for an extended period of time. Shadowing helps build rapport, which is needed to gain access to objects like website analytics, accounting data, phone records, and so on. Shadowing also eliminates the concern of who or what within an organization to follow. In terms of entrepreneurship research, shadowees may find the research appealing to their egos or perceive the research as a possible opportunity. However, this also raises the possibility that the researcher could lose autonomy or have trouble publishing data that is so easily connected to a particular human subject. *Time.* Like traditional ethnographic fieldwork, shadowing is extensive and requires a large investment of time. The amount of data generated from such fieldwork is often overwhelming and, therefore, requires time for analysis. What is more, with the accelerated pace of business, it is likely that research data or findings could become outdated before they are published. One benefit of shadowing, however, is that human shadowees can help the researcher identify things of relevance and the researcher can provide immediate and relevant feedback as quasi-consultants. *Cost.* Linked with time, the cost of shadowing is significant. The cost of shadowing private investigators for the two years I was in the field came to just about $8,000, money spent primarily on travel. Doing research remotely or virtually would certainly reduce these expenses.

Researchers who decide to engage in shadowing research may find savvy routes around these problems. As more researchers conduct and publish shadowing fieldwork on action nets, we will gain a better sense of the benefits and limitations of this growing research approach. I hope neophyte and seasoned researchers will find the orientations and techniques presented in this chapter novel enough to take on the methodological risks. The challenge is not in the methodological procedures—researchers can continue to use the qualitative fieldwork procedures they are comfortable with (e.g., note taking and "thematizing"). The primary challenge for researchers is in modifying where we look, understanding what we are looking at (connections not entities), and changing how we analyze what we observe (and notice but do not see). It is crucial to remember that practices not immediately observed will leave traces of data that reveal what practices and connections matter in particular to the production of objects that are visible.

REFERENCES

Atkinson, P., Coffey, A. J., Delamont, S., Lofland, J., & Loftland, L. H. (Eds.). (2007). *The Sage handbook of ethnography*. Los Angeles, CA: Sage.

Callon, M. (1986). Some elements of a sociology of translation: Domestication of the scallops and the fisherman of Saint Brieuc Bay. In Law, J. (Ed.), *Power, Action, and Belief* (pp. 196–223). London, UK: Routledge.

Cooren, F. (2004). Textual agency: How texts do things in organizational settings. *Organization*, *11*, 373–393. doi:10.1177/1350508404041998

Cooren, F. (2006). The organizational world as a plenum of agencies. In *Communication as Organizing: Empirical and Theoretical Explorations in the Dynamics of Text and Conversation* (pp. 81–100). Mahwah, NJ: Lawrence Erlbaum Associates.

Czarniawska, B. (2000). Organizational translations. In Kalthoff, H., Rottenburg, R., & Wagener, H.-J. (Eds.), *Facts and Figures: Economic Representations and Practices* (pp. 117–142). Marburg, Germany: Metropolis.

Czarniawska, B. (2004). On time, space, and action nets. *Organization*, *11*, 773–791. doi:10.1177/1350508404047251

Czarniawska, B. (2007). *Shadowing and other techniques for doing fieldwork in modern societies*. Liber, Denmark: Copenhagen Business School Press.

Czarniawska, B. (2008). *A theory of organizing*. Cheltenham, UK: Edward Elgar.

Czarniawska, B., & Sevón, G. (2005). Translation is a vehicle, imitation its motor, and fashion sits at the wheel. In Czarniawska, B., & Sevón, G. (Eds.), *Global Ideas: How Ideas, Objects and Practices Travel in a Global Economy* (pp. 7–14). Sweden: Liber AB.

Del Bosco, B., & Misani, N. (2011). Keeping the enemies close: The contribution of corporate social responsibility to reducing crime against the firm. *Scandinavian Journal of Management*, *27*, 87–98. doi:10.1016/j.scaman.2010.10.003

Denzin, N. K., & Lincoln, Y. S. (Eds.). (2005). *The Sage handbook of qualitative research*. Thousand Oaks, CA: Sage.

DiMaggio, P., & Powell, W. W. (1991). *The new institutionalism in organizational analysis*. Chicago, IL: University of Chicago Press.

Driscoll, C., & Gregg, M. (2010). My profile: The ethics of virtual ethnography. *Emotion, Space, and Society*, *3*, 15–20. doi:10.1016/j.emospa.2010.01.012

Fielding, N. G., Lee, R. M., & Blank, G. (2008). *The Sage handbook of online research methods*. Los Angeles, CA: Sage.

Frandsen, A.-C. (2009). From psoriasis to a number and back. *Information and Organization, 19*, 103–128. doi:10.1016/j.infoandorg.2009.02.001

Geertz, C. (1973). Thick description: Toward an interpretive theory of culture. In Geertz, C. (Ed.), *The Interpretation of Cultures: Selected Essays by Clifford Geertz* (pp. 3–30). New York, NY: Basic Books.

Gherardi, S., & Nicolini, D. (2000). To transfer is to transform: The circulation of safety knowledge. *Organization, 7*, 329–348. doi:10.1177/135050840072008

Goodall, H. L. (2000). *Writing the new ethnography*. Walnut Creek, CA: AltaMira Press.

Hammersley, M., & Atkinson, P. (1983). *Ethnography: Principles in practice*. London, UK: Tavistock.

Harper, R. H. (2000). The organisation in ethnography: A discussion of ethnographic fieldwork in CSCW. *Computer Supported Cooperative Work, 9*, 239–264. doi:10.1023/A:1008793124669

Harper, R. P. (1998). *Inside the IMF: An ethnography of documents, technology, and action*. London, UK: Academic Press.

Hine, C. (1994). *Virtual ethnography*. Paper presented at the When Science Becomes Culture International Symposium on Science Literacy Conference. Montreal, Canada. Retrieved from http://www.cirst.uqam.ca/pcst3/PDF/Communications/HINE.PDF.

Hine, C. (2004). *Virtual ethnography revisited*. Paper presented at the Online Research Methods, Research Methods Festival. Oxford, UK. Retrieved from http://www.restore.ac.uk/orm/background/exploringorms/rmf_hine_outline.pdf.

Hine, C. (2008). Virtual ethnography: Modes, varieties, affordances. In Fielding, N., Lee, R. M., & Blank, G. (Eds.), *The Sage Handbook of Online Research Methods* (pp. 257–270). Los Angeles, CA: Sage.

Hjorth, D., & Steyaert, C. (Eds.). (2005). *Narrative and discursive approaches in entrepreneurship: A second movements in entrepreneurship book*. Cheltenham, UK: Edward Elgar.

Korneliussen, T., & Panozzo, F. (2005). From "nature" to "economy" and "culture": How stockfish travels and constructs an action net. In Czarniawska, B., & Sevón, G. (Eds.), *Global Ideas: How Ideas, Objects and Practices Travel in a Global Economy* (pp. 106–125). Sweden: Liber AB.

Kozinets, R. V. (2009). *Netnography: Doing ethnographic research online*. Los Angeles, CA: Sage.

Latour, B. (1986). *The pasteurization of France*. Cambridge, MA: Harvard University Press.

Latour, B. (1994). On technical mediation: Philosophy, sociology, genealogy. *Common Knowledge, 3*, 29–64.

Latour, B. (1999a). On recalling ANT. In Law, J., & Hassard, J. (Eds.), *Actor Network Theory and After* (pp. 15–25). Oxford, UK: Blackwell Publishing.

Latour, B. (1999b). Circulating reference: Sampling the soil in the Amazon Forest. In *Pandora's hope: Essays on the Reality of Science Studies* (pp. 24–79). Cambridge, MA: Harvard University Press.

Latour, B. (2005). *Reassembling the social: An introduction to actor-network-theory*. Oxford, UK: Oxford University Press.

Law, J. (1999). After ANT: Complexity, naming and topology. In Law, J., & Hassard, J. (Eds.), *Actor Network Theory and After* (pp. 1–14). Oxford, UK: Blackwell Publishing.

Lindberg, K., & Czarniawska, B. (2006). Knotting the action net, or organizing between organizations. *Scandinavian Journal of Management, 22,* 292–306. doi:10.1016/j.scaman.2006.09.001

Lindlof, T. R., & Taylor, B. C. (2011). *Qualitative communication research methods* (3rd ed.). Los Angeles, CA: Sage.

Long, S. D. (2010). Preface. In Long, S. D. (Ed.), *Communication, Relationships and Practices in Virtual Work.* Hershey, PA: IGI Global. doi:10.4018/978-1-61520-979-8

Markham, A. N., & Baym, N. K. (Eds.). (2008). *Internet inquiry: Conversations about method.* Los Angeles, CA: Sage.

McDonald, S. (2005). Studying actions in context: A qualitative shadowing method for organizational research. *Qualitative Research, 5,* 455–473. doi:10.1177/1468794105056923

Meunier, D., & Vasquez, C. (2008). On shadowing the hybrid character of actions: A communicational approach. *Communication Methods and Measures, 2,* 167–192. doi:10.1080/19312450802310482

Mintzberg, H. (1970). Structured observation as a method to study managerial work. *Journal of Management Studies, 7,* 87–107. doi:10.1111/j.1467-6486.1970.tb00484.x

Neyland, D. (2007). *Organizational ethnography.* London, UK: Sage.

Prasad, A., & Prasad, P. (2002). The coming age of interpretive organizational research. *Organizational Research Methods, 5,* 4–11.

Prasad, P. (2005). *Crafting qualitative research: Working in the postpositivist traditions.* Armonk, NY: M.E. Sharpe.

Strannegård, L., & Friberg, M. (2002). *Already elsewhere: Play, identity and speed in the business world* (Wilson, D., Trans.). Stockholm, Sweden: Raster Förlag.

Van Maanen, J. (2006). Ethnography then and now. *Qualitative Research in Organizations and Management, 1,* 13–21. doi:10.1108/17465640610666615

Weick, K. (1979). *The social psychology of organizing.* Reading, MA: Addison-Wesley.

Wilson, S. M. (2002). The anthropology of online communities. *Annual Review of Anthropology, 31,* 449–467. doi:10.1146/annurev.anthro.31.040402.085436

Ybema, S., Yanow, D., Wels, H., & Kamsteeg, F. H. (2009). *Organizational ethnography: Studying the complexity of everyday life.* Los Angeles, CA: Sage.

ADDITIONAL READING

Adolfsson, P. (2005). Environment's many faces: On organizing and translating objects in Stockholm. In Latour, B., & Weibel, P. (Eds.), *Making Things Public: Atmospheres of Democracy* (pp. 396–397). Cambridge, MA: MIT Press.

Bruni, A. (2005). Shadowing software and clinical records: On the ethnography of non-humans and heterogeneous contexts. *Organization, 12,* 357–378. doi:10.1177/1350508405051272

Bruyn, S. T. (2002). Studies of the mundane by participant observation. *Journal of Mundane Behavior, 3*(2), 1–9.

Capote, T. (1975). A day's work. In *Music for Chameleons.* London, UK: Abascus.

Cussins, C. (1996). Ontological choreography: Agency through objectification in infertility clinics. *Social Studies of Science, 26,* 575–610. doi:10.1177/030631296026003004

Czarniawska, B. (2008). Organizing: How to study it and how to write about it. *Qualitative Research in Organizations and Management, 3,* 4–20. doi:10.1108/17465640810870364

Lareau, A. (2003). *Unequal childhoods: Class, race, and family life*. Berkeley, CA: University of California Press.

Law, J. (2002). Objects and spaces. *Theory, Culture & Society*, *19*(5/6), 91–105. doi:10.1177/026327602761899165

Miller, D. (1998). *A theory of shopping*. Ithaca, NY: Cornell University Press.

Mintzberg, H. (1973). *The nature of managerial work*. New York, NY: Harper and Row.

Polite, V. C., McClure, R., & Rollie, D. L. (1997). The emerging reflective urban principal: The role of shadowing encounters. *Urban Education*, *31*, 466–489. doi:10.1177/0042085997031005002

Sclavi, M. (2007). *An Italian lady goes to the Bronx* (Martin, H., Trans.). Milan, Italy: IPOC di Pictro Condemi.

Vasquez, C. (2008). *Projecting action: Caught in a dance of agency*. Paper presented at the International Communication Association. Montreal, Canada.

KEY TERMS AND DEFINITIONS

Actants: Any human or non-human object that is said to have agency, or agency-like properties. Actants mobilize practices.

Action Net: A term suggested by Barbara Czarniawska (2004) as a starting point for the social constructivist perspective on organizing. Action net researchers bracket *a priori* assumptions and focus their research on intersecting practices that constitute identities and entities.

Ethnology: The study of humans and objects with the aim of comparing, analyzing, and describing their effects on culture, language, technology, and so on. Ethnographies, or descriptions of cultural and organizational practices, are a typical outcome of the ethnological process.

Hybrid Character of Actions: A term that recognizes that associations among actants within organizational settings are complex. Such associations mobilize the participation of entities with material, discursive, human, and nonhuman ontologies.

Shadowing: A method of study that is similar to ethnology, but with primary focus on following a single person or object (e.g., text) for a period of time.

Textual Agency: A term that seeks to capture the influence of rhetorical and discursive artifacts on humans. In today's technoscape of complex algorithms, it is possible that texts and objects influence each other without human intervention. Francois Cooren (2006) suggests that organizations are comprised solely of agencies (i.e., "a plenum of agencies").

Transaction: An interaction involving transformation of either subject or object, such as in the exchange of information or in the exchange in object possession.

Translation: A term used in actor-network-theory (ANT) to describe the sense-making practices among actors in which something new is produced (e.g., a new relationship, or a new understanding of a subject or object).

Mobilization: A descriptive term that connotes rhetorical influence that "sets in motion" organizing practices.

ENDNOTES

[1] Researchers that study both human and non-human interactions frequently use the term *actant*, which is a better term, "since the word *agent* in the case of nonhumans is uncommon" (Latour, 1994, p. 33).

[2] I am maintaining the numbers I have used in my raw data to track data and protect the identity of research subject.

[3] During my research I only observed one investigative company use Google Docs.

Multiple investigators were working a case and they added their field notes to a report and read others' notes to understand the intelligence that had been collected during the investigation. Cloud computing is relatively new and so this practice will likely increase among professional investigators over time. This example shows how investigators can work virtually (terminal-to-internet environment) but also that virtual work requires more than remote access. They include information gathered by virtual means, but they also gather data gathered through non-virtual means. A researcher can also observe one shadowee by "looking over his or her

shoulder" and, if the Google Doc is being edited by another, can observe "from the other side" by observing how the document changes in the virtual space. The research can make reasonable inferences to the practices on "the other side" of the interaction. Such inferences can be cautiously made within asynchronous situations too. If a private investigator hires a search engine optimization company to design his or her website, even though the website may exist prior to the researcher's presence (and absence at the conclusion of fieldwork), the researcher can reasonably assume what went into the production of the website.

Chapter 3
Teleworkers' Boundary Management:
Temporal, Spatial, and Expectation-Setting Strategies

Kathryn L. Fonner
University of Wisconsin – Milwaukee, USA

Lara C. Stache
University of Wisconsin – Milwaukee, USA

ABSTRACT

Building on boundary theory, this chapter analyzes the open-ended responses of home-based teleworkers (N = 146) to identify the temporal and spatial strategies used by teleworkers to manage the boundary between work and home domains, and the expectation-setting strategies teleworkers use to uphold this boundary with family and work contacts. Teleworkers used temporal routines and physical space to segment work from home domains, but also maintained a degree of permeability between work and home domains in order to preserve the flexible benefits of their work arrangement. Teleworkers employed direct and indirect strategies with their families and colleagues to manage the work-home boundary. Relationships between boundary management choices, demographic variables, work-life conflict, and life-work conflict are also examined.

INTRODUCTION

Telework is a virtual work arrangement in which employees use technology to perform their regular work outside of the organization's physical boundaries (Thatcher & Zhu, 2006). It is increasingly prevalent in the U.S. (World at Work, 2009), and has been lauded for providing employees flex-

ibility and autonomy. While these are clearly desirable job attributes, they also heighten the tension between employees' work responsibilities and personal obligations, and increase the need for effective management of the work-home boundary. This may be especially true for home-based teleworkers, as their work and personal domains occupy the same physical space (Raghuram, Wiesenfeld, & Garud, 2003).

DOI: 10.4018/978-1-4666-0963-1.ch003

To follow, we explore the boundary management strategies home-based teleworkers use to negotiate the boundary between home and work spheres. Building upon boundary theory (Ashforth, Kreiner, & Fugate, 2000), we identify the ways that home-based teleworkers use temporal, spatial, and expectation-setting strategies to establish and sustain the work-home boundary. The goal of this study is to expand current knowledge regarding how teleworkers use time and space to manage the intersection of work and home, as well as to identify the strategies teleworkers use to set expectations with family and work contacts regarding their work-home boundary. The study also extends previous research by examining how demographic variables are associated with the use of temporal and spatial strategies, and how temporal/spatial strategy combinations and expectation-setting strategies are linked to teleworkers' work-life and life-work conflict.

BACKGROUND

Boundary theory provides a theoretical framework for understanding the ways in which individuals create boundaries around work and home role domains in order to facilitate transitions between roles (e.g., Ashforth, et al., 2000; Nippert-Eng, 1996). Boundaries help to delimit the scope and perimeter of an individual's role in a particular domain and can influence their psychological and physical movement between roles (Ashforth, et al., 2000, p. 474). In general, boundaries are defined in terms of their permeability and flexibility. Boundary permeability is the extent to which the domain or role enables an individual to be physically located in one domain but psychologically and behaviorally involved in another domain or role (Pleck, 1977). For example, permeability occurs when a wife accepts phone calls from her husband at work, or a father accepts work-related calls at home (Winkel & Clayton, 2010). Boundary flexibility is the degree to which spatial and

temporal boundaries are pliable (Ashforth, et al., 2000), such that an individual can be cognitively or behaviorally removed from one domain in order to meet the demands of another domain (Bulger, Matthews, & Hoffman, 2007) or can easily transition from one role domain to another (Matthews & Barnes-Farrell, 2010).

To date, boundary management research has largely focused on the ways that boundaries are enacted to either segment or integrate work and family role domains. This research has predominantly been conducted in traditional, or collocated work contexts, with a focus on the management of "boundaries that exist between individuals' work and their (personal) lives outside of work (i.e., work-nonwork boundaries)" (Hecht & Allen, 2009, p. 840). This body of literature has examined how individuals enact boundaries in order to segment and separate home and work roles, or to allow those roles to become integrated and overlap, and the individual and work-related outcomes associated with those role boundary choices. Examples of complete segmentation or integration are rare (Rau & Hyland, 2002), and a range of integration and segmentation approaches represent a viable means to cope with work and personal demands (Edwards & Rothbard, 2000).

Because there may be costs associated with integrating work and family roles, individuals may develop boundary management strategies to separate role demands and expectations into home and work spheres (Ashforth, et al., 2000). Segmentation reduces the blurring of role boundaries and therefore may help individuals cope with different expectations within each role domain (Hewlin, 2003), limit interruptions (Rothbard & Edwards, 2003), diminish the spillover of emotions from one sphere to another (Ilies, Wilson, & Wagner, 2009), and allow for the development of full personal lives (Rothbard, Phillips, & Dumas, 2005). Based on these advantages, individuals may adopt various temporal, spatial, behavioral, and communicative tactics (e.g., Kreiner, Hollensbe, & Sheep, 2009) aimed at segmenting work and home domains. These strategies may include clearly defining work versus personal time and maintaining separate physical spaces for work and personal responsibilities (Kossek, Lautsch, & Eaton, 2006).

However, because transitioning between work and home roles becomes more challenging when strong boundaries are in place, some individuals may prefer an integrated approach (Ashforth, et al., 2000). Integrating strategies enable a more blurred line between home and work spheres, such that role transitions are easy and the barriers between the two domains are not as rigid. Integration allows more flexibility and enables individuals to cope with any issue as it arises in any domain, thus removing the tension of balancing multiple roles (Rothbard, et al., 2003). For these reasons, individuals may prefer integrating strategies such as attending to personal responsibilities during the work day, conducting work after traditional work hours and on weekends, and generally blurring the boundaries around work and personal space and time. Employees with higher work-home integration experience greater spillover of their work attitudes into their personal lives (Ilies, et al., 2009) and greater work-family conflict (Olson & Buchanan, 2006). Additionally, individuals who frequently use communication technologies for work-related purposes during personal time (e.g., "after hours") experience greater work-family interference (Boswell & Buchanan, 2007; Park & Jex, 2011).

Clearly, research in traditional, collocated contexts has shown that there are benefits to segmenting and to integrating the boundary between work and home roles. Although limited research has been conducted to explore the specific boundary management strategies utilized by teleworkers to manage the work-home boundary, some scholars have suggested this is an area ripe for research (e.g., Kossek, et al., 2006; Kreiner, et al., 2009). We propose this is an area that warrants additional investigation.

TELEWORK AND BOUNDARY MANAGEMENT

In any work environment, employees continually negotiate the ongoing tension between professional and personal role responsibilities (Ballard & Gossett, 2007). But teleworkers face a unique challenge, in that their flexibility is coupled with a distance from the structure of daily work routines and interactions, which are useful in establishing and performing organizational roles. In addition, home-based teleworkers face the complexity of managing a work arrangement within their home. This requires teleworkers to make choices about when and where to perform work and personal roles. Thus, a balancing act is required to address the desire for flexibility and the need for structure.

Based on these challenges, we propose it is important to identify and understand the strategies that home-based teleworkers utilize to manage their work-home boundary. In general, telework has been lauded for its many benefits, including increased productivity and work-life balance (Shia & Monroe, 2006). Teleworkers have been found to be less likely to experience work interference in their personal responsibilities, or work-life conflict (e.g., Fonner & Roloff, 2010), and some studies have revealed that telework diminishes both work-life and life-work conflict (e.g., Raghuram & Wiesenfeld, 2004), indicating that teleworkers may structure work and personal boundaries in ways that prevent these domains from conflicting with one another. However, additional research is warranted to identify how employees strike a balance between work and personal responsibilities (Bailey & Kurland, 2002) in order to mitigate potential interruptions and stress. Although teleworkers may experience significantly less stress associated with work-related interruptions and meetings relative to office-based employees (Fonner & Roloff, 2010), non-work-related interruptions inherent in a home work environment can be problematic (Hunton, 2005) and may substantially increase teleworkers' stress (e.g., Konradt, et al., 2003).

Therefore, it is important to evaluate the strategies that home-based teleworkers use to manage and sustain the boundary between work and home in order to successfully manage role transitions and avoid stressful interference between role domains.

Somewhat surprisingly, limited research has investigated the specific ways that teleworkers approach boundary management as they negotiate the work-home interface. Tietze and Musson (2003) conducted interviews with 25 home-based teleworkers in the U.K and discovered that teleworkers and their families negotiated the work-home boundary using various segmenting strategies. These included creating temporal boundaries to regulate work versus personal time, prioritizing the day according to tasks, and managing availability to family members through temporal and spatial boundaries. Based on these 25 interviews, Tietze (2002) presented three case studies representing distinct approaches to "coping" with the shared work-home interface. Teleworkers ranged from managing an integrated, fluid work-home boundary, to sustaining higher segmentation between work and home domains and managing those boundaries through communication, dress, physical space, and temporal routines. In another study, Tietze and Musson (2002) interviewed 20 home-based teleworkers and found that those adopting integrating strategies experienced the benefits of working from home (e.g., flexibility), but also experienced greater stress and chaos associated with balancing multiple roles and blurred boundaries. Alternatively, those using segmenting strategies found their situation to be more "manageable," but their rigid boundaries also created stress as work was often prioritized over family roles (p. 34). A quantitative study by Kossek et al. (2006) supported this, indicating that teleworkers using integrating strategies experienced significantly higher family-work conflict. Although recent research has continued to explore the ways that teleworkers use time, space (Myrie & Daly, 2009; Mustafa, 2010), and technology (Nansen, 2010) to manage the work-home boundary, more research

is warranted to identify the specific strategies that teleworkers utilize, the pervasiveness of strategy use across teleworkers, and the outcomes associated with boundary choices.

Recent research has shown initial evidence that demographic variables may be related to teleworkers' boundary management choices. For example, teleworking mothers face challenges when they integrate their work-home boundary in order to balance work, childcare, and household responsibilities (Hilbrecht, Shaw, Johnson, & Andrey, 2008). Men also struggle to construct their identities as home-based teleworkers and as parents (Marsh & Musson, 2008), and these emotions may shape their boundary choices. In general, gender and having children in the home have been linked with boundary management preferences (Myrie, 2009; Sullivan & Lewis, 2001) and additional demographics such as job and organizational tenure and teleworking extensiveness may also be associated with teleworkers' boundary management preferences.

As telework becomes increasingly prevalent (World at Work, 2009), it will become imperative for organizations and potential teleworkers to understand the complex set of choices that may be involved in working from home and negotiating the work-home boundary. For example, if teleworkers choose to adhere to a particular work schedule, they may still need to determine "to whom to grant access during work hours, how rigidly to maintain these rules of access (as well as to determine what these rules are and how they are to be communicated)" (Tietze, 2002, p. 387). Given the limited research that has been conducted to date, and the relatively small sample sizes that have been evaluated in those studies, we propose an exploratory study with the goal of examining a larger cross-section of teleworkers in order to identify the specific boundary management strategies of home-based teleworkers. To date, scholars have not thoroughly investigated the specific boundary management and expectation-setting strategies used by teleworkers, and have primarily focused on teleworkers' boundary management with their families. In addition, the small sample sizes and interviews used in previous studies have not allowed for an empirical examination of the prevalence of strategy use, the demographics associated with boundary choices, and the outcomes associated with specific strategy combinations and choices. By drawing upon a larger cross-section of teleworkers and analyzing open-ended responses, demographic data, and some closed-ended measures, this study aims to extend future research in several ways.

First, this study will identify specific ways that teleworkers utilize time and space to manage their work-home boundary. We will examine the temporal and spatial strategies teleworkers use to segment or integrate work and home domains, and the extent to which these strategies enable boundary flexibility and permeability. Second, the study will identify the communicative and behavioral expectation-setting strategies teleworkers use with work contacts and family and close personal contacts. Third, the study will examine the extent to which key demographic variables are associated with teleworkers' use of boundary management and expectation-setting strategies. Finally, we will identify how temporal/spatial strategy combinations and expectation-setting strategies are related to work-life and life-work conflict.

Research Questions

Telworkers may adopt segmentation strategies by relying upon temporal structures, such as routines and what they perceive to be "traditional" work hours, in order to remove the overlap in personal and work activities (Kossek, et al., 1999). By adhering to a strict temporal structure, teleworkers may attempt to regulate access to their schedule and "synchronise work and family time" (Tietze & Musson, 2003, p. 447). Alternatively, teleworkers may relish the flexibility of their work arrangement and prefer to adopt a more fluid approach to evaluating time. Indeed, teleworkers may utilize time

in ways that enables or constrains role transitions and the permeability of the work-home boundary.

RQ1: How do teleworkers use temporal structure to manage their work-home boundary?

Teleworkers may also use physical space to negotiate their work-home interface, and to enable or constrain boundary flexibility and permeability. Some may work in separate spaces that are isolated from personal areas of the home, and others may work in spaces that integrate work and personal roles. Teleworkers may also manipulate physical space and manage physical artifacts (Myrie & Daly, 2009) in order to segment or integrate their work-home boundary.

RQ2: How do teleworkers use physical space to manage their work-home boundary?

In order to structure the work-home boundary and to avoid potential boundary violations, teleworkers may utilize various communicative and behavioral expectation-setting strategies to indicate to colleagues, family members, and close personal contacts when and where they will be available to fulfill work and personal roles.

RQ3: How do teleworkers set expectations about the work-home boundary with their family and those with whom they have close personal relationships?
RQ4: How do teleworkers set expectations about the work-home boundary with colleagues and their manager?

Demographic variables such as gender, children in the home, organizational and job tenure, and time spent teleworking may influence teleworkers' use of temporal and spatial strategies, and their choices regarding expectation-setting strategies used with their families, personal contacts, and work contacts.

RQ5: To what extent are demographic differences associated with teleworkers' boundary management choices?

In their *model of work-home boundary work,* Kreiner et al. (2009, p. 711) propose that employees' use of temporal, spatial, communicative, and behavioral boundary tactics will decrease their work-home conflict. Indeed, integration of the work-home boundary has been associated with higher work-family conflict (Olson & Buchanan, 2006) and family-work conflict (Kossek, et al., 2006).

H1: Teleworkers using segmenting strategies will report lower work-life conflict and lower life-work conflict relative to teleworkers using integrative strategies.

METHOD

Sample and Procedure

The study sample consisted of home-based teleworkers (N = 146)[1], including 89 (61%) women and 57 (39%) men (see Table 1 for demographics). The mean age was 41.14 years ($SD = 12.59$). Overall, 35 (24.0%) participants reported that they teleworked 5 days a week, 16 (11.0%) teleworked 4 days, 12 (8.2%) teleworked 3 days, 23 (15.8%) teleworked 2 days, and 42 (28.8%) teleworked 1 day per week[2]. The remaining 18 (12.3%) reported that they teleworked less than 1 day per week, ranging from those teleworking a half day per week to those teleworking only one day per month. Teleworkers were asked to state how long they had been teleworking regularly for at least one day per month. On average, they reported doing so for 5.64 years ($SD = 5.35$).

Three methods were used to recruit participants to complete an online survey. First, a snowball sampling technique was used, by sending emails to personal contacts. Second, a study description and a survey link were posted on two telework websites: www.teleworkexchange.com and www.teleworkadvocacy.com. Third, three upper-division Communication courses at a large Midwestern University offered extra credit to students to recruit qualified participants. Participants were required to be 18 years old, employed, and to telework at least one full day per month. Upon survey completion, participants were given the option to enter a separate website to provide their name for a drawing to win one of two $50 American Express gift cards.

Instrument

Based on qualitative studies focused on the strategies individuals use to manage the boundary between work and home (e.g., Kreiner, et al., 2009; Tietze, 2002; Tietze & Musson, 2003), open-ended survey questions were developed to gauge the temporal, spatial, and expectation-setting strategies home-based teleworkers use to manage their work-home boundary. Respondents were asked to think about the days they telework at home and respond to the following questions.

Q1: When teleworking, how do you use time to structure your day? Are there specific times of day that you specify as "work" or "personal" times of day? Is this up to you, or determined by your employer? Please be as specific as possible.

Q2: Please describe the physical environment in which you telework. For example, do you work in a home office, in the kitchen, etc.? What are your physical surroundings, and are these useful for helping you feel like you are "at work" or "at home"?

Q3: How do you set expectations with your family (or people with whom you have personal relationships) about your work-home boundary? For example, how do you communicate with them about when you are "at work" and "at home" during the day?

Table 1. Demographic information and descriptive statistics

	Teleworking Employees (N = 146)	
	M	SD
Age (years)	41.14	12.59
Organizational Tenure (years)	8.40	7.67
Job Tenure (years)	7.18	6.94
	Frequency	%
Teleworking Voluntary Yes No Other	117 15 13	80.1 10.3 8.9
Gender Male Female	57 89	39.0 61.0
Living Situation Live Alone Roommate/Partner/Spouse Partner/Spouse and Kids (full-time) Partner/Spouse and Kids (part-time) Single Parent and Kids (full-time) Single Parent and Kids (part-time)	14 63 59 2 3 2	9.6 43.2 40.4 1.4 1.4 1.4
Children Living at Home None 1 2 3 4 or more	80 32 26 7 1	54.8 21.9 17.8 4.8 .7
Employment Full-Time Part-Time Independent Contractor	110 17 18	75.3 11.6 12.3
Education Level Graduate Degree University Degree Some College High School Diploma	52 66 25 3	35.6 45.2 17.1 2.1
Type of Organization Privately Owned Publicly Owned Public Education Nonprofit Public Sector/Government Other	79 29 15 10 10 3	54.1 19.9 10.26 6.84 6.84 2.10

Q4: How do you set expectations with your manager and colleagues about your work-home boundary? For example, how do you communicate with them about when you are "at work" at "at home" during the day when you telework?

In addition to responding to a series of demographic questions, teleworkers also responded to questions regarding their work-life and life-work conflict, which were measured using Likert-type scales, from (1) strongly disagree, to (5) strongly agree. Work-life conflict was measured using a

5-item scale (Netemeyer, Boles, & McMurrian, 1996) with items such as, "The demands of my work interfere with my home and family life," and "Things I want to do at home do not get done because of the demands my job puts on me." Life-work conflict was measured using a 5-item scale (Netemeyer, et al., 1996) with items such as, "The demands of my family, spouse, or other personal activities interfere with work-related activities," and "I have to put off doing things at work because of demands on my time at home." Both scales achieved standards of reliability; work-life conflict, α =.92; life-work conflict, α =.89.

Data Analysis

We used grounded theory techniques (Strauss & Corbin, 1998) to guide our analysis, in order to develop thematic categories that represent teleworkers' approaches to managing the work-home boundary. First, we read all open-ended responses to become acquainted with and gain perspective on the data. Second, we performed open coding. Both authors coded the data in a first attempt to condense the data into initial categories, by reading through all open-ended responses line-by-line, making detailed notes, looking for common concepts that emerged, and labeling the data as a part of comparative analysis (Strauss & Corbin, 1998). Open coding allowed us to identify and label concepts that could be applied to broader categories in the next step of analysis.

Next, axial coding was conducted. Keeping the initial codes from open coding in mind, the first author conducted another close-read and took notes on the data again, with the goal of grouping the initial codes into broader categories. A broader set of categories was identified to use for our final analysis. Both authors met to discuss and edit these, and a final set of categories was agreed upon to use for data analysis.

To code the data, each author used the agreed upon categories and read through each line of the data again. A participant's response was coded as 1 if it represented the category, and as 0 if it did not. Upon initial coding, intercoder reliability for nearly all of the categories met or was above the satisfactory level of Cohen's kappa, K =.70 (Cohen, 1968). Those that met the satisfactory criteria ranged from K =.70 to K =.92. However, there were three categories (task-centered approach; constant availability; no need to set expectations with work) that did not meet the intercoder reliability minimum of K =.70. For these, there was evidence that there were slight differences in interpreting the categories. The categories were recorded and upon doing so, these categories achieved a satisfactory intercoder reliability of greater than K =.70. Once intercoder reliability was confirmed for all codes, the authors went through each category to resolve any remaining discrepancies and come to an agreement on the final coding.

Once the coding was final, each boundary management strategy was examined to determine how it was associated with specific demographic variables, work-life conflict, and life-work conflict. Independent samples t-tests were conducted to determine how work-life conflict, life-work conflict, and several demographic variables differed across teleworkers' engagement in temporal, spatial, and expectation-setting strategies.

RESULTS

Teleworkers in this study reported various approaches for managing the work-home interface, ranging from segmenting strategies to integrating strategies. On a whole, teleworkers appeared to have a good deal of flexibility and autonomy, but a subset of the teleworkers reported more binding relationships with their organizations, such that their flexibility in managing temporal boundaries was limited. Teleworkers' temporal and spatial strategies enabled varying degrees of boundary permeability and flexibility (see Table 2). Their expectation-setting strategies consisted of direct

Table 2. Temporal and spatial strategies, work-life conflict, and life-work conflict

	Temporal Strategies		
M(SD)	**Mandated Time** Segmenting Strategy Low Flexibility and Permeability	**Routine but Flexible** Segmenting Strategy Moderate to High Flexibility and Permeability	**Task-Based** Segmenting Strategy Moderate to High Flexibility and Permeability
Work-Life Conflict Life-Work Conflict	2.79 (1.05) 1.21 (.30)	2.79 (1.12) 1.92 (.86)	2.64 (.90) 1.77 (.62)
	Spatial Strategies		
M(SD)	**Home Office** Segmenting Strategy Low Flexibility and Permeability	**Alternative Workspace** Moderately Integrating Strategy High Flexibility and Permeability	**Multiple Workspaces** Integrating or Segmenting Strategy High or Low Flexibility and Permeability
Work-Life Conflict Life-Work Conflict	2.69 (1.15) 1.71 (.90)	2.76 (1.00) 1.71 (.62)	2.82 (1.02) 1.98 (.76)

communicative strategies as well as indirect behavioral strategies (see Table 3). The following are the categories that emerged from the data.

Temporal Strategies

Mandated Temporal Structure

A limited number of teleworkers (14 of 146, 9.6%) reported that their employer determines their daily temporal routine. Most were required to work during "normal working hours" or "office hours" in order to converse and collaborate with their office-based colleagues, customers, and clients.

I have to be online and answering phones and emails between 8am and 5pm. When my boss emails me, he expects me to answer within a few minutes- especially when I am teleworking.

Many of these teleworkers had very little control over their temporal structure, with strict regulation from their employer.

Everything is determined by my employer. Its [sic] just like working in the office. Specific start times and quit times and lunch.

Although a few reported having some flexibility in their schedule, with the ability to take limited breaks during the day, the majority of teleworkers in this category reported they are required to be available and connected to work during specific hours during the day. This renders their work-home boundary more segmented, impermeable, and inflexible, because teleworkers may not be able to enact or transition into personal roles during their work time.

Routine but Flexible Temporal Structure

The majority of the teleworkers in the sample (84 of 146, 57.5%) reported that they use time to structure their day, and this temporal structure was theirs to determine. Some teleworkers employed fairly rigid temporal boundaries, as described in this first response, but the majority appeared to adopt more flexible temporal structures, as described in the second response.

I am very aware of the clock. I make sure I get in the same number of hours that I would if I was in the office. If ever I take more than a few minutes for a personal matter, I find myself "recalculating" my quitting time to ensure I get enough hours

Table 3. Expectation-setting strategies, work-life conflict, and life-work conflict

M(SD)	Family Expectation-Setting Strategies				
	Direct Communication Segmenting Strategy Communicative/Direct	**Spatial Cues** Segmenting Strategy Behavioral/Indirect	**Implicit Under-standing** Segmenting Strategy Behavioral/Indirect	**Selective Response** Segmenting Strategy Behavioral/Indirect	**No Need to Set Expectations with Family**
Work-Life Conflict	2.52 (.96)	2.85 (1.11)	2.57 (1.03)	2.73 (1.26)	2.84 (1.09)
Life-Work Conflict	1.76 (.70)	1.90 (.99)	1.46 (.59)	1.98 (1.27)	1.84 (.69)
M(SD)	Work Expectation-Setting Strategies				
	Use of Technology Segmenting Strategy Communicative/Direct Behavioral/Indirect	**Temporal Routine** Segmenting Strategy Communicative/Direct Behavioral/Indirect	**Constant Availability** Integrating Strategy Behavioral/Indirect	**No Need to Set Expectations with Work**	
Work-Life Conflict Life-Work Conflict	2.64 (1.06) 1.68 (.69)	2.69 (1.10) 1.85 (.75)	3.10 (1.09) 1.85 (1.09)	2.61 (.91) 2.08 (.93)	

in. The timing is definitely up to me and not my employer and it is definitely on the honor system.

I generally use typical "office hours" to structure my day: 9 – noon work, noon – 1 lunch, 1 –5 work. However, I often start late, take long lunches, and/or do errands, and leave early. My employer doesn't really "keep tabs" on me when it comes to my working hours, as long as I hit my quotas, which I have done in spades for him the last several years.

Teleworkers reported a commitment to working a set schedule or a certain number of hours per day, but also noted that these routines were somewhat malleable and could be adjusted, according to personal demands that may arise during the day. They used time to segment work from personal domains, but simultaneously allowed this boundary to remain flexible and permeable, in order to transition between work and personal roles during the day.

I tend to work similar hours when teleworking as I do when I'm working from the office. However, I'm able to switch back and forth between work and personal responsibilities/demands more often than when I am in the office.

Teleworkers acknowledged the necessity of adhering to a temporal routine in order to avoid interruptions and remain productive, while also noting the benefits of flexibility. This included adjusting their temporal routine by working earlier or later than usual to accommodate for personal breaks or other personal responsibilities.

When I work from home, I do specify the hours that I will work and generally try to follow the hours I would have been scheduled in the office for that same day. However, my employer and the type of work allow for the flexibility to adjust start/end times as needed to work around personal obligations. For example, child may have school event in the middle of the day. I will start work earlier to allow for this personal time in the middle of the day.

Clearly, teleworkers appreciated the value of a temporal routine for segmenting work and family domains, but also recognized the significance of maintaining moderate to high degrees of flexibility and permeability. Teleworkers enjoyed managing their telework arrangement to accommodate their personal responsibilities, their need for breaks to keep their mind fresh, and their desire to work during certain times of day over others.

Task-Centered Approach

Rather than utilizing a regulated temporal boundary, teleworkers in this category (38 of 146, 26.0%) reported prioritizing and structuring their day according to task requirements.

The demands of my job dictate the structure of the day; I organize my day and week to get my work done. This is determined by me, and my evaluation of the task at hand.

These teleworkers organized their time around the structuring and completion of tasks rather than around pre-assigned temporal frames. Their schedules were not set on a predetermined routine, but rather, they fluctuated depending on client, customer, or work demands.

I can mix/match as needed and I'm given that flexability [sic]. I have objectives to meet that drive my day, month, etc. so I can spend all day working from home focused soley [sic] on work, or as needed take some time out to attend to personal issues.

These teleworkers evaluated their work time based on when tasks are accomplished rather than by hours worked, but segmented their work and home domains using tasks as the structuring property rather than a temporal frame. Thus, their

ability to address personal and work responsibilities was somewhat negotiable, depending on work priorities and demands. Although some in this category reported intense periods of working where work was prioritized over personal matters, others noted that this approach enabled the ability to balance task and personal roles.

No, I simply have the things I need to do prioritized and do them as I get to them, making sure to take personal breaks for lunch, exercise, running errands, etc.

NO, I do not structure certain times of the day for work vs personal. I prioritize what needs to get done that day based (work or personal) based [sic] on the level of importance ... work does usually win during the week and personal during the weekend.

Overall, a task-centered approach enables teleworkers to adapt their work time according to the daily demands of their work and to accommodate personal needs. Teleworkers use their daily task goals to segment work from home, but these boundaries are pliable and ever-changing based on personal and work demands, and therefore enable moderate to high permeability and flexibility.

Spatial Strategies

Home Office

Many teleworkers (62 of 146, 42.5%) consistently performed their work in a defined workspace within their home, such as a home office or a spare room that doubles as an office or traditionally designated workspace.

I work in an office in my home. This office space is used for nothing else other than my office. I only come in here when working.

Teleworkers' offices were set up to enable their work, and a few noted that the space helped them feel like they are "at work." However, more teleworkers in this category reported that they appreciated their home office because it enabled them to feel like they are "at home" while they are working, including enjoying windows and natural sunlight.

I work in a home office. There's a desk, bookshelves, printer. It feels like a cross between an office and a library. I always feel at home and that's the way I like it.

I have a dedicated home office. This includes a large wraparound desk, book shelves, laptop, printer, fax, copier, plentiful office supplies. There is a couch in the office next to a window, so nice sunlight filters through.

Teleworkers also used their office as a way to avoid the distractions of their home environment.

I have teleworked for a number of years and have also had a dedicated home work office. My current office is secluded from every day activites [sic] in the house with the ability to close the door and have complete privacy.

Although teleworkers clearly enjoyed the benefits of feeling at home and the ability to incorporate aspects of their personal life and "home" into their office environment, the designated home office was primarily used as a segmenting strategy to help teleworkers avoid the distractions and interruptions of the home, as well as to create a boundary around their work. This strategy provides lower boundary flexibility and permeability, as transitioning between roles in a home office poses greater challenges than in other areas of the home.

Alternative Home Workspace

A smaller portion of teleworkers (26 of 146, 17.8%) consistently performed their work in an alternative workspace in the home such as the kitchen table, living room, or bedroom. Rather than choosing a space where they could avoid household distractions, these teleworkers chose their workspace based on their desire to be comfortable and relaxed, enjoy natural lighting, and have ample space.

I work in my living room, sitting in a comfortable chair with my laptop on a tray table. It feels more like a home than workspace. I use the same space to do personal work on my computer.

When I telework I usually sit at my kitchen table. I do this mostly because it is the most convenient place in the house for me to spread out around my laptop.

This category of teleworkers may prefer integration of the work-home boundary, although several did report they would prefer a home office if it were available to them. By working in spaces that are traditionally designated for personal use, these teleworkers can resurrect and remove boundaries as needed during the day to attend to personal and work roles within their physical space. Thus, this strategy enables a relatively high degree of boundary flexibility and permeability, as teleworkers can easily transition into and enact home roles within this space (e.g., fix dinner, clean the living room).

Multiple Workspaces

Many teleworkers (57 of 146, 39.0%) worked in multiple workspaces throughout their home, and a few indicated that they sometimes work outside of their home (e.g., nearby coffee shops).

My environment changes based on the particular project I am working on. I have an office at home that I work in or sometimes I set up my laptop at the kitchen table. If I am reading quite a bit I sit in my cozy chair in the living room.

Primarily, teleworkers appeared to choose their workspace depending on their work demands and where they felt most comfortable and relaxed. They liked feeling "at home" in their work environment, and also appreciated natural light, ample space, and the ability to change locations depending on distractions in the home (e.g., kids coming home from school).

I almost always use my kitchen counter. I have an "office" but it is more comfortable at the counter with more space to spread information out. If I need to print or scan something, I take my computer to the office, print, and then go back downstairs. There is a lot more natural light in the kitchen and I also like that.

I work at home in our family room. Kids and husband are out of the house (husband working, kids at school/daycare) so I am not distracted. If they are home, I will move upstairs to our office. I find it more "comfortable" and relaxing being downstairs in the family room.

In part, teleworkers may use this as an integrating strategy, as working within various locations in the home enables the maintenance of a fluid boundary between the spatial aspects of home and work. With no one physical space ascribed to "work" teleworkers must constantly negotiate spatial boundaries, which enables boundary flexibility and permeability. However, teleworkers may also use this as a segmentation strategy in order to purposefully separate work and home roles by working in a designated workspace away from personal distractions. Teleworkers can use their workspaces to either integrate or segment the work-home boundary, and therefore this approach may afford a high or a low degree of flexibility and permeability.

Expectation-Setting Strategies used with Family Members

Direct Communication

Teleworkers (54 of 140, 38.6%) reported that they directly communicate with their family and personal contacts to set expectations about their work schedule and demands. For example, teleworkers communicate with family and close personal contacts to "let them know" the times they are working or when they are "done for the day" and available for personal roles and responsibilities.

It is only me and my wife. I just tell her I have some work to do and it will take so many hours.

Teleworkers indicated the importance of communicating with their family in order to prevent violations of the work-home boundary. This included communicating to let their families know when they would be available, and when they should not be interrupted.

With my family, I find I just have to communicate clearly when I am really not available. At 9 and 10, my children are appropriately self-centered, so they sometimes interrupt me. I reinforce their interruptions by usually being accessible [sic] to them: if I really cannot be at interrupted that moment, I make it clear, sometimes at the top of my voice if they're not "hearing" me.

Finally, teleworkers also used direct communication to remind their families and personal contacts of the need to segment work and family domains. These teleworkers articulated the distinction between being "at work" and "at home" within the home environment, and through direct communication, strengthened the boundary around their work role.

I make sure I ask the question, "If I were physically at an office would you be asking me to run this errand?" or "I'm at work now, I will be happy to talk with you about this in 45 minutes when my day is over."

I occasionally need to remind partner and friends that I can't answer the home phone even though I am at home working since I may be on a tele-conference or expecting business calls. Also that I am not available for errands or any other activity unless it can be arranged around lunch time and I am free.

Direct communication strategies help tele-workers create segmentation between work and home domains, as they reinforce the need for fam-ily and personal contacts to respect the boundary around the work domain.

Strategic Use of Space and Physical Cues

Teleworkers (31 of 140, 22.1%) also used spatial and physical cues to convey to their family and close personal contacts that they are working and not to be disturbed. For example, teleworkers indicated that they are at "at work" and not avail-able for personal contact by separating themselves from others in the household, working in a home office, and closing the door to their workspace.

I stay up in the office away from them. If I do come down to the "main living area" and other people are around, I keep the conversations short, grab my coffee or food and tell them I have to get back to work. When I come down at the end of the day, I tell them I'm "home from work" so they know that I'm not still in work mode.

In addition to physically separating themselves from others by using another room or closing a door, teleworkers incorporated other physical cues to signal that they are working, such as wearing

a telephone headset, typing at the computer, and wearing earphones.

When I'm wearing the telephone headset it means that I'm in a meeting and shouldn't be disturbed unless there is an emergency.

Headphones are generally a sing [sic] of "I'm working, leave me alone."

Overall, teleworkers strategically manipulated the use of space and physical artifacts in order to reinforce the boundary between work and home domains with family members. These were indi-rect behavioral strategies enacted by teleworkers for the purpose of segmenting the work-home boundary.

Implicit Understanding

Some teleworkers (32 of 140, 22.9%) established an implicit understanding with their family and close personal contacts, who had become accus-tomed to the temporal and spatial flow of their telework arrangement and were able to anticipate when they would be working versus available to fulfill personal roles.

They know that I am at work and when they can/ cannot bother me.

Its [sic] never been necessary for me to set expecta-tions with my family. They have always understood that work is necessary to pay the bills. They tend to leave me alone when I am working but will feel free to interrupt if they need to.

Based on their observation of temporal rou-tines and physical cues, teleworkers' families acknowledged the segmentation of work and home and the boundary that had been constructed by the teleworker. Although it is possible that this implicit understanding is founded on teleworkers' previous communication and expectation-setting regarding the work-home boundary, we propose that as described, this is an indirect, behavioral strategy.

Selective Response

A smaller portion of teleworkers (9 of 140, 6.4%) used a selective response strategy to maintain their work-home boundary. Teleworkers reported screening personal calls using caller ID, allowing personal calls to go to voicemail, and not responding to personal calls and emails until a later time when work demands were too high.

Yes. But thanks for email and caller ID, I'll simply ignore the inbox and the phone when personal notes/calls are coming in. If I do get the phone and it's a personal call during which the caller wants to have a lengthy chat, I've learned simply to explain that I'm working and I'll get back to him or her when I'm done.

Using technology to screen personal communication is an indirect way for teleworkers to indicate their availability, to protect the work boundary, and to maintain segmentation between work and home domains as necessary.

No Need to Set Expectations with Family Members

Some teleworkers (25 of 140, 17.9%) reported that they do not set boundary expectations with family or close personal contacts because they are alone at home during the time that they are working.

Most of the time, my family is out of the home when I am teleworking from home, which makes things easier to manage.

No one is here during the day so that is not an issue....which is part of the reason I feel I can be productive at home.

Having no family or personal contacts in the home during working hours may be useful to teleworkers who prefer to segment work and personal roles. However, there are distractions and interruptions inherent in a home environment that may require strong boundary management, despite not having other people in the home.

Expectation-Setting Strategies used with Work Colleagues

Communicate Availability via Technology

Many teleworkers (61 of 140, 43.6%) communicated their availability for work using technology, such as remaining responsive to their colleagues and manager during the day, acknowledging availability via a shared calendar, setting an "out of office" email or changing their instant messenger status to "unavailable" when they are not available for work, and logging into and out of the company network to indicate their accessibility. Teleworkers used these strategies to transition into and out of work and personal roles during the day—as described in the following first response—as well as to demarcate the beginning and end of the day or to delineate more extended periods of time of working and not working—as described in the second response.

My company gives its employees a lot of flexibility to manage their own schedules and assumes that we are all accountable for how we use our time. If I choose to do something personal during my typical "work hours", I would simply log off the computer or use an out of office message via email or set the status of my instant messanger [sic] to indicate I wasn't working.

I tend to let my manager and co-workers know when I'm logging off or [sic] the day and when I'll be available again for work. Then, I log off my computer and shut it down completely. This makes it harder for them to contact me via instant messenger or email. If they don't see me online they know I'm not available except via telephone for urgent matters.

Some teleworkers noted they did not need to proactively change their "status" or communicate regarding their availability, as the transparency of their organization's virtual system enables their colleagues to know when they are working and available for contact.

We use an instant messaging system and when I am signed on, I am "at work". When I am signed off, I am "at home" and they generally know not to expect an immediate reply.

In general, teleworkers utilize technological strategies to accomplish segmentation, such that their colleagues know when they are available for contact and when they are unavailable. However, there clearly is some boundary flexibility here, as teleworkers often use technology strategically to transition into and out of work and personal roles during the day. Overall, teleworkers segment work and home domains by communicating directly using technology as well as through indirect behavioral methods.

Temporal Structure or Routine

Many teleworkers (37 of 140, 26.4%) reported that an agreed upon or understood schedule acted as a boundary to protect their personal time from work interference. Some teleworkers directly communicated their regular teleworking schedule to colleagues and clients and articulated that they are not available for work outside of these temporal boundaries.

I make it clear that I am available from 7 am to 6 pm.

For me it's my clients that I have to manage... basically I do not accept work calls outside of office hours or on the weekends.

Others maintained this strategy indirectly. They noted that there is an implicit understanding that is respected by their colleagues and clients, who acknowledge the temporal structure and routine of their teleworking arrangement.

Unless it's an emergency or very timely project, most people will only call or expect responses during normal work hours 9-6pm in the time zone you are working.

The routines and temporal schedules set by teleworkers clearly are a tool for segmenting work from personal domains. By maintaining a temporal routine, teleworkers not only diminish interruptions and interference from their family during "work time," they in turn generate an accepted boundary around their personal time that is for the most part respected by colleagues.

Constant Availability

Although many teleworkers benefited from a temporal routine, some teleworkers (16 of 140, 11.4%) reported that they are always available to work and are constantly accessible via communication technologies.

There is no "at home" boundary with work. I am expected to answer emails at all times of day and night and on weekends.

My manager thinks that we are always "at work" and that is his expectation.

These teleworkers strike an integrative approach, as there is little demarcation between work and home, and work is always present even when they are engaged in personal roles and responsibilities. This did not seem to be a preference and there did not appear to be much, if any, direct communication regarding the work-home boundary. Rather, most teleworkers in this category reported that their employers expected or mandated this level of connectedness.

No Need to set Expectations with Work Colleagues

Due to the nature of their work or their relationship with their employer, some teleworkers (22 of 140, 15.7%) indicated that they did not need to set expectations with their colleagues and managers regarding their work-home boundary.

When i'm working there is no difference in communication other than it's not face to face. / If my boss or staff calls me on my personal time there is a good chance there is a problem that needs my attention. I've never had to set boundries [sic] on my personal time, common sense has prevailed here.

I don't need to do this, as my work is quite independent.

These teleworkers either had jobs that were independent and therefore they did not need to set expectations with colleagues or managers, or they felt the boundary around their personal space was fairly well protected and they did not need to communicate or proactively set expectations in order to negotiate that boundary.

Demographics

Next, we examined whether demographic differences were evident in teleworkers' enactment of temporal and spatial boundary management strategies (see Table 4). To do so, we examined teleworkers' simultaneous engagement in temporal and spatial strategies. Several gender differences emerged. Men preferred to utilize the combination of a routine but flexible schedule and a home of-

fice, whereas women preferred the combination of working a routine but flexible schedule in multiple workspaces. In addition, a greater percentage of the female participants reported involvement in strategies that involved mandated time schedules relative to that reported by the male participants, and a greater percentage of the male participants reported involvement in strategies involving task-based approaches compared to females.

Telework extensiveness did not appear to have a major influence on boundary strategy choice. However, living situation appeared to be associated with teleworkers' boundary management choices. Those living alone primarily utilized the routine but flexible time/home office and routine but flexible time/multiple workspace combinations. Those living with just a roommate, partner, or spouse were most likely to utilize the routine but flexible time/home office combination, whereas teleworkers with children living in the home were most likely to utilize the routine but flexible time/multiple workspaces combination. In addition, teleworkers without children living in the home were more likely to utilize task-based approaches relative to those with children.

Two temporal/spatial boundary management strategy combinations were related to job tenure and organizational tenure. The mandated time/alternative workspace and the routine but flexible time/alternative workspace combinations appeared to be embraced by teleworkers who had lower job and organizational tenure relative to teleworkers using other strategy combinations. The difference in teleworkers' organizational tenure for those using mandated time/alternative space and those using task-based time/alternative space, $t(14) = 2.03$, $p = .06$, and task-based time/multiple workspaces, $t(20) = 1.90$, $p = .07$, neared significance. In addition, a near significant difference existed in job tenure between teleworkers using mandated time/alternative workspace and task-based time/alternative workspace combinations, $t(14) = 2.05$, $p < .06$. Significant or nearly significant differences in job tenure emerged

Table 4. Temporal and spatial strategy combinations, work-life and life-work conflict, and demographic variables

	Mandated Time/ Home Office	Mandated Time/ Alternative Workspace	Mandated Time/ Multiple Workspaces	Routine but Flexible Time/ Home Office	Routine but Flexible Time/ Alternative Workspace	Routine but Flexible Time/ Multiple Workspaces	Task-Based Time/ Home Office	Task-Based Time/ Alternate Workspace	Task-Based Time/ Multiple Workspaces
	N = 7	N = 6	N = 1	N = 37	N = 9	N = 37	N = 12	N = 10	N = 16
M(SD)									
W-L Conflict	2.80 (1.06)	2.47 (.85)	4.60 (N/A)	2.76 (1.15)	2.89 (1.39)	2.75 (1.02)	2.38 (.93)	2.72 (.69)	2.78 (.99)
L-W Conflict	1.17 (.37)	1.27 (.24)	1.20 (N/A)	1.85 (.99)	1.82 (.76)	1.96 (.70)	1.60 (.49)	1.86 (.60)	1.85 (.71)
Male	2 (28.6)	1 (16.7)	0	15 (40.5)	4 (44.4)	9 (24.3)	8 (66.7)	5 (50.0)	6 (37.5)
Female	5 (71.4)	5 (83.3)	1 (100.0)	22 (59.5)	5 (55.6)	28 (75.7)	4 (33.3)	5 (50.0)	10 (62.5)
Age	39.50 (5.73)	35.00 (9.17)	56.00 (N/A)	42.71 (14.20)	36.00 (9.06)	41.32 (10.34)	47.25 (14.96)	36.70 (6.04)	39.06 (7.85)
Org Tenure	6.50 (3.99)	3.50 (.71)	11.00 (N/A)	10.02 (9.86)	3.38 (1.89)	7.44 (7.24)	7.95 (5.73)	7.25 (4.44)	10.54 (8.94)
Job Tenure	3.75 (3.16)	3.50 (.71)	6.00 (N/A)	7.46 (7.67)	2.38 (1.80)	7.38 (8.02)	7.75 (5.96)	7.31 (4.46)	9.13 (8.23)
Frequency (Percentage in Category)									
Teleworking Days									
5 per wk	3 (42.9)	1 (16.7)	0	14 (37.8)	2 (22.2)	10 (35.7)	1 (8.3)	0	3 (18.8)
4 per wk	0	1 (16.7)	0	3 (8.1)	0	3 (8.1)	3 (25.0)	3 (30.0)	1 (6.3)
3 per wk	0	0	0	1 (2.7)	0	2 (5.4)	2 (16.7)	2 (20.0)	3 (18.8)
2 per wk	2 (28.6)	0	1 (100.0)	9 (24.3)	1 (11.1)	2 (5.4)	2 (16.7)	2 (20.0)	4 (25.0)
1 per wk	1 (14.3)	3 (50.0)	0	8 (21.6)	4 (44.4)	15 (40.5)	3 (25.0)	3 (30.0)	2 (12.5)
Less than 1	1 (14.3)	1 (16.7)	0	2 (5.4)	2 (22.2)	7 (18.9)	1 (8.3)	0	3 (18.8)
Live Alone	1 (14.3)	2 (33.3)	0	4 (10.8)	0	5 (13.5)	0	0	1 (6.3)
Partner, Spouse, or Roommate	3 (42.9)	3 (50.0)	1 (100.0)	16 (43.2)	7 (77.8)	8 (21.6)	8 (66.7)	5 (50.0)	7 (43.8)
Partner, Spouse (full-time kids)	3 (42.9)	0	0	15 (40.5)	0	23 (62.2)	2 (16.7)	4 (40.0)	5 (31.3)

continued on following page

48

Table 4. Continued

	Mandated Time/ Home Office	Mandated Time/ Alternative Workspace	Mandated Time/ Multiple Workspaces	Routine but Flexible Time/ Home Office	Routine but Flexible Time/ Alternative Workspace	Routine but Flexible Time/ Multiple Workspaces	Task-Based Time/ Home Office	Task-Based Time/ Alternate Workspace	Task-Based Time/ Multiple Workspaces
	N = 7	N = 6	N = 1	N = 37	N = 9	N = 37	N = 12	N = 10	N = 16
Partner, Spouse (part-time kids)	0	0	0	1 (2.7)	0	1 (2.7)	0	0	0
Single Parent (part-time kids)	0	0	0	0	2 (22.2)	0	1 (8.3)	0	1 (6.3)
Single Parent (full-time kids)	0	0	0	0	0	0	0	1 (10.0)	2 (12.5)
Other	0	1 (16.7)	0	1 (2.7)	0	0	1 (8.3)	0	0
Full-time	6 (85.7)	4 (66.7)	1 (100.0)	30 (81.1)	8 (88.9)	24 (64.9)	7 (58.3)	8 (80.0)	11 (68.8)
Part-time	0	0	0	4 (10.8)	1 (11.1)	9 (24.3)	3 (25.0)	0	1 (6.3)
Independent Contractor	1 (14.3)	2 (33.3)	0	3 (8.1)	0	4 (10.8)	2 (16.7)	2 (20.0)	4 (25.0)
Income									
30,000 or less	0	0	0	1 (2.7)	0	4 (10.8)	1 (8.3)	2 (20.0)	1 (6.3)
30,000 –50,000	1 (14.6)	1 (16.7)	0	2 (5.4)	2 (22.2)	0	3 (25.0)	0	5 (31.3)
50,000 –75,000	2 (28.3)	2 (33.3)	0	8 (21.6)	3 (33.3)	12 (32.4)	2 (16.7)	2 (20.0)	2 (12.5)
75,000 –100,000	1 (14.6)	2 (16.7)	1 (100.0)	13 (35.1)	2 (22.2)	11 (29.7)	2 (16.7)	4 (40.0)	2 (12.5)
Over 100,000	3 (42.9)	1 (33.3)	0	13 (35.1)	2 (22.2)	8 (21.6)	4 (33.3)	2 (20.0)	6 (37.5)

between teleworkers using the routine but flexible time/alternative workspace combination and the routine but flexible time/home office, $t(44) =$ 1.96, $p <.06$; flexible time/multiple workspaces, $t(44) = 1.84, p =.07$; task-based time/home office, $t(19) = 2.60$, $p <.05$; task-based time/alternative workspace, $t(17) = 3.09$, $p <.01$; and task-based time/multiple workspaces combinations, $t(23) =$ 2.03, $p =.05$.

Work-Life Conflict and Life-Work Conflict

To identify whether teleworkers' work-life and life-work conflict differed based on the boundary management strategies they utilize, we first examined the levels of work-life and life-work conflict associated with the use of each temporal and spatial strategy (see Table 2). There were no significant differences in teleworkers' work-life conflict across temporal or spatial strategies, indicating that segmenting and integrating strategies did not differ in the degree of work-life conflict they enabled. However, in partial support of H1, life-work conflict was significantly lower for teleworkers using a mandated temporal schedule versus those using a routine but flexible schedule, $t(96) = 3.05, p <.01$, and those using a task-based approach, $t(50)= 3.23$, $p <.01$. The mandated time strategy was clearly the strongest temporal segmenting strategy (e.g., the least permeable) and thus enabled less life-work conflict relative to the other temporal strategies. There was no significant difference in life-work conflict among spatial strategies.

Because teleworkers use temporal and spatial boundary management strategies in tandem, next we explored how combinations of temporal and spatial strategies might be related to work-life and life-work conflict (see Table 4). No participant reported engaging in more than one temporal strategy or more than one spatial strategy, and nearly all participants reported engaging in one temporal and one spatial strategy. This allowed for clear comparisons across strategy combinations. Although teleworkers utilizing the task-based time/home-office combination experienced the lowest work-life conflict, there were no significant differences across work-life conflict levels experienced by teleworkers using the various strategy combinations. The boundary management combinations involving mandated time were associated with the lowest levels of life-work conflict; comparative differences were significant or neared significance. Telworkers utilizing the mandated time/home office combination experienced lower life-work conflict relative to those using the routine but flexible time/alternative space, $t(14)=2.07, p =.057$; task-based time/home office, $t(17) = 1.98$, $p =.06$; routine but flexible time/multiple workspaces, $t(42) = 2.89$, $p <.01$; task-based time/alternative space, $t(15) = 3.24, p =.01$; and task-based time/multiple workspaces combinations, $t(21) = 2.37, p <.03$. Additionally, teleworkers using the mandated time/alternative workspace combination experienced significantly lower life-work conflict relative to those using the routine but flexible time/multiple workspaces combination, $t(41) = 2.37, p <. 01$.

Although all of the family strategies were aimed at segmenting, we examined whether teleworkers using these expectation-setting strategies differed in their work-life and life-work conflict. Direct communication with family was associated with the lowest levels of work-life conflict, but there were no significant differences across strategies for work-life conflict. Overall, teleworkers using an "implicit understanding" expectation-setting strategy with their families and personal contacts had the lowest life-work conflict. Those using the implicit understanding strategy had lower life-work conflict relative to those using direct communication, $t(84) = 2.03$, $p <. 05$; to those using space to set expectations, $t(61) = 2.15, p <.05$; and to those who do not set expectations with family, $t(55) = 2.24, p <.05$.

Those who reported no need to set expectations about the work-home boundary with their work had the lowest work-life conflict, followed by those who used technology to set expectations with work colleagues. However, there was no significant difference in work-life conflict across teleworkers using various strategies. Teleworkers using technology to set expectations with work experienced the lowest life-work conflict, with significantly lower life-work conflict relative to those who reported having no need to set expectations with work, $t(81) = 2.17$, $p < .05$.

Overall, H1 was marginally supported. There were no significant differences among boundary strategies relating to work-life conflict. Teleworkers using a mandated time schedule tended to experience lower life-work conflict relative to those using other temporal strategies, which supports the hypothesis that greater segmentation leads to less life-work conflict. No spatial strategies were more effective than others in diminishing life-work conflict. Of the expectation-setting strategies, all of the family strategies were aimed at segmenting. However, the difference in life-work conflict between teleworkers who use technology to set expectations with work and those who do not set expectations with work colleagues was significant, also lending support to H1.

DISCUSSION

The goal of this study was to extend previous research by exploring home-based teleworkers' management of the work-home boundary. The results of this study build upon and extend the previous boundary management literature. Study findings reveal that (a) teleworkers use a variety of temporal and spatial boundary management strategies that are primarily aimed at segmentation but enable varying degrees of boundary permeability and flexibility; (b) expectation-setting involves communicative/direct and behavioral/ indirect strategies and is also primarily aimed at segmentation; (c) demographic differences exist across spatial/temporal boundary choices; and

(d) work-life conflict does not differ significantly across teleworkers using different temporal/spatial combinations or expectation-setting strategies, but there are limited differences among strategies regarding which are most beneficial toward diminishing life-work conflict. To follow, we highlight primary conclusions drawn from the study.

First, teleworkers utilize a variety of temporal and spatial strategies, which are primarily aimed at segmenting the work-home boundary and afford a range of levels of boundary permeability and flexibility. Overall, teleworkers' use of temporal and spatial boundary strategies reflects the theme of *differential permeability*, or the ability for individuals to "both segment and integrate their work and home domains" (Kreiner, et al., 2009, p. 719) as they determine what should and should not be permitted to permeate their work-home boundary. For example, the theme of differential permeability was dominant in temporal strategies chosen by teleworkers. The overwhelming majority of teleworkers used temporal routines to regulate work, thus enabling the segmentation of the work-home boundary. Teleworkers reported that colleagues "respect the 5:00 whistle" and that their family members develop an implicit understanding of their work times, demonstrating the effectiveness of temporal routines as a segmenting strategy. However, the "routine but flexible" temporal strategy enabled differential permeability as teleworkers maintained a temporal schedule while also sustaining flexibility, blocked segments of time during work for personal needs, and recalibrated their "work time" when they took time out for personal matters. The latter is also similar to the "banking time" temporal strategy identified by Kreiner and colleagues (2009), in which individuals "bank" time from one domain to be used later, so that one domain does not suffer at the expense of the other (p. 720). In general, the routine but flexible temporal strategy enables teleworkers to achieve segmentation through their routine, but also affords some degree of integration through moderate to high boundary flexibility and permeability. Similarly, teleworkers using the task-based approach also segmented their work-home boundary by organizing their time around the structuring and completion of tasks rather than around pre-assigned temporal frames. The task-based approach segments the work-home boundary based on the employee's task, but also allows for permeability and flexibility as there is no space and time consistently attributed to work. Clearly, teleworkers enjoy the benefits of segmenting their time based on a routine or task completion, but also recognize the advantages of maintaining a permeable and flexible boundary that enables some degree of integration.

Differential permeability was also evident in the spatial strategies of teleworkers. Teleworkers were split between the preference to work in a home office—which is a strong segmenting strategy—and a preference to work in multiple workspaces. The multiple workspace strategy demonstrates the theme of differential permeability (Kreiner, et al., 2009), as teleworkers permeate, or integrate, the work-home boundary when they desire to work in a comfortable or "homey" environment, but may segment the boundary by retreating away from distractions to their home office or elsewhere in the house when necessary. Many teleworkers structure their spatial boundaries for segmentation when desired, but permeate those boundaries when they want to feel more "at home" or to reduce the physical distance between work and home domains.

Study findings also extend previous research (e.g., Nansen, 2010) by exploring how teleworkers utilize specific spatial and temporal strategies in tandem. Teleworkers primarily engaged in two combinations of temporal and spatial strategies: routine but flexible time/home office (25%) and routine but flexible time/multiple workspaces (25%). Preference for these strategy combinations reaffirms teleworkers' desire for differential permeability, as both strategy combinations can be used to segment the work-home boundary

but also enable permeation and the enactment of personal roles and responsibilities.

In addition to contributing to the literature regarding teleworkers' use of spatial and temporal strategies, results provide insight regarding the specific communicative and behavioral strategies teleworkers use to set expectations about the work-home boundary. With family, teleworkers primarily used direct communication to segment the work-home boundary in order to establish two goals: to avoid interruptions and to establish or reaffirm the validity of their work arrangement. Indirect behavioral strategies, such as using space to set expectations with family, appeared to reinforce these goals. In general, teleworkers who had achieved an implicit understanding with their families regarding the work-home boundary appeared to have attained these goals, as their life-work conflict was significantly lower compared to teleworkers using other expectation-setting strategies.

With work colleagues and their manager, teleworkers used a combination of direct communicative strategies and indirect behavioral expectation-setting strategies. Using the preferred method of setting expectations through the use of technology, teleworkers communicated directly (e.g., email to indicate a personal break; setting "out of office" email or "not available" instant messenger status) and sent behavioral messages indirectly (e.g., not responding to work correspondence; logging out of work system) regarding their work-home boundary. Surprisingly, using technology to set expectations with work colleagues helped teleworkers reduce their life-work conflict. Teleworkers who used technology to set expectations had significantly less life-work conflict relative to those who reported they had no need to set expectations with work colleagues. Perhaps using this strategy aids teleworkers in their transitions into and out of work and personal roles, therefore diminishing the blurring between domains and limiting the interference of life in their work. In addition to using technological strategies, teleworkers also directly communicated with colleagues about their temporal routine, but primarily allowed their regular temporal routine to indirectly act as an expectation-setting mechanism with their work contacts. In general, these communicative and behavioral strategies helped teleworkers segment work and home domains.

However, 11% of teleworkers reported they were constantly available to their employer, which blurs the boundary between work and home. Although in this sample teleworkers who were constantly connected did not have significantly greater work-life conflict relative to those with more segmented boundaries, it is possible that constant connectivity would generate other negative outcomes such as burnout, lower job satisfaction, and turnover. Indeed, teleworkers' constant connectivity may diminish some of the greatest benefits of their work arrangement, and may lead to stress and constant renegotiation of the work-home boundary with family. Future research should explore the extent to which some segmentation is necessary for positive employee outcomes.

Finally, study findings extend previous research by identifying the demographic differences and the outcomes associated with specific boundary strategies. Overall, data suggest that domestic responsibilities within the home may affect teleworkers' boundary management choices. Specifically, while men and women both favored strategy combinations that involved routine but flexible temporal structures, men primarily worked in a home office, whereas women predominantly worked across multiple workspaces. It is possible that this is related to gender roles in the home. Women tend to place heavy emphasis on fulfilling family and work obligations, whereas men have reported viewing their involvement in domestic roles and family responsibilities as more voluntary (Sullivan & Lewis, 2001). Because teleworking arrangements can be viewed as a means to facilitate women's total domestic responsibility (Hilbrecht, et al., 2008), it is possible that women

desire or need more flexibility in their workspace than do men. This rationale aligns with findings that teleworkers who live with just a roommate, partner, or spouse prefer the routine but flexible time/home office strategy combination, but that teleworkers with children living at home prefer the routine but flexible/multiple workspaces strategy combination. Perhaps women and/or teleworkers with children have more domestic responsibilities, and working in multiple workspaces enables them to integrate and segment work and home domains as necessary to balance multiple roles.

Finally, the study builds upon Kreiner et al.'s (2009) notion that boundary management strategies will be linked to work-life conflict. Although we did not compare teleworkers' work-life and life-work conflict against office-based employees' measures, teleworkers' work-life and life-work conflict levels were relatively low in general. Surprisingly, none of the temporal, spatial, or expectation-setting strategies appeared to be more effective than others at lowering teleworkers' work-life conflict. However, teleworkers utilizing strategies that involved mandated time schedules experienced significantly less life-work conflict relative to teleworkers utilizing other temporal/spatial strategy combinations. Yet despite the benefits of lower life-work conflict that may be gained through a mandated temporal schedule, there are potential drawbacks to this approach. Job autonomy is a major advantage of telework (Gajendran & Harrison, 2007), and teleworkers who work within the constraints of a mandated temporal schedule may not enjoy the full benefits associated with remote work. Thus, rather than requiring teleworkers to maintain a mandated temporal schedule, organizations may instead help teleworkers achieve the utmost benefits of remote work—including lower life-work conflict—by encouraging them to develop an implicit understanding with their families regarding the work-home boundary and to use technology to set expectations with work colleagues.

Overall, this study highlights the temporal, spatial, communicative and behavioral boundary management strategies of home-based teleworkers. It strengthens the findings of previous research on teleworkers' boundary management (e.g., Kossek, et al., 2006; Tietze & Musson, 2003) and sheds new light on the practices teleworkers engage in to set expectations and manage their work-home boundary with their families and colleagues. It also highlights demographic differences regarding strategy use, and highlights the associations between boundary management choices, work-life conflict, and life-work conflict.

RESEARCH AND PRACTICAL IMPLICATIONS

Several practical applications emerge based on study findings. First, we propose that these strategies will be useful for teleworkers and for employees in various contexts, and in particular for those employed in work arrangements where temporal and spatial boundaries may be negotiated to manipulate the work-home boundary (e.g., part-time work, flex-time, job sharing).

Second, we propose that teleworkers should seek a balance between segmentation and integration that affords the benefits of working from home (e.g., flexibility, work-life balance), while also enabling the benefits that are associated with structure (e.g., productivity, lack of distractions). This enables the process of differential permeability of the work-home boundary. For each teleworker this may be a slightly different balance, depending on their organizational, individual, and family situation.

Third, teleworkers should communicate clearly with their families to set expectations regarding the work-home boundary, with the goal of someday attaining an implicit understanding regarding this boundary. They should also utilize technology in order to directly and indirectly set expectations with colleagues regarding the work-home boundary and to help prevent life-work conflict. Teleworkers should be prepared to adjust their work-home boundary as necessary, as these boundaries are co-constructed and negotiated by many people (colleagues, family, friends) and may need to be reevaluated at times in order to determine what works best for all parties involved.

Finally, we propose that organizations need to have greater trust in teleworkers' boundary management choices. Often, there is a concern that home-based interruptions will interfere with teleworkers' ability to work and focus. However, in this study, teleworkers' averages for work-life conflict were higher than their life-work conflict. We suggest that organizations should demonstrate a high degree of trust in teleworkers as they structure their work arrangement based on their unique work and personal situation. According to study findings, most temporal and spatial strategies do not differ significantly in the degree to which they help teleworkers diminish work-life and life-work conflict. In addition, demographic differences (e.g., job tenure, organizational tenure, gender, living situation) may influence teleworkers' work and personal demands and their preferences for the work arrangement structure. Thus, we conclude that teleworkers should be trusted as they are given autonomy to choose the temporal and spatial strategies that work best for their personal and work demands. This recommendation is put forth with the recognition that the employee and employer should continue an open dialogue to ensure a successful work arrangement.

FUTURE RESEARCH DIRECTIONS

We propose three potential directions for future research. First, future research should consider teleworkers' collaborative work when evaluating their boundary management. In an office-environment, managers have been found to have significant control over employees' work-home boundaries (Perlow, 1998), and it will be important to determine the extent to which managers, colleagues, and the overall work team are involved in the boundary management process.

Second, future studies should consider additional work and personal outcomes associated with teleworkers' boundary management choices. For example, segmenting the work-home boundary may lead to overwork and family-related stress, and differential permeability of this boundary may lead to role ambiguity.

Third, studies should examine the effect of individual differences and time on teleworkers' use and the effectiveness of various boundary management and expectation-setting strategies. Workload and job autonomy, organizational culture, family climate, and a variety of other variables may affect the extent to which teleworkers' boundary management choices are effective in their current work and family environments. In addition, teleworkers' boundary management strategies and the strength of those boundaries may change over time, as they evolve in the job or adapt the boundary according to their needs. Individual differences and longitudinal data should be evaluated in future studies.

Continued research should continue to build on the current study, which identifies the temporal, spatial, communicative, and behavioral boundary management strategies of home-based teleworkers, highlights teleworkers' methods of balancing structure with flexibility, and provides new research directions for boundary management research.

ACKNOWLEDGMENT

Funding from the University of Wisconsin-Milwaukee Graduate School supported this study.

REFERENCES

Ashforth, B. E., Kreiner, G. E., & Fugate, M. (2000). All in a day's work: Boundaries and micro role transitions. *Academy of Management Review*, *25*, 472–491.

Bailey, D. E., & Kurland, N. B. (2002). A review of telework research: Findings, new directions, and lessons for the study of modern work. *Journal of Organizational Behavior*, *23*, 383–400. doi:10.1002/job.144

Ballard, D. I., & Gossett, L. M. (2007). Alternative times: Temporal perceptions, processes, and practices defining the nonstandard work relationship. In Beck, C. S. (Ed.), *Communication Yearbook 31* (pp. 275–320). New York, NY: Routledge.

Boswell, W. R., & Buchanan, J. B. (2007). The use of communication technologies after hours: The role of work attitudes and work-life conflict. *Journal of Management*, *33*, 592–610. doi:10.1177/0149206307302552

Bulger, C. A., Matthews, R. A., & Hoffman, M. E. (2007). Work and personal life boundary management: Boundary strength, work/personal life balance, and the segmentation-integration continuum. *Journal of Occupational Health Psychology*, *12*, 365–375. doi:10.1037/1076-8998.12.4.365

Cohen, J. (1968). Weighted kappa: Nominal scale agreement with provision for scaled disagreement of partial credit. *Psychological Bulletin*, *70*, 213–220. doi:10.1037/h0026256

Edwards, J. R., & Rothbard, N. P. (2000). Mechanisms linking work and family: Clarifying the relationships between work and family constructs. *Academy of Management Review*, *25*, 178–199.

Fonner, K. L., & Roloff, M. E. (2010). Why teleworkers are more satisfied with their jobs than are office-based workers: When less contact is beneficial. *Journal of Applied Communication Research, 38*, 336–361. doi:10.1080/00909882.2010.513998

Gajendran, R. S., & Harrison, D. A. (2007). The good, the bad and the unknown about telecommuting: Meta-analysis of psychological mediators and individual consequences. *The Journal of Applied Psychology, 92*, 1524–1541. doi:10.1037/0021-9010.92.6.1524

Hecht, T. D., & Allen, N. J. (2009). A longitudinal examination of the work-nonwork boundary strength construct. *Journal of Organizational Behavior, 30*, 839–862. doi:10.1002/job.579

Hewlin, P. F. (2003). And the award for best actor goes to: Facades of conformity in organizational settings. *Academy of Management Review, 28*, 633–643.

Hilbrecht, M., Shaw, S. M., Johnson, L. C., & Andrey, J. (2008). I'm home for the kids: Contradictory implications for work-life balance of teleworking mothers. *Gender, Work and Organization, 15*, 545–576. doi:10.1111/j.1468-0432.2008.00413.x

Hunton, J. E. (2005). Behavioral self-regulation of telework locations: Interrupting interruptions! *Journal of Information Systems, 19*, 111–140. doi:10.2308/jis.2005.19.2.111

Ilies, R., Wilson, K. S., & Wagner, D. T. (2009). The spillover of daily job satisfaction into employees' daily lives: The facilitating role of work-family integration. *Academy of Management Journal, 52*, 87–102. doi:10.5465/AMJ.2009.36461938

Konradt, U., Hertel, G., & Schmook, R. (2003). Quality of management by objectives, task-related stressors, and non-task related stressors as predictors of stress and job satisfaction among teleworkers. *European Journal of Work and Organizational Psychology, 12*, 61–79. doi:10.1080/13594320344000020

Kossek, E. E., Lautsch, B. A., & Eaton, S. C. (2006). Telecommuting, control, and boundary management: Correlates of policy use and practice, job control, and work-family effectiveness. *Journal of Vocational Behavior, 68*, 347–367. doi:10.1016/j.jvb.2005.07.002

Kossek, E. E., Noe, R. A., & DeMarr, B. J. (1999). Work-family role synthesis: Individual and organizational determinants. *The International Journal of Conflict Management, 10*, 102–129. doi:10.1108/eb022820

Kreiner, G. E., Hollensbe, E. C., & Sheep, M. L. (2009). Balancing borders and bridges: Negotiating work-home interface via boundary work tactics. *Academy of Management Journal, 52*, 704–730. doi:10.5465/AMJ.2009.43669916

Marsh, K., & Musson, G. (2008). Men at work and at home: Managing emotion in telework. *Gender, Work and Organization, 15*, 32–48.

Matthews, R. A., & Barnes-Farrell, J. L. (2010). Development and initial evaluation of an enhanced measure of boundary flexibility for the work and family domains. *Journal of Occupational Health Psychology, 15*, 330–346. doi:10.1037/a0019302

Mustafa, M. (2010). Managing boundaries: The case of home-based self-employed teleworkers. *The International Journal of Business and Management Research, 3*, 55–64.

Myrie, J., & Daly, K. (2009). The use of boundaries by self-employed, home-based workers to manage work and family: A qualitative study in Canada. *Journal of Family and Economic Issues, 30*, 386–398. doi:10.1007/s10834-009-9166-7

Nansen, B., Arnold, M., Gibbs, M., & Davis, H. (2010). Time, space, and technology in the working-home: An unsettled nexus. *New Technology, Work and Employment, 25*, 136–153. doi:10.1111/j.1468-005X.2010.00244.x

Netemeyer, R. G., Boles, J. S., & McMurrian, R. (1996). Development and validation of work-family conflict and family-work conflict scales. *The Journal of Applied Psychology, 81*, 400–410. doi:10.1037/0021-9010.81.4.400

Nippert-Eng, C. (1996). Calendars and keys: The classification of "home" and "work". *Sociological Forum, 11*, 563–582. doi:10.1007/BF02408393

Park, Y., & Jex, S. M. (2011). Work-home boundary management using communication and information technology. *International Journal of Stress Management, 18*, 133–152. doi:10.1037/a0022759

Perlow, L. A. (1998). Boundary control: The social ordering of work and family time in a high-tech corporation. *Administrative Science Quarterly, 43*, 328–357. doi:10.2307/2393855

Pleck, J. H. (1977). The work-family role system. *Social Problems, 17*, 417–427. doi:10.1525/sp.1977.24.4.03a00040

Raghuram, S., & Wiesenfeld, B. (2004). Work-nonwork conflict and job stress among virtual workers. *Human Resource Management, 43*, 259–277. doi:10.1002/hrm.20019

Raghuram, S., Wiesenfeld, B., & Garud, R. (2003). Technology enabled work: The role of self-efficacy in determining telecommuter adjustment and structuring behavior. *Journal of Vocational Behavior, 63*, 180–198. doi:10.1016/S0001-8791(03)00040-X

Rau, B. L., & Hyland, M. A. M. (2002). Role conflict and flexible work arrangements: The effects on applicant attraction. *Personnel Psychology, 55*, 111–136. doi:10.1111/j.1744-6570.2002.tb00105.x

Rothbard, N. P., & Edwards, J. R. (2003). Investment in work and family roles: A test of identity and utilitarian motives. *Personnel Psychology, 56*, 699–730. doi:10.1111/j.1744-6570.2003.tb00755.x

Rothbard, N. P., Phillips, K. W., & Dumas, T. L. (2005). Managing multiple roles: Work- family policies and individuals' desires for segmentation. *Organization Science, 16*, 243–258. doi:10.1287/orsc.1050.0124

Shia, S. M., & Monroe, R. W. (2006). Telecommuting's past and future: A literature review and research agenda. *Business Process Management Journal, 12*, 455–482. doi:10.1108/14637150610678078

Strauss, A., & Corbin, J. (1998). *Basics of qualitative research: Techniques and procedures for developing grounded theory* (2nd ed.). Thousand Oaks, CA: Sage.

Sullivan, C., & Lewis, S. (2001). Home-based telework, gender, and the synchronization of work and family: Perspectives of teleworkers and their co-residents. *Gender, Work and Organization, 8*, 123–145. doi:10.1111/1468-0432.00125

Thatcher, S. M. B., & Zhu, X. (2006). Changing identities in a changing workplace: Identification, identity, enactment, self-verification, and telecommuting. *Academy of Management Review, 31*, 1076–1088. doi:10.5465/AMR.2006.22528174

Tietze, S. (2002). When "work" comes "home": Coping strategies of teleworkers and their families. *Journal of Business Ethics, 41*, 385–396. doi:10.1023/A:1021236426657

Tietze, S., & Musson, G. (2002). Working from home and managing guilt. *Organizations and People*, *9*, 34–39.

Tietze, S., & Musson, G. (2003). The times and temporalities of home-based telework. *Personnel Review*, *32*, 438–533. doi:10.1108/00483480310477524

Winkel, D. E., & Clayton, R. W. (2010). Transitioning between work and family roles as a function of boundary flexibility and role salience. *Journal of Vocational Behavior*, *76*, 336–343. doi:10.1016/j.jvb.2009.10.011

World at Work. (2009). *Telework trendlines 2009*. Retrieved May 1, 2011, from http://www.working-fromanywhere.org/news/Trendlines_2009.pdf.

KEY TERMS AND DEFINITIONS

Telework: A virtual work arrangement in which employees use technology to perform their regular work outside of the organization's physical boundaries.

Boundary Permeability: The extent to which the domain or role enables an individual to be physically located in one domain but psychologically and behaviorally involved in another domain or role.

Boundary Flexibility: The degree to which spatial and temporal boundaries are pliable, such that an individual can easily transition from one role domain to another.

Role Segmentation: Defining work versus personal time and maintaining separate physical spaces for work and personal responsibilities.

Role Integration: Blurring and overlapping the boundary between work and personal time and space.

Work-Life Conflict: The interference of work in one's personal roles and responsibilities.

Life-Work Conflict: The interference of personal roles and responsibilities in one's work.

ENDNOTES

[1] Fifty participants were removed from the sample because they did not complete any of the open-ended responses. The remaining sample was N = 146.

[2] Participants were given the option to respond "other" and fill in the blank. For example, some participants reported they worked an average of 2.5 days per week, or reported they teleworked an average of 1-3 days per week. For the ease of reporting demographics, these were rounded down or averaged (for example, 2.5 became 2; 1-3 days per week became 2). From the "other" category, 1 participant was added to the 1 day per week category, 2 to the 2 days per week, 1 to 4 days per week, and 2 to 5 days per week.

Chapter 4
Thinking Outside the Office:
The Impact of Virtual Work on Creative Workers' Attitudes[1]

Beth A. Rubin
University of North Carolina – Charlotte, USA

April J. Spivack
University of North Carolina – Charlotte, USA

ABSTRACT

This chapter draws on labor process theory and builds on a previous paper by Spivack and Rubin (2011) that explored workplace factors that might diminish the autonomy of creative knowledge workers. Using data from the National Study of the Changing Workforce, this chapter tests hypotheses linking creative workers' ability to work virtually, control their task and temporal autonomy to their well-being, job satisfaction, and commitment. The authors find that creative workers that have spatial autonomy have more positive work attitudes and better mental health. Further, they show that along with task and temporal autonomy, the conditions of the new workplace make spatial autonomy an important consideration. These findings contribute both to literature about the changing workplace and to practitioners concerned with maximizing the well-being of creative knowledge workers.

INTRODUCTION

The contemporary workplace differs dramatically from the industrial workplace of the 20th century. While always international, now it is global; while always employing technologies, now technolo-

gies mediate production in ways unthinkable in previous eras. Likewise, while large bureaucracies still exist, new organizational forms proliferate as do new ways of organizing the productive activity of employees. In addition, where the core of the industrial economy was the manufacture of goods, now, the production of ideas, knowledge and other creative output are the drivers. Finally,

DOI: 10.4018/978-1-4666-0963-1.ch004

where stability and size were associated with organizational success, now it is just as likely that flexibility and networks are so associated (Rubin, 1995). Moreover, the new economy no longer operates within the standardized temporalities of the industrial economy and instead, as a reality of a globalized network of economic transactions, operates 24/7. As many scholars have observed, the global economy is characterized by time-space compression resulting in temporal and spatial restructuring of work.

These characteristics of the contemporary economy require a rethinking of what it means for an employee to *go to work*. The shift from manufacturing to knowledge and creative work for many workers means that productive activity is no longer fixed to a factory floor or office building but can occur anywhere. Not only does the type of work activity in which many workers engage unmoor workers from a workplace, but so too do information technologies that allow workers to "carry" the contents of an entire office with them, remain in communication from almost any locale and otherwise be spatially autonomous.

Contributing to the mobility of work activity is the plethora of "work extending technologies" (Duxbury, Towers, Higgins, & Thomas, 2006; Bittman, Brown, & Wajcman, 2009). These technological innovations allow workers to easily shift the locale in which they work. For knowledge and creative workers, this *untethering* should contribute to greater productivity, satisfaction and well-being. Autonomy is a key criterion to producing creative work as well, so limits to autonomy, spatial, temporal or otherwise, are especially troubling for creative knowledge workers tasked with generating creative solutions—an increasingly important output to organizations given the turbulent environment.

This chapter draws on labor process theory and builds on a previous paper by Spivack and Rubin (2011) that explored workplace factors that might diminish the autonomy of creative knowl-

edge workers. The objective of this chapter is to test hypotheses linking creative workers' ability to work virtually and control their task and temporal autonomy to their well-being, satisfaction and commitment. We use data from the 2008 *National Study of the Changing Workforce* (Work and Families Institute, 2010). Our expectation is that those workers who are required to be creative on their jobs who are able to work virtually are happier, more satisfied and mentally healthy then those who are not.

BACKGROUND

The shift from manufacturing to service and knowledge production in the past several decades has transformed the type of worker that is increasingly important to the contemporary economy. Rather than brawn and physical prowess, high levels of human capital (education, training, and skills) and new kinds of skills prevail (Stewart, 1997). Increasingly, whether in high performance blue collar work (Applebaum & Batt, 1994) or white collar service and knowledge work, employees with "soft skills" and creativity are central to organizational success (Moss & Tilly, 1996; Mumford, 2000).

Additionally, the composition of the workforce has also become increasingly feminized. While women have always been involved in the paid labor force, the percentage of women workers with young children (under the age of 6) has risen from 39% to 64% over the past 40 years (U.S. Bureau of Labor Statistics, 2008). Because parenting is still primarily a responsibility of women, this shift has created new pressures on employers to assist their employees, certainly their knowledge and creative workforce, in their efforts to balance the dual demands of employment and family. This pressure on employers has only increased as the evidence of the negative outcomes related to a failure to institute work-life balance initiatives mounted, including a list of detrimental effects such as higher rates of absenteeism and turnover, stress and illness, loss of productivity, decreased job satisfaction, decreased organizational loyalty and commitment, and increased healthcare costs (Hobson, Delunas, & Kesic, 2001; Rodgers & Rodgers, 1989; Thomas & Ganster, 1995). Importantly, while the burden of combining paid work and household tasks falls more heavily on women, both women and men experience these pressures and negative work-family spillover (Mennino, Rubin, & Brayfield, 1995).

These workforce changes occur, moreover, in the context of organizational and economic restructuring geared towards rendering businesses more flexible so that they may better respond to the heightened competition of the global, 24/7 economy. Flexibility has many dimensions and refers both to the type of organizational restructuring that involves flattening hierarchical structures, debureacratization, and decentralization, as well as work force restructuring. Moreover, it can serve either the needs of employers, the needs of employees and in our view of the best case, both.

Researchers have identified numerical and functional flexibility as two strategies employers have used to make their deployment of work force more flexible (Broschak, Davis-Blake, & Block, 2008; Harrison & Kelley, 1993; Kalleberg, 1977, 2003; Smith, 2001). The first, numerical flexibility, relies on severing the traditional employment contract in which workers have stable, long-term and reliable employment with a single employer as long as they perform well. Instead, increasing numbers of workers have short-term, temporary and contingent employment tied to a firm for the duration of the employer's need (Rubin, 1995; Cappelli, 1997; Smith, 2001; Kalleberg, 2003). Functional flexibility, on the other hand, relies on the creative and knowledge workers with which this study is concerned. Here, employers rely on highly skilled workers that they can easily deploy to accomplish a variety of tasks. These

employees tend to have considerable discretion, autonomy and commitment (Kalleberg, 2003, p. 154; Applebaum & Batt, 1994). Furthermore, as companies debureacratized and flattened, they frequently eliminated departments either by externalizing their functions or by employing workers who are "functionally flexible" (Kalleberg, 2003). Thus, a key transformation is the flattening and debureacratization of organizations that pushes decision-making and discretion down the organizational hierarchy and relies on a skilled, autonomous and functionally flexible workforce (Rubin, 1995; Cappelli, 1997).

Increasing numbers of businesses thus rely on the effort of creative, innovative knowledge workers (e.g. Henard & McFadyen, 2002). How to maximize, encourage and support that creativity creates new sets of problems in the contemporary economy. Increasingly, rather than focus on individual workers' attributes, scholars (Amabile & Gryskiewicz, 1989; Amabile, Conti, Coon, Lazenby, & Herron, 1996; Andriopolous, 2001; Cummings, 1965; LaPierre & Pierre-Giroux, 2003; Woodman, Sawyer, & Griffin, 1993) point to the environment and management strategy as key for generating creativity and innovative output from employees. One of the most widely agreed upon characteristics of an environment that supports creativity is high employee autonomy.

Autonomy, then, is a central component of fostering creative work. Autonomy has long been identified as a central antecedent in many employee outcomes, especially among those workers with high growth needs orientation or white collar jobs. Across social science disciplines (management science, organizational behavior, industrial and organizational psychology, and sociology), researchers have identified the centrality of autonomy to various facets of worker well-being and performance, including job satisfaction (Arches, 1991; Loher, Noe, Moeller, & Fitzgerald, 1985; Kalleberg, 1977; Trow, 1957), organizational commitment (Rubin & Brody, 1995; Cohen, 1992;

Marsh & Mannari, 1977), organizational citizenship behavior (Chien & Chiu, 2009; Peng, Hwang, & Wong, 2010) and well being (Daniels & Guppy, 1994). Moreover, recent research by Kim, Hon, and Grant (2009) have also linked creativity on the job to higher job satisfaction.

Typically, autonomy refers to the degree of control employees have over how they complete their tasks, and, increasingly, when they complete their tasks (e.g., Schieman & Glavin, 2008). While the transition from craft-based to industrial production brought the former to the forefront, the more recent transition to a 24/7 economy (Presser, 2003; Rubin, 2007) has brought the temporal components of autonomy forward. As the work day extends beyond the normative 9-5, five-day-a-week structure, and the boundaries between home and work become increasingly blurred, workers' abilities to work not only how they want, but when they want is contested. Moreover, for many workers, it is not only the extension of the work day but the increasing complexity of that work time as workers "layer" multiple, often widely divergent tasks and attempt to accomplish these in both extended and fragmented work days (Rubin, 2007; Agypt & Rubin, 2011; Agypt, Rubin, & Spivack, 2011).

Facilitating the lengthening of the working day and the layering of tasks within that time are technologies that both free employees from the constraints of their office and, at the same time, tether them to their office 24/7 (Rubin & Brody, 2005; Bittman, Brown, & Wajcman, 2009). Mobile phones, laptop computers, PDAs, fax machines, scanners, conference call software and related technological innovations allow a level of mobility heretofore impossible for a wide array of workers. These technologies, combined with new sorts of work demands (creativity, knowledge and innovation) and increasing numbers of workers who have multiple and competing demands, create new workplace challenges and contested terrains; these are the focus of our study.

AUTONOMY AND VIRTUAL WORK

Labor Process Theory

We argue here that virtual work has emerged out of the combination of factors addressed above and that these changing labor processes create new control issues between employers and their employees. Labor process theory has been particularly important for addressing control in the workplace, but the conditions of the new workplace pose unique challenges for labor process theory. In this section, we provide a brief overview of labor process theory, discuss how the changes above pose challenge to labor process theory and then show its ongoing utility for analyzing worker outcomes in the contemporary knowledge-based economy.

Braverman's (1974) landmark analysis of the transformation of work in the twentieth century identified employers' efforts to control the activities of employees as a key driver of change in the workplace, net of other factors such as competitive pressures. A core observation of labor process analysis is that the "problem of control" emerges out of the indeterminacy of work effort of which employees are capable (Thompson & Smith, 2009). Early labor process theorists, following Braverman's *deskilling* analysis, focused on employers' efforts to use technology to *deskill* workers, a strategy that disempowers them, cheapens them, and makes them relatively interchangeable components of production, thus easier to control.

Edwards (1979) and Burawoy (1979) introduced the missing concept of worker agency and resistance to the Braverman account. Thus, instead of the oddly agentless accounts of workplace transformation present in Braverman, scholars increasingly sought to understand, explain and analyze the ways in which workers' self organization (or lack thereof) confronted the variety of control strategies employers used to extract the maximum amount of effort from employees. What the triumvirate of labor process theorists retained, and what remains at the core of labor process theory, was the tension between labor indeterminacy and struggles for control as driving the transformation of labor processes at *the site of production*.

Importantly, Braverman and his fellow travelers were seeking to understand work in monopoly capitalism, a particular era characterized by the dominance of mass production and the rise of large scale bureaucracies and their growing administrative workforce. Studies of control integrated the role of unions in the blue-collar context and internal labor markets, and their commitment-producing hierarchies, in the white-collar context (Rubin, 1996). Just as scholars recognized the agency of workers, they similarly recognized the duality of control systems that vacillated between command and control as punitive strategies, to commitment seeking and empowering strategies.

Challenges to this perspective emerged from a number of sources (Thompson & Smith, 2009; Halford & Strangleman, 2009). Some contend that the focus of much of labor process theory was on white, male industrial labor and was, therefore, relatively silent to the diversity of work practices and workers. Likewise, much of the early research was overly limited to the focus on economic exploitation and deskilling. That focus on industrial work rendered labor process theory relatively silent to new categories of workers emerging with industrial transformation.

That transformation of the economy posed a second challenge to labor process theory. That is, the shift from industrial manufacturing to service and knowledge-based production called into question the relevance that labor process theory had for the understanding of contemporary work. In answer, however, researchers such as Garson (1994) and Leidner (1993) applying labor process theory to a variety of work settings, including services, sales and professional work, pointed to the continued efforts on the part of workers to maintain control over their labor process in the face of employers' efforts to routinize, standard-

ize, and otherwise control the specifics of labor accomplishment. The changes in the types of work and workers who have become central to contemporary economic success thus pose new challenges both to managers' efforts to exert control and to scholars trying to understand the tensions between control and autonomy in the new economy. Of particular interest and the focus of the next section of this chapter is the emergence of knowledge and creative workers, *virtual* work, and spatial mobility for creative workers.

Task- Temporal- and Spatial-Autonomy

Knowledge and creative workers have emerged as central to the contemporary economy. Rather than produce "things," knowledge and creative workers produce ideas, innovation, and other non-tangible outputs. The nature of their product renders coercive forms of control untenable and instead induces forms of control based on commitment, cooperation and autonomy, the hallmarks of high performance workplaces as well (Applebaum & Batt, 1994). Employers invest in and seek to encourage the creative and productive capacity of workers (O'Doherty & Willmott, 2009, p. 935) in part by providing autonomy not only in task completion and scheduling but also increasingly through spatial autonomy.

For much of the twentieth century, white-collar "knowledge workers" were most likely to work in bureaucratic environments where control over workers and the labor process was embedded in the organizational hierarchy, its rules and reward structures. Bureaucratic control effectively obscured asymmetrical power relations by embedding control in the structure of the organization rather than in an individual (Edwards, 1979). Likewise, the accompanying spatial arrangements reinforced the core organizational components of bureaucracy: centralization of power and authority, formalization and segmentation of work activities. The prototypical office building functions as both a form of structural control as well as a spatial component of bureaucratic control: occupants of offices fill them at precisely defined times delimited by a normative 9 to 5 workday. The office could be understood as "an organizational constant" and work activity "container" (Baldry & Hallier, 2010).

Economic transitions have elevated the importance of flexibility, providing fertile ground for the emergence of new work arrangements, specifically, virtual forms of work (Rubin, 1995). These new virtual work arrangements offer not only flexible scheduling, but also flexible spatial relations, aided by technologies that remove the requirement for spatial and temporal tethering. Thus, as Land and Taylor (2010) point out, work is "… increasingly concerned with communication and social reproduction, and often takes place outside formally designated employment time/space…" (2010, p. 396). The net result is that workers can engage in work activities from any location at any time. Work activities may blend with non-work activities in a number of ways (e.g., writing this chapter in my home office while doing laundry); it may occur in the home, in a "third place" (e.g., Starbucks, cars, subways and pubs) (Bittman, Brown, & Wajcman, 2009, p. 675) or distributed across networks (O'Doherty & Willmott, 2009). Just as work activities are no longer confined to a proto-typical "work-day," it is no longer confined to a work "place."

With this increasing flexibility, however, new challenges for managers have surfaced, since they can no longer rely on old structures, such as fixed space offices, to serve their traditional purposes of control and surveillance. In other words, the freedom to work in virtual offices creates new struggles between employees and their managers who resist relinquishing the control that fixed space offices allow.

While the earlier approaches to management emphasized command and control using standardization, procedures, and measurement (Jackson, Gharavi, & Klobas, 2006), their tendency towards

adversarial relationships is distinctly at odds with the contemporary workplace. Analysts of the flexible knowledge economy and its creative workers suggest that knowledge workers have elevated value, and need flexibility and empowerment rather than control (see, for instance, Albert & Bradley, 1997). Given these new economy requirements of flexibility and empowerment, the former approaches to management would tend to create work structures and environments that inhibit rather than promote the desired outcomes in creative knowledge work.

Further, as scholars envision a workplace that is peopled by creative, autonomous employees who are able to produce their "output" from any place at any time, some argue that managers must shift their effort from *control* to *facilitation* (Albert & Bradley, 1997; Duffy, 2000). Despite these views though, labor process scholars argue that the fundamental challenge, that has not changed at all, is for managers to extract as much effort as possible from their employees and this mandate is no less true for creative knowledge workers. Flexible systems can serve as ways for employers to "remove all obstacles to the extraction of effort" (Thompson & Smith, 2009, p. 919). We view spatial flexibility in these terms.

The challenge for managers of workers with schedule and location flexibility has become balancing the need to provide autonomy with the need to maintain communication and cohesion with and among employees (Richardson, 2010). Indeed, research has demonstrated the ways in which flexible working (temporal and spatial flexibility) is associated with work intensification resulting at least partially from expectations of worker communication availability regardless of time or location, diminishing the boundaries between work and non-work domains (Fleming & Spicer, 2004; Ladner, 2008). The ability to work from home, while frequently sought as a strategy for reconciling work and family demands, often results in intensification (Kaufman-Scarborough, 2006; Hochschild, 1997). Moreover, while it may reduce family-to-work conflict, it does not have the same effect on work-to-family conflict (Redman, Snape, & Ashurst, 2009). Despite this contradiction, studies indicate that there were over 900 million mobile workers in 2009 and that number is estimated to grow to over 1.18 billion, or about 35% of the workforce by 2013 (Ryan, Jaffe, Drake, & Boggs, 2009). All virtual work does not occur at home however, and one of the reasons that virtual forms of work are related to intensification is because, at least for knowledge and creative workers, there is no "dead time" (Bittman, et al., 2009). Employees can continue to "work" no matter where or when they are with the assistance of information and communication technologies (Fleming & Spicer, 2004; Ladner, 2008).

The ability to work from any place poses a contradiction for these workers. Given the voluminous literature on the impact of autonomy on a variety of worker outcomes such as job satisfaction, organizational commitment and sense of well-being, there is every reason to expect that even though having greater spatial flexibility may lead to greater positive feelings about work, it may also serve as a new form of control. The managerial incentive for empowering workers is the extent to which new forms of autonomy boost productivity, commitment to the organization, and its goals. Empowerment initiatives communicate trust by veiling the underlying power relationship between managers and employees, even if only temporarily. We argue, therefore, that managers use this spatial flexibility as a way of generating positive feelings about the workplace and thus minimizing the likelihood that they will lose the effort of valuable employees. These claims lead us to the following hypotheses:

H_1: Employees who are required to be creative in their job who are able to work virtually, are more satisfied with their job than workers who are required to be creative on their job who are not able to work virtually.

H_2: Employees who are required to be creative in their job who are able to work virtually, are more positive about their organization and work than workers who are required to be creative on their job who are not able to work virtually.

H_3: Employees who are required to be creative in their job who are able to work virtually, have greater mental health than workers who are required to be creative on their job who are not able to work virtually.

We turn now to a discussion of research design, findings and implications.

RESEARCH AND PRACTICAL IMPLICATIONS

We use the *2008 National Study of the Changing Workforce* (NSCW) available from the *Families and Work Institute*. The data for the 2008 NSCW were collected by Harris Interactive using an instrument developed by *Families and Work Institute* (Families and Work Institute, 2010). The NSCW is a nationally representative survey of the labor force that is conducted every five years. Harris Interactive, using a CATI system and random digit dialing, drew a national sample that included 3,502 interviews. After stratifying by region, Harris Interactive drew an unclustered random probability sample. To be included in the final sample, respondents had to be 18 years of age or older, working in a paid job or income producing business, residing in the lower 48 states and members of the non-institutionalized civilian labor force (Families and Work Institute, 2010, p. 2). These data are particularly useful for studying the contemporary workplace and the experience of workers in that workplace. The data include measures of a wide range of employee outcomes and working conditions and cover workers across industries and occupations. After weighting, the sample is representative of the labor force on a variety of demographic and economic traits compared to the *Current Population Survey* conducted in the same years (Families and Work Institute, 2010).

We further reduced our sample to include only those individuals employed in occupations that are likely to require creativity on the job. Thus, our analysis includes those workers who are in the following occupations: managers, finance professionals, buyers, purchase agents, marketing and advertising professionals, architects, designers, artists, scientists, mathematicians, and sales professionals.

As a validity check, we compared findings when using the selected occupational groups to the findings when using an item from the survey that asks participants to indicate the extent to which they agree that, "My job requires that I be creative." We selected individuals that rated this item as a 3 or a 4, indicating "agree" or "strongly agree" and performed the same analysis. Similar patterns emerged, therefore we feel confident that our occupational selections were reasonably well-aligned with creative work. A limitation is that we cannot differentiate among types of creativity these workers employ, only whether or not they are creative. We do not, however, see this limitation as overly problematic given the focus of this chapter.

Measures

To test our hypotheses, we selected items from the NSCW dataset that reflected job satisfaction, positive workplace attitudes, and psychological well-being of the individuals.

Job satisfaction. For the measure of job satisfaction, we used three items: (1)"All in all, how satisfied are you with your job—very satisfied, somewhat satisfied, not too satisfied, or not satisfied at all?," (2) "Knowing what you know now, if you had to decide all over again whether to take the job you now have, what would you decide; Would you decide without any hesitation to take the same

job, would you have some second thoughts, or would you decide definitely not to take the same job?," and (3) "If a good friend of yours told you that he or she was interested in working in a job like yours for your employer, what would you tell your friend? Would you strongly recommend your job, would you have doubts about recommending it, or would you strongly advise your friend against working in a job like yours?"

Work attitudes. To assess work attitudes, we used an item to assess turnover intentions and items to assess engagement with the job and employer. Turnover intentions were measured by the item, "Taking everything into consideration, how likely is it that you will make a genuine effort to find a new job with another employer within the next year—very likely, somewhat likely, or not at all likely?" Engagement was assessed through three items: (1) "When I'm at work, time passes very quickly," (2) "I really look forward to going to work most days," and (3) "How much do you agree or disagree with the following statement: I feel I am really a part of the group of people I work with? Do you strongly agree, somewhat agree, somewhat disagree, or strongly disagree?"

Psychological well-being. To measure psychological well-being, we used items to assess mental health, stress, and sleep problems. Mental health was measured through seven items. These items include: (1) "How often in the past month have you been bothered by minor health problems such as headaches, insomnia, or stomach upsets?" (2) "How often in the past month have you had trouble sleeping to the point that it affected your performance on and off the job?" (3) "How often in the past month have you felt nervous and stressed?" (4) "How often in the past month have you felt unable to control the important things in your life?" (5) "How often in the past month have you felt that difficulties were piling up so high you could not overcome them?" (6) "During past month, have you been bothered by feeling down, depressed, or hopeless?" and (7) "During the past month, have you been bothered by little interest or pleasure in doing things?" Stress was measured by the perceived general stress index comprised of five items: (1) How often have you felt nervous and stressed? (2) "How often have you felt that you were unable to control the important things in your life?" (3) "How often have you felt that things were going your way?" (4) "How often have you felt that difficulties were piling up so high that you could not overcome them?" and (5) "Not thinking about work, how stressful has your personal and family life been in recent months—extremely stressful, very stressful, somewhat stressful, not very stressful, or not stressful at all?" Sleep problems were assessed via three items including: (1) "How often have you had trouble sleeping to the point that it affected your performance on and off the job?" (2) "How often have you had trouble falling asleep when you go to bed?" and (3) "How often have you awakened before you wanted to and had trouble falling back asleep?"

Virtual workers. To compare workers that are granted spatial autonomy and are able to work virtually to those employees that are not allowed to work virtually, we identified individuals that answered "yes" versus "no" to the item, "Are you allowed to work part of your regular paid hours at home?" While this item doesn't capture the extent to which workers take advantage of spatial autonomy and participate in a virtual work arrangement, it does capture whether or not they perceive that they have work location options. Since our hypotheses posit outcomes related to whether or not employees are granted spatial/virtual work autonomy, we felt this variable was a sufficient indicator. Also, although virtual work is likely to occur in a wide range of environments, home and work should provide the sharpest contrasts as home is typically defined as the "non-work" domain and is likely to be most qualitatively dissimilar to a main office location.

Results

The descriptive statistics for the selected sample and subset of items from the NSCW dataset are presented in Table 1. Only 25.5% of individuals in the creative occupations sample were allowed to work part of their regular paid hours at home.

We present the correlations among the items in Table 2. All correlations are significant at the $\alpha < .01$ level ($p \leq 0.01$). Strong correlations (values greater than .5) are found between several variable pairs: job autonomy and workplace climate of respect, job autonomy and work-life fit, job autonomy and workplace challenge and learn-

Table 1. Characteristics of individuals in creative occupations

	N	Minimum	Maximum	Mean	Std Dev
Home allow	573	--	--	--	--
Autonomy	590	1.00	4.00	3.17	0.694
Job satisfaction	590	-3.26	0.68	0.01	0.821
Turnover intentions	588	1.00	3.00	1.49	0.726
Engagement	590	1.00	3.00	2.03	0.661
Climate of respect	587	1.00	4.00	3.11	0.790
Work-life fit	529	1.13	4.00	3.30	0.570
Challenge & learning	590	1.00	4.00	3.48	0.581
Mental health	588	-1.44	3.04	-0.09	0.891
Stress	590	1.00	5.00	2.39	0.785
Sleep problems	590	1.00	5.00	2.33	1.047

ing, job satisfaction and engagement, job satisfaction and workplace climate of respect, job satisfaction and work-life fit, job satisfaction and workplace challenge and learning, engagement and a workplace climate of respect, engagement and workplace challenge and learning, workplace climate of respect and work-life fit, mental health and stress, mental health and sleep problems, and stress and sleep problems. The allowance to work at home has a moderately strong correlation with job autonomy (.299), which is the highest correlation this variable has with any other variable in the table.

To test our three hypotheses, we ran Pearson chi-square tests of differences in the outcome variables (job satisfaction, work attitudes, and well-being) based on whether or not the workers were allowed to work at home. Based on these analyses, hypothesis 1 was not supported; job satisfaction was not significantly different between the two groups, $X^2(2, N = 320) = 4.205, p = 0.122$.

Next, we tested whether or not work attitudes were different between workers allowed to work virtually and those that were not and found support for hypothesis 2, when using turnover intentions, level of engagement, and looking forward to going to work as the outcomes. Individuals that were allowed to work from home for part of their regular paid hours were less likely to intend to change employers, $X^2(2, N = 570) = 13.914, p = 0.001$, Cramer's V=.156. Similarly, workers allowed to work from home were more engaged with their jobs and organizations $X^2(2, N= 572) = 15.877$, $p < 0.0001$, Cramer's V=.167, and more likely to look forward to going to work $X^2(3, N = 574)=$ 8.054, $p = 0.045$, Cramer's V=.118.

Third, we tested the groups for differences on mental health, perceived general stress and frequency of sleep problems. For mental health, the difference between groups failed to achieve significance at the α =.05 level, but instead at the .10 level, which has been recognized as still demonstrating a meaningful difference in social sciences, especially when effect sizes are small— here, the effect size given by Cramer's V is .097. The chi-square value for mental health was $X^2(2, N=570) = 5.406, p = 0.067$. In contrast, perceived general stress and frequency of sleep problems provided support for hypothesis 3 by showing significant differences between the workers who are allowed to work from home and those that are not allowed to work from home. For perceived

Table 2. Pearson correlation matrix among spatial autonomy, job autonomy, and outcomes

		1	2	3	4	5	6	7	8	9	10
1	Home allow										
2	Autonomy	.299**									
3	Job sat	.119**	.475**								
4	Turnover	-.140**	-.320**	-.473**							
5	Engagement	.164**	.447**	.526**	-.275**						
6	Respect	.193**	.500**	.548**	-.235**	.505**					
7	Work-life fit	.161**	.517**	.548**	-.399**	.451**	.620**				
8	Challenge	.136**	.540**	.538**	-.345**	.594**	.467**	.437**			
9	Mental health[a]	.120**	.292**	.400**	-.268**	.240**	.278**	.320**	.175**		
10	Stress[a]	.129**	.313**	.398**	-.235**	.267**	.303**	.315**	.183**	.870**	
11	Sleep prob[a]	.162**	.202**	.279**	-.219**	.142**	.273**	.241**	.103**	.710**	.523**

[a]Higher values indicate positive psychological well-being: better mental health, lower stress, fewer sleep problems.
**$p < 0.01$.

general stress, the chi-square value was $X^2(2, N = 573) = 6.650$, $p = 0.036$, Cramer's V =.108. Similarly, frequency of sleep problems were significantly different between the groups at the $\alpha = .01$ level, $X^2(2, N = 503) = 15.980$, $p < 0.001$, Cramer's V = .178. Together, these results provide moderate support for hypothesis 3.

Given our discussion above and small effect sizes (Cramer's V in the .07-.20 range) attributable to the impact of allowing workers to work part of their regular paid hours at home, and the conceptual relationship to job autonomy, we conducted exploratory factor analysis on all items that seem to reflect worker autonomy (these eight items are presented in Table 3). We used factor analysis with the maximum likelihood extraction method and used oblimin rotation to allow for the factors to remain correlated. Examining the scree plot and selecting only those factors with eigenvalues greater than 1.0 revealed two factors. We interpreted the factors and loadings via the pattern matrix (see Table 3); the first factor reflects task autonomy (how work is completed) and explains about 41% of the variance in autonomy scores and an additional factor reflects autonomy regarding where and when work is completed that explains an additional 14.29% of variance in worker autonomy. In sum, these 2 factors explain 55.29% of the variance in autonomy and are still fairly strongly correlated .40. All items reached the minimum factor loading of .30 that indicates at least 10% of the variance in a variable is explained by the factor (see Table 3 for item loadings).

Discussion

Our research answers calls by scholars (Thompson & Smith, 2009) to introduce a spatial component to labor process theory as work becomes untied from a single fixed physical space. The indeterminacy associated with the extraction of work is not just about effort but now increasingly about mobility (Thompson & Smith, 2009, p. 924). LPT is not concerned with how employers maximize work extraction but that they do. This research demonstrates that offering forms of flexibility and empowerment to employees can be effective strategies toward achieving greater organizational commitment and more positive work attitudes in those maximal work extraction efforts, making a contribution to literatures from other disciplines examining command and control and organizational commitment as well.

Together, our results make the case for a relatively new and related dimension of autonomy—that which is related to worker choice of where and when they work. Our findings suggest that this relatively new form of work autonomy has the potential to lead to positive outcomes for workers and the organizations that grant it, providing sup-

Table 3. Pattern matrix with item loadings for autonomy variables

	Factor	
	1	2
Freedom to decide how to work	.746	-.008
Own responsibility to decide how job gets done	.698	.052
Freedom to decide what I do on my job	.631	.174
I have a lot of say about what happens on my job	.584	.314
I feel personally responsible for my work	.443	-.139
I can be myself on the job	.413	.139
Overall how much control in scheduling work hours	-.034	.674
I am allowed to work part of my regular paid hours at home	.130	.421

port for labor process theory. We acknowledge, though, that the effect sizes of spatial autonomy on positive outcomes such as job satisfaction, work attitudes, and psychological well-being were small.

Other recent studies have found similar positive results, but also relatively small effect sizes linking home-based teleworking to organizational commitment and task performance (Hunton & Norman, 2010), and work-life balance and job satisfaction (Fonner & Roloff, 2010; Morganson, Major, Oborn, Verive, & Heelan, 2010; Redman, Snape, & Ashurst, 2009). The small effect sizes can indicate that there are moderating or mediating variables for which this study was unable account that may be hidden when looking at cross-organizational samples and cross-sectional data.

Some researchers have suggested that there may be interference in these positive outcomes due to other simultaneously occurring negative outcomes like social isolation (Morganson, et al., 2010) previously reported to coincide with intensive teleworking (Golden, Veiga, & Dino, 2008), electronic monitoring (Hunton & Norman, 2010), or work intensification (Ladner, 2008; Leonardi, Treem, & Jackson, 2010). Others have also found that the relationship between telecommuting and job satisfaction may not be linear, but an inverted U-shape, which would also cause discrepant findings or weak findings across studies (Virick, DaSilva, & Arrington, 2010). Finally, our measure of virtual work only tapped the ability to work at home not work in other, "third" places, a limitation that also may have affected our results. In sum, these findings indicate a need for further explanation of the relationships between spatial autonomy and organizational and individual outcomes.

FUTURE RESEARCH DIRECTIONS

Based on our extension of LPT and the results of our study and others, we would propose that there is an ongoing tension and continual oscil-lation between efforts to control and empower teleworkers. This tension and oscillation may explain weak findings—as employees negotiate this contradictory process with managers, they are constantly renegotiating their roles and responses; they may find themselves in positions where positive outcomes outweigh the negative outcomes and vice versa at different points in time when the balance of power and resistance shifts.

Some studies have begun to look at the phenomenon of virtual work qualitatively and longitudinally, and have found support for the proposition that spatial and temporal autonomy are persistently granted and taken away through control strategies and tactics to resist them. For example, Richardson (2010, p. 146) found that managers are constantly concerned with the balance of "holding on" by "ensuring appropriate levels of communication, support, and control" and "letting go" by allowing for autonomy and displaying trust. Similarly, increased discretionary effort that often accompanies autonomy also may lead employees to struggle with outcomes of workplace intensification. A variety of factors contribute to that struggle. Employees may desire to comply with professional norms and their internalized professional identity (Fleming & Spicer, 2004; Noble & Lupton, 1998). Likewise, they may experience expectations of "hyper-responsivity" (Ladner, 2008) and/or feelings of guilt when work has penetrated the non-work domain and signals that they have the capability to work and should be working (Noble & Lupton, 1998). In addition, spatial autonomy is often framed as a work benefit and so the question of whether or not there needs to be a policy to restrict work's intrusion on non-work time has gone unasked (Ladner, 2008). Although policy has been lacking, some employees are using tactics to resist being too tightly tethered to the organization, such as by disconnecting their internet access, posting "away" status messages, and scheduling work "travel time" (Leonardi, et al., 2010).

While it may seem that employees' efforts of resistance to management mechanisms of control would harm the organization, it is worth noting that some research suggests that the tactics of resistance were actually tied to improved worker productivity (Leonardi, et al., 2010). Employees' strategies for disconnecting from distracting communications that tether them too tightly to day-to-day organizational phenomena, and instead allow them the time and space to focus on the tasks they were trying to accomplish, actually allow them to be more productive. Managerial efforts to control workers may undermine the very productivity they seek to encourage. Just as tantalizing is the suggestion that workers' resistance to control may produce outcomes that benefit the organization. Some researchers suggest that the boosts to productivity in situations where workers are granted autonomy, despite any efforts by employees to resist control, provide evidence for Gagné and Deci's (2005) proposition that autonomy-supportive work climates facilitate internalization of extrinsic motivation leading to performance that is in line with management's goals (Hunton & Norman, 2010). Together, these findings suggest that allowing employees to work virtually does not compromise employer control; rather it enhances employees' positive feelings about work, their mental health and other indicators of well being. Allowing creative workers flexibility of location contributes to a "win-win" workplace in which both the organization and the actors within it benefit. Moreover, as creative knowledge work becomes an increasingly important part of global businesses, devising proactive strategies that facilitate creative workers' location choice will also position companies to attract and retain the most valuable of their employees.

CONCLUSION

This chapter has introduced spatial autonomy as a new form of autonomy and provided evidence indicating that managers can use spatial autonomy to empower workers in an effort to enhance productivity. The results of our study suggest that workers that are granted spatial autonomy are more likely to have positive attitudes about work, including viewing the work environment as having a greater climate of respect, offering greater challenge and rewards, offering better work-life fit. Workers with the option to work from home for part of their regular paid hours are more likely than those without this option to be engaged with their organization and jobs, have lower turnover intentions, and look forward to going to work. In addition to organization-level benefits, individuals that have the home working option experience benefits to psychological well-being such as lower stress levels and fewer sleep problems.

While this research indicates that spatial autonomy has much to offer for both organizations and individuals, the effect sizes were small and warrant further examination. It is likely that many factors influence these relationships and that there is an on-going process of struggle between control and autonomy with respect to virtual working, as workspace becomes a new contested terrain.

REFERENCES

Agypt, B., & Rubin, B. A. (2011). Time in the new economy: The impact of the interaction of individual and structural temporalities on job satisfaction. *Journal of Management Studies*, *49*(2), 403–428. doi:10.1111/j.1467-6486.2011.01021.x

Agypt, B., Rubin, B. A., & Spivack, A. J. (2012). Thinking outside the clocks: The effect of layered-task time on the creative climate of meetings. *The Journal of Creative Behavior*, *42*, 750–757.

Albert, S., & Bradley, K. (1997). *Managing knowledge*. Cambridge, MA: Cambridge University. doi:10.1017/CBO9780511582486

Amabile, T. M., Conti, R., Coon, H., Lazenby, J., & Herron, M. (1996). Assessing the work environment for creativity. *Academy of Management Journal, 39*(5), 1154–1184. doi:10.2307/256995

Amabile, T. M., & Gryskiewicz, N. (1989). The creative environment scales: The work environment inventory. *Creativity Research Journal, 2,* 231–254. doi:10.1080/10400418909534321

Andriopoulos, C. (2001). Determinants of organisational creativity: A literature review. *Management Decision, 39*(10), 834–840. doi:10.1108/00251740110402328

Applebaum, E., & Batt, R. (1994). *The new American workplace: Transforming work systems in the United States.* Ithaca, NY: ILR Press.

Arches, J. (1991). Social structure, burnout, and job satisfaction. *Social Work, 36*(3), 202–206.

Baldry, C., & Hallier, J. (2010). Welcome to the house of fun: Work space and social identity. *Economic and Industrial Democracy, 31,* 150–172. doi:10.1177/0143831X09351215

Broschak, J. P., Davis-Blake, A., & Block, E. (2008). Nonstatndard, not substandard: The relationship among work arrangements, work attitudes, and job performance. *Work and Occupations, 35*(1), 3–43. doi:10.1177/0730888407309604

Cappelli, P., Bassi, L., Katz, H., Knoke, D., Osterman, P., & Useem, M. (1997). *Change at work.* Oxford, UK: Oxford University Press.

Chen, C. C., & Chiu, S. F. (2009). The mediating role of job involvement in the relationship between job characteristics and organizational citizenship behavior. *The Journal of Social Psychology, 149*(4), 474–494. doi:10.3200/SOCP.149.4.474-494

Cohen, A. (1992). Antecedents of organizational commitment across occupational groups: A meta-analysis. *Journal of Organizational Behavior, 13*(6), 539–558. doi:10.1002/job.4030130602

Cummings, L. (1965). Organizational climates for creativity. *Academy of Management Journal, 8*(3), 220–227. doi:10.2307/254790

Daniels, K., & Guppy, A. (1994). Occupational stress, social support, job control, and psychological well-being. *Human Relations, 47*(12), 1523–1544. doi:10.1177/001872679404701205

Duffy, F. (2000). Design and facilities management in a time of change. *Facilities, 10-12,* 371–375. doi:10.1108/02632770010349592

Edwards, R. (1979). *Contested terrain.* New York, NY: Basic.

Families and Work Institute. (2010). *2008, national study of the changing work force.* Washington, DC: Families and Work Institute.

Fleming, P., & Spicer, A. (2004). You can checkout anytime, but you can never leave: Spatial boundaries in a high commitment organization. *Human Relations, 57*(1), 75–94. doi:10.1177/0018726704042715

Fonner, K. L., & Roloff, M. E. (2010). Why teleworkers are more satisfied with their jobs than are office-based workers: When less contact is beneficial. *Journal of Applied Communication Research, 38*(4), 336–361. doi:10.1080/00909882.2010.513998

Garson, B. (1994). *All the live-long day: The meaning and demeaning of routine work.* New York, NY: Penguin.

Golden, T. D., Veiga, J. F., & Dino, R. N. (2008). The impact of professional isolation on teleworker job performance and turnover intentions: Does time spent teleworking, interacting face-to-face, or having access to communication-enhancing technology matter? *The Journal of Applied Psychology, 93*(6), 1412–1421. doi:10.1037/a0012722

Halford, S., & Strangleman, T. (2009). In search of the sociology of work: Past, present and future. *Sociology, 43*, 811–828. doi:10.1177/0038038509341307

Harrison, B., & Kelley, M. R. (1993). Outsourceing and the search for flexibility. *Work, Employment and Society, 7*(2), 213–255.

Henard, D., & McFadyen, A. M. (2008). Making knowledge workers more creative. *Research-Technology Management, 51*(2), 40–46.

Hobson, C. J., Delunas, L., & Kesic, D. (2001). Compelling evidence of the need for corporate work/life balance initiatives: Evidence from a national survey of stressful life events. *Journal of Employment Counseling, 38*, 38–44. doi:10.1002/j.2161-1920.2001.tb00491.x

Hunton, J. E., & Norman, C. S. (2010). The impact of alternative telework arrangements on organizational commitment: Insights from a longitudinal field experiment. *Journal of Information Systems, 24*(1), 67–90. doi:10.2308/jis.2010.24.1.67

Jackson, P., Gharavi, H., & Klobas, J. (2006). Technologies of the self: Virtual work and the inner panopticon. *Information Technology & People, 19*, 219–243. doi:10.1108/09593840610689831

Kalleberg, A. L. (1977). Work values and job rewards: A theory of job satisfaction. *American Sociological Review, 42*, 124–143. doi:10.2307/2117735

Kalleberg, A. L. (2003). Flexible firms and labor market segmentation: Effects of workplace restructuring on jobs and workers. *Work and Occupations, 30*(2), 154–175. doi:10.1177/0730888403251683

Kaufman-Scarborough, C. (2006). Time use and the impact of technology: Examining workspaces in the home. *Time & Society, 15*, 57–80. doi:10.1177/0961463X06061782

Kim, T.-Y. H., & Grant, A. J. (2009). Proactive personality, employee creativity and newcomer outcomes: A longitudinal study. *Journal of Business and Psychology, 24*(1), 93–103. doi:10.1007/s10869-009-9094-4

Ladner, S. (2008). Laptops in the living room: Mobile technologies and the divide between work and private time among interactive agency workers. *Canadian Journal of Communication, 33*(3), 465–489.

Land, C., & Taylor, S. (2010). Surf's up: Work, life, balance and brand in the a new age capitalist organization. *Sociology, 44*, 395–413. doi:10.1177/0038038510362479

Lapierre, J., & Pierre-Giroux, V. (2003). Creativity and work environment in a high-tech context. *Creativity and Work Environment, 12*(1), 11–23.

Leider, R. (1993). *Fast food, fast talk: Service work and the routinization of everyday life.* Berkeley, CA: University of California Press.

Leonardi, P. M., Treem, J. W., & Jackson, M. H. (2010). The connectivity paradox: Using technology to both decrease and increase perceptions of distance in distributed work arrangements. *Journal of Applied Communication Research, 38*(1), 85–105. doi:10.1080/00909880903483599

Loher, B. T., Noe, R. A., Moeller, N. L., & Fitzgerald, M. P. (1985). A meta-analysis of the relation of job characteristics to job satisfaction. *The Journal of Applied Psychology, 70*(2), 280–289. doi:10.1037/0021-9010.70.2.280

Marsh, R. M., & Mannari, H. (1977). Organizational commitment and turnover: A prediction study. *Administrative Science Quarterly, 22*(1), 57–75. doi:10.2307/2391746

Mennino, S. F., Rubin, B. A., & Brayfield, A. (2005). Home-to job and job-to-home spillover: The impact of demanding jobs, company policies and workplace cultures. *The Sociological Quarterly, 46*, 107–135. doi:10.1111/j.1533-8525.2005.00006.x

Morganson, V. J., Major, D. A., Oborn, K. L., Verive, J. M., & Heelan, M. P. (2010). Comparing telework locations and traditional work arrangements: Differences in work-life balance support, job satisfaction, and inclusion. *Journal of Managerial Psychology, 25*(6), 578–595. doi:10.1108/02683941011056941

Moss, P., & Tilly, C. (1996). Soft skills and race: An investigation of black men's employment problems. *Work and Occupations, 23*(3), 252–276. doi:10.1177/0730888496023003002

Mumford, M. D. (2000). Managing creative people: Strategies and tactics for innovation. *Human Resource Management Review, 10*(3), 313–351. doi:10.1016/S1053-4822(99)00043-1

Noble, G., & Lupton, D. (1998). Consuming work: Computers, subjectivity and appropriation in the university workplace. *The Sociological Review, 46*(4), 803–827. doi:10.1111/1467-954X.00141

O'Doherty, D., & Willmott, H. (2009). The decline of labour process analysis and the future of sociology of work. *Sociology, 43*, 931–951. doi:10.1177/0038038509340742

Peng, Y. P., Hwang, S. N., & Wong, J. Y. (2010). How to inspire university librarians to become "good soldiers"? The role of job autonomy. *Journal of Academic Librarianship, 36*(4), 287–295. doi:10.1016/j.acalib.2010.05.002

Presser, H. (2003). *Working in a 24/7 economy*. New York, NY: Russell Sage Foundation.

Redman, T., Snape, E., & Ashurst, C. (2009). Location, location, location: Does place of work really matter. *British Journal of Management, 20*, S171–S181. doi:10.1111/j.1467-8551.2008.00640.x

Richardson, J. (2010). Managing flexworkers: Holding on and letting go. *Journal of Management Development, 29*(2), 137–147. doi:10.1108/02621711011019279

Rodgers, F., & Rodgers, C. (1989). Business and facts of family life. *Harvard Business Review, 89*, 121–129.

Rubin, B. (1995). Flexible accumulation, the decline of contract and social transformation. *Research in Social Stratification and Mobility, 14*, 297–323.

Rubin, B. (2007). New times redux: Layering time in the new economy. In Rubin, B. A. (Ed.), *Workplace Temporalities: Research in the Sociology of Work* (pp. 527–548). Amsterdam, The Netherlands: Elsevier. doi:10.1016/S0277-2833(07)17017-5

Rubin, B. A., & Brody, C. J. (2005). Contradictions of commitment in the new economy: Insecurity, time and technology. *Social Science Research, 34*, 843–861. doi:10.1016/j.ssresearch.2005.02.002

Ryan, S., Jaffe, J., Drake, S. D., & Boggs, R. (2009). *Worldwide mobile worker population 2009-2013 forecast*. Retrieved May 5, 2011, from www.idc.com/getdoc.jsp?containerId=221309.

Schieman, S., & Glavin, P. (2008). Trouble at the border? Gender, flexibility at work, and the work-home interface. *Social Problems, 55*(4), 590–611. doi:10.1525/sp.2008.55.4.590

Smith, V. (2001). Teamwork versus tempwork: Managers and the dualisms of workplace restructuring. In Campbell, K., Cornfield, D., & McCammon, H. (Eds.), *Working in Restructured Workplaces: New Directions for the Sociology of Work* (pp. 7–28). Thousand Oaks, CA: Sage.

Spivack, A. J., & Rubin, B. A. (2011). *Spaces to control creative output of the knowledge worker: A managerial paradox?* Paper presented at the iConference. Seattle, WA.

Stewart, T. A. (1997). *Intellectual capital: The new wealth of organizations.* New York, NY: Doubleday.

Thomas, L. T., & Ganster, D. (1995). Impact of family-supportive work variables on work-family conflict and strain: A control perspective. *The Journal of Applied Psychology, 80,* 6–15. doi:10.1037/0021-9010.80.1.6

Thompson, P., & Smith, C. (2009). Labour power and the labor process: Contesting the marginality of the sociology of work. *Sociology, 43,* 913–930. doi:10.1177/0038038509340728

Trow, D. B. (1957). Autonomy and job satisfaction in task-oriented groups. *Journal of Abnormal and Social Psychology, 54*(2), 204–209. doi:10.1037/h0041424

U.S. Department of Labor. (2008). *Women in the labor force: A databook.* Washington, DC: US Department of Labor.

Venkatesh, A., & Vitalari, N. (1992). An emerging distributed work arrangement: An investigation of computer-based supplemental work at home. *Management Science, 38,* 1687–1706. doi:10.1287/mnsc.38.12.1687

Virick, M., DaSilva, N., & Arrington, K. (2010). Moderators of the curvilinear relation between extent of telecommuting and job and life satisfaction: The role of performance outcome orientation and worker type. *Human Relations, 63*(1), 137–154. doi:10.1177/0018726709349198

Woodman, R. W., Sawyer, J. E., & Griffin, R. W. (1993). Toward a theory of organizational creativity. *Academy of Management Review, 18*(2), 293–321.

ADDITIONAL READING

Baer, M., & Oldham, G. R. (2006). The curvilinear relation between experienced creative time pressure and creativity: Moderating effects of openness to experience and support for creativity. *The Journal of Applied Psychology, 91*(4), 963–970. doi:10.1037/0021-9010.91.4.963

Bailey, D. E., & Kurland, N. B. (2002). A review of telework research: Findings, new directions, and lessons for the study of modern work. *Journal of Organizational Behavior, 23*(4), 383–400. doi:10.1002/job.144

Baruch, Y. (2000). Teleworking: benefits and pitfalls as perceived by professionals and managers. *New Technology, Work and Employment, 15*(1), 34–49. doi:10.1111/1468-005X.00063

Bharadwaj, S., & Menon, A. (2000). Making innovation happen in organizations: Individual creativity mechanisms, organizational creativity mechanisms or both? *New York, 17,* 424 - 434.

Cappelli, P. (1999). *The new deal at work: Managing the market driven workplace.* Boston, MA: Harvard Business School.

Christensen, K., & Staines, G. L. (1990). Flextime: A viable solution to work/family conflict? *Journal of Family Issues, 11,* 455–476. doi:10.1177/019251390011004007

Cummings, A., & Oldham, G. R. (1997). Enhancing creativity: Managing work contexts for the high potential employee. *California Management Review, 40*(1), 22–38.

Daniels, K., Lamond, D., & Standen, P. (2001). Teleworking: Frameworks for organizational research. *Journal of Management Studies, 38*(8), 1151–1185. doi:10.1111/1467-6486.00276

Donnelly, R. (2004). How 'free' is the free worker? An investigation into the working arrangements available to knowledge workers. *Personnel Review, 35*(1), 78–97. doi:10.1108/00483480610636803

Drazin, R., Glynn, M. A., & Kazanjian, R. K. (1999). Multilevel theorizing about creativity in organizations: A sensemaking perspective. *Academy of Management Review, 24*(2), 286–307.

Felstead, A., Jewson, N., & Walters, S. (2005). *Changing places of work. New York, NY: Palgrave Macmillan. Florida, R. (2002). The rise of the creative class: And how it's transforming work, leisure, community and everyday life*. New York, NY: Basic.

Fenwick, T. (2007). Knowledge workers in the in-between: Network identities. *Journal of Organizational Change Management, 20*(4), 509–524. doi:10.1108/09534810710760054

Fried, M. (1998). *Taking time: Parental leave policy and corporate culture*. Philadelphia, PA: Temple University.

Frolick, M. N., Wilkes, R. B., & Unilever, R. (1993). Telecommuting as a workplace alternative: An identification of significant factors in American firms' determination of work-at-home policies. *The Journal of Strategic Information Systems, 2*(3), 206–222. doi:10.1016/0963-8687(93)90028-9

Gagne, M., & Deci, E. (2005). Self-determination theory and work motivation. *Journal of Organizational Behavior, 26*, 331–362. doi:10.1002/job.322

Gajendran, R., & Harrison, D. (2007). The good, the bad, and the unknown about telecommuting: Meta-analysis of psychological mediators and individual consequences. *The Journal of Applied Psychology, 92*, 1524–1541. doi:10.1037/0021-9010.92.6.1524

Golden, T. D., Veiga, J. F., & Simsek, Z. (2006). Telecommuting's differential impact on work-family conflict: Is there no place like home? *The Journal of Applied Psychology, 91*(6), 1340–1350. doi:10.1037/0021-9010.91.6.1340

Hislop, D., & Axtell, C. (2007). The neglect of spatial mobility in contemporary studies of work: The case of telework. *New Technology, Work and Employment, 22*(1), 34–51. doi:10.1111/j.1468-005X.2007.00182.x

Lewis, T. (2007). Braverman, Foucault and the labor process: Framing the current high-skills debate. *Journal of Education and Work, 20*(5), 397–415. doi:10.1080/13639080701814315

May, T. (1999). From banana time to just-in-time: Power and resistance at work. *Sociology, 33*(4), 767–783.

Mir, A., & Mir, R. (2005). Producing the governable employee. *Cultural Dynamics, 17*(1), 51–72. doi:10.1177/0921374005057601

Oldham, G. R., & Cummings, A. (1996). Employee creativity: Personal and contextual factors at work. *Academy of Management Journal, 39*(3), 607–634. doi:10.2307/256657

Pietrykowski, B. (1999). Beyond the fordist/post-fordist dichotomy: Working through the second industrial divide. *Review of Social Economy, 57*, 177–198. doi:10.1080/00346769900000035

Piore, M., & Sabel, C. (1984). *The second industrial divide: Possibilities for prosperity*. New York, NY: Basic Books.

Shalley, C. E. (1991). Effects of productivity goals, creativity goals, and personal discretion on individual creativity. *The Journal of Applied Psychology, 76*(2), 179–185. doi:10.1037/0021-9010.76.2.179

Vallas, S. (2003). The adventures of managerial hegemony: Teamwork, ideology, and worker resistance. *Social Problems, 50*, 204–225. doi:10.1525/sp.2003.50.2.204

Vanderburg, W. H. (2004). The intellectual assembly line is already here. *Bulletin of Science, Technology & Society, 24*(4), 331–341. doi:10.1177/0270467604267299

KEY TERMS AND DEFINITIONS

Autonomy: Freedom to decide how, when, or where, work gets done.

Control: Managerial efforts to extract maximal productivity from workers by exercising power over them.

Creativity: The process by which novel ideas are generated.

Flexibility: Work arrangements that can vary according to needs of the worker or employer, whether via schedule, location, or other considerations.

Home-Based Telework: A telework arrangement that involves an employee working from home through use of information and communication technologies.

Knowledge Work: Work involving thought processes to generate ideas and other non-tangibles that are hard to measure.

Telework/Virtual Work/Telecommuting: Work arrangements that allow workers to work from a location separate from the main office location through the use of various information and communication technologies.

ENDNOTE

[1] Both authors contributed equally to the research contained in this chapter.

Chapter 5
Virtual Vines:
Using Participatory Methods to Connect Virtual Work with Community–Based Practice

Marianne LeGreco
University of North Carolina at Greensboro, USA

Dawn Leonard
Urban Harvest Greensboro, USA

Michelle Ferrier
Elon University, USA & LocallyGrownNews.com, USA

ABSTRACT

This chapter focuses on the somewhat unexpected relationship between participatory research methods, virtual work, and community-based practices. More specifically, the authors' contribution outlines different conceptual foundations and methodological approaches related to participatory and community-based research. Embedded within this review, they address two key connections between participatory methods and virtual work. First, participatory and community-based methodologies provide a useful set of concepts and practices that can be applied in virtual contexts. Second, virtual work can facilitate participatory initiatives and achieve community-based goals. The chapter also offers two short case studies that illustrate how community-based groups often rely on virtual work to move their local initiatives forward.

INTRODUCTION

Work involves not only paid labor, but also the activities of volunteers and community-based organizations as they work to move their local interests forward. The proliferation of Community-Based and Participatory Research (CBPR) across both organizational and health communication research (e.g., Basu & Dutta, 2008; Deetz, 2009; McDermott, Oetzel, & White 2008) demonstrates that work within communities involves unique and often innovative communication practices in and of themselves. This chapter examines those unique and innovative practices, especially as they

DOI: 10.4018/978-1-4666-0963-1.ch005

pertain to the ways in which community-based work is carried out virtually.

The potential for virtual work to provide a versatile platform for dialogue, interaction, and collaboration across time and space has been well documented (e.g., Long, 2010; Whitman & Woszczynski, 2003). Indeed, the Bureau of Labor Statistics reported data from 2009, claiming that 24% of employed people do all or part of their work from home (U.S. Department of Labor, 2010). Moreover, data from the Pew Research Center suggests that 82% of American adults who also use social network sites—and 85% of Twitter users, in particular—are not just members, but active participants in some form of voluntary group or organization (Rainie, Purcell, & Smith, 2011). In other words, employees are orienting their activities to ever-changing structures of work, and individuals are relying on virtual platforms to meet their needs for community and collaboration. However, our contribution is about much more than the concepts of remote workplaces or virtual communities; rather, we encourage the reader to consider how CBPR methods provide useful resources for scholars and practitioners who study virtual work.

At first glance, CBPR and virtual work might seem like an odd pairing. The former tends to rely on practices of community engagement that imply face-to-face dialogue and interaction, while the latter draws from different Information and Communication Technologies (ICTs) to enable work practices. At the same time, virtual work presents a unique opportunity to engage in participatory and community-based research. By weaving together the relationships between participatory, community-based research and virtual work, this chapter adds a unique and somewhat unexpected take on the spirit of this book. We begin by emphasizing important concepts and techniques that underlie a CBPR methodology. Following this description, we situate those methods alongside virtual work practices, and we offer two mini-case studies as illustrations. Finally, we consider some

of the research implications and future directions of this focus on virtual work and community-based methods.

COMMUNITY-BASED PARTICIPATORY RESEARCH

Before delving into the details of community-based research and virtual work, we find it necessary to situate this chapter in the methodological practices that have given rise to CBPR. As both organizations and individuals realize the need for more inclusive systems of democracy and participation, government agencies and researchers are exploring the possibilities of taking a community-based approach. The United Nations, for example, has considered ways to incorporate the perspectives of non-state actors and community members into their conversations about policy, information, and society (Cogburn, Johnsen, & Bhattacharyya, 2008). Additionally, agencies including the National Institutes of Health and the Robert Wood Johnson Foundation have established funding opportunities that encourage community partnerships in the design and implementation of research projects. CBPR practices have gained a great deal of momentum across disciplines; therefore, it is necessary to mention the research traditions and methodologies that have fueled their development.

The increased interest in CBPR can trace its roots to a range of critical, organizational, and health research trajectories. Early work on action science and research (Argyris, Putnam, & Smith, 1985; Argyris & Schon, 1991) focused on moving research out of controlled laboratory settings to consider how knowledge can solve practical problems in the field. Related methodological positions advocated a co-operative or collaborative research approach through which researchers carry out work "with" participants as opposed to "on" participants (Heron, 1971; Heron & Reason, 1997, 2006; Reason, 1994). Subsequent writings (e.g., Gatenby & Humphries, 2000; Kemmis &

McTaggart, 2000; Whyte, 1991) have developed the language of Participatory Action Research (PAR), which draws from Freire's (1970) critical pedagogy to advocate research practices that enable transformation in the service of human flourishing.

Across these methodologies, scholars tend to agree on their commitment to "bring together broad social analyses: the self-reflective collective self-study of practice, the way language is used, organization and power in a local situation, and action to improve things" (Kemmis & McTaggart, 2000, p. 268). Above all, CBPR methods involve an intense research relationship between researcher and participant (Heron & Reason, 1997). Based on the assumption that participants are not 'cultural dopes' (Giddens, 1979; Kemmis & McTaggart, 2000; Tracy, 2002), CBPR focuses on developing practical knowledge that participants can immediately internalize and apply to solve their own problems in the field. Some of the basic tenets involved in this approach include working with community members to identify those problems (Ashcraft, 1999; Craig & Tracy, 1995; Heron & Reason, 2006; Tracy, 2002); involving participants in the research design, analysis, and evaluation (Heron & Reason, 2006; Reason, 1994); encouraging self-reflexivity on the part of both research and participant (Ashcraft, 1999; Heron & Reason, 1997); and realizing that we as researchers have just as much to learn from our participants as they do from us (Reason, 1994; Trethewey, 2002).

Proponents of these community-based and participatory perspectives are often quick to remind potential scholars that CBPR is a methodology. It does not offer a specific step-by-step method of execution; rather, it presents us with assumptions, philosophies, and goals to take up as part of our research endeavors (McDermott, Oetzel, & White, 2008; Reason, 1994). CBPR promotes a critical subjectivity in which researcher and participant develop a practical knowing about their environment, sense of self, and problems that

they encounter in daily life. To pursue these epistemological and methodological goals, researchers and community members may draw from a range of both qualitative and quantitative resources. For example, researchers can collaborate with community participants to design survey items for a questionnaire or semi-structured questions for an interview guide (Heron & Reason, 2006), to make analytic observations and develop recommendations (LeGreco & Tracy, 2009), or to present research findings to other communities and practitioners (Tracy, 2002).

A community-based approach to research responds to a call from critical and applied scholars across disciplines to take seriously the implications of our research on the participants who might use our results to make everyday decisions. For example, Fine, Weis, Weseen and Wong's (2000) work in low-income neighborhoods compelled them to consider how their own assumptions about power and poverty positioned their relationships with their participants. In doing so, they ultimately came to question how they represented the voices of those participants, as well as how their research might have implications for community members in their everyday lived experiences. Cooperative and participatory perspectives are particularly useful for marginalized groups because of their dual objectives of solving problems in the field and encouraging participants to critically reflect upon their experiences in order to foster their own ways of knowing and navigating social life (Reason, 1994; see also Freire, 1970; Heron & Reason, 2006). Because knowledge is generated and applied from within the research relationship, this style of research does not take the "expert" knowledge from the researcher and apply to an organized setting. Rather, both researcher and participant are considered experts in the collaborative generation and application of knowledge.

Although CBPR practices have the potential to promote multiple stakeholder participation and generate practical solutions to a community's most pertinent problems, they are not without their share of challenges. Considering that the overarching goal of CBPR is to incorporate community perspectives in the pursuit of human flourishing and social change, scholars and community members are often left with outcomes that are difficult to anticipate and even more difficult to measure. This raises a concern among both critics and proponents of CBPR involving the rigor of research design and the capacity for community members to contribute higher order skills to a study (Buchanan, Miller, & Wallerstein, 2007; Freeman, Brugge, Bennett-Bradley, Levy, & Carrasco, 2006). The demands of Institutional Review Boards regarding informed consent and appropriate training can place a burden on CBPR projects that might undermine a research relationship. Moreover, CBPR projects are often directed toward resource-stressed communities with low-education levels, low-literacy rates, and low-income brackets. This can raise ethical paradoxes in CBPR projects by privileging the research over the needs of individuals living within a community or by simply asking them to participate in projects in ways that do not consider their skill sets (Buchanan, Miller, & Wallerstein, 2007; McDermott, Oetzel, & White, 2008).

At the same time, these tensions and paradoxes should not deter the growing interest in CBPR. Indeed, McDermott, Oetzel, and White (2008) argued that working through and reframing those tensions collaboratively can help individuals and groups fulfill their community-based needs. Projects are considered successful when participants can engage in exactly this type of critical self-reflection in order to solve problems within their social relations and practices. As Heron and Reason (1997) clarified, participatory projects enable transformation when participants (and researchers) can synthesize experiential, practical, presentational, and propositional knowledge in order to progress.

Within the field of Communication, CBPR is part of a larger conversation about practical and applied research, social justice, and communication activism. These approaches have been referred to as *Politically Attentive Relational Constructionism* (Deetz, 2009), as especially concerned with how practices "scale up" from local to larger contexts (Conrad, 2004; Keyton, Bisel, & Ozley, 2009), and tend to focus on concepts like transformation and change, dialogue, community, and participation. The organizational and health concepts associated with these perspectives have been applied to a variety of contexts including organizational conferences (Broadfoot, Munshi, & Nelson-Marsh, 2010), online health programs (Ginossar & Nelson, 2010a, 2010b), and policymaking processes (Cogburn, Johnsen, & Bhattacharyya, 2008; LeGreco, 2011). As CBPR practices continue to flourish within a communication context, one area of study that might benefit greatly from a CBPR approach involves virtual work, online collaborations, and community-based transformation. The following section considers this unlikely pairing of CBPR and virtual work.

WORKING VIRTUALLY TO BUILD COMMUNITY

The title for this chapter was inspired by a community-based project called Urban Harvest Greensboro, on which the first and second authors have collaborated to increase access to local food. During the winter of 2011, the second author hosted a community visioning session to help chart the activities for Urban Harvest in the coming year. The 35 people involved in this face-to-face meeting organized a range of possible activities into 11 categories with organically-related titles including "Hearth," "Sprouts," and "Vines." For example, hearth activities included things like cooking classes, whereas vine activities involved building an urban food network. Following this community visioning, a significant amount of work moved online. Urban Harvest relied on Web 2.0 technologies including their website (http://www.urbanharvest-gso.com/), Google Groups and Google Docs (http://groups.google.

com/group/gso-urban-food-networks), and their blog (http://urbanharvestgso.wordpress.com/) to move their interests forward. In other words, their vines became virtual as they attempted to connect resources together and carry out their community-based work.

In this section, we offer our primary contribution to this book on qualitative and quantitative approaches to virtual work by illustrating how the virtual vines enabled by Web 2.0 and ICTs can facilitate the work of community-based researchers and participants. To do so, we focus first on the important concepts and existing literature that demonstrate how these lines of research are already merging. Then, we provide two mini-case studies as exemplars of the connections between community-based and virtual work. We offer more detail on the activities of Urban Harvest, as well as the mobilizing power of LocallyGrownNews.com.

Connecting Community-Based Practices through Virtual Work

The innovative potential for virtual practices to enable community-based change and transformation is beginning to be realized. One need look no further than the 2009 political protests in Iran and the 2011 revolution in Egypt, and the role that social networking sites like Facebook and Twitter played to organize community members to act, to see this potential (Peters, 2011). At the same time, our contribution moves in a direction different than the literature on using social networks to organize social resistance. Rather, we focus on how to connect and study community-based practice through virtual *work*, and we do so by addressing two ways in which those connections have manifested. We consider how CBPR practices might inform the study of virtual work, as well as how virtual workspaces provide a platform to pursue participatory goals. Moreover, we outline some key concepts that highlight both the benefits and challenges of this relationship between CBPR and virtual work.

Situating CBPR and Virtual Work

Initially, CBPR practices are becoming increasingly relevant to the study of virtual contexts. Ginossar and Nelson's (2010a, 2010b) research on internet community-based interventions highlights the potential of bringing these lines of research together. Using a CBPR approach, they worked with community members to design and implement an online health organization in a low-income, Spanish-speaking neighborhood in Albuquerque, New Mexico. They identified and trained *promotoras*—a Spanish word for lay community health educators—to develop online media and health resources for their neighborhood. The purpose of this project was to build technological skills with the women of the neighborhood, promote economic development, and address health disparities in the community. While the focus of Ginossar and Nelson's research was not on virtual work, per se, their community-based project illustrated how the promotoras went through training and socialization practices, made decisions about online materials, and designed their own work with fellow community members. As such, their research provides a nice template for the community-based study of virtual working practices.

Considering that a significant focus of many CBPR projects is to develop job skills and promote economic development, the types of research practices related to its approach could significantly shape the changing world of virtual work. The growth of online resources and ICTs has prompted significant transformations in the way work is carried out, including changes to work structures (Timmerman & Scott, 2006) and knowledge management (Heinz & Rice, 2009). For example, Manpower—the employment services and job placement organization—has been experimenting since 2007 with the Second Life online community program. They have created alternative spaces, like a "virtual beach" for online meetings and interviews or an "orientation trail" to socialize new members to the different trends within the community. Changes like these have given rise to a range of new professional practices, and they have also redefined what counts as work (Broadfood, Munshi, & Nelson-Marsh, 2010; Cheney, Zorn, Planalp, & Lair, 2008; Kisselburgh, Berkelaar, & Buzzanell, 2009). By implementing community-based research practices across these new and changing contexts, we might also take innovative approaches to the study of processes like participation and employee empowerment, as well as other concepts that organizational scholars have warned us of, including increased colonization and work-life conflicts (Deetz, 1992; Fonner & Roloff, 2010).

If community-based and participatory research practices could benefit the study of virtual work, the question remains of how to integrate a CBPR methodology with more specific methods of data collection and analysis. Taking a CBPR approach when it comes to the study of virtual work also presents a unique opportunity for research methods—like discourse tracing (LeGreco & Tracy, 2009) and connective ethnography (Dirksen, Huizing, & Smit, 2010)—that are gaining ground in qualitative circles. For example, discourse tracing could illustrate how the discursive practices of community organizers branch out through online forums and social networking sites to promote changes in workplace practices, health behaviors, or other appropriate contexts. Similarly, connective ethnography could focus on the "inconnection of people and technical systems" (Dirksen, Huizing, & Smit, 2010, p. 1058) as they carry out a range of virtual work practices, like teamwork or socialization. Both methods could incorporate simple CBPR practices including working *with* participants to identify problems in the virtual field, design online interviews, and even train technologically inexperienced participants in the skills necessary to carry out virtual work. CBPR approaches do not require a radical transformation in practice in order to provide useful research

results; rather small changes can often produce the outcomes that this methodology encourages.

In addition to the relevance of CBPR methods to virtual work contexts, virtual work itself is becoming a prominent way to facilitate participatory initiatives and achieve community-based goals. Organizational and health research has illustrated how virtual work can help community members develop innovative practices and accomplish strategic changes within their communities. For example, Broadfoot, Munshi, and Nelson-Marsh's (2010) research on virtual conferencing demonstrates the detailed degrees to which activities had to be coordinated in order to promote multiple stakeholder participation in an online multi-national conference. Their attention to those details paid off, however, as the virtual platform offered a way for the members of a distributed academic community to provide a familiar but transformed conference experience. Practices like paper presentations and feedback sessions could extend well beyond their allotted time in the schedule through virtual chats, a keynote addresses could be accessed at different times depending on one's time zone. This virtual context allowed participants to work more collaboratively, as they moved both their own research interests and those of their community forward.

Further research on virtual and distributed communities only strengthens the case for virtual work as a platform for community-based change. The notion that community organizations would rely on virtual means to promote their initiatives is neither a new nor a novel concept. At the same time, several community members use virtual means to engage in the actual processes of organizing; therefore they rely on virtual work to make decisions, enable teamwork, and coordinate interests across a diverse and often dispersed constituency. La Leche League International, for example, has constructed a web-based community (http://www.llli.org/) that provides health information about breast-feeding to women and families who need it. They also offer peer counselor training and job skill development in order to empower the members of their community. Although La Leche League might not represent an obvious example of a virtual workplace, they are certainly working virtually to move the interests of the organization forward and develop employment for their members.

Virtual space is full of examples of community members organizing to have their interests heard and their needs met. Research on both Ehealth interventions (e.g., Ginossar & Nelson, 2010a; Neuhauser & Kreps, 2010) and grassroots organizing (e.g., Humphreys, 2008) has demonstrated that an increasing amount of community-based activities are moving to online spaces. Virtual work practices, such as online collaboration and teamwork, coordinating activities across distant and distributed space, and providing access to resources help these community initiatives to organize their actions in meaningful ways and bring about the changes which they seek. In doing so, they also enable local community activities to scale up to larger contexts and inspire the actions of an entirely new range of stakeholders.

Conceptualizing CBPR and Virtual Work

Although community-based practices and virtual work hold a great deal of potential benefits for one another, both researchers and participants must also recognize the challenges that this approach will inevitably present. For both of these perspectives on CBPR and virtual work, several sets of concepts require further attention. More specifically, we focus on some of these key concepts in the following pairs: access and training, agency and self-efficacy, publicity and participation.

First, access and training address some of the barriers that CBPR projects must consider when engaging in virtual work. Digital divides and the lack of resources necessary to carry out virtual work are very real and continue to persist among low-income populations (Ginossar & Nelson,

2010b). 2009 U.S. Census data claimed that 68% of households had internet use at home (U.S. Census Bureau, 2010), meaning that community-based researchers cannot always guarantee immediate internet access for almost one-third of the U.S. population. Access has certainly increased in public spaces including libraries and community centers, and community members sometimes have demonstrated a willingness to travel great distances to find a suitable internet connection (Broadfoot, Munshi, & Nelson-Marsh, 2010); however, lack of access raises questions about structural barriers that virtual work projects must address. Lack of access to virtual resources is especially critical in low-income neighborhoods. Data from the Pew Internet and American Life Project report that disparities in computer and internet access for low-income individuals and families are a persistent structural problem (Fox & Vitak, 2008), placing these households at a disadvantage when it comes to engaging in virtual work in the first place. CBPR practices are well-positioned to address these disparities and work with community members to identify creative solutions for moving beyond them.

Simply increasing access to computer, internet, and other virtual resources, however, will not amend those disparities completely. Because CBPR projects are compelled to promote meaningful change and oftentimes economic development, researchers and participants must also commit to training and educational components (Broadfoot, et al., 2008; Cogburn, Johnsen, & Bhattacharyya, 2008). In other words, it is not enough to make sure that every home has a computer and internet access; rather, community-based researchers need to make sure that participants have the skills to enact those resources. Again, we turn to Ginossar and Nelson's (2010a) CBPR project involving online health resources for an example. As part of their community-based project, Ginossar and Nelson worked with members of the community and other health partners to create an online version of the *Salud Manual*, which is a bilingual print guide to health resources for un/underinsured participants. This manual was used by the *promotoras* to train people how to use the online health resources available to them. This example illustrates the potential for CBPR to inform virtual work practices. Not only did the project train participants in the use of virtual resources, it also helped cultivate a marketable skill in participants that could be leveraged to gain future employment.

Second, agency and self-efficacy are concepts related to the issues raised surrounding access and training. Agency and self-efficacy refer to both the capacity for community members to enact the resources made available to them, as well as their perception of that ability to act. In organizational communication, research tends to favor the concept of agency, which addresses how everyday activities are enabled and constrained in relationship to material, communicative, and virtual structures (Giddens, 1984). Concurrently, health communication research focuses more on self-efficacy, which suggests that these structural barriers do not always influence actions directly; rather, they often contribute to perceived barriers that limit the ability to act (Bandura, 1986, 1997; Rains, 2008). In both cases, these concepts draw our attention to additional barriers—beyond access and training—that community members might face when working virtually.

Enabling agency and self-efficacy as a route to human flourishing and transformation is a goal set forth by CBPR projects. At the same time, CBPR projects aimed at studying virtual work have much more to contend with when it comes to the barriers to agency and self-efficacy. For example, extreme poverty and concerns over safety and security have given rise to attitudes and perceptions that often limit community and economic development in low-income neighborhoods (Guttman & Ressler, 2001; see also Ginossar & Nelson, 2010a). Even when community-based projects attempt to promote agency and self-efficacy, the discursive resources used to enable action can obscure classed, gendered, and raced practices

of power and often reproduce the same broken structures (Kuhn, et al., 2008). Working virtually has been identified as a mechanism that has the potential to expand our understandings of work and incorporate more voices in the organization of everyday experience (Broadfoot, et al., 2008; Hylmö, 2006). It also presents an opportunity for CBPR researchers and participants to examine how virtual work has followed through on its promises, especially for individuals and groups with limited resources and perceptions of agency and self-efficacy.

Third and finally, publicity and participation focus on virtual work and its potential to enable and constrain a virtual public sphere (Papacharissi, 2002). As part of his public sphere theory, Habermas (1989) argued that the public sphere was a space for individuals and groups to bring their interests to bear on the state. Subsequent adaptations of his theory have focused on the theory's relevance to work practices (Mumby, 2000), participatory research (Kemmis & McTaggart, 2000), and virtual participation (Dahlberg, 2001; Papacharissi, 2002). The advent of ICTs has helped community-based organizations move some of their work to online forums. As such, virtual resources have systematically changed how individuals and groups do work to secure community-based goals and established a virtual public space for working with multiple stakeholders (Dahlberg, 2001; Soukup, 2006; Wells, 2010). Different web-based programs, like Google Groups, can be designed to make work and other online collaborations publicly viewable through an organization's website. Features like this enable a certain degree of transparency in work practices, and they also allow community-based organizations to increase their social capital and the reach of their networks (Lee & Lee, 2010). In doing so, these virtual resources have also changed what it means for communities to "do work" in a public venue.

These newfound possibilities for publicity and collaboration come with their fair share of tensions, especially when one considers the paradoxes that often accompany participatory practices (Stohl & Cheney, 2001). Although the concept of participation holds the possibility for empowerment and change, CBPR projects and virtual work research are particularly vulnerable to practices that ask participants to act in ways that undermine the goals of the project (Davis, 2010; McDermott, Oetzel, & White, 2008). For example, virtual resources are designed to enable inclusivity in working practices regardless of time and place constraints; at the same time, virtual work practices can be inherently exclusionary based on technological skill level or interest level in the subject matter (Davis, 2010). Even the notion of obtaining informed consent is a paradoxical process, because CBPR practices are set up to empower community members as partners in the research process, as long as they abide by university protocols (McDermott, Oetzel, & White, 2008). To contend with these tensions, Stohl and Cheney offered strategies for managing paradox such as acceptance and reframing, and McDermott and her co-authors opted for a three-step communication process involving recognition, reflection, and reframing. As such, opportunities exist for both living within and working through those paradoxes.

Concepts like the paradoxes of participation, and the others outlined in this section, are presented not to dissuade researchers from taking CBPR approaches to virtual work. Instead the reader should view them as sensitizing concepts for any researcher or community member to consider when embarking on a participatory project, especially when part of their work will be carried out through virtual practices.

Case Studies

Perhaps the best way to demonstrate the connections between community-based, participatory methods and virtual work is to illustrate some of these concepts and arguments through more detailed case studies. We focus on two organiza-

tions based in the Piedmont Triad region of North Carolina that are committed to promoting local food. Urban Harvest is a non-profit organization that helps communities grow their own food. LocallyGrownNews.com is an online news resource that provides a virtual space for conversations about food security, seasonal eating, and sustainability issues in the region. Both organizations rely on Web 2.0 technologies, including social networking sites or Google Groups, which focus on users and participants as active constructors of information as opposed to simply recipients.

At the same, they do so in different ways. Urban Harvest considers itself a community-based organization that operates primarily in a face-to-face capacity, but often uses virtual resources to carry out their work. This case study offers a simple example of how an ICT enabled them to move one of their ideas forward. LocallyGrownNews.com considers itself a hyperlocal online community that provides virtual resources to stakeholders who work in their local food communities. This story outlines the different online resources that they provide to help local food groups organize their efforts. Taken together, these case studies illustrate both of the connections between virtual and community-based work outlined in the previous section. We invite the reader to consider how these exemplars demonstrate those connections.

Urban Harvest

As mentioned previously, Urban Harvest kicked off 2011 with a community visioning session. Participants wanted to keep the conversations going after the meeting had ended, and they requested that Urban Harvest create a listserv. Urban Harvest organizers chose Google Groups as a platform to enable such collaboration— primarily because it was a user-friendly, no-cost mechanism that participants felt comfortable using. It also gave Urban Harvest the opportunity to make the Groups a public dialogue, as all conversations are posted on their website. Using eleven categories that participants created during the visioning session, Urban Harvest organized three groups based on the "Urban Food Networks," "Hearth," and "Vines" categories. Even though we attempted to enable conversation on three of the topics with most interest, the Urban Food Networks Google Group (UFNGG) became the most widely-used channel for communication and virtual work. At the time of publication, 31 members had joined this Google Group, and 12 of those members were active.

One of the ideas that emerged in the visioning session and gained momentum through the UFNGG involved designing and implementing a seed bomb project in Greensboro. Seed bombs are mixtures of dry red clay, compost, water, and seeds. They are designed to be tossed in any open field or empty urban space in the hopes that something beautiful, and possibly nutritious will grow in its place.

In June of 2010, Urban Harvest wrote a blog post about a sidewalk seed bomb project using vintage candy machines in Southern California (http://bit.ly/l0UIwT). During the visioning session, one community member mentioned this seed bomb project again. He also added that he was familiar with retrofitting used gumball machines, and he managed a local coffee bar that could serve as a perfect site for hosting a seed-bomb machine. While neither the seed bomb nor the gumball machine idea was new, this was an ideal time and place for the project to manifest in the community.

The Google Groups were all created within a week of the initial visioning session, and within 2 weeks of the meeting, one member posted the following statement to the UFNGG:

I'm sending this out to see if anyone is interested in helping to make seed balls that will be dispensed in some gumball machines around town. Let me know what kind of interest you have and what day(s) and time(s) works best for making them. Questions, comments, suggestions...feel free to share.

Seven people initially responded to the post with days and times to meet, and one person added more details about his vision for how the project could unfold. The email correspondence was short, quick, and to-the-point—serving more of a scheduling function to set up a face-to-face meeting than anything else.

However, as the group progressed, the virtual work carried out through the Google Group involved gathering and sharing information about seed bomb recipes, making decisions about which recipes to use, coordinating resources and supplies, and soliciting support from other community members who could donate supplies like red clay and compost materials. For example, one member used the site to coordinate materials and let the group know that she had tracked down a resource that had been eluding them:

I am now in possession of a 50-pound bag of dry red clay thanks to [the Art Department]. She also gave me a hunk of mixed-up-stuff, too. I'll bring it tomorrow to the test kitchen.

Another member used the site to brainstorm ways for the Urban Harvest vines to extend their reach deeper into the community:

We could make the seed bomb machines into an actual art project that coincides with one of the First Friday [downtown arts] events...We could most likely work with the Greensboro Arts Counsel or simply approach the various galleries in town. We would enlist artists from the galleries to create their own designs for the machines that could be showcased...hopefully throughout the city.

Although these examples might seem like simple applications of a virtual work approach, the online collaboration achieved through the Google Groups improved the overall functioning of the Urban Harvest initiative. We were able to attend to details that did not require being physically co-present, so we could move more quickly and productively when meeting face-to-face was needed.

A small group of six people met face-to-face initially; however, conversations and meeting notes were still posted to the entire Google Group. This led to an interesting development in the organization of work for the UFNGG. Much of the manual labor (e.g., testing recipes, producing seed bombs) was carried out face-to-face, but much of the organizational and communicative labor (e.g., coordinating resources, brainstorming ideas) was carried out in virtual space. This allowed a much larger group to participate in the process, because members could contribute ideas and make arrangements to deliver materials through an online medium. At least three members, including the second author herself, participated either entirely or almost exclusively online—making the UFNGG an invaluable resource for Urban Harvest to move this community project forward.

The online work carried out through the UF-NGG culminated in two noteworthy deliverables. In March 2011, Urban Harvest participated in a special event hosted at the aforementioned coffee bar. This community-wide market featured local vendors, public speakers, and group activities. Urban Harvest was invited to speak about their work, unveil the first two seed bomb machines, and lead an interactive session about making your own seed bombs. Additionally, Urban Harvest also started a Seed Bomb Greensboro blog (http://seedbombgreensboro.blogspot.com/). This site offers resources like a do-it-yourself guide to making your own seed bombs, as well as an interactive map that helps participants find the ideal location to launch their seeds. The hope is that this site will lead to more interactive maps and web applications that highlight where local food is being grown in the Piedmont Triad.

Based on the virtual work that helped make the seed bomb activity possible, several key observations about access, agency and self-efficacy, and virtual public spaces are possible.

First, the Google Group platform gave members access to resources that enable participation, especially when members could not be physically co-present. At the same time, all of the members who participated were computer literate and had easy access to internet connections. While some members worked with and spoke on behalf of low-income and immigrant communities, and others were students with limited resources, Urban Harvest organizers used this virtual work process to identify the voices that were missing from their conversation. By looking at this case through the lens of CBPR concepts, like access, the members of the UFNGG can draw out the important voices that need to be included as their efforts move forward.

In addition to access, both self-efficacy and agency are also evident in this case. More specifically, the UFNGG provided the structure for individuals to contribute to the seed bomb activity; however, the group still relied on the agency of individuals to enact those structures. Individuals who made active statements through the Google Group often translated those statements into actual events and activities for Urban Harvest; however, those members who made passive statements like, "let me know how I can help," illustrated an uncommitted response. Two members answered this way in response to the very first post about when to meet and start coordinating the project. Ultimately, they were not part of the final project, largely because their passive statements suggested to the rest of the UFNGG that they were not as committed to constructing this project together. In this case, the Google Group operated as a virtual space for the community members to tell Urban Harvest how they planned to get involved and co-construct the seed bomb project. The virtual format did not serve as a forum for Urban Harvest to tell its volunteers what to do. As such, we can see the beginnings of a virtual public sphere that Urban Harvest was starting to carve out. They created access to resources to participate in the seed bomb activity, but they also relied on the agency of their individual members to translate their virtual work into the community-based efforts of the group as a whole.

LocallyGrownNews.com

Community members need resources that raise awareness of the values and pitfalls of sourcing food locally, educate viewers on the issues from farm to fork, and to encourage offline purchasing decisions and actions around local food policy. LocallyGrownNews.com is a hyperlocal, niche online community that provides these sorts of resources for those who are passionate about local food.

Hyperlocal online communities are emerging through the gaps left by the broadcast reach and content breadth and depth of traditional media outlets. While newspapers and broadcast outlets might typically cover a larger, multi-county area, hyperlocal online communities are characterized by a smaller geographic footprint that may represent a few city blocks or a town. Kurpius, Metzgar, and Rowley (2010) suggested:

Hyperlocal media operations are geographically-based, community-oriented, original-news-reporting organizations indigenous to the web and intended to fill perceived gaps in coverage of an issue or region and to promote civic engagement (p. 360).

These small geographic sites—also called hyperlocal sites, Local Online News Communities (LONCs) or placeblogs, are serving ever-smaller audiences with targeted, geographic news and information. Typically these placebloggers will replicate the content of traditional community media, providing news and information on crime, government, education, and other traditional media coverage.

Hyperlocal sites, then, are a subset of social networks focused both on limiting geography

and building social networks both online and off. Kurpius, Metzgar, and Rowley (2010) in their definition of hyperlocal online communities use "civic engagement" to describe the offline activity sought by these site developers. Offline activity in this context may include voting, volunteerism, meet-ups, flash mobs, collaborative projects, petitions or other activity that takes place in the physical world.

In addition to news and information, LocallyGrownNews.com also features an online community where registered members can create a profile and post stories, photos, events and other comments and content to the site. This user-generated content is displayed side by side with staff content; neither is privileged on the web interface.

The website also integrates the online community as well as other online technologies such as Twitter, Facebook, YouTube.com, and Constant Contact email newsletter technologies. Recently, a beta product called Paper.li that aggregates Twitter and Facebook content into a newspaper-like interface, has been added to the technology mix.

In recent years, the focus on local food has been characterized as a "good food movement" or "slow food movement" that encourages residents to purchase food from producers who have grown that food in the resident's local community or county. These movements also challenge conventional agricultural practices through education, action and the creation of alternative local food resources, farmers' markets, community-supported agriculture and local food policy councils. Online networks operate as vehicles for institutional transformation and also they are particularly useful concerning the emergence of alternative institutions (Lin, 2001).

LocallyGrownNews.com uses several functions to generate a sense of community on the website:

• **Profiles:** Users register and upload a picture to the site. New members are prominently displaced with their year of registration. By clicking on a user's image, viewers get a history of the content the user has posted to the site.

- **Events:** A robust calendar sources local events for users, defining relevant community organizations and information to users.
- **Comments/Ratings/Sharing:** Users may post comments to any story, photo and event posted to the site. They can rate the story using a star rating system and can share content using social networking tools such as Twitter, de.li.cious social bookmarking, or Facebook.
- **Forums/Polls:** This discussion board tool allows users to share information on topics of importance to them. Polls engage users by sourcing answers to timely issues.

The website, along with its technological functions, helps to facilitate online activity and serves as an example of how virtual working spaces can be used to pursue community-based goals. The site acts as a resource for conversations around the topic of local food. LocallyGrownNews.com creates the space for users to virtually "meet" other users and connect with a community of like-minded local residents. The site also raises awareness of regional and national food policy issues and educates viewers on how to effect change in their lives and in their community. Online conversations have sparked face-to-face collaborations and vice versa.

In addition, other ICTs such as Twitter and Facebook focus on extending the geographic footprint by providing local food news and information to a broader audience. Using liveblogging, a transcription-like manner of summarizing events and conferences in real time, LocallyGrownNews. com grows its online audience to source fresh content and ideas for its site members. Such an online community is not built through technology alone, however. Such sites require strong, passionate stewards who are out in the com-

munity they serve, meeting users and cultivating new contributors. As an ambassador for the site, the steward facilitates online conversations and brokers partnerships and information offline. Stewards take on an education and advocacy role, encouraging dialogue, participation, action and transformation – engaging in both face-to-face and virtual work.

To provide a more concrete example of how LocallyGrownNews.com connects virtual work to community practice, we turn our attention to local farmers' markets. In early 2011, a local Piedmont farmers' market, at the time managed by the City of Greensboro, was accepting applications for a new market manager or management team. More than 30 individuals and groups were interested in taking over management of the market, resulting in four formal proposals to the City Council and Parks and Recreation Department. The topic of the market's management became a hot-button issue for the city, and LocallyGrownNews.com provided online resources for different community groups to move their interests forward. With more than 850 views, the most-read story on the LocallyGrownNews site summarized the proposal's key points and posted the full text of the proposals. The site also provided an online forum to discuss the proposals and generated an online poll to collect public opinion.

LocallyGrownNews.com became a virtual work resource through which potential market managers could make their case, stakeholders could organize and promote offline meetings, and the community could collaborate to have their needs met. In doing so, they demonstrated how virtual work might be used to enact community-based initiatives. LocallyGrownNews.com promotes access to resources that farmers can use to connect with consumers, and that citizens can use to connect with policymakers on local issues that are important to hyperlocal communities – like which organization should manage a farmers' market. Moreover, the site contributes to a virtual public sphere that organizes local food issues for the Piedmont Triad. By sharing copies of farmer's market proposals through the LocallyGrownNews site, as well as re-posting links to the proposals through Facebook, concerned citizens had more sophisticated resources that they used to influence local city councils and advisory boards. As such, community-based groups can move their initiatives forward by relying on this forum for virtual work.

IMPLICATIONS AND FUTURE DIRECTIONS

The case studies from the previous section highlight some of the opportunities, as well as some of the tensions that organize community-based virtual work. For example, both Urban Harvest and LocallyGrownNews.com incorporated a diversity of stakeholders into their virtual work to promote local food; at the same time, the majority of participants in both community projects had easy access to resources. Only recently have these community-based projects begun more concerted efforts to engage those individuals and groups who have more difficulty accessing and enacting virtual resources. In the closing pages of our chapter, we would like to suggest some of the implications of taking a CBPR approach to study virtual work, as well as points to consider in future research.

Implications for Community-Based Virtual Work

Initially, CBPR and virtual work make an unlikely, yet intriguing pairing; however, virtual work practices will most likely not replace the face-to-face work needed to carry out community-based research and practice completely. Instead, the two will complement each other as community members and researchers draw from a wide range of practices to design projects that meet their needs. As demonstrated in both the Urban Harvest and

LocallyGrownNews.com examples, stakeholders drew from both virtual and face-to-face resources in order plan the seed bomb activity and participate in the farmers' market conversation. Urban Harvest started their project with a face-to-face visioning session, then moved a significant portion of their work online, and finished with another face-to-face community event. LocallyGrownNews.com started as a virtual space, and then helped promote face-to-face meetings and other offline activities. Moreover, some work carried out by these two organizations simply cannot be accomplished online. The goal of Urban Harvest, for instance, is to help communities grow their own food – and not in a virtual "Farmville" sense, but a very real and material sense.

While the possibility exists for CBPR work to be carried out in a completely virtual space, there are physical limitations that will keep certain community projects from moving their work completely online. Furthermore, there seems to be some social support and community-building activity that goes on when community members can meet in physical space (Broadfoot, Munshi, & Nelson-Marsh, 2010). This does not mean that a CBPR project could not be implemented fully online, it simply means that researchers and participants will need to carefully consider which activities are most suitable for which space.

Additionally, our argument in support of community-based virtual work also reminds CBPR researchers to keep the focus on building community. In most cases, stakeholders participate not because they are passionate about the technology, but because they are passionate about the subject matter. As Broadfoot, Munshi, and Nelson-Marsh (2010) learned, some participants were willing travel great distances in order to find a reliable internet connection, because they were committed to the topic of the conference and the potential to collaborate with a diverse set of their peers. For both Urban Harvest and LocallyGrownNews. com, members contributed to the virtual discussions because they were passionate about local food, not because they were particularly fond of Google Groups.

For scholars and communities interested in virtual work, keeping the focus on community is an important reminder. As technology continues to develop at an increasingly rapid pace, both researchers and participants might find it tempting to let the technology lead the research. That temptation is to be avoided, however, because the CBPR methodology requires the research team to return to community needs. Several articles reviewed for this essay referenced Robert Putnam's (2000) book *Bowling Alone* as a justification for encouraging online participation and community development (e.g., Davis, 2010), claiming that virtual spaces provide individuals and groups with resources to reverse the loss of community that Putnam laments. Certainly, the unlikely pairing of CBPR and virtual work can aid in that process, but only in the service of human flourishing and meaningful change.

Future Directions

In many ways, our contribution draws attention to the in-between spaces of virtual work in the field of Communication. As we consider the future directions suggested by our pairing of CBPR and virtual work, we would like to examine those in-between spaces a bit in greater detail. More specifically, this essay moves back and forth between contributions from organizational and health communication scholars in order to make the case for community-based virtual work. We have highlighted conceptual and methodological overlaps regarding CBPR, agency and self-efficacy, and the use of virtual resources to meet community needs. Although organizational communication scholars are more interested in what we would traditionally label as work, and health communication scholars are more inclined to talk about their activities as interventions, they can both inform each other on practices like decision-making, training, and teamwork. The same can be said for our argument

that both qualitative and quantitative methods can inform the development of CBPR practices in the study of virtual work. We would encourage future research to remain committed to this movement along the liminal spaces of organizational and health communication, qualitative and quantitative research, and virtual and face-to-face work.

If, as we suggest, our contribution encourages readers to focus on the in-between spaces of virtual work, then this chapter also calls for more research that addresses the meso-level of social organization. Meso-level research in communication is particularly committed to how discourses and resources are connected across contexts (Alvesson & Karemman, 2000; LeGreco & Tracy, 2009), as well as how local activities scale up and larger structures bear down on the ways in which we organize our practices (Conrad, 2004; Keyton, Bisel, & Ozley, 2009). Virtual work can facilitate this process of coordinating actions and resources across contexts, especially because of its ability to network stakeholders without the same constraints of time and space, as well as its ability to reach a diverse set of individuals and groups. These resources are particularly valuable to community-based projects that often need the support of multiple stakeholders in order to move their initiatives forward. As research in this area continues to develop, we would encourage scholars and participants remain attentive to this meso-level.

CONCLUSION

Increasingly, stakeholders have come to rely on virtual, online, and computer-mediated communication to mobilize new organizational practices like community health initiatives and local policy changes. We believe that teasing out these connections between community-based participatory research and virtual work could be useful for a variety of stakeholders including researchers, community leaders, healthcare providers, policymakers, public health advocates, non-profit organizers, and historically underrepresented individuals and groups. A great deal of power and potential lies in the relationship between CBPR and virtual work. The relationship is not always obvious, nor always comfortable. With the methodological commitments and sensitizing concepts outlined in this chapter, however, we hope to have offered a useful and provocative resource for scholars and citizens who seek to bring about significant changes within their communities.

REFERENCES

Alvesson, M., & Karreman, D. (2000). Varieties of discourse: On the study of organizations through discourse analysis. *Human Relations*, *53*, 1125–1149. doi:10.1177/0018726700539002

Argyris, C., Putnam, R., & Smith, D. M. (1985). *Action science: Concepts, methods, and skills for research and intervention*. Hoboken, NJ: Jossey-Bass.

Argyris, C., & Schon, D. A. (1991). Participatory action research and action science compared. In Whyte, W. F. (Ed.), *Participatory Action Research* (pp. 85–98). London, UK: Sage. doi:10.1177/0002764289032005008

Ashcraft, K. L. (2000). Empowering 'professional' relationships: Organizational communication meets feminist practice. *Management Communication Quarterly*, *13*, 347–393. doi:10.1177/0893318900133001

Bandura, A. (1997). *Self-efficacy: The exercise of control*. New York, NY: Freeman.

Bandura, A. (2006). On integrating social cognitive and social diffusion theories. In Singhal, A., & Dearing, J. (Eds.), *Communication of Innovations: A Journey with Ev Rogers* (pp. 111–135). Beverly Hills, CA: Sage.

Basu, A., & Dutta, M. (2008). The relationship between health information seeking and community participation: The roles of health information orientation and efficacy. *Health Communication*, *23*, 70–79. doi:10.1080/10410230701807121

Broadfoot, K. J., Carlone, D., Medved, C. E., Aakhus, M., Gabor, E., & Taylor, K. (2008). Meaningful work and organizational communication: Questioning boundaries, positionalities, and engagements. *Management Communication Quarterly*, *22*, 152–161. doi:10.1177/0893318908318267

Broadfoot, K. J., Munshi, D., & Nelson-Marsh, N. (2010). COMMUNEcation: A rhizomatic tale of participatory technology, postcoloniality and professional community. *New Media & Society*, *12*, 797–812. doi:10.1177/1461444809348880

Buchanan, D. G., Miller, F. G., & Wallerstein, N. (2007). Ethical issues in community-based participatory research: Balancing rigorous research with community participation in community intervention studies. *Progress in Community Health Partnerships: Research, Education, and Action*, *1*, 153–160. doi:10.1353/cpr.2007.0006

Cheney, G., Zorn, T. E., Planalp, S., & Lair, D. J. (2008). Meaningful work and personal/social well-being: Organizational communication engages the meanings of work. *Communication Yearbook*, *32*, 137–185.

Cogburn, D. L., Finnerup Johnsen, J., & Bhattacharyya, S. (2008). Distributed deliberative citizens: Exploring the impact of cyberinfrastructure on transnational civil society participation in global ICT policy processes. *International Journal of Media and Cultural Politics*, *4*, 27–49. doi:10.1386/macp.4.1.27_1

Conrad, C. (2004). Organizational discourse analysis: Avoiding the determinism–volunteerism trap. *Organization*, *11*, 427–439. doi:10.1177/1350508404042001

Craig, R. T., & Tracy, K. (1995). Grounded practical theory: The case of intellectual discussion. *Communication Theory, 5,* 248–272. doi:10.1111/j.1468-2885.1995.tb00108.x

Dahlberg, L. (2001). The Internet and democratic discourse: Exploring the prospects of online deliberative forums extending the public sphere. *Information Communication and Society, 4,* 615–633. doi:10.1080/13691180110097030

Davis, A. (2010). New media and fat democracy: The paradox of online participation. *New Media & Society, 12,* 745–761. doi:10.1177/1461444809341435

Deetz, S. (1992). *Democracy in an age of corporate colonization.* Albany, NY: SUNY.

Deetz, S. (2009). Politically attentive relational constructionism (PARC) and making a difference in a pluralistic, independent world. In Carbaugh, D., & Buzzanell, P. (Eds.), *Distinctive Qualities in Communication Research.* Oxford, UK: Taylor and Francis.

Dirksen, V., Huizing, A., & Smit, B. (2010). Piling on layers of understanding: The use of connective ethnography for the study of (online) work practices. *New Media & Society, 12,* 1045–1063. doi:10.1177/1461444809341437

Fernback, J. (2005). Information technology, networks and community voices: Social inclusion for urban regeneration. *Information Communication and Society, 8,* 482–502. doi:10.1080/13691180500418402

Fine, M., Weis, L., Weseen, S., & Wong, L. (2000). For whom? Qualitative research, representations, and social responsibilities. In Denzin, N. K., & Lincoln, Y. S. (Eds.), *Handbook of Qualitative Research* (pp. 107–132). Thousand Oaks, CA: Sage.

Fonner, K. L., & Roloff, M. E. (2010). Why teleworkers are more satisfied with their jobs than are office-based workers. *Journal of Applied Communication Research, 38,* 336–361. doi:10.1080/00909882.2010.513998

Fox, S., & Vitak, J. (2008). *Degrees of access.* Retrieved April 25, 2011 from http://www.pewinternet.org/Presentations/2008/Degrees-of-Access-(May-2008-data).aspx.

Freeman, E. R., Brugge, D., Bennett-Bradley, W. M., Levy, J. I., & Carrasco, E. R. (2006). Challenges of conducting community-based participatory research in Boston's neighborhoods to reduce disparities in asthma. *Journal of Urban Health: Bulletin of the New York Academy of Medicine, 83,* 1013–1021. doi:10.1007/s11524-006-9111-0

Freire, P. (1970). *Pedagogy of the oppressed.* New York, NY: Seabury.

Gatenby, B., & Humphries, M. (2000). Feminist participatory action research: Methodological and ethical issues. *Women's Studies International Forum, 23,* 89–105. doi:10.1016/S0277-5395(99)00095-3

Giddens, A. (1984). *The constitution of society: Outline of the theory of structuration.* Berkeley, CA: University of California Press.

Ginossar, T., & Nelson, S. (2010a). La comunidad habla: Using internet community-based information interventions to increase empowerment and access to health care of low income Latino/a immigrants. *Communication Education, 59,* 328–343. doi:10.1080/03634521003628297

Ginossar, T., & Nelson, S. (2010b). Reducing the health and digital divides: A model for using community-based participatory research approach to e-health interventions in low-income Hispanic communities. *Journal of Computer-Mediated Communication, 15,* 530–551. doi:10.1111/j.1083-6101.2009.01513.x

Habermas, J. (1989). *The structural transformation of the public sphere: An inquiry into a category of bourgeois society.* Cambridge, MA: MIT.

Heinz, M., & Rice, R. E. (2009). An integrated model of knowledge sharing in contemporary communication environments. *Communication Yearbook, 33,* 134–175.

Heron, J. (1971). *Experience and method.* Guildford, UK: University of Surrey.

Heron, J., & Reason, P. (1997). A participatory inquiry paradigm. *Qualitative Inquiry, 3,* 274–294. doi:10.1177/107780049700300302

Heron, J., & Reason, P. (2006). The practice of co-operative inquiry: Research "with" rather than "on" people. In Reason, P., & Bradbury-Huang, H. (Eds.), *Handbook of Action Research.* Thousand Oaks, CA: Sage.

Humphreys, S. (2008). Grassroots creativity and community in new media environments: Yarn harlot and the 4000 knitting olympians. *Continuum: Journal of Media & Cultural Studies, 22,* 419–433. doi:10.1080/10304310801989844

Hylmö, A. (2006). Telecommuting and the contestability of choice: Employee strategies to legitimize personal decision to work in a preferred location. *Management Communication Quarterly, 19,* 541–569. doi:10.1177/0893318905284762

Kemmis, S., & McTaggart, R. (2000). Participatory action research. In Denzin, N. K., & Lincoln, Y. S. (Eds.), *Handbook of Qualitative Research* (2nd ed., pp. 567–605). Thousand Oaks, CA: Sage Publications, Inc.

Keyton, J., Bisel, R. S., & Ozley, R. (2009). Recasting the link between applied and theory research: Using applied findings to advance communication theory development. *Communication Theory, 19,* 146–160. doi:10.1111/j.1468-2885.2009.01339.x

Kisselburgh, L. G., Berkelaar, B. L., & Buzzanell, P. M. (2009). Discourse, gender, and the meaning of work. *Communication Yearbook, 33,* 258–299.

Kreps, G. L., & Neuhauser, L. (2010). Editors' introduction, ehealth and health promotion. *Journal of Computer-Mediated Communication, 15,* 527–529. doi:10.1111/j.1083-6101.2010.01526.x

Kuhn, T., Golden, A. G., Jorgenson, J., Buzzanell, P. M., Berkelaar, B. L., & Kisselburg, L. G. (2008). Cultural discourses and discursive resources for meaningful work: Constructing and disrupting identities in contemporary capitalism. *Management Communication Quarterly, 22,* 162–171. doi:10.1177/0893318908318262

Kurpius, D. D., Metzgar, E. T., & Rowley, K. M. (2010). Sustaining hyperlocal media: In search of funding models. *Journalism Studies, 11,* 359–376. doi:10.1080/14616700903429787

Lee, J., & Lee, H. (2010). The computer-mediated communication network: Exploring the linkage between the online community and social capital. *New Media & Society, 12,* 711–727. doi:10.1177/1461444809343568

LeGreco, M., & Tracy, S. J. (2009). Discourse tracing as qualitative practice. *Qualitative Inquiry, 15,* 1516–1543. doi:10.1177/1077800409343064

Lin, N. (2001). *Social capital: A theory of structure and action.* London, UK: Cambridge University.

Long, S. D. (2010). *Communication, relationships and practices in virtual work.* Hershey, PA: IGI Global. doi:10.4018/978-1-61520-979-8

McDermott, V. M., Oetzel, J. G., & White, K. (2008). Ethical paradoxes in community-based participatory research. In Zoller, H. M., & Dutta, M. J. (Eds.), *Emerging Perspectives in Health Communication.* New York, NY: Routledge.

Mumby, D. K. (2000). Communication, organization, and the public sphere: A feminist perspective. In Buzzanell, P. M. (Ed.), *Rethinking Organizational & Managerial Communication from Feminist Perspectives* (pp. 3–23). Thousand Oaks, CA: Sage Publications, Inc.

Neuhauser, L., & Kreps, G. L. (2010). Ehealth communication and behavior change: Promise and performance. *Social Semiotics, 20,* 7–24. doi:10.1080/10350330903438386

Papacharissi, Z. (2002). The virtual sphere: The Internet as a public sphere. *New Media & Society, 4,* 9–27. doi:10.1177/14614440222226244

Peters, M. A. (2011). The Egyptian revolution. *Policy Futures in Education, 9,* 292–295. doi:10.2304/pfie.2011.9.2.292

Putnam, R. (2000). *Bowling alone: The collapse and revival of American community.* New York, NY: Simon & Schuster.

Rainie, L., Purcell, K., & Smith, A. (2011). *The social side of the internet.* Retrieved April 25, 2011 from http://www.pewinternet.org/Reports/2011/The-Social-Side-of-the-Internet.aspx.

Rains, S. A. (2008). Seeking health information in the information age: The role of internet self-efficacy. *Western Journal of Communication, 17,* 1–18. doi:10.1080/10570310701827612

Reason, P. (1994). Three approaches to participative inquiry. In Denzin, N. K., & Lincoln, Y. S. (Eds.), *Handbook of Qualitative Inquiry.* Thousand Oaks, CA: Sage Publications, Inc.

Soukup, C. (2006). Computer-mediated communication as a virtual third place: Building Oldenberg's great good places on the world wide web. *New Media & Society, 8,* 421–444. doi:10.1177/1461444806061953

Stohl, C., & Cheney, G. (2001). Participatory processes/paradoxical practices: Communication and the dilemmas of organizational democracy. *Management Communication Quarterly, 14,* 349–407. doi:10.1177/0893318901143001

Tracy, S. J. (2002). Altered practice, altered stories, altered lives: Three considerations for translating organizational communication scholarship into practice. *Management Communication Quarterly, 16,* 85–91. doi:10.1177/0893318902161005

Trethewey, A. (2002). Translating scholarship into practice. *Management Communication Quarterly, 16,* 81–84. doi:10.1177/0893318902161004

U.S. Census Bureau. (2010). *Internet use in the United States: October 2009.* Retrieved April 26, 2011 from http://www.census.gov/population/www/socdemo/computer/2009.html.

U.S. Department of Labor. (2010). *American time use survey.* Retrieved April 25, 2011 from http://www.bls.gov/news.release/pdf/atus.pdf.

Wells, C. (2010). Citizenship and communication in online youth civic engagement projects. *Information Communication and Society, 13,* 419–441. doi:10.1080/13691180902833208

Whitman, M., & Woszczynski, A. (2003). *The handbook of information systems research.* Hershey, PA: IGI Global. doi:10.4018/978-1-59140-144-5

Whyte, W. F. (1991). *Participatory action research.* London, UK: Sage.

ADDITIONAL READING

Ainsworth, S., Hardy, C., & Harley, B. (2005). Online consultation: E-democracy and e-resistance in the case of the development gateway. *Management Communication Quarterly, 19,* 120–145. doi:10.1177/0893318905276562

Ardichvili, A., Page, V., & Wentling, T. (2003). Motivation and barriers to participation in virtual knowledge-sharing communities of practice. *Journal of Knowledge Management, 7,* 64–77. doi:10.1108/13673270310463626

Boradkar, P. (2010). Transdisciplinary design and innovation in the classroom. In Porter-O'Grady, T., & Malloch, K. (Eds.), *Innovation Leadership* (pp. 109–134). Sudbury, MA: Jones and Bartlett.

Brunarski, D., Shaw, L., & Doupe, L. (2008). Moving toward virtual interdisciplinary teams and a multi-stakeholder approach in community-based return-to-work care. *Work: A Journal of Prevention, Assessment and Rehabilitation, 30,* 329–336.

Davies, R. (2004). Adapting virtual reality for the participatory design of work environments. *Computer Supported Cooperative Work, 13,* 1–33. doi:10.1023/B:COSU.0000014985.12045.9c

Donelle, L., & Hoffman-Goetz, L. (2008). An exploratory study of Canadian aboriginal online health care forums. *Health Communication, 23,* 270–281. doi:10.1080/10410230802056388

Endsley, S. (2010). Innovation in action: A practical system for getting results. In Porter-O'Grady, T., & Malloch, K. (Eds.), *Innovation Leadership* (pp. 59–86). Sudbury, MA: Jones and Bartlett.

Flicker, S., Travers, R., Guta, A., McDonald, S., & Meagher, A. (2007). Ethical dilemmas in community-based participatory research: recommendations for institutional review boards. *Journal of Urban Health, 84,* 478–493. doi:10.1007/s11524-007-9165-7

Ginossar, T. (2008). Online participation: A content analysis of differences in utilization of two online cancer communities by men and women, patients and family members. *Health Communication, 23,* 1–12. doi:10.1080/10410230701697100

Humphreys, L. (2010). Mobile social networks and urban public space. *New Media & Society, 12,* 763–778. doi:10.1177/1461444809349578

Kavanaugh, A., Joon Kim, B., Perez-Quinones, A. P., Schmitz, J., & Isenhour, P. (2008). Net gains in political participation: Secondary effects of Internet on community. *Information Communication and Society, 11,* 933–963. doi:10.1080/13691180802108990

McDaniel, J., Kuhn, T., & Deetz, S. (2008). Voice, participation and the globalization of communications systems. In Ciprut, J. V. (Ed.), *Democratizations: Complex Perspectives, Compound Contexts* (pp. 281–300). Cambridge, MA: MIT Press.

Monge, P. R., Heise, B. R., & Margolin, D. (2008). Communication network evolution in organizational communities. *Communication Theory, 18,* 449–477. doi:10.1111/j.1468-2885.2008.00330.x

Plsek, P. (2010). Directed creativity: How to generate new ideas for transforming health care. In Porter-O'Grady, T., & Malloch, K. (Eds.), *Innovation Leadership* (pp. 87–108). Sudbury, MA: Jones and Bartlett.

Robey, D., & Jin, L. (2003). Studying virtual work in teams, organizations, and communities. In Whitman, M., & Wosczynski, A. (Eds.), *Handbook of Information Systems Research.* Hershey, PA: IGI Global. doi:10.4018/978-1-59140-144-5.ch010

Rohleder, P., Swartz, L., Bozalek, V., Carolissen, R., & Leibowitz, B. (2008). Community, self and identity: Participatory action research and the creation of a virtual community across two South African universities. *Teaching in Higher Education, 13,* 131–143. doi:10.1080/13562510801923187

Schuler, D., & Namioka, A. (1993). *Participatory design: Principles and practices.* Hillsdale, NJ: Lawrence Earlbaum.

Sessions, L. F. (2010). How offline gatherings affect online communities: When virtual community members 'meetup'. *Information Communication and Society*, *13*(3), 375–395. doi:10.1080/13691180903468954

Tremblay, D. G. (2005). Virtual communities of practice: Explaining different effects in two organizational contexts. *Canadian Journal of Communication*, *30*, 367–382.

Vaast, E. (2004). O brother, where art thou? From communities to networks of practice through intranet use. *Management Communication Quarterly*, *18*, 5–44. doi:10.1177/0893318904265125

Wang, C., & Burris, M. (1997). Photovoice: Concept, methodology, and use for participatory needs assessment. *Health Education & Behavior*, *24*, 369–387. doi:10.1177/109019819702400309

KEY TERMS AND DEFINITIONS

Access: The capacity to identify and obtain resources necessary to meet individual or group needs.

Agency: The ability to act in relationship to structural rules and resources.

Community-Based Participatory Research (CBPR): A methodology involving both qualitative and quantitative research methods and incorporates participant voices and skills throughout the research process in the service of transformation and human flourishing.

Information and Communication Technologies (ICTs): A general term for the devices, products, and systems that aid in the coordination of communication practices across time and space, including computer and network hardware, interactive software, and social networking sites.

Paradox: A situation in which the pursuit of a goal requires an individual or group to act in a way that undermines that goal.

Participation: The processes related to decision-making in organizational settings whereby individuals and groups contribute ideas and express opinions in order to exert influence.

Publicity: A concept from Habermas's public sphere theory that involves everyday citizens bringing their interests to bear on an organized system of power (e.g., government, corporation).

Self-Efficacy: A concept related to an individual's perception of his or her own competence.

Training: The process of educating organizational members in order to improve their skill-level and knowledge base.

Virtual Work: Paid or unpaid labor that involves the spatial or temporal displacement of work practices, made possible by information and communication technologies.

Web 2.0: Technologies including social networking sites, blogs, Google, and other web-based innovations that enable individuals and groups to be active participants in the construction of online content.

Chapter 6
Reply Timing and Emotional Strategy in Mobile Text Communications of Japanese Young People:
Replies to Messages Conveying Four Different Emotions

Yuuki Kato
Sagami Women's University, Japan

Shogo Kato
Tokyo Woman's Christian University, Japan

Kunihiro Chida
Toei Animation Institute, Japan

ABSTRACT

In this chapter, the authors present two studies that examine the timing of replies to mobile text messages, especially the behavior of intentionally waiting before replying. As the first step in Study 1, 42 Japanese university subjects were asked by questionnaire survey whether they would wait before replying to mobile text messages they received, and if so, in which situations they would they wait. A large percentage of respondents suggested that they would sometimes wait before replying to a mobile text message. The freeform responses also indicated the involvement of an emotional aspect in most cases where subjects did not immediately reply to a mobile text message, even when they were capable of doing so. For Study 2, 224 Japanese university students were asked to rate on a 6-point scale whether they would wait before replying to mobile text messages from senders conveying each of four emotions: happiness, sadness, anger, and guilt. They were also asked to give a freeform answer as to why they would respond in such a way. The results showed that for each of the four emotional settings, subjects adjust the timing of message replies in order to manipulate the emotions of others or their own emotions, according to the situation. Individual differences were also observed in subjects' thoughts about adjusting reply timing and manipulating emotions.

DOI: 10.4018/978-1-4666-0963-1.ch006

INTRODUCTION

Background

With the spread of e-mail, text-based messages have replaced communications that until now were made by letter or fax and they have now become a normal part of our daily life. It is especially common for Japanese young people to use the mobile email functionality of mobile telephones (hereafter referred to as mobile text messaging) as a form of conversation. Mobile text messaging is also frequently used in Japan when voice communications are difficult or socially unacceptable to make: it is this type of social prohibition that promotes its use. For instance, making and receiving voice calls on public transportation is limited (and in some areas, prohibited) and train, bus, and subway companies make frequent announcements reminding passengers to turn off their phones or change them to silent mode. Many passengers accept these restrictions and turn to mobile text messaging to stay in touch with others while riding the train or subway (Okabe & Ito, 2006).

However, with its limitations in expressing emotions and other non-verbal cues, text communication is said to be susceptible to misunderstandings or miscommunication, especially when attempting to convey emotions (e.g., Short, et al., 1976, Sproull & Kiesler, 1986, Dyer, et al., 1995, Hancock, 2007, Scott, et al., 2009). With the goal of gaining educational insight into how to avoid these kinds of problems in text communication, we focused on various aspects based on the daily experience of users to consider these problems. For example, previous studies on message content or writing style have shown that posing questions to the reader or using emoticons are effective for invoking happiness or positive emotion in the reader (Kato, et al., 2002, 2006a). Previous studies examining the perspective of parties in email conversation considered the impact of text written by persons with a different perspective on reader emotion (Kato, et al., 2006b). The results suggest that familiar expressions in an email from a classmate, or an honest and serious writing style for an email received from a person of seniority, such as an instructor, can invoke positive emotions in student readers. Furthermore, previous studies on the transmission of emotion that investigated which emotional states of a writer would be incorrectly interpreted by the reader (Kato, et al., 2007a, 2007b) found that, compared to positive emotions which were correctly conveyed, emotions such as sadness or anger were difficult to convey and were easily misunderstood. A previous study on emoticons in conveyance of emotion (Kato, et al., 2009) also suggests that mistakes in interpreting emotion were more likely for emoticons that convey negative emotions than emoticons that convey positive ones.

As an example, one of the authors recently heard about the following problem. A university professor working late at night to prepare for class sent an advance email to students' mobile phones with various details about the lecture. However, one of the students objected to the professor's conduct, citing loss of sleep and the need to reply to the professor's mobile text messaging sent late at night as the basis for the complaint. Related to this anecdote, this chapter summarizes the research conducted to date on reply timing for mobile text messaging.

Emotional Strategy

The authors focus on the use of emotional strategy in text communications, taking the Emotional Intelligence (EI) model (Salovey & Mayer, 1990; Mayer, 2000) as a theoretical background. The EI model emphasizes "internal emotional aspects" and addresses "how to deal with emotions that should be suppressed." The authors apply this model to the communication process (Kato, et al., 2008), and use the term "emotional strategy" to refer to the act of manipulating the interaction between "emotional aspects of self and those of another party." When we communicate, we sometimes do not directly convey the emotions we are feeling in order to manipulate the emotions of the other person. In other words, do we sometimes "only correctly convey those emotions that we consider ideal?"

Before we had conducted our previous studies (discussed below), for example, those regarding communication between A and B, the authors had debated the accuracy of emotional transmission with "A's actual emotional state" and "B's interpretation of A's emotional state," and as an extension, the goodness of that interaction. These studies focused on how well the emotion produced by mediated-communication users is conveyed to their partner. One barrier to this process is the possible disconnect between the sender's intended emotion and the actual message they compose (Kato, et al., 2010, 2011a). That is, the sender may be angry, but does not want to project that emotion too strongly or directly to the receiver. In studies related to the expression of emotions in facial expressions, these traits are particularly common among Japanese people. Japanese language and culture place an emphasis on toning down or suppressing one's true feelings to avoid complicating or damaging interpersonal relations (Matsumoto, 1996, Matsumoto & Kudoh, 1993). The authors have now come to believe that it is important to consider ways to intentionally convey emotions which are different from those actually felt in order to manipulate the emotions of others, and to consider whether such attempts result in the other person's emotions being manipulated as planned.

As one example of previous research performed by the authors on the existence of emotional strategies when conveying emotions during communication, a mobile text user relies on various strategies for manipulating his or her own emotions and the emotions of the other person. These are specific strategies, such as to what degree to use emotional expressions, whether to use emoticons, and which medium to use or whether to change the medium (such as responding to a mobile text message with a phone call instead of a text message) (Kato, et al., 2008, Sato, et al., 2008, Kato, et al., 2010, Kato, et al., 2011a). It should be noted that to the authors' knowledge, the only previous studies—both inside and outside of Japan—related to communication by texting that focus on emotional strategies are the authors' own. Therefore, most studies investigate Japanese people in Japan, and there is currently only one published study that compares emotional strategies of Americans and Japanese (Kato, et al., 2011b). This study showed that emotional strategies exist in both countries, and compared to the Japanese, who try more frequently to convey positive emotions such as happiness, Americans tend to convey feelings of anger (not just anger at the other person, but also anger about the situation or something in the discussion). In other words, emotional strategies are thought to be employed both in Japan and overseas, but because there are likely cultural differences in their tendencies, it is necessary to collect and carefully review additional research data.

Finally, in performing this research, the authors collected many strategy-related comments which suggested that people employ a tactic of "waiting before replying" to messages with emotional content (Kato, et al., 2011c). The study we describe here investigates just this aspect of delaying the response (or replying immediately).

Overview of this Chapter

In this chapter, two studies were performed on the timing of replies to mobile text messages, especially on the behavior of intentionally waiting before replying. In Study 1, Japanese university subjects were asked by survey questionnaire whether they would wait before replying to mobile phone emails they received, and if so, in which situations they would they wait. The results showed that most subjects had waited before replying to mobile text messages. The freeform responses also indicated the involvement of an emotional aspect in most cases where subjects did not immediately reply to a mobile text message, even when they were capable of doing so. For this reason, in Study 2, as a more specific situation, a survey questionnaire was administered concerning a situation in which a mobile text message arrives that conveys one of four emotions of the sender (happiness, sadness, anger, or guilt), and asks the subjects whether they would wait before replying in each of these cases and why they would wait. The results showed that for each of the four emotional settings, subjects adjust the timing of their message replies in order to manipulate the emotions of others or their own emotions, according to the situation. Individual differences were also observed in subjects' thoughts about adjusting reply timing and manipulating emotions. This chapter, after describing the above in detail, discusses these results and describes how the results could contribute to actual situations.

OBJECTIVE

In this chapter, two studies were performed on the timing of replies to mobile text messages, especially on the behavior of intentionally waiting before replying. As the first step, in Study 1, 42 Japanese university subjects were asked via survey questionnaire whether they would wait before replying to mobile text messages they received, and if so, in which situations they would they wait. In study 2, study participants were asked to use a questionnaire form to rate to what degree they would wait before replying to mobile text messages from senders conveying each of four emotions, namely happiness, sadness, anger, and guilt, and to explain why they used such an approach.

In analyzing the experimental data obtained, emphasis was placed on what emotional strategy would be employed for manipulating one's own emotions as well as for manipulating the emotions of the other party, with a particular focus on the timing of the reply.

METHOD OF STUDY 1

Subjects

The subjects were 42 second- and third-year university students (23 males, 19 females; mean age 20.17 years [SD 1.22]; range 19–26 years) majoring in arts/humanities who used mobile text messaging on a daily basis. The subjects attended a private university in the suburbs of Tokyo. All subjects were of Japanese nationality. According to Kato, who is one of the authors of this chapter and who leads the class that these students attend, students participating in this study (and actually most Japanese students) says, "nearly all students leave their mobile phones turned on during class, and frequently react to incoming mobile emails. Even during class, some students immediately read the incoming messages and start typing replies." He adds that, of course, students caught doing this are told to put their mobile phones away.

Survey Questionnaire

The questionnaire asked subjects to rate on a 6-point scale (1: never; 2: almost never; 3: infrequently; 4: sometimes; 5: frequently; 6: extremely frequently) how they would respond to the question, "Would you wait before responding to a mobile text message you receive from a friend, even if you are able to immediately respond?" They were also asked to give a freeform answer to the question, "In what situations would you wait before responding?"

RESULTS AND DISCUSSION: STUDY 1

Six-Point Scale Rating Results

The average score for the questionnaire's 6-point scale rating was 3.10. Figure 1 shows the number of responses for each of the six ratings. As shown in Figure 1, although there is variation in frequency, a large majority of respondents gave answers suggesting that they sometimes wait before responding to mobile text messages.

Freeform Response Results

In order to analyze the freeform responses, all responses were categorized according to their meaning and content. This categorization was performed by three researchers, who had sufficient experience in text communications research. In this study, the three researchers "worked together" to discuss each response and then together decided on the category. That is, the categorization method was not one in which each of the three researchers separately chose a category for each response, and then finally made the decision of category based on comparing the categorizations and how well they matched. Working together was beneficial for this study because categories were not predetermined, and it was necessary to generate new categories during the course of the work. Furthermore, because one of the three

researchers was able to contact the subjects of this study, this approach would make it possible to directly verify with a subject the meaning of his or her response if a decision could not be reached during the categorization process. It should be noted here that there were no major differences of opinion during this process, and no cases arose which required direct confirmation with any subject. The freeform response results are shown in Table 1. Additionally, Table 1 shows that depending on the meaning/content of each category, the reasons were largely divided into "my mood," "content of the message," "the other person's mood," "attributes of the other person," "formation of my self-image," and "my mood and the other person's mood."

Many responses indicated that senders would wait before sending the response for reasons due to one's own emotional state, such as "when I am sad" or "when I am angry," the emotional state of the other person, such as "when the other person is angry" or "when the other person is sad," or in consideration of the emotional condition between oneself and the other person, such as

Figure 1. Response distribution for frequency of waiting before replying

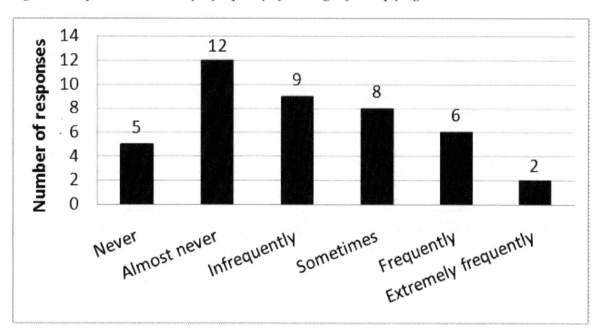

Table 1. Categories of reasons for delaying reply

Situation	
My situation	**Frequency**
When it is burdensome	13
When I am focused on something else	12
When I am feeling down	4
When I am thinking about what to write	3
When I can't think of what to write in my response	2
When I am tired	2
When I am angry	1
When I don't feel like it	1
When I am on the computer	1
Subtotal	39
Message content	**Frequency**
When the content is not urgent	6
When I receive a lengthy mail	2
When the mail is about disparaging someone else	1
When the mail is an apology from someone I was fighting with	1
When I have trouble understanding the message content	1
Subtotal	11
Other person's situation	**Frequency**
When the other person is angry	4
When the other person is sad	3
When the other person is feeling down	1
When the other person is troubled	1
Subtotal	9
Attributes of the other person	**Frequency**
When it is a message from a friend I don't like	2
When it is from someone who usually is late to reply	1
When the other person is the same sex as me	1
Subtotal	4
Formation of my own self-image	**Frequency**
When I don't want people to think I am slow to respond	2
When I don't want the other person to think I am interested in (like) them)	1
Subtotal	3
Both my own and the other person's situations	**Frequency**
When our moods are not in sync (such as receiving a sad message when I am happy)	1
When I receive a message from a person who is in love	1
During a romantic courtship	1
Subtotal	3

"when my feelings and the feelings of the other person are not in sync" or "during a romantic courtship." In other words, the results showed that even when it was possible to immediately respond, subjects were delaying their responses depending on their own emotional state or the emotional state of the other person. Also, subjects sometimes delayed their responses depending on the message content, attributes of the other person, or related to formation of self-image. However, even these circumstances are likely related to emotion, at least by a small degree, such as "when the content is about disparaging someone else," "when the mail is an apology from a person I was fighting with," "it was an email from a friend I don't like," or "when I don't want the other person to think I'm interested in (like) them."

The responses also showed the involvement of an emotional aspect in most cases where subjects did not immediately reply to a mobile text message even when they were capable of doing so. However, because of the small sample size in Study 1, it is not possible to make categorical conclusions from this study. Thus, after increasing the number of subjects, subsequently performed Study 2 investigated the reply timing for several specific instances of receiving a mobile text message which conveyed emotion. It also investigated the reason for choosing the selected timing for each emotional situation. In other words, the aim of Study 2 is to show what strategies are being devised for manipulating the reply timing in order to manipulate one's own feelings or the feelings of the other person.

METHOD OF STUDY 2

Subjects

The subjects were 224 first- and second-year university students (98 males, 126 females; mean age 19.07 years [SD 0.79], range 18–26 years) majoring in arts/humanities who used mobile text

messaging on a daily basis. The subjects attended a private university in the suburbs of Tokyo. All subjects were of Japanese nationality. As in Study 1, subjects were "typical" students who frequently received mobile text messages both inside and outside the classroom.

Four Emotions Selected for This Study

The many emotions we convey in everyday life can, according to some, be sorted into basic emotional categories. For example, Ekman (1992) proposed six basic emotions of happiness, sadness, anger, surprise, fear, and disgust. The authors decided to focus on the basic emotions of happiness, sadness, and anger for this study as they correspond to positive, negative, and hostile emotion, respectively. The authors' previous research has been based on this categorization and the same categorization was adopted for this study as well (Kato, et al., 2008). Special attention was also given to the emotion of guilt as it is closely related to apologizing and could help avoid emotional misunderstandings.

In this study, emotional scenarios were set by asking the subjects to imagine receiving mobile text messages conveying each of the four types of emotions and then to respond to specific questions about the reply strategy they would adopt in each scenario. The examples shown in Table 2 were provided to help subjects visualize specific cases of messages conveying the four types of emotions.

Questionnaire

The questionnaire posed the question, "When you receive a mobile text from a friend conveying each of the four types of emotions, do you wait before responding, even if you are able to immediately respond?" Subjects were instructed to respond using a 6-point rating scale (1: never; 2: almost never; 3: not frequently; 4: occasionally; 5: frequently; 6: every time). They were also asked to

Table 2. Examples of the 4 types of emotional scenarios examined in the study

Happiness
Your friend tells you, "I studied all the right things and passed the test with flying colors."
Sadness
Your friend sadly tells you, "I studied all the wrong things and failed the test."
Anger
Your friend angrily tells you, "I failed the test because you taught me completely the wrong things."
Guilt
Your friend apologetically tells you, "You failed the test because I taught you completely the wrong things."

provide a freeform answer as to why they chose that rating. The freeform question asked subjects who responded 1–3 on the 6-point scale, "Why would you respond immediately?" and asked subjects who responded 4–6, "Why would you wait?"

RESULTS AND DISCUSSION OF STUDY 2

Six-Point Scale Rating Results

First, a one-way repeated measures ANOVA with the four emotional scenarios set as the factor was performed for the 6-point ratings of the questionnaire. A significant difference was shown between the different emotional scenarios ($F(3,669)=2.83$,

$p<0.05$). As seen in Figure 2, there is almost no difference between the four emotional scenarios. However, if a conclusion were to be drawn, out of the four emotional scenarios, the difference is greatest for the anger scenario and guilt scenario. In other words, we can say that subjects tended to wait before responding in the anger scenario and not wait before responding in the guilt scenario. However, as mentioned previously, we conclude overall that the differences between the emotional scenarios were small (e.g., the average difference between anger and guilt was 0.330). Furthermore, in each emotional scenario, the gender differences were not seen in the results that compared the mean between male and female using t-test.

Next, the frequency distribution for the 6-point rating was calculated for each emotional sce-

Figure 2. Comparison of 6-point scale mean scores for each emotional scenario

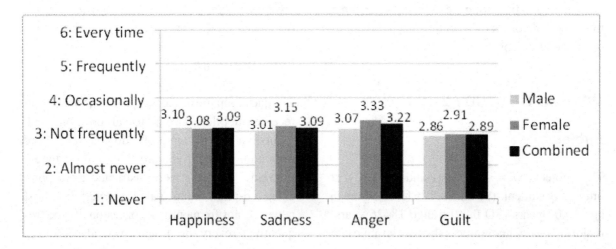

nario. As shown in Figure 3, rating variability was high for all emotional scenarios (SD: happiness 1.33, sadness 1.30, anger 1.51, and guilt 1.50). Figure 3 showed that there were more ratios of "Never" in male subjects than female ones in each emotional scenarios, this suggests that individual views on response timing have a stronger affect than type of emotion, indicating the possible existence of individual differences.

Freeform Response Results

Depending on their rating on the 6-point scale for each emotional scenario, subjects were asked their "reason for immediately replying" or "reason for waiting before replying." For happiness, there were 127 responses for "reason for immediately replying" (of these, 7 responded "no reason") and 97 responses for "reason for waiting before replying" (of these, 15 responded "no reason").

Continuing with the other emotions, the corresponding responses (immediate versus waiting) were as follows: for sadness, 120 responses (4 "no reason") versus 104 responses (6 "no reason"); for anger, 116 responses (2 "no reason") and 108 responses (0 "no reason"); and for guilt, 143 responses (0 "no reason") and 81 responses (4 "no reason").

In order to perform an analysis of the freeform responses regarding reply timing, all responses were categorized according to their meaning and content; a category was created when the same response was received by 2 or more subjects. This categorization was performed by three researchers with sufficient experience in research related to text communication. As for Study 1, the three researchers "worked together" to discuss each response and decide on the category. There were no major differences of opinion during this process, and no cases arose which required

Figure 3. Six-point scale responses for each emotional scenario

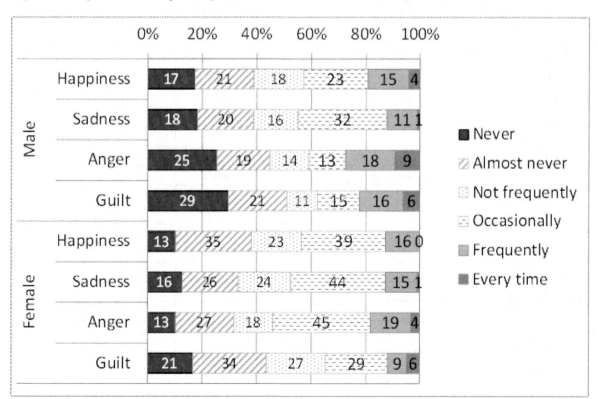

direct confirmation with any subject. Tables 3–6 show the freeform responses and the categories of reasons regarding the reply timing for each of happiness, sadness, anger and guilt, in that order. Response categories are shown in order from most to least common.

Some of the responses in Tables 3–6 reveal that subjects adjust their reply timing to manipulate their own emotions or the emotions of the other party. For happiness, subjects report responding immediately in order to "empathize with the other person" or "reply before the other person's happiness fades." On the other hand, subjects wait before replying when feeling "jealous (at the other person's happiness)" or "to stretch out the happiness (for both parties)." For sadness, subjects

reply immediately in order to "provide encouragement" or "out of sense of concern," although they may wait before replying in order to "wait for the other person's sadness to pass." For anger, subjects reply immediately when "waiting would make the other person feel more angry," but wait to reply in order to "wait for the other person's anger to subside." In the case of guilt, subjects reply immediately in order to "make the other person feel better" or "to let the other person know that they are not mad," but wait before replying to "make the other person think about it more" or "because of their own anger."

Finally, from these tables, the gender differences were mentioned in the following. For happiness, while female subjects report respond-

Table 3. Happiness scenario: reasons for reply timing

Happiness			
	Frequency		
Reason for immediately replying	**Combined**	**Male**	**Female**
To empathize	49	14 (25.0%)	35 (49.3%)
A quick response is polite	25	15 (26.8%)	10 (14.1%)
It is easy to reply	10	4 (7.1%)	6 (8.5%)
To reply before the other person's happiness fades	9	4 (7.1%)	5 (7.0%)
To reply before I forget	9	4 (7.1%)	5 (7.0%)
To kill time	4	3 (5.4%)	1 (1.4%)
To stop the conversation dying down	4	3 (5.4%)	1 (1.4%)
To show my quick reaction	4	3 (5.4%)	1 (1.4%)
Reason for waiting before replying	**Combined**	**Male**	**Female**
I don't feel like it	24	8 (19.0%)	16 (29.1%)
I need to think about it	11	7 (16.7%)	4 (7.3%)
Not urgent	11	4 (9.5%)	7 (12.7%)
The other person might be replying	6	4 (9.5%)	2 (3.6%)
The other person is probably busy	4	3 (7.1%)	1 (1.8%)
Out of jealousy	4	1 (2.4%)	3 (5.5%)
It's customary to wait	3	1 (2.4%)	2 (3.6%)
I don't reply by mail (mobile text)	3	1 (2.4%)	2 (3.6%)
I'm satisfied just reading (the other person's message)	3	0 (0.0%)	3 (5.5%)
To stretch out the happiness	2	1 (2.4%)	1 (1.8%)

ing immediately in order to empathize with the other person more, male subjects more reply immediately because they think that a quick response is polite. For sadness, female subjects report responding immediately in order to provide encouragement more. For anger, female subjects more reply immediately in order to convey a sense of reflection or more wait before replying in order to think about it than male subjects. For guilt, female subjects more report responding immediately in order to put the other person at ease than male subjects.

As the results indicate, reply timing that is adjusted with the intent of manipulating own emotions or those of communication partners are not consistent within an emotional scenario; rather, there are individual differences in deciding whether to "reply immediately" or "wait before replying."

CONCLUSION

Summary of Results

A quantitative analysis of the average values of the 6-point ratings in Study 1 suggests that the majority of subject participants sometimes wait before replying to a mobile text message. A qualitative analysis of the freeform responses also showed an emotional aspect in most cases where subjects did not immediately reply to a mobile text message even when they were capable of doing so.

Table 4. Sadness scenario: reasons for reply timing

Sadness			
	Frequency		
Reason for immediately replying	**Combined**	**Male**	**Female**
To provide encouragement	54	20 (37.0%)	34 (51.5%)
A quick response is polite	15	8 (14.8%)	7 (10.6%)
The other person is troubled	8	3 (5.6%)	5 (7.6%)
I'm worried	8	6 (11.1%)	2 (3.0%)
To ask more details	8	2 (3.7%)	6 (9.1%)
I need to think about it	6	3 (5.6%))	3 (4.5%)
To reply before I forget	4	2 (3.7%)	2 (3.0%)
To empathize	3	2 (3.7%)	1 (1.5%)
To show my quick reaction	3	2 (3.7%)	1 (1.5%)
To kill time	2	2 (3.7%)	0 (0.0%)
Reason for waiting before replying	**Combined**	**Male**	**Female**
I need to think about it	58	22 (50.0%)	36 (60.0%)
I don't feel like it	11	5 (11.4%)	6 (10.0%)
The reply would be troubling	8	2 (4.5%)	6 (10.0%)
I procrastinate	4	1 (2.3%)	3 (5.0%)
I don't reply by mail (mobile text)	4	0 (0.0%)	4 (6.7%)
To provide encouragement	3	3 (6.8%)	0 (2.9%)
To wait until the sadness fades	3	3 (6.8%)	0 (2.9%)
Wait to show that I'm carefully thinking about it	2	1 (2.3%)	1 (1.7%)

Table 5. Anger scenario: reasons for reply timing

Anger			
		Frequency	
Reason for immediately replying	Combined	Male	Female
To convey a sense of reflection	51	22 (37.9%)	29 (50.0%)
To ask more details	17	8 (13.8%)	9 (15.5%)
Waiting would make the other person more angry	8	3 (5.2%)	5 (8.6%)
A quick response is polite	5	3 (5.2%)	2 (3.4%)
Apologizing later would be more difficult	5	2 (3.4%)	3 (5.2%)
I want to know the reason	4	2 (3.4%)	2 (3.4%)
To reply before I forget	3	2 (3.4%)	1 (1.7%)
I need to think about it	2	1 (1.7%)	1 (1.7%)
To get revenge	2	2 (3.4%)	0 (0.0%)
Reason for waiting before replying	Combined	Male	Female
I need to think about it	26	6 (15.0%)	20 (29.4%)
I don't feel like it	24	11 (27.5%)	13 (19.1%)
To wait for the anger to die down	23	10 (25.0%)	13 (19.1%)
I don't reply by mail (mobile text)	9	2 (5.0%)	7 (10.3%)
The reply would be troubling	3	1 (2.5%)	2 (2.9%)
I can't understand the reason for the anger	2	0 (0.0%)	2 (2.9%)
Replying quickly would make things worse	2	1 (2.5%)	1 (1.5%)
To convey a sense of reflection	2	0 (0.0%)	2 (2.9%)

A quantitative analysis of the average values of the 6-point ratings in Study 2 showed a tendency to wait before replying in anger situations and to not wait before replying in guilt situations. Also, a qualitative analysis of the freeform responses showed that in order to manipulate the other person's emotions or one's own emotions, some subjects would choose to wait before responding while others would choose not to wait before responding.

Based on a summary of these two studies, the following conclusion can be drawn: When considering waiting before responding, there is a slight bias to wait before responding in emotional situations, but there is large variability from subject to subject. Whatever the case, the majority of subjects did use reply timing as an emotional strategy. This study thus shows that reply timing is used as an emotional strategy, but that personal differences play a large role in how it is used.

Overall Discussion

The study showed that the timings of replies to mobile text communications are adjusted in order to manipulate own emotions or those of another party. However, individual differences were observed in these adjustments, suggesting the potential for situations where the result of adjusting the reply timing is not as expected. For example, the person waiting for the reply might be expecting a quick reply, while the person doing the replying might think it best to wait before doing so. In such a case, the person waiting for the reply might feel betrayed. Especially for emotionally charged messages such as those considered in

Table 6. Guilt scenario: reasons for reply timing

Guilt			
	Frequency		
Reason for immediately replying	**Combined**	**Male**	**Female**
To put the other person at ease	82	27 (44.3%)	55 (67.1%)
To let the other person know I'm not angry	12	7 (11.5%)	5 (6.1%)
A quick response is polite	12	6 (9.8%)	6 (7.3%)
To resolve the situation quickly	3	0 (0.0%)	3 (3.7%)
To reply before I forget	3	2 (3.3%)	1 (1.2%)
I need to think about it	2	0 (0.0%)	2 (2.4%)
Because I'm angry	2	2 (3.3%)	0 (0.0%)
I don't reply by mail (mobile text)	2	1 (1.6%)	1 (1.2%)
Reason for waiting before replying	**Combined**	**Male**	**Female**
To make the other person think about it more	12	7 (18.9%)	5 (11.4%)
I need to think about it	10	4 (10.8%)	6 (13.6%)
I don't reply by mail (mobile text)	8	2 (5.4%)	6 (13.6%)
Because I'm angry	7	5 (13.5%)	2 (4.5%)
I don't feel like it	7	2 (5.4%)	5 (11.4%)
To put the other person at ease	6	3 (8.1%)	3 (6.8%)
It doesn't really bother me	4	2 (5.4%)	2 (4.5%)

this study, it is likely that individual differences in thoughts about reply timing have an effect on the development of problematic situations.

Without habits or rules that are shared between communication partners, many such subtle emotional strategies are not likely to be successful. In other words, when habits and rules vary across generations or communities, a strategy that would work with one person may not work with another. For example, the anecdote regarding the university professor that was presented earlier may not have caused a problem if the communication partners had a shared set of habits and rules and an understanding about the characteristics of mobile text communication. In the future, information morals education should teach why it is important for media communication partners to understand each other's media habits and rules.

Unlike mobile phone communications (conversations), mobile text messaging is an asynchronous form of communication that does not demand an immediate response. Senders should not have a problem with the recipient reading and responding to their mobile text messages as time allows. However, in mobile text messaging communications between Japanese, especially young Japanese, it has become customary to make an immediate response. For this reason, recipients feel that not responding immediately may risk the sender concluding that the receiver does not deem the message important. Thus, it is reasonable to assume that taking too long to respond can cause problems. For such young Japanese, response timing is a sensitive issue. Even so, these results showed that recipients use response timing differently in different scenarios, even though it is considered good manners (by them) to respond immediately. Different subjects also manipulated response time in different ways. The authors believe that this individual difference in perception toward "sensitive" response timing is an important finding that is worthy of continued study. It is important to address the following questions: Do individual differences affect the occurrence of problems generated by mobile text messaging? If no direct problems are observed, does a separate emotional strategy exist that overcomes these individual differences? Why do individual differences exist? In this study that revealed two groups of individual differences—those who reply immediately and those who wait before replying—which strategy works best? In other words, which strategy leads to matching the intentions of the recipient?

Finally, these results suggest contributions to practical situations, such as virtual work. As a general rule, it is better to respond quickly in communication. This is true for cases where the information being conveyed in communication is "factual" or "matter of fact." Obviously, in actual situations, communication is not always just "factual" or "matter of fact"; there are situations in which bosses admonish or encourage their subordinates. Subordinates may complain about their bosses to coworkers. In other words, communication frequently has emotional content, even in work situations. For example, when a subordinate is slow to respond in a situation where a quick response is usually expected, a boss should see the mere fact that the response is delayed as having become a "media" for conveying emotion. In practical situations, such as virtual work, that are dominated by text communication, smooth operation of the organization will depend on workers not only correctly interpreting the message contained in the communication, but also noting the speed and timing of the reply.

Future Topics

This study considered the reply timing of the person sending a reply message. Future studies should examine how the choice of reply timing is actually perceived by the recipient (the original sender). In addition, this study only considered mobile text messages, and future work should investigate the reply timing of PC email in comparison to that of mobile text messages. Also, the subjects of these two surveys were Japanese people in Japan. Therefore, surveys should be administered in other countries and intercultural comparative studies should be performed.

Finally, this study used a questionnaire to investigate reply timing, but measuring actual reply times is only one possibility. Another possible method could be to send mobile text messages to subjects containing the four types of emotional content shown in Table 1, and measure the time until a reply is received from the subject. However, the authors feel that it would be difficult to experimentally measure reply time, due to problems with writing messages and gathering content in an experiment as well as problems measuring the reaction to the message. It would be necessary to control various factors such as the message delivery timing/time (such as whether it is morning or night or summer vacation), the precise relationship with the other person, and the lifestyles of the other person in addition to the subject (e.g., class schedules, working hours or club activities if they are students). All of these would limit the results that could be obtained. For these reasons, rather than measuring the time until responding, the method chosen for this study was to ask subjects whether they "intentionally" waited before replying. In other words, even when there are differences in the time passed before replying, the aim of this study was to ask whether the delay was intentional and to consider the underlying reasons. However, obtaining quantitative trends in reply timing could be useful in the educational arena, such as choosing the most effective time in e-learning to send messages. There is therefore merit in working on an experimental design to measure actual reply timing.

ACKNOWLEDGMENT

This study was supported by Grant-in-Aid for Young Scientists (B) No. 21700827 and Grant-in-Aid for Young Scientists (B) No. 22700820 from the Ministry of Education, Culture, Sports, Science, and Technology (MEXT) and the Japan Society for the Promotion of Science (JSPS).

REFERENCES

Dyer, R., Green, R., Pitts, M., & Millward, G. (1995). What's the flaming problem? CMC - Deindividuation or disinhibiting? In Kirby, M. A. R., Dix, A. J., & Finlay, J. E. (Eds.), *People and Computers*. Cambridge, MA: Cambridge University Press.

Ekman, P. (1992). An argument for basic emotions. In Stein, N. L., & Oatley, K. (Eds.), *Basic Emotions: Cognition & Emotion* (pp. 169–200). Mahwah, NJ: Lawrence Erlbaum.

Hancock, J. T. (2007). Digital deception: Why, when and how people lie online. In Joinson, A. N., McKenna, K., Postmes, T., & Reips, U. (Eds.), *The Oxford Handbook of Internet Psychology* (pp. 289–301). Oxford, UK: Oxford University Press.

Kato, S., Kato, Y., & Scott, D. J. (2009). Relationships between emotional states and emoticons in mobile phone email communication in Japan. *International Journal on E-Learning Corporate, Government, Healthcare, & Higher Education, 8*(3), 385–401.

Kato, S., Kato, Y., Scott, D. J., & Sato, K. (2008). Selection of ICT in emotional communication for Japanese students: Focusing on emotional strategies and gender differences. In *Proceedings of World Conference on Educational Multimedia, Hypermedia and Telecommunications (ED-MEDIA) 2008*, (pp. 1050-1057). ED-MEDIA.

Kato, Y., Kato, S., & Akahori, K. (2006a). Effects of senders' self-disclosures and styles of writing messages on recipients' emotional aspects in e-mail communication. In *Proceedings of World Conference on E-Learning in Corporate, Government, Healthcare, and Higher Education (E-Learn) 2006*, (pp. 2585-2592). E-Learn.

Kato, Y., Kato, S., & Akahori, K. (2006b). Comparison of emotional aspects in e-mail communication by mobile phone with a teacher and a friend. In *Proceedings of World Conference on Educational Multimedia, Hypermedia and Telecommunications (ED-MEDIA) 2006*, (pp. 425-433). ED-MEDIA.

Kato, Y., Kato, S., & Akahori, K. (2007a). Effects of emotional cues transmitted in e-mail communication on the emotions experienced by senders and receivers. *Computers in Human Behavior, 23*(4), 1894–1905. doi:10.1016/j.chb.2005.11.005

Kato, Y., Kato, S., & Chida, K. (2011c). Investigation of mobile phone email reply time and emotional strategies: Replies to four message-types conveying different emotions. *Journal of Japan Society of Educational Information, 27*(2), 5–12.

Kato, Y., Kato, S., & Scott, D. J. (2007b). Misinterpretation of emotional cues and content in Japanese email, computer conferences, and mobile text messages. In Clausen, E. I. (Ed.), *Psychology of Anger* (pp. 145–176). Hauppauge, NY: Nova Science Publishers.

Kato, Y., Kato, S., Scott, D. J., & Sato, K. (2010). Patterns of emotional transmission in Japanese young people's text-based communication in four basic emotional situations. *International Journal on E-Learning Corporate, Government, Healthcare, & Higher Education, 9*(2), 203–227.

Kato, Y., Kato, S., Sugimura, K., & Akahori, K. (2008). The influence of affective traits on emotional aspects of message receivers in text-based communication -Examination by the experiment using e-mail communication. *Educational Technology Research, 31*(1-2), 85–95.

Kato, Y., Scott, D. J., & Kato, S. (2011a). The influence of intimacy and gender on emotions in mobile phone email. In Gokcay, D., & Yildirim, G. (Eds.), *Affective Computing and Interaction: Psychological, Cognitive and Neuroscientific Perspectives* (pp. 262–279). Hershey, PA: IGI Global. doi:10.4018/978-1-61692-892-6.ch012

Kato, Y., Scott, D. J., & Kato, S. (2011b). Comparing American and Japanese young people's emotional strategies in mobile phone email communication. In *Proceedings of World Conference on Educational Multimedia, Hypermedia and Telecommunications (ED-MEDIA) 2011*, (pp. 170-178). ED-MEDIA.

Kato, Y., Sugimura, K., & Akahori, K. (2002). Effect of contents of e-mail messages on affections. In *Proceedings of International Conference on Computers in Education (ICCE) 2002*, (Vol. 1), (pp. 428-432). ICCE.

Matsumoto, D. (1996). *Unmasking Japan: Myths and realities about the emotions of the Japanese.* Palo Alto, CA: Stanford University Press.

Matsumoto, D., & Kudoh, T. (1993). American-Japanese cultural differences in implicit theories of personality based on smile. *Journal of Nonverbal Behavior, 17*(4), 231–243. doi:10.1007/BF00987239

Mayer, J. D. (2000). Emotion, intelligence, emotional intelligence. In Forgas, J. P. (Ed.), *The Handbook of Affect and Social Cognition* (pp. 410–431). Mahwah, NJ: Lawrence Erlbaum & Associates.

Okabe, D., & Ito, M. (2006). Keitai use in public transportation. In Ito, M., Okabe, D., & Matsuda, M. (Eds.), *Personal, Portable, Pedestrian: Mobile Phones in Japanese Life* (pp. 205–217). Cambridge, MA: MIT Press.

Salovey, P., & Mayer, J. D. (1990). Emotional intelligence. *Imagination, Cognition and Personality, 9*, 185–211.

Sato, K., Kato, Y., & Kato, S. (2008). Exploring emotional strategies in mobile phone email communication: Analysis on the impact of social presence. In *Proceedings of International Conference on Computers in Education (ICCE) 2008*, (pp. 253-260). ICCE.

Scott, D. J., Coursaris, C. K., Kato, Y., & Kato, S. (2009). The exchange of emotional context in business communications: A comparison of PC and mobile email users. In M. M. Head & E. Li (Eds.), *Mobile and Ubiquitous Commerce: Advanced E-Business Methods: Volume 4 of Advances in Electronic Business Series*, (pp. 201-219). Hershey, PA: IGI Global.

Short, J., Williams, E., & Christie, B. (1976). *The social psychology of telecommunications.* London, UK: Wiley.

Sproull, L., & Kiesler, S. (1986). Reducing social context cues: Electronic mail in organizational communication. *Management Science, 32*(11), 1492–1512. doi:10.1287/mnsc.32.11.1492

Chapter 7

Australian Users' Interactions with E-Services in a Virtual Environment

Kamaljeet Sandhu
University of New England, Australia

ABSTRACT

Research into human interaction with computers requires a clear understanding about "user learning experience" on websites that shape user perceptions about virtual work. This chapter investigates issues that impact users' learning based on experience in using the e-services system. This research aims to address some of the important characteristics of user learning experience and how it can positively/ negatively impact user attitudes towards e-service tasks in virtual work. The adoption, use, and then continued use of an e-services system in terms of e-services system characteristics based on service-user interaction will be studied.

INTRODUCTION

E-Services are a focus of research within areas such as Marketing, Management, Information Technology and Information Systems (Parasuraman & Grewal, 2000; Abdelmessih, et al., 2000; Rust & Lemon, 2001; Chea & Lou, 2008; Scupola, 2008; Chellappan, 2008, Li & Liu, 2011). Information

DOI: 10.4018/978-1-4666-0963-1.ch007

Technology usage is a key dependent variable in MIS research (DeLone & McLean, 1992) and users interaction with e-services in a virtual environment. However, little is understood about the adoption process which explores the sequence of activities that lead to the initial adoption and to the continued usage of an IT at the consumer adoption level (Karahanna, et al., 1999). Other researchers argue for identification of what constitutes as successful adoption of a technology (e.g. Brancheau & Wetherbe, 1990; Cooper & Zmud, 1990; Cale & Eriksen, 1994; Prescott & Conger, 1995). However, what is common in different adoption research is the importance of user characteristics that drive the use of a technology such as web-based user services.

This paper specifically investigates issues related to user learning experiences in web-based learning adoption and the process involving continued use of web-based learning services. With technology constantly changing it will subsequently have an effect on the user's learning experience and perception. Web-based user services are generally perceived as being successful, but there has been little evaluation of how well the web meets its user's' primary information requirements in virtual environment tasks (D'Ambra & Rice, 2001). The freedom and flexibility offered by the Internet allow users to connect to other websites of their interest and at the same time build upon their e-learning experience on the web. A number of researchers suggested that flow is a useful construct for describing interactions with websites in virtual tasks (Csikszentmihalyi, 1975; Johnson & Mathews, 1997; Zeithaml, et al., 1993; Zeithaml, et al., 2000; Chea & Lou, 2008). Flow has been described as "the process of optimal experience" (Csikszentmihalyi & LeFevre, 1990) achieved when sufficiently motivated user perceives a balance between their skills and challenges of the interaction, together with focused attention (Hoffman & Novak, 1996).

Earlier studies investigated the adoption of web-based systems in different contexts, but did not provide insight into their acceptance and continued use by users. Though a consumer may use a web-based system for the first time, its continued use relates to the success. The user's web-based learning experience may form an impression of the system in terms of how easy or how difficult it is to operate the system.

Zanna and Rempel (1988) and Karahanna et al. (1999) have distinguished between pre- and post-adoption attitudes, which may be formed based on three general classes of information: information concerning past behaviour, affective information, and cognitive information. Users past behavioural interaction with information forms the initial process that triggers the adoption process, which leads to a user analysing information relevant to the context—and recalling that information in similar situations. In the post-adoption process the user continuously tends to reflect on their past interactions and applies experience that would provide positive outcomes. Karahanna et al. (1999:188) argue that it is reasonable to assume that pre-adoption beliefs are primarily based on indirect experience (effect or cognition) with IT while post-adoption usage beliefs are based on past experience.

BACKGROUND

This study assumes that user's experience with information already exists in the traditional environment (i.e., offline). Understanding the traditional learning complexities of user experience with information and transforming it to the web-based environment is a challenge for both practitioners and researchers. The dimension and scale of such complexity in terms of technology and its alliance with information may provide an integration point where technology requirements may meet with the user's learning experience. Defining user learning experience with information is not an easy and straightforward process. Rather developing an approach to studying the learning experience process on the basis of web-based learning and user interaction is suggested.

User's engaged in web-based learning activities tend to focus on prior information experience and perception of task/s done, especially from the offline environment. The effect of information on user experience in web-based learning on first time user's compared to the frequent user's will vary, a user with no experience can form high (or low) perception, especially via word of mouth communications. Such perceptions may behave differently from those developed via experience. Davidow and Uttal (1989) suggest user's expectation is formed by many uncontrollable factors, from the experience of users' to a user's psychological state. It is argued that a user web-based learning experience is formed and based on wider range of prior experiences that may be recalled or narrowed in a similar situation. The flow of information over the Internet is faster and communication between user's leads in enhanced learning. Understanding the user's web-based learning experience and perception solely on the basis of online or offline experience would tend to limit the research dimension; rather a combination approach is adopted.

The concept of flow is important because it has a clear set of antecedent conditions and consequences that have implications for web-based learning. User's information experience on a website, its impact, retention of that web-based learning experience can be related to the flow concept. For the flow state to be experienced, the user must perceive skills and challenges to be in balance and above a critical threshold and the user must be paying attention. That is a user must be in state of learning. Hoffman and Novak (1996) suggest that the consequences of flow in web-based environments relates to increased learning, increased exploratory and participatory behaviours, and more positive subjective experiences, that a critical objective of a commercial website is to facilitate the flow experience. Karahanna et al. (1999) suggest that user's acquire personal experience and their own source of evaluative information in using the information system. Such an experience can have a strong effect on the user in remembering their learning experience on a particular website.

User information experience in web-based systems learning is an important area that is gradually growing with introduction and adoption of web-based technology (i.e. WebCT, Firstclass, and Blackboard). The information available in web-based systems learning may be one of the determinants which direct the user in achieving the desired objectives that form the purpose of using the system. The user information requirements may be based from prior experience in similar or related traditional learning environment. Information search form the initial need in the activity to achieve the desired objectives, and hence the acquisition of information experience process. Information if not available to users in e-learning or traditional learning environments may direct the user in adopting the search process based on experience.

RESEARCH METHODOLOGY

This research is to understand what affects the adoption, use, and then continued use of an e-services system in terms of e-services system characteristics based on service-user interaction. And the user's attitudes to adopting e-services at different stages based on how user behaviour towards adopting e-services system is influenced: a user's attitudes toward adoption—specific behaviours that are linked to user activities when using e-Services system.

This led to the development of converging lines of inquiry, a process of triangulation (Yin, 1994). In the first instance, discussions were held as a focus group with three senior staff members involved in implementing the web-based e-learning project. Focus group lasted 2 hours. They included the executive director, IT Manager, and an outside consultant. In the second round, separate individual interviews (one-on-one) are conducted with these participants. One-on-one interviews were recorded, each being one hour. One hundred and eighty single-spaced pages of transcribed data was studied by the researcher.

The third round of interviews was conducted with the admissions manager and separate individual interviews with two other staff members. Altogether six separate interviews with participants were held. Though the participant's gender is not a major factor for examination in this research, it coincided to balance, three males and three females. In the first round interviews, the data collected was compared with the second round and third round interview data for consistency, clarity, and accuracy of the information.

Interview data was also compared to test for the factors having effect on users with high and low performance in learning how to use the web-based system. This provided the advantage of not duplicating the data with just one set of evidence. The discussions and interviews were open-ended (Yin, 1994), the researcher in the beginning provided the topic, and the respondents were probed of their opinion about the events.

The questions are directed towards user's learning experience with the web-based system. This led the users in reflecting their recent learning experiences with the system and demonstrating its effectiveness in the web-based task. It provides the opportunity of capturing rich information that is fresh and part of the user-learning interface within the web-based system. It not only provides information about the user's learning experience, but also demonstrates the boundaries of the web-based learning system, in other words the scope of the system in providing enhanced learning is clearly reflected from the data the users provided to what the system was capable of doing within the parameters. This approach took into consideration the users and the system context in understanding the web-based learning process. It provides important information from the user's perspective in the terms of the learning process available in the web-based system.

CASE ANALYSIS

Service quality in e-services environments is expected to change quickly and may differ from user to user. In this context, the level of service quality may not be guaranteed and any unknown interaction occurring between the user and the e-services system that affects e-services is hard to capture. An e-services system's characteristics play an important role—if the system is poorly developed and disorganised and hard to interact with, the user perception of e-services will be low.

The case study examines the web-based framework of the University of Australia (not the real name). International students have the option to lodge an admission application through either of: web-based e-service on the Internet, phone, fax, or in person. On receiving the application a decision is made by the staff on the admission status. Within this process the department is implementing an electronic delivery of its services on the website.

Web-based e-service has been in use for the last two and half years. The complete process involves students making the application and the staff processing applications on the website. The staff is currently using the web-based e-service and the paper-based system in conducting the tasks. Transition from paper-based to web-based e-service is believed by the department to be a significant step in the direction of moving the complete student admission process over the website and gradually removing the paper-based system. The users learning experience in adopting the web-based system is focus of attention in the study.

EXPLORING USERS' INFORMATION EXPERIENCE ON WEBSITES

The user perception of web electronic service is a burden and acted as a barrier to their work. The users learnt that it increased the workload, slowed the work process, and brought in complexity to the task. The department did not implement electronic services or introduce technology into jobs at the same time. The effect on user learning experience in using the e-service is not estimated when the system was being developed. Understanding the task sequence from start to finish, and integrating those functions into web-based learning process is missing. It lacks coherence. Individual users did not have consistent skills in learning how to use the system because of differing levels of expertise (i.e., user category).

The assimilation and dissimulation of learning experience in conducting the web-based e-service task may provide the user an option in retaining that experience which can be remembered easily. A participant claimed:

"Need to rely on paper documents and another database to complete the task... have to use all... "

The information disclosed by the participant point to the fact that the web-based system was short from offering the user a learning process which if available would have gradually build on user's prior information experience, rather the user's were juggling with multiple sources to collect the information that was needed in completing the web-based task.

Specific expertise needed for conducting the task was lacking. Different task requires different skills when done on paper, doing it electronically requires different experience with information and knowing what was happening beyond the user's computer screen. In the paper-based system, it was known to the user how different process of a task and where information was stored and retained when needed, such as the filing, organizing, storing of documentation was systematically interconnected, in case of electronic service little was known by way what constituted as web-based e-service task process beyond the computer screen. Proper documentation providing information to the user's for referencing were either missing or unknown. The users didn't have learning experience in how to operate the system. One participant mentioned:

"Users had no confidence in the system and decision making. "

The users were asked to enter all information directly to the web. To expect a user to start using an electronic service without prior learning the user's experience is not perceive to be appropriate. Despite providing regular training the user resistance to use the electronic system increased. The following quote support this notion:

"There are quite a few fields where we can't use the web-based e-services. "

Martin (1991) suggest that user learning experience evolves, or ranges, from naïve (no system knowledge) through inexperienced to competent and finally to expert. On such basis users can be divided into following categories: novice, intermediate, and experienced. It is important to remember that different categories of users' learning experiences vary at different stages in performing the task. It is anticipated the users are in a learning process and shift from one mode to another, with experience sliding up or down on the learning swing and the user experience varies, till they reach a point (see Figure 1, point A) where the learning experience flow is at the optimum level in doing the task.

The experience attained in online or offline environment is likely to direct the user in retaining the most recent learning experience because this would be much easier to recall, provided that the information is relevant to the current context. Zemke and Connellan (2001) posit that each learning experience, regardless of whether it's online or offline, sets the stage of expectations for future interactions. The user tends to focus on ease of use (more than the usefulness), familiarity, skills needed, website-to-website learning comparison, and on the task complexity. The task complexities can be defined in terms of navigation on the website, information search, transaction processing, and online support (i.e., help). A

Figure 1. Learning-experience swing (Sandhu and Corbitt (2002))

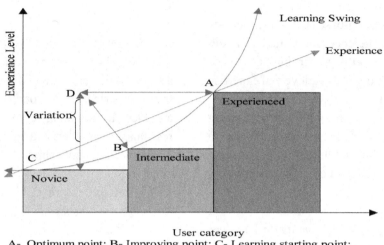

User category
A- Optimum point; B- Improving point; C- Learning starting point;
D- Experience variation point

participant related this in terms of the web-based system as:

"System is not intelligent enough to check simple errors like spell checks, grammar checks..."

The statement referred to the user's learning expectation of the systems capabilities in terms of their prior experience. The users had used this functionality in another system and expected to match with their prior information experience in the web-based system. The users perceived experience about the current system being below its standard and not helpful in doing the task. It did not meet the users' information requirement for the task.

Similarly if the user's needs are met on one dimension and unmet on another, they are actively searching for an alternative on another website or in offline environment. This is supported in our study; the participants reported switching to the paper-based system, as the learning process and its outcome was easier to understand and follow. Zemke and Connellan (2001) suggest that to succeed on the website, it is important to consistently manage the total user learning experience

(i.e. information experience) in the categories in upper three (black) boxes (see Figure 2). They claim to have successfully used the model at Dell Computers in understanding the total user's interaction. However, there is no quantitative data and analysis of the model that suggest how well the model works across web-based e-learning.

User compares similar outcomes on other website or in an offline environment in user transaction process. Zemke and Connellan (2001) claim that the process—the way they are served— is what makes it into learning experience, positively or negatively for users. If the user's needs are not met on the process and outcome axes, they tend to go elsewhere, and hence called defectors. Zemke and Connellan (2001) developed a model (Customer Experience Grid, see Figure 2) to capture the sum total of a user learning experiences. The vertical axis of the user experience grid is the outcome the user receives, and offered on a website. On the horizontal axis the user's goes through the learning process to obtain the outcome, such as navigating the website, printing out information, looking for pricing, ordering a product, etc.

Figure 2. User experience grid (Adapted from Zemke and Connellan (2001))

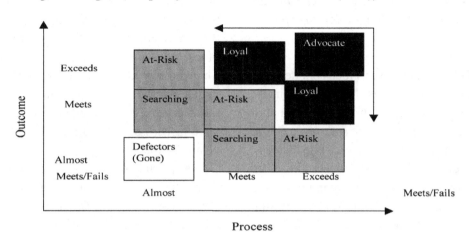

The user's interaction in computer mediated environment is an intense flow being a continuous variable ranging from none to intense (Berthon & Davies, 1999; Foulkes, 1994; Hasher & Zacks, 1984; Chea & Lou, 2008; Chellappan, 2008). The user's purpose of visit to the website may be perceived as more encouraging of exploratory behaviors than others (Trevino & Webster, 1992). If the website meets the primary information need of the user, it may positively affect the user in further progressing with the activity leading to a state of intense flow. It is likely that user's developing a high flow will visit those websites more regularly and for longer duration (Berthon, et al., 1996; Berthon & Davies, 1999). The state of intense learning flow was either missing or faced obstacles. The users weren't able to proceed with the task in the electronic environment. User may tend to reflect on the past experience for future interaction. A participant reflected this in a statement:

"The system is not 100% ready..." "Adds on to the task...increases our task load."

It was believed that the users were losing learning interest in the web-based system due to continuously being put down. To retain interest in a site, there should be enjoyment on the part of the user during the interaction of the site. A participant statement highlights this concern:

"If the system can be fixed it can be fixed, otherwise we will continue using it as it is."

It was known to the users that if the web-based system didn't work they could depend on an alternative system (i.e., paper-bases system) in doing the task. The shifting of learning experience between the paper-based and web-based emerged as a continuum on which the user viewed the web-based system effectiveness before proceeding with the task, which was based on an understanding from past experience. If the user felt the task could be (not only) performed and also completed they went ahead with the web-based system; otherwise they opted for the paper-based system. Any adverse feelings were filtered towards learning the web-based system at that time affecting the decision making to use the web-based system. Those claims were supported by participant statements:

"Verifying information on the Internet is not possible; we still have to check student's education credential in paper form"

"Site needs to be improved with better features and functionality that will make it easier for us to use."

In the flow state, the user's focus or attention is narrowed to a limited stimulus field, and irrelevant thoughts are filtered out. Csikszentmihalyi (1975) suggest that in a flow state the person becomes absorbed in the activity, while increasing his awareness of his own mental processes in the interaction with the web, the computer screen can serve as the limited stimulus field, focusing the individual's attention (Trevino & Webster, 1992). The user faced hurdles during the flow state affecting their learning in doing the task. A participant expressed this:

"Due to time out period that disconnect, the user has to reenter all the information once again... this creates duplicity of information for us...as the same user is reapplying again and it is hard to differentiate between the same application."

As users become more frequent users they place more reliance on learning from internal sources (memory) than external sources (advertisements, word of mouth, etc.) (Johnson & Mathews, 1997). Many researchers have noted the ways in which memory is biased (Foulkes, 1994). Frequent events are easier to recall than infrequent ones (Hasher & Zacks, 1984). Therefore remembering an event is biased by the availability of information within memory (Johnson & Mathews, 1997). The mechanical process of conducting the task with the available tools on the website forms a basis of interactivity for the user and is similar to recalling frequent and infrequent events. Prior research suggests the application of tools to vary across different users from novice to advance (see Martin, 1991).

The development of intelligent agents guiding the user in conducting the task from start to completion tends to improve the user learning interface and reduce uncertainty in learning and problematic experience. This has led to smart software taking over the task, reducing and limiting user's interactivity with the task, and completion of task within a few ticks and clicks of a mouse. The whole process tends to be reduced, removing the intricacies the user can encounter, and at the same time standardizing the users web-based learning across all domain and user developing a positive experience.

Hasher and Zacks (1984) argue that the accuracy with which people encode information increases with the frequency of encoding. Although their research focuses on consumers' exposure to advertising, a parallel can be drawn with consumers' exposure to web-based e-learning. Similarly, Zeithaml et al. (1993, 2000) in their study pointed to information gap on the basis of users learning experience with website that leads to providing incomplete or inaccurate information to the users. It is anticipated that the application of intelligent agents in user interactivity will further enhance and integrate into the user learning experience with information, and become part of the user guidance in conducting web-based task. A participant directed the claim:

"If any information is missed, there is no way to check, there are no compulsory fields to inform of missing information."

The intelligent agent capability in storing and remembering user's transaction details, and displaying on revisits has also reduced the user's need to keep paper record of transaction, making it easier for the user in conducting the task with the availability of past, current and future information records available online. This has an effect on the user learning experience in using the traditional service where the information available is not swift and quick. A reliance on internal search means that the user's memory will have considerable influence on the formation of "learning expectancies" (Foulkes, 1994).

Meuter et al. (2000) report that 80% of the customer complaints are made in person to the company, either by phone or by visiting a service facility. This suggests that the when the user is effected with a problematic experience on web-sites, and to resolve the issue, the user adopts the traditional approach of face-to-face interaction, rather than online approach. The participant in the study evaluated the web-based task, and weighted its effectiveness by comparing it to the paper-based service.

"We can't offer admission letters to higher degree research students on the web-based system, as letter templates are not there; we have to offer it on paper."

The degree of tolerance for web-based system may be intense due to the competitor's service being a click away (Zeithaml, et al., 2000). The users are quick in changing over to paper-based service, which is believed competing with the web-based system. Thus user's tolerance level for web-based system, their immediate reactions to the service failure and their consecutive behavior, are interrelated and forms part of the user learning experience. A participant expressed:

"If the system can be fixed it can be fixed, otherwise we will continue using as it is."

When the web-based system fails it has fallen outside the user's zone of tolerance (Zeithaml, et al., 1993). So far nothing is known about user's tolerance levels of web-based systems, or the user's propensity to complain about online service failures (Riel, et al., 2001), and user's reaction to it. Zeithaml et al. (2000) claim that customers have no expectations, customers have been found to compare web-based service to competitor's services and to brick and mortar stores (Meuter, et al., 2000; Szymanski & Hise, 2000). The de-

gree of user's tolerance is not known. Another participant states:

"They are frightened for asking help if needed... rather they ask for help than provide wrong information."

It seemed there are considerable obstacles the user's developed in their learning experience to use web-based system.

CONCLUSION

This study aims to understand what affects the adoption, use, and then continued use of an e-services system in terms of e-services system characteristics based on service-user interaction. And the user's attitudes to adopting e-services at different stages based on how user behaviour towards adopting e-services system is influenced; a user's attitude to adoption—specific behaviours that are linked to user activities when using e-Services system.

In the preceding discussion, the focus has been on the different user factors that determine the effective use of e-services. An assessment of these factors reveals that user adoption of e-services is process-based and requires considerable attention in specific contexts. User contexts relate to the use of e-services in virtual environments with relevant tasks based on experience and that this probably underpins the practice of continued use of a system. On a theoretical level, the focus has been on user behaviour in effectively using e-services.

The findings of this study can be useful for the practitioners in understanding and avoiding obstacles that may have a negative impact on their experience to use the e-services system. Basic characteristics of the e-services system such as editing text, making corrections, avoiding mistakes, developing letter templates, checking records for accuracy, need to be streamlined and made easy for the users to use.

In understanding the new set of implications, initial research revealed that though uptake and use of this new innovation has been positive, its acceptance and continued use has been limited. The available research though identifies some main issues it lacks in understanding the impact of the critical success factors. Further research will attempt to explore a more structured understanding to web-based systems user learning within a referenced theoretical construct.

From the preceding discussion it has been clear that web-based system adoption is not a simple and straightforward process. Rapid development in technology delivery is gradually shaping the consumer learning in uptake and usage of this new innovation. The level of interaction from traditional services to web-based services and simultaneous use of both has laid a new set of implications for the universities, organizations, government, consumers, practitioners, and researchers.

In line with the preceding discussion it is suggested that web-based systems adoption takes into account the user learning experience that develops with user interaction with the system. Though prior studies even adopted the general technology user models like the TAM model (Davis, 1989; Davis, et al., 1989; Davis, 1993), which is of significance, they do not take into account the user context issues on a commercial situation basis.

To study web-based system from a user learning perspective centered context and combining it with adoption and acceptance models may enhance that understanding. To explore the context further, issues related to situation specific personalization of individual user learning needs in online and offline environment may be used to produce evaluation guidelines that would facilitate the adoption and continuation process.

REFERENCES

Berthon, P., & Davies, T. (1999). Going with the flow: Websites and customer involvement. *Internet Research: Electronic Networking Applications and Policy, 9*(2), 109–116. doi:10.1108/10662249910264873

Berthon, P., Pitt, L., & Watson, R. T. (1996). The world wide web as an advertising medium: Toward an understanding of conversion efficiency. *Journal of Advertising Research, 36*(1), 43–45.

Brancheau, J. C., & Wetherbe, J. C. (1990). The adoption of spreadsheet technology: Testing innovation diffusion theory in the context of end-user computing. *Information Systems Research, 1*(2), 115–143. doi:10.1287/isre.1.2.115

Cale, E. J. Jr, & Eriksen, S. E. (1994). Factors affecting the implementation outcome of a mainframe software package: A longitudinal approach. *Information & Management, 26*, 165–175. doi:10.1016/0378-7206(94)90040-X

Cooper, R. B., & Zmud, R. W. (1990). Information technology implementation research: A technological diffusion approach. *Management Science, 36*(2), 123–139. doi:10.1287/mnsc.36.2.123

Csikszentmihalyi, M. (1975). *Beyond boredom and anxiety.* San Francisco, CA: Jossey-Bass.

Csikszentmihalyi, M., & LeFevre, J. (1990). Optimal experience in work and leisure. *Journal of Personality and Social Psychology, 56*(5), 815–822. doi:10.1037/0022-3514.56.5.815

D'Ambra, J., & Rice, R. E. (2001). Emerging factors in user evaluation of the world wide web. *Information & Management, 38*, 373–384. doi:10.1016/S0378-7206(00)00077-X

Davidow, W. H., & Uttal, B. (1989, July). Service companies: Focus or falter. *Harvard Business Review*, 17–34.

Davis, F. D. (1989). Perceived usefulness, perceived ease of use, and user acceptance of information technology. *Management Information Systems Quarterly*, *13*(2), 319–340. doi:10.2307/249008

Davis, F. D. (1993). User acceptance of information technology: Systems characteristics, user perceptions and behavioral impacts. *International Journal of Man-Machine Studies*, *38*(3), 475–487. doi:10.1006/imms.1993.1022

Davis, F. D., Bagozzi, R. P., & Warshaw, P. R. (1989). User acceptance of computer technology: A comparison of two theoretical models. *Management Science*, *34*(8), 982–1002. doi:10.1287/mnsc.35.8.982

DeLone, W. H., & McLean, E. R. (1992). Information systems success: The quest for the dependant variable. *The Institute of Management Sciences*, *3*(1), 60–95.

Foulkes, V. S. (1994). *How consumers predict service quality: What do they expect? Service Quality, New directions in Theory and Practice.* Thousand Oaks, CA: Sage Publications.

Hasher, L., & Zacks, R. T. (1984). Automatic processing of fundamental information: The case of frequency of occurrence. *The American Psychologist*, *39*, 1372–1388. doi:10.1037/0003-066X.39.12.1372

Hoffman, D. L., & Novak, T. P. (1996). Marketing in hypermedia computer-mediated environments: Conceptual foundations. *JMR, Journal of Marketing Research*, *60*(7), 50–68.

Johnson, C., & Mathews, B. P. (1997). The influence of experience on service expectations. *International Journal of Service Industry Management*, *8*(4), 290–305. doi:10.1108/09564239710174381

Karahanna, E., Straub, D. W., & Chervany, N. L. (1999). Information technology adoption across time: A cross sectional comparison of pre-adoption and post-adoption beliefs. *Management Information Systems Quarterly*, *23*(2), 183–213. doi:10.2307/249751

Li, H., & Liu, Y. (2011). Post adoption behaviour of e-service users: An empirical study on chinese online travel service users. In *Proceedings ECIS 2011*. Retrieved from http://aisel.aisnet.org/ecis2011/56.

Martin, M. P. (1991). *Analysis and design of business information systems.* New York, NY: Macmillan Publishing Company.

Meuter, M. L., Ostrom, A. L., Roundtree, R. I., & Bitner, M. J. (2000). Self-service technologies: Understanding customer satisfaction with technology-based service encounters. *Journal of Marketing*, *64*, 50–64. doi:10.1509/jmkg.64.3.50.18024

Oliver, R. L. (1993). *Service quality: New directions in theory and practice.* Thousand Oaks, CA: Sage.

Prescott, M. B., & Conger, S. A. (1995). Information technology innovations: A classification of IT locus of impact and research approach. *Database*, *26*(2/3), 20–41.

Riel, A. C. R., Liljander, V., & Jurriens, P. (2001). Exploring consumer evaluations of e-services: A portal site. *International Journal of Service Industry Management*, *12*(4), 359–377. doi:10.1108/09564230110405280

Sandhu, K., & Corbitt, B. (2002). *Exploring an understanding of electronic service end-user adoption.* Sydney, Australia: The International Federation for Information Processing.

Scupola, A. (2008). Conceptualizing competences in e-services adoption and assimilation in SMES. *Journal of Electronic Commerce in Organizations*, *6*(2). doi:10.4018/jeco.2008040105

Szymanski, D. M., & Hise, R. T. (2000). E-satisfaction: An initial examination. *Journal of Retailing, 76*(3), 309–322. doi:10.1016/S0022-4359(00)00035-X

Trevino, L. K., & Webster, J. (1992). Flow in computer-mediated communication: Electronic mail and voice evaluation. *Communication Research, 19*(2), 539–573. doi:10.1177/009365092019005001

Yin, R. K. (1994). *Case study research: Design and methods* (2nd ed.). Thousand Oaks, CA: Sage Publications.

Zanna, M. P., & Rempel, J. K. (1988). *Attitudes: A new look at an old concept.* Cambridge, UK: Cambridge University Press.

Zeithaml, V. A., Berry, L., & Parasuraman, A. (1993). The nature and determinants of customer expectations of service. *Journal of the Academy of Marketing Science, 21*(1), 1–12. doi:10.1177/0092070393211001

Zeithaml, V. A., Parasuraman, A., & Malhotra, A. (2000). *A conceptual framework for understanding e-service quality: Implications for future research and managerial practice.* Working Paper. Cambridge, MA: Marketing Science Institute.

Zemke, R., & Connellan, T. (2001). *E-service: 24 ways to keep your customers when the competition is just a click away.* New York, NY: American Management Association.

Chapter 8

High-Touch Interactivity around Digital Learning Contents and Virtual Experiences:
An Initial Exploration Built on Real-World Cases

Shalin Hai-Jew
Kansas State University, USA

ABSTRACT

In high-demand learning, such as in higher education, high-touch interactivity between the subject matter experts and learners is critical as is the mutual creative frictions between the learners themselves. Technological affordances have enabled digital learning contents and immersive spaces to promote high-touch interactivity, intensive long-term conversations, interactions, co-designs, collaborations, and innovations between people. A majority of the digital contents and immersive experiences have been designed for particular purposes; some others are more free-form. In addition, these digital contents may be human-mediated or automated. This chapter examines real-world cases in the uses of digital contents and mediated virtual experiential contents for high-touch interactions.

INTRODUCTION

As learners in higher education specialize in a particular domain field, they engage in complex learning—which often involves ill-structured problem-solving and fresh innovations. A critical element in such learning involves "high-touch interactivity," which refers to intensive social interactions, multi-modal communications, co-designs, collaborations, and innovations. In e-learning, high-touch learning may be encouraged and enhanced by digital learning contents and virtual experiences—most of which are purposively designed for particular aims, and some of which are free-form (created without a particular purpose in mind, unstructured).

DOI: 10.4018/978-1-4666-0963-1.ch008

The concept of high-touch emphasizes the human-to-human collaborative element, but some digital contents and virtual experiences are not human mediated. They may be automated and involve only the learner and the computer-space (as in computer-based trainings). Information and communications technologies have broadened the modes through which people may interact, with a broader range of multimedia response types: textual, auditory, video, multimedia, and various mixed methods. These interchanges may be synchronous, asynchronous, or occurring in mixed-times. Various systems allow enriched intercommunications and knowledge management, with a wider ability to share knowledge through multimedia.

To explore the dynamics of high-touch interactivity around digital learning contents and virtual experiences, this chapter involves analysis of real-world cases of designed digital contents and virtual experiences—and how they enhance high-touch interactivity.

The two main types of digital contents that will be examined involve (1) digital learning contents—which are discrete stand-alone learning objects that may be integrated into a larger sequence or strategy of learning. These objects include audio podcasts, video podcasts, narrated and non-narrated slideshows, videos, interviews, webisodes (Web episodes), digital photo albums, imagery, stories, analytical cases, and other elements. (2) The second main type of contents involves virtual experiences, which tend to be more immersive, or full-sensory and more engaging, and which continue over a certain period of time. These may be shared events like virtual conferences and colloquiums. These may be simulations, scenarios, role plays, digital games, augmented reality experiences, and virtual immersions in virtual worlds, and socio-technical spaces. In other words, virtual experiences tend to be more in-depth for learning, more demanding of the learner, and more involved over time. Both the digital learning contents and the virtual experiences are deployed

through various computing machines: desktop computers, mobile devices and smart phones, handheld devices, smart installations, and others.

REVIEW OF THE LITERATURE

A foundational understanding of interactivity may be drawn from the human perception research in psychology, which conceptualizes interactivity of a human being with his or her environment as a natural part of survival. Interactivity refers to the way people engage the environment to fulfill their needs; interactivity involves gathering information about how the world works. This concept may be applied with multimedia in the sense that the person interacts with the information of the digital environment to learn about the nature of that environment, at one level.

The educational literature offers a range of interpretations of the term "interactivity." One interpretation of media interactivity refers to a media's "potential ability to let the user exert an influence on the content and/or form of the mediated communication" (Jensen, 1999; as cited in Jensen, 2008, p. 129). Jensen describes a typology of interactivity based on four sub-concepts: "transmissional interactivity" (the user's ability to choose from a variety of one-way media); "conversational interactivity" (the media's potential for user-production in a two-way media system, which allows sharing); "consultational interactivity" (a media's potential ability to allow a user to choose "from an existing selection of pre-produced information in a two-way media system with a return-channel"), and "registrational interactivity" (a media's ability to register information from and "also adapt and/or respond to a given user's needs and actions, whether they be the user's explicit choice of communication method or the system's built-in ability to automatically 'sense' and adapt" (Jensen, 2008, p. 129).

This more mechanistic approach in analyzing interactivity has been applied to the design of user interface design—by focusing on the traditional three communications elements: the source or originator of the message, the technological medium or channel through which the content is shared, and message (the content of the communication).

Interactivity situated in any of these three loci of communication can provide cues and affordances that operate either individually or together to capture users' attention and determine the nature and depth of their processing of online content as well as contribute to their perceptions, attitudes and behavioral intentions. This paper discusses psychological mechanisms by which the three classes of interactivity tools affect users, with the specific purpose of drawing out design implications and outlining UI challenges for strategic development of interactive interfaces (Sundar, Xu, & Bellur, 2010, p. 2247).

Interactivity involves give-and-take, a "feedback loop of action-reaction-interaction" which involves "collaboration or exchange" with human-embodied or artificial intelligence computerized agents (Polaine, 2005, p. 151). Researchers suggest that given interactive messages are contingent on user receipt of previous and prior messages, under the so-called "contingency principle," which is a necessary part of sequenced interactivity (Sundar, Xu, & Bellur, 2010, p. 2253).

Another definition of interactivity builds on these issues of user choice by adding "identity-enhancing devices that help individual users to assert their uniqueness" and also which allow customization of the media based on user expertise to help them realize their user agency (such as giving more options and complexity to "power users") (Sundar, Xu, & Bellur, 2010, p. 2253). This conceptualization of interactivity as a way of promoting identity focuses on media affordances made possible by technological advancements and media convergence. Yet another work defines interactivity as a form of human agency or "the

extent to which viewers can exploit their own initiative" (Craven, et al., 2001, pp. 34 - 35). For example, interactive narratives may create "more immersive and transformative experiences for audiences by adding the pleasure of agency" (Hand & Varan, 2009, p. 39). Here, user experiences and preferences may affect the direction of a narrative; audience-member participants help direct and tell the story instead of just interpreting the story.

Built-In Interactivity Affordances in Digital Objects

Interactivity may be seen as a complement to an interactive multimedia artifact; this interactivity is specifically perceivable and describable (Lim, Lee, & Lee, 2009), with unique interactivity attribute mixes per object.

Some types of digital objects are rendered invisible and built into the environment for effective (and unself-conscious) bodily engagements. The authors describe this as "the importance of creating interactive artifacts that do not shield the user from the material and physical environment and the interaction with the social context" (Tholander & Johansson, 2010, p. 4046). (Devices are coming on the market in which game device cameras track players' body movements as a communications tool to the machine to render the players' avatars to engage in a digital 3D space.) Various designs enable movement-based interactivity, which now integrates the mind and body more naturally.

Built-In Interactivity Affordances in Virtual Experiences

Some virtual spaces are almost purely exploratory ones in which individual players interact in an artificial life environment. People engage with the animated life forms around them through multi-sensory experiences—visuals, sounds, and even haptics (in some cases). In some of these spaces, the living creates engage in autopoiesis—or self-creation—based on coded rules of digital artificial "life," which often mimics aspects of the real world albeit in a digital ecosystem. In some virtual experiential spaces, human needs are anticipated and designed for—which suggests limited options both theoretically and in practice (One simple example of this involves the limited in-world physics of most virtual worlds. Another involves the limits to the visual details of the spaces, given the computational expense of rendering and displaying more details.).

Technologically, socio-technical spaces (such as learning / course management systems, groupware, wikis, digital information repositories and referatories, and immersive virtual worlds) have amplified human capabilities of self-expression. People may communicate through text chats, real-time voice, live video, human-embodied avatar appearances and behaviors, whiteboards (2D drawings), and 3D objects; they may pre-record any of these communications and communicate that way, too. In recent years, people have been interacting in content-enriched communications, given the ease of accessing equipment for multimedia capture and sophisticated desktop authoring tools, for user-generated contents (often distributed through rich content spaces). Improved methods of representing and visualizing data enhance users' mental representations. These communications tools afford a greater range of insights of participants' inner states, which may be exteriorized into tangible expressions.

The virtual spaces themselves use a wide range of visual metaphors, with varying degrees of real-world fidelity, to evoke the particular "spaces" around which people interact. Depending on the purposive activity-centric design of the site—whether people are interacting around a simulated social context (speaking in a foreign language in a foreign neighborhood, a virtual graduation, or co-planning virtual land use) or around data (conducting research around a certain problem-solution) or around performance (the enactment of a play using digital avatars) or displays (a virtual gallery art show), each context

involves particular technological affordances and constraints, and rules of interactivity (whether implied or explicit).

A more complex conceptualization of interactivity is open-ended. Virtual immersive spaces that enable human-embodied avatars to express themselves in rich modalities enable this more open-ended interactivity—because the people involved may take a conversation or performance in any direction that they choose. They may script their avatars with various appearances and behaviors. They may co-create 3D objects as a further extension of free-form creativity. Chance encounters may change the direction of a shared endeavor. The individuals participating may improvise and take the work in new directions.

The Benefits of High-Touch Interactivity

In practice, high-touch interactivity refers to the amount of human engagement: the sharing of information, inter-communications, shared collaborations, and endeavors. Interactivity has been found to enhance the user experience in interactive art (Gonzales, Finley, & Duncan, 2009, p. 415). Interactivity between individuals and a company-sponsored site may establish a kind of trust (Yao & Li, 2008). Interactivity with fictional characters has been found to raise audience empathy in interactive narratives (Hand & Varan, 2009, p. 39). Interactivity may enhance artistic experiences (Sundar, Xu, & Bellur, 2010, p. 2247).

In e-learning, interactivity enhances the depth of the learning, as expressed through social cognition and constructivism. Research has found a possible relationship between interactivity and creativity (Shaw, Arnason, & Belardo, 1993), which suggests that complex divergent learning may benefit from selective types of interactivity (such as the interactivity between novices and amateurs with subject matter experts, in the "zone of proximal development"). High-touch interactivity is necessarily linked to complex learning, with wider degrees of freedom—as in the interactions between doctoral students and their faculty advisors—in the design of complex research, analysis, and design.

Figure 1 offers a conceptualization of interactivity on a continuum from low-touch to high-touch. On the low-touch end, the interactivity is pre-designed and limited in terms of actual choices and functions. The learning that occurs there may be rote memorization or practice-based learning. On the other end of the continuum would be high-touch interactivity, which is often human-facilitated and engages complex learning. Theoretically and practically, the interactivity may be unlimited, with open-ended, serendipitous, and complex—because of the high human presence in these interactions. This continuum does not suggest that any sort of interactivity is preferable over another; rather, the level of interactivity should suit the learning objectives, learning context, and learner needs. Basic knowledge of a domain "may be best gained passively, but that knowledge about how to behave and what questions to ask in that domain are best gained through active involvement" (Richards, 2006, p. 59).

Further, the figure shows that the degrees of freedom for users on the low end constrain not only their choices but potentially their conceptualizations of the subject. As their understanding grows, and the scaffolding for the learning diminishes, they may participate as apprentices in the field. This greater level of creative authorship in an interactive work may result in deeper engagement and may lead to the participant's own designs and creativity (Willis, 2006, p. 731). Not only is interactive multimedia richness one potential result of modern Information and Communication Technologies (ICT), but the scope, frequency, intensity, and depth of communications may be enhanced—in both synchronous (real-time) and asynchronous (non-real-time) ways. Communications channels exist for public, semi-public, and private interactions, with both front- and back-channel communications during live web-mediated events. Communications now may be archived for future use; they may be more widely searchable.

In various cases of distributed learning, the distributed cognition is harnessed into interactivity through the uses of digital learning objects and shared mediated experiences. The literature offers little about the way digital contents and experiences are used to evoke interactivity—in the form of conversations, co-creations, information-sharing, collaborations, and simulations.

The building of automated interactions involves a deep level of complexity. Tomlinson points out how linear and interactive animations differ, particularly around the locus of the animated character's decision-making. In traditional linear animations, the animators, writers, and directors "intuit the behavior that the characters should undertake" (Tomlinson, 2005, p. 6). They then create the visuals and sounds and multimedia to convey the decisions. By contrast, interactive animations need to codify those design decisions

Figure 1. Digital object and virtual experience high-touch interactivity continuum

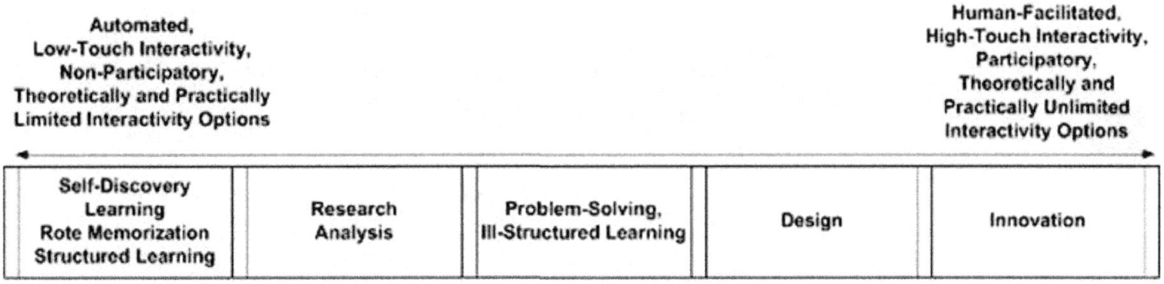

Automated, Low-Touch Interactivity, Non-Participatory, Theoretically and Practically Limited Interactivity Options				Human-Facilitated, High-Touch Interactivity, Participatory, Theoretically and Practically Unlimited Interactivity Options
Self-Discovery Learning Rote Memorization Structured Learning	Research Analysis	Problem-Solving, Ill-Structured Learning	Design	Innovation

into complex computer commands that have digital characters making the same decisions on-the-fly depending on how users interact with the system. Further, Tomlinson describes the concept of negative space, the uses of the blank space around an object to help a draftsperson not draw his or her mental model of a thing but rather the thing itself. Given the generalized stereotypes that exist in most people's heads, many will draw what is in their minds instead of what is actually there. In the same way, individuals who create animated characters define those characters not only by defining who they are but also who they are not (the "negative spaces" around a character).

This notion may be extrapolated to the behavior of animated characters as well. A character is defined not just by what it does, but by what it fails to do or what it is unable to do. In a linear animation, the behavior of each character may be witnessed in its entirety; a linear animator can

see the actions that a character takes and the actions that a character does not take. By thinking about the character's "negative behavior space," the animator may gain another perspective on the character as a whole (Tomlinson, 2005, p. 7).

HIGH-TOUCH INTERACTIVITY IN E-LEARNING

To analyze high-touch interactivity in both (1) digital learning contents and (2) virtual experiences, it will be important to consider both the contents and the virtual experiences—which are actually related. In many cases, digital learning contents are experienced over time as part of a learning sequence. In terms of analysis, looking at contents independently of the learner experience will be over-simplifying the situation. Looking at a virtual experience without considering some of the digital artifacts involved would also be limiting.

Figure 2. Digital Poster Sessions (used by permission of Susan Manning, 2010)

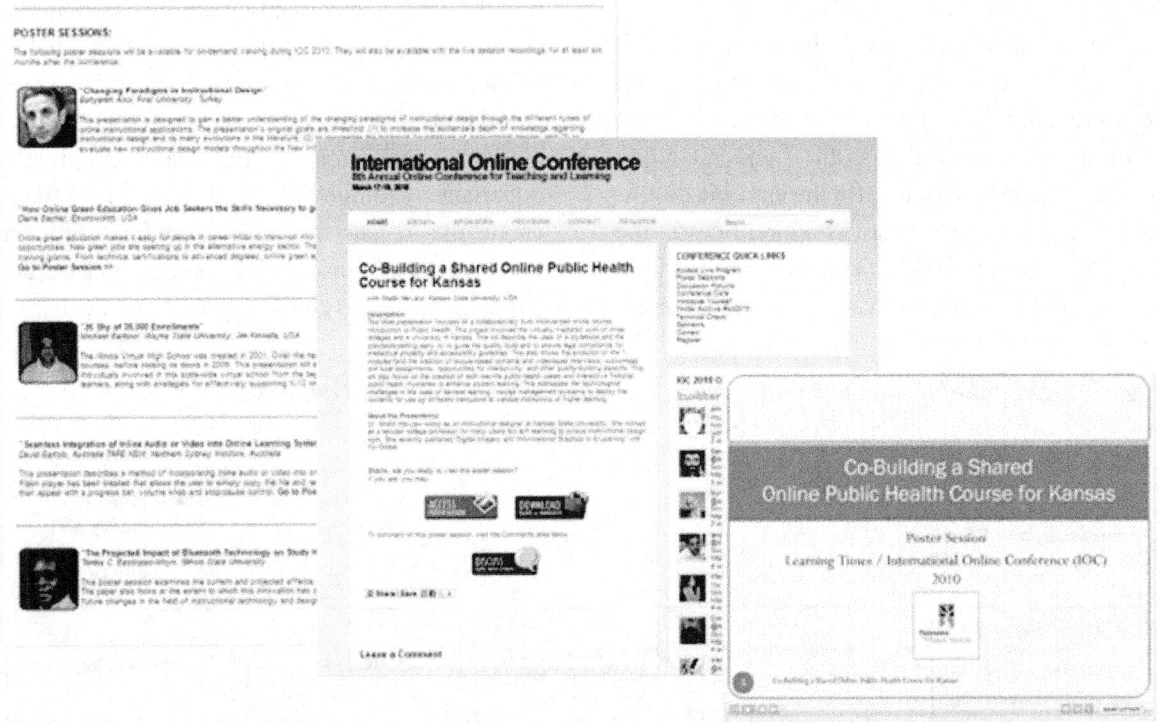

Table 1. Digital contents and virtual experiences that promote high-touch interactivity

Digital Contents and Virtual Experiences			
Digital Contents	**Correlating Virtual Experiences**	**Individual Learning**	**Group Learning**
Knowledge and Knowledge Spaces			
1. Traditional Digital Learning Objects: Videos / podcasts / audio files articles / e-books / publications / blog entries / web documents / displays / digital kiosks (electronic and virtual) / digital art / digital poster sessions	Discussions; Jigsaw exercises (individuals each conduct original research and then share their findings to the group); Research; Paper writing and critique	Data exploration; Individual question consideration; Short answer / short essay analysis Research; Light experiential learning; Informational visualizations	Group discussions; Group case analyses; Group simulations; Group research projects; Group research papers; Group research; Group fieldtrips; Group data exploration; Informational visualizations
2. Digital Repositories and Referatories / Gallery Shows / Collaborative Knowledge Spaces: Digital repositories (multimedia, images, audio files, and others) / publications / digital collections – gallery shows / wikis	Information archival and sharing; Topic-based immersions; Shared digital experiences	Individual research	Communities of practice; networks of practice Collaborative co-learning and co-research; Co-design
3. Information Gathering, Creation, and Analysis: Surveys and questionnaires / data mining / analytical tools / fresh datasets	Research; Experiment setup; The conducting of (usually social) experiments	Information gathering	Analysis and interpretation
Time-Based Events and Sequences			
4. Live Webcasting (Synchronous Events): Webcasts with voice over IP (VOIP / live chat / dual face-to-face and virtual presentations with remote participation of audience members	Synchronous human interactivity; Virtual conference or colloquium participation; Digital poster sessions (complementary to live interactive sequences)	Idea generation, articulation, and sharing; More comprehensive understandings	Idea generation, articulation, and sharing; More comprehensive understandings
5. Discrete Online Courses/ Learning Sequences / Learning Modules: Learning / course management systems (L/ CMSes) and virtual immersive spaces / sequenced and mixed learning activities	Asynchronous human interactivity	Idea generation, articulation, and sharing; More comprehensive understandings	Idea generation, articulation, and sharing; More comprehensive understandings
Virtual and Attentional Immersions			
6. Digital Laboratories and Simulations: Digital laboratories	Digital laboratories and lab learning sequences; Virtual experiment conducting and journaling	Learning of processes and procedures; Hands-on proxy practice; Lab journaling	Learning of processes and collaborations; Lab journaling
7. Digital Stories: Digital storytelling / cases	Digital storytelling; Shared story creation; Shared immersive experiences of storytelling	Design; Storytelling; Self-expression; User-created contents	Participatory design; User-created contents

continued on following page

Table 1. Continued

Digital Contents and Virtual Experiences			
Digital Contents	**Correlating Virtual Experiences**	**Individual Learning**	**Group Learning**
8. Virtual Immersive Spaces: Immersive spaces (recorded) / virtual social events (recorded) / back-end data mining reports / interactive whiteboard / text chat / voice chat / digital poster sessions / human-embodied avatar-mediated interactivity / artificial intelligence-driven avatars	Virtual social events; Assigned collaborations; Immersive spaces	*Machinima* or "machine cinema" (character creation, script writing, set design, directing, video capture, etc.) ; Acculturation; Role plays; Interactions with artificial intelligence (AI) avatars Self-discovery explorations; Creation and design / the building and scripting of 3D digital objects; Problem-based learning; Project-based learning	*Machinima* (character creation, script writing, set design, directing, video capture, etc.); Group acculturation; Social interactions via human-embodied avatars; Digital plays; Foreign language practice; Group simulations; Co-creation and design / the building and scripting of 3D digital object; Problem-based learning; Project-based learning
9. Electronic Games: Objective-based; Serious games; Stand-alone games	Immersive and persistent games; Design of game characters; Continuing storylines; Transferable skills; Parallel universe	Skills practice; Inductive learning;	Team strategizing and play;
Virtual Community			
10. Virtual Community Building with User-Created Contents: Intercommunications; shared histories; unique identities; virtual community building; student portfolios	Learning community building; Student portfolio discussion and analysis	Learner self-expression; Learner analysis of others' works; Acquisition of the language and terminology and practices of the field; Uses of technologies; Socialization into a field	Peer critique; Learner self-expression; Learner analysis of others' works; Acquisition of the language and terminology and practices of the field; Socialization into a field
Mixed Reality Spaces			
11. Mixed Reality / Mobile Learning / Ubiquitous Learning / Geographical Information Systems: Mixed reality (both virtual and physical objects) / digital installations / smart spaces / mobile device objects / locative devices	Augmented reality experiences; Games; Ubiquitous learning experiences (some location-sensitive / some location-insensitive); GIS systems and integrated datasets	Integration of digital information streams in a real-space situation; Navigation in physical space; Multi-sensory explorations; Self-expression; Aesthetic appreciation; Spatial explorations; Decision-making	Multi-sensory exploration; Self-expression; Group spatial exploration; Aesthetic appreciation; Coordination with other team members; Problem-solving; Decision-making

To explore this issue further, it is important to consider the wide ranges of digital contents and virtual experiences. These digital objects and spaces may be designed and created by students, instructors, commercial content creators, subject matter experts, amateurs—or any mix of the above. It is helpful to observe that any of the following may be human-facilitated or not, depending on the complexity of the learning objectives and the divergence of the learning. Table 1 offers a basic conceptualization of these ideas.

Human facilitated guidance of interactivity around contents may involve a variety of learning aims: ascertaining the veracity of information; surfacing information; discussing aesthetics; exploring design solutions; synthesizing informa-

Figure 3. The Instructional Design Open Studio (IDOS) Blog

Figure 4. A Live 3D Weather Simulation by NOAA in Second Life ®

tion across multiple sources; evoking and eliciting personal experiences and insights; analyzing information; inspiring innovations and creations; analyzing live situations, and projecting into the future. Learners may be asked to practice different analytical techniques and analytical frameworks. They may be asked to surface complex ethical insights. The interactions are built to extract and build meaning, to improve the quality of analysis, and to introduce serendipity into the work.

REAL-WORLD EXAMPLES OF HIGH-TOUCH INTERACTIVITY

It is beyond the purview of this chapter to include in-depth examples from all the different types of digital contents and virtual experiences that enhance interactivity. Some real-world cases are lightly introduced below along with some analysis about how these digital learning contents and virtual experiences may be analyzed for high-touch.

Knowledge and Knowledge Spaces

1. Traditional Digital Learning Objects (see Figures 2-4 and Table 2)
2. Digital Repositories and Referatories / Gallery Shows / Collaborative Knowledge Spaces (see Figure 5 and Table 3)
3. Information Gathering, Creation, and Analysis (see Figure 6 and Table 4)

Time-Based Events and Sequences

4. Live Webcasting (Synchronous Events) (See Figure 7 and Table)
5. Discrete Online Courses/ Learning Sequences / Learning Modules (see Figure 8 and Table 6)

Immersions

6. Digital Laboratories and Simulations (see Figure 9 and Table 7)
7. Digital Stories (see Figure 10 and Table 8)
8. Virtual Immersive Spaces (see Figure 11 and Table 9)
9. Electronic Games (see Table 10)

Virtual Community

10. Virtual Community Building with User-Created Contents (see Figure 12 and Table 11)

Mixed Reality Spaces

11. Mixed Reality / Mobile Learning / Ubiquitous Learning / Geographical Information Systems (See Table 12)

DESIGNING FOR HIGH-TOUCH INTERACTIVITY

High-touch learning may enhance learner motivations in their learning; may offer opportunities for more complex learning; may help learners achieve more complex world views and empathetic understandings; and may enhance divergent learning and innovations. This work in analyzing the features that enhance high-touch interactivity in digital content and virtual experience designs highlights some basic elements.

Preliminary Learning and Continuing Support

For high-touch interactivity to work well in online courses, learners need to have clear preliminary learning for the particular topic area. They have to have a clear sense of their respective roles and work. They need to access to resources for their

Figure 5. ELATEwiki (The E-Learning and Teaching Exchange wiki)

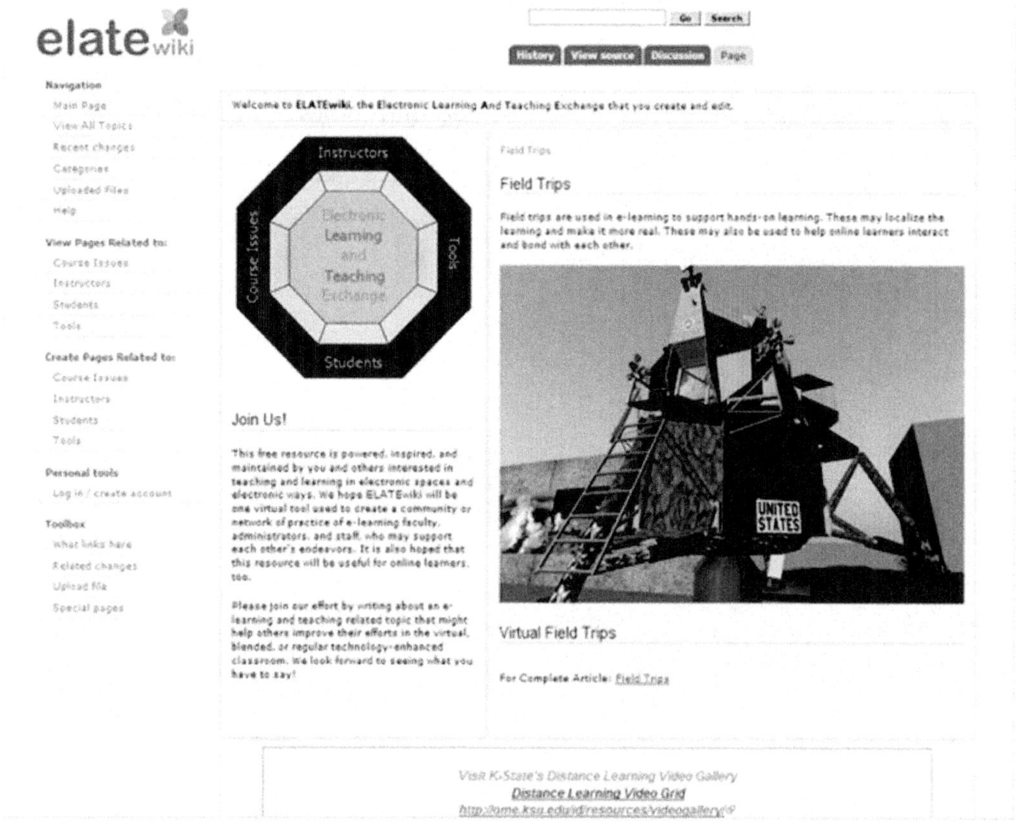

Table 2. Traditional Digital Learning Objects

Analyzing Digital Contents for High-Touch Interactivity	Analyzing Virtual Experiences for High-Touch Interactivity
•Do learners have an opportunity to vote on the digital contents? •Do people comment on the digital contents? (low-touch interactivity) •Do people create counter-multimedia objects in responses to an earlier digital object? •Do the objects spark (inspire) activities among a group of learners? •Do the digital objects spark conversations and debates? Is the digital object real-world? Does it simulate reality?	•Is the learning object used in the context of group learning: A case study? A role play? A simulation? A long-term research project? A field trip? •Does the learning draw on a variety of skill sets by members of a team, who must each rely on the others for the ultimate success of the project? •Do the designed assignments include all necessary information, or do learners have to seek out further information? •Do the learners have to create or design something new from the learning materials as part of a team? •Are the digital learning contents part of an online colloquium, conference, gallery show, or other participatory event?

research, collaborations, designs, and other aspects of learning. They need the necessary facilitation and support in order to enable the ill-structured learning.

Defined Learning Objectives

High-touch interactivity requires a clear integration with the overall learning experience. It clearly has to make sense in the context of the learning; it should not be added on for its own sake. High-

Figure 6. A Screenshot of an Opening Page of a Survey

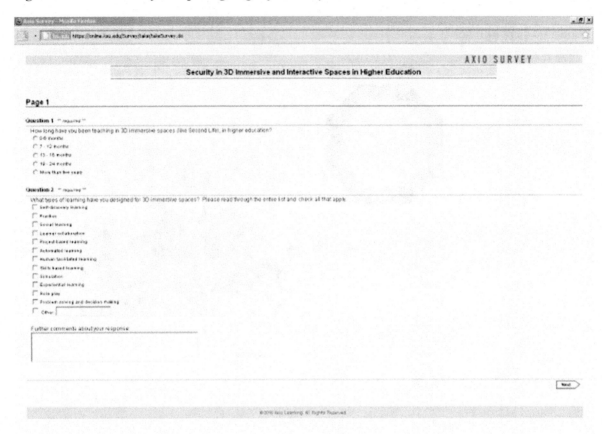

Table 3. Digital Repositories and Referatories / Gallery Shows / Collaborative Knowledge Spaces

Analyzing Digital Contents for High-Touch Interactivity	Analyzing Virtual Experiences for High-Touch Interactivity
•Do learners have a role in creating self-expressive contents for the site or repository or show? •Do learners create new knowledge? •Do learners have a role to analyze and even reverse-engineer the contents? •Do learners build to semi-professional or professional standards? •Do learners conduct research on the site?	•Do the learners co-create contents for the knowledge spaces? •Do the learners share their research with each other? •Do learners co-create contents for the site?

touch interactivity requires investments by both the instructor and the learners. It demands more synchronous time, which is expensive for learners. If high-touch interactivity is non-purposive, learners will not see the value of such an endeavor. If it is ill-defined, learners may be overwhelmed with frustration and not benefit from the learning opportunity.

Figure 7. An Interactive Slide during a Live Web Presentation on Elluminate™ Software through the International Online Conference (2010)

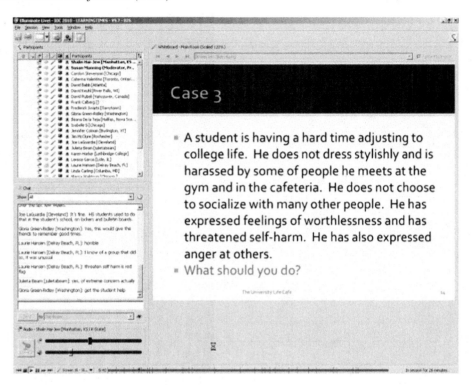

Table 4. Information Gathering, Creation, and Analysis

Analyzing Digital Contents for High-Touch Interactivity	Analyzing Virtual Experiences for High-Touch Interactivity
•Are learners gathering and creating new information for analysis and use? •Does their research work involve interacting with a range of others (such as through surveys and questionnaires, or through aggregated data-mining of socio-technical sites)? •Are the research findings shared with a broader audience?	•Are groups gathering and creating new information for analysis and use? •Are there interdependencies between people who are interacting around information, knowledge, and / or shared interests? •Does the work require mixed skill sets and interdependencies?

Table 5. Live Webcasting (Synchronous Events)

Analyzing Digital Contents for High-Touch Interactivity	Analyzing Virtual Experiences for High-Touch Interactivity
•Are each of the individual participants invited to share their ideas through the text, voice, or other communications channel? •Are there front and back channels? •Are there learning artifacts created by each of the participants? •Is there a wide range of learning objectives for the participants of the live web event?	•Do the participants in the live web event interact with the presenter? •Do the participants in the live web event interact with each other? •Are there shared learning objectives among the participants? Are there diverse learning objectives among the participants? •Has the (projected) audience affected the creation of the presentation contents? •Are the presentation contents real-world? Is the presentation built to meet real-world standards? •Do the participants of the event co-create some responses? Some other contents?

Figure 8. Learning Sequences Maximize the Uses of Time for High-Touch Interactivity

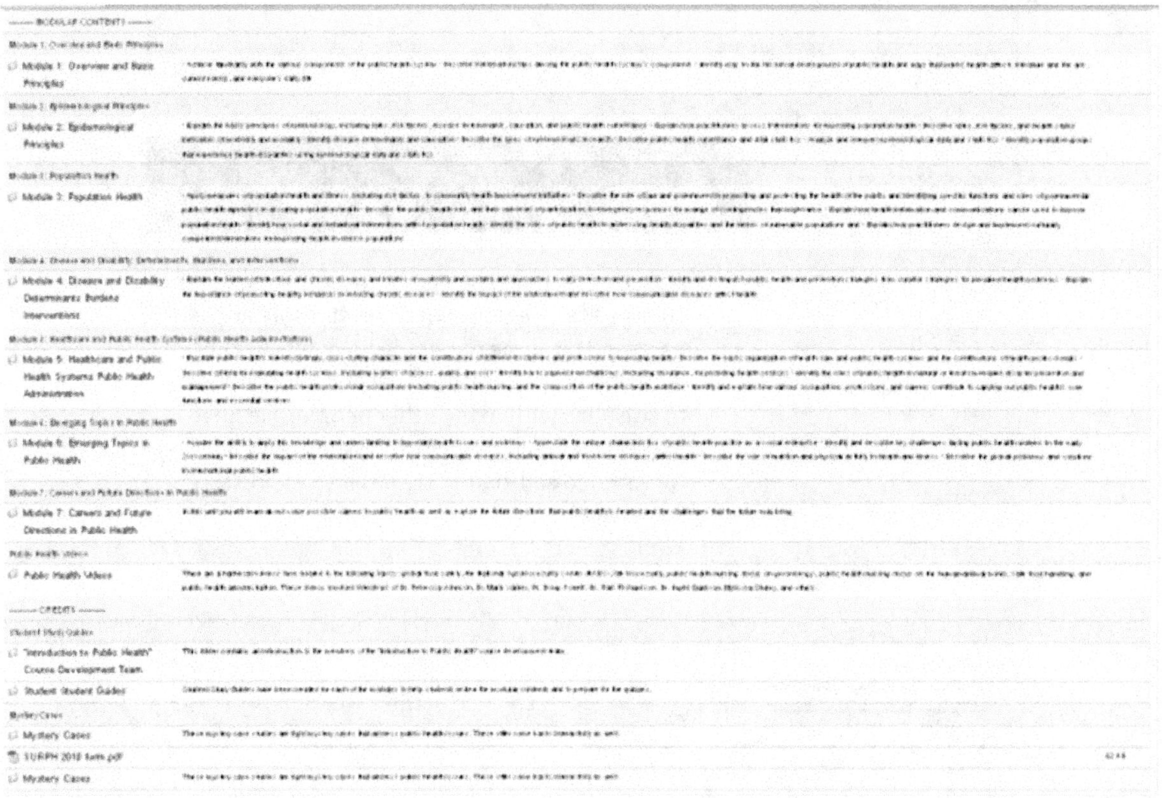

Table 6. Discrete Online Courses/ Learning Sequences / Learning Modules

Analyzing Digital Contents for High-Touch Interactivity	Analyzing Virtual Experiences for High-Touch Interactivity
•Are learners asked to post responses and work that their peers will read and use for their learning? •Do the learners create and share digital artifacts that they have created? Are these artifacts peer-critiqued and analyzed by their peers for learning purposes?	•Are the learners assigned to group work? •Do the learners work together for shared learning, such as through jigsaw research and sharing exercises? •Do the learners interact with the instructor during synchronous interactions? •Do the learners interact with each other during synchronous interactions? •Do the learners create and share digital artifacts demonstrating their learning? Are these artifacts made available semi-publicly or publicly in e-portfolios or through other venues? •Are there ways to tailor messages and collaborations to sub-groups within the larger community? •Are there ways to help members with similar interests to find each other for collaboration? •Are there ways to establish a digital memory of each participant's past behaviors in order to create trust and to enable further constructive interactions? •Is there a way to demonstrate individual telepresence? Group or multi-member social presence?

Figure 9. An Interactive and Fictional Public Health Case Study: "Mystery in a Feedlot"

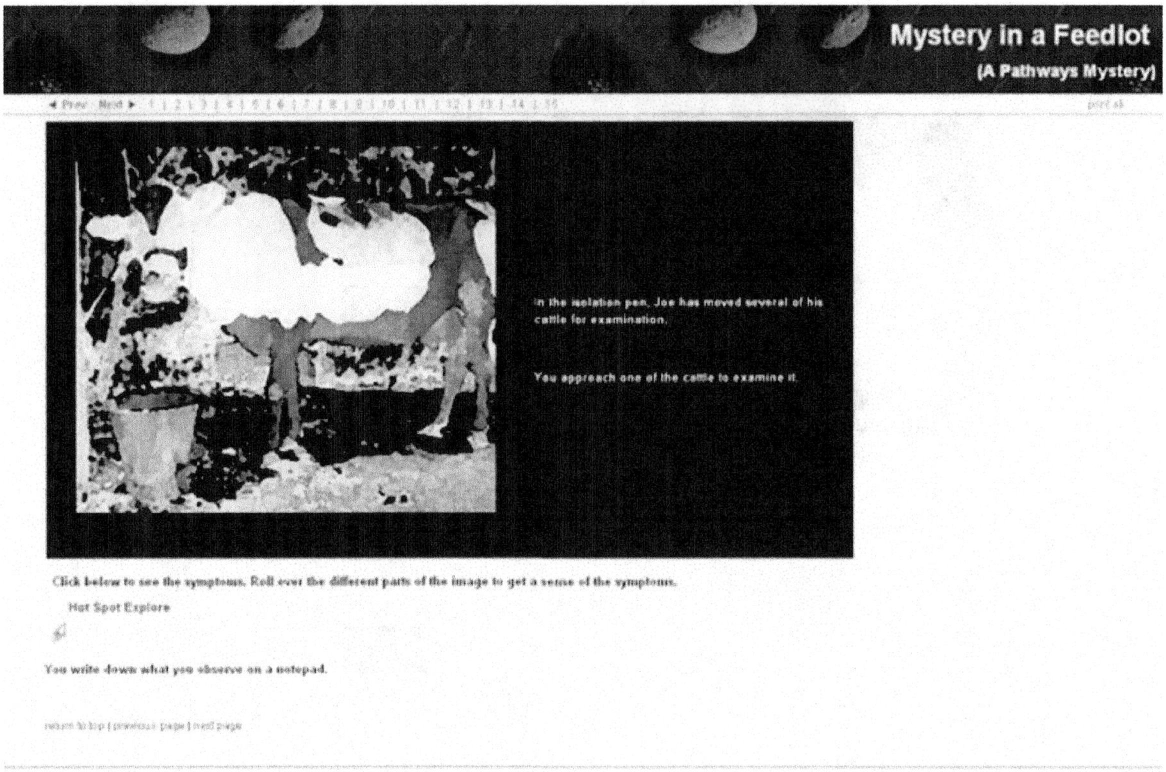

Table 7. Digital Laboratories and Simulations

Analyzing Digital Contents for High-Touch Interactivity	Analyzing Virtual Experiences for High-Touch Interactivity
•Is the learning in the digital laboratory or simulation real-world? •Does the learning involve simulated intelligence agents? •Are there learning artifacts that students create from their uses of the digital laboratories and simulations that benefit the learning of other students? •Do learners interact with their instructor or peers at any point in the digital laboratory / simulation lead-up? During the digital laboratory / simulation? After the digital laboratory / simulation? (These may be synchronous or asynchronous types of interactivity.)	•Do learners have synchronous or asynchronous shared tasks with their peers as part of the digital laboratory or simulation? •Do learners co-create learning artifacts (such as working on a shared wiki) as part of the digital laboratory or simulation experience? •Do learners interact with each other and / or a human facilitator via human-embodied avatars? •Do learners depend on each other's skill sets for their own learning—in an interdependent way? •Do the learners communicate with each other through single or multiple channels before, during, and after the digital laboratories and simulations?

Shared Power in the Learning Context

High-touch interactivity would benefit from the dispersion of power in a learning context. Here, the instructor may expect learners to engage in participatory design of the learning. Here, learners' voices and preferences do matter, and their autonomy, agency, and self-efficacy are emphasized.

Figure 10. The Suzy's Strategies Webisode Series for the University Life Café

Figure 11. Human-Embodied Avatars Interact in Second Life®

Table 8. Digital Stories

Analyzing Digital Contents for High-Touch Interactivity	Analyzing Virtual Experiences for High-Touch Interactivity
•Can learners comment on the stories that they experience? •Do the opinions of learners affect the direction of a story? •Do learners create their own stories? Do they generate user-created contents in various forms (Scripts? Videos? Presentations? Photo slideshows? Others?) •Do learners share their works with each other and comment on each other's works? •Do learners create digital artifacts to enhance the telling of digital stories?	•Do learners co-create the stories by interacting with each other? •Do they create story-derived digital artifacts (such as imaginary learning personas in Facebook™ or fictional digital artifacts or other derivative elements)? •Do learners role-play particular roles to tell certain stories? •Do learners work on teams to co-create digital stories? •Do learners play roles in a certain enactment or re-enactment of a story? Do learners have a wide range of freedom in making decisions about the directions of the story? •Are student works archived for future uses by future learners? By the general public?

Table 9. Virtual Immersive Spaces

Analyzing Digital Contents for High-Touch Interactivity	Analyzing Virtual Experiences for High-Touch Interactivity
•Are there communications channels for asynchronous communications in the virtual immersive space? •Are there communications channels for synchronous communications in the virtual immersive space? •Is there a way to record live interactions for later analysis and observation? •Are learners able to modify their human-embodied avatars for particular styles? •Are the human-embodied avatars given a wide range of freedom of actions in their interactions? •Are human-embodied avatars able to create 3D objects in-world?	•Are human-embodied avatars able to interact with each other in the virtual spaces? •Do the learners interact with each other through their human-embodied avatars in persistent virtual spaces (that last over time)? •Do the human-embodied avatars have to work with other human-embodied avatars to enhance the learning? Do they have shared tasks and interdependencies? •Do the learners have to create new contents from their immersive learning experiences? •Do the learners create new 3D objects in-world? •Are there ways to tailor messages and collaborations to sub-groups within the larger community? •Are there ways to help members with similar interests to find each other for collaboration? •Are there ways to establish a digital memory of each participant's past behaviors in order to create trust and to enable further constructive interactions? •Is there a way to demonstrate individual telepresence? Group or multi-member social presence?

Encouraging Learner Interdependencies

The learning objectives must require human interactions and interdependencies to encourage shared tasks that draw on different learners' various skill sets.

Telepresences and Social Presences

High-touch interactivity requires clear user identities and even a sense of history about each of the learners. There also need to be social presences—or a shared awareness of the various other individuals participating in the high-touch interactivity. Individual learners have to be able to find others with shared interests and to then be able to interact both at the sub-group level and at the larger-group levels in terms of communications and collaborations.

Real-World Constraints

The more real-world the learning is, the more the learning objects must be constrained by professional realities and requirements. These requirements often bring in Subject Matter Experts (SMEs) from a particular domain, to serve

Figure 12. The University Life Café: A Virtual Community to Promote Emotional Well being in University Students

as critics and judges of learner works. These promote high-touch interactivity both within the class and beyond because these draw in people from the larger environment.

High-Level Innovation

There needs to be a higher level of innovation and creativity expected, and often, these created digital learning objects may need to be shared within the

Table 10. Electronic Games

Analyzing Digital Contents for High-Touch Interactivity	Analyzing Virtual Experiences for High-Touch Interactivity
•Does the play include real-time interactivity with live players? •Does the game have implications outside of the game space? Does the game affect life outside the game? (Are there aspects of the game that are real-world?) •Are there channels for the players in the game to communicate and interact?	•Is there competition between live players as part of the gameplay? •Is communication a required element of the gameplay in terms of coordination? •Do learners have to work with other learners in order to achieve their learning aims in the game? •Do the learners create new digital contents as part of the game-play? Are these contents preserved for later use by others?

Table 11. Virtual Community Building with User-Created Contents

Analyzing Digital Contents for High-Touch Interactivity	Analyzing Virtual Experiences for High-Touch Interactivity
•Are participants to a site able to create their own account? Are they able to post messages and digital contents to the site? •Are participants able to see others' postings to the site? Are they able to experience the "social presence" of others to the site? •Are users of a site able to contact those who've created the site to get feedback? Are they able to change the contents of the site based on commentary and feedback given to the originators of the site?	•Are learners interacting with others on the site in terms of communications? •Can users of a site collaborate with others to create contents? •Do the actions of some members of the virtual community affect the lived lives of others? •Are there ways to tailor messages and collaborations to sub-groups within the larger community? •Are there ways to help members with similar interests to find each other for collaboration? •Are there ways to establish a digital memory of each participant's past behaviors in order to create trust and to enable further constructive interactions? •Is there a way to demonstrate individual telepresence? Group or multi-member social presence?

Table 12. Mixed Reality

Analyzing Digital Contents for High-Touch Interactivity	Analyzing Virtual Experiences for High-Touch Interactivity
•Are learners expected to create part (or all) of the mixed-reality display or installation? •Do users provide feedback to the facilitator during the mixed reality experience?	•Are learners co-creating part (or all) of the mixed-reality display or installation? •Do learners have a shared task which is executed with other team members in the mixed reality space? •Do learners communicate with their peers while engaging the physical space?

classroom and even a broader public—possibly even the world. Quality learning objects should be well curated for future use and the preservation of quality work.

Accessibility

Accessibility in high-touch learning may be construed in two critical ways. One is that the learners all have the basic technological infrastructure to connect with and collaborate with peers. The other more legal definition involves accessibility in terms of accommodations for various sensory and symbolic processing disabilities in people.

Some of these features have been built into various digital learning contents and virtual experiences. However, so far, there have not been coherent efforts for building for high-touch interactivity in e-learning. This initial analysis offers some early approaches for building for these very human virtual-collaborative needs.

FUTURE CONSIDERATIONS

More digital contents and virtual experiences are coming online daily. This area provides opportunities for more research and applied design to create richer high-touch interactivity in a higher education context. There are many opportunities for research to answer basic questions.

In specific domain fields, what are strategies for enhancing high-touch interactivity? How may user interfaces be designed to better enhance high-touch interactivity? How may human needs for collaboration be enhanced through new communications and collaboration tools and virtual community spaces? What are ways to harness learning sequences that may make high-touch interactivity more effective? How many people interact more constructively around information and the building of new knowledge? What are some ways to enhance human problem-solving in a high-touch interactive way to benefit the larger publics? What are ways to enhance long-term persistence and learner attention in terms of communities of practice? How may user satisfaction in virtual communities be increased and enhanced from the academic realm into the professional one?

In terms of free-form high-touch interactivity, it would seem that digital contents and virtual experiences will have to be harnessed by those with experiences in constructive interactivity for salience and effective person-to-person interactivity. Online tools may be created to help those with shared interests harness such unformed contents and experiences for mutually beneficial endeavors.

CONCLUSION

High-touch interactivity is critical in online learning, particularly in higher education. Designing various digital content and virtual experiences to improve such human investments in their own and each other's learning and creativity may magnify the efficacy of online learning and virtual community work.

ACKNOWLEDGMENT

Collegial team-based projects for instructional design are the most engaging—and I am grateful to Brent A. Anders, Dr. Deborah J. Briggs, Zachary Caby, Mary Werick, and others for their very fun and collegial work on global public health. Their work showed me that friendship and technologies can really help cut through space-time. This is for R. Max.

REFERENCES

Craven, M., Taylor, I., Drozd, A., Purbrick, J., Greenhalgh, C., & Benford, S. … Hoch, M. (2001). Exploiting interactivity, influence, space and time to explore non-linear drama in virtual worlds. In the *Proceedings of Human Factors in Computer Systems (CHI 2001)*. Seattle, WA: CHI.

Gonzales, A. L., Finley, T., & Duncan, S. P. (2009). (Perceived) interactivity: Does interactivity increase enjoyment and creative identity in artistic spaces. In the *Proceedings of CHI 2009*, (pp. 415-418). Boston, MA: CHI.

Hand, S., & Varan, D. (2009). Interactive stories and the audience: Why empathy is important. *ACM Computers in Entertainment*, 7(3), 1–14. doi:10.1145/1594943.1594951

Jensen, J. F. (2008). The concept of interactivity—Revisited: Four new typologies for a new media landscape. In *Proceedings of the uxTV 2008 Conference*, (pp. 129-132). Silicon Valley, CA: Association of Computing Machinery.

Lim, Y.-K., Lee, S.-S., & Lee, K.-Y. (2009). Interactivity attributes: A new way of thinking and describing interactivity. In the *Proceedings of CHI 2009*, (pp. 105-108). Boston, MA: CHI.

Polaine, A. (2005). The flow principle in interactivity. In the *Proceedings of the Second Australasian Conference on Interactive Entertainment*, (pp. 151-158). Sydney, Australia: ACM.

Richards, D. (2006). Is interactivity actually important? In the *Proceedings of the 3rd Australasian Conference on Interactive Entertainment*, (pp. 59-66). ACM.

Shaw, T., Arnason, K., & Belardo, S. (1993). The effects of computer mediated interactivity on idea generation: An experimental investigation. *IEEE Transactions on Systems, Man, and Cybernetics*, *23*(3), 737–745. doi:10.1109/21.256546

Sundar, S. S., Xu, Q., & Bellur, S. (2010). Designing interactivity in media interfaces: A communications perspective. In the Proceedings of CHI 2010, (pp. 2247-2256). Atlanta, GA: CHI.

Tholander, J., & Johansson, C. (2010). Bodies, boards, clubs, and bugs: A study of bodily engaging artifacts. In the *Proceedings of CHI 2010*, (pp. 4045-4050). Atlanta, GA: CHI.

Tomlinson, B. (2005). From linear to interactive animation: How autonomous characters change the process and product of animating. *ACM Computers in Entertainment*, *3*(1), 1–20.

Willis, K. D. D. (2006). *User authorship and creativity within interactivity. In the Proceedings of Multimedia (MM 2006)* (pp. 731–735). Santa Barbara, CA: ACM.

Yao, G., & Li, Q. (2008). *Exploring the effects of interactivity on consumer trust in e-retailing*. IEEE.

KEY TERMS AND DEFINITIONS

Archival: The long-term storage of digital objects.

Autopoeisic: Self-generating.

Collaboration: The process of working together with others on a shared endeavor.

Engagement: Deep attention.

High-Touch Interactivity: The deep human involvement in intercommunicating and collaborating.

Human-Facilitated: Led or coordinated by a person.

Immersive: Relating to a perceptual experience that involves multiple senses; in-world; the feeling of being submerged or transported (through the human imagination and digitally-evoked sensory details) in a particular experience or virtual space.

Interactivity: The act of communicating and collaborating in close relationship with other people (or with computing machines).

Mediated: Facilitated or made possible by machine or technology as a conduit of information.

Participatory Design: The inclusion of end-users in early and continuing stages of design to ensure the usefulness, aesthetics, and fit of a particular consumer object.

Referatory: A collection or store of links to digital objects and virtual spaces.

Repository: A collection or store of digital objects.

Section 2
Virtual Work Research Methods and Approaches

Chapter 9
The Role of Experiments in the Study of Virtual Groups

Lisa Slattery Walker
University of North Carolina – Charlotte, USA

Anita L. Blanchard
University of North Carolina – Charlotte, USA

Heather Burnett
Bank of America, USA

ABSTRACT

In this chapter, the authors discuss the use of experimental methods in the study of virtual groups. For some time, experimentalists have hoped, as noted in Bainbridge (2007), that virtual worlds would provide a locale for research. The authors discuss practical techniques for doing so, and provide a detailed example of one such experiment as a platform for discussing opportunities and potential pitfalls for conducting research on virtual work groups. For convenience, they divide the steps in creating and conducting an experiment into several stages: design of the experiment, pre-testing, and statistical power of the data it produces. Each stage in any experiment presents challenges and requires decisions on the part of the experimenters; experiments conducted with virtual groups are certainly no exception.

INTRODUCTION

As noted in a recent issue of *Science* (Falk & Heckman, 2009), experiments are a major source of knowledge in the social sciences. Despite some reluctance among social scientists, experiments are gaining prominence. Thye (2007) notes that experiments provide advantages for developing social scientific theory that are unmistakable, such as identifying key processes in theories. Webster and Sell (2007) add that the range of usefulness of experiments in social scientific research has been traditionally understated. Finally, Falk and Heckman (2009) advocate that experiments are an important method to develop causal knowledge.

DOI: 10.4018/978-1-4666-0963-1.ch009

BACKGROUND

When it comes to virtual work, the role of experiments is both less developed but also potentially more promising than in many other areas of social scientific work. Bainbridge (2007) makes this case strongly, urging researchers to consider a variety of virtual settings for their experimental research, including virtual worlds such as Second Life, observational ethnographies online, and analysis of social networks. He views virtual settings as spaces where "people can work and interact in a somewhat realistic setting," which "have great potential as sites for research in the social, behavioral, and economic sciences" (Bainbridge, 2007, p. 317). Even *World of Warcraft*, a very popular massive multiple online role playing game, provides a viable location for examining virtual teams; players of this game cannot advance in any meaningful way without joining with others who have different skills and perspectives. While some online games consist of teams of friends who know each other in "real life," *World of Warcraft* teams are often composed of strangers who do not know each other offline (e.g., Miller, 2007). They can, therefore, provide rich environments for examining distributed teams whose primary mode of interaction is online.

We will leave it to others to explore this variety of virtual settings. Our objectives in this chapter are to describe the role formal experiments can play in the study of virtual work groups and provide some practical advice about conducting such experiments. We include an in-depth description of one such experiment as a case study for lessons learned.

CONDUCTING VIRTUAL GROUP EXPERIMENTS

Design of the Experiment

Experiments, at their best, are about theory-testing and causal knowledge. A researcher designing any experiment, including those conducted in the virtual worlds, should have a prediction about the results, derived from the abstract concepts of a theory (or from several theories). These abstract concepts must be rendered concrete and observable.

Primary among the decisions a researchers must make are: what variables—independent and dependent—will we measure? What will our situation be? What are our conditions and manipulations? There can be a tendency in virtual experiments to be limited to what others have already done (i.e., what others have programmed) without relying on the theoretical constructs to tell us what the most useful questions and answers will be.

Variables and Conditions

It is crucial that researchers are clear from the beginning of the design process just what the variables of interest are and how they will be measured or identified. Clear hypotheses identifying the independent and dependent variables and the exact relationship expected between them will go a long way toward creating a useful experiment.

Hypotheses can be, and often are, stated as "if… then" statements. To be most useful, hypotheses take the form of, "Given situation Z, if X, then Y." Here Z represents the setting or initial conditions under which the cause-effect relationship is expected to hold. X represents the independent variable. X will be introduced in some conditions but not others (or at varying levels across conditions). Y represents the dependent variable which the researcher will measure to compare against predictions derived from the theory.

Once the hypotheses are in place, the number of experimental conditions required can be determined. This process necessitates that the researcher have a good understanding of the variables, the relevant number of levels that each has, and the strength of manipulation (or magnitude of difference between the levels) of the independent variable which should cause a change in the dependent variables. If all relevant levels of the independent variable are not explored or the differences in the levels of the independent variable are not big enough, the resulting data may be meaningless.

Included in this category are experiments where necessary baseline conditions are not conducted or a full cross of the levels of multiple independent variables is not present (i.e., all levels of all independent variables combined together). That is not to say that a full cross or a baseline condition is always necessary; it is important for the researcher to have a theoretical understanding of the various possible levels of independent variables and why either all conditions should be included on only some need to be.

Manipulations

Manipulations are the part of an experiment in which the researchers create their independent variables within the context of the setting. Often for social scientists, this takes the form of some information either provided to or withheld from the participants. Such information can be about the tasks they will undertake, their role in the process, the others with whom they will be working, etc. Sometimes manipulations are simply the behavior of others (co-workers, teammates, the researcher) within that experimental setting.

Manipulations, in particular, require special attention in virtual experiments, as they are often the most nuanced part of an experiment and are also often the most crucial to participant behavior. For example, we are interested in how the technological features of an online group affect the members' perceptions of the viability of the group.

This is much like how the physical environment of, for example, a coffee shop affects the members' perceptions of its opportunities for interaction and comfort. Just as overly highlighting a table and chairs would alert coffee shop patrons that someone was purposefully trying to draw their attention to that area, the technological features of the online group must make sense and be natural in the experimental setting.

Manipulations should be believable, with a reasonable cover story. They should be repeated—all important pieces of differentiation of instructions should be repeated at least three times. MANIPULATIONS SHOULD NOT BE SUBTLE. They should be redundant and noticeable, even while remaining a natural part of the experimental setting. If the variables of interest are technological, rather than social, they are apt to be weaker, necessitating even less subtlety in manipulations. We have this particular challenge in our experiments to make sure that while we do not overly highlight the technological features, they are dramatically different enough to have an effect on the participants' perceptions of the interactivity and identity in the group. Good experiments include manipulation checks as part of their design. Detail is important for painting a full picture, but researchers should take care not to lose the tree for the beautiful, well-described, detailed forest.

Pre-Testing

Creating a successful experiment that creates the social situation desired is a difficult and multi-layered process. A great deal of information needs to be presented to participants in the experiment; some of this is presented explicitly (e.g., instructions on what to do), while other information is presented more subtlety (e.g., who the other participants are). Many factors are involved in enacting independent variables and in measuring dependent variables. Both sets of variables involve both theoretical and operational concepts. When done poorly, an experiment wastes the time and efforts of experimenters and participants and does not inform theory.

Of course, no experiment is perfect, but there are steps that can be taken to ensure that our abstract ideas from theory are realized in our operations in an experiment. In particular, attention can and should be paid to the "experimental instructions," the information presented to participants about the situation, their roles, possible behaviors, and outcomes. For example, in our study, we want our participants to be actively engaged in an online group. Therefore, our instructions are critical in helping develop the psychological realism (Aronson, Willson, & Brewer, 1998) for our participants. Because of the importance of experimental instructions, systematic evaluation of them and how participants interpret them is needed for knowing and standardizing their effects across conditions and even across experiments.

Whatever the particular design of an experiment, the design is communicated to participants through a set of instructions from the experimenter. In most cases of experiments in virtual work group settings, these instructions will be delivered on-screen. All pieces of information need to be presented in such a way, and using such language, that the participants can understand them with a reasonable level of attention. This is easier said than done.

Investigators have identified how experimental instructions can create experimenter effects. Experimenter effects are experimental design processes that can systematically bias results (Rosenthal, 1963). Fortunately, contemporary methods include strategies for identifying, measuring, and controlling these effects (such as pre-testing and computer control).

More recently, other investigators have documented the effects of some technological aspects of experiments such as video and computer technology (e.g., Cohen, 1988; Kiesler, Siegel, & McGuire, 1984; Troyer, 2001, 2002). The concern

of this work is not with how results may be biased for (or against) hypotheses, but instead with making sure that the theoretically-based parts of the experiment are being adequately communicated.

There are two main types of information that need to be conveyed in the experimental instructions: scope conditions (abstract statements of the situations in which a theory is expected to hold), and initial conditions (the features of the experimental situation that participants must understand). Scope conditions in our experimental example include telling the participants that we want them to evaluate a new online group. Initial conditions include telling the participants that this is a community relevant to their interests that they can join and participate in the conversation. For more detail on these types of information and examples of each, see Rashotte, Webster, and Whitmeyer (2005).

Appropriately conveying this information can be very difficult, especially in a virtual setting. The experimenter cannot always accurately judge the attention level and comprehension of the participant. Experiments also require that the experimenter create and maintain an alternate reality for some period of time. In a laboratory setting this is difficult, but in a virtual setting (in which participants may be in the library, a coffee shop, or their dorm room), the challenges of attention and comprehension can be even more difficult to attain.

One important tool used for ensuring that experimental instructions are being correctly interpreted and enacted by participants is through pre-testing. We believe that this tool is especially crucial in the virtual environment as a check on the validity of the design and operations at creating the situation needed. Virtual experiments often create very complicated social situations with multiple conditions, which may vary only slightly (e.g., the presence or absence of a technological feature).

Most experiments do make some attempt at checking for experimental soundness. However, this often does not include explicitly testing the experimental instructions. Further, it is frequently done at the end of a long experiment (sometimes lasting weeks or months), usually by question-naires. While end-of-study questionnaires are useful for examining other elements of a study, they may only tap into a small portion of the in-formation that a thorough pre-test of experimental instructions can provide. Additionally, a pretest of the instructions provides feedback at a time (before many cases have been collected) when it can be most useful.

As noted by Rashotte, Webster, and Whitmeyer (2005), pre-testing may be particularly important when information is delivered through only one medium, such as on-screen instructions to par-ticipants in a virtual setting experiment. These instructions should, but may not always, include repetition of key points. Pre-testing in these types of experiments asks participants to repeat what they have been instructed to do, lest they not be paying attention thoroughly. Without asking them to state the instructions in their own words during pre-testing, the experimenter cannot be sure what it is that the participants are hearing and, therefore, on what they are acting.

Pre-testing can also reveal unanticipated problems in the way the users are engaging in the experiment. During our pre-testing phase, we discovered that nearly half of our participants tried to enact the experiment on their smart phones. The smart phones, while common, cannot adequately support all of the technological features of our online groups. Therefore, we have included in the experimental instructions that participants must use a personal computer and not their smart phones to access our online groups.

Other forms of pre-testing are also important, including measuring instruction characteristics versus a set of target attributes (such as "authori-tative" or "friendly" or any other dimension seen as meaningful to the scope and initial conditions). As noted above, questionnaires at the end of an experiment can also provide useful information,

especially in-depth questionnaires presented to early participants (so that changes can be made if deemed necessary, before too much data has been collected).

Statistical Power

Power analyses are often overlooked, but they are particularly important in messy situations as online groups are apt to be. Statistical power analyses allow experimenters to determine a priori the number of subjects need in various conditions of the experiment before beginning data collection. They are relatively easy statistical computations and online calculators are readily available.

As noted in Keppel (1991), statistical power is best considered as the likelihood of not mak-ing a Type II error. Type II errors occur when one fails to reject a null hypothesis that is not true. As statistical power increases, the likelihood of failing to reject a false null hypothesis decreases. In other words, statistical power helps to make sure that a real effect is not missed.

This is of particular importance in virtual group experiments, where the researchers have less con-trol over the surrounding environment than they would in a laboratory face-to-face experiment. In the lab, one can reduce distractions and increase participants' focus on the task. This is not true if participants are not physically present in a lab, which is much more likely to be the case with virtual groups. One would expect more variation within conditions (i.e., noise) in virtual group experiments than in face-to-face experiments (Of course, sometimes experiments are conducted are virtual groups where everyone comes into a lab and then each participant is isolated physically, but this eliminates much of the benefit of conducting experiments with virtual groups.).

Statistical power depends on three factors: the probability of making a Type I error (the signifi-cance level, the probability of rejecting a null that is true), the size of the differences across conditions, and the sample size (Keppel, 1991). Generally, our statistical tests set the significance level at .05. The size of the differences across conditions in not within the control of the experimenter. The best-case scenario is that the researcher has an adequate way of predicting what the effect size will be, whether this is from theoretically derived predictions, past research, pilot data, or some other method. Thus, tools for calculating statistical power generally focus on determining the number of cases needed per condition.

Since variation within conditions (noise) can affect the detection of differences across conditions, and since there is likely to be more such variation in virtual group experiments than face-to-face experiments, statistical power is especially important. We would recommend that experimenters under-estimate differences between conditions when calculating power for virtual group experiments. In other words, sample sizes should be increased to account for the additional noise provided by the lack of control.

Research and Practical Implications

As an example of the variety of decisions that need to be made is studying a virtual group, we describe a study that investigated the role of entitativity, or the extent to which a group is perceived as a real entity, by manipulating specific cues within a sports-based message board. We consider feelings of entitativity to be an essential component of online work and social work groups and plan a series of experiments to help us understand what affects member perceptions of online group entitativity.

Participants for this particular study were introductory psychology students at a large Southeastern university who volunteered to participate in the study to gain course credit. A total of 128 students completed the experiment. The mean age of the sample was 20.7 (SD = 4.4), and 75% of participants were female. With regard to ethnicity, 68% of the sample was Caucasian,

14% was African-American, 9% was Asian, 5% was Hispanic, and 4% reported another ethnicity.

Data was collected through a web-based survey hosted on an online survey website (SurveyShare). Participants signed up to participate in this experiment through the University's psychology department undergraduate research website. Participants were then shown a message board manipulation. This message board appeared to be a university-specific sports board, with ten pre-posted comments about two sports topics. These participants were randomly assigned to one of two message order conditions (messages grouped by topic or messages grouped by timestamp) and one of three signature file conditions (no signature file [control], topic relevant signature file, or topic irrelevant signature file), resulting in a 2 x 3 (message order vs. signature) experimental design. Participants were instructed that they were going to evaluate a message board in this study.

In the message order condition, participants were shown one of two manipulations. The first manipulation was messages grouped by topics. In this condition, participants can see the progression of conversation regarding each topic within the board. The second condition was messages groups by timestamps. Posts to this board were ordered by time alone, with no differentiation to what topic or thread the user is responding to.

In the signature condition, participants were shown one of three manipulations. The first was a control condition, where all individuals that post to the message board had no signature file. The second was a topic relevant signature file, where the posters' signatures included sports relevant quotes, pictures, and/or countdowns. An example signature is: "10 days until Niner basketball begins!" The third manipulation condition included non-relevant signature files, where the posters' signatures included non-sports related quotes, pictures, and/or countdowns. An example signature would include phrases such as "120 days until LOST Season 5!" or a picture of a Dalmatian.

After viewing the message board manipulation, participants were asked to choose an avatar and username to "join" the message board. Participants were then asked to write one post for either the basketball or football thread. We theorized that active interaction with the message board, as opposed to having participants passively read posts, would cause participants to become more engaged with the group and the study itself, and would more accurately depict a "real-life" virtual group situation.

After completing their post, participants were asked to complete a short, online questionnaire. Participants had access to the message board after they begin the questionnaire, so that they could more accurately judge their overall impressions of the group. This questionnaire measured perceived similarity, interactivity, entitativity, and social identification. Additionally, the questionnaire measured computer experience, message board experience, and sports interest as control variables. Interdependence was measured as a non-equivalent dependent variable. It should not have been affected by the manipulation and should provide strength to the argument presented here, that technical cues affect perceived similarity and interactivity. Demographics were also measured at the end of the questionnaire.

Measured Variables

Identification with Group. Group identification was measured using eight items (Hogg & Hains, 1996). An example item is, "In terms of general attitudes and beliefs, I am very similar to the group as a whole." A 1 (*strongly disagree*) to 5 (*strongly agree*) Likert-type rating scale was used to respond to these items.

Entitativity. Entitativity was measured using three items. An example item is, "This message board qualifies as a group." A 1 (*strongly disagree*) to 5 (*strongly agree*) Likert-type rating scale was used to respond to this item.

Perceived Similarity. Perceived similarity was measured using two items. Items used for this measure were, "Group members appear to be similar to each other" and "Members of this message board appear to have much in common." A 1 (*strongly disagree*) to 5 (*strongly agree*) Likert-type rating scale was used to respond to these items.

Interactivity. Interactivity was measured using three items (Rourke, et al., 1999). An example item is, "Individuals ask questions to other members." A 1 (*strongly disagree*) to 5 (*strongly agree*) Likert-type rating scale was used to respond to these items.

Social Interdependence. Social interdependence was measured using three items adapted from a task interdependence scale (Liden, Wayne, & Bradway, 1997). An example item is, "Group members frequently coordinate their efforts with each other." A 1 (*strongly disagree*) to 5 (*strongly agree*) Likert-type rating scale was used to respond to these items.

Demographics. Measured demographic items included age, gender, ethnicity, and class standing. Each of these variables was measured with a single item and required either selection from a list (ethnicity, class standing, gender) or a fill-in response (age).

Computer Experience. Participants were asked to what extent the following statement describes them: "I have had a lot of previous computer experience." A 1 (*strongly disagree*) to 5 (*strongly agree*) Likert-type rating scale was given to respond to the item.

Message Board Experience. Participants were asked to what extent the following statement describes them: "I have had a lot of previous message board experience." A 1 (*strongly disagree*) to 5 (*strongly agree*) Likert-type rating scale was given to respond to the item.

Sports Interest. Participants were asked to what extent the following statement describes them: "I am interested in sports." A 1 (*strongly disagree*) to 5 (*strongly agree*) Likert-type rating scale was given to respond to the item.

Results from this study indicated that perceived similarity and interactivity did lead to higher entitativity. We found a statistically significant positive relationship between entitativity and identification with the group. In general, the fact that we did observe significant relationships between our main study variables is indicative of an overall sound theory; however, a lack of significant results on other hypotheses indicates that our manipulations were not strong enough to affect the antecedents of entitativity directly.

Additionally, computer experience was found to be a moderator of the relationship between our interactivity manipulation and perceptions of entitativity. This indicates that there may be fundamental differences in how users of differing levels of computer experience perceive our message board exchange manipulations. This finding is similar to earlier research in which the user's computer experience affected research outcomes (Sproull & Kiesler, 1986).

While this study was designed as a first step into the study of entitativity in an online environment, much in its design could be improved. This study provides evidence that perceived similarity and interactivity are important antecedents for entitativity. Additionally, we found that perceiving entitativity within a virtual group can lead to higher perceptions of group identification.

One area we perceived that could be improved was the strength of our manipulation. As we discussed earlier, the technological features in the group are like the environment and can be subtle and in the background, not always attended to by the participants. While this is appropriate so that it does not become clear to the participants what our manipulations actually are, the cues should not be too understated. In our next series of experiments in this area, we include multiple, redundant cues to indicate one of our manipulations: the similarity of group members. We go beyond simply having a signature file with group information available

or not. We also including group relevant (or not) avatars and group relevant (or not) usernames. We also provide additional participant information like tenure and activity level to suggest that this is a longstanding group of interacting similar (or not) individuals.

In future experiments we also will include multiple threads instead of the two we included here. This will make more obvious the arrangement of the threads as grouped by topic or by time stamp. Indeed, more threads and conversations between more participants overall will provide a stronger manipulation by providing a more realistically populated online group.

The results of our previous research project also suggest that future research in this area should further explore computer experience as a moderator of perceptions of entitativity within message boards. Indeed, our results suggest that our manipulations had a much stronger effect on people who had participated in messages boards before the experiment than for participants who had little message board experience. This replicates research findings before (e.g., Sproull & Kiesler, 1986) in which computer experience affected study results.

In order to properly manage these experience effects, future studies could aim at recruiting participants from authentic message board sites. This would ensure that almost all participants have at least a basic level of computer and message board experience. If this is not possible, researchers may want to pre-screen participants for computer experience. Because individuals that regularly use message boards to communicate with others are likely to be more computer-literate than the average individual, removing individuals in a study with very little computer experience should more accurately reflect the target population. This should be taken into consideration especially when studying older generations that may not be as computer-literate as younger, student populations.

FUTURE RESEARCH DIRECTIONS

One of the challenges we foresee as move forward in our research program is designing a system for ongoing group interaction in which we control at least part of either the technologies or the interactions. The design we have presented here is appropriate for us to examine participants' initial impressions about the group's entitativity. However, we are also interested in entitativity and particularly its outcomes that can occur over time. Indeed, we suggest that our model may have recursive relationships related to entitativity (e.g., as members develop an understanding of the "voice" of participants over time, they may develop ideas about the group that can increase or decrease entitativity).

As we approach these research experiments, we anticipate several decision points. First, we could populate the experimental groups with all research participants with particular participation requirements (e.g., how many times they must post in a time frame) and manipulate technological features. We could also have confederates within the experimental groups who either have a strict (or a general) script for posting and responding to topics. While the former is more natural, the latter would make more likely a viable group in order to examine our relevant outcomes.

Our goal is also to create an online system in which we can quickly change technological features or participation types. This goal has particularly challenging to us because of the technological expertise that has been required (i.e., setting up and hosting a viable virtual community). While these host technologies are free and relatively easy to use, they require a level of technological expertise that is hard to come by in sociology and psychology department graduate students, much less their faculty.

We have, therefore, recently teamed with a human computer interaction research team at our university that has provided us with technological expertise while we provide theoretical exposure to our common interests. This provides multiple benefits to our research, not the least of which is the interdisciplinary collaboration that comes from sharing our different perspectives and backgrounds about the same general topic. We strongly encourage other online group researchers to walk around their campus and collaborate across their college boundaries.

We are also considering creating and hosting our own virtual community that we will then use in our ongoing experimental and other virtual community research. By using a popular, free shareware virtual community hosting system (e.g., phpBB) and with the help of our interdisciplinary research team, we plan on creating a "real" sports virtual community around our Division I basketball team and our newly formed football team, whose first season begins in 2012. Similar to MovieLens hosted by the University of Minnesota, we hope that this virtual community will be engaging to the participants while we are able to conduct ongoing research on the group. We suggest this option is available to many virtual work researchers when they initiate interdisciplinary research teams with their computer and information science colleagues.

With a technological system and the subsequent online group environment as we envision it, we could foresee being able to easily test our assumptions as to what affects entitativity over time in online groups. We hope that our experimental system will allow us to repeatedly test multiple technologies and identify which features have the strongest effects on entitativity. Indeed, it is essential that our online group technology be easily modifiable so that we (and hopefully others) can use it for multiple experiments.

CONCLUSION

We look forward to seeing more and more experimental studies of virtual work groups in the future. We echo Bainbridge (2007) in his enthusiasm for the wide variety of social situations that can be studied in the virtual world. Our ability to create engaging, realistic, and complex situations for our experiments has never been greater, due in large part of computer technology and virtual interaction capabilities. However, also echo Bainbridge's caution that there are problems in these endeavors as well. The difficulty in translating abstract, theoretical constructs like those found in the social sciences requires diligence, patience, and careful attention to detail in our any experiments. This is especially true in experiments on virtual work, and we have tried to illustrate the importance of careful experimental design in producing meaningful studies. We hope that this chapter has helped to illuminate some of the difficulties and to envision ways around them.

REFERENCES

Aronson, E., Wilson, T. D., & Brewer, M. B. (1998). Experimentation in social psychology. In Gilbert, D. T., Fiske, S. T., & Lindzey, G. (Eds.), *The Handbook of Social Psychology* (*Vol. 1*, pp. 99–142). Boston, MA: McGraw-Hill.

Bainbridge, W. S. (2007). The scientific research potential of virtual worlds. *Science, 317,* 472–476. doi:10.1126/science.1146930

Cohen, J. C. (1988). *Statistical power analysis for behavioral sciences*. Hillsdale, NJ: Lawrence Erlbaum Associates.

Falk, A., & Heckman, J. J. (2009). Lab experiments are a major source of knowledge in the social sciences. *Science, 326,* 535–538. doi:10.1126/science.1168244

Hogg, M. A., & Hains, S. C. (1996). Intergroup relations and group solidarity: Effects of group identification and social beliefs on depersonalized attraction. *Journal of Personality and Social Psychology, 70,* 295–309. doi:10.1037/0022-3514.70.2.295

Keppel, G. (1991). *Design and analysis: A researcher's handbook*. Englewood Cliffs, NJ: Prentice Hall.

Kiesler, S., Seigel, J., & McGuire, T. (1984). Social psychological aspects of computer-mediated communication. *The American Psychologist, 39*(10), 1123–1134. doi:10.1037/0003-066X.39.10.1123

Liden, R. C., Wayne, S. J., & Bradway, L. K. (1997). Task Interdependence as a moderator of the relation between group control and performance. *Human Relations, 50,* 169–181. doi:10.1177/001872679705000204

Rashotte, L. S., Webster, M. Jr, & Whitmeyer, J. (2005). Pretesting experimental instructions. *Sociological Methodology, 35,* 151–175. doi:10.1111/j.0081-1750.2005.00167.x

Rourke, L., Anderson, T., Garrison, D. R., & Archer, W. (1999). Assessing social presence in asynchronous test-based computer conferencing. *Journal of Distance Education, 14*(2), 50–71.

Sproull, L., & Kiesler, S. (1986). Reducing social context cues: Electronic mail in organizational communication. *Management Science, 32*(11), 1492–1512. doi:10.1287/mnsc.32.11.1492

Thye, S. R. (2007). Logical and philosophical foundations of experimental research in the social sciences. In Webster, M., & Sell, J. (Eds.), *Laboratory Experiments in the Social Sciences*. New York, NY: Elsevier.

Troyer, L. (2001). Effects of protocol differences on the study of status and social influence. *Current Research in Social Psychology, 6,* 182–204.

Troyer, L. (2002). The relation between experimental standardization and theoretical development in group process research. In Szmatka, J., Lovaglia, M., & Wysineska, K. (Eds.), *The Growth of Social Knowledge: Theory Simulation, and Empirical Research in Group Processes*. Westport, CT: Praeger.

Webster, M. Jr, & Sell, J. (2007). Why do experiments? In Webster, M., & Sell, J. (Eds.), *Laboratory Experiments in the Social Sciences*. New York, NY: Elsevier.

ADDITIONAL READING

Rashotte, L. S. (2007). Developing your experiment. In Webster, M., & Sell, J. (Eds.), *Laboratory Experiments in the Social Sciences*. New York, NY: Elsevier.

Walther, J. B. (1995). Relational aspects of computer-mediated communication: Experimental observations over time. *Organization Science*, *6*(2), 186–203. doi:10.1287/orsc.6.2.186

Walther, J. B., & Bunz, U. (2005). The rules of virtual groups: Trust, liking, and performance in computer-mediated communication. *The Journal of Communication*, *55*(4), 828–845. doi:10.1111/j.1460-2466.2005.tb03025.x

Webster, M. Jr, & Sell, J. (2007). *Laboratory experiments in the social sciences*. New York, NY: Elsevier.

KEY TERMS AND DEFINITIONS

Entitativity: Feelings of groupy-ness for members of a group.

Experimental Methods: a set of research techniques designed to understand cause and effect and test theories, accomplished through the manipulation of one variable (or set of variables) to measure the effect on another variable (or set of variables).

Virtual Groups: Groups of people who interact primarily through information and communication technology.

Virtual Work: Work supported by information and communication technology.

Chapter 10
Grounded Theory Approaches to Research on Virtual Work:
A Brief Primer

Danna M. Gibson
Columbus State University, USA

Lynne M. Webb
University of Arkansas, USA

ABSTRACT

This chapter explains how researchers can effectively employ grounded theory to study virtual work. The chapter defines grounded theory, reports the history of its development, describes its data collection and analysis, as well as offers guidelines for writing research reports of grounded theory analyses of human interactions surrounding virtual work.

INTRODUCTION AND BACKGROUND

Unlike its name would imply, grounded theory is *not* a specific theory of social science that describes or predicts the social behavior of human actors. Rather the term "grounded theory" describes a genre of social scientific theory (specifically, theory derived from data) as well as the methodology for the development of such theory. "Grounded theory development (Glaser & Strauss, 1967; Miles & Huberman, 1984) is a methodology that

helps researchers conduct natural observations" for the purpose of discovering emergent insights that can lead to the development of new theory of social behavior (O'Conner, Rice, Peters, & Veryzer, 2003, p. 353). Grounded theory research allows scholars to develop a basic understanding of a phenomenon through allowing informants' understandings to emerge from their accounts.

Grounded theory is perhaps the most commonly cited theoretical paradigm in qualitative research on human interactions surrounding

DOI: 10.4018/978-1-4666-0963-1.ch010

virtual work. Founded as a practical approach to both theory development and data analysis, grounded theory has become a widely used and often misunderstood paradigm (Suddaby, 2006). Its techniques are complex and its principles cannot be readily understood by a casual reader of research reports. The purpose of this chapter is twofold: (a) to explain grounded theory in sufficient detail for readers to understand and critically read grounded theory research as well as (b) to offer a preliminary understanding of grounded theory's purpose and methods so that readers can decide whether to employ a grounded theory approach in their own line of research.

A theory is simply a description of how a phenomenon works. For example, Bandura's (1977) social learning theory describes how individuals learn appropriate social behavior by observing the behavior of others in their social milieu. Social scientific theory describes how human beings think and behave; these detailed descriptions, coupled with rigorous scientific testing of the descriptions, allows for predictions about human behavior. The more valid the theory, the more accurate its descriptions and predictions.

What then is the relationship between theory and research? These two scientific enterprises, theorizing and researching, exist in an on-going symbiotic relationship such that each depends upon and influences the other. A reasonable theory prompts testing; the results of scientific testing prompt revisions and refinement of theory, which in turn prompts further testing. Thus, a good theory is perhaps the most valuable tool at the researcher's disposal, as it can provide guidance in understanding the phenomenon under study and point to the next area ripe for research.

Social science researchers use theory in basically three ways: via deductive reasoning, inductive reasoning, and a combination of deductive and inductive reasoning. Each is described in more detail below. Researchers employ deduc-

tive reasoning in the classic scientific endeavor of testing a theory, often described as positivist thinking. The researcher selects an existing theory and uses a recognized scientific research protocol to test if the identified theory offers a reasonable explanation for the phenomenon under study. Typically, the scientific protocol involves the use of empirical research methods, such as a survey or experiment, yielding numerical data subjected to statistical analysis. For example, Staples and Webster (2007) tested social cognitive theory (Bandura, 2001) by surveying virtual team members; the researchers documented the influence of colleagues' perceptions of effectiveness on team members' own perceived self-efficacy; they analyzed their data using statistical analyses.

Conversely, the researcher can employ inductive reasoning by collecting data and allowing an explanation of the phenomenon under study to emerge from the data. That is, he/she can reason from multiple specific data points to a more general theory about how the phenomenon works. Theories that emerge from data are often described as organic because they are grounded in data. For example, Thompson-Hayes, Gibson, Scott, and Webb (2009) interviewed 20 professors in a variety of disciplines about their online consultations with colleagues around the U. S. Their thematic analysis revealed four dialectical tensions (an interplay of opposing and contradictory forces typically resolved through communication) in such interactions: relational connection and personal autonomy, creativity and the mundane, task and socio-emotional goals, as well as novelty and efficacy.

What then is the place of *grounded theory* in this dichotomy of deductive versus inductive reasoning? Grounded theory offers a third alternative; it uses both kinds of reasoning, first inductive reasoning and then deductive reasoning, to develop detailed, original theories. This "grounded" process of theory development employs the symbiotic relationship earlier described between research and theory by reasoning from data to theory and then checking the accuracy of the tentative theory by comparison to more data. In short, grounded theory researchers use both inductive and deductive reasoning. They employ inductive reasoning to allow preliminary concepts to emerge from the raw data.

Next, grounded theory researchers employ deductive reasoning via complex data analysis to discover the emergent theory. Such data analysis involves multiple steps: Grounded theory researchers form categories from the original concepts and then relationships among the categories, identified via informants' descriptions as well as the researchers' informed understanding of previously published theory and research on the phenomenon. Thus, grounded theory researchers first employ inductive reasoning, and then turn to deductive reasoning to place the emergent concepts and categories into relationships, one with the other.

Grounded theory holds a unique place in the landscape of data analysis and theoretical reasoning because it lies with a foot squarely in both the inductive and deductive reasoning camps. When done well, grounded theory requires complex thinking of multiple types. Further, grounded theory offers a middle ground between the extremes of empirical positivism (which argues for an objective, observable reality that can be discovered through research) and radical interpretivism (which argues that every individual hold a unique view of reality and that all views of reality are equally valid). Instead of these extreme epistemological orientations to theory and research methods in the social sciences, grounded theory claims that individuals interpret their lived reality and then socially construct (Berger & Luckman, 1967) a shared vision of those interpretations— a vision or naïve theory—which the grounded theory researcher attempts to discover in analysis of informants' accounts of their lived experiences.

THE PLACE OF GROUNDED THEORY IN SOCIAL SCIENTIFIC WORK

All three ways of thinking (inductive reasoning, deductive reasoning, and a grounded theory approach) offer rational approaches to generalizing with data. However, the grounded theory approach seems especially well suited for the certain types of research, including those listed below.

- Grounded theory focuses on informants' interpretive process by analyzing "the actual production of meanings and concepts used by social actors in real settings" (Gephart, 2004, p. 457), such as workers employed in virtual tasks. Thus, grounded theory is especially useful in understanding how the people who are experiencing the phenomenon under study understand and think about that phenomenon. Individuals' internal understandings and their interpretative impulses are the key concerns of grounded theory research. In short, a grounded theory approach allows the researcher to discover informants' naïve theories of their experiences. Such an approach is especially useful when the phenomenon under study is not easily observable, such as virtual work.
- Grounded theory research can elicit "fresh understandings about patterned relationships between social actors and how these relationships and interactions actively construct reality" (Suddaby, 2006, p. 636). Thus, grounded theory research is especially well suited to study how individuals construct meaning from their subjective experience and socially constructed realities (Berger & Luckman, 1967), such as collaborative tasks and virtual realities.
- Grounded theory is especially appropriate for studying social knowledge that is widely known but covert and unofficial, such as how workers manage to date colleagues in

the face of organizational policy expressly forbidding such action.

- Grounded theories are frequently developed to describe newer phenomenon where few or no previously published theories exist. Here researchers actively explore how interesting, new phenomenon operate. Clearly, virtual work and the human interaction surrounding it provide new areas of exploration for researchers, as the very phenomenon did not exist 30 years ago.

- Grounded theory can provide insights into an area of contested theoretical thinking or research findings, as it allows researchers to gather data directly from informants—data that explores informants' thinking and experiences on their terms—thus allowing the social actors on the scene to explain what appears to be contradictory behavior or thinking.

- Grounded theory can explicate or illuminate a portion of previously published theory that remains largely understudied by (a) offering a more detailed elaboration of a specific part of the theory, (b) a new understanding of how that theory "works" in a previously unforeseen and undiscussed setting, such as a virtual organization, or (c) with a "new" population, such as virtual workers.

A BRIEF HISTORY OF GROUNDED THEORY

The Discovery of Grounded Theory launched grounded theory as a theory-building methodology (Glaser & Strauss, 1967) that is widely acknowledged as providing a credible alternative to quantitative research (Charmaz, 2006; Thomas & James, 2006). Many contemporary scholars see the two aspects of grounded theory—its research methodology and its theory generative impulse—as inescapably linked. For example, Merrigan and

Huston defined grounded theory as "a methodology that is intended to be used to develop theories by systematically gathering and analyzing field data (Merrigan & Huston, 2004, p. 224).

While grounded theory was introduced in 1967 as a capable qualitative method of theory-building (Glaser & Strauss, 1967; Rupsiene & Pranskuniene, 2010), ways to define and identify grounded theory have changed across time. Indeed, the theory is known by its diverse methodological approaches to data collection and analysis. Rupsiene and Pranskuniene provide an exhaustive and enlightening chronology, detailing the theory's inception and subsequent divergence into multiple approaches and methodologies. However, in all its forms, grounded theory advocates allowing understandings of the phenomenon to emerge from data sets composed of multiple, detailed accounts from informants with first-hand experience with the phenomenon under study. Theory emerges from researchers' analysis of the interplay between informants descriptions of their first-hand experiences and the informants' interpretations of the meaning of these experiences.

Disappointment awaits any researcher seeking a single compartmentalized way to view grounded theory. Glaser and Strauss (1967) initially identified the purpose of grounded theory as generation of substantive, formal theories with specific, narrow application and thus limited generalizability. Later, Strauss and Corbin (1994) identified the heart of the theory as "the capacity to produce conceptually dense data and integrated theory development" (p. 273). While many scholars employ a grounded theory approach that de-emphasizes theory development, others caution against confusing grounded theory with an elaborate methodology that produces rich data for instrument construction, while failing to focus on grounded theory's most valuable inductive theory-building component (Benoliel, 1996; Rupsiene & Pranskuniene, 2010; Wilson & Hutchinson, 1996). Thus, tension exists between viewing grounded theory as a means of theory production via data analysis versus as a means of data analysis per se.

Adding to this pendulum-swing of grounded theory conceptualizations, Strauss and Corbin introduced another variation of its definition: A grounded theory approach can be used for *both* theory and non-theory development (Strauss & Corbin, 1990, 1998). Current literature suggests a trend toward applying an even broader and more generic approach, associating grounded theory with producing "low-level theories" (Rupsiene & Pranskuniene, 2010, p. 15) and labeling it as a *method* to identify theoretical constructs derived from qualitative data analysis (Corbin & Strauss, 2008). Whether the purpose of grounded theory is (a) developing theory, (b) analysis of rich data, or (c) a combination of the two, contemporary scholars recognize grounded theory's ability to guide interpretations that lead to deeper understandings of real-life phenomena. This guidance to deeper understandings is now widely acknowledged as the theory's major contribution and aim, thus placing less emphasis on the generation of formal theory (see McLeod, 2001; Rupsiene & Pranskuniene, 2010; Silverman, 2001; Tavallaei & Talib, 2010) and more emphasis on the outcomes of research projects, thus positioning grounded theory as the theoretical basis for multiple qualitative methodologies that may or may not lead to theory development.

Despite, or maybe because of, the discrepant ways of conceptualizing grounded theory, a long line of research stems from the theory and/or the rich data it produces, including research in the multiple traditions of positivist, interpretive, modern, post-modern, feminist, and critical scholarships (see Charmaz, 2006; Clarke, 2005; Corbin & Strauss, 2008; Rupsiene & Pranskuniene, 2010). Regardless of conceptualization, many scholars view grounded theory as productive (Charmaz, 2009) and assert that grounded theory methods "propose the useful strategies of data collection, management, and analysis" (Rupsiene & Pranskuniene, 2010, p. 12). Indeed,

the primary theoretical foundation for qualitative research methods remains grounded theory. See Birks and Mills (2011) for a detailed review of grounded theory.

In sum, contemporary researchers often describe their methods as "data collection and analysis based on grounded theory approaches" (Pauleen, 2003, p. 227). Further, grounded theory has become so inexorably linked in social scientific work with its methodology that the term "grounded theory" is used to describe the very research methods that produce grounded theory as well as the genre of theory produced by such methods. Thus, a detailed description of grounded theory methodology is appropriate and essential to a fuller understanding of grounded theory. We provide that explanation below.

GROUNDED THEORY METHODOLOGY

The raw data of grounded theory research varies widely in both degree of structure (Franklin, 1996) and specific forms. In the study of the human interaction surrounding virtual work, raw data can be email messages (e.g., Clear & MacDonell, 2011), case studies (Zhang & Poole, 2010), field notes of case studies (Mattarelli & Tagiaventi, 2010), interview transcripts (e.g., Belanger & Watson-Manhein, 2006; Shachaf, 2008), summary reports written by project teams (Davison, Fuller, & Hardin, 2003), as well as multiple data sources (e.g., Maznevski & Chudoba, 2000; Pauleen, 2003; Qureshi, Liu, & Vogel, 2006).

While the purpose of most grounded theory research on human interaction and virtual work is the development of a new theory to explain the phenomenon under study (e.g., Kirkman, Rosen, Gibson, Tesluk, & McPherson, 2002; Pauleen, 2003; Qureshi, Liu, & Vogel, 2006), virtual-work researchers have employed grounded theory methodologies for additional important purposes such as the development of a limited part of a previously published theory (e.g., Mattarelli & Tagliaventi, 2010) and laying the groundwork for future research, often through the development of coding systems used in instrument development (e.g., Davison, Fuller, & Hardin, 2003).

Data analysis typically proceeds in overlapping stages (Dick, 2000), such as the four stages presented below. These stages represent an amalgamation of the methods reported by multiple scholars (Beyers & Hannah, 2002; Davison, Fuller, & Hardin, 2003; Franklin, 1996; O'Conner, et al., 2003; Olson, Daggs, Ellevold, & Rogers, 2007; Mattarelli & Tagiaventi, 2010; Pauleen, 2003; Singh, 1996; Suddaby, 2006; Thompson-Hayes, et al., 2009) who provided detailed descriptions of analyses, as recommended by methodologists (Suddaby, 2006). Below we present the basic goals of the four stages:

Stage 1: Open coding (labeling each concept)
- Identifying preliminary themes, concepts, components, and/or conceptual labels that emerge from the raw data.
- Can be completed on raw data or on summaries of each collection point (e.g., interview).
- Here the researcher identifies concepts that emerge from the data.
- If the researcher stops the analysis here, then the study becomes phenomenological, focused on individuals' interpretations of their subjective experiences, rather than on abstracting those individual experiences into theoretical statements about the lived reality of multiple individuals who share a social milieu in a socially constructed reality (Berger & Luckman, 1967) that can be understood in terms of causal and influential relationship among variables.

Stage 2: Axial coding (developing categories of concepts)

- "The act of relating categories to sub-categories" (Strauss & Corbin, 1998, p. 124)
- Identifying categories (also called "clusters of conceptual codes") that emerge by grouping emergent Step 1 concepts into categories of concepts that occur at a higher level of abstraction. Step 1 concepts are "merged, changed, and occasionally eliminated" (Pauleen, 2003, p. 235) to create the categories of concepts. Using the same process, these categories can be grouped into supra-categories that exist at a higher level of abstraction.
- Such categories or families of concepts can be drawn from previously published theory.
- Drawing connections between categories of concepts that emerge from the data; seeing relationships between the categories or supra-categories, including causal relationships.
- Recognizing one or more core categories that emerge from the data.
- Chronologically ordering categories and supra-categories, if such order emerges from informants' accounts.

Stage 3: Selective coding (completing the coding process)
- Re-examining the raw data to refine and develop additional concepts, categories, or supra-categories that emerge.
- Re-examining the raw data to seek validation for the concepts, categories, supra-categories, relationships, and orders developed in axial coding.
- Re-examining the data to notice how and why the categories, supra-categories, and relationships occur and align with one another to discover both the "story line" of the emerging model

and its inherent logic (e.g., chrono-logical, dialectic).

Stage 4: Emergence of Grounded Theory (pre-senting the emergent model)

  ◦ Map the identified relationships among the emergent and validated categories, including the core concept(s)—the ideas that the model encircles.

  ◦ If relationships and categories did not emerge in axial coding, then identify them now, based on previously published theory and/or research.

  ◦ Present the relationships in a model (typically a path model) that allows for the next step in theory development (i.e., empirical testing of the emergent model).

Given the basic goals of each of the four stages discussed above, we next provide more detailed descriptions of the tasks researchers complete at each stage. Note that in those descriptions below, tasks can overlap between stages and goals can reoccur at multiple stages.

Stage 1: Developing a Coding System

• Coders are first trained to use open coding techniques, the "process of labeling events and ideas represented in the data" (Pauleen, 2003, p. 235). Glaser described open coding as "to absorb the data as data, to be able to step back or distance oneself from it, and then to abstractly conceptualize the data" (Glaser, 1992, p. 11).

• During open coding, researchers attempt to identify common concepts (also called themes) that reoccur across informants' accounts. Many researchers adopt Owen's (1984) three criteria of a theme: recurrence (the concept appears across informants' accounts), repetition (some and perhaps

many individual informants mention the concept more than once), and forcefulness (informants state the concept in a way that emphasizes its importance to their under-standing of the phenomenon under study).

• Next, each coder works independently on a sample of the data. Then they compare their individual analyses in a group meeting, discussing their findings, until they reach a common understanding of the definition of each concept. Thus, the results or findings of the study can emerge from a common understanding of multiple observers' individual observations of the phenomenon under observation.

• Coders typically meet weekly to discuss their individual codings of batches of data, until all data is coded. Disagreements are settled through discussion. The list of discovered emergent concepts continues to grow.

• During coding, analysts may employ one or more data management methods (e.g., color-coding schemes, computer analysis programs such as HYPERQUAL and NUD*IST). Other researchers argue that analysis via computer programs is inconsistent with a grounded theory approach because the creative participation of the researcher in the analysis and interpretation of data cannot be delegated to the computer programmer (Suddaby, 2006).

• At each weekly meeting, such common understandings of the emergent concepts often are reduced to writing and a code book is developed. The advantages of the code book include increased consistency in analysis across coders, easy replication of the study, and ease in training additional coders if and when they are added to the research team.

  ◦ On occasion, a detailed code book can facilitate too fine an analysis to allow main ideas to emerge quickly or readily or the analysis can prove an overwhelming task for a lone researcher; then, the researcher typically writes brief summaries or memos of each data subset (such as each transcript of a virtual team meeting) and analyzes the summaries as a mean of identifying major concepts in the data set (e.g., Singh, 1996).

○ A second concern with the strict application of a code book is the potential loss of the researcher/coders creativity, openness, and sensitivity to the informants' interpretations of their reported experiences. Coders must remain vigilant, in the face of a written codebook, in attempting to accurately represent the data. Such vigilance may result in combining codes, revising codes, relabeling codes, and other changes to increase accuracy of the coding.

• Can data analysis proceed with just a single coder? Yes and in such a case, the coder serves as a textual analyst whose repeated re-readings of the texts serves as hedge against misinterpretation or the introduction of bias in an initial reading (Krusiewicz & Wood, 2001).

• As coding proceeds, the coders use codes developed in previous weeks and also generate additional codes, as needed. Coders introduce potential new codes at weekly staff meetings. Following discussion, accepted new codes are added to the codebook. The addition of new codes may necessitate the recoding of some previously coded data. The back and forth rhythm of coding, as well as the development of new codes during on-going data analysis, constitutes *the constant comparison process* as well as exemplifies the grounded nature of the analysis and resulting theoretical understandings. In this way, "codes" (and codes become themes or concepts that ultimately may appear in the original theory under development) are "tested" by comparing them to new data during analysis. Exemplars of important codes reappear in chunks of data, as they represent concepts central to the informants' understanding of the phenomenon under study.

• The constant comparison process involves moving between the specific data and the emerging concepts, which are more general, and then back to the data. This process of a combination of inductive and deductive reasoning, known as *analytical induction*, can produce theoretical insights that represent new ways of thinking about the phenomenon, and thus yield original theory.

• Coding typically begins during the data collection process. Thus, part of the constant comparison process becomes comparing the current categories to the new data—often necessitating the development of new codes, concepts, or themes. Thus, "theory emerges during actual research, through the continuous interplay between analysis and data collection" (Pauleen, 2003, p. 235). When the coders can develop no new themes from additional data, then data collection ceases as the researcher has achieved *category saturation*. Some researchers continue to collect data for a short while (e.g., conduct a few more interviews) to ensure that no new concepts emerge and to document the achievement of theoretical saturation, but such a step merely provides further validation of saturation and is not essential. Because there is no set and firm amount of data expected in grounded theory research, the standard for judging sample is size is whether the researcher achieved categorical saturation.

Stage 2: Discovering Emergent Central Concepts and Relationships

- The *central concept* or category provides "analytic power" to "pull the other categories together to form an explanatory whole" (Strauss & Corbin, 1998, p. 146). The central concept or variable typically appears in the center of the model representing the emergent, new theory. All of other variables in the model are mapped in relation to the central concept. Typically, the central concept is the most frequently occurring concept in the data set and/or holds a place of importance in the process described by the informants.
- If the relationships between concepts or categories of concepts are not self-evident, the researchers can complete a reading of the data set looking specifically for causal and associated linkages described by the informants.
- When concepts, categories, and relationships emerge, the ordering of the relationships (which appears first in the model, which appears next in the model, etc.) many not be obvious. In such cases, the researchers can complete a reading of the data set looking specifically for ordering of causal and associated linkages described by the informants.
- Ordering of relationships represents change across time. Such change can be discovered in multiple ways including collecting data across time, including coding informants descriptions of such changes, conducting multiple interviews with the same set of informants across time (e.g., Beyer & Hannah, 2002), or examining communicative artifacts, such as email, that informants created across time (Clear & MacDonell, 2011).

- Thus, the quality of the theory will depend in large part on the researchers' interpretative skills. Researchers who provide a "sensitive read" of the data easily discern connections between informants' accounts as well as their connotative meanings that moves beyond a cursory "read" of the interactive situation.

Stage 3: Reaching Saturation

- While this stage serves as verification for the results that emerge in Stages 1 and 2, it also allows further development of and/ or refinement of concepts, categories, and connections.
- In this stage, conflicting findings can be resolved (perhaps through the realization of the existence of dialectical tensions).
- Here the researcher moves between the data, the emerging concepts, and the final theoretical model. Such back and forth movement continues until no additional refinements emerge.
- The goal of this stage is to "exhaust whatever insights the variations across respondents and time could provide" (Beyer & Hannah, 2002, p. 640), thus providing further evidence of *category saturation*.
- Saturation can be verified in multiple ways including (a) collecting more data to discover if additional concepts or categories emerge and (b) comparing concepts and categories that emerge from two cohorts; if concepts/categories match, saturation has been achieved (Beyer & Hannah, 2002). This latter technique for documenting saturation can be especially useful for data sets that include groups of informants that comprise cohort groups, such as virtual workers from two organizations in the same industry.

- Saturation occurs when the limitations of three contributing factors converge: (a) the variation within the data, (b) the coders' ability to discover variations in the data set, as well as (c) "the integration and density of the [emerging] theory" (Glaser & Strauss, 1967, p. 62).

Stage 4: Describing the Emergent Theory

- The goal Stage 4 is creation of a model containing the emergent central core concept, the emergent concepts and/or categories that appear related to it, and the relationships between them.
- Such relationships may include "causal and contextual conditions that influence the phenomenon, the actions or strategies that individuals make in response to the conditions, and the outcomes or consequences of those actions (Strauss & Corbin, 1998)" (Olson, et al., 2007, p. 233).
- The researcher seeks to develop the most complete, accurate, and concise representation of the informants' understandings of the phenomenon under study.
- To this end, the researcher freely adds ideas from previously published theories and research, if they represent the informants' experiences as described in the data.
- The researcher often constructs a variety of preliminary models refining the accuracy and simplicity of the model with each draft.
- In the end, the final model presents the researcher's best understanding of the informants' ideas, including a core concept, the additional major concepts and/or categories, and the relationships between them.
- Prior to publication, researchers often share their model with a sample of their informants to discover if the model "rings

true" as representing the informants' lived experiences.
- The usefulness of the theory "is judged primarily by the fit and relevance to the research participants' local situation" (Pauleen, 2003, p. 235).

REPORTING GROUNDED THEORY

Many scholars have described the collection and analysis of data using grounded theory approaches (e.g., Browning, 1978; Corbin & Morse, 2003; Corbin & Strauss, 1990; Eisenhardt, 1989; Hamilton & Bowers, 2006; Kazmer & Xie, 2008; Mann & Stewart, 2002; Martin & Turner, 1986; McCoyd & Kerson, 2006; Miles & Huberman, 1994; Murray & Sixsmith, 1998; O'Conner, et al., 2003). However, few offer advice on how to report the resultant findings and/or theory. Social scientific journals continue to follow the format originally designed to report empirical research in the conventional four-section format (theory and literature review, methods, results, discussion/interpretation). Grounded theory researchers who desire to see their work published in these same journals must employ this same four-section format. Over time, grounded theory researchers have developed often used modifications of the traditional content of each section to allow for appropriate descriptions of their research efforts. Because such modifications are not always obvious and rarely articulated, we offer below specific suggestions for reporting grounded theory research in conventional, social-scientific journals.

Introduction and Literature Review

The literature review should be minimal and painted in broad strokes. It may reference and explain a previously published theory, if the purpose of the study is to augment understanding of a specific aspect of that theory. More typically, however, no previously published theory is articulated and instead the theory emerges from the data; the researcher reports the emergent theory in results section of the paper and explains in more detail in discussion. Often the literature review section contains a statement explaining the researchers' use of inductive reasoning at this point, as exemplified below:

As is customary in grounded theory research, we used only a few central ideas and theories to inform the design and execution of our data collection (Eisenhardt 1989, Strauss & Corbin, 1990). However, as our analysis of the data proceeded, we searched the literature for other research that was pertinent to the theoretical issues emerging from the data. We will discuss the initial ideas and the theories we brought to the research in this section and will introduce other pertinent literature as we present and discuss our findings (Beyer & Hannah, 2002, p. 636)

The purpose statement and research questions typically appear in this opening section of the manuscript. The purpose statement might reasonable reflect one or more of the purposes described earlier in this chapter in the section labeled "The Place of Grounded Theory in Social Scientific Work." The research questions reflect the researcher's understanding of a socially constructed (Berger & Luckman, 1967) versus objective reality under study. Often one general research question is employed; for example, Mattarelli and Tagliaventi asked "What is the interplay between members' organizational and professional identities in intraorganizational knowledge-intensive GDTs [globally distributed teams], and what are its consequences for GDTs? " (Mattarelli & Tagliaventi, 2010, p. 419).

Methods

In the methods section, "the process of data analysis, including coding techniques and category creation, should be apparent to the reader" (Suddaby,

2006, p. 637). Methods should be reported in sufficient detail to allow the reader to understand how the researcher generated conceptual categories from the data. Tables or appendices can be used to provide a timeline of the evolution of the conceptual categories as well as examples of codes and illustrative quoted data. Steps to ensure rigor in methodology can be explicated in a transparent way, specifically describing sampling techniques, the constant comparison process, and evidence of saturation. Finally, authors should employ the technical language of grounded theory in a way that demonstrates understanding of grounded theory methodology.

Results

In the Results section, the researcher reports his/her findings in a way that welcomes new (and sometimes unexpected) findings and interpretations, in combination with previously published view points, when appropriate. Results should be reported in a way that demonstrates sensitivity to subtly and detail in informants' interpretations. Results should reflect the researchers' ability to make thoughtful theoretical sense of the new ideas beside the old as well as the specific findings in light of the generalizations that are drawn from them. Occasionally, the axial and selective coding reveal such dramatic findings that researchers report the analysis process in two phases (e.g., Thompson-Hayes, 2009).

Discussion

In the Discussion section, the researcher places his/her emergent theory and/or results in the context of previously published knowledge about the phenomenon under study. A skillful placement demonstrates the researcher's openness to new ideas coupled with an impulse to integrate new ideas into the on-going development of advanced theoretical understandings of the phenomenon under study. Indeed, excellence in grounded theory research depends in large part on the researcher maintaining an on-going understanding of both the lived experience of the phenomenon as well as the published scholarship on the subject. Such knowledge allows for more accurate data analysis and interpretation.

CONCLUSION

Skill at grounded theory research is developmental (Suddaby, 2006). The more knowledge and experience a researcher acquires, the more skilled he/she becomes at the process of grounded theory research. This chapter provides readers with exposure to common understandings of grounded theory research methods and thus contributes to skill development. In sum, the chapter defined grounded theory, provided a history of its development, identified appropriate uses of grounded theory methods, described grounded theory methods in detail, and finally offered advice on how to report the findings of such research. With this knowledge, the reader can understand and critically read grounded theory research as well as decide if he/she desires to employ a grounded theory approach in his/her own line of research.

ACKNOWLEDGMENT

The authors acknowledge their equal contributions to the research, writing, and editing of this chapter. Further, the authors thank their colleagues Kerk F. Kee (Chapman University) and Marceline Thompson-Hayes (Arkansas State University) for their assistance, generosity, and understanding surrounding preparation of this manuscript.

REFERENCES

Bandura, A. (1977). *Social learning theory*. Englewood Cliffs, NJ: Prentice-Hall.

Bandura, A. (2001). Social cognitive theory: An agentic perspective. *Annual Review of Psychology, 52*, 1–26. doi:10.1146/annurev.psych.52.1.1

Belanger, F., & Watson-Manheim, M. B. (2006). Virtual teams and multiple media: Structuring media use to attain strategic goals. *Group Decision and Negotiation, 15*, 299–321. doi:10.1007/s10726-006-9044-8

Benoliel, J. Q. (1996). Grounded theory and nursing knowledge. *Qualitative Health Research, 6*, 406–428. doi:10.1177/104973239600600308

Berger, P., & Luckman, T. (1967). *The social construction of reality: A treatise in the sociology of knowledge and commitment in American life*. Garden City, NY: Anchor.

Beyer, J. M., & Hannah, D. R. (2002). Building on the past: Enacting established personal identities in a new work setting. *Organization Science, 13*, 636–652. doi:10.1287/orsc.13.6.636.495

Birks, M., & Mills, J. (2011). *Grounded theory: A practical guide*. Thousand Oaks, CA: Sage.

Browning, L. D. (1978). A grounded organizational communication theory derived from qualitative data. *Communication Monographs, 45*, 93–109. doi:10.1080/03637757809375957

Charmaz, K. (2006). *Constructing grounded theory: A practical guide through qualitative analysis*. London, UK: Sage.

Charmaz, K. (2009). Shifting the grounds: Constructivist grounded theory methods. In Morce, J., Stern, P. J., Corbin, J., Bowers, B. K., Charmaz, K., & Clarke, A. (Eds.), *Developing Grounded Theory: The Second Generation*. Walnut Creek, CA: Left Coast Press.

Clarke, A. E. (2005). *Situational analysis: Grounded theory mapping after the postmodern turn*. Thousand Oaks, CA: Sage.

Clear, T., & MacDonell, S. G. (2011). Understanding technology use in global virtual teams: Research methodologies and methods. *Information and Software Technology*, *53*, 994–1011. doi:10.1016/j.infsof.2011.01.011

Corbin, J., & Morse, J. (2003). The unstructured interview: Issues of reciprocity and risks when dealing with sensitive topics. *Qualitative Inquiry*, *9*, 335–354. doi:10.1177/1077800403009003001

Corbin, J., & Strauss, A. (1990). Grounded theory research: Procedures, canons, and evaluative criteria. *Qualitative Sociology*, *13*, 3–21. doi:10.1007/BF00988593

Corbin, J., & Strauss, A. (2008). *Basics of qualitative research* (3rd ed.). Thousand Oaks, CA: Sage.

Davison, R., Fuller, M., & Hardin, A. (2003). E-consulting in virtual negotiations. *Group Decision and Negotiation*, *12*(6), 517–534. doi:10.1023/B:GRUP.0000004256.03294.e3

Dick, B. (2000). *Grounded theory revisited*. Retrieved from http://www.scu.edu.au/schools/gcm/ar/arm/op026.html.

Eisenhardt, K. M. (1989). Building theories from case study research. *Academy of Management Review*, *14*, 532–550.

Franklin, C. (1996). Learning to teach qualitative research: Reflections of a quantitative researcher. In Gilgun, J. F., & Sussman, M. B. (Eds.), *The Methods and Methodologies of Qualitative Family Research* (pp. 241–274). Binghamton, NY: Haworth.

Gephart, R. P. (2004). Qualitative research and the Academy of Management Journal. *Academy of Management Journal*, *47*, 454–462. doi:10.5465/AMJ.2004.14438580

Glaser, B., & Strauss, G. (1967). *The discovery of grounded theory: Strategies for qualitative work*. Chicago, IL: Aldine.

Glaser, B. G. (1992). *Basics of grounded theory analysis: Emergence versus forcing*. Mill Valley, CA: Sociology Press.

Hamilton, R. J., & Bowers, B. J. (2006). Internet recruitment and e-mail interviews in qualitative studies. *Qualitative Health Research*, *16*, 821–835. doi:10.1177/1049732306287599

Kazmer, M. M., & Xie, B. (2008). Qualitative interviewing in internet studies: Playing with the media, playing with the method. *Information Communication and Society*, *11*, 257–278. doi:10.1080/13691180801946333

Kirkman, B. L., Rosen, B., Gibson, C. B., Tesluk, P. E., & McPherson, S. O. (2002). Five challenges to virtual team success: Lessons from Sabre, Inc. *The Academy of Management Executive*, *16*, 67–79. doi:10.5465/AME.2002.8540322

Krusiewicz, E. S., & Wood, J. T. (2001). He was our child from the moment we walked in that room: Entrance stories of adoptive parents. *Journal of Social and Personal Relationships*, *18*, 785–803. doi:10.1177/0265407501186003

Mann, C., & Stewart, F. (2002). Internet interviewing. In Gulbrium, J. F., & Holstein, J. A. (Eds.), *Handbook of Interview Research: Context and Method* (pp. 603–628). Thousand Oaks, CA: Sage.

Martin, P. Y., & Turner, B. A. (1986). Grounded theory and organizational research. *The Journal of Applied Behavioral Science*, *22*, 141–157. doi:10.1177/002188638602200207

Mattarelli, E., & Tagliaventi, M. R. (2010). Work-related identities, virtual work acceptance and the development of globalized work practices in globally distributed teams. *Industry and Innovation*, *17*, 415–443. doi:10.1080/13662716.2010.496247

Maznevski, M. L., & Chudoba, K. M. (2000). Bridging space over time: Global virtual team dynamics and effectiveness. *Organization Science, 11*, 473–492. doi:10.1287/orsc.11.5.473.15200

McCoyd, J. L. M., & Kerson, T. S. (2006). Conducting intensive interviews using email. *Qualitative Social Work, 5*, 389–406. doi:10.1177/1473325006067367

McLeod, J. (2001). *Qualitative research in counseling and psychotherapy*. London, UK: Sage.

Merrigan, G., & Huston, C. L. (2004). *Communication research methods*. Belmont, CA: Thomson Wadsworth.

Miles, M. B., & Huberman, A. M. (1994). *Qualitative data analysis: An expanded sourcebook* (2nd ed.). Thousand Oaks, CA: Sage.

Murray, C., & Sixsmith, J. (1998). E-mail: A qualitative research medium for interviewing? *International Journal of Social Research Methodology, 1*, 103–121.

O'Conner, G. C., Rice, M. P., Peters, L., & Veryzer, R. W. (2003). Managing interdisciplinary, longitudinal research teams: Extending grounded theory-building methodologies. *Organization Science, 14*, 353–373. doi:10.1287/orsc.14.4.353.17485

Olson, L. N., Daggs, J. L., Ellevold, B. L., & Rogers, T. K. K. (2007). Entrapping the innocent: Toward a theory of child sexual predators' luring communication. *Communication Theory, 17*, 231–251. doi:10.1111/j.1468-2885.2007.00294.x

Owen, W. F. (1984). Interpretive themes in relational communication. *The Quarterly Journal of Speech, 70*, 274–287. doi:10.1080/00335638409383697

Pauleen, D. J. (2003). An inductively derived model of leader-initiated relationship building with virtual team members. *Journal of Management Information Systems, 20*, 227–256.

Qureshi, S., Liu, M., & Vogel, D. (2006). The effects of electronic collaboration in distributed project management. *Group Decision and Negotiation, 15*, 55–75. doi:10.1007/s10726-005-9006-6

Rupsiene, L., & Pranskuniene, R. (2010). The variety of grounded theory: Different versions of the same method or different methods? *Socialiniai Mokslai, 4*(70), 7–20.

Shachaf, P. (2008). Cultural diversity and information and communication technology impacts on global virtual teams: An exploratory study. *Information & Management, 45*, 131–142. doi:10.1016/j.im.2007.12.003

Silverman, D. (2001). *Interpreting qualitative data, methods for analyzing talk, text and interaction* (2nd ed.). Thousand Oaks, CA: Sage.

Singh, S. (1996). Money, marriage and the computer. In Gilgun, J. F., & Sussman, M. B. (Eds.), *The Methods and Methodologies of Qualitative Family Research* (pp. 369–398). Binghamton, NY: Haworth.

Staples, D. S., & Webster, J. (2007). Exploring traditional and virtual teams' members' "best practices": A social cognitive theory perspective. *Small Group Research, 38*, 60–97. doi:10.1177/1046496406296961

Strauss, A. J., & Corbin, J. (1994). Grounded theory methodology. In Denzin, N. K., & Lincoln, Y. S. (Eds.), *Handbook of Qualitative Research* (pp. 53–65). Thousand Oaks, CA: Sage.

Strauss, A. L., & Corbin, J. (1990). *Basics of qualitative research: Grounded theory procedures and techniques*. Newbury Park, CA: Sage.

Strauss, A. L., & Corbin, J. (1998). *Basics of qualitative research: Techniques and procedures for developing grounded theory* (2nd ed.). Thousand Oaks, CA: Sage.

Stroh, M. (2000). Qualitative interviewing. In Burton, D. (Ed.), *Research Training for Social Scientists: A Handbook for Postgraduate Researchers* (pp. 196–217). London, UK: Sage.

Suddaby, R. (2006). From the editors: What grounded theory is not. *Academy of Management Journal, 49*, 633-642.

Tavallaei, M., & Talib, M. A. (2010). A general perspective on role of theory in qualitative research. *Journal of International Social Research, 3*, 570–577.

Thomas, G., & James, D. (2006). Reinventing grounded theory: Some questions about theory, ground and discovery. *British Educational Research Journal, 32*, 767–795. doi:10.1080/01411920600989412

Thompson-Hayes, M., & Gibson, D., M., Scott, A. T. & Webb, L. M. (2009). Professorial collaborations via CMC: Interactional dialectics. *Computers in Human Behavior, 25*, 208–216. doi:10.1016/j.chb.2008.09.003

Wilson, H. S., & Hutchinson, S. A. (1996). Methodologic mistakes in grounded theory. *Nursing Research, 45*, 122–124. doi:10.1097/00006199-199603000-00012

Zhang, H., & Poole, M. S. (2010). Virtual team identity construction and boundary maintenance. In Long, S. (Ed.), *Communication, Relationships and Practices in Virtual Work* (pp. 100–122). Hershey, PA: IGI Global. doi:10.4018/978-1-61520-979-8.ch006

Corbin, J., & Strauss, A. (2008). *Basics of qualitative research* (3rd ed.). Thousand Oaks, CA: Sage.

Edley, P. P., & Houston, R. (2011). The more things change, the more they stay the same: The role of ICTs in work and family connections. In Wright, K. B., & Webb, L. M. (Eds.), *Computer Mediated Communication in Personal Relationships* (pp. 194–221). New York, NY: Peter Lang Publishers.

Morse, J. M., Stern, P. N., Corbin, J., Bowers, B., Clarke, A. E., & Charmaz, K. (2009). *Developing grounded theory: The second generation*. Walnut Creek, CA: Left Coast Press.

Strauss, A. J., & Corbin, J. (1994). Grounded theory methodology. In Denzin, N. K., & Lincoln, Y. S. (Eds.), *Handbook of Qualitative Research* (pp. 53–65). Thousand Oaks, CA: Sage.

Strauss, A. L., & Corbin, J. (1990). *Basics of qualitative research: Grounded theory procedures and techniques*. Newbury Park, CA: Sage.

Strauss, A. L., & Corbin, J. (1998). *Basics of qualitative research: Techniques and procedures for developing grounded theory* (2nd ed.). Thousand Oaks, CA: Sage.

Tavallaei, M., & Talib, M. A. (2010). A general perspective on role of theory in qualitative research. *Journal of International Social Research, 3*, 570–577.

Thomas, G., & James, D. (2006). Reinventing grounded theory: Some questions about theory, ground and discovery. *British Educational Research Journal, 32*, 767–795. doi:10.1080/01411920600989412

ADDITIONAL READING

Birks, M., & Mills, J. (2011). *Grounded theory: A practical guide*. Thousand Oaks, CA: Sage.

Charmaz, K. (2006). *Constructing grounded theory: A practical guide through qualitative analysis*. Thousand Oaks, CA: Sage.

KEY TERMS AND DEFINITIONS

Analytical Induction: Using of a combination of inductive and deductive reasoning to move between data and emerging, more abstract ideas as a means of identifying concepts, categories, relationships, and/or theories that describe the informants' thinking as recorded in the data.

Category Saturation: Comparing the concepts emerging from data to new data, often prompting the development of new codes, concepts, or themes. When no new ideas emerge from additional data, then data collection ceases as the researcher has achieved category saturation.

Coding: To develop categories for ideas that emerge from a data set.

Concept, Category, Supra-Category: Ideas that emerge from data at increasing levels of abstraction.

Constant Comparison Process: Moving between the specific data and the emerging concepts, which are more general, and then back to the data. The primary mode of analysis in the constant comparison process is analytic induction, defined above.

Deductive Reasoning: To reason from the general to the specific.

Forcefulness: The strength of an informant's statement; the extent to which he/she indicts that an idea is important.

Grounded Theory: Allowing the central ideas within a text to emerge through the reading, rereading, and repetitive mention of those ideas within the text; then explaining the object of study via the central, emergent ideas.

Inductive Reasoning: To reason from the specific to the general.

Qualitative Research: Assessing ideas and understandings rather than measuring a perceived objective reality typically via quantitative measures.

Theme: A central idea that emerges from a text-based data set.

Theory: A description of how a phenomenon works.

Chapter 11
Exploring Organizational Cultures through Virtual Survey Research

Eletra S. Gilchrist
The University of Alabama – Huntsville, USA

Pavica Sheldon
The University of Alabama – Huntsville, USA

ABSTRACT

The survey is regarded as the most commonly used methodological tool in gathering information. There are many types of surveys, but this chapter discusses how to conduct and analyze quantitative and qualitative survey research in virtual environments via online or computer-administered surveys. Corporations are increasingly relying on virtual surveys to acquire knowledge about their employees' morale, satisfaction, and productivity. Hence, this chapter is intended as a tutorial guide for exploring organizational cultures through virtual survey research. This chapter explains in detail how to design survey questionnaires, sample subjects, analyze data both quantitatively and qualitatively, and finally how to interpret survey results. Strengths and limitations associated with using virtual surveys are highlighted. The chapter also considers future directions for understanding employees' needs through virtual survey research.

INTRODUCTION

Picture these scenarios: The chief executive officer of a Fortune 500 company wants to know how to motivate his or her employees to double company profits within the next five years. A manager of a

DOI: 10.4018/978-1-4666-0963-1.ch011

small, yet profitable company has recently noticed that the employees seem uninspired and apathetic; hence, the manager desires to understand what is impacting worker morale. A boss at a newly established corporation seeks to unearth employees' perceptions of the strengths and limitations of communicating virtually. These are just some of the many questions that confront upper management on a regular basis. With these questions in mind, corporations must explore possible avenues for answering these important questions.

At its most fundamental level, research is defined as the process of asking questions and finding answers to those questions (Keyton, 2011). When questions are answered, investigators can use the answers to make necessary decisions. In the first scenario, for example, if research revealed that employees would be motivated to increase their level of productivity if the company offered more flexible working hours, then the CEO might be motivated to implement some flexibility in the work schedule. Likewise, as stated in the second scenario, if research suggested that the manager could improve worker morale and satisfaction by personally visiting with the employees more often, then the manager might be willing to schedule monthly or at least quarterly face-to-face meetings. In reference to the third scenario, if research indicated employees perceive that the strengths of communicating virtually far outweigh the limitations, then the boss might become a strong advocate for virtual work. In other words, when company leaders take on the role of detective by asking questions and seeking answers to those questions, they allow themselves to track down the information needed to make decisions (Keyton, 2011).

Researchers have explored a plethora of important topics related to employees, including organizational climate and employee engagement (Langford, 2009), relational limitations intrinsic to virtual work (Gilchrist, 2010), job satisfaction (Tsair-Wei, Wen-Pin, Chih-Wei, Weng-Chung, Shih-Chung, Hsien-Yi, & Shih-Bin, 2011) and perceptions of safety (Carder, 2003; O'Toole & Nalbone, 2011). These topics have been instrumental in enhancing our understanding of employees' needs and facilitating a more productive work environment. Though these topics have varied in their overall methodology, each of them has used surveys as the prime methods for data collection. Because surveys, in particular those administered

virtually, are readily used to acquire data about employees in the field of organizational communication, this chapter explores survey research and virtual work. Specifically, the chapter addresses conducting and analyzing quantitative and qualitative survey research in a virtual environment, while exploring the strengths and limitations associated with both approaches.

BACKGROUND

Psychologist James Cattell (1860-1944) is one of the pioneers of survey research. Cattell started using mental measures to examine college students and, thus, established psychology as a legitimate science. According to Reinard (2008), the term *survey* involves "the process of looking at something in its entirety" in order to scrutinize "the complete scope of something" (p. 346). Wrench, Thomas-Maddox, Richmond, and McCroskey (2008) add that a survey is "a social scientific method for gathering quantifiable information about a specific group of people..." (p. 214). However, in social scientific research, the terms *survey* and *questionnaire* are often used interchangeable and refer to the use of questions for the purpose of discovering descriptive characteristics about phenomena (Reinard, 2008). More specifically, a questionnaire is "a form containing a series of questions and mental measures that is given to a group of people in an attempt to gain statistical information about the group as part of a survey" (Wrench, et al., 2008, p. 215). This chapter uses the terms *survey* and *questionnaire* to refer to the tools used in survey research.

The survey is regarded as the most commonly used methodological tool in gathering information (Keyton, 2011), and it is frequently done at a single point in time, though multi-time research is also available via the survey (Watt & van den Berg, 1995). Surveys are especially useful when gathering information about populations that are too large for everyone in the population to be studied (Frey, Botan, & Kreps, 2000). Hence, the objective of surveys is to collect data from a representative sample that can be generalized to the population from which the respondents were selected (Keyton, 2011). By asking questions with surveys, researchers can collect data that can be used to describe, compare, or explain attitudes or behaviors about the population in question (Fink, 1995b).

There are many types of surveys, but the most common ones include in-person or face-to-face, telephone, mail, and online or computer-administered surveys (Keyton, 2011; Watt & van den Berg, 1995). Because this chapter focuses on the use of survey research in virtual work, a deeper discussion of online or computer-administered surveys is warranted. As the name suggests, computer-administered surveys are conducted virtually via computers and have become increasingly popular because of online survey sites, such as SurveyMonkey.com and QuestionPro.com. These programs have revolutionized virtual surveys by making it easy to design and collect data. Many researchers have used these programs to collect virtual survey data, such as Inungu, Mumford, Younis, and Langford (2009) who used Survey Monkey to distribute an anonymous questionnaire to 1,000 students about their HIV knowledge, sources of information, attitudes toward people living with HIV/AIDS, and their sexual behaviors. Online survey sites can be especially appealing when they allow researchers to collect data free of charge. However, many of the free versions have limits regarding the number of items that can be asked and the number of respondents that can complete the survey. Thus, it is important for researchers to consider other methods for conducting online survey research.

Researchers often rely on three alternatives to free online survey programs. First, surveys may be included in an email, where respondents simply note their answers in a reply message. Alternately, the respondents may receive a survey attached to an email that requires them to open the attach-ment, type and save their responses, then send the document back to the researcher for analysis. Gilchrist (2011) used this method when she emailed an open-ended survey to a purposive sample of African-American women professors and solicited their responses to questions regarding their interactions with majority-race students. Though this approach can be effective, the responses are not anonymous because the researchers will know who said what based on return email addresses.

A second method involves the participants completing a survey that was created with HTML and posted as a web page with a unique URL. With this method, the researcher can instruct potential respondents to go to the URL and complete the survey online. As stated by Keyton (2011), "the respondent comes to the survey rather than the survey going to the respondent" (p. 163). Kath, Magley, and Marmet (2009) used this method to survey 599 employees from 97 workgroups across a New England grocery store chain about the relationships between safety climate, trust, and organizational outcomes.

Third, the researcher may decide to hire a professional survey company, such as Pew Research, The Gallop Corporation, or The Selzer Company. This method has been used by corporations who seek to better understand employees' needs, concerns, and perceptions relative to a mix of issues, such as employee engagement. According to Flander (2008), "employee engagement is becoming top of mind for CEOs and boards at the nation's largest companies" (para. 1). Northrop Grumman recently hired The Gallop Corporation to administer an employee engagement survey to assess one-third of its 122,000 employees (Hegeman, 2011).

Not only can researchers use a myriad of methods for getting virtual surveys to respondents, researchers also have many forms of virtual surveys at their disposal. The most common form is the *self-report* or *self-administered* survey, where individuals answer questions about themselves. In contrast, *proxy responses* or *other-reports* ask respondents to report information about other people. There are strengths and limitations associated with both methods. For example, a strength of self-reports is the freedom individuals have in revealing information about themselves, and it is presumed that people do not know others as well as they know themselves. However, just because individuals know themselves and how they feel about particular topics does not mean they will share that information with researchers. Hence, lying or failing to reveal candid information with researchers is a limitation of self-reports. Other-reports are useful in that other individuals may be more willing to share truthful information about others, but Blair, Menon, and Bickart (1991) warn that people acquire information about themselves and others differently. Thus, information perceived to be true about others may actually vary dramatically from the actual information or individuals' accounts of that information. For this reason, self-reports are more commonly used compared to other-reports.

Whether surveys are designed for self or other reporting, according to Reinard (2008), all survey research involves six steps: (1) selecting questions and providing instructions, (2) formatting the survey, (3) determining reliability and validity, (4) sampling subjects, (5) administering the survey, and (6) analyzing and interpreting the results. The ensuing section expounds upon each of these six steps in the contexts of quantitative and qualitative survey methods.

SURVEY RESEARCH AND VIRTUAL WORK

An Overview of Quantitative and Qualitative Survey Research

At its most fundamental level, quantitative research is science through numbers. Specifically, it refers to the systematic and empirical investigation of human behavior and social phenomena through statistical procedures. As stated by Bashi (2004), quantitative research aims to "summarize trends and test hypotheses that describe samples and predict the likelihood of event occurrences" (p. 40). While experiments and surveys comprise the two major branches of quantitative research (Reinard, 2008), this chapter only addresses surveys.

In its most basic form qualitative research is scientific inquiry that expresses data through words and descriptions. Ragin, Nagel, and White (2004) add that the primary goal of qualitative research is to "make the facts understandable" through detailed knowledge of specific cases (p. 10). There are many approaches to qualitative research, including grounded theory, focus groups, autoethnography, ethnography, observations, interviews etc. This chapter focuses specifically on the interview or open-ended survey form of qualitative research.

Selecting Questions and Providing Instructions

Survey research begins with picking questions (Reinard, 2008). There is no single best way to select questions, as the type of questions will be dictated by the research question(s) or the problem(s) the researcher is trying to solve. Generally, questions will reflect one of the four levels of measurement: nominal, ordinal, interval, or ratio. *Nominal* level questions are great for determining descriptive statistics of the research sample (Wrench, et al., 2008). Those might include questions about biological sex, ethnicity, religious affiliation, or political party. *Ordinal* level questions are less often used in survey research, but they are useful for determining rank orders, such as respondents' socioeconomic status or rank in a company. The most common type of questions seen on quantitative questionnaires involves *interval* level questions. These questions not only rank order, but assume equal distance between the data points, such as with Likert and semantic differential scales. Likert-type scales were developed by psychologist Rensis Likert (1932) to identify the extent of a person's beliefs, attitudes, or feelings toward some object. The traditional scale asks respondents the extent to which they agree or disagree with a set of statements by choosing one response category generally on a 5, 7, or 9-point scale that ranges from "strongly agree" to "strongly disagree" (Frey, et al., 2000). Likert-type scales are variations of a traditional scale and might include different answer categories than range from agree to disagree, important to unimportant, or always to never. The semantic differential scale was developed by Osgood (1952) and asks respondents to rate their opinion on a linear scale between two endpoints that have opposite meanings (e.g., good/bad or weak/strong) (Wrench, et al., 2008). The stimulus is identified at the top of the scale and may be a word, phrase, statement, or picture. For example, employees may be asked to rate their feelings toward a new software program installed on their computers with response categories ranging from "low quality" (1) to "high quality" (7). The fourth type of questions includes *ratio* level questions, where there exists a true zero in the data. Normally there are not many questions that a researcher will ask using a ratio level of measurement (Wrench, et al., 2008), though they could be useful if a corporation wanted to see how many times employees have been reprimanded or fired.

Survey questions measured at the nominal, ordinal, interval, and ratio levels can often be formatted as closed-ended or open-ended questions. *Closed-ended* questions are those in which respondents have a fixed amount of choices to use in answering a question or responding to a statement, such as *yes* or *no*. These questions are often used when conducting quantitative survey research. An example of a closed-ended question might be: "Are you satisfied with the company's current fringe benefits package?" Closed ended questions should be used if there is agreement on what the response set should be and statistical

analysis and reporting of the data are desirable or necessary (Keyton, 2011).

Although closed-ended questions limit response options, *open-ended* questions allow for maximum lei-way in responding because respondents choose their own replies (Keyton, 2011), and they give the researcher data from the respondents' point of view rather than the researcher's (Fink, 1995a). Qualitative survey research, in particular, uses open-ended questions. Open-ended questions are effective when exploring new topics or if detailed information is required from the respondents. For example, if a manager wants to explore the company's technological deficiencies, open-ended questions might be warranted. An example might include: "In what areas of technology should our company expand?" According to Keyton (2011), five conditions justify the use of open-ended questions: (1) respondents' own words are important and the researcher wants direct quotes; (2) respondents are willing and can answer questions in their own words; (3) the set of response choices is unknown; (4) the researcher is willing to analyze the text of responses; and (5) the reporting needs are best met by open-ended responses.

Choosing the most appropriate type of question is not the only thing a researcher has to be careful about when designing a questionnaire. Creating clear instructions is important as well. Watt and van den Berg (1995) contend that instructions should be as short and simple as possible, not exceeding three or four sentences. Wrench et al. (2008) also encourage researchers to offer participants dummy questions (e.g., example questions) before they begin filling out the questionnaire so that the participants will understand what is expected of them.

Formatting the Survey

One of the most challenging questions for a researcher is where to place a question in the overall survey. According to Reinard (2008), formatting the questionnaire is the second step in survey research. Fowler (2009) argues that survey questions should be straightforward or concrete, which is achieved when the questions are precise and unambiguous. Each item should be one complete thought written in sentence or question format and worded in such a precise manner that the respondents know how to answer. As stated by Keyton (2011), "How you word survey or questionnaire items is crucial to obtaining the information you desire" (p. 167).

Wrench et al. (2008) suggest grouping similar questions together when formatting a survey. For example, a set of Likert-type questions (i.e., disagree, neutral, agree) should be placed together. Nominal level questions (e.g., age and gender) are easiest to answer and are, therefore, most effective if placed at the end of a longer survey when participants start feeling fatigue (Wrench, et al., 2008). Because people assume that the first item the researcher has on a questionnaire reflects what the study is about, controversial or sensitive questions should also be placed toward the end of the survey, thus, allowing participants to get comfortable with the study by answering the easier questions first (Wrench, et al., 2008).

When formatting the survey, researchers should also consider the length of the survey. As stated by Watt and van den Berg (1995), "filling out a questionnaire is work" (p. 368). Respondents tend to comply less with long and demanding surveys, and the fatigue that comes from filling out long surveys may interfere with the responses. Hence, it is recommended that surveys require no more than 15-minutes to complete (van den Berg, 1995).

In Web surveys, question text can be supplemented with a variety of visual elements, including graphics, color, and interactive features. Those elements, however, have to be used with great care in order to facilitate and not distract respondents from the task of completing the survey (Couper, Traugott, & Lamias, 2001).

Though there are many factors to carefully consider when formatting a survey, novice re-searchers may find it easier to use established surveys. For example, *Communication Research Measures II: A Sourcebook* edited by Rubin, Rubin, Graham, Perse, and Seibold (2009) is a collection scales that measure communication phenomena in a variety of settings, including organizations. In addition to providing the scales, the book also gives the reliability and validity measures of each scale; reliability and validity are expounded on in the following section.

Determining Reliability and Validity

Data collected through questionnaires are worthwhile only if they are recorded in accurate ways. Developing a reliable and valid instrument is, therefore, a primary concern for all researchers (Frey, et al., 2000). Reinard (2008) argues that the third step in survey research involves determining if the questionnaire is reliable and valid. Though it is beyond the scope of this chapter to fully explore reliability and validity, reliability and validity give survey findings credibility. Specifically, *reliability* involves measuring something in a consistent and stable manner, and *validity* is concerned with how well researchers measure what they intend to measure (Frey, et al., 2000). The more reliable a measurement is, the more dependable it is because it leads to similar outcomes when applied to different people, texts, and contexts. The most popular method for determining reliability with a quantitative survey is Cronbach's alpha or the alpha coefficient, which is a number that ranges from 0 to 1.00. However, measurement validity has no meaningful number attached to it; instead, researchers have to argue at the conceptual level that a measurement technique assesses accurately what it is supposed to assess (Frey, et al., 2000).

The credibility of qualitative survey research is enhanced through *triangulation,* which is the use of multiple data collection methods (Denzin & Lincoln, 2005). For example, if a corporation used an online open-ended survey to collect data from its employees, the corporation could also conduct in-person focus groups with its employees to ensure that the information gathered from the surveys truly captured the essence of the employees' perceptions. In other words, by triangulating or using methods in addition to the online surveys, organizational leaders can be more confident about their findings and conclusions (Denzin & Lincoln, 2005).

Sampling Subjects

After the questionnaire is designed, the researcher is tasked with selecting participants for the study—hence, the fourth step in conducting survey research (Reinard, 2008). Because it is impossible to collect data from every member of a given population (including corporations), researchers select a number of participants who are representative members of the population they desire to study. Participants can be *randomly* selected, which means that each member of the population has an equal chance of being selected, or they can be selected in a *nonrandom* manner, which means that each member of the population does not have an equal chance of being selected. Examples of random sampling methods for obtaining participants include simple, cluster, stratified, and systematic samples, whereas examples of nonrandom methods include convenience, volunteer, purposive, quota, and network samples (for descriptions see Frey, et al., 2000). It is generally best if researchers have a random sample because this type of sample makes it possible for researchers to calculate the sampling error or the degree to which the sample might be different from the population it represents (Wrench, et al., 2008). However, research that occurs within organizations usually involves nonrandom samples because the researchers desire responses from very specific and purposive samples (e.g., Gilchrist, 2010; Kath, Magley, & Marmet, 2009).

Regardless of whether a random or nonrandom sample is used, all respondents should have access to the information needed to answer the questions

(Keyton, 2011). Respondents who lack the knowledge or ability to answer the survey questions should not be asked to participate in the survey. Thus, it is important for corporate leaders to make sure they are asking the appropriate questions to each type of employee. For example, it would be ineffective to ask a newly hired employee how the workplace climate has changed over the past decade; veteran employees would be more suited for answering these types of questions. In sum, the success of survey research depends, in part, on asking the right questions to the right people.

Administering the Survey

Once the survey is created, the researcher must determine the best way to administer the survey or place it into the hands of the representative sample, which is step number five in the survey research process (Reinard, 2008). Before researchers administer the survey to a huge sample of their target population, it is advisable to *pretest* or *pilot test* the survey, which involves distributing the survey to a small group of participants from the target population and analyzing the data to see if changes are needed (Frey, et al., 2000). For example, if a management team asks its employees to "rate the respect of your immediate boss," pretesting might reveal that the question is too general, and a clearer question would ask the employees to "rate how well your boss communicates respect to customers, suppliers, and competitors." Pretesting should especially be done if researchers develop their own questions or use only some of the items from an established survey (Keyton, 2011). Once researchers have pretested the survey and made any necessary changes, they can proceed with administering the survey to the targeted population.

The most common way of disseminating questionnaires is through self-administration. This includes mass administration or handing out a survey to a large group of people in a stable physical environment. Self-administration is the cheapest and fastest method and generally results in a high response rate. As previously mentioned, this chapter focuses on surveys that are self-administered virtually. The ensuring sections segue into the implications of virtual survey research.

Analyzing and Interpreting the Results

The essence of conducting survey research in virtual environments rests upon researchers acquiring data that can be used to better understand and enhance organizational cultures. Before such information can be obtained, it is imperative that the data are appropriately analyzed and interpreted. Data analysis is the final step in the process of survey research (Reinard, 2008).

Data obtained from quantitative surveys are analyzed using a variety of statistical tests that transform data into useful information that can be shared with others. There are two types of statistical data analysis: descriptive statistical data analysis and inferential statistical data analysis. *Descriptive statistics* include summary statistics or numerical indicators that summarize the data. Measures of central tendency, such as mean, median, and mode, are descriptive statistics that summarize the center of a data set. In other words, there is one number that summarizes all the scores on a variable. On the other hand, measures of dispersion, such as range, variance, and standard deviation, are descriptive statistics that report how much scores vary from each other or how far they are spread around the center point of a data set (Frey, et al., 2000). Managers might calculate descriptive statistics if they wanted to assess employees' average feelings about an impending company downsize.

Inferential statistics is the second type of statistical data analysis. There are many types of tests, including chi-squares, t-tests, correlations, ANOVAs, regressions etc. Each test has its own detailed formula that may be found by consulting any number of statistics books (e.g., Frey, et al.,

2000; Keyton, 2011; Reinard, 2008; Wrench, et al., 2008). Inferential statistics are used to infer or estimate the characteristics of a population based on data collected from the sample. Inferential statistics are concerned with significance testing, which means that they examine how likely differences between groups and relationships between variables occur by chance (Frey, et al., 2000). For instance, if a company's CEO wanted to examine if a relationship exists between employee grievances at the middle and upper management levels, it would be appropriate for the CEO to use a correlation as the correct inferential statistical test.

As previously stated, qualitative survey research uses open-ended questions that allow for maximum lei-way in responding. Because the results can be so varied, "responses to open questions are difficult to translate into numerical equivalents for use in statistical tests" (Keyton, 2011, p. 172). So, instead of analyzing data with descriptive statistics or inferential statistical tests, data obtained from open-ended surveys are often analyzed with qualitative content analysis, which is useful when exploring the meaning of messages (Frey, et al., 2000). Specifically, a qualitative approach focuses both on "explicit and implicit concepts and empowers the researcher to use his or her judgment in determining, on a case by case basis, whether a particular linguistic token references a particular concept in the given context" (Bazerman & Prior, 2004, p. 15). Qualitative content analysis further allows researchers to act as tools for analyzing the data (Hoepfl, 1997).

Before the qualitative data can be analyzed, however, the researcher must determine the units to be coded through a process called *unitizing* (Frey, et al., 2000). There are many types of units, but the ones that are especially relevant to content analysis of a qualitative nature include: syntactical, propositional, and thematic. *Syntactical units* involve discrete units of language, such as unique words, phrases, or sentences. For example, a manager who wants to examine the current state of employee morale might unitize employees' comments syntactically, looking for how many times the employees say they are "satisfied" or "dissatisfied" with their work. *Propositional units* are assertions about a phenomenon that are polar opposites, such as positive or negative. This unitizing method would be useful if a boss wanted to gage employees' perceptions of a new software program. Once the employees wrote their responses, the boss could examine how many positive and negative references were made relative to the software. Lastly, *thematic units* consist of the topics or themes found within messages. Repeating ideas characterized into *thematic constructs* include abstract concepts that organize a group of themes by placing them into a theoretical framework (Auerbach & Silverstein, 2003). Thematic unitizing might be used if a CEO wanted a holistic view of how employees perceive an impending company merger.

Each type of unitizing involves human judgments (Watt & van den Berg, 1995), where researchers examine written text and look for *repeating ideas*, which are defined as concepts "expressed in relevant texts by two or more research participants" (Auerbach & Silverstein, 2003, p. 54). Because the researcher comprises the prime mode of data analysis with qualitative content analysis, the researcher must determine the amount of unreliability that is introduced by differences in judgment (Watt & van den Berg, 1995). Hence, it is recommended that two coders are used to analyze the data and the *intercoder reliability coefficient* is calculated. Though there are a number of ways to calculate intercoder reliability (for examples see Frey, et al., 2000; Reinard, 2008; Watt & van den Berg, 1995), each formula connotes an intercoder correlation of .80 or higher as acceptable reliability.

Once the quantitative or qualitative survey data are appropriately analyzed, the final step involves interpreting the results. Keyton (2011) cautions researchers to interpret the data ethically and consider the data as a whole, rather than focusing on individual responses. The goal of research is to make sense of the data and examine the findings holistically. Luckily, many Fortune 500 companies seem to be getting it right. According to Ian V. Ziskin, corporate vice president and chief human resource and administrative officer at Northrop Grumman, a major defense and aerospace contractor, "The single biggest thing to focus on is not the actual scores or the response rates—that's a means to an end. The end is, do you really understand what the issues are in your business, and what are the actions you're taking to improve them?" (Flander, 2008, para. 22).

IMPLICATIONS OF SURVEY RESEARCH AND VIRTUAL WORK

It is not by coincidence that surveys are the most commonly used method for gathering information about populations (Keyton, 2011). Surveys have been especially relied upon to collect data about employees, and many of these surveys have been administered virtually (see Carder, 2003; Gilchrist, 2010; Kath, Magley, & Marmet, 2009; Langford, 2009; Tsair-Wei, et al., 2011). Whether the surveys take on a quantitative or qualitative orientation, there is a wealth of strengths associated with using virtual surveys to examine organizational cultures.

Strengths of Survey Research in Virtual Work

One issue with administering face-to-face surveys is that the presence of the survey distributor may result in *social desirability bias,* which means that the respondents may answer in ways that are perceived to be favorable (Marlowe & Crowne, 1960). In contrast, administering surveys virtually in a secure and anonymous environment removes the presence of the survey distributor, which should subsequently facilitate more open responses from the survey participants.

Besides minimizing the effects of social desirability bias, computer-administered surveys allow the researcher to prepare an extensive set of questions, yet respondents are directed to answer only the questions that are relevant to them (Keyton, 2011; Watt & van den Berg, 1995). For example, if a company is exploring employees' perceptions of the company's benefits package, an early question might be "Do you think our current benefits package meets employees' needs?" Respondents who answer *yes* can be given one set of questions, whereas respondents who answer *no* can be given an alternate set of questions. The computer's ability to pick and choose relevant questions based on prior responses is called *adaptive interviewing* (Watt & van den Berg, 1995). An additional, yet commonly overlooked, benefit of Internet survey research is the ease with which a survey can be quickly modified. For example, early data returns may suggest additional questions that the employer should ask. Changing questions in the middle of the data collection process would be impossible with many other survey methods, including the mail questionnaire (Watt, 1997). Online surveys also commonly display a progress indicator, which is used to signal how much of a task is completed (Yan, Conrad, Tourangeau, & Couper, 2010). Studies have shown (e.g., Couper, et al., 2001; Crawford, Couper, & Lamias, 2001) that respondents are more likely to complete a self-administered web questionnaire if they know how much remains.

Time efficiency marks another benefit associated with survey research administered virtually. Because replies to the survey questions are entered directly on the computer keyboard, the data are quickly retrieved from the respondents and can be immediately analyzed. Virtual survey research is also cost effective because the expenses associated with hiring someone to key in data are eliminated. In addition, reminder emails can be sent to nonrespondents if questionnaires are not returned in the allotted time period.

Internet questionnaires can also be made visually pleasing with attractive fonts and graphics. In some cases, audio and video components could be added to the questionnaire (Watt, 1997). For example, an employee might be asked to watch a video about unethical work practices, after which he or she would answer a set of questions related to that video.

Limitations of Survey Research in Virtual Work

Though the strengths associated with survey research in virtual environments are plentiful, limitations also abound. Whether the surveys are quantitatively or qualitatively oriented, research has noted that with online surveys there is an increased chance of acquiring low-quality data. Specifically, research has found that respondents tend give more "don't know" and "nonresponse" answers, resulting in less variation of the data (Heerwegh & Loosveldt, 2008).

Keyton (2011) noted four additional disadvantages to conducting survey research virtually: (1) challenges in identifying populations and samples, (2) concerns of computer security, (3) researcher must be skilled at creating web pages or will need to purchase survey software services, and (4) must have accurate email addresses or contact information of potential respondents. Moreover, there tends to be a response bias linked to online surveys in that only people who are comfortable using computers and the Internet tend to respond to questions administered virtually (Couper, 2000). Another problem is the absence of an interviewer to motivate the respondents or provide guidance on how to answer each question (Schwarz, 1995, 1996). With the absence of an interviewer, the respondents must seek such information from the instrument itself. Hence, researchers should pay special attention to the visual elements of virtual survey design.

While this chapter duly notes the limitations intrinsic to not only working virtually, but also conducting research virtually, previous studies have noted that employees are comfortable with virtual work and often prefer it to more traditional face-to-face methods (e.g., Gilchrist, 2010). Hence, it is our position that despite the limitations, conducting survey research in virtual environments is feasible, beneficial, and can provide company leaders with invaluable information.

FUTURE RESEARCH DIRECTIONS

Corporations are increasingly relying on virtual surveys to acquire knowledge about their employees. As this method of inquiry continues to advance, considerations of important future directions are warranted. Initially, future research should focus on how to create and also protect web-based survey data so that employees feel more confident that their responses will be kept confidential. This is necessary as studies (e.g., Borg, Braun, & Baumgartner, 2008) have found that employees who have a low commitment to their work, low job satisfaction, and a negative attitude toward the company's leadership were less likely to provide demographic information such as their full name and address when surveyed by the company. This is one of the reasons many employee web-based surveys today have demographic information filled out automatically by the personnel information system (Borg, et al., 2008). In addition, future studies should inquire about issues pertaining to work, personality, or other factors that influence employees' compliance or noncompliance with web-based survey requests. These factors should be examined across time and cultures using both quantitative and qualitative methods.

Past studies have found contradictory findings about the usefulness of video and audio features in survey design. For example, the graphic progress indicator helps respondents stay motivated to complete an online survey, but at the same time, it might take longer to download the image. These features might also distract the respondent from answering the questions accurately and honestly (Couper, et al., 2001). All these possibilities require further research.

Considering the increasing use and popularity of social networking sites and corporate blogs in American workplaces, future research should also assess organizations' use of social media for conducting surveys online. For example, Facebook has its own Zoomerang Application that allows users to create surveys or polls. Some companies have used Facebook groups to post the links to conventional online surveys hosted outside Facebook (e.g., Skittles Bubble Gum). For a relatively small fee, a firm can pose a question to a Facebook audience of a specified size and receive an answer within hours (Poynter, 2008). Facebook and other social networking sites allow companies to target the audience very specifically—based on traditional demographic models (e.g., age, gender, type of work, etc.). Future studies should, therefore, investigate the potentials of Facebook and other similar social media in acquiring data about employees working virtually.

CONCLUSION

Virtual work has become a staple in many of today's corporations. When Gilchrist (2010) surveyed a sample of engineers about the strengths and limitations of working virtually, the engineers noted many limitations associated with virtual work, including (1) less personal, (2) lack of nonverbal cues, (3) increased miscommunications, (4) more noise/interference, and (5) reduced interpersonal competence. Yet, though the engineers were cognizant of these relational limitations, they consistently reported that the benefits of working virtually outweighed the limitations because virtual work (1) overcomes geographical distances, (2) cuts costs, (3) expedites meeting times, (4) permits flex time, (5) is convenient, and (6) easy to use. Findings from Gilchrist (2010) suggest that engineers are not only comfortable with virtual work, but prefer it more than traditional methods, such as face-to-face communication. In fact, virtual communication is now perceived to facilitate task and social exchanges comparatively as well as more traditional communication forms (Walther & Parks, 2002).

Just as companies are becoming increasingly aware of the benefits linked to working virtually, it is important for organizational leaders to use advancements in technology to better understand their employees' needs and maintain a more productive working environment. Toward that end, this chapter has examined survey research in virtual environments. By unearthing the means of conducting, analyzing, and evaluating quantitative and qualitative survey research in virtual environments, this chapter provides organizational leaders with tools that not only can facilitate a better understanding of employee concerns, but can potentially transform holistic organizational cultures.

REFERENCES

Auerbach, C. F., & Silverstein, L. B. (2003). *Qualitative data: An introduction to coding and analysis.* New York, NY: New York University Press.

Bashi, V. (2004). Improving qualitative research proposal evaluation. In C. C. Ragain, J. Nagel, & P. White (Eds.), *Workshop on Scientific Foundations of Qualitative Research,* (pp. 39-43). Washington, DC: National Science Foundation.

Bazerman, C., & Prior, P. (2004). *What writing does and how it does it: An introduction to analyzing texts and textual practices.* Mahwah, NJ: Lawrence Earlbaum.

Blair, J., Menon, G., & Bickart, B. (1991). Measurement effects in self vs. proxy responses to survey questions: An information-processing perspective. In Biemer, P. P., Groves, R. M., Lyberg, L. E., Mathiowetz, N. A., & Sudman, S. (Eds.), *Measurement Errors in Surveys* (pp. 145–166). New York, NY: Wiley. doi:10.1002/9781118150382. ch9

Borg, I., Braun, M., & Baumgartner, M. K. (2008). Attitudes of demographic item nonrespondents in employee surveys. *International Journal of Manpower, 29,* 146–160. doi:10.1108/01437720810872703

Carder, B. (2003). A survey-based system for safety measurement and improvement. *Journal of Safety Research, 34*(2), 157–163. doi:10.1016/ S0022-4375(03)00007-0

Couper, M. P. (2000). Web surveys: A review of issues and approaches. *Public Opinion Quarterly, 64,* 464–481. doi:10.1086/318641

Couper, M. P., Traugott, M. W., & Lamias, M. J. (2001). Web survey design and administration. *Public Opinion Quarterly, 65,* 230–253. doi:10.1086/322199

Crawford, S. D., Couper, M. P., & Lamias, M. J. (2001). Web surveys: Perception of burden. *Social Science Computer Review, 19,* 146–162. doi:10.1177/089443930101900202

Crowne, D. P., & Marlowe, D. (1960). A new scale of social desirability independent of psychopathology. *Journal of Consulting Psychology, 24,* 349–354. doi:10.1037/h0047358

Denzin, N. K., & Lincoln, Y. S. (2005). *The Sage handbook of qualitative research* (3rd ed.). Thousand Oaks, CA: Sage.

Fink, A. (1995a). *How to ask survey questions* (*Vol. 1*). Thousand Oaks, CA: Sage.

Fink, A. (1995b). *The survey handbook* (*Vol. 1*). Thousand Oaks, CA: Sage.

Flander, S. (2008). Terms of engagement. *Human Resource Executive Online*. Retrieved from http://www.hreonline.com/HRE/story.jsp?storyId=59866490.

Fowler, F. J. Jr. (2009). *Survey research methods* (4th ed.). Thousand Oaks, CA: Sage.

Frey, L., Botan, C., & Kreps, G. (2000). *Investigating communication: An introduction to research methods* (2nd ed.). Boston, MA: Allyn & Bacon.

Gilchrist, E. S. (2010). Employees' perceptions of relational limitations inherent in virtual work. In Long, S. D. (Ed.), *Communication, Relationships, and Practices in Virtual Work* (pp. 224–238). Hershey, PA: IGI Global. doi:10.4018/978-1-61520-979-8.ch013

Gilchrist, E. S. (2011). One of these things is not like the others: African American women professors' experiences with majority-race students. In Niles, M. N., & Gordon, N. (Eds.), *Still Searching for Our Mothers' Gardens: Experiences of New, Tenure Track Faculty of Color at 'Majority' Institutions* (pp. 213–233). Lanham, MD: University Press of America.

Heerwegh, D., & Loosveldt, G. (2008). Face-to-face versus web surveying in a high-internet-coverage population. *Public Opinion Quarterly, 72*, 836–846. doi:10.1093/poq/nfn045

Hegeman, J. (2011). Currents. *Northrop Grumman Shipbuilding-Newport News*. Retrieved from http://www.huntingtoningalls.com/nns/employees/currents/2011/011011.pdf.

Hoepfl, M. (1997). Choosing qualitative research: A primer for technology education researchers. *Journal of Technology Information, 9*, 47–63.

Inungu, J., Mumford, V., Younis, M., & Langford, S. (2009). HIV knowledge, attitudes, and practices among college students in the United States. *Journal of Health and Human Services Administration, 32*(3), 259–277.

Kath, L. M., Magley, V. J., & Marmet, M. (2009). The role of organizational trust in safety climate's influence on organization outcomes. *Accident; Analysis and Prevention, 42*(5), 1488–1497. doi:10.1016/j.aap.2009.11.010

Keyton, J. (2011). *Communication research: Asking questions, finding answers* (3rd ed.). New York, NY: McGraw-Hill.

Langford, P. H. (2009). Measuring organisational climate and employee engagement: Evidence for a 7 Ps model of work practices and outcomes. *Australian Journal of Psychology, 61*(4), 185–198. doi:10.1080/00049530802579481

Likert, R. (1932). A technique for the measurement of attitudes. *Archives de Psychologie, 140*, 1–55.

O'Toole, M., & Nalbone, D. P. (2011). Safety perception surveys what to ask, how to analyze. *Professional Safety, 56*(6), 58–62.

Osgood, C. E. (1952). The nature and measurement of meaning. *Psychological Bulletin, 49*, 197–237. doi:10.1037/h0055737

Poynter, R. (2008). Facebook: The future of networking with customers. *International Journal of Market Research, 50*, 11–12.

Ragin, C. C., Nagel, J., & White, P. (2004). *Workshop on scientific foundations of qualitative research*. Washington, DC: National Science Foundation. Retrieved from www.nsf.gov/pubs/2004/nsf04219/start.htm.

Reinard, J. C. (2008). *Introduction to communication research* (4th ed.). New York, NY: McGraw-Hill.

Rubin, R. B., Rubin, A. M., Graham, E. E., Perse, E. M., & Seibold, D. R. (2009). *Communication research measures II: A sourcebook*. New York, NY: Routledge.

Schwarz, N. (1995). What respondents learn from questionnaires: The survey interview and the logic of conversation. *International Statistical Review, 63*, 153–168. doi:10.2307/1403610

Schwarz, N. (1996). *Cognition and communication: Judgmental biases, research methods, and the logic of conversation.* Mahwah, NJ: Erlbaum.

Tsair-Wei, C., Wen-Pin, L., Chih-Wei, L., Weng-Chung, W., Shih-Chung, C., Hsien-Yi, W., & Shih-Bin, S. (2011). Web-based computer adaptive assessment of individual perceptions of job satisfaction for hospital workplace employees. *BMC Medical Research Methodology, 11*(1), 47–54. doi:10.1186/1471-2288-11-47

Watt, J. H. (1997). Using the internet for quantitative survey research. *Quirk's Marketing Research Review.* Retrieved from http://www.unt.edu/rss/class/survey/watt.htm.

Watt, J. H., & van den Berg, S. (1995). *Research methods for communication science.* Needham Heights, MA: Allyn & Bacon.

Wrench, J. S., Thomas-Maddox, C., Richmond, V. P., & McCroskey, J. C. (2008). *Quantitative research methods for communication: A hands-on-approach.* New York, NY: Oxford University Press.

ADDITIONAL READING

Auerbach, C. F., & Silverstein, L. B. (2003). *Qualitative data: An introduction to coding and analysis.* New York, NY: New York University Press.

Bailey, C. (1997). Managerial factors related to safety program effectiveness: An update on the Minnesota perception survey. *Professional Safety, 42*(8), 33–35.

Bazerman, C., & Prior, P. (2004). *What writing does and how it does it: An introduction to analyzing texts and textual practices.* Mahwah, NJ: Lawrence Earlbaum.

Bryden, M., & McCorkle, D. (2005). Virtual engineering. *Mechanical Engineering (New York, N.Y.), 127*, 138–167.

eWeek. (2007). Emerging technology disappointments. *eWeek, 24*, 46.

Fowler, F. (1995). *Improving survey questions: Design and evaluation.* Thousand Oaks, CA: Sage.

Fowler, F. J. Jr. (2009). *Survey research methods* (2nd ed.). Thousand Oaks, CA: Sage.

Frey, L., Botan, C., & Kreps, G. (2000). *Investigating communication: An introduction to research methods* (2nd ed.). Boston, MA: Allyn & Bacon.

Hinds, P., & Kiesler, S. (1995). Communication across boundaries: Work, structure, and use of communication technologies in a large organization. *Organization Science, 6*, 373–393. doi:10.1287/orsc.6.4.373

Hoepfl, M. (1997). Choosing qualitative research: A primer for technology education researchers. *Journal of Technology Information, 9*, 47–63.

Jones, S. (Ed.). (1997). *Virtual culture: Identity and communication in cybersociety.* Thousand Oaks, CA: Sage.

Keyton, J. (2011). *Communication and organizational culture: A key to understanding work experiences* (2nd ed.). Thousand Oaks, CA: Sage.

Keyton, J., Beck, S. J., Messersmith, A. S., & Bisel, R. S. (2010). Ensuring communication research makes a difference. *Journal of Applied Communication Research, 38*, 306–309. doi:10.1080/00909882.2010.490844

Keyton, J., & Shockley-Zalabak, P. (Eds.). (2010). *Case studies for organizational communication: Understanding communication processes* (3rd ed.). New York, NY: Oxford University Press.

Kirkby, H. M., Wilson, S., Calvert, M., & Draper, H. (2011). Using e-mail recruitment and an online questionnaire to establish effect size: A worked example. *BMC Medical Research Methodology*, *11*(1), 89–92. doi:10.1186/1471-2288-11-89

Liu, Y., Wu, A. D., & Zumbo, B. D. (2007). The impact of outliers on cronbach's coefficient alpha estimate of reliability: Ordinal/rating scale item responses. *Educational and Psychological Measurement*, *67*(4), 620–634. doi:10.1177/0013164406296976

Peet, T., & Kren, L. (2005). Online communities and discussion boards are critical to today's design engineers. *Machine Design*, *77*, 133.

Pettey, C. (2007). *Gartner says number of identity theft victims has increased more than 50 percent since 2003*. Retrieved April 25, 2009, from www.gartner.com/it/page.jsp?id=501912.

Rubin, R. B., Palmgreen, P., & Sypher, H. E. (1994). *Communication research measures: A sourcebook*. New York, NY: Routledge.

Stefanick, L., & LeSage, E. J. (2005). Limitations to developing virtual communities in the public sector: A local government case study. *Canadian Public Administration*, *48*, 231–250. doi:10.1111/j.1754-7121.2005.tb02189.x

Tennant, A., & Pallant, J. (2006). Unidimensionality matters. *Rasch Measurement Transactions*, *20*, 1048–1051.

Toepoel, V., Das, M., & Van Soest, A. (2008). Effects of design in web surveys: Comparing trained and fresh respondents. *Public Opinion Quarterly*, *72*, 985–1007. doi:10.1093/poq/nfn060

Toepoel, V., Das, M., & Van Soest, A. (2009). Design of web questionnaires: The effects of the number of items per screen. *Field Methods*, *21*, 200–213. doi:10.1177/1525822X08330261

Walther, J. B., & Parks, M. R. (2002). Cues filtered out, cues filtered in: Computer-mediated communication and relationships. In Knapp, M. L., & Daly, J. A. (Eds.), *Handbook of Interpersonal Communication* (3rd ed., pp. 529–563). Thousand Oaks, CA: Sage.

Williams, R., & Rice, R. E. (1983). Communication research and new media technologies. In Bostrom, R. (Ed.), *Communication Yearbook* (pp. 200–224). Beverly Hills, CA: Sage Publications.

Witmer, B. G., & Singer, M. J. (1998). Measuring presence in virtual environments: A presence questionnaire. *Presence (Cambridge, Mass.)*, *7*, 225–240. doi:10.1162/105474698565686

Wood, A. F., & Smith, M. J. (2001). *Online communication: Linking technology, identity, and culture*. Mahwah, NJ: Lawrence Erlbaum Associates.

Wright, B. D., & Masters, G. N. (1982). *Rating scale analysis*. Chicago, IL: MESA Press.

KEY TERMS AND DEFINITIONS

Descriptive Statistics: Statistical tests used to describe the shape of a dataset; it includes summary statistics, standard scores, and visual displays of data.

Inferential Statistics: Statistical tests that allow researchers to make references about some unknown aspect of a population from a sample.

Other-Report/Proxy Responses: Survey format where individuals answer questions about other individuals.

Qualitative Content Analysis: Analysis procedure used with open-ended survey that explores the meaning of messages.

Qualitative Survey Research: Open-ended survey research where participants have maximum lei-way in responding.

Quantitative Survey Research: Survey research characterized by closed-ended, Likert, or semantic differential questions that limit the choices presented to respondents.

Research: An investigative process involving a research asking questions about a phenomenon and seeking answers to those questions.

Self-Administered/Self-Report: Survey format where individuals answer questions about themselves.

Social Desirability Bias: Occurs when a researcher's presence leads respondents to answer in ways that are perceived to be favorable to the researcher.

Survey Research: Terms that in social scientific research commonly refer to the use of questionnaires for the purpose of discovering descriptive characteristics of phenomena.

Triangulation: Combination of several research methodologies in the study of the same phenomenon.

Chapter 12
Conducting Effective Interviews about Virtual Work:
Gathering and Analyzing Data Using a Grounded Theory Approach

Kerk F. Kee
Chapman University, USA

Marceline Thompson-Hayes
Arkansas State University, USA

ABSTRACT

This chapter explicates interviewing as a viable research method for studying virtual work. The chapter begins with a review of the existing interdisciplinary scholarship on qualitative interviewing along with three modes of interviewing, interviewing techniques, formats, and rigor. Next, the chapter reviews exemplary research reports on virtual work to illustrate best practices in interviewing and data analysis. Finally, suggestions for collecting, analyzing, and interpreting interview data about virtual work are discussed.

INTRODUCTION AND BACKGROUND

"Qualitative research is an umbrella term that encompasses several philosophical or theoretical orientations" (Merriam, 2002, p. 15); it includes methodologies such as biography, case study, ethnography, and phenomenology (Creswell, 1998; Merriam, 2002). Qualitative research provides a viable alternative to the limits imposed by the positivist research model and empirical analyses. A major strength of qualitative inquiry lies in its ability to provide a depth of understanding about the phenomenon under study (Rubin, 2000). Qualitative methods provide rich accounts of human experiences and, of particular interest to social scientists, how interactants apply meanings

DOI: 10.4018/978-1-4666-0963-1.ch012

to those experiences (Fossey, Harvey, McDermott, Davidson, 2002; Rubin & Rubin, 2005). The most popular qualitative research methods include interviews, observation, and archival studies (Bowen, 2005). Of the many qualitative data collection methods, interviewing provides the most direct, research-focused interaction between researcher and participant (Kvale, 1996; Rubin & Rubin, 2005; Stroh, 2000). Interviewing is widely valued by multiple disciplines as a primary research tool that allows for initial exploration of a previously uninvestigated phenomenon. Conversely, interviewing can provide fresh insights into a well-explored but complicated phenomenon surrounded by theoretical controversy or conflicting findings.

The body of research on organizational behavior and the research literature examining online behavior both enjoy a rich tradition of qualitative methodologies, including interviewing. Thus, it comes as no surprise that interviewing emerges as a prominent research methodology in the study of virtual work. The purpose of this chapter is to explicate interviewing as a research methodology and its application to the study of virtual work. The chapter contains four distinct sections: First, we provide a brief literature review on qualitative interviewing along with a brief discussion of three specific modes of interviews (i.e., face-to-face, telephone, and online). Then we explain basic interviewing techniques, formats, and rigor. The third section provides multiple case studies of published research reports to illustrate the techniques and types of interviewing methods employed in the study of virtual work. Finally, we offer advice on how to conduct effective interview studies of virtual work by providing specific recommendations for data collection, analysis, and interpretation.

INTERVIEWING

Scholars have attempted to define the method of interviewing with different emphases. Rubin and Rubin (1995) refer to interviewing as the art of hearing data. They further explain, "Qualitative interviewing is a way of finding out what others feel and think about their worlds. Through qualitative interviews you can understand experiences and reconstruct events in which you did not participate" (p. 1). Furthermore, interviewing involves many choices. Hookway (2008) argues that the interviewing method for data collection depends on participants' willingness to generously share their feelings, thoughts, and experiences. On the other hand, Kvale (1996) maintains, "Interviewing is a craft: It does not follow content- and context-free rules of method, but rests on the judgments of a qualified researcher" (Kvale, 1996, p. 105). In both statements, the subjective choices by the participants and the researcher play an important role in data collection and interpretation.

Lastly, Seidman (1998) argues that interviewing is a method that "provides access to the context of people's behavior and thereby provides a way for researchers to understand the meaning of that behavior... Interviewing allows us to put behavior in context and provides access to understanding their action" (p. 4). This definition highlights the need to understand participants' meaning making and the context in which meaning making take place. Overall, qualitative interviewing involves hearing the data, finding out the feelings and thoughts of the informants, researchers' making active interpretations and decisions, as well as understanding the meaning and context that prompted informants' behaviors. Given this overview of the different definitions of interviewing, we will discuss three particular modes of interviewing modalities.

Face-to-Face Interviewing: Conducting an interview in person has several advantages. First, meeting face-to-face allows the researcher to pick up subtle nonverbal cues, such as hand gestures, body positioning, eye contact, facial expression, etc. (Holt, 2010). These nonverbal cues may provide useful insights for later data analysis, interpretation, and coding. Second, informants often provide more detailed responses during face-to-face interviews, compared to telephone interviews (Sturges & Hanrahan, 2004).Therefore, conducting interviews in person is likely to yield more data for the researchers to work with. Third, assuring informants of anonymity and confidentiality can be better achieved when meeting face-to-face, and this is especially true in intercultural situations (Harvey, 2011). This argument points out the relational and rapport building needs for conducting effective interviews. While many traditional qualitative researchers believe that face-to-face interviews are the only path to best and authentic data (Silverman, 2001), this assumption can be challenged (Hookway, 2008). In fact, Sturges and Hanrahan (2004) argue that telephone interviews yield comparable data quality as face-to-face interviews. We will discuss telephone interviewing next.

Telephone Interviewing: Due to time constraints and the costs involved, sometimes it is not possible and not feasible for researchers to travel to multiple people and places to conduct face-to-face interviews (Gratton & O'Donnell, 2011). The first alternative is telephone interviewing. telephone interviews can be more time efficient for both the researcher and the informants (Stephens, 2007). Instead of coordinating and traveling for an appointment for a face-to-face interview, a phone interview will help both the researcher and participant save time. Moreover, qualified informants and willing participants may not be many in the immediate vicinity of a researcher. By expanding the data collection method to using the phone, the researcher could greatly increase participation in the project (Harvey, 2011). Additionally, telephone interviewing can often help reduce the impact of the researchers and the informants, such as their race and ethnicity, during the interview (Holt, 2010). In some interview projects, the superficial identification, thus stereotypical assumption, of participants and researchers as perceived by each other, can distract both parties' attention away from the central topic of interests. Given all the

advantages discussed, Holt (2010) argue that phone interviewing could be considered a better choice over the traditional method under certain circumstances, and it should not be regarded as the 'second-best' option to the more familiar face-to-face approach. Here we will discuss yet another alternative to face-to-face interviewing, given the proliferation of Internet-based communication technologies.

Online Interviewing: Hine (2010) suggests that one way to define online interviewing is research that utilizes the Internet as its medium. Moreover, James and Busher (2006) refer to web-based approaches to interviewing as online interviewing. In today's world, the Internet provides many synchronous (i.e., skype, IM, etc.) and asynchronous communication (i.e., emails, webpages, etc.) technologies that makes online interviewing and information searching a viable choice for qualitative research. In a latter piece of work, James and Busher (2009) argue that the Internet is a complex phenomenon that involves dynamic social, spatial, and temporal dimensions that shape the relationships and context underlying a research project. In other words, online interviewing is a research method that deserves a careful discussion.

Under the category of online interviewing, one particular technique is email interviewing. James and Busher (2006) discuss several important advantages of this approach. First, participants decide when they want to respond to the interviewing questions via emails. This gives participants control in the research process. Second, email interviewing is less stressful for participants, because they can pace themselves and choose to respond at a time that is most suitable for them. Third, because there can be more time to compose one's response, the answers provided via emails are often more reflective and thoughtful. These three arguments provide a useful framework for comparing asynchronous online interviewing with face-to-face, telephone, and synchronous online interviewing.

INTERVIEWING METHODS

The goal of any qualitative research is to obtain a depth of understanding that provides a clearer and more comprehensive picture of the phenomenon under study (Cresswell, 1994: Rupsiene & Pranskuniene, 2010). As one of many qualitative data collection methods, interviewing provides a direct, research-focused interaction between researcher and participant (Kvale, 1996; Stroh, 2000; Rubin & Rubin, 2005) and is widely valued as a primary research tool by multiple disciplines (Rubin & Rubin, 2005). Indeed, interviewing is recognized both as an academic and practical research tool (Rubin & Rubin, 2005).

Basic Interviewing Techniques

As previously discussed, an interview traditionally takes the form of a one-on-one, Face-to-Face (FtF) conversation in which a researcher poses inquiries to a single respondent from a pre-prepared protocol containing questions or talking points about the topic under study. A researcher typically presents carefully scripted inquiries with appropriate probes and improvisation. Interviews tend to be relaxed conversations where the researcher primarily listens rather than questions aggressively. A researcher will conduct a series of such conversations with specific types of individuals about specific subject matter. Typically, interviews are audio- or video-taped and then transcribed for later analysis. Usually the transcription of the formal interview constitutes the "meat" of an interview study.

Interviewing can provide and increase understanding of experiences and/or events even when the researcher did not personally participate in the experiences (Rubin & Rubin, 2005). For example, interviews with virtual workers from Joplin, Missouri may provide the researcher with insights into post-tornado work life without the researcher being at ground zero during the tornado. Interviewing allows participants to describe their experiences

and thus affords researchers opportunities to explore meanings reflective of multiple participant views (Misheler, 1986; Murray & Sixsmith, 1998). During interviews, researchers can become involved with participants who become "partners rather than objects of research" (Rubin & Rubin, 2005, p. 10).

The concepts of multiple and socially-created realities (Berger & Luckman, 1967) is presumed in the nature of the interview (Corbin & Strauss, 2008; Denzin, 1998; Denzin & Lincoln, 1998). The issue becomes how the researcher can best facilitate the informants to reveal their perceived realities. While facilitating the revelation of meaning via the questions asked, the interviewer responds with neutral, accepting comments, thus maintaining the topical focus of conversation on the object of study (Denzin, 1998) and facilitating the informant to reveal his/her vision of reality concerning the phenomenon under study. After the interviews are completed, the transcripts provide researchers a text they can analyze for emergent themes. Such themes provide an understanding of "what is going on" for the participants.

Interviewing Formats

Interviewing formats range from the highly structured to the semi-structured and unstructured (where the participant tells his / her story, thus, assisting the researcher to identify areas of importance to the participant). Interviews have been described as conversations designed to provide researchers insight into the realities or worldviews of their informants (Kvale, 1996) and, as such, carry an unpredictable nature as the informants reveal their socially constructed meanings (Berger & Luckman, 1967). Regardless of the formality of the interviews, researchers and participants engage in conversations that allow meanings to emerge through interaction (Corbin & Morse, 2003; Corbin & Strauss, 2008; Rubin & Rubin, 2005).

Interviews can be conducted with individuals, focus groups, or both. For example, in a study of a global software team, Gibbs (2009) conducted both one-on-one and focus group interviews to yield rich data about how distributed workers negotiate dialectical tensions across time, space, and culture when they balance between a mix of face-to-face and virtual work arrangements during the project period. Interviews can take many forms including oral histories, life histories, and evaluations (Rubin & Rubin, 2005). Interviews can employ multiple communication modalities and formats, including many technologically-assisted channels of communication, as discussed in detail below.

Rigor in Interviewing

Rigor in interviewing may require engaging in lengthy interviews (rather than relying on brief conversations) and opting for more (rather than less) follow-up interviews as ways to allow and improve the interviewer's chances of overcoming potential social desirability biases (Merriam, 2002; Padgett, 1998; Rubin, 2000). Interviewing multiple participants aids in theme emergence and often involves collecting and presenting multiple stories to illustrate themes that emerge across interviews (Merriam, 2002; Rubin & Rubin, 2005).

Padgett (1998) suggested multiple methods of increasing the trustworthiness of the interview: auditing, prolonged engagement, triangulation of data, peer debriefing and support, member checking, and negative case analysis (where researchers conduct a thorough search for consistencies and inconsistencies). The goal of qualitative interviewing is not to eliminate inconsistencies but, rather, to provide information that increases understanding of inconsistencies and why they occur (Rubin & Rubin, 2005). Bowen (2005) suggested triangulating the interview data from numerous sources as a way to corroborate researcher(s) discovery, thereby, adding confidence to the trustworthiness of the conclusions.

Moran-Ellis et al. (2006) argue that triangulation can be understood as using multiple methods to "to reveal the different dimensions of a phenomenon and to enrich understandings of the multi-faceted, complex nature of the social world" (p. 48). In other words, insights in different forms can be complementary to each other in providing a fuller picture of the phenomenon of interests (Greene, et al., 1989). Researchers have acknowledges that triangulation is important because it helps us better get at the multiplex and contingent nature of social world (Fielding & Fielding, 1986). Later in this chapter, we extend these arguments to the use of various forms of online interviewing data, including online interviews, IM, emails, web pages, online profiles, etc.

Transparency involves leaving an audit trail of raw data (interview transcripts) that other researchers can use to determine if findings are reproducible and verifiable (Rubin, 2000, p. 175). Further, transparency in reporting involves providing a thorough and detailed methodological description that acknowledges strengths and weaknesses of the study (Rubin). In addition to transparency, Rubin and Rubin (2005) suggest that researchers must explain the consistencies or inconsistencies of themes, individuals, and across cases; such explanations communicate a description of what it means to be in the particular situation studied. Interviewing is a valuable way to build a "consistent portrait that is close to the evidence" through which readers can be persuaded the evidence is credible (Rubin & Rubin, p. 92).

In summary, qualitative interviewing provides researchers with a useful method for collecting, managing, and analyzing data that can be used to generate theory or discover themes and patterns within a data set. Interviewing is a particularly advantageous approach, given its conversational nature that can tap participants' socially constructed meanings (Berger & Luckman, 1967). The next section of the chapter focuses on conducting online interviews.

Conducting Online Interviews

A plethora of research recognizes the impact Computer-Mediated Communication (CMC) can have on personal, social, and professional relationships (see Wright & Webb, 2011). CMC has been recognized as an effective social support medium (Burleson, Albrecht, & Satason, 1994; Pennebaker & Traue, 1993) that can promote a socially created, friendly environment that assists in overcoming many barriers common to FtF interactions (Kazmer, 2007; Thompson-Hayes, Gibson, Scott, & Webb, 2009; Rheingold, 1991, 1993). CMC has been recognized for its potential to provide an effective interview platform and has served as the methodology for multi-faceted lines of research exploring technology-mediated work (e.g., internet, telephone, teleconference, Instant Messenger [IM], Skype) as well as the opportunities and challenges of virtual work (Davis, Bolding, Hard, Sherr, & Elford, 2004; Kazmer & Xie, 2010; Thompson-Hayes, et al., 2009).

According to Kazmar and Xie (2008), researchers increasingly rely on online interviewing such as interviews conducted via email or IM. For example, email interviewing is becoming increasingly common; McCoyd and Kerson (2006) argue that there is an emerging body of literature indicating an "acceptance of email interviewing as a legitimate research technology despite the scarcity of methodological analysis in the literature" (p. 392).

Using CMC to conduct interviews brings with it both obvious (and not-so-obvious) opportunities and challenges. Research suggests that CMC (e.g., e-mail, IM, teleconferencing, Skype, chat and team rooms, e-meetings) can be a valuable asset in the qualitative research process by helping to bridge and mitigate space, time, cultural, social, and educational differences (Kazmer & Xie, 2008; Thompson-Hayes, et al., 2009). Furthermore, CMC can encourage collaboration on interactive projects that, heretofore, only could be done FtF

(Ramirez, Walther, Burgoon, & Sunnafrank, 2002; Thompson-Hayes, et al., 2009; Walther, Loh, & Granka, 2005; Walther & Parks, 2002).

Opportunities. The flexibility of online interviews in text, voice, and video formats (Kazmer & Xie, 2008; Mann & Stewart, 2002) can accommodate the needs of both researcher and the participant (e.g., asynchronous or synchronous, public or semi-private). Similarly, email can help overcome difficulties in data transcription, provide access (e.g., ease in collaborating across geographical areas and time zones), and expand data gathering opportunities (Kazmer & Xie, 2008; Thompson-Hayes, et al., 2009). As a medium for interviews, CMC is not perceived to be less emotional or less personally involving medium than FtF interaction (Derks, Fisher, & Bos, 2008). Research suggests increased collaboration among geographically distant coworkers who use IM for data collection and analysis (Cameron & Webster, 2005).

Challenges. Despite the numerous possible communication technology options available for use in a single research project, most researchers prefer to use only a few types of CMC technology per study (Initial, 2011; Thompson-Hayes, et al., 2009), believing that switching from one technology to another may impede the collaboration process (Initial, 2011; Kazmer & Xie, 2008; Ramierz & Zhang, 2007). Further, researchers may be wary about mixing data obtained from differing interview modalities (e.g., telephone, IM interviews), believing that inherent inconsistencies between modes may contaminate data sets (Kramer & Xie, 2008; Wiesenfeld, Raghuram, & Garud, 2001).

Fewer Non-verbal Cues. While not posing insurmountable problems, among the most frequently reported challenges to virtual interviewing versus FtF interviewing is the reduced number of nonverbal cues available for decoding (Kazmer & Xie, 2008; Thompson-Hayes, et al., 2009). In their research on how professors use CMC to enact their scholarly partnerships, Thompson-Hayes et al. suggest that, given the demands of virtual intellectual teams, multiple forms of communication technologies may be required to complete collaboration projects; the type of technology employed may vary depending upon the nature of the task. For example, edited documents are typically conveyed via email, whereas problematic topics (e.g., disagreements) and creative work (e.g., theorizing, developing a research design) typically are discussed in richer modes such as FtF interactions, Skype, or telephone conversations. Similarly, researchers may prefer richer modes of online interviewing, such as Skype or telephone conversations.

Lack of Access to or Hesitancy to Use Technologies. While electronic interfaces such as email may work well for less complicated tasks, email alone is not sufficient to complete complex virtual work tasks (Barile & Durson, 2002). Despite the numerous CMC options available for interviewing, commonly occurring challenges and frustrations identified in the research include lack of access to (Jankowski, et al., 2001) or hesitancy to use technology, often due to discomfort with the technology (Ingram, Hathorn, & Evans, 2000; Shedletsky & Aitken, 2001; Walther, et al., 2005) as well as the belief that the data gathered will be inferior to data collected via FtF interviewing (Initial, 2011; Kazmer & Xie, 2008). For example, in their study of how professors used CMC in their professional writing partnerships, Thompson-Hayes et al. (2009) discovered that few professors utilized IM technologies. However, this limitation seems less likely to occur in interviews with virtual workers, except perhaps for those new to the job.

Potential Ethical Dilemmas. Because online interviewing can prompt researchers to examine all steps in the research process, additional attention may be paid to how participants are recruited to participate in the research. Traditional methods of assuring confidentiality do not necessarily apply when conducting qualitative research via CMC. Thus, online interviewing poses potential ethical dilemmas in recruiting, obtaining signed consent, and scheduling to interviews (Flicker, Haas, & Skinner, 2004; Hamilton & Bowers, 2006, Kazmer & Xie, 2008; Shachaf, 2008) as well as assuring confidentiality of *both* participant and researcher. For example, the researcher must consider (and attempt to safeguard against) the potential implications of confidential information that is distributed online as such material may potentially reach people other than, or in addition to, the intended interview participant (Hamilton & Bowers, 2006). Especially for researchers comfortable with technology, the convenience of conducting online interviews often outweighs the drawbacks, as many problems traditionally associated with FtF and telephone interviews (e.g., geographically distant, difficulty scheduling mutually convenient times, cultural differences in transcribing interviews) can be overcome through online interviewing (Shachaf, 2008; Thompson-Hayes, et al., 2009). Additionally, online interviews can supplement data from telephone and FtF interviews. Indeed, multiple modes offer multiple opportunities to gather unique data sets—each with distinct advantages—that can be used to triangulate results (Kazmer & Xie, 2008; Shachaf, 2008; Thompson-Hayes, et al., 2009), as discussed in more detail in a later section.

Given the challenges and advantages of online interviewing, its effective use may not be obvious. To provide clarity and to illustrate effective use of interviewing to study virtual work, including online interviewing, the next section provides in-depth descriptions of multiple case studies, specifically, multi-disciplinary published research on virtual work environments. Relevant methodological details are discussed to illuminate how researchers from a variety of disciplines employed interviewing to study virtual work.

CASE STUDIES OF BEST PRACTICES TO EFFECTIVELY STUDY VIRTUAL INTERACTIONS

Interviewing methods have been used to study virtual work and online interactions in three ways: in conjunction with surveys, to generate theory, and as data analytic tools. These three methods have been used individually as well as in combination to successfully conduct research on virtual work that has led to publication. This section of the chapter discusses three such research reports to illustrate these methods: Wiesenfeld, Raghuran, and Garad (2001), Shachaf (2008), and Thompson-Hayes et al. (2009).

Interviews in Conjunction with Surveys. Interview data can be used in conjunction with survey data—both as a first step in survey research and as a means of interpreting survey results. In their study of organizational identification among virtual workers, Wiesenfeld et al. (2001) employed semi-structured interviews in two ways (1) to generate survey items measuring work-based social support and (2) to interpret the results of their subsequent survey. To develop new survey instruments, the authors modified existing survey instruments measuring social support based, in part, on their interview data: "We rephrased the items [of the work-based social support scale] slightly based on our preliminary interviews and pretests" (p. 220). The authors included interview items in an appendix. Questions that appear to tap into work-based social support included "Has your relationship with your manager changed? How? Has your relationship with your coworkers changed? How? and do you feel you received all the support you needed to telecommute?" (p. 277).

Although the authors did not report a thematic analysis of their interview data in this article, they interpreted their survey results in relationship to the interview data. For example, their survey data revealed that participants' need for affiliation was positively correlated with organizational identification. The authors interpreted this result as "consistent with themes that emerged in our interviews with virtual workers" (p. 221). Thus, Wiesenfeld et al.'s (2001) study provides an example of how quantitative and qualitative data co-mingle and how interview data can supplement survey research.

Interviews to Generate Theory. Interview data can be used to generate theory or theoretical models. This approach is aligned with grounded theory, a topic discussed by Gibson and Webb in another chapter in this book. For example, Shachaf (2008) conducted 41 interviews with members of Global Virtual Teams (GVTs) from nine countries to develop a model of the impact of cultural diversity, information, and technology on communication in decision-making. Shachaf developed an interview protocol from a review of relevant literature, conducted interviews, transcribed recordings of the interviews, and then analyzed the transcripts via "open coding" (i.e., identifying initial categories that emerge from the data by examining the data in minute detail without imposing a priori categories) to generate basic themes.

Next, Shachaf (2008) undertook "pattern coding" (i.e., breaking down abstract, thematic categories into smaller, more concrete categories) to further analyze the data through the use of the "constant comparison" process (i.e., comparing data to emerging thematic categories throughout the analysis process). To identify relationships among the variables, Shachaf used the "search and retrieve" function of NVIVO 1.3 software and developed a matrix of co-occurring ideas or themes (variables). Her research produced a model of relationships among variables that is grounded in and emerged from interview data. Specific findings from the study were that participants believed that (1) GVT projects are enhanced by multiple viewpoints and an array of skills that diverse members bring to a project. (2) Diversity can have the negative effect of producing misunderstandings due to language, verbal, and nonverbal differences. (3) Information and communication technology (e.g., email, teleconferencing, Internet chat) can mitigate the negative effects of cultural diversity, while enhancing the positive effects. For example, participants said they could spend more time constructing an email to make the message clear and reduce misunderstandings.

Data-Analytic Tool with Interview Transcripts. Finally, qualitative analysis can be applied to interview data, where interview data is processed interpretively without the explicit intent of developing theory. In this circumstance, researchers look for patterns and themes in a dataset, while *not* building a theory or theoretical model. This inductive approach would simply shed light on *what is there* in the data without imposing meanings on the data.

Such approaches normally employ grounded theory techniques such as open coding. However, interview data also can be processed to supplement, extend, or expand existing theory in a more deductive process. For example, Thompson-Hayes et al. (2009) successfully used both approaches in their study of professorial collaborations. They conducted 20 semi-structured telephone interviews and subsequent email interviews with university professors to examine the role of CMC in their professional collaborations. Telephone interviews were conducted first and centered around an 11-item interview protocol based on suggestions from experts in qualitative interviewing (i.e., Fontana & Frey, 1998; Kvale, 1996). Next, the authors emailed a four-item, open-ended questionnaire to participants to follow up on specific areas of inquiry. The telephone interviews were independently conducted by three researchers on the four-person team. Each interviewer transcribed her interviews verbatim, then read and reread the transcripts to identify themes within her dataset through inductive analysis. Next, the three researchers met via one two-hour conference telephone call to discuss themes across the entire sample. As a validation procedure, a deliberate attempt was made to consider negative evidence

for the identified themes, in accordance with Miles and Huberman (1994) guidelines.

This interpretive process produced six discrete themes concerning CMC professorial collaborations: (1) limited technology (i.e., professors in the sample used primarily email for its ease of use and familiarity and few other technologies), (2) expanded opportunities (i.e., professors cited the convenience that CMC affords to work on projects that would have been difficult or impossible FtF), (3) instrumentality (i.e., professors indicated that CMC did not replace FtF communication but served as a value tool for working out the mechanical aspects of collaboration such as sharing edits), (4) nonverbal deficit (i.e., professors reported compensating for the lack of nonverbal elements inherent in CMC by using emoticons and strategic language to address potential misunderstandings or socio-emotional aspects of a message), (5) relational connection (i.e., professors indicated that they preferred to work with others they could trust), and (6) personal autonomy (i.e., while many professors appreciated working collaboratively, they liked the independence that CMC allowed). As a validation procedure, the fourth member of the research team independently examined randomly selected samples of the data set to confirm that each theme appeared in more than one transcript across at least two interviewers.

The lack of conceptual overlap along the emergent themes together with the discovery of two themes that formed a dialectic (i.e., relational connection and personal autonomy) prompted the fourth team member to organize the initial themes into dialectical tensions (i.e., relational connection vs. autonomy, creativity vs. mundane tasks, task vs. social emotional goals, novelty vs. efficacy of CMC). Then, the researchers undertook a secondary analysis: The three team members who served as the interviewers and original coders re-examined the interview transcripts to verify the presence of the proposed dialectics in the transcripts of the interviews they conducted as well as in the transcripts of the other two interviewers. The fourth coder reviewed random sections of each transcript and verified the presence of at least one dialectical tension in each transcript and multiple dialectics in multiple transcripts of individual interviews.

The Thompson-Hayes et al. (2009) study provides an example of how multiple interview methods can be mixed to achieve complex research goals. The study combined inductive as well as deductive approaches to processing interview data. Grounded theory procedures were used to identify initial themes; then a theory-driven, deductive approach was used in the second level of analysis to verify the emergent dialectics. The second level of analysis was unanticipated as the dialectics emerged from the grounded data analysis. Due to this development, a literature review on relational dialectics was not included in the beginning of the paper. In fact, a sentence in the "Discussion" section reads, "We did not anticipate finding dialectical tensions at the onset of this project and thus we here provide a brief explanation of communication and dialectics" (p. 213). Thus, although some scholars may argue that theory driven (deductive) versus data driven (more inductive) approaches are not compatible, we assert that sometimes the data speak to the researchers, and that the messages from the data can lead researchers to work within the parameters of an existing theory.

Further, the Thompson-Hayes et al. (2009) study employed a "mixed" methodological data set; telephone and email interview data were collected separately from the same set of participants and yet analyzed as one data set. Some researchers are reluctant to "trust" interview data from a "mixed" data set, believing that the findings will be "messy" or will lack depth and richness. FtF interviews may have the advantage of appearing "rich" but they pose serious potential drawbacks as well (e.g., geographic distance, scheduling mutually convenient times for the interviews, labor-intensive transcription process). We could locate no evidence that interview data collected via differing communication channels produced data sets of different quality or content. In fact, Kruisiewicw and Wood (2001) noted that "A comparison of face-to-face and email interviews revealed no notable differences in length, detail, disclosiveness, anecdotal content, and personal tone or substantive richness" (p. 790). Furthermore, it is increasingly common for virtual work researchers to report results from interview data collected via multiple communication channels (e.g., Gibbs, 2009; Kee & Browning, 2010).

Moreover, people who work in virtual environments may be more comfortable with online data collection. Online chat, email, and telephone interviews may be an *ideal* ways to supplement or replace FtF interviews with virtual workers. Further, if data collection progresses through stages, it may be advantageous to use one data set to guide protocols for the next data set.

The three case studies discussed above (i.e., Wiesenfeld, et al., 2001; Shachaf, 2008; Thompson-Hayes, et al., 2009) demonstrate the ways in which interviews have been used in published research on virtual work environments. The next section offers practical advice and specific strategies for collecting and interpreting interview data using GT techniques.

EFFECTIVE USE OF INTERVIEWING AS A RESEARCH METHOD

Given the above interdisciplinary overview of interviewing as well as the in-depth discussion of illustrative research studies of virtual work conducted via interviews, we here offer specific recommendations to researchers of every discipline who study virtual work and desire to employ interview methodologies. We organize these recommendations into subsections based on the stages of data collection, data analysis, and data interpretation.

Data Collection

The formal interview, whether synchronous (as in FtF, Skype, phone calls) or asynchronous (as in emails or to a certain extent, IM, because of some lag time), often constitutes the "meat" of research data about virtual work. During a formal interview, a researcher presents carefully scripted questions with appropriate probes and improvisation. This part of the interview produces research data. To gather rich interview data for studying the complex phenomenon of virtual work, we recommend that the researcher consider triangulating data by, in addition to conducting interviews, gathering data from additional sources such as organizational websites, individual online profiles, recruitment emails exchanges, follow-up communication, and organizational internal communication and/or listservs. We elaborate on these potential data sources in more detail below.

Organizational Websites. Virtual workers and their organizations often maintain a strong online presence. Today's organizational websites and social media sites typically provide information about the companies and their employees. Furthermore, many virtual workers have strong social media presences, using web 2.0 tools such as LinkedIn, Twitter, and Facebook. Information displayed on these organizational and individual sites is often public. Therefore, information extracted from these sites could be used as the first type of data for studying virtual work. For example, Kee and Browning (2010) analyzed information from the website of the government agency that funds a distributed network of scientists and technologists; they compared the website information to their interview data to reveal a dialectical tension between investing in building a technological infrastructure to support virtual scientific work or to advancing the technology itself. This dialectical tension was discovered only as the result of incorporating information from the web into an interview study.

Communiqué with Participants as Data. Researchers today often approach potential research participants via recruitment emails. If a virtual worker agrees to participate in the study, a series of email exchanges typically clarifies the purpose of the study, verifies the fit of the potential participant with the study, and explains the research protocol. Thus, an informal interview has started with the first recruitment email. We suggest treating these email exchanges as research data, after receiving the participant's consent to do so. Obviously, researchers of virtual work should keep careful records of emails with research participants. If there are short phone calls before and/or after the formal interviews, notes should be taken immediately as part of field notes. Such communiqué may prove useful as data (e.g., Kee, 2010).

Post-Interview Correspondence as Data. After a formal interview, a researcher often sends a thank-you email to the participant to show appreciation for his/her time and contribution to the study. Such an email may prompt the participant to provide additional information and/or engage in further conversation about the study. When a thank you email or follow-up email generates replies, we recommend the researcher seek consent from the participant to include the email as a part of research data for the study. For example, Kee and Browning's (2010) study of virtual scientific work incorporated follow-up emails as a part of their data. When a participant used the numbers "4, 8, 12" during an interview, she did not explain the numbers. A follow-up email clarified that she was referencing "4, 8, 12 processors." The word "processor" was then added in brackets to the transcript and ultimately to the data presentation in the published article.

Listserv Posts as Data. Some organizations and professional communities maintain a completely or semi-public listserv. To further sensitize the researcher to a particular virtual worker's situation and to further contextualize the study, a researcher may consider joining such a listserv (if permission is granted by gatekeepers). Information gathered from observing the listserv could be documented in the researcher's field notes. If a researcher gains access to internal listservs and intranets, the observational data of internal communication could shed light on the phenomenon under study. For example, in her study of a global software team, Gibbs (2009) joined the company as an intern and thus gained access to internal intranet, including listserv messages.

Data Analysis

Given the rich and multi-dimensional data available from a range of public websites, private emails, formal interviews, follow-up conversations, internal organizational information, and field notes, we now explain two approaches to data analysis: thematic analysis and grounded theory analysis.

Thematic Analysis. The first approach discussed is thematic analysis, and it can follow a series of sorting steps discussed by McCracken (1988) and a set of qualitative criteria articulated by Owen (1994). To begin sorting, McCracken's (1988) procedure has the researcher follow these steps: (a) sort out important data from unimportant data; (b) examine the slices of data for logical relationships and contradictions; (c) re-read the transcripts to confirm or disconfirm emerging relationships and to scan for the general properties of the data; (d) identify the general themes and sort the themes in a hierarchical fashion, while discarding those that prove useless in the organization; and (e) review the emergent themes for each of the transcripts and determines how they can synthesized into a still wider set of overarching themes.

During the sorting process, researchers can apply Owen's (1984) criteria. According to Owen, themes are "a limited range of interpretations used to conceive of and constitute relationships" (p. 274), which means that the data are reduced by looking for outstanding properties. He presents

three criteria of thematic analysis: recurrence, repetition, and forcefulness.

First, *recurrence* refers to the resurfacing of "salient meanings" (p. 275); this search for reoccurrence accepts that (a) the actual wordings that reflect the meanings may vary and that (b) the same theme can be stated in different ways by communicators and that they (c) move in and out of each other's foreground and background in any given instance. In fact, it is in the various wordings that a salient theme or meaning is discovered and established. Owen explains, "This criterion allowed salient meanings to be discovered in the foreground of a report—a theme, while other meanings remained in the background" (p. 275). Second, *repetition* simply refers to the frequency at which key words, phrases, or sentences are being repeated in a report. The criterion of repetition is an extension of recurrence. However, repetition points to the repeated usage of the exact wordings used to communicate a theme.

Third, *forcefulness* refers to the vocal or visual accents placed on certain utterances offered in verbal or written forms. Vocal accents could be "vocal inflection, volume, or dramatic pauses" (p. 275) and visual accents could be "underlying of words and phrases, the increased size of print or use of colored marks circling or otherwise focusing on passages in the written reports" (pp. 275-276). In other words, forcefulness calls attention to the "the *form* of … discourse" (p. 276). Van Manen (1990) describes the thematization process as an attempt to give "shape to the shapeless" (p. 88). Forcefulness refers to the style of the communication (Brummett, 2008).

Grounded Theory (GT) Analysis. The second approach of data analysis is guided by Grounded Theory. Although there is a separate chapter on grounded theory by Gibson and Webb in this book, we simply provide a brief discussion on five coding strategies researches can use to study virtual work: open coding, axial coding, process coding, selective coding, and cluster coding (also called "clustering").

Open Coding. Open coding is the analytic fracturing and systematic interpretation of raw data (Corbin & Strauss, 1990). Thoughts, actions, events, and incidents in raw data are compared to identify similarities and differences. Similar concepts collapse to form meta-categories, categories, and subcategories. In GT analyses, preliminary open coding begins with the first interview as it is conducted and/or transcribed. Because a researcher is informed and guided by preliminary concepts and categories, he or she is able to ask generative and comparative questions with the next interview or during the next observation. Asking generative questions enables the researcher to recognize the implications/theoretical possibilities and to gather data to provide specificity to each category. Then, the properties and dimensions of each derived concept can be analyzed. Additional fieldwork can add specification to the concepts obtained.

Axial Coding. Axial coding is a process in which "categories are related to their subcategories, and the relationships [are] tested against data" (Corbin & Strauss, 1990, p. 13). This process is similar to the pattern coding and constant comparison process mentioned earlier in this chapter. Axial coding and its related strategies are an ongoing process, in which the researcher continues to develop and revise identified categories by paying close attention to how conditions, contexts, strategies (action/interaction), and consequences influence the relationships between subcategories and their meta-category. The researcher's goal is to identify relationships tying concepts with conditions, contexts, strategies, and consequences. A researcher also can search for variations in the patterns and exceptions to the rules, using a constant comparison process. Once identified, categories can be revised with greater specificity until no variations and exceptions can be found in the data. Using this form of analysis, outliers lead to new, provisional, conditional categories. In this way, the researcher develops a theory conceptually denser, and identifies the linkages among concepts that

are increasingly more specific. A researcher may conclude, "Under these conditions, action takes this form, whereas under these other conditions, it takes another" (Corbin & Strauss, 1990, p. 14).

Process Coding. Because it is often overlooked by researchers, Baxter and Babbie (2003) separate and emphasize process coding in GT data analysis. They explain that process coding is the linking of sequences or flow of events, actions, interactions, and reactions *over time* to explain a social phenomenon. The temporal sequence and flow of concepts/categories derived from axial coding are important in GT because they can focus the researcher's attention on the evolution of a social phenomenon.

We believe process coding can be especially important to the study of virtual work because such a work arrangement is rapidly emerging. When close attention is paid to how events, actions, interactions, and reactions are connected across time, such attention can provide a clearer understanding of the phenomenon of virtual work and enable more accurate descriptions. For example, a worker new to virtual work may struggle with managing multiple technologies in collaboration with multiple remote colleagues. However, over time, this worker may gain confidence and competence with the technologies and excel at virtual work. Without paying attention to the across-time learning process, the researcher's explanation of the virtual work experience is incomplete.

Selective Coding. Selective coding often occurs during later stages of an investigation, when categories converge to reveal a core (or root) category. The core category is often the focal phenomenon of interest in a GT study. One way to integrate categories is diagramming (Corbin & Strauss, 1990). In a diagram, multiple categories can appear in relation to the core category, as conditions, contexts, strategies, and consequences change. A strong theory with explanatory power usually has categories and subcategories with high conceptual density. Poorly developed categories will be identified during selective coding, and subsequently divided or merged. Thus, a weak theory can be strengthened by revisions of initial concepts, categories, and relationships. The newly revised theory can be verified by collection and analysis of additional data.

Cluster Coding or Clustering. In his work on grounded organizational communication theory, Browning (1978) takes GT techniques and selective coding to the next level by proposing that core categories can form "postulates" (p. 102) or general statements about the data and the phenomenon of interest. He calls this approach "generating theoretical clusters" (p. 93). Given clusters of core categories and postulates about a social phenomenon in virtual world, a researcher can propose hypothetical statements about the relationships between core categories emerging from selective coding about virtual work. In that case, the final GT of a social phenomenon concerning virtual work becomes a complex collection of hypothetical statements linking the core categories, evolving processes, conceptual variations, and theoretical concepts for a more robust explanation. We encourage interested readers to consult the chapter by Gibson and Webb on grounded theory for a detailed discussion.

Data Interpretation

Because qualitative interviewing is a rich and evolving approach to research and theory building, it is appropriate for studying the emerging phenomenon of virtual work. To explicate the connection between qualitative interviewing and virtual work research, we make two observations about data interpretation specific to research about virtual work.

Multiple Modes of Interviewing. While consistency of interviewing modes and data formats has been a methodological concern in traditional qualitative research (Kramer & Xie, 2008; Wiesenfeld, et al., 2001), we argue the new social phenomenon of virtual work could benefit

from exploration via a variety of interviewing modes and data formats. Because virtual work is a complex phenomenon that involves formal and informal communication (Long, 2010) and a mix of mediated and FtF communication (Kee & Browning, 2010), a grounded theorist of virtual work should not ignore a piece of data simply because it is not in the same format as the remaining data. Conversely, limiting research data to a single format may limit the richness of a robust GT. To avoid such an outcome, data interpretation can involve triangulation of data sets gathered via multiple modes of interviewing (e.g., Gibbs, 2009; Kee & Browning, 2010); online interview data be treated as equally valid or as supplement to traditional FtF interview data.

Online Interviewing. Because virtual workers may be more comfortable with online interviewing techniques (Kazmer & Xie, 2008), a researcher can rely on participants' technical competence and allow their voices to emerge via online data collection. Shuy (2002) calls this allowing for "contextual naturalness" (p. 538). For example, Kazmer and Xie argue that textual data, such as comments in a participant's email allow the researchers to bear witness to participants' voices in their preferred venue, thus giving a participant power in their representation in the study. They cited the example of "MAC," "mac," or "Mac" for Macintosh, and argue that the variations can impact readers' perceptions of the participant in a study. Such variations and choices of representation would not be possible in an audio or video interview transcript because the researcher determines the written form of the message during transcription. Therefore, we argue that researchers of virtual work could and should take advantage of the opportunity to allow participants to perform their identities in studies of virtual work via online data collection. As discussed earlier in the section on virtual interviewing, such an approach could allow participants to become research partners rather than mere informants or objects of study.

CONCLUSION: RECOMMENDATIONS FOR NOVICE RESEARCHERS

This chapter reviewed qualitative interviewing along with three modes of qualitative interviewing, explained interviewing techniques, formats, and rigor, introduced illustrative case studies, and provided suggestions for researchers collecting interview data to study virtual work. We end with "bullet point" suggestions for researcher using interviewing to study virtual work. The bullet points represent a brief summary of the key points for the effective use of interviewing generally, as well as the specific stages of data collection, data analysis, and data interpretation in research on virtual work.

- Be curious, be open-minded, and pursue the social phenomenon of interest and participants through multiple online and offline channels (i.e., triangulation).
- Keep a careful record of all information, communication, and observation about a social phenomenon of interest and participants involved in the study.
- Begin making sense of information about the social phenomenon (i.e., open coding) with the first interview and/or observation. Constantly compare and contrast initial/tentative codes with every new piece of data (i.e., axial coding).
- As you draw tentative conclusions, pay attention to how the contexts (i.e., conditional matrix) and timing (i.e., process coding) influence participants' behaviors and explanations.
- Allow conceptual categories to converge (i.e., selective coding) and connect (i.e., cluster coding or clustering) to generate a robust framework to explain the phenomenon of interest.
- Whenever possible, allow participants to self-represent in the data. Invite willing participants to co-construct data into meaning (Berger & Luckman, 1967).
- Avoid immediately disregarding voices that differ from the majority of the participants. Allow "forcefulness" to alert you to minority and/or outliers' insights. GT is ongoing. Follow the participants' lead by including forceful minority/outliners' voices.
- Observe how the social phenomenon under study evolves over time under changing conditions.
- Allow clustered postulates to guide any quantitative extension of the study.

In conclusion, qualitative interviewing offers many advantages for studying virtual work. Interviewing offers a rich way to collect and organize data, by following the techniques and procedures discussed in this chapter, researchers can interpret data in ways that build theory, identify themes, reveal patterns, and/or serve as a first step in building quantitative survey instruments. Although interviewing can produce massive amounts of data and thus can seem overwhelming, the practical tips provided in this chapter will assist both the novice and experienced researcher in making sense of resultant data sets. Given the complexity of virtual work, qualitative interviewing, including online interviewing, provides a viable methodological option for research on virtual work.

REFERENCES

Barile, A. L., & Durso, F. T. (2002). Computer-mediated communications in collaborative writing. *Computers in Human Behavior*, *18*(2), 173–190. doi:10.1016/S0747-5632(01)00040-1

Baxter, L. A., & Babbie, E. (2003). *The basics of communication research*. Boston, MA: Wadsworth.

Benoliel, J. Q. (1996). Grounded theory and nursing knowledge. *Qualitative Health Research, 6*, 406–428. doi:10.1177/104973239600600308

Berger, P., & Luckman, T. (1967). *The social construction of reality: A treatise in the sociology of knowledge and commitment in American life*. Garden City, NY: Anchor.

Birks, M., & Mills, J. (2011). *Grounded theory: A practical guide*. Thousand Oaks, CA: Sage.

Bowen, G. A. (2005). Preparing a qualitative research-based dissertation: Lessons learned. *The Qualitative Report, 10*, 208-222.

Browning, L. D. (1978). A grounded organizational communication theory derived from qualitative data. *Communication Monographs, 45*(2), 93–109. doi:10.1080/03637757809375957

Brummett, B. (2008). *A rhetoric of style*. Carbondale, IL: Southern Illinois University Press.

Burleson, B. R., Albrecht, T. L., & Satason, I. G. (Eds.). (1994). *Communication of social support*. Newbury Park, CA: Sage.

Cameron, A. F., & Webster, J. (2005). Unintended consequences of emerging technologies: Instant messaging in the workplace. *Computers in Human Behavior, 21*(1), 85–103. doi:10.1016/j.chb.2003.12.001

Charmaz, K. (2006). *Constructing grounded theory: A practical guide through qualitative analysis*. London, UK: Sage.

Charmaz, K. (2009). Shifting the grounds: Constructivist grounded theory methods. In Morce, J., Stern, P. J., Corbin, J., Bowers, B. K., Charmaz, K., & Clarke, A. (Eds.), *Developing Grounded Theory: The Second Generation*. Walnut Creek, CA: Left Coast Press.

Clarke, A. E. (2005). *Situational analysis: Grounded theory mapping after the postmodern turn*. Thousand Oaks, CA: Sage.

Corbin, J., & Morse, J. (2003). The unstructured interview: Issues of reciprocity and risks when dealing with sensitive topics. *Qualitative Inquiry, 9*, 335–354. doi:10.1177/1077800403009003001

Corbin, J., & Strauss, A. (1990). Grounded theory research: Procedures, canons, and evaluative criteria. *Qualitative Sociology, 13*(1), 3–21. doi:10.1007/BF00988593

Corbin, J., & Strauss, A. (2008). *Basics of qualitative research* (3rd ed.). Thousand Oaks, CA: Sage.

Cresswell, J. W. (1998). *Qualitative inquiry and research design: Choosing among five traditions*. Thousand Oaks, CA: Sage.

Davis, M., Bolding, G., Hard, G., Sherr, L., & Elford, J. (2004). Reflecting on the experience of interviewing online: Perspectives from the internet and HIV study in London. *AIDS Care: Psychological and Socio-Medical Aspects of AIDS / HIV, 16*, 944-952.

Denzin, N. K. (1998). The art and politics of interpretation. In Denzin, N. K., & Lincoln, Y. (Eds.), *Handbook of Qualitative Research* (pp. 313–371). Thousand Oaks, CA: Sage.

Denzin, N. K., & Lincoln, Y. S. (1998). *Collecting and interpreting qualitative materials*. Thousand Oaks, CA: Sage.

Derks, D., Fischer, A. H., & Bos, A. E. R. (2008). The role of emotion in computer-mediated communication: A review. *Computers in Human Behavior, 24*(3), 766–785. doi:10.1016/j.chb.2007.04.004

Dilley, P. (2004). Interviews and the philosophy of qualitative research. *The Journal of Higher Education, 75*(1), 127–132. doi:10.1353/jhe.2003.0049

Fielding, N. G., & Fielding, J. L. (1986). *Linking data: The articulation of qualitative and quantitative methods in social research*. Beverly Hills, CA: Sage.

Flicker, S., Haas, D., & Skinner, H. (2004). Ethical dilemmas in research on Internet communities. *Qualitative Health Research*, *14*, 124–134. doi:10.1177/1049732303259842

Fontana, A., & Frey, J. H. (1998). Interviewing: The art of science. In Denzin, N. K., & Lincoln, Y. S. (Eds.), *Collecting and Interpreting Qualitative Materials* (pp. 47–78). Thousand Oaks, CA: Sage.

Fossey, E., Harvey, C., McDermott, F., & Davidson, L. (2002). Understanding and evaluating qualitative research. *The Australian and New Zealand Journal of Psychiatry*, *36*, 717–732. doi:10.1046/j.1440-1614.2002.01100.x

Gibbs, J. (2009). Dialectics in a global software team: Negotiating tensions across time, space, and culture. *Human Relations*, *62*, 905–935. doi:10.1177/0018726709104547

Glaser, B., & Strauss, G. (1967). *The discovery of grounded theory: Strategies for qualitative work*. Chicago, IL: Aldine.

Gratton, M., & O'Donnell, S. (2011). Communication technologies for focus groups with remote communities: A case study of research with first nations in Canada. *Qualitative Research*, *11*(2), 159–175. doi:10.1177/1468794110394068

Greene, J., Benjamin, L., & Goodyear, L. (2001). The merits of mixing methods in evaluation. *Evaluation*, *7*(1), 25–44. doi:10.1177/13563890122209504

Hamilton, R. J., & Bowers, B. J. (2006). Internet recruitment and e-mail interviews in qualitative studies. *Qualitative Health Research*, *16*, 821–835. doi:10.1177/1049732306287599

Harvey, W. S. (2011). Strategies for conducting elite interviews. *Qualitative Research*, *11*(4), 431–441. doi:10.1177/1468794111404329

Hine, C. (2010). Book Review: Natalita James and Hugh Busher, online interviewing. *Qualitative Research*, *10*(4), 502–504. doi:10.1177/1468794110010004606

Holt, A. (2010). Using the telephone for narrative interviewing: A research note. *Qualitative Research*, *10*(1), 113–121. doi:10.1177/1468794109348686

Hookway, N. (2008). Entering the blogosphere: Some strategies for using blogs in social research. *Qualitative Research*, *8*(1), 91–113. doi:10.1177/1468794107085298

Ingram, A. L., Hathorn, L. G., & Evans, A. D. (2000). Beyond chat on the Internet. *Computers & Education*, *35*, 21–35. doi:10.1016/S0360-1315(00)00015-4

James, N., & Busher, H. (2009). *Online interviewing*. London, UK: Sage.

Kazmer, M. M. (2007). Beyond CUL8R: Disengaging from online social worlds. *New Media & Society*, *9*(1), 111–138. doi:10.1177/1461444807072215

Kazmer, M. M., & Xie, B. (2008). Qualitative interviewing in internet studies: Playing with the media, playing with the method. *Information Communication and Society*, *11*, 257–278. doi:10.1080/13691180801946333

Kee, K. F. (2010). *The rationalities behind the adoption of cyberinfrastructure for e-science in the early 21st century USA*. Unpublished Doctoral Dissertation. Austin, TX: University of Texas.

Kee, K. F., & Browning, L. D. (2010). The dialectical tensions in the funding infrastructure of cyberinfrastructure. *Computer Supported Cooperative Work*, *19*, 283–308. doi:10.1007/s10606-010-9116-9

Krusiewicz, E. S., & Wood, J. T. (2001). He was our child from the moment we walked in that room: Entrance stories of adoptive parents. *Journal of Social and Personal Relationships*, *18*, 785–803. doi:10.1177/0265407501186003

Kvale, S. (1996). *Interviews: An introduction to qualitative research interviewing*. Thousand Oaks, CA: Sage.

Kvale, S. (1996). *InterViews: An introduction to qualitative research interviewing*. Thousand Oaks, CA: Sage.

Long, S. (Ed.). (2010). *Communication, relationships and practices in virtual work*. Hershey, PA: IGI Global. doi:10.4018/978-1-61520-979-8

Mann, C., & Stewart, F. (2002). Internet interviewing. In Gulbrium, J. F., & Holstein, J. A. (Eds.), *Handbook of Interview Research: Context and Method* (pp. 603–628). Thousand Oaks, CA: Sage.

McCoyd, J. L. M., & Kerson, T. S. (2006). Conducting intensive interviews using email. *Qualitative Social Work*, *5*, 389–406. doi:10.1177/1473325006067367

McLeod, J. (2001). *Qualitative research in counseling and psychotherapy*. London, UK: Sage.

Merriam, S. B. (Ed.). (2002). *Qualitative research in practice*. San Francisco, CA: Jossey-Bass.

Miles, M. B., & Huberman, A. M. (1994). *Qualitative data analysis: An expanded sourcebook* (2nd ed.). Thousand Oaks, CA: Sage.

Misheler, E. G. (1986). *Research interviewing: Context and narrative*. Cambridge, MA: Harvard University Press.

Moran-Ellis, J., Alexander, V. D., Cronin, A., Dickinson, M., Fielding, J., Sleney, J., & Thomas, H. (2006). Triangulation and integration: Processes, claims and implications. *Qualitative Research*, *6*(1), 45–59. doi:10.1177/1468794106058870

Murray, C., & Sixsmith, J. (1998). E-mail: A qualitative research medium for interviewing? *International Journal of Social Research Methodology*, *1*, 103–121.

Owen, W. F. (1984). Interpretive themes in relational communication. *The Quarterly Journal of Speech*, *70*, 274–287. doi:10.1080/0033563840938369

Padgett, D. K. (1988). *Qualitative methods in social work*. Thousand Oaks, CA: Sage.

Pennebaker, J. W., & Traue, H. C. (1993). Inhibition and psychosomatic processes. In Traue, H. C., & Pennebaker, J. W. (Eds.), *Emotion Inhibition and Health* (pp. 146–163). Seattle, WA: Hogrefe & Huber.

Ramierz, A. Jr, & Zhang, S. (2007). When online meets offline: The effect of modality switching on relational communication. *Communication Monographs*, *74*, 287–310. doi:10.1080/03637750701543493

Ramirez, A. Jr, Walther, J. B., Burgoon, J. K., & Sunnafrank, M. (2002). Information-seeking strategies, uncertainty, and computer-mediated communication: Toward a conceptual model. *Human Communication Research*, *28*, 213–228.

Rheingold, H. (1991). Reviews the book Virtual Reality. *Science News*, *140*, 322–323.

Rheingold, H. (1993). Cold knowledge and social warmth. *Newsweek*, *122*(10), 49–50.

Rubin, A. (2000). Standards for rigor in qualitative inquiry. *Research in the Sociology of Work*, *10*, 173–178.

Rubin, H. J., & Rubin, I. S. (1995). *Qualitative interviewing: The art of hearing data*. Thousand Oaks, CA: Sage.

Rubin, H. J., & Rubin, I. S. (2005). *Qualitative interviewing: The art of hearing data* (2nd ed.). Thousand Oaks, CA: Sage.

Rupsiene, L., & Pranskuniene, R. (2010). The variety of grounded theory: Different versions of the same method or different methods? *Socialiniai Mokslai*, *4*(70), 7–20.

Seidman, I. (1998). *Interviewing as qualitative research: A guide for researchers in education and the social sciences* (2nd ed.). New York, NY: Teachers College Press.

Shachaf, P. (2008). Cultural diversity and information and communication technology impacts on global virtual teams: An exploratory study. *Information & Management, 45*, 131–142. doi:10.1016/j.im.2007.12.003

Shedletsky, L. J., & Aitken, J. E. (2001). The paradoxes of online academic work. *Communication Education, 50*, 206–217. doi:10.1080/03634520109379248

Shuy, R. W. (2002). In-person versus telephone interviewing. In Gubrium, J. F., & Holstein, J. A. (Eds.), *Handbook of Interview Research: Context and Method* (pp. 537–555). Thousand Oaks, CA: Sage.

Silverman, D. (2001). *Interpreting qualitative data: Methods for analyzing talk, text, and interaction.* London, UK: Sage.

Silverman, D. (2001). *Interpreting qualitative data, methods for analyzing talk, text and interaction* (2nd ed.). Thousand Oaks, CA: Sage.

Square Methodology. (2011, January 28). *Initial thoughts on interview via Skype.* Retrieved from http://www.squaremethodology.com.

Stephens, N. (2007). Collecting data from elites and ultra elites: Telephone and face-to-face interviews with macroeconomists. *Qualitative Research, 7*(2), 203–216. doi:10.1177/1468794107076020

Strauss, A. J., & Corbin, J. (1994). Grounded theory methodology. In Denzin, N. K., & Lincoln, Y. S. (Eds.), *Handbook of Qualitative Research* (pp. 53–65). Thousand Oaks, CA: Sage.

Stroh, M. (2000). Qualitative interviewing. In Burton, D. (Ed.), *Research Training for Social Scientists: A Handbook for Postgraduate Researchers* (pp. 196–217). London, UK: Sage.

Sturges, J. E., & Hanrahan, K. J. (2004). Comparing telephone and face-to-face qualitative interviewing: A research note. *Qualitative Research, 4*(1), 107–118. doi:10.1177/1468794104041110

Tavallaei, M., & Talib, M. A. (2010). A general perspective on role of theory in qualitative research. *Journal of International Social Research, 3*, 570–577.

Thomas, G., & James, D. (2006). Reinventing grounded theory: Some questions about theory, ground and discovery. *British Educational Research Journal, 32*(6), 767–795. doi:10.1080/01411920600989412

Thompson-Hayes, M., Gibson, D. M., Scott, A. T., & Webb, L. (2009). Professorial collaborations via CMC: Interactional dialectics. *Computers in Human Behavior, 25*, 208–216. doi:10.1016/j.chb.2008.09.003

Tierney, W. G., & Dilley, P. (2002). Interviewing in education. In Gubrium, J. F., & Holstein, J. A. (Eds.), *Handbook of Interview Research: Context & Method* (pp. 453–471). Thousand Oaks, CA: Sage.

Walther, J. B., Loh, T., & Granka, L. (2005b). Let me count the ways: The interchange of verbal and nonverbal cues in computer-mediated and face-to-face affinity. *Journal of Language and Social Psychology, 24*, 36–65. doi:10.1177/0261927X04273036

Walther, J. B., & Parks, M. R. (2002). Cues filtered out, cues filtered in: Computer mediated communication and relationships. In Knapp, M. L., Daley, J. A., & Miller, G. R. (Eds.), *The Handbook of Interpersonal Communication* (3rd ed., pp. 529–563). Thousand Oaks, CA: Sage.

Wiesenfeld, B. M., Raghuram, S., & Garud, R. (2001). Organizational identification among virtual workers: The role of need for affiliation and perceived work-based social support. *Journal of Management, 27*, 213–229.

Wilson, H. S., & Hutchinson, S. A. (1996). Methodologic mistakes in grounded theory. *Nursing Research, 45*(2), 122–124. doi:10.1097/00006199-199603000-00012

Wright, K. B., & Webb, L. M. (Eds.). (2011). *Computer mediated communication in personal relationships*. New York, NY: Peter Lang Publishers.

ADDITIONAL READING

Birks, M., & Mills, J. (2011). *Grounded theory: A practical guide*. Thousand Oaks, CA: Sage.

Corbin, J., & Morse, J. (2003). The unstructured interview: Issues of reciprocity and risks when dealing with sensitive topics. *Qualitative Inquiry, 9*, 335–354. doi:10.1177/1077800403009003001

Corbin, J., & Strauss, A. (2008). *Basics of qualitative research* (3rd ed.). Thousand Oaks, CA: Sage.

Kazmer, M. M., & Xie, B. (2008). Qualitative interviewing in internet studies: Playing with the media, playing with the method. *Information Communication and Society, 11*, 257–278. doi:10.1080/13691180801946333

Mann, C., & Stewart, F. (2002). Internet interviewing. In Gulbrium, J. F., & Holstein, J. A. (Eds.), *Handbook of Interview Research: Context and Method* (pp. 603–628). Thousand Oaks, CA: Sage.

McCoyd, J. L. M., & Kerson, T. S. (2006). Conducting intensive interviews using email. *Qualitative Social Work, 5*, 389–406. doi:10.1177/1473325006067367

Misheler, E. G. (1986). *Research interviewing: Context and narrative*. Cambridge, MA: Harvard University Press.

Murray, C., & Sixsmith, J. (1998). E-mail: A qualitative research medium for interviewing? *International Journal of Social Research Methodology, 1*, 103–121.

Rubin, A. (2000). Standards for rigor in qualitative inquiry. *Research in the Sociology of Work, 10*, 173–178.

Rubin, H. J., & Rubin, I. S. (2005). *Qualitative interviewing: The art of hearing data* (2nd ed.). Thousand Oaks, CA: Sage.

Shachaf, P. (2008). Cultural diversity and information and communication technology impacts on global virtual teams: An exploratory study. *Information & Management, 45*, 131–142. doi:10.1016/j.im.2007.12.003

Shuy, R. W. (2002). In-person versus telephone interviewing. In Gubrium, J. F., & Holstein, J. A. (Eds.), *Handbook of Interview Research: Context and Method* (pp. 537–555). Thousand Oaks, CA: Sage.

Silverman, D. (2001). *Interpreting qualitative data, methods for analyzing talk, text and interaction* (2nd ed.). Thousand Oaks, CA: Sage.

Thompson-Hayes, M., Gibson, D. M., Scott, A. T., & Webb, L. (2009). Professorial collaborations via CMC: Interactional dialectics. *Computers in Human Behavior, 25*, 208–216. doi:10.1016/j.chb.2008.09.003

Wiesenfeld, B. M., Raghuram, S., & Garud, R. (2001). Organizational identification among virtual workers: The role of need for affiliation and perceived work-based social support. *Journal of Management, 27*, 213–229.

KEY TERMS AND DEFINITIONS

Coding: To develop categories for ideas that emerge from a data set.

Forcefulness: The strength of an informant's statement; the extent to which he/she indicts that an idea is important.

Grounded Theory: Allowing the central ideas within a text to emerge through the reading, rereading, and repetitive mention of those ideas within the text; then explaining the object of study via the central, emergent ideas.

Interviewing: A focused conversation between a researcher and participant in which the researcher posed queries about a specific subject matter and listens as the informant provides an explanation of his/her understanding of that subject matter.

Qualitative Research: Assessing ideas and understandings rather than quantitative measures.

Theme: A central idea that emerges from a text-based data set.

Virtual Interview: An interview conducted, not in a face-to-face format, but rather via a medium such as telephone, Skype, IM, and email.

Chapter 13
Virtual Matters:
Exploring the Communicative Accomplishment of Virtual Work and Virtual Ethnography

Natalie Nelson-Marsh
Boise State University, USA

ABSTRACT

Recent research highlights the complexity of virtual work and calls on researchers to examine virtual work as more than simply doing a job, but as negotiating a state of being virtual (Leonardi, Jackson, & Marsh, 2004; Long, 2010). A similar call has been made by virtual ethnographers to move away from cataloguing the differences between virtual ethnographic practices and co-located ethnographic practices and instead reflexively reconsider how and why to conduct a virtual ethnography (Hine, 2005). This chapter responds to both calls by exploring how virtual workers communicatively construct distance not as geographical absence, but as presence (Leonardi, et al., 2004; Broadfoot, Munshi, & Nelson-Marsh, 2010). Based on this knowledge, the chapter then develops a heuristic methodological framework that embraces reflexivity as a starting point and privileges communication as the mode through which virtual work is constituted and through which academics arrive at a deeper understanding of both virtual work and virtual ethnography.

INTRODUCTION

Scholars interested in organizing claim that virtual work "fundamentally redefines" the nature of organization (Donaldson & Weiss, 1998, p. 25). Those who aim to understand this fundamental redefinition often begin with the assumption that virtual work is different from co-located work re-sulting in studies that catalogue the characteristics that make virtual work, and virtual organizing, unique (Warner & Witzel, 2004). Scholars interested in methods used to research virtual work also often begin from a position of difference by characterizing the benefits and limitations of using conventional methods as compared with the innovation of new methods for the unique conditions of virtual work (Mann & Stewart, 2000).

DOI: 10.4018/978-1-4666-0963-1.ch013

Recent scholarship demonstrates the complexity of virtual work (Long, 2010; Leonardi, Treem, & Jackson, 2010; Nelson Marsh, 2006) and calls upon scholars to reflexively reconsider not only the position of difference, but also what we know of virtual work (Long, 2010) and how we research virtual work (Hine, 2000; Hine 2005).

This chapter takes up this call and provides a different starting position that examines the mode through which all organizing (virtual or co-located) and all research (conventional or innovative) occurs: communication. Focusing on communication as a generative mechanism that constitutes virtual work and virtual methods moves away from examining the differences between virtual and co-located work and research practices, to examining what these practices mean and why these practices matter in the context of virtual organizing.

This chapter explores virtual ethnography in particular because, as Hine (2005) notes, "our knowledge of the Internet as a cultural context is intrinsically tied up with the application of ethnography. The method and the phenomenon define one another in a relationship of mutual dependence" (p. 8). This chapter argues our knowledge of virtual work as a cultural context is also intrinsically tied up with the application of ethnography. In order to reconsider the mutually defining relationship of virtuality and ethnography, Hine proposes the "Sociology of Cyber-Social-Scientific Knowledge" (SCSSK). Hine (2005) notes that SCSSK is "not a catchy term, but worth practicing" for

SCSSK offers the opportunity to seize upon the power of reflexivity to examine methods afresh and to open up possibilities for new designs and approaches...It also prompts us to be wary of the risks of over-asserting difference between virtual methods and their traditional counterparts (p. 9-10).

What Hine conceptualizes, this chapter extends by engaging current controversies in ethnographic

research of virtual work and providing a different kind of methodological framework for the ethnographic study of virtual work.

In order to develop this framework, the chapter emerges in two parts. The chapter will first discuss how recent scholarship that challenges what virtual work means and our knowledge of virtual work based on the experiences of virtual workers (Leonardi, Jackson, & Marsh, 2004). In particular, the chapter discusses how virtual workers construct *distance* to mean *presence* (Broadfoot, Munshi, & Nelson-Marsh, 2010; Hine, 2000; Leonardi, Jackson, & Marsh, 2004). Based on these understandings of virtual work, the chapter then provides a heuristic methodological framework comprised of three constructs that guide researchers in reflexively reconsidering, designing, and conducting virtual ethnographies. These three constructs also emerge as communicative modes of research and include: Identification, Presentation, and Representation. Each mode has two dimensions: a conceptual dimension as a construct and a practical dimension as the construct emerges in various ethnographic practices (both established practices and innovative practices).

In essence, this chapter takes the position that virtuality is a social accomplishment (Miller & Slater, 2000). This chapter extends this idea by focusing on communication as a generative mechanism that enables scholars to produce interesting knowledge about virtual work emphasizing what virtual work and virtual ethnography mean and why virtual work and virtual ethnography matter.

BACKGROUND: VIRTUAL WORK MATTERS

Asking the question "what is different about virtual work" leads researchers down a path of cataloguing characteristics that aid in recognizing virtual work in contrast to more traditional work. However, as Long (2010) emphasizes

Virtual work is much more than just "doing" something. Virtual work is a state of being in a dislocated space operating under a new and emerging (and always changing) social contract between the organization and its members (p. xvi).

From this perspective, understanding the complexity of virtual work involves not only noting the practices that illustrate virtual work, but also examining the dynamic negotiation of what it *means* to "be" virtual.

The dynamic negotiation of human being in both co-located or dislocated organizational spaces is often taken-for-granted. Virtual work simply accentuates the idea that organizations are fundamentally communicative (Nelson Marsh, 2006). Therefore, focusing on communication enables researchers to understand both how and why people virtually work in particular ways by focusing upon both practices (in talk or text) and the interpretations of the meanings manifest in these practices.

Yet, if there is one factor researchers hold true regarding virtual work, it is that virtual work occurs at a physical distance. This is objectively true; virtual work emerges when workers are dislocated spatially. Information and Communication Technologies (ICTs) then are often examined as the new, objective mechanisms through which workers manage distance (Daft & Lengel, 1986). However, recent scholars claim that distributed organizing across geographical distance is not a new concept; it has existed as a practice for centuries (King & Frost, 2002; Nelson Marsh, 2006; O'Leary, Orlikowski, & Yates, 2002; see also DeSanctis & Monge, 1999). As O'Leary, Orlikowski, and Yates (2002) emphasize, "distributed work and virtual organizations are currently the object of considerable attention from the academic and popular presses…but such organizations are far from modern. In fact, with *virtual* defined in terms of geographic dispersion, virtual organizations are quite ancient" (p. 27; see also King &

Frost, 2002). For example, the Roman Catholic Church (King & Frost, 2002) and the Hudson Bay Company (O'Leary, Orlikowski, & Yates, 2002) illustrate two organizations that have survived centuries distributed across vast geographical space. Moreover, if the geographical dispersion of organizations is "quite ancient," so too is the use of varying Information and Communication Technologies through which participants interact across space and time (King & Frost, 2002; Hughes, 1987). These researchers challenge the idea that ICTs are the new, electronic mechanisms that neutrally negotiate space. Instead, they define communication technologies broadly, emphasizing the material functionality of devices such as the physical pen or printing press as well as the patterns of interpretation through which humans know how to use these technologies (King & Frost, 2002; Nelson Marsh, 2006).

If organizations have long been distributed across time and space and organizations have long been communicating technologically, then what is next for researchers interested in virtual work? It is intriguing to focus upon the taken-for-granted choices virtual workers (and virtual ethnographers) make when negotiating a social contract regarding how and why to work (and research) in some ways and not others. This chapter aims to provide a methodological framework that enables researchers, particularly ethnographers, to understand this dynamic negotiation of the social contract between people and how this negotiation emerges as a recognizable organization. This begins by challenging the nature of distance as simply the objective physical dislocation between workers. Virtual workers are distributed, but how do they interpret distance? Virtual work does include utilizing technologies to accomplish their work, but *why* do virtual workers work as they do? What influences their choices? If we assume virtual work is more than physical distribution across time and space and consider virtual work as a state of being, and more specifically a state of being constantly negotiated through various communication processes, then what "distance" and "presence" means depends upon the negotiation between virtual workers.

Distance and Presence

Beginning from the assumption that distance equals geographical space privileges the material world as responsible for dictating how and why virtual workers act or work as they do. Virtual workers actions then become means to mimic face-to-face co-presence. Therefore, assuming distance equals geographical dispersion also privileges face to face interactions as the standard that should guide virtual workers when making choices about how and why to work in particular ways. In essence, from this perspective, distance equals absence (Gergen, 2002). A focus on absence assumes there is something missing from interaction. For example, researchers argue what is missing in virtual interaction is significance, depth, intimacy, authenticity, or the ability to truly establish culture (Gergen, 1991; Robins, 1999; Robins & Webster, 1999). Virtual interaction is banal and superficial at a minimum (Robins and Webster, 1999) and a threat to constructing deep, meaningful culture (Gergen, 1991; Robins, 1999) at a maximum. Yet, even as these critiques argue that distance is something to overcome, they invoke the idea that distance is negotiated, in that they, as researchers, have assigned value to distance as a threat to establishing culture. In creating a meaning for distance, these critiques propose an opportunity to reflexively reconsider distance as more than simple dislocation and instead question what distance means.

Problematizing what distance means lends to a perspective that distance is a state of being negotiated communicatively (Leonardi, Jackson, & Marsh, 2004). As Leonardi et al. (2004) state, "distance is enacted, conveyed, and managed communicatively. In other words, distance workers

constitute distance through communication" (p. 165). While the work setting for a virtual worker may differ, organizational members communicatively construct and negotiate what distance and presence mean symbolically. To focus this claim, how virtual workers negotiate distance depends upon how they, as a collective group of workers, interpret distance. What distance means emerges not from one individual, but in relationship with others.

Distance then, represents more than geographic dislocation and emerges as a cultural construct created by organizational members that aid members in knowing how to categorize or understand how and why to work in particular ways. How these constructs are interpreted leads to different communicative practices or strategies that both constitute how to do a job virtually and construct why these ways are legitimate ways to work (Leonardi, et al., 2004).

Problematizing distance enables researchers to explore the richer nature of distance and in particular to demonstrate how interpretations of distance by those in virtual work situations actually accentuate connective participation (Leonardi, et al., 2004; Broadfoot, et al., 2010). Specifically, distance was "a feeling of connection to a group of individuals as one's 'presence' in a location" (Leonardi, et al., 2004, p. 162). Negotiating meanings for distance becomes an interpretive form of presence. Distance, as connection or presence, emerges through communicative practices or strategies such as creating special occasions for interaction as with virtual lunches or simply actively seeking out frequent conversation with others to establish and maintain a feeling of connection (Leonardi, et al., 2004). Distance, for virtual workers, is not constituted by space but by interpretations of connectedness with others that emerge in collective communication strategies. What distance is for virtual workers depends on what virtual workers co-construct virtual work to mean. Virtual work is not bound by physical space or time (Bhabha, 1994; Bhabha, 1996) but is bound by the communicatively constructed meanings.

Presence then also emerges as a conceptual construct that influences how members categorize how and why to work in particular ways. Interpretations of presence manifest in various communication strategies that establish a sense of connection with others. The frequency of interaction whether planned or spontaneous creates a *sense* of presence or co-presence (Broadfoot, et al., 2010). Distance as presence provides the opportunity to "express situated personal experiences, needs, and problems, and [thus undermines] the clichéd distinction between 'virtual' and 'real' (Feenberg & Bakardjieva, 2004, p. 40). Virtual workers emerge as "present" as they present themselves in rich, meaningful, and interactive ways (Broadfoot, et al., 2010). Thus, distance and presence are created, "conveyed and managed communicatively" (Leonardi, 2004, p. 165). However, these communication practices strategically respond to the perceived interpretation of others. Who I am as a virtual worker emerges in relationship to other workers—something that occurs in both co-located and virtual spaces.

Distance and presence are cultural constructs that cannot be measured as varying degrees of absence. Rather, distance and presence emerge in a variety of communicative practices and strategies. Understanding distance and presence as constructs moves researchers away from simply focusing on how people virtually work in contrast to co-located work, to why people work in these ways. What do these work practices mean? Characterizing distance and presence as cultural constructs, I aim to provide a heuristic *conceptual* framework that focuses on the patterns of virtual work as meaningful. Drawing inspiration from these constructs I move to developing a heuristic *methodological* framework that enables researchers to recognize not only how and why virtual workers work as they do, but how and why virtual ethnographers

work (i.e. research) virtual work as they do. Below, I first develop the controversies revolving around virtual ethnography as they parallel the controversies in studying virtual work. I then draw on the development of distance and presence and what has been learned from previous studies of virtual work to create this methodological framework for researchers interested in conducting a virtual ethnography.

VIRTUAL ETHNOGRAPHY MATTERS

As with research on virtual work, much of the research surrounding how to conduct a virtual ethnography begins from a premise that virtual ethnography takes place at a physical distance. Recent calls by virtual ethnographers argue a different starting place is needed (Hine, 2005) in order to understand the complexity of virtual ethnographic work. A new starting place would provide a perspective that reflexively reconsiders what virtual ethnography means and how this meaning emerges in ethnographic practice.

This chapter responds to this call by first exploring the current controversies regarding virtual ethnographic methods. The chapter then draws on and reflexively reconsiders "distance and presence" as *conceptual* heuristic constructs that aid in developing three *methodological* heuristic constructs: Identification, Presentation, and Representation. These methodological constructs aim to help future ethnographers (virtual and co-located) in reflexively conceptualizing methods they believe will enable them to understand the virtual, cultural work they study. The benefit of this heuristic model is the reflexivity involved in research development, design, implementation, and revision. Research methods become more that just doing virtual research work to communicatively negotiating and co-constructing what it means to be a virtual worker *and* a virtual researcher.

Virtual Ethnography: Perpetuating the Crises of Legitimation and Representation

Virtual ethnographers who write about virtual groups or the methods involved in studying these groups often begin by explaining the difference or innovativeness of these new methodological practices. Much like studies of virtual work that focus on distinguishing virtual and co-located work practices, virtual ethnographers focus on distinguishing traditional methods with new or innovative methods (Hine, 2005). Hine (2005) captures this idea when she states:

we seem to feel the need to speak of virtual groups, online ethnography, cyber research, and web experiments to distinguish old familiar methods from their new offspring. This usage marks the air if innovation around the fields and also provides for a sense of anxiety. The formulation of the online world as new territory for social research also creates the perception that nothing can be taken for granted (p. 5).

However, critics and advocates of virtual ethnography do not simply debate the work practices of ethnographers, but the assumptions manifest in these methods. For example, both co-located and virtual ethnographers demonstrate three agreed upon ethnographic commitments. First, ethnographers identify with the necessity to experience a social group first-hand as participant observers and to document these interactions and their significance as they are meaningful to local actors in the form of "thick description" (Atkinson, Coffey, Delemont, Lofland, and Lofland, 2001; Geertz, 1973). Second, ethnographers identify the need engage and interact with members (Atkinson, et al., 2001). Third, ethnographers write up their interpretations for a larger, academic audience (Atkinson, et al., 2001; Lindlof & Taylor, 2002). It would appear that these commitments are clear-cut practices: participate and observe, engage, and

author interpretations. However, ethnographers have historically debated the symbolic meaning of these commitments and how these meanings emerge in a diversity of practices claimed to be ethnographic (Atkinson, et al., 2001). These debates are embedded in the history of ethnography and have been labeled the dual crises of legitimation and representation (Atkinson, et al., 2001). Both crises emerge due to the challenges different ethnographies present in their assumptions about what participant observation means, what engagement means, and what authorship or representation of a culture means.

A simplified summary of the historic controversies in ethnographies focuses first upon ethnographers who assume that empirical data unproblematically represents a culture. Therefore, descriptive field notes present an accurate and objective accounting of the culture. These realist assumptions lead to claims of legitimacy and a standard of social scientific truth in ethnographic methods and findings (Brown, 1977; Clifford and Marcus, 1986). In contrast, with the Interpretive turn, scholars reflexively questioned these realist assumptions and problematized both the orthodoxy and assumed universality of methods and the privileging of the authorial voice in representing, in a totalizing manner, the experiences of others (Clifford & Marcus, 1986). Introducing these challenges leads to the crisis of legitimation of methods (whose methods are right) and the crisis of representation in authorial writing (whose voice is privileged) about a culture. These dual crises invoke arguments of the "right" way to work as an ethnographer in the field and the "right" way to work as authors in a disciplinary field.

While some ethnographers posit there is an orthodox or traditional method for ethnographers, others posit ethnography as a reflexive endeavor open to new and innovative methods (Denizen, 1997; Atkinson, et al., 2001). As Denizen (1997) argues, there was never a traditional ethnographic order and to argue such "insists on marginalizing the new order of things, always defining it as an aberrant variation on the traditional way of doing things" (p. 251). In other words, ethnography has always been open to interpretation and has "never been a stable entity" (Atkinson, et al., 2001, p. 4). Thus, when a researcher invokes the term ethnography this does not imply a single set of methods for data collection, data analysis (Lindlof & Taylor, 2010; Lindlof & Taylor, 2004, Atkinson, et al., 2001), or data presentation in the form of authorship (Bochner & Ellis, 1996). Ethnography includes a wide-range of diverse methods that incorporate qualitative and even quantitative methods (Lindlof & Taylor, 2004). As Lindlof and Taylor (2004) state, "basically ethnographers will turn to any method that will help them to achieve success…[in] describing and interpreting observed relationships between social practices and the systems of meaning in a particular cultural milieu" (p. 16.).

Virtual ethnographies exemplify the ongoing nature and the legacy of the dual crises of legitimation and representation. Both advocates and critics of the legitimacy of virtual ethnographic methods begin from the premise that geographic distance between participants means absence. According to critics, geographic dispersion of virtual communities, cultures, and members means absence or a lack of authentic or genuine interaction (Hine, 2000). Given this lack, virtual interaction is argued to be superficial, banal, and therefore participants lack in the ability to create substantive, deep, cultural relationships (Robins & Webster, 1999). Thus, such superficiality results in less authoritative claims by virtual ethnographer regarding the "culture" of virtual groups.

Yet, we have now entered a phase where advocates of virtual ethnography have established the legitimacy of virtual worlds as social and cultural contexts (Baym, 1995, Rheingold, 1993) and in doing so challenge the assumption that distance means absence. As Hine (2005) argues, virtual ethnographers illustrate in their representation both the legitimacy of virtual ethnographic methods and the richness of virtual interactions that construct virtual cultures. In essence,

it is possible to go so far and to suggest that our knowledge of the Internet as a cultural context is intrinsically tied up with the application of ethnography. The method and the phenomena define one another in a relationship of mutual dependence. The online context is defined as a cultural context by the demonstration that ethnography can be applied to it (Hine, 2005, p. 8).

Anxiety and tension will continue to exist because there is no standard method that serves as a foundation upon which to judge the correctness of a virtual ethnology because ethnographies have always been diverse (Atkinson, et al., 2004; Hine, 2000; Hine, 2005). Rather than try to alleviate and resolve the tension with another argument about the legitimacy of virtual ethnography, it is more interesting to sit in the tension and engage in the reflexive moment as researchers reconsidering what we take for granted about the nature of research, conceptual and practical, the nature of the cultural contexts we study, and the nature of the knowledge we claim to be justified by our research.

This reflexive moment demonstrates more than the crisis of legitimation and representation, but a crisis of praxis (Denizen, 1997). Engaging the tension or anxiety and reflexively reconsidering the conceptual constructs that guide research practices is an opportunity to learn about virtual ethnography and virtual work and present new knowledge about both. Hine (2005) characterizes this reflexive engagement with the term "Sociology of Cyber-Social-Scientific-Knowledge" (SCSSK). SCSSK is a conceptual framework that reminds the researcher to sit in the tension and reflexively examine the "epistemological and methodological commitments of ethnography and explore the possibilities for research designs and approaches" (p. 9). While a cumbersome term, the sentiment for reflexive engagement provides an opportunity to explore how, through communication, both virtual ethnographers and virtual workers constitute the phenomenon of virtual work in relationships of mutual dependence.

Despite Hine's framing SCSSK in the introduction of her edited book, as she notes, the chapters in her book do not directly take up this framework but instead explore a series of methods for studying online spaces. Thus, the opportunity to take up SCSSK is ripe. Based on what was learned from previous studies of virtual work as developed above, taking up the SCSSK also involves considering what distance and presence mean for virtual ethnographers and the role of communication in constituting the meaning and practice of distance and presence in virtual ethnographic work practices. Rather than propose another set of diverse methodological practices or designs (traditional, innovative, or a mixture of both), this chapter moves next into creating a different kind of ethnographic framework, a heuristic methodological framework that develops cultural constructs that aid researchers in a) reflexively reconsidering the assumptions that guide why they research in a particular way and b) based on this reflexivity, consider which diverse practices to include in the design and implementation of research methods.

A Communication Methodological Framework for Virtual Ethnography

Virtual organizations and virtual ethnographies are fundamentally communicative. Virtual workers and virtual ethnographers negotiate what it means to be virtual through symbolic communication practices with others. Communication is also the generative and constitutive mode through which knowledge of virtual work emerges. Therefore, reconsidering the commitments of virtual ethnographers involves reflexively examining communication processes through which virtual ethnographers constitute both virtual work and virtual ethnography.

This section focuses on three communicative processes that constitute the texture of virtual ethnography: Identification, Presentation, and Representation. As heuristic constructs Identification, Presentation, and Representation are abstract and ambiguous. As abstract constructs, there are no standard practices that universally apply when conducting a virtual ethnography. Virtual ethnographers may choose from or create a variety of methods for data collection, data analysis, or data articulation in order to describe and interpret symbolic virtual work practices. Therefore, a diversity of research practices can be utilized in and across various contexts of virtual work. The ambiguous meanings associated with the heuristic constructs leaves room for multiple interpretations by researchers who may choose either traditional or innovative methods based upon their assumptions. By not proposing specific methodological practices, these constructs ask researchers to consider why they might embody and perform certain research practices over others.

Identification

The first construct, Identification, does not signify the first stage of research. The boundaries between these constructs blend and blur. Identification is a construct that emerges in all stages of ethnographic research and is a construct to which the researcher should regularly attend in order to maintain a state of reflexivity during the research process. Identification is a position of constantly questioning with what socialized meanings the researcher identifies and how the researcher presents and represents these meanings through communicative practices.

Virtual workers and virtual ethnographers do not simply do virtual work (Long, 2010) they reflexively monitor their own and others interactions as symbolic of the right or potentially the wrong way to virtually work (Nelson Marsh, 2006). This includes with what meanings the researcher identifies as a professional ethnographer (Wellin & Fine, 2001) and the meanings with which research participants identify (Lindlof & Taylor, 2010). More specifically, by engaging the Identification construct, virtual ethnographers ask the questions: 'with what do I identify (as a professional and as a participant observer)?' 'What am I paying attention to and why?' and 'How am I identifying?' Questions like these, asked at various stages of ethnographic research, help in sustaining a space of reflexivity by asking the researcher to analyze and reconsider the meanings that guide the choices made about which research methods to implement and how to articulate what is learned in writing. In essence, Identification becomes a means of consciously recognizing how to interact with participants and other academic peers and why to engage in this way. Identification then, emerges in a variety of communication practices in which participants perform an identity and reflexively monitor the identity of others (Kuhn & Nelson, 2002; Scott, Corman, & Cheney, 1998; see also Giddens, 1984).

For example, if a virtual researcher believes that in order to be legitimate, engagement with participates must include semi-structured interviews, then by conducting a semi-structured interview the researcher both identifies or reproduces a particular understanding of ethnographic engagement and presents the role as ethnographer to participants and other professional ethnographers. If the researcher adheres to a belief that semi-structured interviews need to be spontaneous in order to be considered more legitimate, s/he may opt for a telephone or video conference interview or even travel to the participant. However, if the researcher believes that a semi-structured interview is legitimate when it captures the virtual experiences of participants, s/he might opt for an electronic text-based email or instant message interview (Kivits, 2001). Through the communicative practice of interviewing—which may take many forms—the researcher establishes symbolic assumptions about the right way to establish presence with virtual workers. The Identification construct is important in that it creates a space in the research process to

reflect upon with what meanings the ethnographer identifies and how these identifications shape the method and content of the ethnography. The methods of engagement such as interview, casual conversation, document collection, and so on vary. Recognizing what meanings guide the choice to use one method or another aids the researcher in making the choice in the first place, articulating why the choice was made to others, and/or choosing an alternative method after reflection and reconsideration.

Presentation

The communication construct Presentation draws upon the understandings of distance as presence developed above in that distance in virtual work does not equal geographic distance or absence. Rather, distance is a cultural construct negotiated through the communicative performances that establish presence. In other words, as virtual workers *and* ethnographers participate and connect through communication with participants, they present or perform their work. Goffman's (1959) development of performance nicely captures this idea in that a performance includes all activity of a person as it occurs/emerges during a period of time "marked by his (sic) continuous presence before a partial set of observers which has some influence on the observer" (p. 24). In reflexively reconsidering the role of the researcher as a participant observer, "being there" or being present is not enough (Hine, 2000). It is necessary also to engage in interaction with participants (Hine, 2000). Initial and ongoing participation and presentation as a researcher with participants is an ongoing and negotiated performance. The construct presentation highlights the flexibility in considering how to present to others, why to present in this way, and how to continue to negotiate presence with others.

A helpful way to organize these thoughts is to keep in mind the questions: 'what is going on here?' 'How do I present myself as a researcher in this context?' (Lindlof & Taylor, 2004), and 'How do I negotiate and perform as a researcher in this context?' Researchers make a choice (even if taken-for-granted) regarding how to act and how to perform and present for participants. Even if this choice is deliberate, the choice itself is significant. By asking what is going on here and how do I negotiate this role, ethnographic researchers begin orienting to how participants normally communicate and thus how to connect with one another virtually.

A variety of methods can make manifest virtual ethnographers' interpretations of the "right" way to present. For example, virtual ethnographers may begin by lurking as a means to ascertain, through participant presentations or performances, who the gatekeepers might be or what the norms of presentation are. In a study of the virtual workers responsible for the development of the Internet (Nelson Marsh, 2006) newcomers were expected to lurk in order to understand the norms and how to negotiate the norms so as not to impede the process of Internet infrastructure development. Newcomers who broke established norms were often ostracized. While not presenting verbally, the researcher may establish presence through distance using electronic cues such as login identification in instant message chats.

Presentation also involves how to engage as an ethnographer *with* participants, again, guided by the questions 'what is going on here?' and 'how do present myself as a researcher in this context?' involves noticing how the researcher and participants perform their roles in relationship with others. For example, what communicative practices perform or signify formal roles such as Engineer or informal roles such as virtual office gossip? What are the routine interactions and what interactions stand out (Lindlof & Taylor, 2002)? In turn, the researcher also considers the formal and informal interactions that emerge when presenting the role of ethnographer. What communication practices emerge between participants and ethnographer?

For example, the ethnographer may interact with participants as a student asking questions about why things are done in particular ways. Why do these practices and not others establish presence? Perhaps an ethnographer participates by providing work services. Each choice for negotiating presence depends upon the interpretations of what presentation will mean in context.

By considering and practicing the nuances of presentation in virtual work contexts, virtual workers and virtual ethnographers socially construct an understanding of virtual work. Presentation, as an ambiguous and abstract construct, enables researchers to recognize how and why to observe and participate in some ways and not others. Participant observation even in co-located ethnography is not a singular process. Not confined to a set of practices, the emphasis becomes reflexive communication in the form of presentation both for others and with others.

Representation

The third construct, Representation, explores what is considered another essential part of ethnography: describing, documenting, and authoring the observations of practices and the interpreted meaning of these practices for others. Not only do virtual ethnographers gain access, present, immerse, and identify in virtual, social contexts, so too do they re-present these worlds or "inscribe" these worlds (Geertz, 1973, p. 19). Both virtual participants and virtual ethnographers practice representation in texts as a performative communicative process. Thus, reflexively reconsidering the choices people make in what to represent becomes an important part of the virtual work of virtual ethnographers.

The construct representation engages the reflexivity of the researcher in three ways. First virtual ethnographers reflexively consider and ask: what is the role of text in virtual ethnographer and how do I participate and make sense of studying textual and other interactions? Second, virtual ethnographers might ask what to document and how to document their observations and interpretations? Third, virtual ethnographers should ask how do I author and represent the culture of virtual work to an academic audience? For all three of these areas of interest, the idea of distance as presence becomes particularly important. Representation as it emerges in field notes, sense-making interaction with participants, and authoring academic texts, inherently involves negotiating distance as connection and presence.

For example, data collection from participant observation involves textual interaction in virtual worlds. Virtual work takes many forms including video conferencing, telephone calls, email, instant message, travel to meet face-to-face, etc. Yet textual interaction is a large component of negotiating what it means to be a virtual worker and a virtual ethnographer. For example, writing a text (email, instant message) in order to present or engage with participants is not a neutral task, but laden with meaning. It is important for the virtual ethnographer to reflexively consider not only the content of the text, but also how the text is situated in a context that makes it meaningful (Thompson, 1995). Texts do not stand alone, isolated, but emerge as patterned interactions that contextualize virtual work for the ethnographer to study. As Thompson (1995) contends, observing the presentation of texts ethnographically requires identifying how those texts connect to a particular group and why they connect in a meaningful way. How participants and the ethnographer identify the meaning of the text *in relation* to other texts enables the researcher to more deeply understand (and re-present) the culture of virtual work. However, textual interaction is always incomplete and partial as it invokes other texts in order for the larger significance to make sense.

This complexity and partiality makes sense to a virtual ethnographer who, in participating and observing, also documents interactions in field notes. These field notes make sense of the culture

textually when the ethnographer analyzes the field notes or textual representation in relation to one another. The virtual ethnographer makes choices in regards to what to document (the content of the text) and how to document such as the frame of the text, the presentation as fact, stories, or meanings, etc. (see Emerson, Fretz, & Shaw, 2001). Reflexivity focuses on the choices made regarding what to document and how to document which shapes the claims made about virtual work. The analysis methods differ and might focus on themes, metaphors, codes or categories (Strauss, 1987). How the researcher chooses to make connections shapes what is re-presented as the culture to others. What virtual work is proclaimed to be culture emerges in the choices virtual ethnographers make when analyzing the relationship between field note texts and representing these interpretations in articles, books, or other documents, for a discipline.

Finally, representation also involves reflexively understanding the meaningful choices involved in how a virtual researcher chooses to re-present the culture of virtual work to others. The author may choose to invoke a voice of authority communicating observations as factual or true. The author may work to weave the voice of participants together to tell the story of their virtual work lives. The author may choose to focus on the personal voice and account, in the form of autoethnography, for an individual interpretation so as not to impose meanings upon the participants (Bochner & Ellis, 1996). Each choice impacts what is known about virtual work.

As a construct, Representation aids researchers in conceptually categorizing the practice of observing texts, engaging and interacting through texts, and authoring field notes and formal texts in a way that reflexively considers why certain choices were made and how these choices impact what is known about virtual work.

Each of the three communication constructs presented in this chapter act as part of an overall heuristic methodological framework that embraces reflexivity as a starting point for researchers and privileges communication as the generative means through which virtual work is constituted and through which academics arrive at a deeper understanding of both virtual work and virtual ethnography.

FUTURE RESEARCH DIRECTIONS

When research on virtuality begins from a premise of difference, the discussion tends toward either criticizing whether virtual worlds are banal spaces (Robins & Webster, 1999) or cultural spaces (Baym, 1993; Rheingold, 1999). Similarly, researchers who write about utilizing virtual ethnographic methods who begin from a premise of difference tend toward defending virtual spaces as legitimate spaces to engage in traditional ethnographic methods while others propose the need to innovate new methods for these spaces (Hine, 2005). In order to progress knowledge about virtual work it is time to reconsider our starting place as virtual ethnographers (Hine, 2005). While Hine proposed a starting place that embraced reflexivity with her Sociology of Cyber-Social-Scientific Knowledge (SCSSK) construct, her edited book did not develop this model. In taking up Hine's call, this chapter proposes an innovative and untested methodological framework. Therefore, future research could involve exploring and extending the proposed framework in one of three ways.

First, utilizing this framework for the empirical study of virtual work would position the researcher as a reflexive co-participant in constituting knowledge of virtual work. This framework would provide a means of designing a virtual ethnography that embraces diversity by incorporating traditional and innovative methods in order to examine the complexity of virtual work. For example, as an ethnographer reflexively considers with what professional meanings s/he identifies, s/he may decide to first develop and implement a survey to ascertain expectations of participants' normal practices and meanings for these practices. S/he may then decide to present and connect with participants through instant messaging conversation, observe email listservs, and conduct telephone interviews. Finally, the ethnographer may develop a manuscript that accounts for the meanings that guided his/her choices and the resulting understanding of the virtual culture studied. The development and implementation of a diversity of methods emerges from consideration of what is meaningful to participants *and* to the researcher as guided by the heuristic methodological constructs.

A second research direction might focus on the experience of researchers who have experimented with the proposed methodological framework in a research project. Having experimented with this heuristic methodological framework, the author might add to knowledge about virtual ethnography through an analysis of what worked with this framework and what did not, extending the framework so as to aid future researchers. For example, the heuristic constructs proposed are not exhaustive. Therefore, the researcher might add other heuristic constructs that emerges in communicative practices.

Finally, because the heuristic methodological framework proposed in this chapter is a new creation, it is open for conceptual critique as well. This framework is shaped by the author's assumptions as a virtual ethnographer from the communication discipline. For example, this heuristic model advances a decentering of virtual ethnography and virtual organization as objective phenomena. Instead, this chapter proposes a model that assumes virtual work is discursively co-constructed by virtual workers and virtual ethnographers. Virtual ethnographers might engage this framework in a debate by exploring the assumptions that shaped its development, and discuss the benefits and limitations of this model in order to strengthen the method when it is utilized in practice.

CONCLUSION

Current controversies regarding virtual ethnographies argue that distance de-legitimizes the practice of virtual ethnography and de-legitimizes the claims made by virtual ethnographies about the symbolic nature of virtual work. By challenging the assumption that distance means absence, researchers of virtual work demonstrate the need to move beyond comparing virtual with co-located work or virtual ethnographies with co-located ethnographies. Beginning instead with an understanding that distance means presence and connection, this chapter develops a heuristic methodological framework that consists of three communication constructs: Identification, Presentation, and Representation. By providing this framework, this chapter creates a space for virtual ethnographers to reflexively consider the symbolic meanings that guide how virtual ethnographers *and* virtual workers interact as they do across time and space because as Hine (2005) accentuates, turning the lens on ethnography aids in understanding how the method and the phenomenon "define one another in a relationship of mutual dependence" (p. 8). This chapter demonstrates how our knowledge of virtual work as a cultural context is also intrinsically tied up with the application of ethnography and proposes a model to continue exploring the complexity of virtual work as a communicative accomplishment.

REFERENCES

Atkinson, P., Coffey, A., Delamont, S., Lofland, J., & Lofland, L. (2001). Editorial introduction. In Atkinson, P., Coffey, A., Delamont, S., Lofland, J., & Lofland, L. (Eds.), *Handbook of Ethnography*. Thousand Oaks, CA: Sage Publishing.

Baym, N. K. (1995). From practice to culture on usenet. In Star, S. L. (Ed.), *The Cultures of Computing*. Cambridge, UK: Blackwell Publishers.

Bhabha, H. K. (1994). *The location of culture*. London, UK: Routledge.

Bhabha, H. K. (1996). Culture's in-between. In Hall, S., & du Gay, P. (Eds.), *Questions of Cultural Identity* (pp. 53–60). London, UK: Sage Publications.

Bochner, A. P., & Ellis, E. M. (1996). Taking ethnography into the twenty-first century. *Journal of Contemporary Ethnography*, *25*, 3–5. doi:10.1177/089124196025001001

Broadfoot, K., Munshi, D., & Nelson-Marsh, N. (2009). COMMUNEcation: A rhizomatic tale of participatory technology, postcoloniality and professional community. *New Media & Society*, *12*(5), 797–812. doi:10.1177/1461444809348880

Brown, R. H. (1977). *A poetic for sociology*. Cambridge, UK: Cambridge University Press.

Clifford, J., & Marcus, G. E. (1986). *Writing culture: The poetics and politics of ethnography*. Berkeley, CA: University of California Press.

Daft, R. L., & Lengel, R. (1986). Organizational information requirements, media richness, and structural design. *Management Science*, *32*(5), 554–571. doi:10.1287/mnsc.32.5.554

Denizen, N. K. (1997). *Interpretive ethnography: Ethnographic practices for the 21st century*. Thousand Oaks, CA: Sage Publications.

DeSanctis, G., & Monge, P. (1999). Introduction: Communication processes for virtual organizations. *Organization Science*, *10*, 693–703. doi:10.1287/orsc.10.6.693

Donaldson, S. I., & Weiss, R. (1998). Health, well-being, and organizational effectiveness in the virtual workplace. In Iberia, M., & Tan, M. (Eds.), *The Virtual Workplace*. Hershey, PA: IGI Global.

Emerson, R. M., Fretz, R. I., & Shaw, L. L. (2001). Participant observation and fieldnotes. In Atkinson, P., Coffey, A., Delamont, S., Lofland, J., & Lofland, L. (Eds.), *Handbook of Ethnography*. Thousand Oaks, CA: Sage Publishing.

Feenberg, A., & Bakardjieva, M. (2004). Virtual community: No "killer implication". *New Media & Society*, *6*(1), 37–43. doi:10.1177/1461444804039904

Geertz, C. (1973). *The interpretation of cultures: Selected essays*. New York, NY: Basic Books.

Gergen, K. (1991). *The saturated self: Dilemmas of identity in contemporary life*. New York, NY: Basic Books.

Gergen, K. (2002). The challenge of absent presence. In Katz, J. E., & Aakhus, M. A. (Eds.), *Perpetual Contact: Mobile Communication, Private Talk, Public Performance*. Cambridge, UK: Cambridge University Press.

Giddens, A. (1984). *The constitution of society: Outline and theory of structuration*. Berkeley, CA: University of California Press.

Goffman, E. (1959). *The presentation of self in everyday life*. Harmondsworth, UK: Penguin.

Hine, C. (2000). *Virtual ethnography*. Thousand Oaks, CA: Sage Publications.

Hine, C. (2005). Virtual methods and the sociology of cyber-social-scientific knowledge. In Hine, C. (Ed.), *Virtual Methods: Issues in Social Research on the Internet*. New York, NY: Oxford International Publishers.

Hughes, T. P. (1987). The evolution of large technological systems. In W. E. Bijker, T. P. Hughes, &, T. J. Pinch (Eds.), *The Social Construction of Technological Systems: New Direction in the Sociology and History of Technology*. Cambridge, MA: The MIT Press.

King, J. L., & Frost, R. L. (2002). Managing distance over time: The evolution of technologies of disambiguation. In Hinds, P., & Kiesler, S. (Eds.), *Distributed Work*. Cambridge, MA: The MIT Press.

Kivits, J. (2005). Online interviewing and the research relationship. In Hine, C. (Ed.), *Virtual Methods: Issues in Social Research on the Internet*. New York, NY: Oxford International Publishers.

Kuhn, T., & Nelson, N. (2002). Reengineering identity: A case study of multiplicity and duality in organizational identification. *Management Communication Quarterly*, *16*, 5–39. doi:10.1177/0893318902161001

Leonardi, P. M., Jackson, M. J., & Marsh, N. (2004). The strategic use of "distance" among virtual team members: A multi-dimensional communication model. In Godar, S. H., & Ferris, S. P. (Eds.), *Virtual and Collaborative Teams: Process, Technologies, and Practice*. Hershey, PA: IGI Global. doi:10.4018/978-1-59140-204-6.ch009

Leonardi, P. M., Treem, J. W., & Jackson, M. H. (2010). The connectivity paradox: Using technology to both decrease and increase perceptions of distance in distributed work arrangements. *Journal of Applied Communication Research*, *38*, 85–105. doi:10.1080/00909880903483599

Lindlof, T. R., & Taylor, B. C. (2004). *Qualitative communication research methods* (2nd ed.). Thousand Oaks, CA: Sage.

Lindlof, T. R., & Taylor, B. C. (2010). *Qualitative communication research methods* (3rd ed.). Thousand Oaks, CA: Sage.

Long, S. (2010). *Communication, relationships and practices in virtual work*. Hershey, PA: IGI Global. doi:10.4018/978-1-61520-979-8

Mann, C., & Stewart, F. (2000). *Internet communication and qualitative research: A handbook for researching online*. Thousand Oaks, CA: Sage Publishing.

Miller, D., & Slater, D. (2000). *The internet: An ethnographic approach*. New York, NY: Oxford International Publishers.

Nelson-Marsh, N. (2006). *Reconsidering the conceptual relationship between organizations and technology: A study of the internet engineering task force as a virtual organization*. Unpublished Doctoral Dissertation. Boulder, CO: University of Colorado at Boulder.

O'Leary, M., Orlikowski, W., & Yates, J. (2002). Distributed work over the centuries: Trust and control in the Hudson's bay company, 1670-1826. In Hinds, P., & Kiesler, S. (Eds.), *Distributed Work*. Cambridge, MA: The MIT Press.

Rheingold, H. (1993). *The virtual community: Homesteading on the electronic frontier*. Reading, MA: Addison-Wesley.

Robins, K. (1999). Against virtual community: For a politics of distance. *Journal of the Theoretical Humanities*, *4*, 163–170. doi:10.1080/09697259908572045

Robins, K., & Webster, F. (1999). *Times of technoculture: From the information society to the virtual life*. New York, NY: Routledge.

Scott, C. R., Corman, S. R., & Cheney, G. R. (1998). Development of a structurational model of identification in the organization. *Communication Theory*, *8*(3), 298–336. doi:10.1111/j.1468-2885.1998.tb00223.x

Strauss, A. L. (1987). *Qualitative analysis for social scientists*. Cambridge, UK: Cambridge University Press. doi:10.1017/CBO9780511557842

Thompson, J. B. (1995). *Other floors, other voices: A textography of a small university building*. Mahway, NJ: Lawrence Erlbaum.

Warner, M., & Witzel, M. (2004). *Managing in virtual organizations*. London, UK: Thompson.

Wellin, C., & Fine, G. A. (2001). Ethnography as work: Career socialization, settings and problems. In Atkinson, P., Coffey, A., Delamont, S., Lofland, J., & Lofland, L. (Eds.), *Handbook of Ethnography*. Thousand Oaks, CA: Sage Publishing.

ADDITIONAL READING

Abu-Lughod, L. (1997). The interpretation of culture(s) after television. *Representations (Berkeley, Calif.)*, *59*, 109–130. doi:10.1525/rep.1997.59.1.99p0026o

Allvesson, M., & Deetz, S. (1996). Critical theory and postmodernism: Approaches to organizational studies. In Clegg, S. R., Hardy, C., & Nord, W. R. (Eds.), *Handbook of Organization Studies*. Thousand Oaks, CA: Sage.

Anderson, J. A. (2001). The challenge of writing the interpretive inquiry. In Alexander, A., & Potter, W. J. (Eds.), *How to Publish your Communication Research: An Insider's Guide*. Thousand Oaks, CA: Sage. doi:10.4135/9781412990066.d8

Anderson, J. A., & Meyer, T. P. (1988). *Mediated communication: A social action perspective*. Newbury Park, CA: Sage.

Apgar, M. (1982). Toward and ethnographic language. *American Anthropologist*, *84*, 779–795. doi:10.1525/aa.1982.84.4.02a00030

Atkinson, P. A. (1992). *Understanding ethnographic texts*. Newbury Park, CA: Sage.

Burkhalter, B. (1999). Reading race online: Discovering racial identity in Usenet discussions. In Smith, M. A., & Kollock, P. (Eds.), *Communities in Cyberspace*. London, UK: Routledge.

Button, G. (1993). The curious case of the vanishing technology. In Button, G. (Ed.), *Technology in Working Order: Studies of Work, Interaction and Technology*. London, UK: Routledge.

Correll, S. (1995). The ethnography of an electronic bar: The lesbian café. *Journal of Contemporary Ethnography*, *24*(3), 270–298. doi:10.1177/089124195024003002

Fernback, J. (1997). The individual within the collective: Virtual ideology and the realization of collective principles. In Jones, S. G. (Ed.), *Virtual Culture: Identity and Communication in Cybersociety*. Thousand Oaks, CA: Sage.

Flew, T. (2005). *New media: An introduction*. Melbourne, Australia: Oxford University Press.

Hammersley, M., & Atkinson, P. (1995). *Ethnography: Principles in practice* (2nd ed.). London, UK: Routledge.

Jackson, M. H. (1997). Assessing the structure of communication on the world wide web. *Journal of Computer-Mediated Communication*, *3*(1).

Jones, S. G. (1997). The internet and its social landscape. In Jones, S. G. (Ed.), *Virtual Culture: Identity and Communication in Cybersociety*. Thousand Oaks, CA: Sage.

Kozinets, R. V. (2001). *The field behind the screen: Using the method of netnography to research market-oriented virtual communities*. Retrieved March 3, 2011, from http://www.nyu.edu/classes/bkg/methods/netnography.pdf.

Lindlof, T. R., & Shatzer, M. J. (1998). Media ethnography in virtual space. *Journal of Broadcasting & Electronic Media*, *42*(2), 170–189. doi:10.1080/08838159809364442

Mann, C., & Stewart, F. (2000). *Internet communication and qualitative research: A handbook for researching online*. Thousand Oaks, CA: Sage.

Markham, A. (1998). *Life online: Researching real experience in virtual space*. Walnut Creek, CA: AltaMira.

Miller, D., & Slater, D. (2000). *The internet: An ethnographic approach*. New York, NY: Berg.

Poster, M. (1998). Virtual ethnicity: Tribal identity in an age of global communication. In Jones, S. G. (Ed.), *Cybersociety 2.0: Revisiting Computer-Mediated Communication and Community*. Thousand Oaks, CA: Sage.

Rosen, M. (1999). I get by with a little help with my cyber-friends sharing stories of good and bad times on the web. *Journal of Computer-Mediated Communication, 4*. Retrieved May 9, 2011, from http://jcmc.indiana.edu/vol4/issue4/rosson.html.

Sassen, S. (1999). Digital networks and power. In Featherstone, M., & Lash, S. (Eds.), *Spaces of Culture*. London, UK: Sage.

Schwartz, C. R. (1987). How the refrigerator got its hum. In Bijker, W. E., Hughes, T. P., & Pinch, T. (Eds.), *The Social Construction of Technological Systems*. Cambridge, MA: MIT Press.

Stone, A. R. (1991). Will the real body please stand up? Boundary stories about virtual cultures. In Benedikt, M. (Ed.), *Cyberspace: First Steps*. Cambridge, MA: MIT Press.

Van Maanen, M. (1995). An end to innocence: The ethnography of ethnography. In Van Maanen, J. (Ed.), *Representation in Ethnography*. Thousand Oaks, CA: Sage Publications.

KEY TERMS AND DEFINITIONS

Construct: A symbolic assumption or belief that derives from social interaction. This belief influences how humans categorize people and practices and influences how humans act in relationship with these people in patterned ways.

Distance: The interpretation of the space between people.

Ethnography: A qualitative research method that involves participating and observing a culture in order to understand that culture from the perspective of participants.

Legitimation: The communicative interactions through which a group of people decide what counts as the "right" way and what counts as "wrong" way to do something.

Negotiation: Sometimes overt and sometimes taken-for-granted, negotiation is the ongoing communication practices involved in managing multiple meanings that emerge when a diversity of people need to work together toward some collective goal.

Presence: A state of being sensed and interpreted by others communicatively.

Reflexive: The thoughtful practice of critically thinking about why we act as we do. Having critically assessed why we act as we do, acting with awareness to what assumptions and meanings guide how we interact and how our interactions affect others.

Chapter 14

Mapping a Typology for Identifying the Culturally–Related Challenges of Global Virtual Teams:
A Research Perspective

Norhayati Zakaria
University of Wollongong in Dubai, UAE

Andrea Amelinckx
University of Lethbridge, Canada

David Wilemon
Syracuse University, USA

ABSTRACT

This chapter presents and synthesizes the culturally oriented challenges of managing distributed projects by Global Virtual Teams (GVTs) and examines the distinctive issues intrinsic to GVT work structures from a research perspective. In the first section, the authors define the concept of the global virtual team and explore the differences between global virtual teams and traditional co-located team structures. In the second section, they draw upon the cross-cultural theories (Hall, 1976; Hofstede, 1984) as a framework to explore the unique aspects of managing GVTs and then further develop a cultural typology illustrating the challenges of GVTs. Next, the authors discuss the research approaches to examine the cultural impacts on the success of GVTs, as well as highlight the practical implication in the light of the wide-ranging training programs needed by multinational corporations. In the final section, they assert that in order to be effective, GVTs need to develop new patterns of communication, team structure, knowledge exchange, and project management capabilities, and thus, the authors conclude with the future research directions.

DOI: 10.4018/978-1-4666-0963-1.ch014

INTRODUCTION

In this era of increased globalization and complex work integration, Global Virtual Teams (GVTs) have become widely accepted innovative work structures that transcend boundaries of time and space. Such structure brings together diverse professionals to collaborate through computer-mediated communication technologies. While the usage of the GVTs has risen exponentially over the last decade, its success as an effective organizational tool depends, in part, on *why* it is formed – its mandate and mission and *how* it is formed, managed and integrated into the organization. GVTs individually and as a group, cope with very different challenges than do traditional team structures and their work environments, communication strategies, and collaborative arrangements pose unique opportunities and challenges (Lee-Kelley & Sankey, 2008). As virtual teams engage in their collaborative efforts, they often face challenges arising from team members' divergent cultural differences, mental maps, leadership views, and technologies. To be successful, GVTs need an external environment that is conducive to its existence, namely, adequate organizational, managerial, and technological support. Managers need to understand the cultural and social complexities of such teams and provide the socio-technical infrastructure, intercultural training, and support in order to facilitate team efficacy and success. Concurrently, teams also need a conducive internal environment which promotes trust and intra-team member support while members actively engage in new patterns of communication, collaboration, knowledge, and social exchange and social loafing in a computer-mediated environment (Alnuaim, Robert, & Maruping, 2010; Powell, Piccoli, & Ives, 2004; Jarvenpaa, Shaw, & Staples, 2004; Duarte & Snyder, 2006; Sarker, Sarker, & Jana, 2010).

This chapter presents the challenges of managing distributed projects by GVTs and examines the distinctive issues intrinsic to GVT work structures.

In the first section, we define the concept of the global virtual team; note the growing phenomenon of GVTs and their managerial implications. We also explore the difference between GVTs and traditional co-located team structures. In the second section, we discuss the use of cross-cultural theories as the basis to explore cultural-attuned challenges that inherently faced by GVTs in multinational corporations. Next, we develop a cultural typology to explore the complex management aspects of using GVTs as well as the unique challenges of synchronizing elements such as distance, time, and culture. In the fourth section, the implications of using GVTs for distributed projects are discussed in light of research propositions on how to examine cultural issues related to GVTs and practical implications in respect to the wide-ranging training programs needed for multinational corporations. In the conclusion, we provide a summary and future research directions by addressing the culturally-attuned challenges of managing GVTs. We postulate that in order to be effective, GVTs need to develop new patterns of communication, cohesive team structure, enhanced knowledge exchange, and supportive organizational culture with compatible and supportive leadership. Multinational corporations must understand the cultural and social complexities of such teams and understand the factors that contribute or detract from team efficacy. In addition, they need to provide the socio-technical infrastructure, intercultural training, and support needed to facilitate team success.

Defining Global Virtual Teams and Collocated Teams

We define a global team as a distinct entity that is organizationally dispersed and whose members come from different geographical locations, do not necessarily have a common cultural or linguistic background, and collaborate using asynchronous and synchronous ICT technologies. When considering GVTs, one must recognize that such teams differ in many aspects from traditional teams but fundamentally diverge on two distinct dimensions - the sophistication of their communication tools and the time spent working apart (Griffith & Neale, 2001; Powell, et al., 2004). The purest global virtual team is the one that collaborates while team members are situated in different locales, totally working apart, and depending entirely on computer-mediated communication tools. We will specifically address the challenges of collaborating with team members who are strangers to one another. In short, team members are basically 'strangers' when people work in a pure virtual environment—i.e. members may have never met with one another face-to-face at any point of time, be it prior, during or after the project is completed. This type of virtual collaboration results in heightened challenges for organizations to manage and such teams also differ on managerial requirements and strategies from the onset and throughout the team's life cycle (Maznevski & Chudoba, 2000; Furst, Reeves, Rosen, & Blackburn, 2004; Montoya, Massey, & Lockwood, 2011).

Historically, collocated teams are defined as team members that work side by side in the same project area or work space (Crow, 1996), for instance in the same building, department, organization, or geographic location. Members contribute different levels of knowledge and expertise that is shared in order to develop a product or service (Crow, 1996; Maznevski & Chudoba, 2000). Collocation can also occur in the virtual sense when members are geographically distributed yet connected to each other through the use of computer-mediated communication tools (Mark, Grudin, & Poltrock, 1999) as emphasized by us with the concept of GVTs.

Differences between Global Virtual Teams and Collocated Teams

In order to begin to appreciate how GVTs function, it is necessary to understand that such teams

fundamentally differ from traditional teams in how they work together (Becker-Beck, Wintermantel, & Borg, 2005; Hoegl, Ernst, & Proserpio, 2007). Creating and sustaining effective intra-team work relations over time is often difficult even when team members are in the same locale, for GVTs, due to their geographic dispersal and communication medium, it proves even more challenging to maintain momentum and motivation. Differences between the two types of teams are noted in Table 1. Dealing with conflicts between team members that are virtually collocated requires specific cultural communication competencies to overcome a variety of problems. Not only does distance matter as well as time differences in this new working structure, but additionally cultural differences further intensify the problems of working apart or virtually collocated and are key problems faced by GVTs.

As noted above, global virtual team members face very different challenges than do their counterparts in traditional teams; they are more likely to experience difficulty in developing swift trust, relationship and team conflicts, communication breakdown, and etc. (Bjørn & Ngwenyama, 2009; Wakefield, Leidner, & Garrison, 2008; Kankanhalli, Tan, & Kwok Kee, 2007). In this case, team members need to embrace the concept of shared minds (Bjørn & Ngwenyama, 2009; Schrage, 2000) and build the 'team-learning' climate (Chih-Jou & Shiu-Wan, 2010) by creating common ground among members in order to effectively manage globally distributed collaboration. Not only does distance matter, time also matter in this new working structure, but additionally cultural differences further intensify the problems of working apart or virtually collocated. Barriers of developing trust due to geographical distance and time dimension are also one of the key problems faced by GVTs (Dubé & Robey, 2009; Robert, Dennis, & Hung, 2009).

In summary, global teams and global virtual teams can be differentiated based on the medium of communication and collaboration that they used.

Table 1. Differences between global virtual teams vs. collocated teams (adopted from Lipnack & Stamps, 1997)

Category	Global Virtual Teams	Collocated Teams
1. Definition	A distinct entity, whose members come from different geographical locations, may not have a common background, are organizationally dispersed, collaborate using asynchronous and synchronous technologies, and often are on assemble on an ad-hoc basis.	Team members that work side by side in the same project area or work space for instance in the physical sense such as same building, departments, or geographic location.
2. Characteristics	Depend largely on computer-mediated communication technologies, e.g. email, videoconferencing, instant messaging, and etc.	Less dependent on computer-mediated communication technologies
	Composition of members are based on different cultural backgrounds—heterogeneous group members	Composition of members is based either on different or similar cultural backgrounds—usually comprise of homogeneous group members as well as heterogeneous members
	Members are geographically disperse or distributed	Members are located in the same geographic area
	Work within different time-dimensions	Work within same or different time dimensions
3. Challenges	Managing incompatibility between technology fit vs. cultural fit	False consensus among team members
	Maintaining the momentum of working together apart	Unresolved overt conflict and underground conflict
	Managing differences stages of group learning	Closure avoidance among team members
	Marketing team's products to key stakeholders	Uneven participation
	Maintaining senior management support and interest	Lack of accountability, and forgetting the customer
		Providing effective training to members

In particular the primary difference lies in factors such as geographically dispersed and time zone differences that separate the team members due to the use of ICT. The same criteria can be applied in understanding the concepts of collocated and non-collocated teams (refer to Table 1).

CROSS-CULTURAL THEORETICAL FRAMEWORK

In this section, we will provide an overview of the key cross-cultural theories to provide a basic understanding of culturally-attuned challenges for GVTs. These cross-cultural theories are well recognized in the field of intercultural communication and cross-cultural management. In the late 1970s, an anthropologist Edward T. Hall (1976) examined factors that influence intercultural understanding which either facilitate or inhibit effective communication between individuals from different cultural backgrounds. His initial

approach in cross-cultural study was based on a qualitative method where he conducted numerous participant observations. As a result, he introduced a key cultural dimension called "context." Context explains the way people evaluate and interpret the meaning of information that they receive. Hall and Hall (1990) stipulates that context comprises a system of meaning for information exchanges between group of people or within a group of people. It provides a framework that enables people to comprehend communication forms ranging from purely non-verbal such as hand gestures, body language, facial expressions, and tone of voice to purely verbal aspects such as written text or spoken words. In his work, he presents context as a continuous variable that reflects how much reliance a culture places on non-verbal cues in order to communicate: the heavier the reliance, the higher the culture's context. Additionally, it is important to note that Hall also argues that although people may use both high context and low context communication, only one style is predominant at any given moment (Gudykunst, Ting-Toomey, & Nishida, 1996). Hall also suggests when a society ascribes to high context culture, they will put less emphasis on the content. Instead, they will sensitize their communication behaviours to '*what is not spoken or written*,' in which non-verbal cues are taken seriously. On the other hand, the low context society often prefer to put their reliance on communicative behaviours which are content-based—i.e. high bearing on '*what is said and/or endorsed on paper.*' In essence, high context can also be recognized as 'content independent,' while low context is known as 'context independent' (Zakaria & Cogburn, 2010). Examples of countries that fall under high context are such as China, Japan, Thailand, India, etc. while countries that fall under low context are UK, Canada, US, etc.

As the need for cross-cultural understanding arise, in the early of 1980s, Geert Hofstede (1984) pioneered cross-cultural workplace research by studying the attitudes of employees from fifty countries and three regions. His scholarly work is the most widely cited and replicated model in cross-cultural management literature for examining cultural differences across nations. He offers a multidimensional cultural model through quantitative measurements, and proposes that national culture and values affect the work environment and its management on five dimensions: (1) power distance, (2) individualism-collectivism, (3) uncertainty avoidance, (4) masculinity-femininity, and (5) Confucian dynamism. Based on data collected from 116,000 IBM employees from over 50 countries, he found that there were significant cultural and management differences between nations. Using statistical techniques such as factor analysis, his research distilled the major differences into five main dimensions in which a country can be ranked along a continuum; similar to Hall's 'context' dimension which is from low to high. Hofstede described the dimensions as:

- **Power Distance:** the degree of inequality which the population of a country considers as normal.
- **Uncertainty Avoidance:** the degree to which people in a country prefer structured over unstructured situations.
- **Individualism vs. collectivism:** the degree to which people in a country prefer to act as individuals rather than as members of groups.
- **Masculinity/Femininity:** the degree to which values like assertiveness, performance, success and competition, which in nearly all societies are associated with the role of men, prevail over values like the quality of life, maintaining warm personal relationships, service, care for the weak and solidarity, which in nearly all societies are more associated with the role of women.
- **Time Orientation** is a dimension in which nations can be considered as being either short-term or long-term in orientation.

The concepts of high context and low context complements other cross-cultural dimensions such as individualism versus collectivism (Hofstede, 1980), associative versus abstractive (Glenn, 1981), and specific versus diffuse (Trompenaars & Hampden-Turner, 2000). Out of the five dimensions introduced by Hofstede, the individualism and collectivism constructs are the most similar to the high context and low context constructs (Gudykunst, Ting-Toomey, & Chua, 1988, Korac-Kakabadse, et al., 2001). Hofstede's empirical findings suggested that low context people are predominantly individualist while high context people are predominantly collectivist. This was further supported in a study conducted by Levine (1985) on the use of direct versus indirect and certainty versus ambiguity categories in communication. According to Korac-Kakabadse et al. (2001), Levine's study suggested that directness and certainty characterizes the individualist culture and hence correspondingly describes the low context communication style. On the other hand, indirectness and ambiguity characterizes the collectivist culture, which in turn relates to the high context communication style (Kapoor, Hughes, Baldwin, & Blue, 2003).

DEVELOPING A CULTURAL TYPOLOGY FOR GLOBAL VIRTUAL TEAMS

Based on the underlying cross-cultural theoretical lens (Hall, 1976, 1990; Hofstede, 1984), we develop a cultural typology which underlines the management practices of the GVTs–building trust (in-group and out-group), power orientation, (maintain senior management support, principle of control), source of cohesion (teamwork momentum), and leadership and management styles. Both national and organizational cultures have strong effects on GVT formation, interaction, and achievement. One must recognize the complexity, range, and distinctiveness of each culture and consider their impact, which may act as a stimulus or constraint. One must also consider how divergent individual team members are from each other when considering the extent of challenges such teams may face. In essence, the following are the key challenges that need to be addressed since it is difficult for team members to be effective and efficient given two key factors—diverse cultural backgrounds and geographical distance. The challenges described below are arguments made in light of crucial factors such as (1) no past collaboration, (2) short-term projects, and (3) cultural distance is large (e.g. USA vs. Japan, compared to Malaysia vs. Indonesia). For GVTs, many of the distributed project management challenges emerge from four issues such as (1) managing trust based on different stages of team learning, (2) managing team stress and conflict, (3) managing the role of leadership to maintain team momentum, and (4) developing a conducive

organizational culture that maintains senior management support and interest. Under this section, we will present four different challenges that are potentially encountered by managers at multinational corporations when managing GVTs. These challenges will be presented based on a cultural typology that are useful to be discussed based on four different aspects—trust, stress and conflicts, leadership, and organizational culture.

It is useful to note that in the *formation stage* of any teamwork structure, many factors influence the performance of team members. For example, when a team first forms, members will undergo a learning process regarding team dynamics, role assignments, shared expertise and contribution expectations, and project management. However, over time, cultural differences may become secondary while task orientation becomes more important. Other than that, cultural values also shape important management tasks such as decision making, negotiating, organizing, planning, and coordinating.

Factors that can exacerbate the challenges that GVTs face include, (1) no past collaboration experience, (2) limited group allegiance due to the transitory nature of the group, and (3) if societal cultural distance between group members is great. According to Lojeski and Reily (2008) cultural distance is defined as "...the function of differences in values and communication styles that are rooted in culture (demographics or organizational)" (p. 665).

Based on Hall (1976) and Hofstede (1984) cultural dimensions, we present the cultural typology which highlights the key challenges that need to be addressed (see Table 2). The following four aspects of management practices are--trust, team cohesion, leadership, and organizational culture.

Managing Team Trust: In-Group vs. Out-Group

For GVTs, effective knowledge sharing and group learning requires more than computer technol-

Table 2. A cultural typology for managing global virtual teams (adopted from Hall, 1976; Hofstede, 1984; Trompenaars, 1997)

Cultural Typology (Hofstede, 1984; and Hall, 1976, 1990)	
Team & Trust	**Team & Cohesiveness**
Challenges: *Establishing trust and building rapport*	Challenges: *Managing Conflict and Stress*
1. Who can team members trust? –in-group vs. out-group	1. What facilitates team cohesion?
2. What is the condition for team members to aquire a trusting environment?	2. How do team members achieve cohesiveness based on distance and cultural diversity?
3. How quick can trust to be developed among team members?	3. Why is cohesiveness and cooperation important?
Team & Leadership	**Team & Organizational Culture**
Challenges: *Team momentum and high collegiality*	Challenges: *Creating a supportive organizational culture*
1. Who is in charge of directing team goals? –Assigned or volunteer leader?	1. What is the organizational culture for GVTs?
2. How do you motivate and influence the team members?	2. What kind of support is needed from top management?
3. What sustains the motivation among team members for collegiality?	3. How does organizational culture shape the knowledge sharing among teams?

ogy; it is predicated on the ability to create and sustain a team-learning climate within a virtual work structure and requires both the motivation to connect and share within the team and the cross-cultural competencies to succeed. In order for such a climate to occur, as well as to be sustained, members must be able to trust each other and be confident that they can rely on one another, particularly when it comes to project coordination and task completion. Team learning cannot occur without intra-team trust and is predicated on effective communication from the onset.

Team learning acknowledges the importance of knowledge retention, group dynamics, and the interplay of intra-team knowledge transfer. Team learning is prefaced on the assumption that transmitting experiences and/or data—the process of communication—occurs. Unfortunately, an unimpeded communication process in the global virtual team context cannot be assumed as the process of sharing experience rests on the team's

ability to effectively communicate despite differences in culture, language, and technology.

During the team formation period, members begin to understand cultural difference and start to develop trusting intra-team relationships based on collaboratively negotiated communication protocols. This is of particular importance as research has shown that cultural differences in particular, can affect communication and team relations (Lee-Kelly & Sankey, 2008; Strikova & Rayna, 2008). The establishment of trust-based intra-team relations can foster dialogue, debate, knowledge sharing and group-mediated solutions. As Holton (2001) notes, "The challenge to team building in a virtual environment is that of creating avenues and opportunities for team members to have the level and depth of dialogue necessary to create a shared future" (p. 2).

Moreover, initial relationship building between members faces more challenges, as does the establishment of intra-team trust. Jarvenpaa, Knoll, and Leidner (1998) posit that virtual teams have no time to gradually develop trust and therefore require a high degree of "swift trust" to be demonstrated by enthusiastic and proactive team member behaviour. It should be noted that Jarvenpaa (later questioned the role of trust in global virtual team relations noting that trust may have an initial direct positive effect on the perception of team cohesion but may later act as a moderator and indirectly impact team dynamics depending on the situation (Jarvenpaa, Shaw, & Staples, 2004).

Team members evolve and mature over time. As they continue to work with each other, they learn to know each other, then relationships are developed, and eventually trust emerges. However, in certain cultures such as those that are described as "high context" (Hall, 1976), people need additional time to develop trust because they need to build comfortable working relationships. Unfortunately in the global virtual setting, sometimes, the project needs to be completed in a short time, thus trust needs to be accomplished quickly. Conversely, for low context cultures, they are more concerned with task orientation, that developing relationship becomes secondary. In such case, swift trust may be possible because productivity and performance is the essence of the relationship among team members. In essence, trust plays out differently for high vs. low context cultures (Hall, 1976). It all depends on the role, function, meaning, and purpose.

Thus, to reiterate, the challenge faced by GVTs is on trust formation with several key questions such as what are the possibilities of developing swift trust given the non-collocated challenges, and how does the in group vs. out-group concept challenge the ability for team members to quickly trust others when working in projects?

Managing Team Cohesion: Conflicts and Stress

If working within a single culture can be stressful at times, working with others different from ourselves also can increase the anxiety, stress, and conflicts experienced. Managing team stress and conflict is never easy; for a cross-cultural team, it can be far more difficult than with a culturally homogeneous team since the manifestations of tension and discord vary. In part, conflict is determined and defined by culture-specific norms. Similarly, how conflict is addressed –either by avoidance, direct or indirect means, is also culturally defined.

All cultures develop strategies to prevent or minimize types of behaviour that are seen likely to provoke conflicts. In different cultures, disputes are communicated differently, can have diverse meaning, and can be initiated for various reasons. For example, collectivistic cultures normally prefer to deal with conflicts in a harmonious approach—using non-confrontational, accommodating, and risk-averse methods (Ketrow, 1999; Hodgets & Luthan, 2003), while individualistic societies often prefer to state their views, opinions, and feelings openly and are more likely to use competitive and confrontational approaches (Hofstede, 1980). Teams need to have the ability to perceive and address a dispute whenever possible before it becomes a full-blown conflict. When disputes are not resolved or cannot be resolved they often deteriorate into conflicts which have a negative and damaging effect on both the team as well as the overall organization.

Diversity can cause communication problems (Steinfield, et al., 2001). Thus, it should not be surprising that miscommunication and misinterpretations between team members are a prevalent source of conflict for GVTs. "Low social presence generally is unsatisfying and leaves people in some situations, such as those involving conflict, unable to resolve differences effectively or meet their goals" (Triandis, 1995, p. 272). Another source of conflict is a clash between team members culturally-defined work values. Conflicts may arise from contradicting work preferences—whether that be how social loafing is defined or a preference of individual work or more collectivistic collaboration.

Distributed work design can also provide challenges when dealing with different cultural backgrounds of the team members. For example, for collectivistic /high context cultures, people prefer to build relationship first before they can undertake tasks. In contrast, for individualistic / low context/ culture, task orientation takes precedence over relationship building. Thus, managers need to utilize technology that enables those members from collectivistic cultures to develop trust and thus engage in relationship building before they can work at a distance. Email may not be the best solution as it does not provide many non-verbal (contextual) cues that are needed for relationship building by collectivistic culture (Fujimoto, Bahfen, Fermelis, & Hartel, 2007). For those members from individualistic cultures, on the other hand, using email seems appropriate because it can be used to carry out tasks effectively at a distance as it is based primarily on texts and words (Bovée, Thill, & Schatzman, 2003). In a nutshell, some inherent challenges faced by GVTs are employing appropriate and effective conflict management to ensure source of cohesion can be clearly identified and cohesiveness among team members are achieved.

Managing Team and Leadership: Teamwork and Momentum

Creating and sustaining effective intra-team work relations over time is often difficult even when team members are in the same locale. It proves even more challenging to maintain momentum and motivation when team members are separated by distance and culture and to some extent, language. Research on both virtual teams and global teams indicates that team members face very different challenges than do their counterparts in traditional teams. They are more likely to experience information overload, social isolation and uneven power distributions - domination of certain group members over others - within the team (Lipnack & Stamps, 1997). Conversely, Baan and Maznevski (2008) note that the restrictions that computer-mediated communication technology imposes on the users may actually filter out the noise and distractions of social activity and result in more meaningful communication.

Successful virtual team management is heavily reliant on effective leadership and organizational support (Berry, 2011). Not only that the type of leadership styles need to be aligned with the teams, more importantly is the level of trust that needs to be developed between leaders and subordinates in ensuring the projects move towards the agreed direction (Thomas & Bostrom, 2010). Preventing inertia and team apathy from setting in is one of the major tasks that a team leader faces. Leaders have multiple functions in the virtual team environment and will invariably act as coach, facilitator, task manager, and intermediary when conflicts arise. Since ICTs (define) eliminate the verbal and social cues that are prerequisite to certain cultures, leaders must help team members build and maintain trust, ease the transition process, select and use appropriate electronic media and collaboration technologies, and manage performance without the traditional forms of feedback.

Certain researchers maintain that face-to-face meetings should still be used periodically for GVTs (Robbins, 2001). Despite the convenient use of information communication technologies, studies have shown that teams that wholly rely on online communication using email, video conferencing, instant messaging communicate, etc., replacing all face to face communication, report less satisfaction with group interaction. Maznevski and Chudoba (2000) note that face-to-face team meetings continue to play in important role for virtual teams throughout their existence and can re-invigorate team energy and mark transition points.

Organizational support is equally significant for maintaining the momentum since team members are also organizational members and require institutional legitimacy. Apart from national culture, organizational culture has a strong effect on management systems. Organizational culture may act as a barrier or restraint to information communication technology usage or provide the necessary support in regards to technology, time, and infrastructure to actively foster it. To sum up, the challenge in managing GVTs lies on building and capitalizing on the roles of leadership so that momentum and spirit and collegiality among members are maintained. Difficulty faced by leaders to understand which leadership style can be used to manage teams who come from diverse cultural backgrounds. 'One size fits all' may not be applicable.

Managing Organizational Culture: Senior Management Support

The organizational culture of multinational corporations can play a large role in the success or failure of its GVTs. A key challenge for senior management as leaders is to recognize the role that the larger organization plays in building a more conducive work environment. Most GVTs projects are initiated by members of senior management. If a project is not singly initiated by the managers, then it needs to have the support of senior management. Hence, organizational culture is crucial in inculcating a conducive team environment that expands into virtual work structure. The new organizational culture needs to take into account the element of vast geographical distance, distinctive cultural values, and different time management capabilities (Shachaf, 2008).

Hence, creating and then maintaining project visibility is important in that management has many responsibilities and interests that can change rapidly. Therefore, it is important to keep the project on management's "radar screen." The GVT leader and even team members can help maintain visibility by supplying periodic reports; by demonstrating the project to management and by regularly communicating performance accomplishments. Accessibility of a global virtual team

implies having the ability to discuss project issues with senior management and sponsors.

When there is a lack of accessibility, the project may suffer from a lack of visibility and also communication may get distorted if there are multiple layers of management which 'filter' the GVTs' communication and information sharing. Thus, when an important issue develops the team and especially the leader needs to be able to have access to key decision-makers. When a GVTs' project is being planned it can be important to predetermine the communication links between the GVTs and management. This is an issue that is far better accomplished at the front-end of a project.

The final area we consider especially important in developing and maintaining effective relationships with senior management is the GVTs' credibility. In other words, are the project leader, the team, and the project credible with the GVTs' sponsors? In one situation we are aware of a global virtual team leader was selected due to her track record and accomplishments. In summary, all of the four abovementioned areas are at play in dealing with globally distributed team management. The astute GVT learns that all four factors are important to create and maintain unity, consistency, and cohesion. Also, effective teams understand that these four variables are correlated. The loss of visibility or credibility, for example, can clearly affect priority, while the loss of accessibility can diminish the GVTs' priority.

RESEARCH PERSPECTIVES ON EXPLORING CULTURAL CHALLENGES OF GLOBAL VIRTUAL TEAMS

The following section briefly discusses the research perspectives when exploring and understanding the culturally-attuned challenges of GVTs (refer to Table 2). With the growth of globalization and the increasing demand for the GVT work structure, a greater understanding is needed in order to effectively manage globally distributed collaboration of teams. This conceptual paper aims at addressing the following gaps, as evident in the literature, which demand further empirical exploration, such as:

- The few empirical studies that exist have not provided consistent findings or offered definite answers regarding cultural impacts GVTs;
- The effects of different behavioural patterns arising from the presence of diverse cultural values have been insufficiently explored and the application of cross-cultural theories to explain the cultural effects on globally distributed collaboration is fairly limited (Mohd Yusof & Zakaria, 2012; David, Chand, Newell, & Resende-Santos, 2008; Shachaf, 2008; Riemer, 2008; Hanisch & Corbitt, 2007; Cousins, Robey, & Zigurs, 2007).

It is clearly noted in the field of cross-cultural management, culture is an intricate and complex concept. Decades ago, two renowned scholars—Kroeber and Kluckhorn (1952)—critically reviewed the concept of culture and they have identified over 164 varied definitions; thus making it tremendously difficult to measure such concept objectively. This has also led other more recent researchers to use multi-dimensional and multi-level approaches to conduct cross-cultural research such as Fischer (2009) and Fontaine (2008). On the other hand, it is equally difficult to measure culture subjectively when it is embedded in human behaviours, either observable (overt) or hidden (tacit). Schneider and Barsoux (1998) provide a framework for understanding the multiple layers of culture and its methods of discovery. The different layers include artifacts and behaviours, beliefs and values, and basic assumptions. The layers move from the most easily and readily observed to the most challenging to access and understand. Each layer requires different methods of exploration. (Refer to Figure 1).

Figure 1. A research framework for exploring cultural influence on GVTs (adapted from Zakaria, 2006; Schneider & Barsoux, 1998)

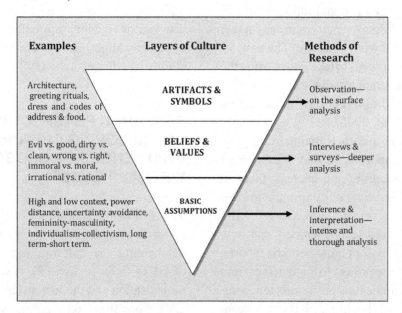

The first layer, artifacts and behaviours, can be directly observed and may be the easiest form of analysis. Although some behaviours are clearly visible making observation an appropriate method of discovery, the roots of many behaviours are unobservable or hidden, which makes them harder to discover. Thus, at times observations can be confusing, misleading, and conflicting, resulting in more misinterpretations or problems rather than understanding. The second layer, beliefs and values, probes deeper by asking individuals to explain the meaning of their behaviours; common investigative methods are interviews and surveys. Again, this poses some problems if certain observed behaviours are not consciously explicable by the respondents. A person can only tell the researcher what he or she knows, or will only tell what he or she wants to tell. For example, surveys can only investigate concepts and explanations that the respondents are already aware of and understand; a survey cannot go deeper than the respondent's own conscious knowledge. In a similar vein, using the interview method, a researcher can only learn about a behaviour that is culturally rooted if the informant wants (or is able) to describe the experience to the researcher. The third layer, basic assumptions, focuses on understanding the hidden cultural assumptions that emerge from the observed artefacts and behaviours. In analysing answers and explanations, patterns emerge from which a researcher derives inferences, interpretations, and ultimately a coherent theory.

In this chapter, we are proposing to explore the culturally-attuned challenges of GVTs based on the qualitative research method by means of in-depth and semi-structured interviews with GVTs. According to Osland and Bird (2003), the appreciation and understanding of a culture needs to be bounded in a context to uncover the paradoxes of behaviours, instead of a sophisticated stereotyping. They suggested a model called '*cultural sense-making*' which is comprised of sequential events such as indexing context (identifying and notic-

ing cues about a situation encountered), making attributes (drawing inferences based on identity and experiences), and selecting scheme (enacting appropriate behavioural scripts by reflecting one's cultural values and cultural history. Hence, by allowing the respondents (GVTs) to make sense of their own cultural experiences, they would be able to articulate such varied cultural paradoxes in an elaborated manner.

Based on such data, we will then conduct the analysis based on deductive approach by using the two abovementioned cultural theoretical frameworks to understand the challenges stemming from the teams' behaviours. As such, the assumptions are more attuned to the cultural sense making, thus establishing a relationship between the expected behaviours and the observed behaviours. Although the behaviours being observed and the values being explained may be consistent, the underlying assumptions may be counterintuitive and complex. Hence, interpreting and making inferences can be challenging without an understanding of the underpinning theories. However, we are also interested in observing patterns of behaviours that are unique which are rooted not only from the national culture of team members, but also from the organizational culture developed by the different multinational organizations across the world. In essence, the aim of the proposed research topic is to obtain illuminating and rich descriptions based on the multi-layers dimensions where culture can be observed in respect to the GVTs' thinking, feeling, and actions.

PRACTICAL IMPLICATIONS OF GLOBAL VIRTUAL TEAMS

In order to be successful, GVTs need to consider three inter-related issues—how to manage themselves, their environment, and their relationship to the organization. Having positive visibility within the organization cannot be sustained if internal team issues exist and are not addressed.

GVTs must have appropriate membership that is willing and able to work in a virtual workplace and have appropriate technology to function. For example, we suggest that in the selection of team members, organizations need to take into account temperament, culture and personality along with technical expertise. Although the choice and variety of information communication technology media plays a role in virtual teamwork, intra-team relations tends to be a greater factor in team coherence, performance, and work output. While team efficacy does not routinely follow when positive team relations exist, it remains a necessary precursor.

There are many ways that project managers of multinational corporations can manage their GVTs. One of the most important activities is to provide clear, compelling goals for the entire organization besides providing key resources such as financial funding, knowledge and expertise, and training. These goals become the context for GVTs. Unless clear goals are present, others are likely to 'second guess' the work of a GVT. Senior management need to develop a culture which supports global virtual teamwork. This can be particularly rewarding for global virtual team members in far-flung operations who may feel neglected and isolated. Closely related is the importance of empowering teams and giving them sufficient autonomy.

Development teams also need a clear charter and the empowerment and responsibility to accomplish their assigned tasks. A minimum of meddling and "micro-managing" by senior management also is helpful in supporting a GVT. Finally, it is important for senior managers to model effective teamwork. If people see effective teamwork demonstrated at the top of their own organizations, they are more likely to value and engage in teamwork at the level of GVTs. Finally, we suggest that senior management as leaders can provide a number of training and/or educational programs for GVTs. These training suggestions are in addition to the needed information technology skills, which are necessary for a GVT to function effectively and better manage project of GVTs.

FUTURE RESEARCH DIRECTIONS

As previously noted, both national and organizational cultures have strong effects on GVT formation, interaction and achievement. One must recognize the complexity, range, and distinctiveness of each culture and consider their impact which may act as a stimulus or constraint. The responsibilities faced by these types of teams are often too important not to have sufficient organizational planning and consideration prior to team development and must include sufficient organizational support. GVTs are used by many organizations and this trend will continue to grow and expand—necessitating thoughtful deliberation regarding team development, structure, team member's roles and the team's significance to the organization.

Based on our work on the cultural and managerial challenges associated with GVTs, we suggest that there are several opportunities for future research, which can add to our growing body of knowledge in this area. These future research areas focus primarily on GVT team leaders and their relationship with senior management. Some of the ideas we suggest have been addressed but too often, they are based on anecdotal evidence or single studies. The research areas we advance can be performed either by qualitative or quantitative studies. In many cases, we recommend fieldwork, interviews, and case studies as a first step followed by rigorous quantitative work. Both research approaches have their obvious strengths and limits. We suggest these research topics:

1. What qualities do high-performing global virtual team leaders possess? How do they compare to leaders who are less effective conducting similar work?

2. Does stress from global teamwork affect team members differently based on their cultural background? Does such stress manifest itself differently and, if so, what impact does it have on the team?

3. Do assignments on GVTs impact future managerial opportunities? If so, how?

4. How does mentoring and coaching occur in GVTs? Is informal or spontaneous mentoring more effective than formal or assigned roles?

5. How do age, gender, and/or other aspects of status or difference influence intra-team relations and team relations?

6. What is the impact of unsuccessful or ineffective GVTs on team members' assignments to future virtual teams? How is blame assigned when challenges arise and how does perceived culpability affect team members?

7. Do senior managers with no previous experience with GVTs manage such teams differently and with different expectations than to managers with personal experience in or with such teams? If so, how do the differences affect team morale, team relations, and output?

8. What deficiencies, if any, do GVTs not in achieving higher performance levels? What might be the implications for designing global virtual team training/educational programs?

REFERENCES

Alnuaim, O. A., Robert, L. P. Jr, & Maruping, L. M. (2010). Team size, dispersion, and social loafing in technology-supported teams: A perspective on the theory of moral disengagement. *Journal of Management Information Systems*, *27*(1), 203–230. doi:10.2753/MIS0742-1222270109

Amant, K. S. (2002). When cultures and computer collide: Rethinking computer-mediated communication according to international and intercultural communication expectations. *Journal of Business and Technical Communication*, *16*(2), 196–214. doi:10.1177/1050651902016002003

Baan, A., & Maznevski, M. (2008). Training for virtual collaboration: Beyond technical competencies. In Nemiro, J., Beyerlein, M., Bradley, L., & Beyerlein, S. (Eds.), *The Handbook of High Performance Virtual Teams: A Toolkit for Collaborating across Boundaries* (pp. 345–365). San Francisco, CA: Jossey-Bass.

Becker-Beck, U., Wintermantel, M., & Borg, A. (2005). Principles of regulating interaction in teams practicing face-to-face communication versus teams practicing computer-mediated communication. *Small Group Research*, *36*(4), 499–536. doi:10.1177/1046496405277182

Berry, G. R. (2011). A cross-disciplinary literature review: Examining trust on virtual teams. *Performance Improvement Quarterly*, *24*(3), 9–28. doi:10.1002/piq.20116

Bjørn, P., & Ngwenyama, O. (2009). Virtual team collaboration: Building shared meaning, resolving breakdowns and creating translucence. *Information Systems Journal*, *19*(3), 227–253. doi:10.1111/j.1365-2575.2007.00281.x

Bovée, C. L., Thill, J. V., & Schatzman, B. E. (2003). *Business communication today* (7th ed.). Upper Saddle River, NJ: Prentice Hall.

Chen, C.-J., & Hung, S.-H. (2010). To give or to receive? Factors influencing members' knowledge sharing and community promotion in professional virtual communities. *Information & Management*, *47*(4), 226–236. doi:10.1016/j.im.2010.03.001

Cousins, K. C., Robey, D., & Zigurs, I. (2007). Managing strategic contradictions in hybrid teams. *European Journal of Information Systems*, *16*(4), 460–478. doi:10.1057/palgrave.ejis.3000692

Crow, K. (2006). *Enabling product development teams with collocation*. Retrieved on 10/27/2011 from http://www.npd-solutions.com/collocation.html.

Dabbish, L., & Kraut, R. (2008). Awareness displays and social motivation for coordinating communication. *Information Systems Research, 19*(2), 221–238. doi:10.1287/isre.1080.0175

Daft, R. L., & Lengel, R. H. (1986). Organizational information requirements, media richness and structural design. *Management Science, 32*(5), 554–571. doi:10.1287/mnsc.32.5.554

Duarte, D., & Snyder, N. (1999). *Mastering virtual teams: Strategies, tools, and techniques that succeed*. San Francisco, CA: Jossey-Base Publisher.

Duarte, D. L., & Snyder, N. T. (2006). *Mastering virtual teams: Strategies, tools, and techniques that succeed* (3rd ed.). San Francisco, CA: Jossey-Bass.

Dubé, L., & Robey, D. (2009). Surviving the paradoxes of virtual team work. *Information Systems Journal, 19*(1), 3–30. doi:10.1111/j.1365-2575.2008.00313.x

Fischer, R. (2009). Where is culture in cross-cultural research? An outline of a multilevel research process for measuring culture as a shared meaning system. *International Journal of Cross Cultural Management, 9*(1), 25–49. doi:10.1177/1470595808101154

Fontaine, J. R. (2008). Traditional and multilevel approaches in cross-cultural research: An integration of methodological frameworks. In van de Vijver, F. J. R., van Hermert, D. A., & Poortinga, Y. (Eds.), *Individuals and Cultures in Multilevel Analysis*. Mahwah, NJ: Lawrence Erlbaum Associates.

Fujimoto, Y., Bahfen, N., Fermelis, J., & Hartel, C. E. J. (2007). The global village: Online cross-cultural communication and HRM. *Cross Cultural Management, 14*, 7–22. doi:10.1108/13527600710718804

Furst, S. A., Reeves, M., Rosen, B., & Blackburn, R. S. (2004). Managing the life cycle of virtual teams. *The Academy of Management Executive, 18*(4), 6–20. doi:10.5465/AME.2004.13837468

George, A. M. (2003). Teaching culture: The challenges and opportunities of international public relations. *Business Communication Quarterly, 66*(2), 97–113. doi:10.1177/108056990306600212

Glenn, E. S. (1981). *Man and mankind*. Ablex, NJ: Norwood.

Griffith, T. L., & Neale, M. A. (2001). Informational processing in traditional, hybrid, and virtual teams: From nascent knowledge to transactive memory. *Research in Organizational Behavior: An Annual Series of Analytical Essays and Critical Reviews, 23*, 379–421. doi:10.1016/S0191-3085(01)23009-3

Gudykunst, W. B., Ting-Toomey, S., & Chua, E. G. (Eds.). (1988). *Intercultural communication theory: Interpersonal communication*. Beverly Hills, CA: Sage.

Gudykunst, W. B., Ting-Toomey, S., & Nishida, T. (Eds.). (1996). *Communication in personal relationships across cultures*. Thousand Oaks, CA: Sage.

Guffey, M. E. (2003). *Business communication: Process and product* (4th ed.). Mason, OH: South-Western/Thomson Learning.

Hall, E. (1976). *Beyond culture*. Garden City, NY: Anchor Press.

Hall, E., & Hall, M. (1990). *Understanding cultural differences: Germans, French, and Americans*. Boston, MA: Intercultural Press.

Hammer, M. (2004). The intercultural conflict style inventory: A conceptual framework and measure of intercultural conflict approaches. In *Proceedings of IACM, 17th Annual Conference.* Retrieved from http://ssrn.com/abstract=601981.

Hanisch, J., & Corbitt, B. (2007). Impediments to requirements engineering during global software development. *European Journal of Information Systems, 16*(6), 793–805. doi:10.1057/palgrave. ejis.3000723

Hellriegel, D., Slocum, J., & Woodman, R. (2001). *Organizational behavior* (9th ed.). Mason, OH: South Western College Publishing.

Hodgets, R., & Luthan, F. (2003). *International management* (5th ed.). New York, NY: McGraw Hill.

Hoegl, M., Ernst, H., & Proserpio, L. (2007). How teamwork matters more as team member dispersion increases. *Journal of Product Innovation Management, 24*(1), 156–165. doi:10.1111/j.1540-5885.2007.00240.x

Hofstede, G. (1984). *Culture's consequences.* Beverly Hills, CA: Sage.

Holton, J. A. (2001). Building trust and collaboration in virtual teams. *Team Performance Management, 7*(3-4), 36–47. doi:10.1108/13527590110395621

Jarvenpaa, S., Knoll, K., & Leidner, D. (1998). Is anybody out there? Antecedents of trust in global virtual teams. *Journal of Management Information Systems, 14*(4), 29–64.

Jarvenpaa, S., Shaw, T., & Staples, D. (2004). Toward contextualized theories of trust: The role of trust in global virtual teams. *Information Systems Research, 15*(3), 250–268. doi:10.1287/isre.1040.0028

Kankanhalli, A., Tan, C. Y., & Kwok-Kee, W. (2007). Conflict and performance in global virtual teams. *Journal of Management Information Systems, 23*(3), 237–274. doi:10.2753/MIS0742-1222230309

Kapoor, S., Hughes, P. C., Baldwin, J. R., & Blue, J. (2003). The relationship of individualism–collectivism and self-construal to communication styles in India and India and the United States. *International Journal of Intercultural Relations, 27*(6), 683–700. doi:10.1016/j.ijintrel.2003.08.002

Kerzner, H. (2006). *Project management: A systems approach to planning, scheduling and controlling* (9th ed.). New York, NY: John Wiley and Sons.

Ketrow, S. (1999). Nonverbal aspects of group communication. In Frey, L. R. (Ed.), *The Handbook of Group Communication Theory and Research* (pp. 251–287). Thousand Oaks, CA: Sage.

Korac-Kakabadse, N., Kouzmin, A., Korac-Kakabadse, A., & Savery, L. (2001). Low- and high-context communication patterns: Toward mapping cross-cultural encounters. *Cross Cultural Management, 8*(2), 3–24. doi:10.1108/13527600110797218

Kroeber, A. L., & Kluckhohn, C. (1952). *Culture: A critical review of concepts and definitions.* Cambridge, MA: Harvard University Press.

Lee-Kelley, L., & Sankey, T. (2008). Global virtual teams for value creation and project success: A case study. *International Journal of Project Management, 26*(1), 51–62. doi:10.1016/j.ijproman.2007.08.010

Levine, D. (1985). *The flight from ambiguity.* Chicago, IL: Chicago University Press.

Lipnack, J., & Stamps, J. (1997). *Virtual teams - Reaching across space, time and organizations with technology.* New York, NY: John Wiley and Sons.

Locker, K., & Kaczmarek, S. (2001). *Business communication: Building critical skills*. Boston, MA: McGraw-Hill Irwin.

Lojeski, K. S., & Reily, R. R. (2008). Understanding effective e-collaboration through virtual distance. In *Encyclopedia of E-Collaboration* (pp. 660–665). Hershey, PA: Idea Group Publishing.

Mark, G., Grudin, J., & Poltrock, S. E. (1999). Meeting at the desktop: An empirical study of virtually collocated teams. In *Proceedings of ECSCW 1999, the 6th European Conference on Computer Supported Cooperative Work*, (pp. 159-178). Copenhagen, Denmark: CSCW.

Maznevski, M., & Chudoba, K. (2000). Bridging space over time: Global virtual-team dynamics and effectiveness. *Organization Science, 11*, 273–492. doi:10.1287/orsc.11.5.473.15200

Mohd Yusof, S. A., & Zakaria, N. (2012). *Exploring the state of discipline on the formation of swift trust within global virtual teams*. Paper presented at the 45th Hawaii International Conference on System Sciences (HICSS). Hawaii, HI.

Montoya, M., Massey, A. P., & Lockwood, N. S. (2011). 3D collaborative virtual environments: Exploring the link between collaborative behaviors and team performance. *Decision Sciences, 42*(2), 451–476. doi:10.1111/j.1540-5915.2011.00318.x

Olaniran, B. (2001). The effects of computer-mediated communication on transculturalism. In Milhouse, V. H., Asante, M. K., & Nwosu, P. O. (Eds.), *Transcultural Realities: Interdisciplinary Perspectives on Cross-Cultural Relations* (pp. 55–70). Thousand Oaks, CA: Sage.

Osland, J. S., & Bird, A. (2003). Beyond sophisticated stereotyping: Cultural sensemaking in context. In Thomas, D. C. (Ed.), *Readings and Cases in International Management: A Cross-Cultural Perspective* (pp. 58–70). Thousand Oaks, CA: Sage. doi:10.5465/AME.2000.2909840

Powell, A., Piccoli, G., & Ives, B. (2004). Virtual teams: A review of current literature and directions for future research. *The Data Base for Advances in Information Systems, 35*(1), 6–36. doi:10.1145/968464.968467

Riemer, K., & Klein, S. (2008). Is the V-form the next generation organisation? An analysis of challenges, pitfalls and remedies of ICT-enabled virtual organisations based on social capital theory. *Journal of Information Technology, 23*(3), 147–162. doi:10.1057/palgrave.jit.2000120

Robbins, S. (2001). *Organizational behaviour* (9th ed.). Upper Saddle River, NJ: Prentice Hall.

Robert, L. P. Jr, Dennis, A. R., & Yu-Ting, C. H. (2009). Individual swift trust and knowledge-based trust in face-to-face and virtual team members. *Journal of Management Information Systems, 26*(2), 241–279. doi:10.2753/MIS0742-1222260210

Rogers, E., & Albritton, M. (1995). Interactive communication technologies in business organizations. *Journal of Business Communication, 32*(2), 177. doi:10.1177/002194369503200206

Sarker, S., Sarker, S., & Jana, D. (2010). The impact of the nature of globally distributed work arrangement on work-life conflict and valence: The Indian GSD professionals' perspective. *European Journal of Information Systems, 19*(2), 209–224. doi:10.1057/ejis.2010.20

Schneider, S. C., & Barsoux, J. (1997). *Managing across cultures*. London, UK: Prentice Hall.

Schrage, M. (2000). *Serious play: How the world's best companies simulate to innovate*. Boston, MA: Harvard Business School Press.

Shachaf, P. (2008). Cultural diversity and information communication technology impacts on global virtual teams: An exploratory study. *Information & Management, 45*, 131–142. doi:10.1016/j.im.2007.12.003

Singh, N., Zhao, H., & Hu, X. (2003). Cultural adaptation on the web: A study of American companies' domestic and Chinese websites. *Journal of Global Information Management, 11*(3), 63–81. doi:10.4018/jgim.2003070104

Steinfield, C., Huysman, M., Kenneth, D., Chyng, Y., & Poot, J. Huis,... Cabrera, A. (2001). New methods for studying global virtual teams: Towards a multi-faceted approach. In *Proceedings of the 34th Annual Hawaii International Conference on System Sciences (HICSS-34)*. Hawaii, HI: HICSS.

Striukova, L., & Rayna, T. (2008). The role of social capital in virtual teams and organisations: Corporate value creation. *International Journal of Networking and Virtual Organisations, 5*(1), 103–119. doi:10.1504/IJNVO.2008.016005

Thomas, D., & Bostrom, R. (2010). Building trust and cooperation through technology adaptation in virtual teams: Empirical field evidence. *EDPACS, 42*(5), 1–20. doi:10.1080/07366981.2010.537182

Triandis, H. C. (1995). *Individualism and collectivism*. Boulder, CO: Westview Press.

Trompenaars, F., & Hampden-Turner, C. (2000). *Building cross-cultural competence: How to create wealth from conflicting values*. New Haven, CT: Yale University Press.

Wakefield, R. L., Leidner, D. E., & Garrison, G. (2008). A model of conflict, leadership, and performance in virtual teams. *Information Systems Research, 19*(4), 434–455. doi:10.1287/isre.1070.0149

Warekentin, M., Sayeed, L., & Hightower, R. (1997). Virtual teams versus face-to-face teams: An exploratory study of a web-based conference system. *Decision Sciences, 28*(4), 975–996. doi:10.1111/j.1540-5915.1997.tb01338.x

Zakaria, N. (2006) *Culture Matters?: The Impact of Context on Globally Distributed Civil Society Decision Making Processes during WSIS*. Unpublished dissertation: Syracuse University.

Zakaria, N., Amelinckx, A., & Wilemon, D. (2004). Working together apart? Building a knowledge-sharing environment for global virtual teams. *Creativity and Innovation Management, 13*(1), 15–29. doi:10.1111/j.1467-8691.2004.00290.x

Zakaria, N., & Cogburn, D. L. (2010). Context-dependent vs. content-dependent: An exploration of the cultural behavioural patterns of online intercultural communication using e-mail. *International Journal of Business and System Research, 4*(3), 330–347. doi:10.1504/IJBSR.2010.032954

KEY TERMS AND DEFINITIONS

Collocated Teams: Team members that work side by side in the same project area or work space for instance in the physical sense such as same building, departments, or geographic location.

Global Virtual Teams: A distinct entity, whose members come from different geographical locations, may not have a common background, are organizationally dispersed, collaborate using asynchronous and synchronous technologies, and often are on assemble on an ad-hoc basis.

In-Group: A cohesive social group united by shared beliefs, attitudes, or interests towards which individual group members feel allegiance and loyalty, i.e. spouse, family members, close friends.

National Culture: Ways of thinking, feeling and behaving which members of a society learn, share, and pass on to succeeding generations.

Organizational Culture: A set of beliefs, values, and norms which are shared among the workforce members in an organization.

Out-Group: A group of people excluded from or not belonging to the in-group, i.e. acquaintances, strangers.

Teamwork: The collaborative work efforts of a group of people to achieve a common goal.

Trust: An act and/or relationship based on assured reliance on another's ability, competence, and/or dependability.

Chapter 15
Considering Phenomenology in Virtual Work Research

Shawn D. Long
University of North Carolina – Charlotte, USA

Cerise L. Glenn
University of North Carolina – Greensboro, USA

ABSTRACT

Phenomenology provides a framework for understanding the dynamic, complex processes of everyday lived experiences. We suggest that the virtual work environment is fertile ground to utilize a phenomenological approach. Centralizing the lived experiences of organizational members frames the utility of this method throughout this chapter. A historical discussion of the roots of phenomenology, its application to the virtual work environment, a potential research study, and recommended uses and limitations of this approach are offered in this chapter.

INTRODUCTION AND BACKGROUND

The virtual workplace is an important site for extensive qualitative studies. Examining the "lived" experiences of those organizational members engaged in virtual work is of critical importance as organizations experience a radical structural shift in how work is constructed and accomplished. This chapter offers a critical need of using a phenomenological approach to the study of virtual work in all of its forms.

Phenomenology describes the meaning of the lived experiences for several individuals about a concept or the phenomenon (Creswell, 1998). Phenomenology is primarily concerned with exploring the structures of consciousness in human experiences (Polkinghorne, 1989). With the rapid expansion of the virtual workplace due to the internet and remote connectivity, organizations are taking new shapes and forms due to the increasing opportunities afforded by innovative and practical communication technologies. Organizational

DOI: 10.4018/978-1-4666-0963-1.ch015

members no longer need to physically be in the same place to accomplish work goals. This rapid transition is fertile ground for qualitative researchers interested in phenomenological studies. By bringing sharp focus to the lived experiences of virtual workers, scholars and practitioners have an opportunity to forge new knowledge areas about virtual work and its impact on virtual employees and the organization.

What is Phenomenology? Husserl's Approach to Understanding Everyday Lived Experiences

Phenomenology provides a framework for understanding the dynamic, complex processes of everyday lived experiences. Simply put, phenomenology refers to the study of phenomena in the manner in which they are experienced by people. The experiences of the "everyday" significantly impact how people understand and respond to a variety of social phenomena. This approach challenges the belief in a single, objective external reality (see Craig, 1999; Craig & Muller, 2007). Phenomenologists believe that our sense of reality is rooted in our daily experiences. Through these experiences, we create our understanding of the world and can continually adjust these understandings as we have new and different experiences. Thus, reality is socially constructed and cannot be understood solely through detached, "objective" modes of study. From this perspective, events, ideas and concepts that were once conceived as natural are indeed products of human thought (Craig, 1999).

Although there are multiple lines of phenomenological inquiry, this perspective has conceptual foundations in German philosophy, particularly Husserl. Husserl challenged positivist notions of an external reality, but also eschewed ideas of a purely mentalist perspective that does not believe in a material reality (Baker, Wuest, & Noerager Stern, 1992; Husserl, 1962; Spielberg,

1975). Our social experiences combine both objective *and* subjective positionalities that impact our conscious understandings of the numerous interactions we have with others. Our objective and subjective experiences cannot be understood in isolation, but in conjunction with each other. Phenomenology "links a phenomenon and being in an inseparable way: there is a phenomenon only when there is a subject who experiences the phenomenon" (Sadala & Adorno, 2002, p. 282). This perspective of the world, however, creates a paradox of consciousness relating to our objective and subjective perceptions of the social world. We have a concrete understanding of our own subjectivities, but understand others as objects (Husserl, 1962). We understand our experiences subjectively in the context of our experiences; however, we view the actions of others from a more detached stance as we attempt to make meaning of their actions.

Husserl sought ways to critically engage how we negotiate this paradox, as well as how he could frame ways to reintegrate what he labels the science world and the life world. He uses the notion of the life world to explain the prereflexive and preobjective world. Our experiences drive our understandings of the "objective" world; therefore, before there can be pregiven knowledge or laws, there must be some type of experience drawn from to create social laws that can be empirically tested. Our common experiences of this world generate laws pertaining to particular phenomena. We use the laws generated from our experiences to categorize them by patterns and repetition associated with these phenomena and integrate them into our understanding of how they work or operate. We then repeat these patterns as we continue to experience the phenomena in the future.

Husserl asserts that we can understand how others make sense of their world through intentionality of consciousness and phenomenological reduction. All communicative actions have meaning, including both verbal utterances and gestures. We understand these meanings and use them with conscious intent to share our meanings with others. Without shared understanding of these verbal and nonverbal interactions, it would not be possible to discuss an object or understand its "essence" (Husserl, 1962; Sadala & Adorno, 2002). According to Husserl, "Whenever we light upon the passive contents of consciousness, upon the 'essence' side of meaning, a process of free creativity occurs, in which there spring forth in our minds new categorical Activity" (Schutz, 1967, p. 282). Although we at times interact with others through utilizing and repeating the behaviors of others as we create shared constructions of meaning, we also have the ability to reflect upon our behaviors and generate new types of meaning that we associate with our own experiences and the experiences of others.

Individuals discover the intentionality of consciousness that people have through the process of phenomenological reduction. This entails the process of bracketing, or identifying key assumptions and judgments about a phenomenon being studied. Once those assumptions are identified, they can be set aside to attempt to prevent them from influencing the researcher's openness in examining aspects of experiences. Understanding preconceptions allows us to recognize them when examining the experiences of others so we do not let our own experiences influence how we make sense of those of others. The characteristics of the phenomenon under investigation can then be identified and its attributes can then be continually reduced until the essential essence of the phenomenon is uncovered (Baker, et al., 1992; Sadala & Adorno, 2002; Merleau-Ponty, 2002). The process of reduction entails locating the phenomenon in contexts to remove characteristics that may be influenced by those contexts. Removing the unessential elements and searching for constant aspects of experiences allows the researcher to understand the essential and unvarying elements of the phenomenon under study (Husserl, 1962; Sadala & Adorno, 2002; Merleau-Ponty, 2002).

Schutz Connects Phenomenology and the Social Sciences

Since phenomenology has roots in philosophy, generally considered a humanistic field of study, it can often be difficult to see how this perspective works in conjunction with inquiry in applied fields. Scholars, such as Schutz, have advanced philosophical understandings of phenomenology to create frameworks for gathering data of people's experiences and connecting them to the subjective/objective paradox, as well as in application to specific fields and industries. Schutz' work in the area of interpretive sociology builds upon the ideas of Husserl and Weber (a German sociologist) to create ways to connect phenomenology to human action.

Like Husserl, Schutz examines the dialectical relationship between people (subjects) and their outside world (objects); however, his approach extends Weber's notion of ideal types (ways in which we categorize, compare, and order phenomenon in the social world). This school of thought asserts that we cannot describe the objective **or** subjective world, but only examine the subjective world from the position and experiences of the subject to understand human action as opposed to merely understanding human behavior. He contends that social scientific approaches that define constructs narrowly and in a pre-determined fashion to be tested through hypotheses do not fully account for understanding the reflexive nature of human beings.

Schutz (1967) also connects the notion of consciousness to action by exploring concepts such as motivation and flowing consciousness (also termed stream of consciousness). He separates the notion of experiences into two different types, "one can define the context of experience as (a) the totality of meaning-configurations brought together within one moment or (b) as a meaning-context of a higher order" (p. 76). This then creates more than one type of consciousness that Husserl explicates. Schutz argues that there is a total context of experiences that consists of *real* and *ideal* objects. Over time, the totality of experiences creates lower ordering of patterns that become taken for granted and we utilize them in our daily interactions with others without questioning the very constructs upon which these experiences are based. He explains, "This reserve stock of knowledge is preserved in the form of mere passive content" (p. 77). He further explains that these types of experiences can be "unfrozen" and brought back to a more active state of consciousness through reflection. Reflection allows us to retrospectively distinguish our different experiences, thus creating a higher level of consciousness. The ability to distinguish between our experiences adds a temporal dimension to phenomenology in addition to differentiating higher and lower levels of consciousness (Schutz, 1967). For instance, consider how you learn to interact with a new supervisor at work-Shauna Jones. You may first watch the behaviors of others to see how they interact with her. Do your new co-workers call her Shauna or Ms. Jones? Or do they refer to her by her title in the organization coupled with her first or last name? If you hear your co-workers refer to her as Ms. Jones and do the same when you meet her, you are participating in the behavioral patterns at work as you have observed them. You address her as Ms. Jones whenever you see her in the office, so this becomes a pattern repeated regularly enough that it no longer requires much conscious thought and feels like an automatic behavior. One day you talk to a colleague in the hallway who tells you that he overheard her tell a new employee to call her Shauna. This new experience generates more active thought about how to address her at work. With this new "light" do you change the way you address her or continue to repeat the patterns of interaction you see with your co-workers?

In the example above, take a minute to think about what you consider appropriate ways to address a supervisor. Do you think using Ms. Jones is too formal? Or does it show respect? Perhaps you think it reflects power imbalances within the workplace and prefer everyone be called by their first name regardless of their position. Maybe you think you should "go with the flow" and mirror what others do to fit into the organizational culture. Engaging in this activity causes you to momentarily pause your stream of experiences and reflect upon them. Through reflection, we can retrospectively make sense of how we have adopted patterns of behavior. It also allows us to consider and perhaps change our behavior as we have new experiences related to interacting with supervisors at work. Schutz' explication of intersubjective understanding allows us to problematize the notion of shared meanings of understandings that Husserl discusses, particularly as they relate to the object-subject paradox. In our own stream of consciousness, we can pinpoint the context of our experiences and beliefs regarding how to address a supervisor.

We do not understand the experiences of others, yet often act as if another's stream of consciousness and lived experiences should cause this person to behave in the same manner we do based on our own experiences with the same phenomenon (in this instance interacting with supervisors at work). We view our experiences subjectively through the totality of our experiences, yet view others as objects through their manifestations of their thoughts through behavior. Even when we try to understand the experiences of others, we can engage in the fallacy of what Schutz terms the projective theory of empathy. We attempt to understand others by projecting our lived experiences unto them. By beginning with Husserl's notion of bracketing, we can identify our own preconceptions and then set them aside when trying to understand the actions of others. This allows us to bring openness to understanding others, what Schutz terms as the beginning of genuine intersubjective understanding. This process entails two steps: studying the "genuine understanding of actions which are performed *without any communicative intent...*second we would examine cases where such communicative intent was present" (Schutz, 1967, p. 113). In the first step, we observe behavior without analyzing intent. We watch the actions of another person to understand patterns of action. Only after learning about these patterns of behavior can we then observe how people interact with others across various instances and contexts to understand their communicative intent.

Schutz and Husserl's phenomenological framework creates possibilities for multiple interpretations that are non-exclusionary. Furthermore, it allows us to critically examine deeply imbedded assumptions that have been framed in other modes of thought as "natural" and universal. The openness to multiple interpretations provides opportunities to discover the common meanings that undergird phenomena deemed natural, as well as a way to understand variations in the understandings of empirically tested laws and rules. Phenomenological inquiry creates space to challenge the "natural" order of the world to provide new insights into the various ways in which people experience and make sense of their lives. Additionally, phenomenology provides a frame for exploring how numerous aspects of people's lives simultaneously influence each other.

PHENOMENOLOGY AND VIRTUAL WORK

The utility of applying phenomenology to the study of virtual work cannot be overstated. Long (2010) defined virtual work as:

The value-laden, politically rich, nuanced form of organizational functioning that has significant ecological considerations and implications. Virtual work is complicated by the constant energy given to tasks, social concerns, information and formal communication, labor (emotional, psychological and physical), impression management, face-saving techniques, virtual dramaturgy, *managing up and down, motivating employees, rewarding and punishing virtual work behaviors, decision-making, socializing, organizational change, diversity issues, leading a virtual work team/group, among other things" (p. xvi).*

Long's definition lays the foundation for critical phenomenological studies. Understanding the organizational members lived experiences of engaging in these ecological virtual work features are salient for legacy and future virtual workers and managers. Although several traditional (e.g. surface) workplace concepts and methods may adequately apply to the virtual work environment, several may not. The absence of constant non-verbal cues, lack of managements' physical presence, reduction of the physical informal work/ social network and regular physical presence and engagement with other organizational members may greatly impact and influence the work experience of individuals.

OPPORTUNITIES FOR PHENOMENOLOGY IN VIRTUAL WORK

In light of the definition of virtual work highlighted above, phenomenology is a key qualitative methodological approach in understanding the virtual workers' perceptions, behaviors, and communication in virtual work. There are a number of phenomenological studies ripe for virtual work including studying the lived experiences of virtual employees, managers' perceptions of virtual work and the influence of virtual work on employee/manager relations, client/worker relations and other critical workplace interpersonal interactions.

Due to the increasing reliance on information technology and the inexpensive costs of assessing an individual's work experience through online questionnaires, telephone interviews and other social network tools, applying a virtual work phenomenological approach is an ideal methodology. Contemporary data collection software systems allow for quick and robust responses to semi structured questions about an individual's virtual work experience, while eliminating the need for extensive transcriptions of audio tapes.

Engaging in electronic forums to conduct focus groups or remote individual interview (with transcription services included) also allows for immediate data analysis of the participants' responses. These data gathering techniques certainly do not preclude a researcher from the traditional face-to-face methods of data collection such as interviews and focus groups, but given the source population of virtual workers and where they primarily traffic, leveraging virtual methodologies is a salient and critical evolution in better understanding a phenomenon, phenomenological studies included. Contemporary and innovative communication technologies facilitate rapid and robust information gathering opportunities for researchers, scholars and practitioners interested in the health and well being of virtual organizational members.

A Case Study: Understanding Human Experiences as Part of the Everyday World of Work

Since phenomenology has not been heavily applied in the context of virtual work, connecting everyday lived experiences to technology in the workplace provides an exemplar for understanding how virtual work influences and impacts the lived experiences of virtual workers. As a case example, a new manager at a technology firm attempted to train an employee on utilizing new technological tools when working remotely with clients in different locations. Rather than the traditional face-to-face team approach of getting work done, the organizational technology would allow workers to complete tasks independently and completely to serve their respective clients. This was both a cost-saving strategy as well as a client relation strategy of having one person re-

sponsible for the full execution of tasks. Despite extensive training to learn the new system, a long term employee was unable to complete the new tasks as effectively and efficiently as directed by the manager. The manager felt that the employee's deficiencies were less a matter of age, but more centrally tied to his lack of abstract technological skills, independent task competence, and more importantly a lack of desire to change the way he had always done his work, which was primarily face-to-face and handing off aspects of the job to another person. Unfortunately, the manager had to step in to complete his work for him due to the time sensitive nature of the work. This resulted in an overage of billable hours to the client, as well as created a high cost to the firm. Management decided to offer early retirement to the employee so he would not have to be terminated. He was replaced with a younger, cheaper worker who worked more quickly, eagerly and independently.

This created a shift in organizational culture for the workers in this environment. As more employees were offered early retirement and newer (and fewer) employees with more technological aptitude were hired and offered the flexibility to work remotely, away from the office. Tensions rose between the incumbent (surface workers) and newly hired virtual workers (preferred to work from home). The older employers began to label the younger ones as the "invisible" workers because they had little work or social contact with them. The younger employees could not figure out why the incumbent workers wanted to come to the office daily with the commute and deal with the office politics when all of their work could be accomplished at "home" or a "coffee shop." They often called the legacy employees "dinosaurs." When physical meetings were convened, the newer or virtual workers did not sit next to the incumbent employees, many of which still worked at the physical office daily despite being offered an opportunity to work at home.

Although technology has the ability to increase effectiveness and productivity, it can also create divisions (e.g. demographic, work function, spatial, etc.) that demarcate perceptions of fit and belonging to various organizations. Technology is certainly influencing the way we do work and it is dramatically shifting work cultures, regardless of industry or sector. Furthermore, it influences perceptions of performance, desire and ability, which has an effect on upward mobility, job satisfaction, organizational commitment, among other organizational issues. Applying phenomenology to the study of various virtual work organizational issues is of great importance as we continue to make sense of the lived experiences of organizational members. As previously noted, individual interviews and focus groups have been traditionally utilized in phenomenological inquiry. In this case it may be helpful to conduct focus groups with the newer employees who eagerly accept remote working environments, as well as with those who are more reticent to do so. Individual interviews also provide in-depth understanding to the lived experiences in the changing world of virtual work. This fosters space for participants to tell their stories in their own words without being influenced by the ideas of others. Virtual spaces create opportunities to conduct research remotely. Newer technologies, such as webcams and digital workspaces, allow the researcher to interact with others without traveling to numerous locations.

CHALLENGES OF USING PHENOMENOLOGY IN VIRTUAL WORK

Virtual work phenomenology is not without inherent challenges. There are five immediate issues when using a phenomenological approach in the study of virtual work. First, the researcher requires a firm foundation in the philosophical underpinnings of phenomenology. As the historical review of phenomenology reflects, there is a long and storied history associated with this approach and a researcher should be familiar with the spirit of this approach before haphazardly applying this tradition to a study.

Second, the participants in the study should be carefully selected to include those who have actually experienced the phenomenon. To achieve the "essence" of a phenomenon, a participant should respond from a position of authority to authenticate the phenomenon under investigation. Third party accounting is not sufficient to assess the "lived experience" of an individual.

Third, a researcher must have the ability (often times) to suspend judgment or bracket his or her personal experiences in order to respect the narrative or experiences of the participant in the study. This can be sometimes difficult, particularly if the researcher is inclined to study this phenomenon based upon his or her own lived experience with the topic. For example, a researcher who experienced a hostile virtual work environment, primarily due to the dislocated nature of the work, may have difficulty suspending his or her negative judgments about telework if their biases are not conscious, checked and direct.

Fourth, conducting a phenomenological study virtually has significant privacy and trust implications. When designing a phenomenological study, a researcher should be aware that asking participants to share their lived experiences in an electronic format may be problematic for a number of reasons including archival data, electronic trail, privacy and security trust issues, among other concerns. This issue may prevent a participant from fully disclosing all information associated with his or her experiences or cause them to severely self-censor their responses. Depending on the sensitivity of the topic and the comfort level of the participants, different data collection techniques may be more appropriate than others (e.g. face to face interviews, focus groups, etc.).

Fifth, permission to access and collect data may be an issue in conducting research in virtual spaces if the research is being conducted through participation in "live" time with people from multiple locations. Obtaining permission from

Institutional Review Boards (IRB) can be problematic due to the rapid growth and development of virtual work in organizations. "Ownership" of virtual spaces may complicate understanding how permission should be obtained and from whom it should be obtained. For instance, a virtual meeting can take place online with people in various locations (domestic and abroad). Crossing national borders, even virtual ones, may result in further steps needed to receive approval to conduct research. Consulting with your IRB well before you plan to begin data collection will assist with issues obtaining permission.

FUTURE RESEARCH DIRECTIONS

Despite the previously discussed challenges, phenomenology provides a useful theoretical framework for understanding how virtual work influences perceptions of the everyday world of work. Future research studies could examine how virtual work influences organizational identity and identification. Perceptions of organizational fit and belonging include focus areas such as examining how and if people feel they belong to organizations, how organizations can foster identification, and the strength of the perception of the sense of belonging to a particular organization (Glenn & Jackson, 2010). Work in this area could contribute to understanding how virtual work processes affect the way in which employees feel connected to the organizational environment or separated from it. This provides opportunities to examine and develop ways to make employees feel connected to their work environments to foster stronger feelings of organizational commitment.

Along with the studying the perceptions of the employees from a phenomenological perspective, an interesting, and much needed, research area could be to examine the lived experiences of managers supervising virtual workers. There is a

dearth of literature on virtual work leadership and the challenges and opportunities associated with this way of working. Applying phenomenology to this research domain is fertile ground for future and salient research.

CONCLUSION

Virtual work is here to stay. Organizations are increasing their virtual workforce and the subsequent scholarship and research in this area must continue to grow and develop. Centralizing phenomenological approaches to the study of virtual work is a critical step in fully understanding individuals' lived experiences in the electronic domain. This chapter provides a historical, current and future approach to phenomenology from traditional and contemporary perspectives.

We find that phenomenology is an interesting and salient methodological tool and approach to use when investigating virtual work. We hope that more scholarship emerges using this important research method.

REFERENCES

Baker, C., Wuest, J., & Noeranger Stern, P. (1992). Method slurring: The grounded theory/phenomenological example. *Journal of Advanced Nursing*, *17*, 1355–1360. doi:10.1111/j.1365-2648.1992.tb01859.x

Craig, R. T. (1999). Communication theory as a field. *Communication Theory*, *9*, 119–161.

Craig, R. T., & Muller, H. L. (Eds.). (2007). *Theorizing communication: Readings across traditions*. Thousand Oaks, CA: Sage Publications.

Creswell, J. W. (1998). *Qualitative inquiry and research design: Choosing among five traditions*. Thousand Oaks, CA: Sage.

Glenn, C. L., & Jackson, R. L. II. (2010). Re-negotiating identity in the field of communication. In Allan, S. (Ed.), *Rethinking Communication: Keywords In communication Research* (pp. 137–149). Cresskill, NJ: Hampton Press.

Husserl, E. (1962). *The foundations of phenomenology* (Farber, M., Trans.). New York, NY: Paine-Whitman.

Long, S. D. (Ed.). (2010). *Communication, relationships and practices in virtual work.* Hershey, PA: IGI Global. doi:10.4018/978-1-61520-979-8

Merleau-Ponty, M. (2002). *Husserl at the limits of phenomenology.* Evanston, IL: Northwestern University Press.

Sadala, M., & Ferreira, R. (2002). Phenomenology as a method to investigate the experience lived: A perspective from Husserl and Merleau Ponty's thought. *Journal of Advanced Nursing, 37*(3), 282–293. doi:10.1046/j.1365-2648.2002.02071.x

Schutz, A. (1967). *The phenomenology of the social world* (Walsh, G., & Lehnert, F., Trans.). Evanston, IL: Northwestern University Press.

Spielberg, H. J. (1975). *Doing phenomenology.* Dordrecht, The Netherlands: Martinus Nijhoff.

KEY TERMS AND DEFINITIONS

Intentionality of Consciousness: Learning the meanings of communicative actions and the way we intend to convey them with others in social interactions.

Phenomenological Reduction: A methodological process for bracketing preconceived thoughts and ideas about research phenomena and analyzing data until they are reduced to their essential elements.

Phenomenology: A framework for understanding the dynamic, complex processes of everyday lived experiences.

Virtual Work: The value-laden, politically rich, nuanced form of electronic organizational functioning that has significant ecological considerations and implications.

Chapter 16
Case Study Findings from Human Interaction with Web E-Services:
Qualitative Data Analysis

Kamaljeet Sandhu
University of New England, Australia

ABSTRACT

Case study findings may provide a deeper insight into human interaction with web e-services. The qualitative data that was captured in this study suggests that human interaction with web e-services may make the user task difficult, and that the user expectation about the system not meeting user requirements may downgrade the system's use. Introducing an e-services system without integrating the user-friendly characteristics may have the effect of introducing complexity. Initial staff impressions of the system were formed on the basis of their expectations. When task outcomes did not meet their expectations, staff tried and then avoided its use.

INTRODUCTION

The implications of using e-services are significant for business (Xue, et al., 2004). Customer participation in and acceptance of e-services provides them with a broader choice of services that meet their requirements. In some organisations this has led to the overhaul of the service delivery system (Xue, et al., 2004; Al-Ajeeli & Al-Bastaki, 2011). It is therefore important to understand the user roles in e-services system development. User-e-services interaction behaviour on websites is unique in the sense that the interface takes place in

DOI: 10.4018/978-1-4666-0963-1.ch016

cyberspace within a short time. It is important for business to understand what influences the use of an e-services system with in that short time frame (Grönroos, et al., 2000). End-user requirements is one of the core themes driving the success/failure of e-services systems.

Organisations engaged in e-business are providing e-services such as banking, airline ticket booking, car rental, management consulting, and the selling of music and software. Educational institutions are increasingly opting for interactive, e-services system delivery to meet user demand (Forrest & Mizerski, 1996). E-services system offer advantages such as instant and 24 X 7 access, immediate feedback and receipting, effective and immediate ordering etc, to business and government organisations delivering online services. For example, Hewlett Packard is rapidly transforming their after-sales service to e-services system business units (McCarthy, 1999; Ruyter, et al., 2001). Organisations have realised it would be easier for both businesses and their customers to put information up on the web than to answer repeated requests from users (Berners-Lee, 1999, p. 65).

With the development of information technology allowing user participation in service delivery on websites, customers' roles in the e-services process have become more important. Therefore, it can be argued that researchers need to pay more attention to customers' and users' evaluations of technology-based services (Parasuraman & Grewal, 2000; Chea & Lou, 2008; Chellappan, 2008).

In general, existing research suggests that e-services system translate into fast delivery of services on websites and portals without the users investing much time or effort. The flexibility in service delivery offered by e-services system provides users with quick selection of the best services available, choice from a wider range of service providers, the availability of interaction in their own time and space, easier access to several related services, access to unlimited content, and excellent retrieval facilities (van Riel, et al., 2001).

Organisations and governments worldwide have established e-services system on websites, including services as diverse as bill paying, taxation, online delivery of education, medical information, legal consultancy, business consultancy, cultural awareness, real estate buying and selling, and transport information on timetables and registration (for example www.firstgov.com in the USA; www.europa.eu.int in Europe; www.ukonline.gov.uk in the UK; www.fed.gov.au in Australia; www.gov.sg in Singapore; and www.gov.hk in Hong Kong).

LITERATURE REVIEW

The Technology Acceptance Model (TAM) represents an important theoretical contribution toward understanding Information Systems (IS) usage and IS acceptance behaviour (Davis, et al., 1989; Robey & Sahay, 1996). Similarly Venkatesh (2000) argues that perceived usefulness and useability of IT are major determinants of IT usage. Previous research demonstrates that this model is valid across a wide variety of IS studies (e.g. Adams, et al., 1992; Chin & Gopal, 1993; Hendrickson, et al., 1993; Chin & Todd, 1995; Davis, 1993; Davis & Venkatesh, 1996; Gefen & Straub, 1997; Iqbaria, et al., 1997; Mathieson, 1991; Segars & Grover, 1993; Subramanian, 1994; Szajna, 1994, 1996; Taylor & Todd, 1995; Venkatesh & Davis, 1996; Venkatesh, 1999; Venkatesh & Morris, 2000; Legris, et al., 2003). Applying TAM is a useful means of investigating user requirements with regard to usefulness and user friendliness in this study as they apply to e-Services (Pedersen & Methlie, 2001). Davis (1989) argues that the role of perceived usefulness and perceived ease of use determines user acceptance of a technology. Perceived ease of use is the extent to which a user believes that using a technology will be free of effort; whereas usefulness is linked to a user's assessment of the effort involved in using the system (Davis, 1989; Venkatesh, 2000). In the context of e-Services system, the application of ease of use and usefulness from the user experience perspective may be relevant.

Parasuraman et al. (2005) developed the means-end framework as a theoretical foundation, shown in Figure 1, that conceptualizes, constructs, refines, and tests a multiple-item scale (E-S-QUAL) for measuring the service quality delivered by Web sites on which customers shop online. The authors suggest that to deliver superior service quality, managers of companies with Web presences must first understand how consumers perceive and evaluate e-Services.

Heijden (2000) conducted an empirical study to predict e-Services system usage on websites. The independent constructs (i.e. perceived usefulness and perceived ease of use) were found to influence the dependent variable, which was e-Services system usage, in order to measure usage independent of the user. In the study Heijden (2000) reports: 1) that an extended version of TAM (Davis 1989, 1993) settings with respect to entertainment value supports high correlations between e-Services system usage and e-Services system usefulness; 2) that ease-of-use does not influence e-Services system usage directly, but indirectly through usefulness; and 3) that attractiveness does not influence e-Services system usage directly, but indirectly through entertainment value.

Heijden (2000) argues that usefulness and entertainment value are the first-order drivers, ease-of-use and attractiveness being second-order. An implication of this finding is that antecedents of entertainment and usefulness deserve more attention. This is directly relevant to the current research investigating factors affecting the acceptance of e-Services system and their continued use. Heijden (2000) concedes that the results of his study were limited to evaluation of one e-Services system and the original model was not fully supported with the new data.

Both Venkatesh (2000) and Hackbarth et al. (2003) explore the role of user experience in the ease of use construct. User experience to use a technology may be the first phase in understanding the user e Services interface process. At the current level of understanding, it would be reasonable to expect that user experience to use a technology may be based both on previous interactions and the level of contact the user attains in the process. For example, it can be argued that the minimum expectation for e-Services system to be effectively used would constitute a user spending adequate time understanding the features that contribute to the e-Services system functioning.

Figure 1. A means-end framework for understanding the domain and consequences of e-SQ (Parasuraman, et al., 2005)

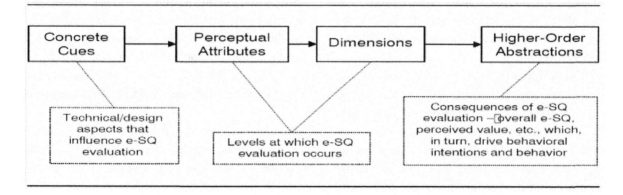

Motivation-ability-opportunity framework explains user attitudes to perform specific behaviours when using e-Services to buy financial products (e.g. Ramaswami, et al., 2001). The basic constructs in the model includes website purchase, website information search, and antecedent levels of motivation, ability and opportunity. Ramaswami et al. (2001) propose that: 1) users who search e-Services system websites for financial information may also buy them on websites; and 2) user buying and search activities will be influenced by their motivation to examine alternatives to the traditional channel (i.e. offline), their ability (i.e. confidence) to take care of their financial affairs without the help of a sales agent, and their opportunity to use the e-Services system website to buy financial products. However, due to the sample size limitation, age was used as a co-variate to ensure that its effects were controlled and did not provide information about different age-group users and their tendency to use and buy financial e-Services on websites.

INSIGHT TO THE RESEARCH PROBLEM

This study aims to understand what affects the adoption, use, and then continued use of an e-Services system in terms of e-Services system characteristics based on service-user interaction, the user's attitudes to adopting e-Services at different stages based on how user behaviour towards adopting e-Services system is influenced, and user attitudes to adoption—specific behaviours that are linked to user activities when using e-Services system.

The problem facing the international admission department is that the staff is not accepting the web electronic service system in processing the student admission application; instead continue to use the old system that is a traditional paper-based service. Printing documents, storing in folders, processing, and correspondence with

students are through traditional mail and central to the workflow system. Reliance on paper-based service tends to duplicate and increase task load leading to errors and confusion. As a result of this, the department lags behind in providing good service to its clients (students), resulting in considerable backlog. This is shown in Figure 2.

The case study examines the Web Electronic Service framework of the University of Australia (not the real name). The department is in the process of developing and implementing Web-based e-service system. International students have the option to lodge the admission application through either of any: web-based e-service system on the World Wide Web, phone, fax, or in person. On receiving the application, a decision is made by the staff on the admission status. The department is implementing the electronic delivery of its services on the website. The web electronic service is believed to be in use for approximately last two and half years. The e-service process involves students making the application and the staff processing application on the website.

The department introduced the web electronic service to catch up with the increasing backlog and to improve the service. The staff indicated their resistance to accept web-based e-service system on the basis of factual information such as: it added additional load to their current task, lack of confidence, fear of providing wrong information on the web, and not seeking help when required.

The Department has always used a paper-based administrative processing system to file information enquiries, process applications, and support potential and existing overseas students at the university. With the volume of enquiries and numbers of applications increasing at 30% per year for the past 3 years, there has been a need to increase efficiency. The IT Manager said:

It is a pretty big area. When starting the enquiries we are looking at...there are probably about 30,000 individual records and many come down

Figure 2. Past-present situation and future goals

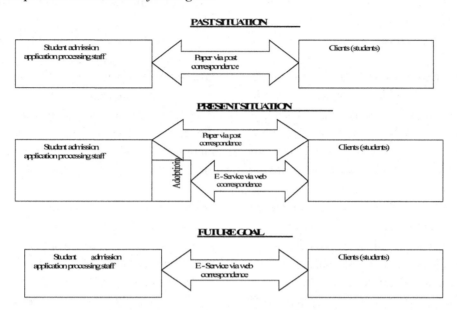

to applications…but you are probably dealing with a number a lot less than that.

As a result, the Manager of the Department initiated the development of an e-Services system to undertake all of the tasks previously done manually. The system has now been in place for 2 years. The Management envisaged that this new e-Services system would create new business opportunities by providing international students with an electronic platform for sending and receiving information. The system would also enable the Department to achieve its aim to provide quality customer service to these students and deliver all services electronically. The primary aim of the Department's Managers for the e-Services system was to reduce paper processes and provide quicker and more efficient service to its clients (i.e. international students). Management expected the staff to use the e-Services system in their regular work so that they could use it to manage and make day-to-day work more efficient and more significant in managing workflow.

One of the user's reaction to e-services prior to its implementation:

E-service has been a long time coming and there has been a lot of talk about it and finally when it was launched it didn't work. And that is discouraging people from actively using it and being excited about it anymore.

One of the user's reaction to e-services during its implementation:

The e-Services system, which is entirely not ready to work, creates all sorts of difficulties. I think it is discouraging people from actively using it and learning about it. Every time it shuts down the staff looses interest and also confidence in using the system. The system has not been able to connect to the staff. That bond doesn't exist or it might have at the beginning but after being constantly put down it has faded.

One of the user's reaction to e-services after its implementation:

I think obviously there is resistance to using the e-Services system because the staff feel that they were never consulted on the system's development so they are quite insulted. I mean it is a very obvious thing that the system should be able to do basic functions. Staff need to be consulted about this.

The senior staff outlined the department goals as: (1) processing all application by web electronic service on the Internet; (2) respond to student correspondence by web electronic service within 24 hours (and in peak time within 48 hours); and (3) diverting more students towards adopting the web electronic service application.

The theme of the case study is to investigate the uptake of web electronic services system amongst end-users especially based on user requirements. The benefits that the readers are expected to receive from reading this article is to understand the development process of e-services system from the user side (i.e. albeit reducing the technical focus), the use of qualitative data in solving the problem that can have an impact on e-services project, and the transition gap from paper-based to web-based e-services system.

The staff is using the web electronic service system along with another database system (which will be referred as DA system in this study). DA system is accessible only to the internal staff processing student applications, and offers all the functions in complementing the paper-based system in conducting the task. In simple terms, it is known as the paper-based service system. It is believed to be in use approximately for last eight years. The DA system does not interact and neither offers its functionality directly with web electronic system. The staff at the time was using both systems to do the task. The transition from paper-based to web-based e-service system is anticipated by the department to be a significant step in the direction of moving the service process over the website and gradually removing the paper-based system.

Case Analysis of the Problem

One of the staff reported that the attributes of the interface with the system, such as navigation and task button functionalities, were unclear despite being given some training. DeLone and McLean (1992) claim that the systems quality is one of the important characteristics for measuring Information Systems success. For example that staff member noted:

We have very little experience in the working of the e-services system. We don't know how it is supposed to function and what we can expect out of it. From our past experience in using e-services we know that it cannot be used in all areas of our work and it is still being developed and is incomplete. It is not 100% complete yet and there is a risk involved with its use.

Staff were asked to enter all information directly into the e-services system. Even with some training, staff resistance to using the e-services system appeared to increase over the case study period and in follow ups with staff over the next 12 months. This emerged as an issue because of different levels of confusion caused by the lack of complete functionality of the new systems and poor integration with the other systems in use at the Department. One staff member said:

There are quite a few fields where we can't use the e-services system. It just doesn't work. We have to use the paper-based system to complete the work, and that adds on to our workload to use both systems at same time. It takes a lot of time especially when we want to get a simple task done. The two systems are not compatible to each other and we have to depend on both and sometimes it is confusing to know which one works better than the other.

There was a consistent view amongst staff that the e-services system was inadequate and it was obvious in all of the interviews and in discussions with staff that no staff member believed that the training given was adequate. Land (1999) suggested that the skills in using the system can be acquired, providing an incremental learning experience exists. In its absence in this case study, staff were juggling with multiple paper-based sources to gather information needed to complete the e-services system task. One staff member added:

We need to rely on paper documents and another database to complete the tasks...we have to use both systems (i.e. paper-based and e-services based)...and sometimes we are busy; it is too much. We need to gather more expertise about using the system rather than the system helping us in our work. There are paper-based records, which have no connection with the e-services system. We keep using them as well. Plus we use another database, which is not connected to the e-services system, but the IT Manager told us that it should soon start working with the e-services system. It's been quite long and that hasn't happened yet.

In the discussions and interviews with the staff, they focused on issues of systems familiarity, work comparison with both systems, and on the task complexity when doing their work.

Electronic services system were perceived by Management to provide benefits including less paperwork, quick delivery of information, easy editing and updating of information. Parthasarathy and Bhattacherjee (1998) suggest that the utilization levels of e-services is through the user's ability to realise expected benefits via appropriate utilisation of their superior technological skills and ability to mobilise effort and resources to learn the innovation. Student evaluation of e-services acceptance is based on time they spent in doing work on the e-services system; money (dollars) spent in using the e-services, and proposed benefits in student's work to use e-services. Performing

different tasks simultaneously on e-services system such as information searches, downloading information and emailing, may provide the user with a positive perception of the benefits. There was significant emphasis on the introduction of e-services system technology to improve efficiency and effectiveness of the staff and their operations within the Department.

The Management envisaged that this new e-services system would create new business opportunities by providing international students with an electronic platform for sending and receiving information. The system would also enable the Department to achieve its aim to provide quality customer service to these students and deliver all services electronically. The primary aim of the Department's Managers for the e-services system was to reduce paper processes and provide quicker and more efficient service to its clients (i.e. international students). Management expected the staff to use the e-services system in their regular work so that they could use it to manage and make day-to-day work more efficient and more significant in managing workflow.

The staff and Management acceptance of the e-services system and its use in processing international student's admission applications is considered a major organisational requirement to meet Departmental targets in the university's Strategic Plans. However, the Executive Director noted:

"One of our problems is that we have a lot of trouble with our staff coping with the new e-services system. To get them to work with the two systems is troublesome for them. But actually we have 'realised' that the e-services system is part of everyday work. And it probably deserves more attention instead of paper-based print applications in many ways. Our e-services practices had to change."

Electronic services system were perceived by Management to provide benefits including less paperwork, quick delivery of information, easy editing and updating of information. Rogers (1995) argue that attributes of the innovation should be compatible to the organisation. At the same time Management realised that new systems challenge staff on implementation.

Rogers (1995) suggests that complexity of systems implementation, trialability of the system, and ease of observability are the perceived characteristics of innovation. Through prior analysis of the situation, the Management's perception of introducing the new technology was based on the belief that such technology would have a positive impact on staff work when the advantages were reflected in their work.

RESEARCH METHODOLOGY

Multiple sources are used in data collection (Yin, 1994)—documentation, archival records, open-ended interviews, direct observation, participant-observation, and physical artifacts. This is a major strength of case study data collection to use many different sources of evidence (Yin, 1994) providing real life information on the existing problem. Information on the current system provided insight on the obstacles in the user acceptance in systems development and implementation process. This led to the development of converging lines of inquiry, a process of triangulation (Yin, 1994) in processing information from a number of sources.

In the first instance discussions are held with three senior staff members involved in implementing the web-based e-service system. They included the executive director, IT Manager, and an outside Consultant. In the second round separate individual interview are conducted with these participants. The third round of interviews is conducted with the admissions manager and separate individual interviews with two other staff members. Altogether six separate interviews with participants are undertaken. In the study they are referred to as Participant 1, Participant 2, and

so forth, due to participant confidentiality and their identity not disclosed in the study. Though the participant gender is not a major factor for introspection, it coincided to be balanced, three males and three females.

In the first round interview the data collected and compared with the second round and third round interview data, for consistency, clarity and accuracy of the information. Participant 5 and 6 interview data were contrasted to test for the factors having effect on users with high and low performance in using the system. This provided the advantage of not duplicating the data with just one set of evidence.

The discussions and interviews were open-ended (Yin, 1994), the researcher in the beginning provided the topic, and the respondents were probed of their opinion about the events. A reasonable approach was taken to verify the responses with information from other sources (Yin, 1994). The respondents were encouraged to provide their own insight into the problem and this was later converged with responses from other respondents and sources pointing to the fact. The researcher avoided following the sequence of a certain set of questions only, as it would have limited the scope of study and may not have provided important and rich information. This is shown in Figure 3.

ANALYSIS OF THE QUALITATIVE EVIDENCE

The objective of this research is to examine the user acceptance and use of an e-services system. User's acceptance to use e-services relates to the initial use when users trial the use of e- Services system and evaluate its effectiveness in meeting their objectives for visiting the e- Services system. This is shown in Figure 4. For example, a student may use e-services system on a university website for emailing but its effective use can only be determined if such activities meet with

Figure 3. Triangulation-convergence of multiple sources of evidence (adapted from Yin, 1994)

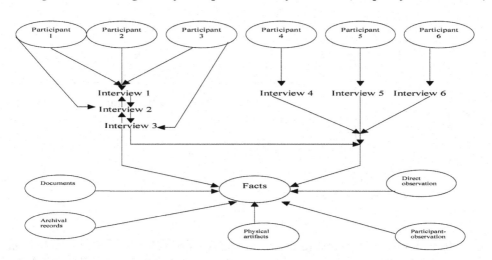

the student's objectives. If the objectives are not met, the student is unlikely to accept e-services.

This case study follows the theoretical propositions that led to the case study (Yin, 1994). The original objectives and design of the case study were based on propositions, which reflected on research questions, review of literature, and the conceptual model. The central problem in the case study coincided with the research problem under investigation. This helped the researcher to focus attention on certain data and ignore other data (Yin, 1994), due to the scope of the study, limited time, and resources.

TAM has been applied in a variety of end-user studies on the world-wide-web (Heijden, 2000; Gefen & Straub, 2000; Venkatesh, 2000; Wright & Granger, 2001). These studies investigated the application of TAM in conjunction with one or more factors (i.e., experience, motivation, and usage frequency). Currently research on web-based e-services focus on understanding those factors that influence how successfully and rapidly users adopt web-based e-service. The Technology Acceptance Model (TAM) of Davis (1989, 1993) represents an important theoretical contribution toward understanding IS usage and IS acceptance behaviour (Davis, et al., 1989, 1992) (see Figure 5).

Figure 4. End-users web electronic usage and acceptance

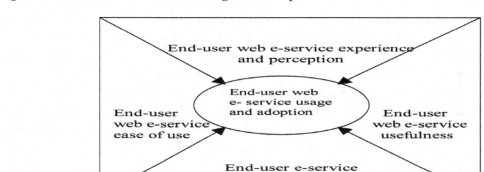

Figure 5. The technology acceptance model (Davis, 1989)

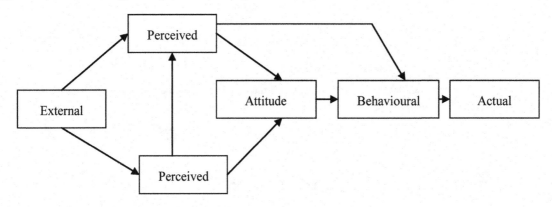

Löfstedt (2007) suggests that Swedish research on e-services focuses on citizens, communication, the development of e-services, the design of e-services, the maintenance of e-services, e-participation, the quality of services, evaluation, organisational changes, interactions between different e-services, usability, cooperation, inter-organisational co-operation, accessibility, e-Health, the development of methods, and process orientation.

The staff experience of the web-based system to have high controls, lesser flexibility, and it is not intelligent to detect simple task errors. This remarkably reflects on prior experience and perception in doing the task with ease with the paper-based system. Though the web-based e-services system offers usefulness but users perceptions is it lacks ease of use. The web-based system isn't prototyped and tested for efficiency, performance and the bugs need fixing.

The user resistance in accepting web-based system also implicates some degree of perceived ease of use and perceived usefulness (Davis, 1989; Chea, 2008; Chellappan, 2008) among staff in using the e-services. It is unveiled that the paper-based system is popular among staff, due to its ease of use and usefulness in conducting the task. It offers users with better control, self-service, and support, than the web-based system.

GAP BETWEEN THE PAPER BASED SYSTEM AND E-SERVICES SYSTEM

The gap between paper-based and web-based e-service system are identified emerging due to information gap, design gap, communication, and fulfillment gap. Zeithaml et al. (2000) in their study pointed to each of these gaps on the basis of users experience with the website. Information gap leads to providing incomplete or in accurate information to the users. The initial design of a website not meeting the user's requirement may result in design gap. The presence of an information gap would exacerbate the design gap because incomplete or incorrect understanding of users might adversely affect the design of the website, therefore compounding user's frustration (Zeithaml, et al., 2000).

Similarly communication gap reflects on a lack of accurate understanding about the websites features, capabilities, and limitations. Sometimes users are made promises that cannot be met, that contribute to the fulfillment gap. In the systems gap situation when the users expectations are not met their reactions is that of frustration. Although emotions such as anger and frustration are expressed when users report on problems arising from web electronic service quality, these appear to be less tense than those associated with traditional service quality experience (Zeithaml, et al., 2000). It can be suggested that the contrast in being "less tense" may be due to the users perception of conveying their problem on web e-services system is relatively new and any expression will need further user experience.

The Figure 6 points to the factors effecting users in paper-based and web-based systems. User experience in paper-based service is considered as one of the factors having significant effect. Such experience is formed of different characteristics. One such contemporary characteristic is the email correspondence. Paper-based service has long been in existence before the web-based system, the user expertise is more concentrated and central to using the paper-based service. The web-based e-service is viewed as an alternative, which will replace the paper-based service but is far from matching user's expectation of the system when compared to the paper-based service system. This is believed to increase the gap. The two systems offer different functionality based on their system characteristics and functionality, at the same time meeting user's expectation of the system is critical to successful acceptance and continued use.

The emerging systems gap at the time is anticipated to be growing. Introducing new changes in web electronic workflow entirely without transferring the user-friendly characteristics (e.g., ease of use) of paper-based system is started effecting users motivation and usage frequency in using web-based e-service. There is underlying resistance in acceptance of the web-based e-service system and increasing negativity towards it features and usage. Low user perception and experience of the electronic system reflects in lower motivation to work with the new system and hence lower usage, which results in doing less work within the web electronic framework and more through paper-based system. As a result lower productivity resulted in web e-service system. Users had less confidence (i.e., low motivation) in the web-based e-service, which is intrinsic as well as extrinsic. Low intrinsic motivation reflects on the desire to use the web e-service, which at times is at its lowest. Conducting task on paper-based systems is considered easy to do, known to the users, less complicated, systematic, and the users know what they are doing. Such consistent pattern of characteristics is missing and not known (though it existed) to the users in the web-based e-service workflow.

An important feature of web e-service system is its usefulness, and the users are familiar with, but the ease of use of the new system is regarded

Figure 6. Web-based e-service systems gap

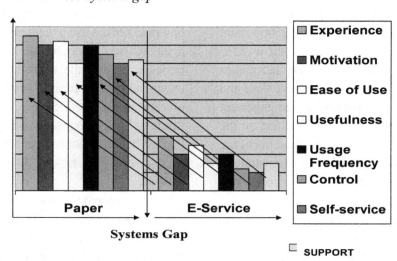

complicated. Simultaneous use of both the system, stemming from the task requirement further complicated the use of web electronic service as the user has to revert repeatedly to the paper based system to complete the web-based e-service task. The web-based system is believed not to be self-sufficient and being developed and updated from time to time, and in those times the users has to rely on the paper-based service system for information.

The scope of web-based system functionality isn't defined and the user didn't have a good experience from the beginning. Establishing the web electronic workflow frame within the system, after the system was developed, resulted in adjusting the other features of the system, and hence adjusting the user experience, which was not an easy and straightforward process. Though the user may have taken the new features into their experience but it formed an initial perception of the system as "being inadequate to perform the web electronic service task." Such early perception may have a down side effect on acceptance and further usage of the web electronic service.

User's guidelines in transferring work from paper-based system to web-based system may have greatly enhanced user's experience. Although such user experience already existed and transferring to the web-based system may have been easy. Users are aware of the guidelines that were verbally conveyed, written guidelines are either missing or unknown to the users. Important information that is not conveyed to the users is "how the new web-based e-service system makes their work easier to perform and save time and effort." Though this is not considered important at the time, it may have a positive effect on the user if known. A list outlining the benefits of the web-based e-service system may demonstrate to the users of their performance improvement when using the system.

Developing a system without involving the users is not based on a good System Development Life Cycle (SDLC) principle. User participation in the development of the new system (i.e., web-based system) is very crucial before and after the system development. Such interaction allows the system to be custom made meeting the users expectations of what the system can do and not the other way around. Adding new features and upgrades to the existing system also requires close interaction with the user group, for testing and demonstrating its effectiveness, before finally integrating to the existing system.

THE MIRROR EFFECT

The web-based system is not tested with the users for its effectiveness before final deployment. It is important to know "what is expected from the web-based system," or which characteristics that can be migrated from the old system to the new one, even the ones that didn't work in the old system may be improved and tested and offered to the user with a better experience in the new system (Figure 7). This would have greatly enhanced the web electronic workflow system. Understanding and relating the users motivation and usage frequency characteristics from the old system (i.e. paper-based) into the new (i.e. web electronic) may have offered the user with the same look and feel within the new system.

A different approach may not been appropriate in developing users experience based on the system (and not the user) requirement, this discouraged the users from parting their prior (old) experience. Rather the users examined the new experience (on the basis of system requirements) as rigid and not effective in the current electronic task. Keeping aside ones prior experience that has been developed over a period of time and used in everyday task is difficult to forget or separate.

A good system will complement and integrate user's prior experience within the new framework. For example a typist using a typewriter has prior experience developed over a period of time and is

Figure 7. The mirror effect for the two systems

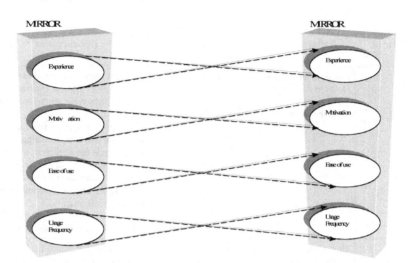

proficient with its use. If the typist is asked to use a personal computer without using prior typing skills may offer resistance in acceptance of the personal computer and its future usage. Precautions may be taken not to relate the negative effects from one system to another (i.e. paper-based to web-based system). Such negative effects can be scrutinized and tested for improvement for their effect in the new system which is shown is Table 1.

IMPLICATIONS AND DISCUSSIONS FOR RESEARCH

The experiences learnt from the e-services system development are:

1. The users need to be involved in the systems development from a very early stage.
2. The use of qualitative data from users in e-services systems implementation need not be underestimated. No user group (e.g. administration staff, academic staff, and senior management staff) should be ignored.
3. Detail conceptualization of the e-services systems needs to be developed and mapped and shown to the user group and ask for their

input. Any changes to that process needs to be implemented at that stage.

The approach that was adapted for this development was just the opposite. Very few users were involved in the e-services systems development. The use of qualitative data was ignored. No detail conceptualization of the e-services system was solicited from the user group.

User's effective role in determining the contents of service and its outcome may require moderate levels of input in the form of information from users to deliver the service. Though such participation in developing the service in paper-based system was present its applicability in web-based e-service system is either missing or very low. Defining user jobs and managing the diverse user groups requires an initiative at the system development stage, which at its very central may be integrated with the workflow process.

The key learning points for this article is to know the users effective role in using the e-services system based on user requirements, implement those requirements within the e-services system by reducing technical complexities and increasing task simplicity on the computer screen. Further, understanding the systems gap and the impact

Table 1. Perceived dimensions, attributes, and concrete cues for web-based e-service system development and selected illustrative quotes from participants

Dimension of Web-based System	Facets of Web-based E-Service Systems Dimension	Evidence from Selected Quotes
Reliability	Site is up and running Helps in doing the task Error checks Does the site meet all the task needs	"The system is not 100% ready…" "Adds on to the task…increases task load." "the system is not connected to the financial system" "If the system can be fixed it can be fixed, otherwise we will continue using it as it is." "System is not intelligent to check simple errors like spell checks, grammar checks." "If any information is missed, there is no way to check, there are no compulsory fields to inform of missing information." "Need to rely on paper documents and another database to complete the task… have to use all."
Responsiveness	Help available if there was a problem Support Manuals, guidelines, online help When the system doesn't work Information search	"It is available...but if the system cannot do certain things, we have to do it manually." "Mine has been chucked out...haven't seen one." "Sometimes have frustration with the system when it doesn't work, of what we expect of it... it brings the motivation down, and when it works, it bounces the motivation up…tell everyone how well it works" "At home I am more motivated in using the system, as I am relaxing; at work I am hurrying as I have to do this quick…do that." "The site doesn't have a search engine...if there was one; information search would have been easier." "Students with high level of literacy good English language skills will be confident to use the site a lot."
Access	To the site Login to the site Site update	"Too many log in screens…" "Speed needs to be improved, needs to be faster." "Due to time out period that disconnect, the user has to reenter all the information once again…this creates duplicity of information for us...as the same user is reapplying again and it is hard to differentiate between the same application."
Flexibility	Choice of ways to do the task Available	"Verifying information on the Internet is not possible, we still have to check students education credential in paper form" "We need more control…we can get report, but that's only in numbers, whereas the other databases has more information providing us with more control over information…this makes the work easier." "When students are filling the forms online...it is not compulsory for them to write email address… we can't proceed or get in contact if email address is not provided."
Ease of navigation	Easy to find what I need Easy to get anywhere on the website Contains a site map with links to everything on the site Has a search engine	"When I am in between different tasks it logs off... have to login number of times...due to time out period, loose work when login back…it's irritating"

continued on following page

Table 1. Continued

Dimension of Web-based System	Facets of Web-based E-Service Systems Dimension	Evidence from Selected Quotes
Efficiency	Simple to use Site that contains just the basics Doesn't require me to input a lot of information Structured properly Gives information in reasonable hunks Gives information on command rather than all at once No scrolling from side to side No fine print that is difficult to read and hard to find	"Site needs to be improved with better features and functionality that will make it easier for us to use."
Site Aesthetics	Good pictures of items Color of items same as what it is on the screen Eye Catching Color is intriguing Brightness rather than dark background Simple Free of distraction Uncluttered Clean, not too busy No flashing things going across the screen	"Lot of pictures…in some countries computer is slower; it would take a long time to download images." "Screen is fine, fonts are too small, and trying to fit everything in one page…people whose first language is not English would like the fonts to be bigger in size."
Customization and Personalization	Site that help me find exactly what I want Easy to customize	"Can't change or edit letter templates, can't do anything, everything is fixed…whereas with the other system lets you do"

(Adapted from Zeithaml, et al., 2000; Parasurman, et al., 2005)

it can have on the e-services project, by tapping into the users knowledge about the features of the previous system (i.e. paper-based) and building those features into the new e-services system that would make the transition easy for the user.

This study contributes to more effective design and development by implementing the important elements of dimension for a web-based e-services system (e.g. Table 1) based on qualitative evidence from participants. The facets of web-based e-service systems dimension (e.g. Table 1, column 2) are only understood when the system has been developed and runing, thus capturing users understanding of the systems deficiency. This research differs from the previous literature by suggesting that the important aspects of the e-services dimension need to be 'early on designed and tested' and built into the system development cycle. This would reduce the negative impact on the users

attitude towards e-services system performance. E-services system are user driven, features that enhances the systems design will have an effect on the user adoption of e-services. This research also identifies the need to integrate qualitative data into the design for e-services system development projects.

The level of user's participation that may be increased or decreased depending on the user's experience thus shifting the complicated and repetitive task on technology, other task requiring minimum input can be done by the user, making the process easier for the user to complete. Such an understanding if applied may greatly enhanced user task. The senior staff had the view of "we don't want them to create things" which was getting to be difficult when user wanted to customize features such as letter templates, screen fonts size, other changes, that were not allowed within the web-based systems parameters. This may have brought in a sense of disconnected feeling among the users, as one participant put it "they (i.e. users) see themselves as backroom people and not front room they need to be in the front room."

From the service context it is encouraged to have user's participation in service evolving process as much as possible, which adds on users experience, motivation, and decision-making. The user's comment about the web-based e-service system is "we are not consulted and no one ever speaks to us about the online web processing system, it just suddenly appeared and we have to use it." One participant even went a step further and said, "they (the users) don't feel they have any ownership from the beginning" and "we are slowly trying to introduce that sense of ownership among users." Such experience may have been frequently shared among colleagues who were using the web-based system, and the overall general perception of the system is perceived to be low not as a result of its characteristics (not this time) but due to the intense downside collective feeling against accepting the system, due to lack of contribution in its development, participation, and consultation process.

General models of employee behavior suggest that behavior is determined by role of clarity, ability to perform, and motivation to perform (Zeithaml & Bitner, 2000; Sandhu & Corbitt, 2008; Sandhu, 2009). Similarly, user behavior in a service production and delivery situation is facilitated when (1) users understand their roles and know how they are expected to perform, such as clearly defining their task; (2) users are able to perform as expected, that is the minimum standard expected to do the task; and (3) there are valued rewards for performing as expected (Schneider & Bowen, 1990), that is users will be motivated individually and collectively for their achievements. While working with both systems users had forgotten their actual roles within the systems.

A participant disclosed this as "when marketing managers are told to handle an inquiry, the reaction is, it isn't their job." This clearly demonstrated that either the users are shifting their task to their sub-ordinates or they didn't understand their contribution and responsibilities in the web-based system. No minimum standard is set for each task; rather the complete service output is taken as a final delivery of service. This has reduced the sense of user ownership, and the minimum standard expected in doing the task.

It is not known whether the user are proficient in using the web-based database system, rather it is assumed on the basis of their past experience and interface with the paper based system. Working with a database system requires certain level of expertise, for which the users are not tested. It may not be possible for the user to understand the essential requirements of the task and what was expected from it. There weren't any rewards set for the expected performance because nothing is stated as "expected performance." The user isn't encouraged by the rewards rather they processed output on the basis of input.

CONCLUSION

Users need to be educated of their roles and their inputs so that they can perform the task effectively. To understand what is expected of them and the expertise to accomplish the task needs evaluation and feedback of their abilities necessary to perform within a specified context. Users education program can take the form of formal orientation programs, training, written literature provided to users (or manual, that were either missing or unknown), directional cues and signage in the service environment, learning from colleagues and customers, and personal experience. User's performing a specific task requires understanding of the task process (for example: What is needed? How to progress? What is user supposed to do?).

Observing other users doing the same task (brings confidence), exchanging information with other users, enhances users experience. Rewarding the users performing their roles effectively motivates the users and influences others in doing their task well, provides confidence, increases motivation, and job satisfaction. Rewards are likely to come in the form of increased control over the web-based e-service delivery process, timesaving, monetary savings, and psychological or physical benefits.

Users did not recognize the benefits and rewards of effective participation unless they are specifically informed about its benefits, ease of use, and usefulness. The users are not informed about the accrued benefits not only to them, but also to their colleagues, the department, and the whole organization. All users are not motivated with the same types of rewards, efforts to include individualized rewards may be considered. Some may value the increased access and timesaving they can gain by performing their service roles effectively. Others may value recognition, monetary benefits, or still other may be looking for a promotion, autonomy, or greater personal control over the service outcome. If users are not satisfied and their motivation is lacking, it will result in negative outcomes such as, not understanding the service process, slowing down the change process, resistance to change affecting each other (i.e. their colleagues) as well as the customer.

The users may have been clearly informed about their contribution in developing the web-based e-service. Different user's contribution in forming the end-service requires a clear understanding of each user participation and contribution to the process. Interconnected task of different users may demonstrate the start and completion of each user task and responsibilities. Whatever the case, the expected level of user participation required to be communicated verbally or in writing in order to perform their roles.

REFERENCES

Adams, D. A., Nelson, R. R., & Todd, P. A. (1992). Perceived usefulness, ease of use, and usage on information technology: A replication. *Management Information Systems Quarterly, 16*(2), 227–250. doi:10.2307/249577

Al-Ajeeli, A., & Al-Bastaki, Y. (2011). Handbook of research on e-services in the public sector: E-government strategies and advancements. *IGI Global*. Retrieved from http://www.igi-global.com/book/handbook-research-services-public-sector/37290.

Chea, S., & Lou, M. (2008). Post-adoption behaviors of e-service customers: The interplay of cognition and emotion. *International Journal of Electronic Commerce, 12*(3), 29–56. doi:10.2753/JEC1086-4415120303

Chellappan, C. (2008). *E-services: The need for higher levels of trust by populace*. Chennai, India: Anna University.

Chin, W. W., & Gopal, A. (1993). An examination of the relative importance of four belief constructs on the GSS adoption decision: A comparison of four methods. In *Proceedings 26th Hawaii International Conference on Systems Science*. Hawaii: HICSS.

Chin, W. W., & Gopal, A. (1993). An examination of the relative importance of four belief constructs on the GSS adoption decision: A comparison of four methods. In *Proceedings of the 26th Hawaii International Conference on Systems Sciences*. Hawaii: HICSS.

Chin, W. W., & Todd, P. A. (1995). On the use, usefulness, and ease of use of structural equation modelling in MIS research: A note of caution. *Management Information Systems Quarterly, 19*(2), 237–246. doi:10.2307/249690

Davis, F. D. (1989). Perceived usefulness, perceived ease of use, ånd user acceptance of information technology. *Management Information Systems Quarterly, 13*(2), 319–340. doi:10.2307/249008

Davis, F. D. (1993). User acceptance of information technology: System characteristics, user perceptions and behavioural impacts. *International Journal of Man-Machine Studies, 38*(3), 475–487. doi:10.1006/imms.1993.1022

Davis, F. D., Bagozzi, R. P., & Warshaw, P. R. (1989). User acceptance of computer technology: A comparison of two theoretical models. *Management Science, 34*(8), 982–1002. doi:10.1287/mnsc.35.8.982

Davis, F. D., Bagozzi, R. P., & Warshaw, P. R. (1992). Extrinsic and intrinsic motivation to use computers in the workplace. *Journal of Applied Social Psychology, 22*(14), 111–132. doi:10.1111/j.1559-1816.1992.tb00945.x

Davis, F. D., & Venkatesh, V. (1996). A critical assessment of potential measurement biases in the technology acceptance model: Three experiments. *International Journal of Human-Computer Studies, 45*, 19–45. doi:10.1006/ijhc.1996.0040

DeLone, W. H., & McLean, E. R. (1992). Information systems success: The quest for the dependant variable. *The Institute of Management Sciences, 3*(1), 60–95.

Forrest, E., & Mizerski, R. (1996). *Interactive marketing, the future present*. Chicago, IL: American Marketing Association.

Gefen, D., & Straub, D. (1997). Gender differences in perception and adoption of email: An extension to the technology acceptance model. *Management Information Systems Quarterly, 21*(4), 389–400. doi:10.2307/249720

Gefen, D., & Straub, D. (2000). The relative importance of perceived ease of use in IS adoption: A study of e-commerce adoption. *Journal of the Association for Information Systems, 1*(8), 1–20.

Grönroos, C., Heinonen, F., Isoniemi, K., & Lindholm, M. (2000). The netoffer model: A case example from the virtual marketplace. *Management Decision, 38*(4), 243–252. doi:10.1108/00251740010326252

Hackbarth, G., Grover, V., & Yi, M. Y. (2003). Computer playfulness and anxiety: Positive and negative mediators of the system experience effect on perceived ease of use. *Information & Management, 40*, 221–232. doi:10.1016/S0378-7206(02)00006-X

Heijden, H. (2000). *Using the technology acceptance model to predict website usage: Extensions and empirical test. Research Memorandum 2000-25*. Amsterdam, The Netherlands: Vrije Universiteit.

Hendrickson, A. R., Massey, P. D., & Cronan, T. P. (1993). On the test-retest reliability of perceived usefulness and perceived ease of use scales. *Management Information Systems Quarterly, 17*(2), 227–230. doi:10.2307/249803

Igbaria, M. A., Zinatelli, N., Cragg, P., & Cavaye, A. L. M. (1997). Personal computing acceptance factors in small firms: A structural equation model. *Management Information Systems Quarterly, 21*(3), 279–305. doi:10.2307/249498

Land, F. (1999). *The management of change: Guidelines for the successful implementation of information systems*. London, UK: London School of Economics and Political Science.

Legris, P., Ingham, J., & Collerette, P. (2003). Why do people use information technology? A critical review of the technology acceptance model. *Information & Management, 40*, 191–204. doi:10.1016/S0378-7206(01)00143-4

Löfstedt, U. (2007). Public e-services research-A critical analysis of current research in Sweden. *International Journal of Public Information Systems, 2.*

Mathieson, K. (1991). Predicting user intentions: Comparing the technology acceptance model with the theory of planned behaviour. *Information Systems Research, 2*(3), 173–191. doi:10.1287/isre.2.3.173

McCarthy, V. (1999). *HP splits in two to focus on enterprise, e-services.* Retrieved from http://www.hpworld.org/hpworldnews/hpw903/news/01.html.

Parasuraman, A., & Grewal, D. (2000). The impact of technology on the quality-value-loyalty chain: A research agenda. *Journal of the Academy of Marketing Science, 28*(1), 168–174. doi:10.1177/0092070300281015

Parasuraman, A., Zeithaml, V., & Malhotra, A. (2005). E-S-QUAL: A multiple-item scale for assessing electronic service quality. *Journal of Service Research, 7*(10), 1–21. Retrieved from http://public.kenan-flagler.unc.edu/faculty/malhotra/E-S-QualJServRsch.pdf

Parthasarathy, M., & Bhattacherjee, A. (1998). Understanding post-adoption behaviour in the context of online services. *Information Systems Research, 9*(4), 362–379. doi:10.1287/isre.9.4.362

Pedersen, P. E., & Methlie, L. B. (2001). *Understanding mobile commerce end-user adoption: A triangulation perspective and suggestions for an exploratory service evaluation framework.* Working Paper. Agder, Norway: Agder University College.

Ramaswami, S. N., Strader, T. J., & Brett, K. (2000). Determinants of on-line channel use for purchasing financial products. *International Journal of Electronic Commerce, 5*(2), 95–118.

Ramaswami, S. N., Strader, T. J., & Brett, K. (2001). Identifying potential customers for on-line financial services. *The Journal of Internet Banking and Commerce.* Retrieved from http://www.arraydev.com/commerce/JIBC/9806-05.htm.

Robey, D., & Sahay, S. (1996). Transforming work through information technology: A comparative case study of geographical information systems in county government. *Information Systems Research, 7*(1), 93–110. doi:10.1287/isre.7.1.93

Rogers, E. M. (1995). *Diffusion of innovations.* New York, NY: The Free Press.

Ruyter, K. D., Wetzels, M., & Kleijnen, M. (2001). Customer adoption of e- services: an experimental study. *International Journal of Service Industry Management, 12*(2), 184–207. doi:10.1108/09564230110387542

Sandhu, K. (2009). Measuring the performance of electronic services acceptance model (E-SAM). *International Journal of Business Information Systems, 5*(4).

Sandhu, K., & Corbitt, B. (2008). A framework for electronic services system. *International Journal of Electronic Customer Relationship Management, 2*(1). doi:10.1504/IJECRM.2008.019568

Segars, A. H., & Grover, V. (1993). Re-examining perceived ease of use and usefulness: A confirmatory factor analysis. *Management Information Systems Quarterly, 17*(4), 517–525. doi:10.2307/249590

Subramanian, G. H. (1994). A replication of perceived usefulness and perceived ease of usefulness measurement. *Decision Sciences, 25*(5), 863–874. doi:10.1111/j.1540-5915.1994.tb01873.x

Szajna, B. (1994). Software evaluation and choice: Predictive validation of the technology acceptance instrument. *Management Information Systems Quarterly, 18*(3), 319–324. doi:10.2307/249621

Szajna, B. (1996). Empirical evaluation of the revised technology acceptance model. *Management Science, 42*(1), 85–92. doi:10.1287/mnsc.42.1.85

Taylor, S., & Todd, P. (1995). Assessing IT usage: The role of prior experience. *Management Information Systems Quarterly, 19*(4), 561–571. doi:10.2307/249633

Taylor, S., & Todd, P. A. (1995). Understanding information technology usage: A test of competing models. *Information Systems Research, 6*(2), 144–176. doi:10.1287/isre.6.2.144

van Riel, A. C. R., Liljander, V., & Jurriëns, P. (2001). Exploring consumer evaluations of e-services: A portal site. *International Journal of Service Industry Management, 12*(40), 359–377. doi:10.1108/09564230110405280

Venkatesh, V. (1999). Creation of favourable user perceptions: Exploring the role of intrinsic motivation. *Management Information Systems Quarterly, 23*(2), 239–260. doi:10.2307/249753

Venkatesh, V. (2000). Determinants of perceived ease of use: Integrating control, intrinsic motivation, and emotion into the technology acceptance model. *Information Systems Research, 11*(4), 342–365. doi:10.1287/isre.11.4.342.11872

Venkatesh, V., & Davis, F. D. (1996). A model of the antecedents of perceived ease of use: Development and test. *Decision Sciences, 27*(3), 451–482. doi:10.1111/j.1540-5915.1996.tb01822.x

Venkatesh, V., & Morris, M. G. (2000). Why don't men ever stop to ask for directions? Gender, social influence, and their role in technology acceptance and user behaviour. *Management Information Systems Quarterly, 24*, 115–139. doi:10.2307/3250981

Wright, K. M., & Granger, M. J. (2001). Using the web as a strategic resource: An applied classroom exercise. In *Proceedings of the 16th Annual Conference of the International Academy for Information Management.* New Orleans, LA: IAIM.

Xue, M., Harker, P. T., & Heim, G. R. (2004). *Incorporating the dual customer roles in e-service design.* The Working Paper Series. New York, NY: The Wharton Financial Institutions Center.

Yin, R. K. (1994). *Case study research: Design and methods.* Thousand Oaks, CA: Sage Publications.

Zeithaml, V. A., & Bitner, M. J. (2000). *Services marketing: Integrating customer focus across the firm.* New York, NY: Irwin McGraw-Hill.

Zeithaml, V. A., Parasuraman, A., & Malhotra, A. (2000). *A conceptual framework for understanding e-service quality: Implications for future research and managerial practice.* Working Paper. Boston, MA: Marketing Science Institute.

Chapter 17
Applying Dramaturgy to Virtual Work Research

Shawn D. Long
University of North Carolina – Charlotte, USA

Frances Walton
University of North Carolina – Charlotte, USA

Sayde J. Brais
University of North Carolina – Charlotte, USA

ABSTRACT

Dramaturgy as a research approach is a creative and useful tool to fully understand the complex dynamics of individuals interacting in a virtual work environment. Following Goffman's seminal dramaturgical research techniques, this chapter applies the principles and tenants of dramaturgy to virtual work. The authors examine the historical and theoretical underpinnings of dramaturgy and offer a potential research design integrating this methodological approach. The chapter extends the dramaturgical approach to offer challenges and opportunities of using this research approach in an electronic work domain.

INTRODUCTION

Dramaturgy is a sociological approach with roots in symbolic interactionism that accounts for social interactions in everyday life. Erving Goffman (1959) in his seminal book, *The Presentation of Self in Everyday Life,* argues that human actions are dependent upon time, place and audience. Goffman offers a theatrical metaphor to capture this method in that individuals present themselves to others based on cultural values, norms, and expectations. Individuals are viewed as actors, the scene is viewed as the situation and the audience is the intended target for this performance. The ultimate goal of the presentation is acceptance from the audience through carefully conducted performance.

Dramaturgy, as a research tool, is an important methodological approach that allows researchers to better understand human performances in daily interactions, particularly in the workplace. As technology becomes more prevalent, accessible and sophisticated- many organizations are leveraging technological advances to facilitate the shift

DOI: 10.4018/978-1-4666-0963-1.ch017

from a face-to-face work environment to one that is increasingly remote. Work that was traditionally performed in a physical face-to-face environment can now be accomplished in a geographically dispersed digital environment. The time and space boundaries of the traditional workplace are being eradicated and replaced with less restrictive boundaries facilitated by technology.

This dramatic shift is reconstituting how we define and make sense of our work. A critical feature of the human condition is our ability to present, understand, display and interpret the communication and behavior of ourselves and others. Our expressions are our being. Goffman, a seminal scholar in dramaturgy, argued that all human interactions are very much like a grand play (Kivisto & Pittman, 2007). He eloquently posited that all human interactions and displays are performances that are acted out, observed, interpreted, and replayed between humans. The spirit of Goffman's scholarship was not solely concerned with the broad human experience, but also with the micro-level interactions between individuals that in its cumulative form embodies the lived human condition (Kivisto & Pittman, 2007). Human performances are identifiable in our constant physical interactions with others across a number of contexts. However, with the rapid explosion of information technology, particularly in the workplace, understanding, seeing, and interpreting virtual interactions as actual performances is not as easily transparent nor subject to this theatrical gaze that dramaturgy provides us.

This chapter centralizes the dramaturgical approach as a critical methodological tool for researchers to better understanding the experiences of organizational members in a virtual work environment. Long (2010) defined "virtual work" as a complex organizational phenomenon that is not easily defined, nor bounded to task-related considerations. He further explains that virtual work is a value-laden, politically rich, nuanced form of organizational functioning that has significant ecological considerations and implica-

tions. Moreover, virtual work is complicated by the constant attention to tasks, social concerns, informal and formal communication, emotional labor (as well as psychological and physical), impression management, face-saving techniques, surveillance, mentoring, decision-making, among other considerations. Long's (2010) definition of virtual work lays the methodological foundation to facilitate further exploration of virtual work from a dramaturgical perspective. Virtual work is primarily a performance bounded within the organizational context.

PHILOSOPHICAL AND THEORETICAL BACKGROUND OF DRAMATURGY

Humans are equipped with the ability to choose their actions (German, 2009; Goffman, 1959). Goffman finds that it is these interactions that can be read and understood through the lens of a staged play. At the core of these interactions are human agency and this agency leads scholars to consider everyday human interaction as comparable to a drama or performance (Burke, 1952; German, 2009; Goffman, 1959; Mitchell, 1978; Panteli & Duncan, 2004). The theoretical framework of dramaturgy centralizes the persuasive effect of selective staging of symbols and symbolic interaction (Manning, 1996). This framework is found across disciplines such as sociology, literary criticism, political science, rhetoric, organizational communication, philosophy, as well as interpersonal communication (German, 2009). Dramaturgy attempts to describe human interaction (Mitchell, 1978), while also acknowledging the world as "a symbolic creation of drama in which language is strategic and motivated by response to specific situations" (German, 2009, p. 1). Gardner (1992) envisions life as a drama wherein people carry out the role of actors on a stage. These staged dramas dictate how individuals, groups, and organizations carry out their behavior through acting, which serves as a mechanism to influence and persuade (German, 2009; Goffman, 1959).

Goffman used the dramaturgy metaphor as a way to clarify human action by viewing people as though they were actors (Mitchell, 1978). His view, unlike Burke (1952), is not a literal translation of drama. This social behavior consists of an over-arching performance between actors (Goffman, 1959; Mitchell, 1978; Panteli &Duncan, 2004) who purposefully aim to mold expressions they give and give off so the impression is in line with who they claim to be (Clark & Mangham, 2004; Goffman, 1959; Mitchell, 1978; Whittle & Mueller, 2009). Face management is constantly being negotiated (Metts, 2009) because as Goffman asserts, "performers can stop giving expressions, but cannot stop giving them off" (Goffman, 1959, p. 108). These performances occur in different settings specialized for their intended audience in order to shape the situational definition (Panteli & Duncan, 2004).

Components of Dramaturgical Approach

Like a theatrical play, dramaturgy consists of actors, audience, stage, scripts, situation, as well as an overall performance. An *actor* is an individual who carries out acts and actions in situations in order to persuade their audience to form a certain impression of him or herself. The *audience,* the intended target of the performance, through their response and point of view contribute to defining the interaction (Goffman, 1959; Panteli & Duncan, 2004). Clark and Mangham (2004) and Whittle and Mueller (2009) describe the stages as both front and back stage. Back stage is considered the behind the scenes, unpolished, and practice for the front stage self. The front stage is the actual performance with other actors and audience members. The back stage grants the actor a place for them to be "off-stage" and expose their true selves (Lin, Wu, & Hsieh, 2009).

In preparation for the front stage, actors often correct mistakes (Goffman, 1959) and may even perform illegitimate tasks while, "not on" (Mitchell, 1978) stage or in the back stage. These tasks may include working through various scenarios and reactions to varying degrees of the truth. A critical dimension of the back stage is privacy (Whittle & Mueller, 2009). For example, one's home or an apartment can be viewed as the back stage. It is the behind the scenes region in which the actor dresses the part, can rehearse lines, and gather props all in preparation for their front stage interaction with another person or an audience of people (Goffman, 1959; Metts, 2009).

Physical environments in which the front and back stage behaviors take place constitute the *setting* (Kivisto & Pittman, 2007). A home setting according to Goffman (1959) contains both the front stage living room area as well as the back stage bathroom quarters. Specified locations within these settings and their accompanying props foster public and private interactions (Goffman, 2007). Props such as a couch or a locking mechanism aid in the distinction between the front and back stage regions (Goffman, 1959).

The refined public performance is considered the "front stage" display or presentation (Goffman, 1959; Whittle & Mueller, 2009). The front stage is the space where the actor is in the presence of others who have the ability to judge whether a performance is authentic (Mitchell, 1978). The setting in the front stage includes the environmental features of the location in which the performance takes place (Goffman, 1959), such as the workplace, on a date, in other public venues. Goffman describes the personal front of the front stage as the expressive equipment purposefully or unintentionally exhibited by an actor while performing. In other words, the personal front is a combination of individual appearance as well as the manner in which the actor approaches the interaction. These items include individual characteristics that come attached to the actor. They include, but are not limited to, age, rank, or race, among other demographic markers.

Dramaturgical concepts have often been applied to a number of workplaces (Gardner, 1992; Goffman, 1959; Kivisto & Pittman, 2007; Panteli & Duncan, 2007; Whittle & Mueller, 2009). A hospital, office, retail store, or car dealership are examples of work settings where dramaturgical performances has been studied (Kivisto & Pittman, 2007, Meyrowitz, 1990). The public or private exchanges employees engage in define what is front stage and what is back stage behavior (Kivisto & Pittman, 2007). Whittle and Mueller's (2009) application of dramaturgy to work environments considers the back stage region as interactions that occur between employees when clients are not present. It is the sharing of private information between team members that deems it back stage interaction (Panteli & Duncan, 2007). Meyrowitz (1990) brings attention to a case wherein a doctor utilizes that space to complain about work stress to her colleagues outside of the view of the general public.

Another component of dramaturgy is the *script*. Scripts are reference points for how an actor should guide their behavior. Norms, rituals, as well as expected conduct in social settings, guide scripted behavior in actors (Lin, Wu, & Hsieh, 2009). In the workplace, a script can be a job contract that defines the socially acceptable work duties that an employee is to follow (Panteli & Duncan, 2004).

The next aspect of dramaturgy is *performance*. A performance consists of an actor's speech, paralanguage, artifacts and behaviors (Gardner, 1992). Goffman (1959) emphasizes the importance of upholding a balanced front stage performance. Manner, settings, and appearances must align to make a performance appear legitimate (Goffman, 1959; Mitchell, 1978). Inconsistencies in performance call the actor's credibility into question. The expectation of a judge is to dress in a black robe and sit high on the bench, (Meyrowitz, 1990) whereas a judge sitting on the floor wearing a red robe would make their performance questionable.

The next aspect of dramaturgy is the *situation*. The situation is the meeting space between the actor and audience (Goffman, 1963). For Goffman (1963) there are spatial and temporal dimension to situations. First, participants must be in the physical presence of one another. Second, the performance begins with two or more people and ends the instant one leaves the situation. Traditionally, dramaturgy only considers face-to-face interaction as the sole setting for a performance dates the theory to some extent. However, extending this approach to the virtual environment allows for contemporary application of dramaturgy to virtual work research.

Meyrowitz (1990) broadened dramaturgy to including communications media such as the radio, telephone, television, as well as the computer. These media provides an audience presence beyond the typical face-to-face interaction. These mediums extend the performer's behavior to that of virtual behavior. This is viewed as virtuality.

Pantelli and Duncan (2004) describe virtuality as a host of performances. In the electronic domain the setting becomes an altered space. According to Meyrowitz (1990), mediated presence is a prioritized setting (Meyrowitz, 1990). For example a phone call conversation may make the participants feel closer to one another than the people sharing their actual physical space. Meyrowitz suggests that there is a blurring of the front and back stage areas in mediated interactions. He terms this blurring the "middle region" (Meyrowitz, 1990, p. 92). The middle region has become all the more apparent in the current technological environment. The application of dramaturgy in virtual environments creates a space for social science disciplines to understand the many facets of computer mediated human interaction.

Virtual Work and Dramaturgy Research

Uses of Goffman's (1959) presentation of self concepts such as dramaturgy, impression management, and face-work have been applied to organizational and management studies research (Mangham & Overington, 1987; Rosenfeld, et al., 1995; Gardner & Avolio, 1998; as cited in Whittle & Mueller, 2009). Panteli and Duncan (2004) acknowledge dramaturgy is a salient way to make sense of face-to-face and virtual organizational practices. Dramaturgy in organizations involves how a person presents themselves, their activity, as well as their motives to others (Goffman, 1959). Presentation of self for organizational members is important in organizations because it involves a number of key dramaturgical components in a richly nuanced atmosphere of goal motivated tasks affecting informal and formal communication.

In the workplace, an organizational member performs based on scripts guided by member norms, behaviors and work culture (Goffman, 1959; Panteli & Duncan, 2004). Mitchell (1978) in an earlier writing believes that a consistent bureaucratic approach should be considered to provide a consistent performance each time. However, as we move from a face-to-face communal organizational setting to a more virtual work-oriented community, more dramaturgical research needs to be done in order to understand situational and performance changes that accompany virtual work.

Virtual dramaturgy is defined and highlighted in a few studies. Whittle and Mueller (2009) applied the dramaturgical perspective to telework and working from home. Panteli and Duncan (2004) observed trust in temporary virtual work teams using dramaturgy. The virtual space is defined as a site for dramaturgical research, "virtuality takes the role of theatre that hosts the performance. It is the place where various "plays" commence where actors engage in performances, different roles, and different scripts" (Panteli & Duncan, 2004, p. 428). Dramaturgy in virtual work also offers opportunities for self-presentation and impression management (Panteli & Duncan, 2004).

Several questions arise when considering virtual work dramaturgy as an approach. What is considered the front stage in Computer Mediated Communication (CMC)? Does the asynchronous nature of virtual work affect an actor's performance in managing impressions? Do scripts for face-to-face organizations apply to CMC work places? Do the same dramaturgical organizational issues such as an employee's investment in managing the perception of their role overshadow the actual work they put forth?

VIRTUAL WORK DRAMATURGICAL METHODOLOGY

It is clear that the electronic connection associated with virtual work enables us to re-imagine how work is constructed, executed, interpreted, and communicated. This new electronic work arrangement lays the methodological foundation for researchers to rethink how traditional methods of assessing employee well being and organizational effectiveness is conducted. Old ways of studying employees and the work environment should be updated to reflect the new virtual workplace. Dramaturgy is one methodological approach that has been and should continue to be translated in this new sphere.

Virtual work dramaturgy extends the work of traditional dramaturgy to the virtual work environment. Goffman's (1956) original dramaturgy concepts of actors, audience, stage, scripts, situation, and overall performance can be applied to the virtual work environment.

Although the core components of traditional dramaturgy can be applied to virtual work dramaturgy, the electronic environment may actually change the way people perform and do their work. Due to the electronic nature of virtual work, there are innate risks associated with performance behaviors. For example, performances in the virtual work environment are more easily archived, documented, substantiated, reinforced, replicated, and interrogated than in the traditional face-to-face work environment. The denial face-to-face performance, especially when between only two actors is eliminated from virtual work because there is a real-time and historical electronic trail documenting every act performed online. This has serious implications for the actors and their performance. The situation and setting is of great importance as it is not perishable like traditional face-to-face interactions.

Increased surveillance associated with working virtually also has a significant influence on employee performance (Long, Goodman, & Clow, 2010). Current communication technologies have the potential to monitor every keystroke, visited websites, time on tasks, phone calls and emails originating from an employee. This increased surveillance may change the way people work and how they communicate and perform their work with others within and beyond the organization. Virtual work, in its entirety, becomes the performance and situation for examining virtual work behavior and the employees, management and other organizational members (e.g. vendors, board members, customers).

POTENTIAL RESEARCH STUDIES

As mentioned earlier, Goffman's dramaturgy originates from social interactionism thought, which believes that people have the ability to shape their reality. Dramaturgical methodology analyzes interaction through a theatrical lens. Thus researchers decode situations in terms analogous to theater such as actor, script, stage, performance, and audience in order to understand the motivations behind human behavior.

When applying the dramaturgical framework to a study there are a multiple approaches a researcher can take to decipher interaction. A micro lens observes internal and external motivations for an actor's behavior. A macro lens might approach an institution to understand how actors, audiences, and scripts shape their structure. When trying to layout groundwork for a relatively new application

of dramaturgy it is best to begin with definitions of the theatrical terms in regards to the study.

We suggest the study of virtual work through a dramaturgical lens by examining the usage of various social media (i.e. Linkedin, Facebook, Twitter, Foursquare, etc.). Social media is the ideal avenue for the study of intertwined concepts of virtual work and dramaturgy for a number of reasons. First, social media is growing in popularity and in usage by people of all ages and professions. Second, social media is a logical playground for the observation of virtual work, professionally and socially. Lastly, social media is often used in professional interactions for both private and/or personal purposes. Thus we feel that the social media platform allows researchers an opportunity to examine the performances of organizational actors. For example, a study could examine the various scripts that emerge on the professional pages versus the private pages of organizational members. How are these people talking? What language do they use on each page? Who are their audiences?

A researcher may conduct observations and analyses of social media pages to determine the commonality of persons having both professional and private pages and the differences between both pages. That may include a focus on a particular organization and its members who use social media. Observations may also made to determine whether a member has a Linkedin account (social medium specifically created to network professionally) for professional reasons, and also having a Facebook or Twitter account for personal reasons.

Other qualitative methods may include electronic focus groups, which may be conducted with individuals, who participate in the front and back stages of the social media world, to talk about their reasoning for doing so, specific experiences and personal feelings. Focus groups typically contain around five to eight participants and one moderator. The format involves the moderator asking a series of questions (open-ended) to the participants and leaving the discussion up to those who choose to discuss. From there, the moderator takes the data and analyzes it for specific themes and patterns which may lend to the study's research questions or hypotheses directly. Similarly, in-depth interviews can be conducted to retrieve detailed accounts from participants on their experiences with partaking in the front and back stages of social media.

The options to study virtual work through a dramaturgical lens are extensive. We offer potential research questions as viable considerations for dramaturgical research using contemporary communication technologies. As indicated earlier, there are studies that have effectively used the dramaturgical approach to better understand work in the virtual environment.

RECOMMENDATIONS

To study virtual work through a dramaturgical lens, it is important to define and relate as many elements of dramaturgy as possible to the virtual work arena. Studies should include involvement and analysis of elements such as: actors, audience, stages, scripts, etc. All of these elements are applicable and equally as important to the study of virtual work and virtual communication.

Consequently, virtual work, mainly electronic communication, centralizes written communication, with the exception of videoconferencing and telephone conferencing, which limits the ability of paralanguage. Emotional cues, voice inflection, tone, and nonverbal signals work simultaneously for the actor in a physical environment in persuading his or her audience. Examining the techniques actors use in their virtual performance and the audience reaction to this performance is an interesting area of for future inquiry.

Since virtual work takes place in the electronic domain, understanding leadership approaches and organizational members' various personality types is a salient dramaturgical study. Leadership

development using dramaturgical analysis is of interest. In this new era, leaders may develop who would not otherwise because they flourish in a computer-mediated environment. The actor's performance in face-to-face interactions could potentially counter their front stage performance in the virtual workplace.

Additionally, it may be beneficial to compare dramaturgical elements in face-to-face work interactions to virtual work interactions. This comparative approach could determine the major differences and similarities between the two environments.

Finally, future studies could examine the communication patterns of effective and ineffective employee-management communication. Virtual work has the potential to be a high stakes work environment, due to the increased surveillance, distance from organizational campus and the boundary-flexible infrastructure. This infrastructure may privilege some types of organizational members and disadvantaging others. A closer look at the communication strategies of successful versus unsuccessful interactions is an ideal virtual work dramaturgical study.

CHALLENGES WITH VIRTUAL WORK DRAMATURGY

As with any method, there are particular challenges or limitations associated with applying dramaturgy to virtual work research. Given the nature of traditional dramaturgy, it particularly lends itself well to qualitative approaches. Dramaturgy seeks to describe, rather than predict human behavior. Although social patterns are important, generalizability of the results of a dramaturgical study may be difficult to achieve. This is due in part to the typically small sample size that does not claim to represent the general population. For example, an analysis of virtual workers theatrical back stage performance is more indicative of that particular set of actors under investigation, rather than the entire population of virtual workers. Circumstances, settings, situation, scripts and actors are contingent on the sample and claims beyond that sample should be met with a great deal of caution.

Another concern is the validity of the interpretations. The researcher is the primary analytic tool and their interpretation of the performance is subjective, rather than objective, in many cases. This certainly is the case with virtual work dramaturgy. Although there is a significant amount of data to observe, catalog and analyze in a virtual work environment, due to the archival and storage nature of digital work, it is still a matter of researcher bias and subjectivity that is central to the tenants of dramaturgy. This research is from a particular point of view and while this approach is celebrated in some circles, it is still considered a scholarly limitation.

Finally, but not exhaustively, the authenticity of the performances is a concern for researchers. This should be considered a limitation. As individuals work more closely with technology, there is an inherent implicit social contract that is emerging that suggests that if one works with technology, they are giving up a great deal of privacy and anonymity. Technology, as mentioned throughout, has the potential for increased surveillance, archiving information, time stamps, keystroke monitoring, along with a number of other technological advancements. This new norm of being constantly under surveillance and monitored may alter an individual's behavior in a number of ways. Individuals may not express how they genuinely feel about work issues and they may significantly alter their virtual performance to fit an acceptable norm. This may prevent the researcher from understanding the individual nuances of organizational members' performance in the virtual environment. This creates a false marker of human behavior in virtual work.

CONCLUSION

Applying dramaturgical principles to virtual work is an important methodological tool for researchers across various disciplines and industries. Work performance is more than just a bottom line productivity accounting; it is the micro, macro and overall performances of organizational members that constitute work. The virtual work environment is fertile ground for integrating innovative approaches to better understand individuals' engagement with dislocated work arrangements. By bringing sharp focus to dramaturgy as an important and critical research approach to be used to make sense of the lived experiences of virtual organizational members, the role of communication and performance in understanding engagement in this new work space is a salient feature of organizational life.

REFERENCES

Burke, K. (1952). A dramatistic view of the origins of language. *The Quarterly Journal of Speech*, *38*, 251–264. doi:10.1080/00335635209381782

Clark, T., & Mangham, I. (2004). From dramaturgy to theatre as technology: The case of corporate theatre. *Journal of Management Studies*, *41*(1), 37–59. doi:10.1111/j.1467-6486.2004.00420.x

Gardner, W. I. (1992). Lessons in organizational dramaturgy: The art of impression management. *Organizational Dynamics*, *1*, 33–47. doi:10.1016/0090-2616(92)90084-Z

Gardner, W. L., & Avolio, B. J. (1998). The charismatic relationship: A dramaturgical perspective. *Academy of Management Review*, *23*(1), 32–58.

German, K. M. (2009). Dramatism and dramatistic pentad. *Encyclopedia of Communication Theory*. Thousand Oaks, CA: Sage Publications. Retrieved from http:sage-ereference.com/communicationtheory/Article_n119.html.

Goffman, E. (1959). *The presentation of self in everyday life*. New York, NY: Doubleday.

Goffman, E. (1963). *Behavior in public places*. New York, NY: The Free Press.

Kivisto, P., & Pittman, D. (2007). Goffman's dramaturgical sociology: Personal sales in a commodified world. In Kivisto, P. (Ed.), *Illuminating Social Life* (pp. 271–290). Thousand Oaks, CA: Pine Forge Press.

Lin, C., Wu, H., & Hsieh, C. (2009). A world of paradox: Is that the public statement or private talk in virtual community. *Pacific Asia Conference on Information Systems*. Retrieved from http://aisel.aisnet.org/pacis2009/5.

Long, S. D. (Ed.). (2010). *Communication, relationships and practices in virtual work*. Hershey, PA: IGI Global. doi:10.4018/978-1-61520-979-8

Long, S. D., Goodman, R. A., & Clow, C. (2010). The electronic panopticon: Organizational surveillance in virtual work. In Long, S. D. (Ed.), *Communication, Relationships and Practices in Virtual Work*. Hershey, PA: IGI Global. doi:10.4018/978-1-61520-979-8.ch005

Mangham, I. L., & Overington, M. A. (1987). *Organizations as theatre: A social psychology of dramatic appearances*. Chichester, UK: John Wiley & Sons.

Manning, P. K. (1996). Dramaturgy, politics and the axial media event. *The Sociological Quarterly*, *24*(2), 261–278. doi:10.1111/j.1533-8525.1996.tb01749.x

Metts, S. (2009). Impression management. *Encyclopedia of Communication Theory*. Thousand Oaks, CA: Sage Publications. Retrieved from http://sage-ereference.com/communicationtheory/Article_n189.html.

Meyrowitz, J. (1990). Redefining the situation: Extending dramaturgy into a theory of social change and media effects. In Riggins, S. H. (Ed.), *Beyond Goffman: Studies on Communication, Institution and Social Interaction* (pp. 65–97). Berlin, Germany: Mouton de Gruyter. doi:10.1515/9783110847291.65

Mitchell, J. (1978). *Social exchange, dramaturgy and ethnomethodology*. Oxford, UK: Elsevier.

Panteli, N., & Duncan, E. (2004). Trust and temporary virtual teams: Alternative explanations and dramaturgical relationships. *Information Technology & People*, *17*(4), 423–441. doi:10.1108/09593840410570276

Rosenfeld, P. R., Giacalone, R. A., & Riordan, C. A. (1995). *Impression management in organizations: Theory, measurement, and practice*. New York, NY: Routledge.

Whittle, A., & Mueller, F. (2009). I could be dead for two weeks and my boss would never know: Telework and the politics of representation. *New Technology, Work and Employment*, *24*(2), 131–143. doi:10.1111/j.1468-005X.2009.00224.x

KEY TERMS AND DEFINITIONS

Dramaturgy: Dramaturgy is a sociological approach with roots in symbolic interactionism that accounts for social interactions in everyday life.

Social Interactionism: A theoretical perspective that centralizes social processes from human interaction. It is the study of individuals and how they act within society.

Virtual Work: The value-laden, politically rich, nuanced form of electronic organizational functioning that has significant ecological considerations and implications.

Compilation of References

Adams, D. A., Nelson, R. R., & Todd, P. A. (1992). Perceived usefulness, ease of use, and usage on information technology: A replication. *Management Information Systems Quarterly, 16*(2), 227–250. doi:10.2307/249577

Agypt, B., & Rubin, B. A. (2011). Time in the new economy: The impact of the interaction of individual and structural temporalities on job satisfaction. *Journal of Management Studies, 49*(2), 403–428. doi:10.1111/j.1467-6486.2011.01021.x

Agypt, B., Rubin, B. A., & Spivack, A. J. (2012). Thinking outside the clocks: The effect of layered-task time on the creative climate of meetings. *The Journal of Creative Behavior, 42*, 750–757.

Al-Ajeeli, A., & Al-Bastaki, Y. (2011). Handbook of research on e-services in the public sector: E-government strategies and advancements. *IGI Global.* Retrieved from http://www.igi-global.com/book/handbook-research-services-public-sector/37290.

Albert, S., & Bradley, K. (1997). *Managing knowledge.* Cambridge, MA: Cambridge University. doi:10.1017/CBO9780511582486

Alnuaim, O. A., Robert, L. P. Jr, & Maruping, L. M. (2010). Team size, dispersion, and social loafing in technology-supported teams: A perspective on the theory of moral disengagement. *Journal of Management Information Systems, 27*(1), 203–230. doi:10.2753/MIS0742-1222270109

Alvesson, M., & Karreman, D. (2000). Varieties of discourse: On the study of organizations through discourse analysis. *Human Relations, 53*, 1125–1149. doi:10.1177/0018726700539002

Amabile, T. M., Conti, R., Coon, H., Lazenby, J., & Herron, M. (1996). Assessing the work environment for creativity. *Academy of Management Journal, 39*(5), 1154–1184. doi:10.2307/256995

Amabile, T. M., & Gryskiewicz, N. (1989). The creative environment scales: The work environment inventory. *Creativity Research Journal, 2*, 231–254. doi:10.1080/10400418909534321

Amant, K. S. (2002). When cultures and computer collide: Rethinking computer-mediated communication according to international and intercultural communication expectations. *Journal of Business and Technical Communication, 16*(2), 196–214. doi:10.1177/1050651902016002003

Andriopoulos, C. (2001). Determinants of organisational creativity: A literature review. *Management Decision, 39*(10), 834–840. doi:10.1108/00251740110402328

Applebaum, E., & Batt, R. (1994). *The new American workplace: Transforming work systems in the United States.* Ithaca, NY: ILR Press.

Arches, J. (1991). Social structure, burnout, and job satisfaction. *Social Work, 36*(3), 202–206.

Argyris, C., Putnam, R., & Smith, D. M. (1985). *Action science: Concepts, methods, and skills for research and intervention.* Hoboken, NJ: Jossey-Bass.

Argyris, C., & Schon, D. A. (1991). Participatory action research and action science compared. In Whyte, W. F. (Ed.), *Participatory Action Research* (pp. 85–98). London, UK: Sage. doi:10.1177/0002764289032005008

Aronson, E., Wilson, T. D., & Brewer, M. B. (1998). Experimentation in social psychology. In Gilbert, D. T., Fiske, S. T., & Lindzey, G. (Eds.), *The Handbook of Social Psychology* (Vol. 1, pp. 99–142). Boston, MA: McGraw-Hill.

Ashcraft, K. L. (2000). Empowering 'professional' relationships: Organizational communication meets feminist practice. *Management Communication Quarterly, 13,* 347–393. doi:10.1177/0893318900133001

Ashforth, B. E., Kreiner, G. E., & Fugate, M. (2000). All in a day's work: Boundaries and micro role transitions. *Academy of Management Review, 25,* 472–491.

Atkinson, P., Coffey, A. J., Delamont, S., Lofland, J., & Loftland, L. H. (Eds.). (2007). *The Sage handbook of ethnography*. Los Angeles, CA: Sage.

Atkinson, P., Coffey, A., Delamont, S., Lofland, J., & Lofland, L. (2001). Editorial introduction. In Atkinson, P., Coffey, A., Delamont, S., Lofland, J., & Lofland, L. (Eds.), *Handbook of Ethnography*. Thousand Oaks, CA: Sage Publishing.

Auerbach, C. F., & Silverstein, L. B. (2003). *Qualitative data: An introduction to coding and analysis*. New York, NY: New York University Press.

Baan, A., & Maznevski, M. (2008). Training for virtual collaboration: Beyond technical competencies. In Nemiro, J., Beyerlein, M., Bradley, L., & Beyerlein, S. (Eds.), *The Handbook of High Performance Virtual Teams: A Toolkit for Collaborating across Boundaries* (pp. 345–365). San Francisco, CA: Jossey-Bass.

Bailey, D. E., & Kurland, N. B. (2002). A review of telework research: Findings, new directions, and lessons for the study of modern work. *Journal of Organizational Behavior, 23,* 383–400. doi:10.1002/job.144

Bainbridge, W. S. (2007). The scientific research potential of virtual worlds. *Science, 317,* 472–476. doi:10.1126/science.1146930

Baker, C., Wuest, J., & Noeranger Stern, P. (1992). Method slurring: The grounded theory/phenomenological example. *Journal of Advanced Nursing, 17,* 1355–1360. doi:10.1111/j.1365-2648.1992.tb01859.x

Baldry, C., & Hallier, J. (2010). Welcome to the house of fun: Work space and social identity. *Economic and Industrial Democracy, 31,* 150–172. doi:10.1177/0143831X09351215

Ballard, D. I., & Gossett, L. M. (2007). Alternative times: Temporal perceptions, processes, and practices defining the nonstandard work relationship. In Beck, C. S. (Ed.), *Communication Yearbook 31* (pp. 275–320). New York, NY: Routledge.

Bandura, A. (1977). *Social learning theory*. Englewood Cliffs, NJ: Prentice-Hall.

Bandura, A. (1997). *Self-efficacy: The exercise of control*. New York, NY: Freeman.

Bandura, A. (2001). Social cognitive theory: An agentic perspective. *Annual Review of Psychology, 52,* 1–26. doi:10.1146/annurev.psych.52.1.1

Bandura, A. (2006). On integrating social cognitive and social diffusion theories. In Singhal, A., & Dearing, J. (Eds.), *Communication of Innovations: A Journey with Ev Rogers* (pp. 111–135). Beverly Hills, CA: Sage.

Barile, A. L., & Durso, F. T. (2002). Computer-mediated communications in collaborative writing. *Computers in Human Behavior, 18*(2), 173–190. doi:10.1016/S0747-5632(01)00040-1

Bashi, V. (2004). Improving qualitative research proposal evaluation. In C. C. Ragain, J. Nagel, & P. White (Eds.), *Workshop on Scientific Foundations of Qualitative Research,* (pp. 39-43). Washington, DC: National Science Foundation.

Basu, A., & Dutta, M. (2008). The relationship between health information seeking and community participation: The roles of health information orientation and efficacy. *Health Communication, 23,* 70–79. doi:10.1080/10410230701807121

Baxter, L. A., & Babbie, E. (2003). *The basics of communication research*. Boston, MA: Wadsworth.

Baym, N. K. (1995). From practice to culture on usenet. In Star, S. L. (Ed.), *The Cultures of Computing*. Cambridge, UK: Blackwell Publishers.

Bazerman, C., & Prior, P. (2004). *What writing does and how it does it: An introduction to analyzing texts and textual practices*. Mahwah, NJ: Lawrence Earlbaum.

Becker-Beck, U., Wintermantel, M., & Borg, A. (2005). Principles of regulating interaction in teams practicing face-to-face communication versus teams practicing computer-mediated communication. *Small Group Research, 36*(4), 499–536. doi:10.1177/1046496405277182

Belanger, F., & Watson-Manheim, M. B. (2006). Virtual teams and multiple media: Structuring media use to attain strategic goals. *Group Decision and Negotiation, 15*, 299–321. doi:10.1007/s10726-006-9044-8

Benoliel, J. Q. (1996). Grounded theory and nursing knowledge. *Qualitative Health Research, 6*, 406–428. doi:10.1177/104973239600600308

Berger, P., & Luckman, T. (1967). *The social construction of reality: A treatise in the sociology of knowledge and commitment in American life*. Garden City, NY: Anchor.

Berry, G. R. (2011). A cross-disciplinary literature review: Examining trust on virtual teams. *Performance Improvement Quarterly, 24*(3), 9–28. doi:10.1002/piq.20116

Berthon, P., & Davies, T. (1999). Going with the flow: Websites and customer involvement. *Internet Research: Electronic Networking Applications and Policy, 9*(2), 109–116. doi:10.1108/10662249910264873

Berthon, P., Pitt, L., & Watson, R. T. (1996). The world wide web as an advertising medium: Toward an understanding of conversion efficiency. *Journal of Advertising Research, 36*(1), 43–45.

Beyer, J. M., & Hannah, D. R. (2002). Building on the past: Enacting established personal identities in a new work setting. *Organization Science, 13*, 636–652. doi:10.1287/orsc.13.6.636.495

Bhabha, H. K. (1994). *The location of culture*. London, UK: Routledge.

Bhabha, H. K. (1996). Culture's in-between. In Hall, S., & du Gay, P. (Eds.), *Questions of Cultural Identity* (pp. 53–60). London, UK: Sage Publications.

Birks, M., & Mills, J. (2011). *Grounded theory: A practical guide*. Thousand Oaks, CA: Sage.

Bjørn, P., & Ngwenyama, O. (2009). Virtual team collaboration: Building shared meaning, resolving breakdowns and creating translucence. *Information Systems Journal, 19*(3), 227–253. doi:10.1111/j.1365-2575.2007.00281.x

Blair, J., Menon, G., & Bickart, B. (1991). Measurement effects in self vs. proxy responses to survey questions: An information-processing perspective. In Biemer, P. P., Groves, R. M., Lyberg, L. E., Mathiowetz, N. A., & Sudman, S. (Eds.), *Measurement Errors in Surveys* (pp. 145–166). New York, NY: Wiley. doi:10.1002/9781118150382.ch9

Bochner, A. P., & Ellis, E. M. (1996). Taking ethnography into the twenty-first century. *Journal of Contemporary Ethnography, 25*, 3–5. doi:10.1177/089124196025001001

Borg, I., Braun, M., & Baumgartner, M. K. (2008). Attitudes of demographic item non-respondents in employee surveys. *International Journal of Manpower, 29*, 146–160. doi:10.1108/01437720810872703

Boswell, W. R., & Buchanan, J. B. (2007). The use of communication technologies after hours: The role of work attitudes and work-life conflict. *Journal of Management, 33*, 592–610. doi:10.1177/0149206307302552

Bovée, C. L., Thill, J. V., & Schatzman, B. E. (2003). *Business communication today* (7th ed.). Upper Saddle River, NJ: Prentice Hall.

Bowen, G. A. (2005). Preparing a qualitative research-based dissertation: Lessons learned. *The Qualitative Report, 10*, 208-222.

Brancheau, J. C., & Wetherbe, J. C. (1990). The adoption of spreadsheet technology: Testing innovation diffusion theory in the context of end-user computing. *Information Systems Research, 1*(2), 115–143. doi:10.1287/isre.1.2.115

Broadfoot, K. J., Carlone, D., Medved, C. E., Aakhus, M., Gabor, E., & Taylor, K. (2008). Meaningful work and organizational communication: Questioning boundaries, positionalities, and engagements. *Management Communication Quarterly, 22*, 152–161. doi:10.1177/0893318908318267

Broadfoot, K. J., Munshi, D., & Nelson-Marsh, N. (2010). COMMUNEcation: A rhizomatic tale of participatory technology, postcoloniality and professional community. *New Media & Society, 12,* 797–812. doi:10.1177/1461444809348880

Broschak, J. P., Davis-Blake, A., & Block, E. (2008). Nonstatndard, not substandard: The relationship among work arrangements, work attitudes, and job performance. *Work and Occupations, 35*(1), 3–43. doi:10.1177/0730888407309604

Brown, L. (2009). *European agriculture: Farming in Europe from 1500 to 1815.* Retrieved from http://www.suite101.com/content/european-agriculture-a114546.

Browning, L. D. (1978). A grounded organizational communication theory derived from qualitative data. *Communication Monographs, 45*(2), 93–109. doi:10.1080/03637757809375957

Brown, R. H. (1977). *A poetic for sociology.* Cambridge, UK: Cambridge University Press.

Brummett, B. (2008). *A rhetoric of style.* Carbondale, IL: Southern Illinois University Press.

Buchanan, D. G., Miller, F. G., & Wallerstein, N. (2007). Ethical issues in community-based participatory research: Balancing rigorous research with community participation in community intervention studies. *Progress in Community Health Partnerships: Research, Education, and Action, 1,* 153–160. doi:10.1353/cpr.2007.0006

Bulger, C. A., Matthews, R. A., & Hoffman, M. E. (2007). Work and personal life boundary management: Boundary strength, work/personal life balance, and the segmentation-integration continuum. *Journal of Occupational Health Psychology, 12,* 365–375. doi:10.1037/1076-8998.12.4.365

Burke, K. (1952). A dramatistic view of the origins of language. *The Quarterly Journal of Speech, 38,* 251–264. doi:10.1080/00335635209381782

Burleson, B. R., Albrecht, T. L., & Satason, I. G. (Eds.). (1994). *Communication of social support.* Newbury Park, CA: Sage.

Cale, E. J. Jr, & Eriksen, S. E. (1994). Factors affecting the implementation outcome of a mainframe software package: A longitudinal approach. *Information & Management, 26,* 165–175. doi:10.1016/0378-7206(94)90040-X

Callon, M. (1986). Some elements of a sociology of translation: Domestication of the scallops and the fisherman of Saint Brieuc Bay. In Law, J. (Ed.), *Power, Action, and Belief* (pp. 196–223). London, UK: Routledge.

Cameron, A. F., & Webster, J. (2005). Unintended consequences of emerging technologies: Instant messaging in the workplace. *Computers in Human Behavior, 21*(1), 85–103. doi:10.1016/j.chb.2003.12.001

Cappelli, P., Bassi, L., Katz, H., Knoke, D., Osterman, P., & Useem, M. (1997). *Change at work.* Oxford, UK: Oxford University Press.

Carder, B. (2003). A survey-based system for safety measurement and improvement. *Journal of Safety Research, 34*(2), 157–163. doi:10.1016/S0022-4375(03)00007-0

CDW. (2008). *Telework report: Feds stuck in second gear: Private sector puts the pedal to the metal.* Retrieved from http://webobjects.cdw.com/webobjects/media/pdf/2008-CDW-Telework-Report.pdf.

Center for Democracy and Technology & Earnest and Young. (2008). *Risk at home: Privacy and security risks in telecommuting.* Retrieved from http://www.cdt.org/privacy/20080729_riskathome.pdf.

Charmaz, K. (2006). *Constructing grounded theory: A practical guide through qualitative analysis.* London, UK: Sage.

Charmaz, K. (2009). Shifting the grounds: Constructivist grounded theory methods. In Morce, J., Stern, P. J., Corbin, J., Bowers, B. K., Charmaz, K., & Clarke, A. (Eds.), *Developing Grounded Theory: The Second Generation.* Walnut Creek, CA: Left Coast Press.

Chea, S., & Lou, M. (2008). Post-adoption behaviors of e-service customers: The interplay of cognition and emotion. *International Journal of Electronic Commerce, 12*(3), 29–56. doi:10.2753/JEC1086-4415120303

Chellappan, C. (2008). *E-services: The need for higher levels of trust by populace.* Chennai, India: Anna University.

Chen, C. C., & Chiu, S. F. (2009). The mediating role of job involvement in the relationship between job characteristics and organizational citizenship behavior. *The Journal of Social Psychology, 149*(4), 474–494. doi:10.3200/SOCP.149.4.474-494

Chen, C.-J., & Hung, S.-H. (2010). To give or to receive? Factors influencing members' knowledge sharing and community promotion in professional virtual communities. *Information & Management, 47*(4), 226–236. doi:10.1016/j.im.2010.03.001

Cheney, G., Zorn, T. E., Planalp, S., & Lair, D. J. (2008). Meaningful work and personal/social well-being: Organizational communication engages the meanings of work. *Communication Yearbook, 32*, 137–185.

Chin, W. W., & Gopal, A. (1993). An examination of the relative importance of four belief constructs on the GSS adoption decision: A comparison of four methods. In *Proceedings 26th Hawaii International Conference on Systems Science*. Hawaii: HICSS.

Chin, W. W., & Todd, P. A. (1995). On the use, usefulness, and ease of use of structural equation modelling in MIS research: A note of caution. *Management Information Systems Quarterly, 19*(2), 237–246. doi:10.2307/249690

Clarke, A. E. (2005). *Situational analysis: Grounded theory mapping after the postmodern turn*. Thousand Oaks, CA: Sage.

Clark, T., & Mangham, I. (2004). From dramaturgy to theatre as technology: The case of corporate theatre. *Journal of Management Studies, 41*(1), 37–59. doi:10.1111/j.1467-6486.2004.00420.x

Clear, T., & MacDonell, S. G. (2011). Understanding technology use in global virtual teams: Research methodologies and methods. *Information and Software Technology, 53*, 994–1011. doi:10.1016/j.infsof.2011.01.011

Clifford, J., & Marcus, G. E. (1986). *Writing culture: The poetics and politics of ethnography*. Berkeley, CA: University of California Press.

Cogburn, D. L., Finnerup Johnsen, J., & Bhattacharyya, S. (2008). Distributed deliberative citizens: Exploring the impact of cyberinfrastructure on transnational civil society participation in global ICT policy processes. *International Journal of Media and Cultural Politics, 4*, 27–49. doi:10.1386/macp.4.1.27_1

Cohen, A. (1992). Antecedents of organizational commitment across occupational groups: A meta-analysis. *Journal of Organizational Behavior, 13*(6), 539–558. doi:10.1002/job.4030130602

Cohen, J. (1968). Weighted kappa: Nominal scale agreement with provision for scaled disagreement of partial credit. *Psychological Bulletin, 70*, 213–220. doi:10.1037/h0026256

Cohen, J. C. (1988). *Statistical power analysis for behavioral sciences*. Hillsdale, NJ: Lawrence Erlbaum Associates.

Conrad, C. (2004). Organizational discourse analysis: Avoiding the determinism–volunteerism trap. *Organization, 11*, 427–439. doi:10.1177/1350508404042001

Cooper, R. B., & Zmud, R. W. (1990). Information technology implementation research: A technological diffusion approach. *Management Science, 36*(2), 123–139. doi:10.1287/mnsc.36.2.123

Cooren, F. (2004). Textual agency: How texts do things in organizational settings. *Organization, 11*, 373–393. doi:10.1177/1350508404041998

Cooren, F. (2006). The organizational world as a plenum of agencies. In *Communication as Organizing: Empirical and Theoretical Explorations in the Dynamics of Text and Conversation* (pp. 81–100). Mahwah, NJ: Lawrence Erlbaum Associates.

Corbin, J., & Morse, J. (2003). The unstructured interview: Issues of reciprocity and risks when dealing with sensitive topics. *Qualitative Inquiry, 9*, 335–354. doi:10.1177/1077800403009003001

Corbin, J., & Strauss, A. (1990). Grounded theory research: Procedures, canons, and evaluative criteria. *Qualitative Sociology, 13*(1), 3–21. doi:10.1007/BF00988593

Corbin, J., & Strauss, A. (2008). *Basics of qualitative research* (3rd ed.). Thousand Oaks, CA: Sage.

Couper, M. P. (2000). Web surveys: A review of issues and approaches. *Public Opinion Quarterly, 64,* 464–481. doi:10.1086/318641

Couper, M. P., Traugott, M. W., & Lamias, M. J. (2001). Web survey design and administration. *Public Opinion Quarterly, 65,* 230–253. doi:10.1086/322199

Cousins, K. C., Robey, D., & Zigurs, I. (2007). Managing strategic contradictions in hybrid teams. *European Journal of Information Systems, 16*(4), 460–478. doi:10.1057/palgrave.ejis.3000692

Coyle, D. (1999). *The weightless world: Strategies for managing the digital economy.* Cambridge, MA: The MIT Press.

Craig, R. T. (1999). Communication theory as a field. *Communication Theory, 9,* 119–161.

Craig, R. T., & Muller, H. L. (Eds.). (2007). *Theorizing communication: Readings across traditions.* Thousand Oaks, CA: Sage Publications.

Craig, R. T., & Tracy, K. (1995). Grounded practical theory: The case of intellectual discussion. *Communication Theory, 5,* 248–272. doi:10.1111/j.1468-2885.1995.tb00108.x

Craven, M., Taylor, I., Drozd, A., Purbrick, J., Greenhalgh, C., & Benford, S. … Hoch, M. (2001). Exploiting interactivity, influence, space and time to explore non-linear drama in virtual worlds. In the *Proceedings of Human Factors in Computer Systems (CHI 2001).* Seattle, WA: CHI.

Crawford, S. D., Couper, M. P., & Lamias, M. J. (2001). Web surveys: Perception of burden. *Social Science Computer Review, 19,* 146–162. doi:10.1177/089443930101900202

Cresswell, J. W. (1998). *Qualitative inquiry and research design: Choosing among five traditions.* Thousand Oaks, CA: Sage.

Creswell, J. W. (1998). *Qualitative inquiry and research design: Choosing among five traditions.* Thousand Oaks, CA: Sage.

Crow, K. (2006). *Enabling product development teams with collocation.* Retrieved on 10/27/2011 from http://www.npd-solutions.com/collocation.html.

Crowne, D. P., & Marlowe, D. (1960). A new scale of social desirability independent of psychopathology. *Journal of Consulting Psychology, 24,* 349–354. doi:10.1037/h0047358

Csikszentmihalyi, M. (1975). *Beyond boredom and anxiety.* San Francisco, CA: Jossey-Bass.

Csikszentmihalyi, M., & LeFevre, J. (1990). Optimal experience in work and leisure. *Journal of Personality and Social Psychology, 56*(5), 815–822. doi:10.1037/0022-3514.56.5.815

Cummings, L. (1965). Organizational climates for creativity. *Academy of Management Journal, 8*(3), 220–227. doi:10.2307/254790

Czarniawska, B. (2000). Organizational translations. In Kalthoff, H., Rottenburg, R., & Wagener, H.-J. (Eds.), *Facts and Figures: Economic Representations and Practices* (pp. 117–142). Marburg, Germany: Metropolis.

Czarniawska, B. (2004). On time, space, and action nets. *Organization, 11,* 773–791. doi:10.1177/1350508404047251

Czarniawska, B. (2007). *Shadowing and other techniques for doing fieldwork in modern societies.* Liber, Denmark: Copenhagen Business School Press.

Czarniawska, B. (2008). *A theory of organizing.* Cheltenham, UK: Edward Elgar.

Czarniawska, B., & Sevón, G. (2005). Translation is a vehicle, imitation its motor, and fashion sits at the wheel. In Czarniawska, B., & Sevón, G. (Eds.), *Global Ideas: How Ideas, Objects and Practices Travel in a Global Economy* (pp. 7–14). Sweden: Liber AB.

Dabbish, L., & Kraut, R. (2008). Awareness displays and social motivation for coordinating communication. *Information Systems Research, 19*(2), 221–238. doi:10.1287/isre.1080.0175

Daft, R. L., & Lengel, R. (1986). Organizational information requirements, media richness, and structural design. *Management Science, 32*(5), 554–571. doi:10.1287/mnsc.32.5.554

Dahlberg, L. (2001). The Internet and democratic discourse: Exploring the prospects of online deliberative forums extending the public sphere. *Information Communication and Society*, *4*, 615–633. doi:10.1080/13691180110097030

D'Ambra, J., & Rice, R. E. (2001). Emerging factors in user evaluation of the world wide web. *Information & Management*, *38*, 373–384. doi:10.1016/S0378-7206(00)00077-X

Daniels, K., & Guppy, A. (1994). Occupational stress, social support, job control, and psychological well-being. *Human Relations*, *47*(12), 1523–1544. doi:10.1177/001872679404701205

Davidow, W. H., & Uttal, B. (1989, July). Service companies: Focus or falter. *Harvard Business Review*, 17–34.

Davis, M., Bolding, G., Hard, G., Sherr, L., & Elford, J. (2004). Reflecting on the experience of interviewing online: Perspectives from the internet and HIV study in London. *AIDS Care: Psychological and Socio-Medical Aspects of AIDS / HIV*, *16*, 944-952.

Davis, A. (2010). New media and fat democracy: The paradox of online participation. *New Media & Society*, *12*, 745–761. doi:10.1177/1461444809341435

Davis, F. D. (1989). Perceived usefulness, perceived ease of use, and user acceptance of information technology. *Management Information Systems Quarterly*, *13*(2), 319–340. doi:10.2307/249008

Davis, F. D. (1993). User acceptance of information technology: System characteristics, user perceptions and behavioural impacts. *International Journal of Man-Machine Studies*, *38*(3), 475–487. doi:10.1006/imms.1993.1022

Davis, F. D., Bagozzi, R. P., & Warshaw, P. R. (1989). User acceptance of computer technology: A comparison of two theoretical models. *Management Science*, *34*(8), 982–1002. doi:10.1287/mnsc.35.8.982

Davis, F. D., Bagozzi, R. P., & Warshaw, P. R. (1992). Extrinsic and intrinsic motivation to use computers in the workplace. *Journal of Applied Social Psychology*, *22*(14), 111–132. doi:10.1111/j.1559-1816.1992.tb00945.x

Davis, F. D., & Venkatesh, V. (1996). A critical assessment of potential measurement biases in the technology acceptance model: Three experiments. *International Journal of Human-Computer Studies*, *45*, 19–45. doi:10.1006/ijhc.1996.0040

Davison, R., Fuller, M., & Hardin, A. (2003). E-consulting in virtual negotiations. *Group Decision and Negotiation*, *12*(6), 517–534. doi:10.1023/B:GRUP.0000004256.03294.e3

Deetz, S. (1992). *Democracy in an age of corporate colonization*. Albany, NY: SUNY.

Deetz, S. (2009). Politically attentive relational constructionism (PARC) and making a difference in a pluralistic, independent world. In Carbaugh, D., & Buzzanell, P. (Eds.), *Distinctive Qualities in Communication Research*. Oxford, UK: Taylor and Francis.

Del Bosco, B., & Misani, N. (2011). Keeping the enemies close: The contribution of corporate social responsibility to reducing crime against the firm. *Scandinavian Journal of Management*, *27*, 87–98. doi:10.1016/j.scaman.2010.10.003

DeLone, W. H., & McLean, E. R. (1992). Information systems success: The quest for the dependant variable. *The Institute of Management Sciences*, *3*(1), 60–95.

Denizen, N. K. (1997). *Interpretive ethnography: Ethnographic practices for the 21st century*. Thousand Oaks, CA: Sage Publications.

Denzin, N. K. (1998). The art and politics of interpretation. In Denzin, N. K., & Lincoln, Y. (Eds.), *Handbook of Qualitative Research* (pp. 313–371). Thousand Oaks, CA: Sage.

Denzin, N. K., & Lincoln, Y. S. (1998). *Collecting and interpreting qualitative materials*. Thousand Oaks, CA: Sage.

Denzin, N. K., & Lincoln, Y. S. (2005). *The Sage handbook of qualitative research* (3rd ed.). Thousand Oaks, CA: Sage.

Derks, D., Fischer, A. H., & Bos, A. E. R. (2008). The role of emotion in computer-mediated communication: A review. *Computers in Human Behavior*, *24*(3), 766–785. doi:10.1016/j.chb.2007.04.004

DeSanctis, G., & Monge, P. (1999). Introduction: Communication processes for virtual organizations. *Organization Science, 10*, 693–703. doi:10.1287/orsc.10.6.693

Dick, B. (2000). *Grounded theory revisited*. Retrieved from http://www.scu.edu.au/schools/gcm/ar/arm/op026.html.

Dilley, P. (2004). Interviews and the philosophy of qualitative research. *The Journal of Higher Education, 75*(1), 127–132. doi:10.1353/jhe.2003.0049

DiMaggio, P., & Powell, W. W. (1991). *The new institutionalism in organizational analysis*. Chicago, IL: University of Chicago Press.

Dirksen, V., Huizing, A., & Smit, B. (2010). Piling on layers of understanding: The use of connective ethnography for the study of (online) work practices. *New Media & Society, 12*, 1045–1063. doi:10.1177/1461444809341437

Donaldson, S. I., & Weiss, R. (1998). Health, well-being, and organizational effectiveness in the virtual workplace. In Iberia, M., & Tan, M. (Eds.), *The Virtual Workplace*. Hershey, PA: IGI Global.

Driscoll, C., & Gregg, M. (2010). My profile: The ethics of virtual ethnography. *Emotion, Space, and Society, 3*, 15–20. doi:10.1016/j.emospa.2010.01.012

Drucker, F. P. (1993). *Post capitalist society*. New York, NY: HarperCollins.

Duarte, D. L., & Snyder, N. T. (2006). *Mastering virtual teams: Strategies, tools, and techniques that succeed* (3rd ed.). San Francisco, CA: Jossey-Bass.

Dubé, L., & Robey, D. (2009). Surviving the paradoxes of virtual team work. *Information Systems Journal, 19*(1), 3–30. doi:10.1111/j.1365-2575.2008.00313.x

Dudley, W. (Ed.). (1998). *The industrial revolution opposing viewpoints*. San Diego, CA: Greenhaven Press, Inc.

Duffy, F. (2000). Design and facilities management in a time of change. *Facilities, 10-12*, 371–375. doi:10.1108/02632770010349592

Dyer, R., Green, R., Pitts, M., & Millward, G. (1995). What's the flaming problem? CMC - Deindividuation or disinhibiting? In Kirby, M. A. R., Dix, A. J., & Finlay, J. E. (Eds.), *People and Computers*. Cambridge, MA: Cambridge University Press.

Economist. (2011a, February 10). *Print me a Stradivarius: How a new manufacturing technology will change the world*. Retrieved from http://www.economist.com.

Economist. (2011b, February 10). *Three-dimensional printing from digital designs will transform manufacturing and allow more people to start making thing*. Retrieved from http://www.economist.com.

Edwards, J. R., & Rothbard, N. P. (2000). Mechanisms linking work and family: Clarifying the relationships between work and family constructs. *Academy of Management Review, 25*, 178–199.

Edwards, R. (1979). *Contested terrain*. New York, NY: Basic.

Eisenhardt, K. M. (1989). Building theories from case study research. *Academy of Management Review, 14*, 532–550.

Ekman, P. (1992). An argument for basic emotions. In Stein, N. L., & Oatley, K. (Eds.), *Basic Emotions: Cognition & Emotion* (pp. 169–200). Mahwah, NJ: Lawrence Erlbaum.

Emerson, R. M., Fretz, R. I., & Shaw, L. L. (2001). Participant observation and fieldnotes. In Atkinson, P., Coffey, A., Delamont, S., Lofland, J., & Lofland, L. (Eds.), *Handbook of Ethnography*. Thousand Oaks, CA: Sage Publishing.

Falk, A., & Heckman, J. J. (2009). Lab experiments are a major source of knowledge in the social sciences. *Science, 326*, 535–538. doi:10.1126/science.1168244

Families and Work Institute. (2010). *2008, national study of the changing work force*. Washington, DC: Families and Work Institute.

Feenberg, A., & Bakardjieva, M. (2004). Virtual community: No "killer implication". *New Media & Society, 6*(1), 37–43. doi:10.1177/1461444804039904

Fernback, J. (2005). Information technology, networks and community voices: Social inclusion for urban regeneration. *Information Communication and Society, 8*, 482–502. doi:10.1080/13691180500418402

Fielding, N. G., & Fielding, J. L. (1986). *Linking data: The articulation of qualitative and quantitative methods in social research*. Beverly Hills, CA: Sage.

Fielding, N. G., Lee, R. M., & Blank, G. (2008). *The Sage handbook of online research methods*. Los Angeles, CA: Sage.

Fine, M., Weis, L., Weseen, S., & Wong, L. (2000). For whom? Qualitative research, representations, and social responsibilities. In Denzin, N. K., & Lincoln, Y. S. (Eds.), *Handbook of Qualitative Research* (pp. 107–132). Thousand Oaks, CA: Sage.

Fink, A. (1995a). *How to ask survey questions (Vol. 1)*. Thousand Oaks, CA: Sage.

Fink, A. (1995b). *The survey handbook (Vol. 1)*. Thousand Oaks, CA: Sage.

Fischer, R. (2009). Where is culture in cross-cultural research? An outline of a multilevel research process for measuring culture as a shared meaning system. *International Journal of Cross Cultural Management, 9*(1), 25–49. doi:10.1177/1470595808101154

Flander, S. (2008). Terms of engagement. *Human Resource Executive Online*. Retrieved from http://www.hreonline.com/HRE/story.jsp?storyId=59866490.

Fleming, P., & Spicer, A. (2004). You can checkout anytime, but you can never leave: Spatial boundaries in a high commitment organization. *Human Relations, 57*(1), 75–94. doi:10.1177/0018726704042715

Flicker, S., Haas, D., & Skinner, H. (2004). Ethical dilemmas in research on Internet communities. *Qualitative Health Research, 14*, 124–134. doi:10.1177/1049732303259842

Fonner, K. L., & Roloff, M. E. (2010). Why teleworkers are more satisfied with their jobs than are office-based workers. *Journal of Applied Communication Research, 38*, 336–361. doi:10.1080/00909882.2010.513998

Fontaine, J. R. (2008). Traditional and multilevel approaches in cross-cultural research: An integration of methodological frameworks. In van de Vijver, F. J. R., van Hermert, D. A., & Poortinga, Y. (Eds.), *Individuals and Cultures in Multilevel Analysis*. Mahwah, NJ: Lawrence Erlbaum Associates.

Fontana, A., & Frey, J. H. (1998). Interviewing: The art of science. In Denzin, N. K., & Lincoln, Y. S. (Eds.), *Collecting and Interpreting Qualitative Materials* (pp. 47–78). Thousand Oaks, CA: Sage.

Forrest, E., & Mizerski, R. (1996). *Interactive marketing, the future present*. Chicago, IL: American Marketing Association.

Fossey, E., Harvey, C., McDermott, F., & Davidson, L. (2002). Understanding and evaluating qualitative research. *The Australian and New Zealand Journal of Psychiatry, 36*, 717–732. doi:10.1046/j.1440-1614.2002.01100.x

Foulkes, V. S. (1994). *How consumers predict service quality: What do they expect? Service Quality, New directions in Theory and Practice*. Thousand Oaks, CA: Sage Publications.

Fowler, F. J. Jr. (2009). *Survey research methods* (4th ed.). Thousand Oaks, CA: Sage.

Fox, S., & Vitak, J. (2008). *Degrees of access*. Retrieved April 25, 2011 from http://www.pewinternet.org/Presentations/2008/Degrees-of-Access-(May-2008-data).aspx.

Frandsen, A.-C. (2009). From psoriasis to a number and back. *Information and Organization, 19*, 103–128. doi:10.1016/j.infoandorg.2009.02.001

Franklin, C. (1996). Learning to teach qualitative research: Reflections of a quantitative researcher. In Gilgun, J. F., & Sussman, M. B. (Eds.), *The Methods and Methodologies of Qualitative Family Research* (pp. 241–274). Binghamton, NY: Haworth.

Freeman, E. R., Brugge, D., Bennett-Bradley, W. M., Levy, J. I., & Carrasco, E. R. (2006). Challenges of conducting community-based participatory research in Boston's neighborhoods to reduce disparities in asthma. *Journal of Urban Health: Bulletin of the New York Academy of Medicine, 83*, 1013–1021. doi:10.1007/s11524-006-9111-0

Freire, P. (1970). *Pedagogy of the oppressed*. New York, NY: Seabury.

Frey, L., Botan, C., & Kreps, G. (2000). *Investigating communication: An introduction to research methods* (2nd ed.). Boston, MA: Allyn & Bacon.

Fujimoto, Y., Bahfen, N., Fermelis, J., & Hartel, C. E. J. (2007). The global village: Online cross-cultural communication and HRM. *Cross Cultural Management, 14*, 7–22. doi:10.1108/13527600710718804

Furst, S. A., Reeves, M., Rosen, B., & Blackburn, R. S. (2004). Managing the life cycle of virtual teams. *The Academy of Management Executive, 18*(4), 6–20. doi:10.5465/AME.2004.13837468

Gajendran, R. S., & Harrison, D. A. (2007). The good, the bad and the unknown about telecommuting: Meta-analysis of psychological mediators and individual consequences. *The Journal of Applied Psychology, 92,* 1524–1541. doi:10.1037/0021-9010.92.6.1524

Gardner, W. I. (1992). Lessons in organizational dramaturgy: The art of impression management. *Organizational Dynamics, 1,* 33–47. doi:10.1016/0090-2616(92)90084-Z

Gardner, W. L., & Avolio, B. J. (1998). The charismatic relationship: A dramaturgical perspective. *Academy of Management Review, 23*(1), 32–58.

Garson, B. (1994). *All the live-long day: The meaning and demeaning of routine work.* New York, NY: Penguin.

Gatenby, B., & Humphries, M. (2000). Feminist participatory action research: Methodological and ethical issues. *Women's Studies International Forum, 23,* 89–105. doi:10.1016/S0277-5395(99)00095-3

Geertz, C. (1973). *The interpretation of cultures: Selected essays.* New York, NY: Basic Books.

Geertz, C. (1973). Thick description: Toward an interpretive theory of culture. In Geertz, C. (Ed.), *The Interpretation of Cultures: Selected Essays by Clifford Geertz* (pp. 3–30). New York, NY: Basic Books.

Gefen, D., & Straub, D. (1997). Gender differences in perception and adoption of email: An extension to the technology acceptance model. *Management Information Systems Quarterly, 21*(4), 389–400. doi:10.2307/249720

Gefen, D., & Straub, D. (2000). The relative importance of perceived ease of use in IS adoption: A study of e-commerce adoption. *Journal of the Association for Information Systems, 1*(8), 1–20.

George, A. M. (2003). Teaching culture: The challenges and opportunities of international public relations. *Business Communication Quarterly, 66*(2), 97–113. doi:10.1177/108056990306600212

Gephart, R. P. (2004). Qualitative research and the Academy of Management Journal. *Academy of Management Journal, 47,* 454–462. doi:10.5465/AMJ.2004.14438580

Gergen, K. (1991). *The saturated self: Dilemmas of identity in contemporary life.* New York, NY: Basic Books.

Gergen, K. (2002). The challenge of absent presence. In Katz, J. E., & Aakhus, M. A. (Eds.), *Perpetual Contact: Mobile Communication, Private Talk, Public Performance.* Cambridge, UK: Cambridge University Press.

German, K. M. (2009). Dramatism and dramatistic pentad. *Encyclopedia of Communication Theory.* Thousand Oaks, CA: Sage Publications. Retrieved from http:sage-ereference.com/communicationtheory/Article_n119.html.

Gherardi, S., & Nicolini, D. (2000). To transfer is to transform: The circulation of safety knowledge. *Organization, 7,* 329–348. doi:10.1177/135050840072008

Gibbs, J. (2009). Dialectics in a global software team: Negotiating tensions across time, space, and culture. *Human Relations, 62,* 905–935. doi:10.1177/0018726709104547

Giddens, A. (1984). *The constitution of society: Outline and theory of structuration.* Berkeley, CA: University of California Press.

Gilchrist, E. S. (2010). Employees' perceptions of relational limitations inherent in virtual work. In Long, S. D. (Ed.), *Communication, Relationships, and Practices in Virtual Work* (pp. 224–238). Hershey, PA: IGI Global. doi:10.4018/978-1-61520-979-8.ch013

Gilchrist, E. S. (2011). One of these things is not like the others: African American women professors' experiences with majority-race students. In Niles, M. N., & Gordon, N. (Eds.), *Still Searching for Our Mothers' Gardens: Experiences of New, Tenure Track Faculty of Color at 'Majority' Institutions* (pp. 213–233). Lanham, MD: University Press of America.

Ginossar, T., & Nelson, S. (2010a). La communidad habla: Using internet community-based information interventions to increase empowerment and access to health care of low income Latino/a immigrants. *Communication Education, 59,* 328–343. doi:10.1080/03634521003628297

Ginossar, T., & Nelson, S. (2010b). Reducing the health and digital divides: A model for using community-based participatory research approach to e-health interventions in low-income Hispanic communities. *Journal of Computer-Mediated Communication, 15*, 530–551. doi:10.1111/j.1083-6101.2009.01513.x

Glaser, B. G. (1992). *Basics of grounded theory analysis: Emergence versus forcing*. Mill Valley, CA: Sociology Press.

Glaser, B., & Strauss, G. (1967). *The discovery of grounded theory: Strategies for qualitative work*. Chicago, IL: Aldine.

Glenn, E. S. (1981). *Man and mankind*. Ablex, NJ: Norwood.

Glenn, C. L., & Jackson, R. L. II. (2010). Re-negotiating identity in the field of communication. In Allan, S. (Ed.), *Rethinking Communication: Keywords In communication Research* (pp. 137–149). Cresskill, NJ: Hampton Press.

Goffman, E. (1959). *The presentation of self in everyday life*. Harmondsworth, UK: Penguin.

Goffman, E. (1963). *Behavior in public places*. New York, NY: The Free Press.

Golden, T. D., Veiga, J. F., & Dino, R. N. (2008). The impact of professional isolation on teleworker job performance and turnover intentions: Does time spent teleworking, interacting face-to-face, or having access to communication-enhancing technology matter? *The Journal of Applied Psychology, 93*(6), 1412–1421. doi:10.1037/a0012722

Gonzales, A. L., Finley, T., & Duncan, S. P. (2009). (Perceived) interactivity: Does interactivity increase enjoyment and creative identity in artistic spaces. In the *Proceedings of CHI 2009*, (pp. 415-418). Boston, MA: CHI.

Goodall, H. L. (2000). *Writing the new ethnography*. Walnut Creek, CA: AltaMira Press.

Gratton, M., & O'Donnell, S. (2011). Communication technologies for focus groups with remote communities: A case study of research with first nations in Canada. *Qualitative Research, 11*(2), 159–175. doi:10.1177/1468794110394068

Greene, J., Benjamin, L., & Goodyear, L. (2001). The merits of mixing methods in evaluation. *Evaluation, 7*(1), 25–44. doi:10.1177/13563890122209504

Griffith, T. L., & Neale, M. A. (2001). Informational processing in traditional, hybrid, and virtual teams: From nascent knowledge to transactive memory. *Research in Organizational Behavior: An Annual Series of Analytical Essays and Critical Reviews, 23*, 379–421. doi:10.1016/S0191-3085(01)23009-3

Grönroos, C., Heinonen, F., Isoniemi, K., & Lindholm, M. (2000). The netoffer model: A case example from the virtual marketplace. *Management Decision, 38*(4), 243–252. doi:10.1108/00251740010326252

Gudykunst, W. B., Ting-Toomey, S., & Chua, E. G. (Eds.). (1988). *Intercultural communication theory: Interpersonal communication*. Beverly Hills, CA: Sage.

Gudykunst, W. B., Ting-Toomey, S., & Nishida, T. (Eds.). (1996). *Communication in personal relationships across cultures*. Thousand Oaks, CA: Sage.

Guffey, M. E. (2003). *Business communication: Process and product* (4th ed.). Mason, OH: South-Western/Thomson Learning.

Habermas, J. (1989). *The structural transformation of the public sphere: An inquiry into a category of bourgeois society*. Cambridge, MA: MIT.

Hackbarth, G., Grover, V., & Yi, M. Y. (2003). Computer playfulness and anxiety: Positive and negative mediators of the system experience effect on perceived ease of use. *Information & Management, 40*, 221–232. doi:10.1016/S0378-7206(02)00006-X

Halford, S., & Strangleman, T. (2009). In search of the sociology of work: Past, present and future. *Sociology, 43*, 811–828. doi:10.1177/0038038509341307

Hall, E. (1976). *Beyond culture*. Garden City, NY: Anchor Press.

Hall, E., & Hall, M. (1990). *Understanding cultural differences: Germans, French, and Americans*. Boston, MA: Intercultural Press.

Hamilton, R. J., & Bowers, B. J. (2006). Internet recruitment and e-mail interviews in qualitative studies. *Qualitative Health Research, 16*, 821–835. doi:10.1177/1049732306287599

Hammer, M. (2004). The intercultural conflict style inventory: A conceptual framework and measure of intercultural conflict approaches. In *Proceedings of IACM, 17th Annual Conference*. Retrieved from http://ssrn.com/abstract=601981.

Hammersley, M., & Atkinson, P. (1983). *Ethnography: Principles in practice*. London, UK: Tavistock.

Hancock, J. T. (2007). Digital deception: Why, when and how people lie online. In Joinson, A. N., McKenna, K., Postmes, T., & Reips, U. (Eds.), *The Oxford Handbook of Internet Psychology* (pp. 289–301). Oxford, UK: Oxford University Press.

Hand, S., & Varan, D. (2009). Interactive stories and the audience: Why empathy is important. *ACM Computers in Entertainment, 7*(3), 1–14. doi:10.1145/1594943.1594951

Hanisch, J., & Corbitt, B. (2007). Impediments to requirements engineering during global software development. *European Journal of Information Systems, 16*(6), 793–805. doi:10.1057/palgrave.ejis.3000723

Harper, R. H. (2000). The organisation in ethnography: A discussion of ethnographic fieldwork in CSCW. *Computer Supported Cooperative Work, 9*, 239–264. doi:10.1023/A:1008793124669

Harper, R. P. (1998). *Inside the IMF: An ethnography of documents, technology, and action*. London, UK: Academic Press.

Harrison, B., & Kelley, M. R. (1993). Outsourceing and the search for flexibility. *Work, Employment and Society, 7*(2), 213–255.

Harvey, W. S. (2011). Strategies for conducting elite interviews. *Qualitative Research, 11*(4), 431–441. doi:10.1177/1468794111404329

Hasher, L., & Zacks, R. T. (1984). Automatic processing of fundamental information: The case of frequency of occurrence. *The American Psychologist, 39*, 1372–1388. doi:10.1037/0003-066X.39.12.1372

Hecht, T. D., & Allen, N. J. (2009). A longitudinal examination of the work-nonwork boundary strength construct. *Journal of Organizational Behavior, 30*, 839–862. doi:10.1002/job.579

Heerwegh, D., & Loosveldt, G. (2008). Face-to-face versus web surveying in a high-internet-coverage population. *Public Opinion Quarterly, 72*, 836–846. doi:10.1093/poq/nfn045

Hegeman, J. (2011). Currents. *Northrop Grumman Shipbuilding-Newport News*. Retrieved from http://www.huntingtoningalls.com/nns/employees/currents/2011/011011.pdf.

Heijden, H. (2000). *Using the technology acceptance model to predict website usage: Extensions and empirical test. Research Memorandum 2000-25*. Amsterdam, The Netherlands: Vrije Universiteit.

Heinz, M., & Rice, R. E. (2009). An integrated model of knowledge sharing in contemporary communication environments. *Communication Yearbook, 33*, 134–175.

Hellriegel, D., Slocum, J., & Woodman, R. (2001). *Organizational behavior* (9th ed.). Mason, OH: South Western College Publishing.

Henard, D., & McFadyen, A. M. (2008). Making knowledge workers more creative. *Research-Technology Management, 51*(2), 40–46.

Hendrickson, A. R., Massey, P. D., & Cronan, T. P. (1993). On the test-retest reliability of perceived usefulness and perceived ease of use scales. *Management Information Systems Quarterly, 17*(2), 227–230. doi:10.2307/249803

Heron, J. (1971). *Experience and method*. Guildford, UK: University of Surrey.

Heron, J., & Reason, P. (1997). A participatory inquiry paradigm. *Qualitative Inquiry, 3*, 274–294. doi:10.1177/107780049700300302

Heron, J., & Reason, P. (2006). The practice of co-operative inquiry: Research "with" rather than "on" people. In Reason, P., & Bradbury-Huang, H. (Eds.), *Handbook of Action Research*. Thousand Oaks, CA: Sage.

Hewlin, P. F. (2003). And the award for best actor goes to: Facades of conformity in organizational settings. *Academy of Management Review, 28*, 633–643.

Hilbrecht, M., Shaw, S. M., Johnson, L. C., & Andrey, J. (2008). I'm home for the kids: Contradictory implications for work-life balance of teleworking mothers. *Gender, Work and Organization, 15*, 545–576. doi:10.1111/j.1468-0432.2008.00413.x

Hine, C. (1994). *Virtual ethnography*. Paper presented at the When Science Becomes Culture International Symposium on Science Literacy Conference. Montreal, Canada. Retrieved from http://www.cirst.uqam.ca/pcst3/PDF/Communications/HINE.PDF.

Hine, C. (2004). *Virtual ethnography revisited*. Paper presented at the Online Research Methods, Research Methods Festival. Oxford, UK. Retrieved from http://www.restore.ac.uk/orm/background/exploringorms/rmf_hine_outline.pdf.

Hine, C. (2000). *Virtual ethnography*. Thousand Oaks, CA: Sage Publications.

Hine, C. (2005). Virtual methods and the sociology of cyber-social-scientific knowledge. In Hine, C. (Ed.), *Virtual Methods: Issues in Social Research on the Internet*. New York, NY: Oxford International Publishers.

Hine, C. (2008). Virtual ethnography: Modes, varieties, affordances. In Fielding, N., Lee, R. M., & Blank, G. (Eds.), *The Sage Handbook of Online Research Methods* (pp. 257–270). Los Angeles, CA: Sage.

Hine, C. (2010). Book Review: Natalita James and Hugh Busher, online interviewing. *Qualitative Research, 10*(4), 502–504. doi:10.1177/14687941100100040606

Hjorth, D., & Steyaert, C. (Eds.). (2005). *Narrative and discursive approaches in entrepreneurship: A second movements in entrepreneurship book*. Cheltenham, UK: Edward Elgar.

Hobson, C. J., Delunas, L., & Kesic, D. (2001). Compelling evidence of the need for corporate work/life balance initiatives: Evidence from a national survey of stressful life events. *Journal of Employment Counseling, 38*, 38–44. doi:10.1002/j.2161-1920.2001.tb00491.x

Hodgets, R., & Luthan, F. (2003). *International management* (5th ed.). New York, NY: McGraw Hill.

Hoegl, M., Ernst, H., & Proserpio, L. (2007). How teamwork matters more as team member dispersion increases. *Journal of Product Innovation Management, 24*(1), 156–165. doi:10.1111/j.1540-5885.2007.00240.x

Hoepfl, M. (1997). Choosing qualitative research: A primer for technology education researchers. *Journal of Technology Information, 9*, 47–63.

Hoffman, D. L., & Novak, T. P. (1996). Marketing in hypermedia computer-mediated environments: Conceptual foundations. *JMR, Journal of Marketing Research, 60*(7), 50–68.

Hofstede, G. (1984). *Culture's consequences*. Beverly Hills, CA: Sage.

Hogg, M. A., & Hains, S. C. (1996). Intergroup relations and group solidarity: Effects of group identification and social beliefs on depersonalized attraction. *Journal of Personality and Social Psychology, 70*, 295–309. doi:10.1037/0022-3514.70.2.295

Holt, A. (2010). Using the telephone for narrative interviewing: A research note. *Qualitative Research, 10*(1), 113–121. doi:10.1177/1468794109348686

Holton, J. A. (2001). Building trust and collaboration in virtual teams. *Team Performance Management, 7*(3-4), 36–47. doi:10.1108/13527590110395621

Hookway, N. (2008). Entering the blogosphere: Some strategies for using blogs in social research. *Qualitative Research, 8*(1), 91–113. doi:10.1177/1468794107085298

Hughes, T. P. (1987). The evolution of large technological systems. In W. E. Bijker, T. P. Hughes, &, T. J. Pinch (Eds.), *The Social Construction of Technological Systems: New Direction in the Sociology and History of Technology*. Cambridge, MA: The MIT Press.

Humphreys, S. (2008). Grassroots creativity and community in new media environments: Yarn harlot and the 4000 knitting olympians. *Continuum: Journal of Media & Cultural Studies, 22*, 419–433. doi:10.1080/10304310801989844

Hunton, J. E. (2005). Behavioral self-regulation of telework locations: Interrupting interruptions! *Journal of Information Systems, 19*, 111–140. doi:10.2308/jis.2005.19.2.111

Hunton, J. E., & Norman, C. S. (2010). The impact of alternative telework arrangements on organizational commitment: Insights from a longitudinal field experiment. *Journal of Information Systems, 24*(1), 67–90. doi:10.2308/jis.2010.24.1.67

Husserl, E. (1962). *The foundations of phenomenology* (Farber, M., Trans.). New York, NY: Paine-Whitman.

Hylmö, A. (2006). Telecommuting and the contestability of choice: Employee strategies to legitimize personal decision to work in a preferred location. *Management Communication Quarterly, 19*, 541–569. doi:10.1177/0893318905284762

Igbaria, M. A., Zinatelli, N., Cragg, P., & Cavaye, A. L. M. (1997). Personal computing acceptance factors in small firms: A structural equation model. *Management Information Systems Quarterly, 21*(3), 279–305. doi:10.2307/249498

Ilies, R., Wilson, K. S., & Wagner, D. T. (2009). The spillover of daily job satisfaction into employees' daily lives: The facilitating role of work-family integration. *Academy of Management Journal, 52*, 87–102. doi:10.5465/AMJ.2009.36461938

Ingram, A. L., Hathorn, L. G., & Evans, A. D. (2000). Beyond chat on the Internet. *Computers & Education, 35*, 21–35. doi:10.1016/S0360-1315(00)00015-4

International Telecommunication Union. (2010). *Internet user.* Retrieved from http://www.itu.int.

Inungu, J., Mumford, V., Younis, M., & Langford, S. (2009). HIV knowledge, attitudes, and practices among college students in the United States. *Journal of Health and Human Services Administration, 32*(3), 259–277.

Jackson, P., Gharavi, H., & Klobas, J. (2006). Technologies of the self: Virtual work and the inner panopticon. *Information Technology & People, 19*, 219–243. doi:10.1108/09593840610689831

James, N., & Busher, H. (2009). *Online interviewing.* London, UK: Sage.

Jarvenpaa, S., Knoll, K., & Leidner, D. (1998). Is anybody out there? Antecedents of trust in global virtual teams. *Journal of Management Information Systems, 14*(4), 29–64.

Jarvenpaa, S., Shaw, T., & Staples, D. (2004). Toward contextualized theories of trust: The role of trust in global virtual teams. *Information Systems Research, 15*(3), 250–268. doi:10.1287/isre.1040.0028

Jensen, J. F. (2008). The concept of interactivity—Revisited: Four new typologies for a new media landscape. In *Proceedings of the uxTV 2008 Conference,* (pp. 129-132). Silicon Valley, CA: Association of Computing Machinery.

Johnson, C., & Mathews, B. P. (1997). The influence of experience on service expectations. *International Journal of Service Industry Management, 8*(4), 290–305. doi:10.1108/09564239710174381

Kalleberg, A. L. (1977). Work values and job rewards: A theory of job satisfaction. *American Sociological Review, 42*, 124–143. doi:10.2307/2117735

Kalleberg, A. L. (2003). Flexible firms and labor market segmentation: Effects of workplace restructuring on jobs and workers. *Work and Occupations, 30*(2), 154–175. doi:10.1177/0730888403251683

Kankanhalli, A., Tan, C. Y., & Kwok-Kee, W. (2007). Conflict and performance in global virtual teams. *Journal of Management Information Systems, 23*(3), 237–274. doi:10.2753/MIS0742-1222230309

Kapoor, S., Hughes, P. C., Baldwin, J. R., & Blue, J. (2003). The relationship of individualism–collectivism and self-construal to communication styles in India and India and the United States. *International Journal of Intercultural Relations, 27*(6), 683–700. doi:10.1016/j.ijintrel.2003.08.002

Karahanna, E., Straub, D. W., & Chervany, N. L. (1999). Information technology adoption across time: A cross sectional comparison of pre-adoption and post-adoption beliefs. *Management Information Systems Quarterly, 23*(2), 183–213. doi:10.2307/249751

Kath, L. M., Magley, V. J., & Marmet, M. (2009). The role of organizational trust in safety climate's influence on organization outcomes. *Accident; Analysis and Prevention, 42*(5), 1488–1497. doi:10.1016/j.aap.2009.11.010

Kato, S., Kato, Y., Scott, D. J., & Sato, K. (2008). Selection of ICT in emotional communication for Japanese students: Focusing on emotional strategies and gender differences. In *Proceedings of World Conference on Educational Multimedia, Hypermedia and Telecommunications (ED-MEDIA) 2008*, (pp. 1050-1057). ED-MEDIA.

Kato, Y., Kato, S., & Akahori, K. (2006a). Effects of senders' self-disclosures and styles of writing messages on recipients' emotional aspects in e-mail communication. In *Proceedings of World Conference on E-Learning in Corporate, Government, Healthcare, and Higher Education (E-Learn) 2006*, (pp. 2585-2592). E-Learn.

Kato, Y., Kato, S., & Akahori, K. (2006b). Comparison of emotional aspects in e-mail communication by mobile phone with a teacher and a friend. In *Proceedings of World Conference on Educational Multimedia, Hypermedia and Telecommunications (ED-MEDIA) 2006*, (pp. 425-433). ED-MEDIA.

Kato, Y., Scott, D. J., & Kato, S. (2011b). Comparing American and Japanese young people's emotional strategies in mobile phone email communication. In *Proceedings of World Conference on Educational Multimedia, Hypermedia and Telecommunications (ED-MEDIA) 2011*, (pp. 170-178). ED-MEDIA.

Kato, Y., Sugimura, K., & Akahori, K. (2002). Effect of contents of e-mail messages on affections. In *Proceedings of International Conference on Computers in Education (ICCE) 2002*, (Vol. 1), (pp. 428-432). ICCE.

Kato, S., Kato, Y., & Scott, D. J. (2009). Relationships between emotional states and emoticons in mobile phone email communication in Japan. *International Journal on E-Learning Corporate, Government, Healthcare, &. Higher Education, 8*(3), 385–401.

Kato, Y., Kato, S., & Akahori, K. (2007a). Effects of emotional cues transmitted in e-mail communication on the emotions experienced by senders and receivers. *Computers in Human Behavior, 23*(4), 1894–1905. doi:10.1016/j.chb.2005.11.005

Kato, Y., Kato, S., & Chida, K. (2011c). Investigation of mobile phone email reply time and emotional strategies: Replies to four message-types conveying different emotions. *Journal of Japan Society of Educational Information, 27*(2), 5–12.

Kato, Y., Kato, S., & Scott, D. J. (2007b). Misinterpretation of emotional cues and content in Japanese email, computer conferences, and mobile text messages. In Clausen, E. I. (Ed.), *Psychology of Anger* (pp. 145–176). Hauppauge, NY: Nova Science Publishers.

Kato, Y., Kato, S., Scott, D. J., & Sato, K. (2010). Patterns of emotional transmission in Japanese young people's text-based communication in four basic emotional situations. *International Journal on E-Learning Corporate, Government, Healthcare, &. Higher Education, 9*(2), 203–227.

Kato, Y., Kato, S., Sugimura, K., & Akahori, K. (2008). The influence of affective traits on emotional aspects of message receivers in text-based communication -Examination by the experiment using e-mail communication. *Educational Technology Review, 31*(1-2), 85–95.

Kato, Y., Scott, D. J., & Kato, S. (2011a). The influence of intimacy and gender on emotions in mobile phone email. In Gokcay, D., & Yildirim, G. (Eds.), *Affective Computing and Interaction: Psychological, Cognitive and Neuroscientific Perspectives* (pp. 262–279). Hershey, PA: IGI Global. doi:10.4018/978-1-61692-892-6.ch012

Kaufman-Scarborough, C. (2006). Time use and the impact of technology: Examining workspaces in the home. *Time & Society, 15*, 57–80. doi:10.1177/0961463X06061782

Kazmer, M. M. (2007). Beyond C U L8R: Disengaging from online social worlds. *New Media & Society, 9*(1), 111–138. doi:10.1177/1461444807072215

Kazmer, M. M., & Xie, B. (2008). Qualitative interviewing in internet studies: Playing with the media, playing with the method. *Information Communication and Society, 11*, 257–278. doi:10.1080/13691180801946333

Kee, K. F. (2010). *The rationalities behind the adoption of cyberinfrastructure for e-science in the early 21st century USA.* Unpublished Doctoral Dissertation. Austin, TX: University of Texas.

Kee, K. F., & Browning, L. D. (2010). The dialectical tensions in the funding infrastructure of cyberinfrastructure. *Computer Supported Cooperative Work, 19*, 283–308. doi:10.1007/s10606-010-9116-9

Kemmis, S., & McTaggart, R. (2000). Participatory action research. In Denzin, N. K., & Lincoln, Y. S. (Eds.), *Handbook of Qualitative Research* (2nd ed., pp. 567–605). Thousand Oaks, CA: Sage Publications, Inc.

Keppel, G. (1991). *Design and analysis: A researcher's handbook*. Englewood Cliffs, NJ: Prentice Hall.

Kerzner, H. (2006). *Project management: A systems approach to planning, scheduling and controlling* (9th ed.). New York, NY: John Wiley and Sons.

Ketrow, S. (1999). Nonverbal aspects of group communication. In Frey, L. R. (Ed.), *The Handbook of Group Communication Theory and Research* (pp. 251–287). Thousand Oaks, CA: Sage.

Keyton, J. (2011). *Communication research: Asking questions, finding answers* (3rd ed.). New York, NY: McGraw-Hill.

Keyton, J., Bisel, R. S., & Ozley, R. (2009). Recasting the link between applied and theory research: Using applied findings to advance communication theory development. *Communication Theory, 19*, 146–160. doi:10.1111/j.1468-2885.2009.01339.x

Kiesler, S., Seigel, J., & McGuire, T. (1984). Social psychological aspects of computer-mediated communication. *The American Psychologist, 39*(10), 1123–1134. doi:10.1037/0003-066X.39.10.1123

Kim, T.-Y. H., & Grant, A. J. (2009). Proactive personality, employee creativity and newcomer outcomes: A longitudinal study. *Journal of Business and Psychology, 24*(1), 93–103. doi:10.1007/s10869-009-9094-4

King, J. L., & Frost, R. L. (2002). Managing distance over time: The evolution of technologies of disambiguation. In Hinds, P., & Kiesler, S. (Eds.), *Distributed Work*. Cambridge, MA: The MIT Press.

Kirkman, B. L., Rosen, B., Gibson, C. B., Tesluk, P. E., & McPherson, S. O. (2002). Five challenges to virtual team success: Lessons from Sabre, Inc. *The Academy of Management Executive, 16*, 67–79. doi:10.5465/AME.2002.8540322

Kisselburgh, L. G., Berkelaar, B. L., & Buzzanell, P. M. (2009). Discourse, gender, and the meaning of work. *Communication Yearbook, 33*, 258–299.

Kivisto, P., & Pittman, D. (2007). Goffman's dramaturgical sociology: Personal sales in a commodified world. In Kivisto, P. (Ed.), *Illuminating Social Life* (pp. 271–290). Thousand Oaks, CA: Pine Forge Press.

Kivits, J. (2005). Online interviewing and the research relationship. In Hine, C. (Ed.), *Virtual Methods: Issues in Social Research on the Internet*. New York, NY: Oxford International Publishers.

Konradt, U., Hertel, G., & Schmook, R. (2003). Quality of management by objectives, task-related stressors, and non-task related stressors as predictors of stress and job satisfaction among teleworkers. *European Journal of Work and Organizational Psychology, 12*, 61–79. doi:10.1080/13594320344000020

Korac-Kakabadse, N., Kouzmin, A., Korac-Kakabadse, A., & Savery, L. (2001). Low-and high-context communication patterns: Toward mapping cross-cultural encounters. *Cross Cultural Management, 8*(2), 3–24. doi:10.1108/13527600110797218

Korneliussen, T., & Panozzo, F. (2005). From "nature" to "economy" and "culture": How stockfish travels and constructs an action net. In Czarniawska, B., & Sevón, G. (Eds.), *Global Ideas: How Ideas, Objects and Practices Travel in a Global Economy* (pp. 106–125). Sweden: Liber AB.

Kossek, E. E., Lautsch, B. A., & Eaton, S. C. (2006). Telecommuting, control, and boundary management: Correlates of policy use and practice, job control, and work-family effectiveness. *Journal of Vocational Behavior, 68*, 347–367. doi:10.1016/j.jvb.2005.07.002

Kossek, E. E., Noe, R. A., & DeMarr, B. J. (1999). Work-family role synthesis: Individual and organizational determinants. *The International Journal of Conflict Management, 10*, 102–129. doi:10.1108/eb022820

Kozinets, R. V. (2009). *Netnography: Doing ethnographic research online*. Los Angeles, CA: Sage.

Kreiner, G. E., Hollensbe, E. C., & Sheep, M. L. (2009). Balancing borders and bridges: Negotiating work-home interface via boundary work tactics. *Academy of Management Journal, 52*, 704–730. doi:10.5465/AMJ.2009.43669916

Kreps, G. L., & Neuhauser, L. (2010). Editors' introduction, ehealth and health promotion. *Journal of Computer-Mediated Communication, 15*, 527–529. doi:10.1111/j.1083-6101.2010.01526.x

Kroeber, A. L., & Kluckhohn, C. (1952). *Culture: A critical review of concepts and definitions*. Cambridge, MA: Harvard University Press.

Krusiewicz, E. S., & Wood, J. T. (2001). He was our child from the moment we walked in that room: Entrance stories of adoptive parents. *Journal of Social and Personal Relationships, 18*, 785–803. doi:10.1177/0265407501186003

Kuhn, T., Golden, A. G., Jorgenson, J., Buzzanell, P. M., Berkelaar, B. L., & Kisselburg, L. G. (2008). Cultural discourses and discursive resources for meaningful work: Constructing and disrupting identities in contemporary capitalism. *Management Communication Quarterly, 22*, 162–171. doi:10.1177/0893318908318262

Kuhn, T., & Nelson, N. (2002). Reengineering identity: A case study of multiplicity and duality in organizational identification. *Management Communication Quarterly, 16*, 5–39. doi:10.1177/0893318902161001

Kurpius, D. D., Metzgar, E. T., & Rowley, K. M. (2010). Sustaining hyperlocal media: In search of funding models. *Journalism Studies, 11*, 359–376. doi:10.1080/14616700903429787

Kvale, S. (1996). *Interviews: An introduction to qualitative research interviewing*. Thousand Oaks, CA: Sage.

Ladner, S. (2008). Laptops in the living room: Mobile technologies and the divide between work and private time among interactive agency workers. *Canadian Journal of Communication, 33*(3), 465–489.

Land, C., & Taylor, S. (2010). Surf's up: Work, life, balance and brand in the a new age capitalist organization. *Sociology, 44*, 395–413. doi:10.1177/0038038510362479

Land, F. (1999). *The management of change: Guidelines for the successful implementation of information systems*. London, UK: London School of Economics and Political Science.

Langford, P. H. (2009). Measuring organisational climate and employee engagement: Evidence for a 7 Ps model of work practices and outcomes. *Australian Journal of Psychology, 61*(4), 185–198. doi:10.1080/00049530802579481

Lapierre, J., & Pierre-Giroux, V. (2003). Creativity and work environment in a high-tech context. *Creativity and Work Environment, 12*(1), 11–23.

Latour, B. (1986). *The pasteurization of France*. Cambridge, MA: Harvard University Press.

Latour, B. (1994). On technical mediation: Philosophy, sociology, genealogy. *Common Knowledge, 3*, 29–64.

Latour, B. (1999a). On recalling ANT. In Law, J., & Hassard, J. (Eds.), *Actor Network Theory and After* (pp. 15–25). Oxford, UK: Blackwell Publishing.

Latour, B. (1999b). Circulating reference: Sampling the soil in the Amazon Forest. In *Pandora's hope: Essays on the Reality of Science Studies* (pp. 24–79). Cambridge, MA: Harvard University Press.

Latour, B. (2005). *Reassembling the social: An introduction to actor-network-theory*. Oxford, UK: Oxford University Press.

Law, J. (1999). After ANT: Complexity, naming and topology. In Law, J., & Hassard, J. (Eds.), *Actor Network Theory and After* (pp. 1–14). Oxford, UK: Blackwell Publishing.

Lee, J., & Lee, H. (2010). The computer-mediated communication network: Exploring the linkage between the online community and social capital. *New Media & Society, 12*, 711–727. doi:10.1177/1461444809343568

Lee-Kelley, L., & Sankey, T. (2008). Global virtual teams for value creation and project success: A case study. *International Journal of Project Management, 26*(1), 51–62. doi:10.1016/j.ijproman.2007.08.010

LeGreco, M., & Tracy, S. J. (2009). Discourse tracing as qualitative practice. *Qualitative Inquiry, 15*, 1516–1543. doi:10.1177/1077800409343064

Legris, P., Ingham, J., & Collerette, P. (2003). Why do people use information technology? A critical review of the technology acceptance model. *Information & Management, 40*, 191–204. doi:10.1016/S0378-7206(01)00143-4

Leider, R. (1993). *Fast food, fast talk: Service work and the routinization of everyday life*. Berkeley, CA: University of California Press.

Leonardi, P. M., Jackson, M. J., & Marsh, N. (2004). The strategic use of "distance" among virtual team members: A multi-dimensional communication model. In Godar, S. H., & Ferris, S. P. (Eds.), *Virtual and Collaborative Teams: Process, Technologies, and Practice*. Hershey, PA: IGI Global. doi:10.4018/978-1-59140-204-6.ch009

Leonardi, P. M., Treem, J. W., & Jackson, M. H. (2010). The connectivity paradox: Using technology to both decrease and increase perceptions of distance in distributed work arrangements. *Journal of Applied Communication Research, 38*(1), 85–105. doi:10.1080/00909880903483599

Levine, D. (1985). *The flight from ambiguity*. Chicago, IL: Chicago University Press.

Li, H., & Liu, Y. (2011). Post adoption behaviour of e-service users: An empirical study on chinese online travel service users. In *Proceedings ECIS 2011*. Retrieved from http://aisel.aisnet.org/ecis2011/56.

Liden, R. C., Wayne, S. J., & Bradway, L. K. (1997). Task Interdependence as a moderator of the relation between group control and performance. *Human Relations, 50*, 169–181. doi:10.1177/001872679705000204

Likert, R. (1932). A technique for the measurement of attitudes. *Archives de Psychologie, 140*, 1–55.

Lim, Y.-K., Lee, S.-S., & Lee, K.-Y. (2009). Interactivity attributes: A new way of thinking and describing interactivity. In the *Proceedings of CHI 2009*, (pp. 105-108). Boston, MA: CHI.

Lin, C., Wu, H., & Hsieh, C. (2009). A world of paradox: Is that the public statement or private talk in virtual community. *Pacic Asia Conference on Information Systems*. Retrieved from http://aisel.aisnet.org/pacis2009/5.

Lindberg, K., & Czarniawska, B. (2006). Knotting the action net, or organizing between organizations. *Scandinavian Journal of Management, 22*, 292–306. doi:10.1016/j.scaman.2006.09.001

Lindlof, T. R., & Taylor, B. C. (2010). *Qualitative communication research methods* (3rd ed.). Thousand Oaks, CA: Sage.

Lin, N. (2001). *Social capital: A theory of structure and action*. London, UK: Cambridge University.

Lipnack, J., & Stamps, J. (1997). *Virtual teams - Reaching across space, time and organizations with technology*. New York, NY: John Wiley and Sons.

Lister, K., Harnish, T., & Nille, J. M. (2009). *Undress for success -- The naked truth about making money at home*. New York, NY: John Wiley & Sons.

Locker, K., & Kaczmarek, S. (2001). *Business communication: Building critical skills*. Boston, MA: McGraw-Hill Irwin.

Löfstedt, U. (2007). Public e-services research-A critical analysis of current research in Sweden. *International Journal of Public Information Systems, 2*.

Loher, B. T., Noe, R. A., Moeller, N. L., & Fitzgerald, M. P. (1985). A meta-analysis of the relation of job characteristics to job satisfaction. *The Journal of Applied Psychology, 70*(2), 280–289. doi:10.1037/0021-9010.70.2.280

Lojeski, K. S., & Reily, R. R. (2008). Understanding effective e-collaboration through virtual distance. In *Encyclopedia of E-Collaboration* (pp. 660–665). Hershey, PA: Idea Group Publishing.

Long, S. (Ed.). (2010). *Communication, relationships and practices in virtual work*. Hershey, PA: IGI Global. doi:10.4018/978-1-61520-979-8

Long, S. D., Goodman, R. A., & Clow, C. (2010). The electronic panopticon: Organizational surveillance in virtual work. In Long, S. D. (Ed.), *Communication, Relationships and Practices in Virtual Work*. Hershey, PA: IGI Global. doi:10.4018/978-1-61520-979-8.ch005

Mangham, I. L., & Overington, M. A. (1987). *Organizations as theatre: A social psychology of dramatic appearances*. Chichester, UK: John Wiley & Sons.

Mann, C., & Stewart, F. (2000). *Internet communication and qualitative research: A handbook for researching online*. Thousand Oaks, CA: Sage Publishing.

Mann, C., & Stewart, F. (2002). Internet interviewing. In Gulbrium, J. F., & Holstein, J. A. (Eds.), *Handbook of Interview Research: Context and Method* (pp. 603–628). Thousand Oaks, CA: Sage.

Manning, P. K. (1996). Dramaturgy, politics and the axial media event. *The Sociological Quarterly, 24*(2), 261–278. doi:10.1111/j.1533-8525.1996.tb01749.x

Mark, G., Grudin, J., & Poltrock, S. E. (1999). Meeting at the desktop: An empirical study of virtually collocated teams. In *Proceedings of ECSCW 1999, the 6th European Conference on Computer Supported Cooperative Work*, (pp. 159-178). Copenhagen, Denmark: CSCW.

Markham, A. N., & Baym, N. K. (Eds.). (2008). *Internet inquiry: Conversations about method*. Los Angeles, CA: Sage.

Marsh, K., & Musson, G. (2008). Men at work and at home: Managing emotion in telework. *Gender, Work and Organization, 15*, 32–48.

Marsh, R. M., & Mannari, H. (1977). Organizational commitment and turnover: A prediction study. *Administrative Science Quarterly, 22*(1), 57–75. doi:10.2307/2391746

Martin, M. P. (1991). *Analysis and design of business information systems*. New York, NY: Macmillan Publishing Company.

Martin, P. Y., & Turner, B. A. (1986). Grounded theory and organizational research. *The Journal of Applied Behavioral Science, 22*, 141–157. doi:10.1177/002188638602200207

Mathieson, K. (1991). Predicting user intentions: Comparing the technology acceptance model with the theory of planned behaviour. *Information Systems Research, 2*(3), 173–191. doi:10.1287/isre.2.3.173

Matsumoto, D. (1996). *Unmasking Japan: Myths and realities about the emotions of the Japanese*. Palo Alto, CA: Stanford University Press.

Matsumoto, D., & Kudoh, T. (1993). American-Japanese cultural differences in implicit theories of personality based on smile. *Journal of Nonverbal Behavior, 17*(4), 231–243. doi:10.1007/BF00987239

Mattarelli, E., & Tagliaventi, M. R. (2010). Work-related identities, virtual work acceptance and the development of globalized work practices in globally distributed teams. *Industry and Innovation, 17*, 415–443. doi:10.1080/13662716.2010.496247

Matthews, R. A., & Barnes-Farrell, J. L. (2010). Development and initial evaluation of an enhanced measure of boundary flexibility for the work and family domains. *Journal of Occupational Health Psychology, 15*, 330–346. doi:10.1037/a0019302

Mayer, J. D. (2000). Emotion, intelligence, emotional intelligence. In Forgas, J. P. (Ed.), *The Handbook of Affect and Social Cognition* (pp. 410–431). Mahwah, NJ: Lawrence Erlbaum & Associates.

Maznevski, M. L., & Chudoba, K. M. (2000). Bridging space over time: Global virtual team dynamics and effectiveness. *Organization Science, 11*, 473–492. doi:10.1287/orsc.11.5.473.15200

McCarthy, V. (1999). *HP splits in two to focus on enterprise, e-services*. Retrieved from http://www.hpworld.org/hpworldnews/hpw903/news/01.html.

McCoyd, J. L. M., & Kerson, T. S. (2006). Conducting intensive interviews using email. *Qualitative Social Work, 5*, 389–406. doi:10.1177/1473325006067367

McDermott, V. M., Oetzel, J. G., & White, K. (2008). Ethical paradoxes in community-based participatory research. In Zoller, H. M., & Dutta, M. J. (Eds.), *Emerging Perspectives in Health Communication*. New York, NY: Routledge.

McDonald, S. (2005). Studying actions in context: A qualitative shadowing method for organizational research. *Qualitative Research, 5*, 455–473. doi:10.1177/1468794105056923

McLeod, J. (2001). *Qualitative research in counseling and psychotherapy*. London, UK: Sage.

Mennino, S. F., Rubin, B. A., & Brayfield, A. (2005). Home-to job and job-to-home spillover: The impact of demanding jobs, company policies and workplace cultures. *The Sociological Quarterly, 46*, 107–135. doi:10.1111/j.1533-8525.2005.00006.x

Merleau-Ponty, M. (2002). *Husserl at the limits of phenomenology*. Evanston, IL: Northwestern University Press.

Merriam, S. B. (Ed.). (2002). *Qualitative research in practice*. San Francisco, CA: Jossey-Bass.

Merrigan, G., & Huston, C. L. (2004). *Communication research methods*. Belmont, CA: Thomson Wadsworth.

Metts, S. (2009). Impression management. *Encyclopedia of Communication Theory.* Thousand Oaks, CA: Sage Publications. Retrieved from http://sage-ereference.com/communicationtheory/Article_n189.html.

Meunier, D., & Vasquez, C. (2008). On shadowing the hybrid character of actions: A communicational approach. *Communication Methods and Measures, 2,* 167–192. doi:10.1080/19312450802310482

Meuter, M. L., Ostrom, A. L., Roundtree, R. I., & Bitner, M. J. (2000). Self-service technologies: Understanding customer satisfaction with technology-based service encounters. *Journal of Marketing, 64,* 50–64. doi:10.1509/jmkg.64.3.50.18024

Meyrowitz, J. (1990). Redefining the situation: Extending dramaturgy into a theory of social change and media effects. In Riggins, S. H. (Ed.), *Beyond Goffman: Studies on Communication, Institution and Social Interaction* (pp. 65–97). Berlin, Germany: Mouton de Gruyter. doi:10.1515/9783110847291.65

Miles, M. B., & Huberman, A. M. (1994). *Qualitative data analysis: An expanded sourcebook* (2nd ed.). Thousand Oaks, CA: Sage.

Miller, D., & Slater, D. (2000). *The internet: An ethnographic approach.* New York, NY: Oxford International Publishers.

Mintzberg, H. (1970). Structured observation as a method to study managerial work. *Journal of Management Studies, 7,* 87–107. doi:10.1111/j.1467-6486.1970.tb00484.x

Misheler, E. G. (1986). *Research interviewing: Context and narrative.* Cambridge, MA: Harvard University Press.

Mitchell, J. (1978). *Social exchange, dramaturgy and ethnomethodology.* Oxford, UK: Elsevier.

Mohd Yusof, S. A., & Zakaria, N. (2012). *Exploring the state of discipline on the formation of swift trust within global virtual teams.* Paper presented at the 45th Hawaii International Conference on System Sciences (HICSS). Hawaii, HI.

Montoya, M., Massey, A. P., & Lockwood, N. S. (2011). 3D collaborative virtual environments: Exploring the link between collaborative behaviors and team performance. *Decision Sciences, 42*(2), 451–476. doi:10.1111/j.1540-5915.2011.00318.x

Moran-Ellis, J., Alexander, V. D., Cronin, A., Dickinson, M., Fielding, J., Sleney, J., & Thomas, H. (2006). Triangulation and integration: Processes, claims and implications. *Qualitative Research, 6*(1), 45–59. doi:10.1177/1468794106058870

Morganson, V. J., Major, D. A., Oborn, K. L., Verive, J. M., & Heelan, M. P. (2010). Comparing telework locations and traditional work arrangements: Differences in work-life balance support, job satisfaction, and inclusion. *Journal of Managerial Psychology, 25*(6), 578–595. doi:10.1108/02683941011056941

Moss, P., & Tilly, C. (1996). Soft skills and race: An investigation of black men's employment problems. *Work and Occupations, 23*(3), 252–276. doi:10.1177/0730888496023003002

Mumby, D. K. (2000). Communication, organization, and the public sphere: A feminist perspective. In Buzzanell, P. M. (Ed.), *Rethinking Organizational & Managerial Communication from Feminist Perspectives* (pp. 3–23). Thousand Oaks, CA: Sage Publications, Inc.

Mumford, M. D. (2000). Managing creative people: Strategies and tactics for innovation. *Human Resource Management Review, 10*(3), 313–351. doi:10.1016/S1053-4822(99)00043-1

Murray, C., & Sixsmith, J. (1998). E-mail: A qualitative research medium for interviewing? *International Journal of Social Research Methodology, 1,* 103–121.

Mustafa, M. (2010). Managing boundaries: The case of home-based self-employed teleworkers. *The International Journal of Business and Management Research, 3,* 55–64.

Myrie, J., & Daly, K. (2009). The use of boundaries by self-employed, home-based workers to manage work and family: A qualitative study in Canada. *Journal of Family and Economic Issues, 30,* 386–398. doi:10.1007/s10834-009-9166-7

Nansen, B., Arnold, M., Gibbs, M., & Davis, H. (2010). Time, space, and technology in the working-home: An unsettled nexus. *New Technology, Work and Employment, 25,* 136–153. doi:10.1111/j.1468-005X.2010.00244.x

Nelson-Marsh, N. (2006). *Reconsidering the conceptual relationship between organizations and technology: A study of the internet engineering task force as a virtual organization.* Unpublished Doctoral Dissertation. Boulder, CO: University of Colorado at Boulder.

Netemeyer, R. G., Boles, J. S., & McMurrian, R. (1996). Development and validation of work-family conflict and family-work conflict scales. *The Journal of Applied Psychology, 81,* 400–410. doi:10.1037/0021-9010.81.4.400

Neuhauser, L., & Kreps, G. L. (2010). Ehealth communication and behavior change: Promise and performance. *Social Semiotics, 20,* 7–24. doi:10.1080/10350330903438386

Neyland, D. (2007). *Organizational ethnography.* London, UK: Sage.

Nippert-Eng, C. (1996). Calendars and keys: The classification of "home" and "work". *Sociological Forum, 11,* 563–582. doi:10.1007/BF02408393

Noble, G., & Lupton, D. (1998). Consuming work: Computers, subjectivity and appropriation in the university workplace. *The Sociological Review, 46*(4), 803–827. doi:10.1111/1467-954X.00141

O'Conner, G. C., Rice, M. P., Peters, L., & Veryzer, R. W. (2003). Managing interdisciplinary, longitudinal research teams: Extending grounded theory-building methodologies. *Organization Science, 14,* 353–373. doi:10.1287/orsc.14.4.353.17485

O'Doherty, D., & Willmott, H. (2009). The decline of labour process analysis and the future of sociology of work. *Sociology, 43,* 931–951. doi:10.1177/0038038509340742

O'Leary, M., Orlikowski, W., & Yates, J. (2002). Distributed work over the centuries: Trust and control in the Hudson's bay company, 1670-1826. In Hinds, P., & Kiesler, S. (Eds.), *Distributed Work.* Cambridge, MA: The MIT Press.

O'Toole, M., & Nalbone, D. P. (2011). Safety perception surveys what to ask, how to analyze. *Professional Safety, 56*(6), 58–62.

Okabe, D., & Ito, M. (2006). Keitai use in public transportation. In Ito, M., Okabe, D., & Matsuda, M. (Eds.), *Personal, Portable, Pedestrian: Mobile Phones in Japanese Life* (pp. 205–217). Cambridge, MA: MIT Press.

Olaniran, B. (2001). The effects of computer-mediated communication on transculturalism. In Milhouse, V. H., Asante, M. K., & Nwosu, P. O. (Eds.), *Transcultural Realities: Interdisciplinary Perspectives on Cross-Cultural Relations* (pp. 55–70). Thousand Oaks, CA: Sage.

Oliver, R. L. (1993). *Service quality: New directions in theory and practice.* Thousand Oaks, CA: Sage.

Olson, L. N., Daggs, J. L., Ellevold, B. L., & Rogers, T. K. K. (2007). Entrapping the innocent: Toward a theory of child sexual predators' luring communication. *Communication Theory, 17,* 231–251. doi:10.1111/j.1468-2885.2007.00294.x

Osgood, C. E. (1952). The nature and measurement of meaning. *Psychological Bulletin, 49,* 197–237. doi:10.1037/h0055737

Osland, J. S., & Bird, A. (2003). Beyond sophisticated stereotyping: Cultural sensemaking in context. In Thomas, D. C. (Ed.), *Readings and Cases in International Management: A Cross-Cultural Perspective* (pp. 58–70). Thousand Oaks, CA: Sage. doi:10.5465/AME.2000.2909840

Owen, W. F. (1984). Interpretive themes in relational communication. *The Quarterly Journal of Speech, 70,* 274–287. doi:10.1080/00335638409383697

Padgett, D. K. (1988). *Qualitative methods in social work.* Thousand Oaks, CA: Sage.

Panteli, N., & Duncan, E. (2004). Trust and temporary virtual teams: Alternative explanations and dramaturgical relationships. *Information Technology & People, 17*(4), 423–441. doi:10.1108/09593840410570276

Papacharissi, Z. (2002). The virtual sphere: The Internet as a public sphere. *New Media & Society, 4,* 9–27. doi:10.1177/14614440222226244

Parasuraman, A., & Grewal, D. (2000). The impact of technology on the quality-value-loyalty chain: A research agenda. *Journal of the Academy of Marketing Science, 28*(1), 168–174. doi:10.1177/0092070300281015

Parasuraman, A., Zeithaml, V., & Malhotra, A. (2005). E-S-QUAL: A multiple-item scale for assessing electronic service quality. *Journal of Service Research, 7*(10), 1–21. Retrieved from http://public.kenan-flagler.unc.edu/faculty/malhotra/E-S-QualJServRsch.pdf

Park, Y., & Jex, S. M. (2011). Work-home boundary management using communication and information technology. *International Journal of Stress Management, 18*, 133–152. doi:10.1037/a0022759

Parthasarathy, M., & Bhattacherjee, A. (1998). Understanding post-adoption behaviour in the context of online services. *Information Systems Research, 9*(4), 362–379. doi:10.1287/isre.9.4.362

Pauleen, D. J. (2003). An inductively derived model of leader-initiated relationship building with virtual team members. *Journal of Management Information Systems, 20*, 227–256.

Pedersen, P. E., & Methlie, L. B. (2001). *Understanding mobile commerce end-user adoption: A triangulation perspective and suggestions for an exploratory service evaluation framework.* Working Paper. Agder, Norway: Agder University College.

Peng, Y. P., Hwang, S. N., & Wong, J. Y. (2010). How to inspire university librarians to become "good soldiers"? The role of job autonomy. *Journal of Academic Librarianship, 36*(4), 287–295. doi:10.1016/j.acalib.2010.05.002

Pennebaker, J. W., & Traue, H. C. (1993). Inhibition and psychosomatic processes. In Traue, H. C., & Pennebaker, J. W. (Eds.), *Emotion Inhibition and Health* (pp. 146–163). Seattle, WA: Hogrefe & Huber.

Perlow, L. A. (1998). Boundary control: The social ordering of work and family time in a high-tech corporation. *Administrative Science Quarterly, 43*, 328–357. doi:10.2307/2393855

Peters, M. A. (2011). The Egyptian revolution. *Policy Futures in Education, 9*, 292–295. doi:10.2304/pfie.2011.9.2.292

Pleck, J. H. (1977). The work-family role system. *Social Problems, 17*, 417–427. doi:10.1525/sp.1977.24.4.03a00040

Polaine, A. (2005). The flow principle in interactivity. In the *Proceedings of the Second Australasian Conference on Interactive Entertainment*, (pp. 151-158). Sydney, Australia: ACM.

Powell, A., Piccoli, G., & Ives, B. (2004). Virtual teams: A review of current literature and directions for future research. *The Data Base for Advances in Information Systems, 35*(1), 6–36. doi:10.1145/968464.968467

Poynter, R. (2008). Facebook: The future of networking with customers. *International Journal of Market Research, 50*, 11–12.

Prasad, A., & Prasad, P. (2002). The coming age of interpretive organizational research. *Organizational Research Methods, 5*, 4–11.

Prasad, P. (2005). *Crafting qualitative research: Working in the postpositivist traditions.* Armonk, NY: M.E. Sharpe.

Prescott, M. B., & Conger, S. A. (1995). Information technology innovations: A classification of IT locus of impact and research approach. *Database, 26*(2/3), 20–41.

Presser, H. (2003). *Working in a 24/7 economy.* New York, NY: Russell Sage Foundation.

Putnam, R. (2000). *Bowling alone: The collapse and revival of American community.* New York, NY: Simon & Schuster.

Qureshi, S., Liu, M., & Vogel, D. (2006). The effects of electronic collaboration in distributed project management. *Group Decision and Negotiation, 15*, 55–75. doi:10.1007/s10726-005-9006-6

Raghuram, S., & Wiesenfeld, B. (2004). Work-nonwork conflict and job stress among virtual workers. *Human Resource Management, 43*, 259–277. doi:10.1002/hrm.20019

Raghuram, S., Wiesenfeld, B., & Garud, R. (2003). Technology enabled work: The role of self-efficacy in determining telecommuter adjustment and structuring behavior. *Journal of Vocational Behavior, 63*, 180–198. doi:10.1016/S0001-8791(03)00040-X

Ragin, C. C., Nagel, J., & White, P. (2004). *Workshop on scientific foundations of qualitative research.* Washington, DC: National Science Foundation. Retrieved from www.nsf.gov/pubs/2004/nsf04219/start.htm.

Rainie, L., Purcell, K., & Smith, A. (2011). *The social side of the internet.* Retrieved April 25, 2011 from http://www.pewinternet.org/Reports/2011/The-Social-Side-of-the-Internet.aspx.

Rains, S. A. (2008). Seeking health information in the information age: The role of internet self-efficacy. *Western Journal of Communication, 17*, 1–18. doi:10.1080/10570310701827612

Ramaswami, S. N., Strader, T. J., & Brett, K. (2001). Identifying potential customers for on-line financial services. *The Journal of Internet Banking and Commerce*. Retrieved from http://www.arraydev.com/commerce/JIBC/9806-05.htm.

Ramaswami, S. N., Strader, T. J., & Brett, K. (2000). Determinants of on-line channel use for purchasing financial products. *International Journal of Electronic Commerce, 5*(2), 95–118.

Ramierz, A. Jr, & Zhang, S. (2007). When online meets offline: The effect of modality switching on relational communication. *Communication Monographs, 74*, 287–310. doi:10.1080/03637750701543493

Ramirez, A. Jr, Walther, J. B., Burgoon, J. K., & Sunnafrank, M. (2002). Information-seeking strategies, uncertainty, and computer-mediated communication: Toward a conceptual model. *Human Communication Research, 28*, 213–228.

Rashotte, L. S., Webster, M. Jr, & Whitmeyer, J. (2005). Pretesting experimental instructions. *Sociological Methodology, 35*, 151–175. doi:10.1111/j.0081-1750.2005.00167.x

Rau, B. L., & Hyland, M. A. M. (2002). Role conflict and flexible work arrangements: The effects on applicant attraction. *Personnel Psychology, 55*, 111–136. doi:10.1111/j.1744-6570.2002.tb00105.x

Reason, P. (1994). Three approaches to participative inquiry. In Denzin, N. K., & Lincoln, Y. S. (Eds.), *Handbook of Qualitative Inquiry*. Thousand Oaks, CA: Sage Publications, Inc.

Redman, T., Snape, E., & Ashurst, C. (2009). Location, location, location: Does place of work really matter. *British Journal of Management, 20*, S171–S181. doi:10.1111/j.1467-8551.2008.00640.x

Reed, B. (2007). Co-working: The ultimate in teleworking flexibility: Co-working sites make space, build community for telecommuters. *Network World*. Retrieved from http://www.networkworld.com/news/2007/102307-coworking.html.

Reinard, J. C. (2008). *Introduction to communication research* (4th ed.). New York, NY: McGraw-Hill.

Rheingold, H. (1993). Cold knowledge and social warmth. *Newsweek, 122*(10), 49–50.

Rheingold, H. (1991). Reviews the book Virtual Reality. *Science News, 140*, 322–323.

Rheingold, H. (1993). *The virtual community: Homesteading on the electronic frontier*. Reading, MA: Addison-Wesley.

Richards, D. (2006). Is interactivity actually important? In the *Proceedings of the 3rd Australasian Conference on Interactive Entertainment*, (pp. 59-66). ACM.

Richardson, J. (2010). Managing flexworkers: Holding on and letting go. *Journal of Management Development, 29*(2), 137–147. doi:10.1108/02621711011019279

Riel, A. C. R., Liljander, V., & Jurriens, P. (2001). Exploring consumer evaluations of e-services: A portal site. *International Journal of Service Industry Management, 12*(4), 359–377. doi:10.1108/09564230110405280

Riemer, K., & Klein, S. (2008). Is the V-form the next generation organisation? An analysis of challenges, pitfalls and remedies of ICT-enabled virtual organisations based on social capital theory. *Journal of Information Technology, 23*(3), 147–162. doi:10.1057/palgrave.jit.2000120

Robbins, S. (2001). *Organizational behaviour* (9th ed.). Upper Saddle River, NJ: Prentice Hall.

Robert, L. P. Jr, Dennis, A. R., & Yu-Ting, C. H. (2009). Individual swift trust and knowledge-based trust in face-to-face and virtual team members. *Journal of Management Information Systems, 26*(2), 241–279. doi:10.2753/MIS0742-1222260210

Robey, D., & Sahay, S. (1996). Transforming work through information technology: A comparative case study of geographical information systems in county government. *Information Systems Research, 7*(1), 93–110. doi:10.1287/isre.7.1.93

Robins, K. (1999). Against virtual community: For a politics of distance. *Journal of the Theoretical Humanities*, *4*, 163–170. doi:10.1080/09697259908572045

Robins, K., & Webster, F. (1999). *Times of technoculture: From the information society to the virtual life*. New York, NY: Routledge.

Rodgers, F., & Rodgers, C. (1989). Business and facts of family life. *Harvard Business Review*, *89*, 121–129.

Rogers, E. M. (1995). *Diffusion of innovations*. New York, NY: The Free Press.

Rogers, E., & Albritton, M. (1995). Interactive communication technologies in business organizations. *Journal of Business Communication*, *32*(2), 177. doi:10.1177/002194369503200206

Rosenfeld, P. R., Giacalone, R. A., & Riordan, C. A. (1995). *Impression management in organizations: Theory, measurement, and practice*. New York, NY: Routledge.

Rothbard, N. P., & Edwards, J. R. (2003). Investment in work and family roles: A test of identity and utilitarian motives. *Personnel Psychology*, *56*, 699–730. doi:10.1111/j.1744-6570.2003.tb00755.x

Rothbard, N. P., Phillips, K. W., & Dumas, T. L. (2005). Managing multiple roles: Work- family policies and individuals' desires for segmentation. *Organization Science*, *16*, 243–258. doi:10.1287/orsc.1050.0124

Rourke, L., Anderson, T., Garrison, D. R., & Archer, W. (1999). Assessing social presence in asynchronous test-based computer conferencing. *Journal of Distance Education*, *14*(2), 50–71.

Rubin, A. (2000). Standards for rigor in qualitative inquiry. *Research in the Sociology of Work*, *10*, 173–178.

Rubin, B. (1995). Flexible accumulation, the decline of contract and social transformation. *Research in Social Stratification and Mobility*, *14*, 297–323.

Rubin, B. (2007). New times redux: Layering time in the new economy. In Rubin, B. A. (Ed.), *Workplace Temporalities: Research in the Sociology of Work* (pp. 527–548). Amsterdam, The Netherlands: Elsevier. doi:10.1016/S0277-2833(07)17017-5

Rubin, B. A., & Brody, C. J. (2005). Contradictions of commitment in the new economy: Insecurity, time and technology. *Social Science Research*, *34*, 843–861. doi:10.1016/j.ssresearch.2005.02.002

Rubin, H. J., & Rubin, I. S. (2005). *Qualitative interviewing: The art of hearing data* (2nd ed.). Thousand Oaks, CA: Sage.

Rubin, R. B., Rubin, A. M., Graham, E. E., Perse, E. M., & Seibold, D. R. (2009). *Communication research measures II: A sourcebook*. New York, NY: Routledge.

Rupsiene, L., & Pranskuniene, R. (2010). The variety of grounded theory: Different versions of the same method or different methods? *Socialiniai Mokslai*, *4*(70), 7–20.

Ruyter, K. D., Wetzels, M., & Kleijnen, M. (2001). Customer adoption of e- services: an experimental study. *International Journal of Service Industry Management*, *12*(2), 184–207. doi:10.1108/09564230110387542

Ryan, S., Jaffe, J., Drake, S. D., & Boggs, R. (2009). *Worldwide mobile worker population 2009-2013 forecast*. Retrieved May 5, 2011, from www.idc.com/getdoc.jsp?containerId=221309.

Sadala, M., & Ferreira, R. (2002). Phenomenology as a method to investigate the experience lived: A perspective from Husserl and Merleau Ponty's thought. *Journal of Advanced Nursing*, *37*(3), 282–293. doi:10.1046/j.1365-2648.2002.02071.x

Salovey, P., & Mayer, J. D. (1990). Emotional intelligence. *Imagination, Cognition and Personality*, *9*, 185–211.

Sandhu, K. (2009). Measuring the performance of electronic services acceptance model (E-SAM). *International Journal of Business Information Systems*, *5*(4).

Sandhu, K., & Corbitt, B. (2002). *Exploring an understanding of electronic service end-user adoption*. Sydney, Australia: The International Federation for Information Processing.

Sandhu, K., & Corbitt, B. (2008). A framework for electronic services system. *International Journal of Electronic Customer Relationship Management*, *2*(1). doi:10.1504/IJECRM.2008.019568

Sarker, S., Sarker, S., & Jana, D. (2010). The impact of the nature of globally distributed work arrangement on work-life conflict and valence: The Indian GSD professionals' perspective. *European Journal of Information Systems*, *19*(2), 209–224. doi:10.1057/ejis.2010.20

Sato, K., Kato, Y., & Kato, S. (2008). Exploring emotional strategies in mobile phone email communication: Analysis on the impact of social presence. In *Proceedings of International Conference on Computers in Education (ICCE) 2008*, (pp. 253-260). ICCE.

Schieman, S., & Glavin, P. (2008). Trouble at the border? Gender, flexibility at work, and the work-home interface. *Social Problems*, *55*(4), 590–611. doi:10.1525/sp.2008.55.4.590

Schneider, S. C., & Barsoux, J. (1997). *Managing across cultures*. London, UK: Prentice Hall.

Schrage, M. (2000). *Serious play: How the world's best companies simulate to innovate*. Boston, MA: Harvard Business School Press.

Schutz, A. (1967). *The phenomenology of the social world* (Walsh, G., & Lehnert, F., Trans.). Evanston, IL: Northwestern University Press.

Schwarz, N. (1995). What respondents learn from questionnaires: The survey interview and the logic of conversation. *International Statistical Review*, *63*, 153–168. doi:10.2307/1403610

Schwarz, N. (1996). *Cognition and communication: Judgmental biases, research methods, and the logic of conversation*. Mahwah, NJ: Erlbaum.

Scott, D. J., Coursaris, C. K., Kato, Y., & Kato, S. (2009). The exchange of emotional context in business communications: A comparison of PC and mobile email users. In M. M. Head & E. Li (Eds.), *Mobile and Ubiquitous Commerce: Advanced E-Business Methods: Volume 4 of Advances in Electronic Business Series*, (pp. 201-219). Hershey, PA: IGI Global.

Scott, C. R., Corman, S. R., & Cheney, G. R. (1998). Development of a structurational model of identification in the organization. *Communication Theory*, *8*(3), 298–336. doi:10.1111/j.1468-2885.1998.tb00223.x

Scupola, A. (2008). Conceptualizing competences in e-services adoption and assimilation in SMES. *Journal of Electronic Commerce in Organizations*, *6*(2). doi:10.4018/jeco.2008040105

Segars, A. H., & Grover, V. (1993). Re-examining perceived ease of use and usefulness: A confirmatory factor analysis. *Management Information Systems Quarterly*, *17*(4), 517–525. doi:10.2307/249590

Seidman, I. (1998). *Interviewing as qualitative research: A guide for researchers in education and the social sciences* (2nd ed.). New York, NY: Teachers College Press.

Shachaf, P. (2008). Cultural diversity and information and communication technology impacts on global virtual teams: An exploratory study. *Information & Management*, *45*, 131–142. doi:10.1016/j.im.2007.12.003

Shapiro, R. J. (2008). *Futurecast: How superpowers, populations, and globalization will change the way you live and work*. New York, NY: St. Martin's Press.

Shaw, T., Arnason, K., & Belardo, S. (1993). The effects of computer mediated interactivity on idea generation: An experimental investigation. *IEEE Transactions on Systems, Man, and Cybernetics*, *23*(3), 737–745. doi:10.1109/21.256546

Shedletsky, L. J., & Aitken, J. E. (2001). The paradoxes of online academic work. *Communication Education*, *50*, 206–217. doi:10.1080/03634520109379248

Shia, S. M., & Monroe, R. W. (2006). Telecommuting's past and future: A literature review and research agenda. *Business Process Management Journal*, *12*, 455–482. doi:10.1108/14637150610678078

Short, J., Williams, E., & Christie, B. (1976). *The social psychology of telecommunications*. London, UK: Wiley.

Shuy, R. W. (2002). In-person versus telephone interviewing. In Gubrium, J. F., & Holstein, J. A. (Eds.), *Handbook of Interview Research: Context and Method* (pp. 537–555). Thousand Oaks, CA: Sage.

Silverman, D. (2001). *Interpreting qualitative data, methods for analyzing talk, text and interaction* (2nd ed.). Thousand Oaks, CA: Sage.

Singh, N., Zhao, H., & Hu, X. (2003). Cultural adaptation on the web: A study of American companies' domestic and Chinese websites. *Journal of Global Information Management, 11*(3), 63–81. doi:10.4018/jgim.2003070104

Singh, S. (1996). Money, marriage and the computer. In Gilgun, J. F., & Sussman, M. B. (Eds.), *The Methods and Methodologies of Qualitative Family Research* (pp. 369–398). Binghamton, NY: Haworth.

Smith, V. (2001). Teamwork versus tempwork: Managers and the dualisms of workplace restructuring. In Campbell, K., Cornfield, D., & McCammon, H. (Eds.), *Working in Restructured Workplaces: New Directions for the Sociology of Work* (pp. 7–28). Thousand Oaks, CA: Sage.

Soukup, C. (2006). Computer-mediated communication as a virtual third place: Building Oldenberg's great good places on the world wide web. *New Media & Society, 8*, 421–444. doi:10.1177/1461444806061953

Spielberg, H. J. (1975). *Doing phenomenology.* Dordrecht, The Netherlands: Martinus Nijhoff.

Spivack, A. J., & Rubin, B. A. (2011). *Spaces to control creative output of the knowledge worker: A managerial paradox?* Paper presented at the iConference. Seattle, WA.

Sproull, L., & Kiesler, S. (1986). Reducing social context cues: Electronic mail in organizational communication. *Management Science, 32*(11), 1492–1512. doi:10.1287/mnsc.32.11.1492

Square Methodology. (2011, January 28). *Initial thoughts on interview via Skype.* Retrieved from http://www.squaremethodology.com.

Staples, D. S., & Webster, J. (2007). Exploring traditional and virtual teams' members' "best practices": A social cognitive theory perspective. *Small Group Research, 38*, 60–97. doi:10.1177/1046496406296961

Steinfield, C., Huysman, M., Kenneth, D., Chyng, Y., & Poot, J. Huis,... Cabrera, A. (2001). New methods for studying global virtual teams: Towards a multi-faceted approach. In *Proceedings of the 34th Annual Hawaii International Conference on System Sciences (HICSS-34).* Hawaii, HI: HICSS.

Stephens, N. (2007). Collecting data from elites and ultra elites: Telephone and face-to-face interviews with macroeconomists. *Qualitative Research, 7*(2), 203–216. doi:10.1177/1468794107076020

Stewart, T. A. (1997). *Intellectual capital: The new wealth of organizations.* New York, NY: Doubleday.

Stohl, C., & Cheney, G. (2001). Participatory processes/paradoxical practices: Communication and the dilemmas of organizational democracy. *Management Communication Quarterly, 14*, 349–407. doi:10.1177/0893318901143001

Strannegård, L., & Friberg, M. (2002). *Already elsewhere: Play, identity and speed in the business world* (Wilson, D., Trans.). Stockholm, Sweden: Raster Förlag.

Strauss, A. J., & Corbin, J. (1994). Grounded theory methodology. In Denzin, N. K., & Lincoln, Y. S. (Eds.), *Handbook of Qualitative Research* (pp. 53–65). Thousand Oaks, CA: Sage.

Strauss, A. L. (1987). *Qualitative analysis for social scientists.* Cambridge, UK: Cambridge University Press. doi:10.1017/CBO9780511557842

Strauss, A. L., & Corbin, J. (1990). *Basics of qualitative research: Grounded theory procedures and techniques.* Newbury Park, CA: Sage.

Strauss, A. L., & Corbin, J. (1998). *Basics of qualitative research: Techniques and procedures for developing grounded theory* (2nd ed.). Thousand Oaks, CA: Sage.

Striukova, L., & Rayna, T. (2008). The role of social capital in virtual teams and organisations: Corporate value creation. *International Journal of Networking and Virtual Organisations, 5*(1), 103–119. doi:10.1504/IJNVO.2008.016005

Stroh, M. (2000). Qualitative interviewing. In Burton, D. (Ed.), *Research Training for Social Scientists: A Handbook for Postgraduate Researchers* (pp. 196–217). London, UK: Sage.

Sturges, J. E., & Hanrahan, K. J. (2004). Comparing telephone and face-to-face qualitative interviewing: A research note. *Qualitative Research, 4*(1), 107–118. doi:10.1177/1468794104041110

Subramanian, G. H. (1994). A replication of perceived usefulness and perceived ease of usefulness measurement. *Decision Sciences*, *25*(5), 863–874. doi:10.1111/j.1540-5915.1994.tb01873.x

Suddaby, R. (2006). From the editors: What grounded theory is not. *Academy of Management Journal*, *49*, 633-642.

Sullivan, C., & Lewis, S. (2001). Home-based telework, gender, and the synchronization of work and family: Perspectives of teleworkers and their co-residents. *Gender, Work and Organization*, *8*, 123–145. doi:10.1111/1468-0432.00125

Sundar, S. S., Xu, Q., & Bellur, S. (2010). Designing interactivity in media interfaces: A communications perspective. In the Proceedings of CHI 2010, (pp. 2247-2256). Atlanta, GA: CHI.

Szajna, B. (1994). Software evaluation and choice: Predictive validation of the technology acceptance instrument. *Management Information Systems Quarterly*, *18*(3), 319–324. doi:10.2307/249621

Szajna, B. (1996). Empirical evaluation of the revised technology acceptance model. *Management Science*, *42*(1), 85–92. doi:10.1287/mnsc.42.1.85

Szymanski, D. M., & Hise, R. T. (2000). E-satisfaction: An initial examination. *Journal of Retailing*, *76*(3), 309–322. doi:10.1016/S0022-4359(00)00035-X

Tavallaei, M., & Talib, M. A. (2010). A general perspective on role of theory in qualitative research. *Journal of International Social Research*, *3*, 570–577.

Taylor, S., & Todd, P. (1995). Assessing IT usage: The role of prior experience. *Management Information Systems Quarterly*, *19*(4), 561–571. doi:10.2307/249633

Taylor, S., & Todd, P. A. (1995). Understanding information technology usage: A test of competing models. *Information Systems Research*, *6*(2), 144–176. doi:10.1287/isre.6.2.144

Telework Research Network. (2011). *How many people telecommute*. Retrieved from http://www.teleworkresearchnetwork.com/research/people-telecommute.

Thatcher, S. M. B., & Zhu, X. (2006). Changing identities in a changing workplace: Identification, identity, enactment, self-verification, and telecommuting. *Academy of Management Review*, *31*, 1076–1088. doi:10.5465/AMR.2006.22528174

Tholander, J., & Johansson, C. (2010). Bodies, boards, clubs, and bugs: A study of bodily engaging artifacts. In the *Proceedings of CHI 2010*, (pp. 4045-4050). Atlanta, GA: CHI.

Thomas, D., & Bostrom, R. (2010). Building trust and cooperation through technology adaptation in virtual teams: Empirical field evidence. *EDPACS*, *42*(5), 1–20. doi:10.1080/07366981.2010.537182

Thomas, G., & James, D. (2006). Reinventing grounded theory: Some questions about theory, ground and discovery. *British Educational Research Journal*, *32*(6), 767–795. doi:10.1080/01411920600989412

Thomas, L. T., & Ganster, D. (1995). Impact of family-supportive work variables on work-family conflict and strain: A control perspective. *The Journal of Applied Psychology*, *80*, 6–15. doi:10.1037/0021-9010.80.1.6

Thompson-Hayes, M., & Gibson, D., M., Scott, A. T. & Webb, L. M. (2009). Professorial collaborations via CMC: Interactional dialectics. *Computers in Human Behavior*, *25*, 208–216. doi:10.1016/j.chb.2008.09.003

Thompson, J. B. (1995). *Other floors, other voices: A textography of a small university building*. Mahway, NJ: Lawrence Erlbaum.

Thompson, P., & Smith, C. (2009). Labour power and the labor process: Contesting the marginality of the sociology of work. *Sociology*, *43*, 913–930. doi:10.1177/0038038509340728

Thye, S. R. (2007). Logical and philosophical foundations of experimental research in the social sciences. In Webster, M., & Sell, J. (Eds.), *Laboratory Experiments in the Social Sciences*. New York, NY: Elsevier.

Tierney, W. G., & Dilley, P. (2002). Interviewing in education. In Gubrium, J. F., & Holstein, J. A. (Eds.), *Handbook of Interview Research: Context & Method* (pp. 453–471). Thousand Oaks, CA: Sage.

Tietze, S. (2002). When "work" comes "home": Coping strategies of teleworkers and their families. *Journal of Business Ethics, 41*, 385–396. doi:10.1023/A:1021236426657

Tietze, S., & Musson, G. (2002). Working from home and managing guilt. *Organizations and People, 9*, 34–39.

Tietze, S., & Musson, G. (2003). The times and temporalities of home-based telework. *Personnel Review, 32*, 438–533. doi:10.1108/00483480310477524

Tomlinson, B. (2005). From linear to interactive animation: How autonomous characters change the process and product of animating. *ACM Computers in Entertainment, 3*(1), 1–20.

Touré, H. I. (2011). *ITU telecom world 2011 forum closing speech*. Retrieved from http://www.itu.int/en/osg/speeches/Pages/2011-10-27.aspx.

Tracy, S. J. (2002). Altered practice, altered stories, altered lives: Three considerations for translating organizational communication scholarship into practice. *Management Communication Quarterly, 16*, 85–91. doi:10.1177/0893318902161005

Trethewey, A. (2002). Translating scholarship into practice. *Management Communication Quarterly, 16*, 81–84. doi:10.1177/0893318902161004

Trevino, L. K., & Webster, J. (1992). Flow in computer-mediated communication: Electronic mail and voice evaluation. *Communication Research, 19*(2), 539–573. doi:10.1177/009365092019005001

Triandis, H. C. (1995). *Individualism and collectivism*. Boulder, CO: Westview Press.

Trompenaars, F., & Hampden-Turner, C. (2000). *Building cross-cultural competence: How to create wealth from conflicting values*. New Haven, CT: Yale University Press.

Trow, D. B. (1957). Autonomy and job satisfaction in task-oriented groups. *Journal of Abnormal and Social Psychology, 54*(2), 204–209. doi:10.1037/h0041424

Troyer, L. (2001). Effects of protocol differences on the study of status and social influence. *Current Research in Social Psychology, 6*, 182–204.

Troyer, L. (2002). The relation between experimental standardization and theoretical development in group process research. In Szmatka, J., Lovaglia, M., & Wysineska, K. (Eds.), *The Growth of Social Knowledge: Theory Simulation, and Empirical Research in Group Processes*. Westport, CT: Praeger.

Tsair-Wei, C., Wen-Pin, L., Chih-Wei, L., Weng-Chung, W., Shih-Chung, C., Hsien-Yi, W., & Shih-Bin, S. (2011). Web-based computer adaptive assessment of individual perceptions of job satisfaction for hospital workplace employees. *BMC Medical Research Methodology, 11*(1), 47–54. doi:10.1186/1471-2288-11-47

U.S. Census Bureau. (2010). *Internet use in the United States: October 2009*. Retrieved April 26, 2011 from http://www.census.gov/population/www/socdemo/computer/2009.html.

U.S. Department of Labor. (2008). *Women in the labor force: A databook*. Washington, DC: US Department of Labor.

U.S. Department of Labor. (2010). *American time use survey*. Retrieved April 25, 2011 from http://www.bls.gov/news.release/pdf/atus.pdf.

Van Maanen, J. (2006). Ethnography then and now. *Qualitative Research in Organizations and Management, 1*, 13–21. doi:10.1108/17465640610666615

van Riel, A. C. R., Liljander, V., & Jurriëns, P. (2001). Exploring consumer evaluations of e-services: A portal site. *International Journal of Service Industry Management, 12*(40), 359–377. doi:10.1108/09564230110405280

Venkatesh, A., & Vitalari, N. (1992). An emerging distributed work arrangement: An investigation of computer-based supplemental work at home. *Management Science, 38*, 1687–1706. doi:10.1287/mnsc.38.12.1687

Venkatesh, V. (1999). Creation of favourable user perceptions: Exploring the role of intrinsic motivation. *Management Information Systems Quarterly, 23*(2), 239–260. doi:10.2307/249753

Venkatesh, V. (2000). Determinants of perceived ease of use: Integrating control, intrinsic motivation, and emotion into the technology acceptance model. *Information Systems Research*, *11*(4), 342–365. doi:10.1287/isre.11.4.342.11872

Venkatesh, V., & Davis, F. D. (1996). A model of the antecedents of perceived ease of use: Development and test. *Decision Sciences*, *27*(3), 451–482. doi:10.1111/j.1540-5915.1996.tb01822.x

Venkatesh, V., & Morris, M. G. (2000). Why don't men ever stop to ask for directions? Gender, social influence, and their role in technology acceptance and user behaviour. *Management Information Systems Quarterly*, *24*, 115–139. doi:10.2307/3250981

Virick, M., DaSilva, N., & Arrington, K. (2010). Moderators of the curvilinear relation between extent of telecommuting and job and life satisfaction: The role of performance outcome orientation and worker type. *Human Relations*, *63*(1), 137–154. doi:10.1177/0018726709349198

Wakefield, R. L., Leidner, D. E., & Garrison, G. (2008). A model of conflict, leadership, and performance in virtual teams. *Information Systems Research*, *19*(4), 434–455. doi:10.1287/isre.1070.0149

Walther, J. B., Loh, T., & Granka, L. (2005b). Let me count the ways: The interchange of verbal and nonverbal cues in computer-mediated and face-to-face affinity. *Journal of Language and Social Psychology*, *24*, 36–65. doi:10.1177/0261927X04273036

Walther, J. B., & Parks, M. R. (2002). Cues filtered out, cues filtered in: Computer mediated communication and relationships. In Knapp, M. L., Daley, J. A., & Miller, G. R. (Eds.), *The Handbook of Interpersonal Communication* (3rd ed., pp. 529–563). Thousand Oaks, CA: Sage.

Warekentin, M., Sayeed, L., & Hightower, R. (1997). Virtual teams versus face-to-face teams: An exploratory study of a web-based conference system. *Decision Sciences*, *28*(4), 975–996. doi:10.1111/j.1540-5915.1997.tb01338.x

Warner, M., & Witzel, M. (2004). *Managing in virtual organizations*. London, UK: Thompson.

Watt, J. H. (1997). Using the internet for quantitative survey research. *Quirk's Marketing Research Review*. Retrieved from http://www.unt.edu/rss/class/survey/watt.htm.

Watt, J. H., & van den Berg, S. (1995). *Research methods for communication science*. Needham Heights, MA: Allyn & Bacon.

Webster, M. Jr, & Sell, J. (2007). Why do experiments? In Webster, M., & Sell, J. (Eds.), *Laboratory Experiments in the Social Sciences*. New York, NY: Elsevier.

Weick, K. (1979). *The social psychology of organizing*. Reading, MA: Addison-Wesley.

Wellin, C., & Fine, G. A. (2001). Ethnography as work: Career socialization, settings and problems. In Atkinson, P., Coffey, A., Delamont, S., Lofland, J., & Lofland, L. (Eds.), *Handbook of Ethnography*. Thousand Oaks, CA: Sage Publishing.

Wells, C. (2010). Citizenship and communication in online youth civic engagement projects. *Information Communication and Society*, *13*, 419–441. doi:10.1080/13691180902833208

Wells, W. (2003). *American capitalism, 1945-2000: Continuity and change from mass production to the information society*. Chicago, IL: Ivan R. Dee.

Whitman, M., & Woszczynski, A. (2003). *The handbook of information systems research*. Hershey, PA: IGI Global. doi:10.4018/978-1-59140-144-5

Whittle, A., & Mueller, F. (2009). I could be dead for two weeks and my boss would never know: Telework and the politics of representation. *New Technology, Work and Employment*, *24*(2), 131–143. doi:10.1111/j.1468-005X.2009.00224.x

Whyte, W. F. (1991). *Participatory action research*. London, UK: Sage.

Wiesenfeld, B. M., Raghuram, S., & Garud, R. (2001). Organizational identification among virtual workers: The role of need for affiliation and perceived work-based social support. *Journal of Management*, *27*, 213–229.

Willis, K. D. D. (2006). *User authorship and creativity within interactivity. In the Proceedings of Multimedia (MM 2006)* (pp. 731–735). Santa Barbara, CA: ACM.

Wilson, H. S., & Hutchinson, S. A. (1996). Methodologic mistakes in grounded theory. *Nursing Research, 45*(2), 122–124. doi:10.1097/00006199-199603000-00012

Wilson, S. M. (2002). The anthropology of online communities. *Annual Review of Anthropology, 31*, 449–467. doi:10.1146/annurev.anthro.31.040402.085436

Wilson, S., & Franzen, J. (2002). *The man in the gray flannel suit*. New York, NY: Da Capo Press.

Winkel, D. E., & Clayton, R. W. (2010). Transitioning between work and family roles as a function of boundary flexibility and role salience. *Journal of Vocational Behavior, 76*, 336–343. doi:10.1016/j.jvb.2009.10.011

Woodman, R. W., Sawyer, J. E., & Griffin, R. W. (1993). Toward a theory of organizational creativity. *Academy of Management Review, 18*(2), 293–321.

World at Work. (2009). *Telework trendlines 2009*. Retrieved May 1, 2011, from http://www.workingfromanywhere.org/news/Trendlines_2009.pdf.

Wrench, J. S., Thomas-Maddox, C., Richmond, V. P., & McCroskey, J. C. (2008). *Quantitative research methods for communication: A hands-on-approach*. New York, NY: Oxford University Press.

Wright, K. M., & Granger, M. J. (2001). Using the web as a strategic resource: An applied classroom exercise. In *Proceedings of the 16th Annual Conference of the International Academy for Information Management*. New Orleans, LA: IAIM.

Wright, K. B., & Webb, L. M. (Eds.). (2011). *Computer mediated communication in personal relationships*. New York, NY: Peter Lang Publishers.

Xue, M., Harker, P. T., & Heim, G. R. (2004). *Incorporating the dual customer roles in e-service design*. The Working Paper Series. New York, NY: The Wharton Financial Institutions Center.

Yao, G., & Li, Q. (2008). *Exploring the effects of interactivity on consumer trust in e-retailing*. IEEE.

Ybema, S., Yanow, D., Wels, H., & Kamsteeg, F. H. (2009). *Organizational ethnography: Studying the complexity of everyday life*. Los Angeles, CA: Sage.

Yin, R. K. (1994). *Case study research: Design and methods* (2nd ed.). Thousand Oaks, CA: Sage Publications.

Zakaria, N., Amelinckx, A., & Wilemon, D. (2004). Working together apart? Building a knowledge-sharing environment for global virtual teams. *Creativity and Innovation Management, 13*(1), 15–29. doi:10.1111/j.1467-8691.2004.00290.x

Zakaria, N., & Cogburn, D. L. (2010). Context-dependent vs. content-dependent: An exploration of the cultural behavioural patterns of online intercultural communication using e-mail. *International Journal of Business and System Research, 4*(3), 330–347. doi:10.1504/IJBSR.2010.032954

Zanna, M. P., & Rempel, J. K. (1988). *Attitudes: A new look at an old concept*. Cambridge, UK: Cambridge University Press.

Zeithaml, V. A., Parasuraman, A., & Malhotra, A. (2000). *A conceptual framework for understanding e-service quality: Implications for future research and managerial practice*. Working Paper. Boston, MA: Marketing Science Institute.

Zeithaml, V. A., Berry, L., & Parasuraman, A. (1993). The nature and determinants of customer expectations of service. *Journal of the Academy of Marketing Science, 21*(1), 1–12. doi:10.1177/0092070393211001

Zeithaml, V. A., & Bitner, M. J. (2000). *Services marketing: Integrating customer focus across the firm*. New York, NY: Irwin McGraw-Hill.

Zemke, R., & Connellan, T. (2001). *E-service: 24 ways to keep your customers when the competition is just a click away*. New York, NY: American Management Association.

Zhang, H., & Poole, M. S. (2010). Virtual team identity construction and boundary maintenance. In Long, S. (Ed.), *Communication, Relationships and Practices in Virtual Work* (pp. 100–122). Hershey, PA: IGI Global. doi:10.4018/978-1-61520-979-8.ch006

About the Contributors

Shawn D. Long (Ph.D., University of Kentucky; M.P.A., Tennessee State University) is Chair of the Department of Communication Studies and former Director of the Communication Studies Graduate Program at the University of North Carolina at Charlotte. He is currently Associate Professor of Communication Studies and Associate Professor of Organizational Science at the University of North Carolina at Charlotte. An organizational scholar with numerous peer-reviewed publications, Dr. Long's teaching and research spans organizational communication, organizational science, virtual work, diversity communication, virtual- team assimilation, and socialization, and health communication. Dr. Long studies the utility and development of communication practices and processes in virtual work. He has consulted several organizations on communication, technology, culture, diversity, and structure. He has written, presented, and published several peer-reviewed papers around issues of organizational technology, diversity, virtual work in organizations, health communication, and organizational culture. He has appeared as a featured guest on several media outlets including the National Public Radio and the Canadian Broadcast Corporation. His most recent research appears in *Communication Monographs, Journal of National Medical Association, Clinical Transplantation, Health Communication, Journal of Health Psychology, Journal of Health Communication, Communication Teacher, Health Communication, Information and Science Technology, The Encyclopedia of Organizational/Industrial Psychology, Case Studies for Organizational Communication: Understanding Communication Processes,* and *Virtual and Collaborative Teams.* His book, *Communication, Relationships and Practices in Virtual Work* (2010) was nominated for two Outstanding Book Awards in two divisions of the National Communication Association. He is currently guest editor of a special issue of the *Journal of Information Technology Research.* He serves on a number of journal editorial boards. Dr. Long is immediate past-Chair of the African American Communication and Culture Division of the National Communication Association. Prior to arriving at UNC-Charlotte, Dr. Long was a Southern Regional Educational Board Doctoral Scholar and Lyman T. Johnson Doctoral Scholar at the University of Kentucky. He has been recognized with several professional awards including the 2011 Southern States Communication Association Outreach Award, 2009 Organizational Science Outstanding Service Award, 2010 Southern States Communication Association Minority and Retention Award, Chancellor's Award for Outstanding Teaching at the University of Kentucky, The Multicultural Summer Fellowship at the University of Nebraska-Lincoln, Outstanding Teaching Assistant in the College of Communication and Information Studies at the University of Kentucky, Outstanding Graduate Teaching Assistant recognized by the International Communication Association, and Who's Who Among American Teachers.

* * *

Andrea Amelinckx, J.D., is the Director of the International Programs Office, the Chair of the International Management Area, and the Director of the First Nations Governance Program at the University of Lethbridge, Faculty of Management in Lethbridge, Alberta, Canada. Her research interests are in the areas of cross-cultural management, indigenous studies, and virtual global team relations. She currently teaches such courses as cross-cultural study in Malaysia, cross-cultural management practices, and Canadian culture and management. Currently, she is working with an interdisciplinary team on First Nations, studying community and corporate relations and involvement in the natural resource sector.

Anita Blanchard is Associate Professor of Psychology and Organization Science at the University of North Carolina Charlotte. She has her PhD from Claremont Graduate University in Organizational Psychology. Her research interests include how successful virtual communities function, particularly within organizations. She examines the application of behavior setting theories to virtual communities, the effects of virtual community participation on face-to-face communities' trust and social capital, the development and experience of a sense of community within virtual communities, and how virtual groups come to be experiences as "groups."

Sayde J. Brais is an M.A. Candidate in the Communication Studies program at the University of North Carolina at Charlotte. Previously, she earned a B.A. in International Public Relations from UNC Charlotte. Her research interests are in organizational communication which includes socialization and membership negotiation in church settings, identity formation in organizational settings, diversity communication, and virtual work. She has served as a graduate teaching and research assistant for nearly two years in the program. Upon graduating, she plans to pursue a Ph.D.

Heather D. Burnett earned her Master's in Industrial and Organizational Psychology from The University of North Carolina at Charlotte. While there, she worked closely with Dr. Anita Blanchard in the Virtual Communities Research Lab and investigated how users perceive the entitativity (or "groupiness") of virtual groups and communities as well as how users identify with these virtual groups through the management of specific technological design features. After obtaining her degree, Heather joined Bank of America, where she has held a number of consulting roles in the Staffing and Leadership Development functions of Global Human Resources.

Kunihiro Chida is a Professional Japanese Animation Artist in Toei Animation Institute. His main work is many background pictures for internationally-renowned animations, "One Piece," "Dragon Ball," "Dr. Slump," and so on. His general research interests are applications to computer-mediated communications of "Image BG," a technique for expressing the emotional states of animated characters in background images.

Craig L. Engstrom is Assistant Professor in the Department of Communication Arts and Sciences at Elmhurst College, where he teaches Business and Organizational Communication from Interpretive and Rhetorical Perspectives. His research currently focuses on writing accounts of institutional and prosaic practices, specifically those of professionals, and exploring the role of rhetoric and interpretation in enacting professional and entrepreneurial opportunities. His research has appeared in *Qualitative Research* *in Organizations and Management, TransFormations, Journal of Critical Organizational Inquiry,* and *Communication Quarterly.* He provides a variety of consulting services to small business and professionals, including search engine optimization, website and social networking design and maintenance, and résumé consulting. When he's detached from virtual environments, he enjoys travelling internationally, cycling, and baking.

Michelle Ferrier is founder and publisher of LocallyGrownNews.com, a hyperlocal online community platform for local food advocates. She is an Associate Professor in the School of Communications at Elon University, where she teaches Journalism, Magazine Publishing, Interactive Media, and Online Community Development. Ferrier holds a Ph.D. from the University of Central Florida in Texts and Technology with special emphasis on Online Communities, Online Learning, and New Media Technologies. She also holds a M.S. from the University of Memphis in Journalism. For more than 20 years, Ferrier has been experimenting with and developing content for a variety of digital platforms. She has been a beta tester and early adopter of such technologies as page layout software, direct-to-plate printing, content management systems, website development, online learning, and other digital communication technologies.

Kathryn L. Fonner (Ph.D., Northwestern University) is an Assistant Professor in the Department of Communication at the University of Wisconsin-Milwaukee. Her research focuses on telework and alternative work arrangements, work-life balance, and the changing nature of the relationship between customers and service providers. Her work has appeared in journals such as *Communication Monographs, Journal of Applied Communication Research,* and *Management Communication Quarterly.*

Danna M. Gibson (PhD, The University of Memphis, 2001) is Professor of Communication at Columbus State University in Columbus, GA, where she currently serves as interim chair of the Communication Department and directs the Non-Profit and Civic Engagement Academic Center (NPaCE). She has received numerous teaching, research, and community awards for her work with nonprofits and workforce development. Her research interests explore ways communication can help to create and maintain healthy relational communities. Dr. Gibson has written numerous literacy and workforce development grants, has authored numerous convention presentations, co-authored an on-line public speaking textbook, entitled *Empowering Your Public Voice,* and has published essays in *Computers in Human Behavior* and *Communication Law Review.* Dr. Gibson is recognized for her work with student service learning and community partnership formation.

Cerise L. Glenn (PhD, Howard University) is an Assistant Professor in the Department of Communication Studies at the University of North Carolina at Greensboro. She examines how various aspects of social identity, especially race/ethnicity, gender, and socioeconomic status, intersect in various contexts. Her research and teaching interests center on social constructions of difference (diversity), particularly identity negotiation and representations of underrepresented groups in organizational, intercultural/ international, and mass-mediated contexts.

Shalin Hai-Jew works as an instructional designer at Kansas State University. She has BAs in English and psychology, an MA in English (from the University of Washington) and an Ed.D. from Seattle University. She teaches for WashingtonOnline through Walla Walla Community College. She reviews for *Educause Quarterly* and *JOLT of MERLOT*.

Marceline Hayes (PhD, University of Memphis, 2000) is an associate professor of communication and interim department chair at Arkansas State University. Her research interests include many facets of interpersonal communication and qualitative research methods.

Shogo Kato is an Assistant Professor in the School of Arts and Sciences, Tokyo Woman's Christian University, Japan, and a part-time instructor in the Faculty of Economics, Dokkyo University, Japan. He earned a Ph.D. from Tokyo Institute of Technology in 2005. His general research interests include educational technology and the application of behavior science, psychology, and Information and Communication Technology (ICT) to educational scenes. Dr. Kato is particularly interested in the emotional aspects in virtual community, such as Internet bullying.

Yuuki Kato is an Assistant Professor at Sagami Women's University, Faculty of Arts and Sciences, Department of Information and Media Studies, Japan. He earned a Ph.D. from Tokyo Institute of Technology in 2005. His general research interests include educational technology and the application of behavior science, psychology, and Information and Communication Technology (ICT) to educational scenes. Dr. Kato is particularly interested in the emotional aspects in technology-mediated human communications.

Kerk F. Kee (Ph.D., University of Texas at Austin) is an Assistant Professor in the Department of Communication Studies, Chapman University, Orange, California, USA. He actively conducts research in the areas of emerging technologies and social media as well as organizational and health communication. His recent work appears in journals such as *Journal of Computer-Mediated Communication, Computer Supported Cooperative Work, CyberPsychology, Behavior, & Social Networking*, and *IEEE Computer* as well as the *Oxford Handbook of Positive Organizational Scholarship*. His current projects include looking at cyberinfrastructure adoption in scientific organizations, organizational use of social media for distributed collaboration and virtual organizing, as well as how social media data can be used to identify social aggregates to aid in the diffusion of health interventions.

Marianne LeGreco is an Assistant Professor in the Department of Communication Studies at the University of North Carolina at Greensboro. Her work focuses on community-based and participatory research methods, food, and nutrition programming in low-income neighborhoods, and the application of organizational communication concepts in health communication contexts. LeGreco earned her PhD in Communication from the Hugh Downs School of Human Communication at Arizona State University, with an emphasis on organizational and health communication. Her current research focuses on refining a qualitative research method called discourse tracing, developing concepts and practices related to kitchen literacy, as well as managing at Food Policy Think Tank at UNCG. She is particularly interested in concepts and theories related to access to resources, policy, and participation.

Dawn Leonard is the Co-Founder of Urban Harvest Greensboro. In her role as Executive Director, she organized and oversaw day-to-day activities at the community garden including: hosting volunteer groups of all ages; running the CSA (Community Supported Agriculture); and outreach to foster activity at and around the garden. As ED of Urban Harvest, she built a network of support for projects relating to urban agriculture and food access in Greensboro. Dawn graduated from Iowa State University in 2002 with a BFA in Graphic Design and a minor in music. She completed the Yoga Alliance 200-hr teacher-training program in 2008 and is now working on her 500-hr certification. Since the dissolution of Urban Harvest, Dawn leads the dual life of Yoga Instructor at Guilford College and other Greensboro locations, and Web Manager for First Presbyterian Church.

Natalie Nelson-Marsh (Ph.D., University of Colorado at Boulder, 2006) is an Associate Professor in the Department of Communication at Boise State University. Her main research interests include the study of non-traditional organizations focusing on virtual organizations in particular, organizational culture, information and communication technologies, organizational stability and change, and qualitative research methods. Her work has appeared in journals including *Management Communication Quarterly* and *New Media and Society*.

Beth A. Rubin is Professor of Sociology and Organizational Science and Adjunct Professor of Management at UNC-Charlotte. She held prior appointments at the National Science Foundation, Tulane University, and Cornell University. Dr. Rubin has published numerous articles in leading academic journals on organizational, economic, and workplace transformation, on the re-employment of displaced workers, labor unions, homelessness, and social policy and social theory. She has also published three books, *Research in the Sociology of Work: Workplace Temporalities* (2007); *Beside the Golden Door: Policy, Politics, and the Homeless* (1998, with James Wright and Joel Devine) and *Shifts in the Social Contract* (1996). Rubin's current research is on generational differences in the workplace; the impact on organizational and workplace transformation on employee creativity, commitment, and well-being; gender differences in organizations; time in organizations; organizational and workplace restructuring; and various types of inequality and employee outcomes in the United States and China.

Kamaljeet Sandhu is a Senior Lecturer of Accounting and Information Systems at the School of Business, Economics, and Public Policy of the University of New England. He earned his Ph.D. in Information Systems from Deakin University, Melbourne. His teaching and research expertise are in electronic services and services management at universities, corporate governance, accounting information systems, management accounting, asset management, and e-learning.

April J. Spivack is a Ph.D. Candidate in the Transdisciplinary Organizational Science program at the University of North Carolina at Charlotte. She has earned a B.S. in Zoology from the University of Florida, an MBA in Marketing Management from Syracuse University, and a Masters in Industrial/Organizational Psychology from UNC-Charlotte. Her research interests include the changing nature of how people work—specifically the impact of autonomy and work environments on worker creativity and well-being. She has several publications including a chapter on trends in environmental psychology, papers published in the *Journal of Creative Behavior*, *Entrepreneurship Theory and Practice*, and the *Journal of Small Business and Entrepreneurship*. She has served a term as Assistant Editor for the

Journal of Business and Psychology. Currently, she serves as the Student Representative to the Board of the Environmental Design and Research Association (EDRA), where she also serves as co-chair of the Work Environments Network.

Lara C. Stache (M.A., Northeastern Illinois University) is a doctoral student in the Department of Communication at the University of Wisconsin-Milwaukee. Her research focuses on how alternative groups use technology and online spaces to create a rhetoric that defines the alternative identity and purpose, while allowing for inclusion of those that fit the alternative definition.

Lisa Slattery Walker (formerly Rashotte) received her Ph.D. in Sociology from the University of Arizona in 1998. She joined the UNC Charlotte faculty as Assistant Professor of Sociology in 1998, and was promoted to Professor in 2010. Her research focuses on small group interaction, nonverbal behaviors, identity, emotions, gender, and expectations. Her work has appeared in *Social Psychology Quarterly*, *Social Science Research*, *Social Forces*, *Sex Roles* and numerous other journals. She has been PI or Co-PI on four NSF-funded projects. Recently, she has conducted projects on altering the status meaning of gender and, with Murray Webster, on the effect of behaviors on inequality structures in small groups. A current laboratory project, also with Dr. Murray Webster, addresses how characteristics come to have status value. Current work with Dr. Anita Blanchard examines how groups develop in online environments.

Frances Walton has a B.A. in Communication Studies from the University of North Carolina at Greensboro. She recently obtained an M.A in Communication Studies with an International Public Relations concentration from the University of North Carolina at Charlotte. Frances presently holds a part-time lecturer position at UNC Charlotte as a Business Communication and Public Speaking instructor.

Wendy Wang, Ph.D., is Associate Professor of Information Systems at the College of Business Administration, Trident University International. Her research interests include natural language processing, text abstraction and extraction, IT adoption, ERP implementation, online education, virtual workforce and organizations, etc. She has published in academic journals such as *American Society for Information Science and Technology*, and has made many presentations in international and national information systems conferences. Prior to her current position, she has been an Assistant Professor at Management of Information Systems, College of Business, San Jose State University, California.

Lynne M. Webb (PhD, University of Oregon, 1980) is Professor of Communications, University of Arkansas, and previously held tenured appointments at the University of Florida and the University of Memphis. She has published two scholarly readers, including *Computer Mediated Communication in Personal Relationships*, and over 50 essays including work in *Journal of Applied Communication Research* and *Computers in Human Behavior*. Dr. Webb is known as an applied scholar and groundbreaking researcher in social media and in family communication, who has published multiple theories, research reports, and pedagogical essays. Dr. Webb has received numerous service and teaching awards during her 30+ years as a college professor. She served as President of the Southern States Communication Association and on the governing board of the National Communication Association.

David Wilemon, PhD., is Emeritus Professor of Innovation Management and Entrepreneurship in the Whitman School of Management at Syracuse University. He is the co-founder of the Entrepreneurship and Emerging Enterprises Program and the Innovation Management Program at Syracuse. He is a co-founder of the Product Development and Management Association and served as its president. He is widely recognized for his research on new product development, innovation management, corporate venturing, project management, and high performing teamwork and has published widely in journals such as the *Academy of Management Journal, Engineering Management Review, R&D Management, Journal of Marketing, Sloan Management Review, Journal of Management Studies, Research Management, Columbia Journal of World Business,* Transactions *on Engineering Management, Project Management Journal, Research-Technology Management, Organizational Dynamics,* and the *California Management Review.* He has been the recipient of the Syracuse University Scholar/Teacher of the Year Award; the Outstanding Contribution Award to the Whitman School of Management; Outstanding Whitman Scholar; and named the Snyder Professor of Innovation Management and Entrepreneurship in 2000. He was named as one of the most prolific scholars in the area of innovation management and in technology management by the *Journal of Product Innovation Management* and the *R&D Management Journal.*

Norhayati Zakaria, PhD., is an Associate Professor in the Faculty of Business and Management at the University of Wollongong in Dubai. For the past six years, she has also been a Research and Teaching Associate at the Center of Collaboratory on Technology Enhanced Learning Communities Lab (CO-TELCO) at American University and Syracuse University, USA, in which she has been leading a global virtual team for a globally distributed collaboration research project. Dr. Zakaria graduated with a Ph.D. in Information Science and Technology and MPhil. in Information Transfer from Syracuse University, USA, and a MSc. Management from Rensselaer Polytechnic Institute, USA. Since both schools focus on interdisciplinary programs, her area of expertise bridges two distinct fields—cross-cultural management and information communication technology. Her research program builds on a key question "what are the effective strategies to manage human resources in a virtual environment given the cultural and distance barriers?" Her key areas of expertise include designing training programs for developing cultural intelligence and competencies of expatriates, managers, and multicultural teams when working in culturally diverse environments, managing organizational decision making processes in globally distributed collaboration contexts, and building models of effectiveness and best practices of using global virtual teams in group learning environments in international organizations.

Index

A

actants 10-11, 17-22, 29
action net 10, 12, 15, 17, 19-24, 27-29
Action Research (PAR) 80
analytical induction 167, 174
autoethnography 179, 223
autopoiesis 129
axial coding 38, 165-166, 203-204, 206

B

boundary flexibility 32, 35, 42-43, 46, 51, 56, 58
boundary management research 32, 55
boundary permeability 32, 38, 51, 58
boundary theory 31-32

C

category saturation 167-168, 175
cluster coding 203, 205-206
collectivism 234, 245, 247
collectivist culture 235
Community-Based and Participatory Research (CBPR) 78-86, 88, 91-93, 98
community-based work 79, 82, 86
computer-mediated communication 92, 94-96, 126, 158-159, 190, 197, 207, 209, 228, 231-232, 238, 243, 246
constant comparison process 167, 170, 175, 204
consultational interactivity 128
content-enriched communications 130
conversational interactivity 128
coworking 6
creative knowledge workers 59-60, 64
cyberethnography 11

D

debureacratization 61
deductive reasoning 161-162, 167, 174-175
descriptive statistics 37, 67, 179, 183, 190
differential permeability 51-52, 54-55
digital learning contents 127-128, 132, 136, 145
digital objects 129, 134, 147
dramaturgy 252, 277-285

E

Ehealth interventions 84
e-learning 112-113, 116-117, 120, 122, 127, 130, 132, 137, 145
emoticons 100-101, 113, 200
Emotional Intelligence (EI) model 100
emotional strategy 99-100, 102, 110, 112
emotional transmission 99, 101, 113
empirical positivism 162
employee autonomy 61
entitativity 154-157, 159
e-services system 115, 117-118, 123, 257-264, 266-267, 269, 271
Ethnography
traditional 11, 25
virtual 10-12, 26-27, 213-214, 217-220, 224-226
expectation-setting strategies 31-32, 34-36, 38, 40, 43, 45, 50-53, 55

F

functional flexibility 61

G

Global Virtual Teams (GVTs) 199, 230-231
Google AdWords 14, 17, 23-24

grounded theory 38, 57, 160-164, 166-167, 169-175, 179, 192, 199-201, 203, 205, 207-212, 255

H

high-demand learning 127
high-touch interactivity 127-128, 130-133, 136-138, 140-141, 143-147
hybrid character of actions 10, 17-18, 21-22, 28-29
hyperlocal communities 90

I

ill-structured learning 127, 137
inductive reasoning 161-162, 170, 175
industrial revolution 1, 3-8
inferential statistics 183, 190
information experience 115-120
initial conditions 150, 152-153
intentionality of consciousness 249-250, 256
interactivity 122, 127-134, 136-138, 140-141, 143-147, 151, 155-156
intercoder reliability 38, 184
intercultural training 231
interpretive shadowing 10-11, 17
interviewing 193
IT security 1-2, 6

K

knowledge workers 5-6, 59-61, 63-64, 73, 75-76

L

labor process theory 59-60, 62-63, 69-70
learning-experience swing 115, 120
legitimation 218-219, 229
life-work conflict 31-33, 35-40, 48, 50-54, 58
Local Online News Communities (LONCs) 89

M

mass manufacturing 4, 6
mixed reality 136, 145
mobile text messaging 99-100, 102, 105, 111-112
mobilization 29

N

national culture 234, 238, 241, 247
netnography 11, 27, 228
network ethnography 11
nomadic work 6-7

numerical flexibility 61

O

open coding 38, 165-166, 199-200, 203-204, 206
organizational culture 13, 55, 189, 231, 235, 239, 241, 247, 251, 253

P

pattern coding 199, 204
phenomenological reduction 249-250, 256
phenomenology 192, 248-256
pilot test 182
post-industrial society 4-5, 7
power distance 234
pre-testing 149, 151-153, 182
private investigations 10, 15, 18, 24
process coding 203-204, 206
promotoras 82, 85

Q

qualitative inquiry 10-11, 95-96, 172, 192, 207, 209, 211, 255
qualitative research 10-12, 17, 25-26, 28, 57, 94-95, 160, 164, 172-175, 179, 187-189, 192-195, 197-198, 205, 207-212, 227-229, 241
qualitative survey 176-177, 179-181, 183-184, 187, 191
quantitative survey 180-181, 189, 191, 206

R

radical interpretivism 162
registrational interactivity 128
reply timing 99-100, 102, 105, 107-112
role integration 58
role segmentation 58

S

scope conditions 152
selective coding 165, 170, 203-206
self-report 178, 191
shadowers 10, 18-19, 25
smart phones 12, 128, 153
social desirability bias 184, 191
social interactionism 282, 285
social scientific research 149, 177, 191
social scientific theory 149, 160-161
Sociology of Cyber-Social-Scientific Knowledge (SCSSK) 214, 224, 226

socio-technical spaces 128, 130
spatial autonomy 59, 63, 67-68, 70-71
System Development Life Cycle (SDLC) principle 268

T

Technology Acceptance Model (TAM) 124, 258, 265
telecommuting 1-2, 5-8, 56-57, 70, 75-77, 95
telework 1-2, 7-9, 31, 33-34, 36-37, 41-42, 44, 47, 53, 55-58, 73-77, 254, 281, 285
Telework Enhancement Act 7
teleworkers 31-47, 50-57, 70, 72, 94
temporal autonomy 59-60, 70
textual agency 21-22, 26, 29
time orientation 234
transmissional interactivity 128
triangulation 117, 181, 191, 196, 205-206, 209, 264, 275

U

uncertainty avoidance 234
user interaction 115-116, 124
user learning experience 115-116, 118-120, 122-124

V

video conferencing systems 5
virtual beach 82
virtual dramaturgy 252, 281
virtual ethnography 10-12, 26-27, 213-214, 217-220, 224-226

virtual experiences 127-129, 131-134, 136, 145-146, 221
virtual groups 149, 153, 159, 218-219
virtual interaction 158, 216, 219
virtual interview 212
virtual organization 1, 163, 224, 227
virtual organizing 213-214
virtual platforms 79
virtual private networks 5
virtual resources 84-86, 91-92
virtual survey research 176, 183, 185
virtual surveys 176, 178, 184, 186
virtual teams 150, 171-173, 199, 210-211, 230-233, 235-239, 241, 243-247, 285
virtual work 1, 8, 10-11, 15, 17-19, 21, 23-25, 28, 30-31, 58-59, 62-65, 67, 70, 73, 77-79, 81-93, 95, 97-98, 112, 115, 149-150, 152, 157-164, 172, 174, 177-179, 184-188, 192-193, 196-199, 201-206, 209, 213-226, 236, 239, 248-249, 252-256, 277-278, 280-285
Voice over IP 5

W

web-based learning adoption 116
web-based systems learning 117
work extending technologies 60
work-life conflict 31, 33, 36-40, 50-51, 53-55, 58, 246
workplace management 4
workspaces 42-43, 47, 50, 52-53, 73, 82, 254